THE WRITINGS

OF

THOMAS PAINE

COLLECTED AND EDITED BY

MONCURE DANIEL CONWAY

AUTHOR OF " THE LIFE OF THOMAS PAINE," " OMITTED CHAPTERS OF HISTORY
DISCLOSED IN THE LIFE AND PAPERS OF EDMUND RANDOLPH,"
" GEORGE WASHINGTON AND MOUNT VERNON," ETC.

VOLUME IV.

AMS Press, Inc.
New York
1967

Reprinted from the edition of 1894–1896, New York
First AMS edition published in 1967
2 nd printing , 1972
Library of Congress Catalog Card Number:
International Standard Book Number:
Set Number: 0-404-04870-6
Volume 4   : 0-404-04874-9

Manufactured in the United States of America

AMS PRESS INC.
NEW YORK, N. Y. 10003

THE WRITINGS

OF

THOMAS PAINE

VOLUME IV.

AMS PRESS
NEW YORK

CONTENTS.

GENERAL INTRODUCTION,

WITH LAST GLEANINGS, HISTORICAL AND BIOGRAPHICAL.

BEFORE sending out this final volume, I have rambled again in some of the fields harvested in my seven years' labour on the Life and Works of Thomas Paine, and present the more important gleanings in these preliminary pages.

I recently obtained from a solicitor of Rotherham, Mr. Rising, a letter (on whose large seal part of the P remains), written by Paine from London to Thomas Walker, Esq., a member of the firm which manufactured the large model of the iron bridge invented by the author, and exhibited at Paddington in June, 1790. The letter is dated February 26, 1789, and the first part, which relates to the bridge, is quoted in Appendix E. The political part, here given, relates to the controversy which arose on the insanity of George III., in which Mr. Fox and the Opposition maintained that the crown passed to the Prince of Wales by hereditary right, while the Pitt Ministry maintained that the Prince had no right during the King's lifetime, more than any other person, though it was "expedient" to select him as the Regent, with restrictions on his power imposed by the two Houses of Parliament. Paine writes :

"With respect to News and Politics, the King is certainly greatly amended, but what is to follow from it is a matter of much uncertainty. How far the Nation may be safe with a man of a deranged mind at the head of it, and who, ever since he took up the notion of quitting England and going to live in Hanover, has been continually planning to entangle England with German connections, which if followed must end in a war, is a matter that

will occasion various opinions. However unfortunate it may
have been for the sufferer, the King's malady has been no disser-
vice to the Nation ; he was burning his fingers very fast in the
German war, and whether he is enough in his senses to keep out
of the fire is a matter of doubt.

"You mention the Rotherham Address as complimenting Mr.
Pitt on the success of his administration, *and for asserting and
supporting the Rights of the People.* I differ exceedingly from you
in this opinion, and I think the conduct of the Opposition much
nearer to the principles of the Constitution, than what the conduct of the Ministry was. So far from Mr. Pitt asserting and
supporting the Rights of the people, it appears to me taking them
away—but as a man ought not to make an assertion without giving his reasons, I will give you mine.

"The English Nation is composed of two orders of men—
Peers and Commoners. By Commoners is properly meant every
man in the Nation not having the title of Peer. And it is the
existence of those two orders, setting up distinct and opposite
Claims, the one hereditary and the other elective, that makes it
necessary to establish a third order, or that known by the name
of the Regal Power, or the Power of the Crown.

"The Regal Power is the Majesty of the Nation collected to a
center, and residing in the person exercising the Regal Power.
The Right therefore of the Prince is a Right standing on the
Right of the whole Nation. But Mr. Pitt says it stands on the
Right of Parliament. Is not Parliament composed of two houses,
one of which is itself hereditary, and over which the people have
no controul, and in the establishment of which they have no election ; and the other house the representative of only a small part
of the nation ? How then can the Rights of the People be
asserted and supported by absorbing them into an hereditary
house of Peers ? Is not one hereditary power or Right as dangerous as the other ? And yet the Addressers have all gone on
the Error of establishing Power in the house of Peers, over whom,
as I have already said, they have no controul, for the inconsistent
purpose of opposing it in the prince over whom they have some
controul.

"It was one of those Cases in which there ought to have been
a National Convention for the express purpose : for if Government be permitted to alter itself, or any of the parts be permitted

to alter the other, there is no fixed Constitution in the Country. And if the Regal Power, or the person exercising the Regal Power, either as King or Regent, instead of standing on the universal ground of the Nation, be made the meer Creature of Parliament, it is, in my humble opinion, equally as inconsistent and unconstitutional as if Parliament was the meer Creature of the Crown.

" It is a common Idea in all countries that to take Power from the Prince is to give liberty to the people. But Mr. Pitt's conduct is almost the reverse of this : his is to take power from one part of the Government to add it to another ; for he has encreased the Power of the Peers, not the Rights of the People.—I must give him credit for his ingenuity if I do not for his principles, and the less so because the object of his conduct is now visible, which was to [keep] themselves in pay after they should be out of f[avour], by retaining, thro' an Act of Parliament of their own making, between four and five hundred thousand pounds of the Civil List in their own hands. This is the key of the whole business ; and it was for this and not for the Rights of the people that he set up the Right of Parliament, because it was only by that means that the spoil could be divided. If the restrictions had been that he should not declare war, or enter into foreign alliances without the consent of Parliament, the objects would have been national and would have had some sense in them ; but it is, that he should not have *all the money.* If Swift was alive he would say—'S—— on such Patriotism.'

" How they will manage with Ireland I have no opportunity of learning, as I have not been at the other end of the Town since the Commission arrived. Ireland will certainly judge for itself, and not permit the English Parliament or Doctors to judge for her.—Thus much for Politics."

The letter just quoted is the more remarkable because the Prince Regent was particularly odious to Paine. The reader will find this issue of the Regency dealt with in the " Rights of Man " (ii., p. 371 of this edition), but it may be remarked in passing that this supposed purblind enemy of thrones was found in 1789 maintaining that the monarch, however objectionable, was more related to the people than a non-representative Parliament, and that in 1793 he pleaded for the life of Louis XVI.

The last paragraph in the above extract shows that Paine was already in sympathy with Irish discontent. I have a little scrap of his writing (early 1792) which appears to be from the draft of a note to one of the associations in London, respecting the Society of United Irishmen, whose Declaration was issued in October, 1791:

"I have the honour of presenting the Gentlemen present a letter I have received from the United Irishmen of Dublin informing me of my having been elected an honorary member of their Society. By this adoption of me as one of their body I have the pleasure of considering myself on their"——[*cætera desunt*].

The tremendous effect produced in Ireland by Paine's answer to Burke is indicated in the Charlemont Papers (Hist. MSS. Com. 1894). Mr. Thomas Shore first called attention to the items concerning Paine in the London *Freethinker*, March and April, 1896. Although Charlemont had been made an earl for quelling an insurrection in Ulster, 1763, he was a Liberal Whig. In 1791 (April 11) Sheridan writes from Downpatrick to Charlemont:

"I find from the newspapers that the Whigs of the capital (a society of which I am a member, and into which I entered with the best intentions) have, in my absence, and without my knowledge, named and published me one of a committee for disseminating Mr. Paine's pamphlet in reply to Mr. Burke's 'Reflections on the French Revolution.' I have read that pamphlet; it appears to me designed to level all distinction, and to have this object in view—a total overthrow of the Constitution. With this opinion I must naturally feel it indecent, in my public situation as a member of parliament, a citizen, a barrister and (what I value least) one of his majesty's counsel, to disseminate that work, but I am at a loss how to act. My first intention was to contradict it publicly. I fear a misinterpretation of my motives, and I dislike public differences with men in whose cause I am an humble assistant."

Two days later Charlemont replies:

" Thinking exactly as you do of Paine's very entertaining, very ingenious, but very dangerous performance . . . yet how to advise upon this occasion I do not well know. A serious public contradiction would not be pleasant, and possibly not innoxious. Perhaps the best method may be to expostulate between jest and earnest with some of your brethren on the liberty they have taken, and to declare in all companies, without being too serious, your real opinion of the tendency of the pamphlet, giving it, however, its due praise, for much merit it certainly has. . . . Men connected with the popular party will often be brought into scrapes of this sort, as the people who sometimes do not go too far will seldom go far enough."

It is evident that Paine had a powerful following, and that it was not at that time prudent for a Whig politician to repudiate him. Soon after we find Earl Charlemont writing from Dublin, May 9, 1791, to Dr. Alexander Haliday, Belfast: " I did, indeed, suppose that Paine's pamphlet, which is, by the way, a work of great genius, would be well received in your district ; yet, in my opinion, it ought to be read with some degree of caution. He does, indeed, tear away the bandage from the public eye ; but in tearing it off there may be some danger of injuring the organ." In reply to a radical outburst from Haliday, Charlemont writes (July 30, 1791): " Though I admire Mr. Paine, I am by no means a convert to his doctrine concerning our constitution, and cannot help thinking that some approbation of this constitution, as it ought to be, should at all times be joined with the applause which we so justly bestow on the emancipation of a great people from utter slavery." Charlemont was a friend and correspondent of Burke, and frankly expressed his differences of opinion, but Haliday gave him proofs of a dishonourable proceeding on Burke's part, eleven years before (borrowing a manuscript play of Haliday's in confidence, showing it to Sheridan, and never returning it, professing that it was lost), and pronounced him (Burke) a snake in the grass. Thereafter no communication appears between Charlemont and Burke.

The prosecution of the second Part of the " Rights of

Man," and the panic caused by massacres in France, thinned
the ranks of Paine's eminent friends, while the popularity of
his work increased.   Malone, writing from London to Charlemont, December 3, 1792, says : " For several weeks past not
less than four thousand per week of Paine's despicable and
nonsensical pamphlet have been issued forth, for almost
nothing, and dispersed all over the kingdom.   At Manchester the innovators bribe the poor by drink to hear it read."
And on December 22, four days after Paine's trial, Malone
has the satisfaction of reporting : " That vain fellow Erskine
has been going about this month past, saying he would make
a speech in defence of Paine's nonsensical and impudent
libel on the English constitution, that would astonish the
world, and make him to be remembered when Pitt and Fox
and Burke, etc., were all forgotten.   After speaking for four
hours, and fainting in the usual form, the jury, without
suffering the attorney-general to reply, found Paine guilty."
Malone (Edmund, the Shakespearian) was an admirable
Irishman, but he seems to have been taken off his feet by
the court-panic in London.   There is a touch of comedy
in finding him bringing out a quarto with a republican
publisher.

"This person," he tells Charlemont, November 15, 1793, " a
Mr. George Robinson, is unluckily too a determined republican,
on which account alone I am sorry that I have employed him. In
consequence of his political phrenzy he at this moment is apprehensive of judgment being pronounced against him by the king's
bench for selling Paine's pamphlet, and may probably be punished
for his zeal in the ' good old cause,' as they called it in the last
century, by six months' imprisonment. I shall not have the
smallest pity for him. To do any act whatever that may tend to
forward the principles maintained by the diabolical ruffians in
France is so highly criminal that I hope the chief justice will
inflict the most exemplary punishment on all the favourers of that
vile system, whenever he can lay hold on them."

Robinson had been found guilty August 10, and when
called up for judgment seems to have escaped with a fine

(Sherwin's " Paine," p. 138). Before leaving the Charlemont Papers it may be remarked that in no case does the Earl respond to Malone's acrimonious language against Paine, and even when the good Catholic has before him the author's direst offences, he limits himself in writing to Haliday (long since scared) to a mild sentence: " So Paine has now attacked Washington! No wonder; he has lately dared to attack heaven."

From the papers of Francis Place (British Museum), it appears that the work of repressing political discussion was begun by the Lord Mayor, who on November 27, 1792, closed the debating society which had been meeting at the King's Arms, Cornhill. (By the diary of Paine's friend, John Hall, I find that after the information had been lodged against Paine, all of the debating societies in London were intimidated, and the King's Arms debate had come down to the question, " Whether a husband obstinate and ignorant, or a man of parts, though tyrannical, was the most eligible for a woman of refined sensibilities?" Hall adds : " Did not stay to the end, but it seemed to be going in favour of the sensible man, the tyrant." Whether the Lord Mayor scented sedition in such questions or not, John Hall, after some absence from London, enters in his diary, November 26, " Could not find where Debating Society met.")

In the Francis Place MSS., 27, 809, p. 268, there is a list of the prosecutions in 1793 ; and in 27, 812, pp. 10, 12, are documents showing that about the middle of June, 1792, subscriptions had been opened, for the defence of Paine, by both the " London Corresponding Committee " and the " Constitutional Society." In MSS. 27, 817, p. 24, " Mr. Payne " (*sic*) and Rickman are in the list of those who met in the London Coffee House, May 9, 1792, and founded the " Society of Friends of the People."

Paine was elected a member of the French National Convention by four departments—Oise, Puy-de-Dôme, the Somme, and Pas-de-Calais, and decided to sit for the latter. Among the manuscripts of Genet, the first Minister sent by the Convention to the United States, confided to me by his

son, George Clinton Genet of New York, I find a memorandum of great historical interest, which may be inserted here
in advance of the monograph I hope to prepare concerning
that much-wronged ambassador. In this memorandum Genet
—a brother of Madame Campan—states that his appointment to the United States was in part because of the position his family had held at Court, and with a view to the
banishment of the royal family to that country. (It had
already been arranged that Paine should move for this in the
Convention.) I now quote Genet :

Roux Facillac, who had been very intimate in my father's
family at Versailles, met me one morning [January 14, 1793] and
wished me to spend the evening at Le Brun's, where I had been
invited. He accompanied me there and we met Brissot, Guadet,
Leonnet, Ducos, Fauchet, Thomas Paine, and most of the Gironde
leaders. . . . Tom Paine, who did not pretend to understand
French, took no part in the conversation, and sat quietly sipping
his claret. " Ask Paine, Genet," said Brissot, " what effect the
execution of Capet would have in America ? " Paine replied to
my enquiry by simply saying " bad, very bad." The next day
Paine presented to the Convention his celebrated letter demand-
ing in the name of Liberty, and the people of the United States,
that Louis should be sent to the United States. Vergniaux enquired of me what effect I thought it would have in Europe. I
replied in a few words that it would gratify the enemies of France
who had not forgiven Louis the acceptance of the Constitution
nor the glorious results of the American Revolution. . . .
" Genet," continued Le Brun, " how would you like to go to the
United States and take Capet and his family with you ? "

The next day, January 15, Genet was appointed by Le
Brun (Minister of Foreign Affairs), and Paine's appeal was
made in the Convention ; but there is reason to believe that
Le Brun's servant was a spy ; and the conversation, reported
to the Jacobins soon after its occurrence, " contributed,"
Genet believed, " to the early fall of Louis."
I will now call attention to a passage in " The Journal of
a Spy in Paris during the Reign of Terror," recently pub-

lished, and will place it beside an extract from Paine's memorial to Monroe while in prison.

The Spy.	Paine, 1794.
" April 2, 1793. He [Paine] is said to be moving heaven and earth to get himself recognized as an *American Citizen,* and thereon liberated. . . The Minister of the American States [Gouverneur Morris] is too shrewd to allow such a fish to go over and swim in his waters, if he can prevent it ; and avows to Robespierre that he knows nothing of any rights of naturalization claimed by Paine."	" However discordant the late American Minister Gouverneur Morris and the late French Committee of Public Safety were, it suited the purpose of both that I should be continued in arrestation. The former wished to prevent my return to America that I should not expose his misconduct ; and the latter, lest I should publish to the world the history of its wickedness. Whilst that Minister and the Committee continued I had no expectation of liberty. I speak here of the Committee of which Robespierre was a member."

Here then is corroboration, were it needed, of the criminal treachery of Morris to both Paine and Washington, of which I have given unanswerable documentary evidence (vol. iii., chap. 21), although I had not then conceived that Morris' guilt extended to personal incitements of Robespierre against Paine.

Morris knew well that " naturalization," though an effective word to use on Robespierre, had nothing to do with the citizenship acquired at the American Revolution by persons of alien birth, such as Paine, Hamilton, Robert Morris,—to name three who had held high offices in the United States. But, as Monroe stated, all Americans of 1776 were born under the British flag, and needed no formal process to make them citizens.

Mr. J. G. Alger, author of " Englishmen in the French Revolution," and " Glimpses of the French Revolution," whose continued researches in Paris promise other original and striking works, has graciously sent me a document of much interest just discovered by him in the National Archives, where it is marked U 1021. It is the copy of a " Declaration " made by Paine, the original being buried away in the chaos of Fouquier-Tinville documents. The Declaration was made on October 8, 1794, in connection with the trial of Denis Julien, accused of having been a Spy of Robespierre and his party in the Luxembourg prison. It was proved that on June 29, 1794, Julien had been called on in the prison, where he was detained, to inform the revolutionary tribunal concerning the suspected conspiracy among the prisoners. He said that he knew nothing ; that his room was at the extremity of the building divided off from the mass of prisoners, and he could not pronounce against any one. (Wallon's " Hist. Tribunal Révolutionnaire," iv., p. 409.) Wallon, however, had not discovered this document found by Mr. Alger, which shows that Paine was long a room-mate of Julien in the prison where his (Paine's) Declaration was demanded and given as follows :

" Denis Julien was my room mate from the time of his entering the Luxembourg prison at the end of the month of Ventose [about the middle of March] till towards the end of Messidor [about the middle of July], at which date I was visited with a violent fever which obliged me to go into a room better suited to the condition I was in. It is for the time when we were room mates that I shall speak of him, as being within my personal knowledge. I shall not go beyond that date, because my illness rendered me incapable of knowing anything of what happened in the prison or elsewhere, and my companions on their part, all the time that my recovery remained doubtful, were silent to me on all that happened. The first news which they told me was of the fall of Robespierre. I state all this so that the real reason why I do not speak of any of the allegations preferred against Julien in the summoning of him as a witness before the revolutionary tribunal, in the case of persons accused of conspiracy, may be clearly known, and that my silence on that case may not be attributed to any unfavourable reticence. Of his conduct during the time of our room intimacy, which lasted more than four months, I can speak fully. He appeared to me during all that time a man of strict honour, probity, and humanity, incapable of doing anything repugnant to those principles. We found ourselves in entire agreement in the horror which we felt for the character of Robespierre, and in the opinion which we formed of his hypocrisy, particularly on the occasion of his harangue on the Supreme Being, and on the atrocious perfidy which he showed in proposing the bloody law of the 22 Prairial [June 10, 1794] ; and we communicated our opinions to each other in writing, and these confidential notes we wrote in English to prevent the risk of our being understood by the prisoners, and for our own safety we threw them into the fire as soon as read. As I knew nothing of the denunciations which took place at the Luxembourg, or of the judgments and executions which were the consequence, until at least a month after the event, I can only say that when I was informed of them, as also of the appearance of Julien as a witness in that affair, I concluded from the opinion which I had already formed of him that he had been an unwilling witness, or that he had acted with the view of rendering service to the accused, and I have now no reason to believe otherwise. That the accused were not guilty of any anti-revolutionary conduct is also what I believe, but the fact was that all the prisoners saw themselves shut up like sheep in a pen to be sacrificed in turn just as they daily saw their companions were, and the expression of discontent which the misery of such a situation forced from them was converted into a conspiracy by the spies of Robespierre who were posted in the prison.—Luxembourg, 17 Vendemiaire, Year 3."

Julien was discharged without trial. The answers he had given to the Revolutionary Committee, quoted above, unknown of course to Paine, justified his opinion of Julien, though the fact of his being summoned at all looks as if Julien had been placed with Paine as an informer. In the companionship of the author Julien may have found a change of heart ! Mr. Alger in a note to me remarks, " What a picture of the prisoners' distrust of each other ! " The document also brings before us the notable fact that, though at its date, fourteen weeks after the fall of Robespierre, the sinister power of Gouverneur Morris' accomplices on the Committee of Public Safety still kept Paine in prison, his testimony to the integrity of an accused man was called for and apparently trusted.

The next extract that I give is a clipping from a London paper of 1794, the name not given, preserved in a scrap-book extending from 1776 to 1827, which I purchased many years ago at the Bentley sale.

"GENERAL O'HARA AND MR. THOMAS PAYNE.—These well-known Gentlemen are at Paris—both kept at the Luxembourg— imprisoned, indeed, but in a mitigated manner as to accommodations, apartments, table, intercourse, and the liberty of the garden —which our well-informed readers know is very large. The ground plan of the Luxembourg is above six acres. In this confinement General O'Hara and Mr. Thomas Payne have often met, and their meeting has been productive of a little event in some sort so unexpected as to be added to the extraordinary vicissitudes of which the present time is so teeming. The fact was that General O'Hara wanted money ; and that through Mr. Thomas Payne he was able to get what he wanted. The sum was 200*l.* sterling. The General's bill, through other channels tried in vain, was negociated by Mr. Thomas Payne."

The story of this money, and how Paine contrived to keep it, is told in vol. iii., p. 396, n. The mitigations of punishment alluded to in the paragraph did not last long ; the last months of Paine's imprisonment were terrible. O'Hara, captured at Toulon and not released until August, 1795, was the General who carried out the sword of Cornwallis for surrender at Yorktown.

Charles Nodier, in his "Souvenirs de la Révolution et de l'Empire" (Paris, 1850), has some striking sketches of Paine and his friends in the last years of the eighteenth century. Nodier had no sympathy with Paine's opinions, but was much impressed by the man. I piece together some extracts from various parts of his rambling work.

"One of our dinners at Bonneville's has left such an impression on me that when I am thinking of these things it seems like a dream. There were six of us in the Poet's immense sitting room.

It had four windows looking on the street. The cloth was spread on an oblong table, loaded at each end with bronzes, globes, maps, books, crests, and portraits. The only one of the guests whom I knew was the impenetrable Seyffert, with his repertory of ideas a thousand times more profound, but also a thousand times more obscure, than the cave of Trophonius. . . Old Mercier came in and sat down with his chin resting on his big ivory-topped cane. . . The fifth guest was a military man, fifty years of age, with a sort of inverted curled up face, reserved in conversation, like a man of sense, common in manners, like a man of the people. They called him a Pole. The last guest was an Anglo-American, with a long, thin, straight head, all in profile as it were, without any expression ; for gentleness, benevolence, shyness, give little scope for it. . . This Anglo-American was Thomas Payne, and the Tartar with sullen looks was Kosciusko. . . Thomas Payne, whom I seldom saw, has left on me the impression of a well-to-do man, bold in principle, cautious in practice ; liable to yield himself up to revolutionary movements, incapable of accepting the dangerous consequences ; good by nature, and a sophist by conviction. . . . On the whole an honest and unpretending person who, in the most fatal day of our annals, exhibited every courage and virtue ; and of whom history, in order to be just to his memory, ought to forget nothing but his writings."

At a somewhat later period Paine was met in Paris by the eminent engraver, Abraham Raimbach, Corresponding Member of the Institute of France, whose " Recollections," privately printed, were loaned me by Mr. Henry Clifton. I am permitted by Mr. W. L. Raimbach, grandson of the engraver, to use this family volume. Raimbach probably had met Paine between 1800 and 1802, and writes :

" He was at this time constantly to be seen at an obscure *cabaret* in an obscure street in the fauxbourg St. Germain (Café Jacob, rue Jacob). The scene as we entered the room from the street—it was on the ground floor—was, under the circumstances, somewhat impressive. It was on a summer's evening, and several tables were occupied by men, apparently tradesmen and mechanics, some playing at the then universal game of dominoes, others drinking their bottle of light, frothy, but pleasant beer, or their little glass of liqueur, while in a retired part of the room sat the once-dreaded demagogue, the supposed conspirator against thrones and altars, the renowned Thomas Paine ! He was in conversation with several well-dressed Irishmen, who soon afterwards took leave, and we placed ourselves at his table. His general appearance was mean and poverty-stricken. The portrait of him engraved by Sharp from Romney's portrait is a good likeness, but he was now much withered and careworn, tho' his dark eye still retained its sparkling vigour. He was fluent in his speech, of mild and gentle demeanour, clear and distinct in enunciation, and his voice exceedingly soft and agreeable. The subject of his talk being of course political, resembled very much his printed opinions ; and the dogmatic form in which he delivered them seemed to evince his own perfect self-conviction of their truth."

Raimbach mentions having afterwards understood that Colonel Bosville, of Yorkshire, was very kind to him, and enabled Paine to return to America. Lewis Goldsmith says that Sir Francis Burdett and Mr. William Bosville made him a present of 300 louis d'ors, with which he remunerated Bonneville, with whom he had resided nearly six years. Goldsmith's article on Paine (*Anti-Gallican Monitor*, February 28, 1813) contains a good many errors, but some shrewd remarks :

" From what I knew of this man, who once made such a noise in this country and America, I judge him to have been harmless and inoffensive ; and I firmly believe that if he could have imagined that his writings would have caused bloodshed he would never have written at all. . . . He never was respected by any party in France, as he certainly was not an advocate of (what was falsely called) French liberty,—that system which enforced Republican opinions by drowning, shooting, and the guillotine. . . . He even saw several foreigners, who like himself were staunch admirers of the French Revolution, led to the scaffold—such as Anacharsis Clootz, Baron Trenk, etc.—and had Robespierre lived eight days longer Paine would have certainly followed them, as his name was already on the Proscribed list of the Public Accuser. . . . I have no doubt that if

Paine, on his return to America, had found the head of the government of that country [Jefferson] to be that stern Republican which he professed to be, he would have written some account of the French Revolution, and of the horrid neglect which he experienced there from Robespierre as well as from Buonaparte ; for if the former designed to take away his life, the latter refused him the means of living. . . . I must in justice to him declare that he left France a decided enemy to the Revolution in that country, and with an unconquerable aversion to Buonaparte, against whom he indulged himself in speaking in severe terms to almost every person of his acquaintance in Paris."

The last of my gleanings were gathered at Bromley, in Kent, where Paine went on April 21, 1792, " to compose," says his friend Hall, " the funeral sermon of Burke," but local tradition says, to write the " Age of Reason." Paine, as a private letter proves, was anxious for a prosecution of his " Rights of Man," which Burke had publicly proposed, and no doubt began at Bromley his pamphlet with the exposure of Burke's pension. However, when Paine sought refuge from the swarm of radicals and interviewers besetting him in his London lodgings, it is highly probable that he wished to continue his meditations on religious subjects and add to his manuscripts, begun many years before, ultimately pieced together in the " Age of Reason." Under the guidance of Mr. Coles Childs, present owner of Bromley Palace, I visited Mr. How, an intelligent watchmaker, who remembers when a boy of twelve hearing his father say that Paine occupied " Church Cottage," and there wrote the " Age of Reason." There is also a local tradition that Paine used to write on the same work while seated under the " Tom Paine Tree," which is on the palace estate. " Church Cottage " was ecclesiastical property, may even have been the Vicarage, and Paine would pass by the beautiful palace of the Bishops of Rochester to his favourite tree. The legend which has singled out the heretical work of Paine as that which was written in an ecclesiastical mansion, and in an episcopal park, is too picturesque for severe criticism. The " Tom Paine

Tree " is a very ancient oak, solitary in its field, and very
noble. Mr. Childs pointed out to me some powerful but
much rusted wires, amid the upper branches, showing that it
had been taken care of. The interior surface of the trunk,
which is entirely hollow, is completely charred. The girth
at the ground must be twenty-five feet. Not a limb is dead :
from the hollow and charred trunk a superb mass of foliage arises. I think Paine must have remembered it when
writing patriotic songs for America in the Revolution,—
" The Liberty Tree," and the " Boston Patriot's Song," with
its lines—

> " Our mountains are crowned with imperial oak,
>   Whose roots like our Liberty ages have nourished."

From this high and clear spot one may almost see the
homestead of Darwin who, more heretical than Paine, has
Westminster Abbey for his monument ; and whose neigh-
bor, the Rev. Robert Ainslie, of Tromer Lodge, kept in his
house the skull and right hand of Thomas Paine ! Of the
remains of Paine, exhumed by Cobbett in America, the
brain came into the possession of Rev. George Reynolds,
the skull into that of Rev. Robert Ainslie, both orthodox at
the time, both subsequently unorthodox, possibly through
some desire to know what thoughts had played through the
lamp whose fragments had come into their hands. The
daughter of Mr. Ainslie, the first wife of the late Sir Rus-
sell Reynolds, wrote me that she remembered the relics, but
could not find them after her father's death ; if ever discovered they might well be given quiet burial or cremation at
the foot of this " Tom Paine Tree." However that may
be, it is a Talking Oak, if one listens closely, and tells true
fables of the charred and scarred and storm-beaten man,
rooted deep in the conscience and soul of England, whose
career, after its special issues are gone, is still crowned with
living foliage. That none can doubt who witnessed the
large Paine Exhibition in South Place Chapel, in December, 1895, or that in the Bradlaugh Club, January 29, 1896,
and observes the steady demand for his works in England

and America. Yet it is certain that comparatively few of those who cherish relics of Paine, and read his books, agree with his religious opinions, or regard his political theories as now practicable. Paine's immortality among the people is derived mainly from the life and spirit which were in him, consuming all mean partitions between man and man, all arbitrary and unreal distinctions, rising above the cheap Jingoism that calls itself patriotism, and affirming the nobler State whose unit is the man, whose motto is " My country is the world, to do good my religion."

Personally I place a very high value on Paine's writings in themselves, and not simply for their prophetic genius, their humane spirit, and their vigorous style. While his type of deism is not to me satisfactory, his religious spirit at times attains sublime heights ; and while his republican formulas are at times impaired by his eagerness to adapt them to existing conditions, I do not find any writer at all, not even the most modern, who has equally worked out a scheme for harmonizing the inevitable rule of the majority with individual freedom and rights. Yet it is by no means on this my own estimate of Paine's ideas that I rest the claims of his writings to attention and study. Their historical value is of the highest. Every page of Paine was pregnant with the life of his time. He was the *enfant terrible* of the times that in America, England, France, made the history that is now our international heritage : he was literally the only man who came out with the whole truth, regardless of persons: his testimony is now of record, and the gravest issues of to-day cannot be understood until that testimony is mastered.

I especially invoke to the study of Paine's Life, and of these volumes of his Writings, the historians, scholars, statesmen of the mother of nations—England. I have remarked a tendency in some quarters to preserve the old odium against Paine, no longer maintainable in respect of his religion or his character, by transferring it to his antagonism to the government of England in the last century. And it is probable that this prejudice may be revived by the republication in this edition of several of his pamphlets, notably that on the " Invasion of England " in the Appendix (to which some of Paine's most important works have been relegated). But if thinking Englishmen will rid themselves of that counterfeit patriotism now called " Jingoism," and calmly study those same essays, they will begin to understand that while Paine arraigned a transient misgovernment of England, his critics arraign England itself by treating attacks on minions of George III. as if hostile to the England of Victoria. The widespread hostility to England recently displayed in America has with some justice been traced to the kind of teaching that has gone on for nearly four generations in American schools under the name of history; but what remedy can there be for this disgraceful situation so long as English historians are ignorantly keeping their country, despite the friendship of its people for Americans, in the attitude of a party to a *vendetta* transmitted from a discredited past? And much the same may be said concerning the strained relations between England and France, which constitute a most sad, and even scandalous, feature of our time. About a hundred years ago an English government was instigating parochial mobs to burn " Tom Paine " in effigy for writing the " Rights of Man," little reflecting that it was making the nation it misgoverned into an effigy for American and French democrats to burn, on occasion, for a century to come. Paine, his name and his personal wrongs, passed out of the case altogether, like the heart of the hollow " Tom Paine Tree " at Bromley: but like its living foliage the principles he represented are still renewed, and flourish under new names and forms. But old names and forms are coined in prejudices. The Jeffersonian in America and the Girondin in France are now in power, and are sometimes victimized by a superstition that George III. is still monarch of England, and Pitt still his Minister. Meanwhile the credit of English Literature commands the civilized world. The next great writer will be the historian who shall without flattery, and with inflexible justice and truth, examine and settle these long-standing accounts with the past ; and to him I dedicate

in advance these volumes, wherein he will find valuable resources and materials.

Here then close my labours on the history and the writings
of the great Commoner of Mankind, founder of the Republic
of the World, and emancipator of the human mind and heart,.
THOMAS PAINE.

THE AGE OF REASON.

EDITOR'S INTRODUCTION.

WITH SOME RESULTS OF RECENT RESEARCHES.

In the opening year, 1793, when revolutionary France had beheaded its king, the wrath turned next upon the King of kings, by whose grace every tyrant claimed to reign. But eventualities had brought among them a great English and American heart—Thomas Paine. He had pleaded for Louis Capet—" Kill the king but spare the man." Now he pleaded,—" Disbelieve in the King of kings, but do not confuse with that idol the Father of Mankind ! "

In Paine's Preface to the Second Part of " The Age of Reason " he describes himself as writing the First Part near the close of the year 1793. " I had not finished it more than six hours, in the state it has since appeared, before a guard came about three in the morning, with an order signed by the two Committees of Public Safety and Surety General, for putting me in arrestation." This was on the morning of December 28. But it is necessary to weigh the words just quoted—" in the state it has since appeared." For on August 5, 1794, François Lanthenas, in an appeal for Paine's liberation, wrote as follows : " I deliver to Merlin de Thionville a copy of the last work of T. Payne [The Age of Reason], formerly our colleague, and in custody since the decree excluding foreigners from the national representation. This book was written by the author in the beginning of the year '93 (old style). I undertook its translation before the revolution against priests, and it was published in French about the same time. Couthon, to whom I sent it, seemed offended with me for having translated this work."

Under the frown of Couthon, one of the most atrocious colleagues of Robespierre, this early publication seems to have been so effectually suppressed that no copy bearing that date, 1793, can be found in France or elsewhere. In Paine's letter to Samuel Adams, printed in the present volume, he says that he had it translated into French, to stay the progress of atheism, and that he endangered his life " by opposing atheism." The time indicated by Lanthenas as that in which he submitted the work to Couthon would appear to be the latter part of March, 1793, the fury against the priesthood having reached its climax in the decrees against them of March 19 and 26. If the moral deformity of Couthon, even greater than that of his body, be remembered, and the readiness with which death was inflicted for the most theoretical opinion not approved by the " Mountain," it will appear probable that the offence given Couthon by Paine's book involved danger to him and his translator. On May 31, when the Girondins were accused, the name of Lanthenas was included, and he barely escaped ; and on the same day Danton persuaded Paine not to appear in the Convention, as his life might be in danger. Whether this was because of the " Age of Reason," with its fling at the " Goddess Nature " or not, the statements of author and translator are harmonized by the fact that Paine prepared the manuscript, with considerable additions and changes, for publication in English, as he has stated in the Preface to Part II.

A comparison of the French and English versions, sentence by sentence, proved to me that the translation sent by Lanthenas to Merlin de Thionville in 1794 is the same as that he sent to Couthon in 1793. This discovery was the means of recovering several interesting sentences of the original work. I have given as footnotes translations of such clauses and phrases of the French work as appeared to be important. Those familiar with the translations of Lanthenas need not be reminded that he was too much of a literalist to depart from the manuscript before him, and indeed he did not even venture to alter it in an instance (presently considered) where it was obviously needed. Nor would Lanthenas have omitted any of the paragraphs lacking in his translation. This original work was divided into seventeen chapters, and these I have restored, translating their headings into English. The "Age of Reason" is thus for the first time given to the world with nearly its original completeness.

It should be remembered that Paine could not have read the proof of his "Age of Reason" (Part I.) which went through the press while he was in prison. To this must be ascribed the permanence of some sentences as abbreviated in the haste he has described. A notable instance is the dropping out of his estimate of Jesus the words rendered by Lanthenas "trop peu imité, trop oublié, trop meconnu." The addition of these words to Paine's tribute makes it the more notable that almost the only recognition of the human character and life of Jesus by any theological writer of that generation came from one long branded as an infidel.

To the inability of the prisoner to give his work any revision must be attributed the preservation in it of the singular error already alluded to, as one that Lanthenas, but for his extreme fidelity, would have corrected. This is Paine's repeated mention of six planets, and enumeration of them, twelve years after the discovery of Uranus. Paine was a devoted student of astronomy, and it cannot for a moment be supposed that he had not participated in the universal welcome of Herschel's discovery. The omission of any allusion to it convinces me that the astronomical episode was printed from a manuscript written before 1781, when Uranus was discovered. Unfamiliar with French in 1793, Paine might not have discovered the *erratum* in Lanthenas' translation, and, having no time for copying, he would naturally use as much as possible of the same manuscript in preparing his work for English readers. But he had no opportunity of revision, and there remains an *erratum* which, if my conjecture be correct, casts a significant light on the paragraphs in which he alludes to the preparation of the work. He states that soon after his publication of "Common Sense" (1776),

he " saw the exceeding probability that a revolution in the
system of government would be followed by a revolution in
the system of religion," and that " man would return to the
pure, unmixed, and unadulterated belief of one God and no
more." He tells Samuel Adams that it had long been his
intention to publish his thoughts upon religion, and he had
made a similar remark to John Adams in 1776. Like the
Quakers among whom he was reared Paine could then
readily use the phrase " word of God " for anything in the
Bible which approved itself to his " inner light," and as he
had drawn from the first Book of Samuel a divine condemnation of monarchy, John Adams, a Unitarian, asked him if he
believed in the inspiration of the Old Testament. Paine
replied that he did not, and at a later period meant to publish his views on the subject. There is little doubt that he
wrote from time to time on religious points, during the
American war, without publishing his thoughts, just as he
worked on the problem of steam navigation, in which he had
invented a practicable method (ten years before John Fitch
made his discovery) without publishing it. At any rate it
appears to me certain that the part of " The Age of Reason "
connected with Paine's favorite science, astronomy, was
written before 1781, when Uranus was discovered.

Paine's theism, however invested with biblical and Christian phraseology, was a birthright. It appears clear from
several allusions in " The Age of Reason " to the Quakers
that in his early life, or before the middle of the eighteenth
century, the people so called were substantially Deists. An
interesting confirmation of Paine's statements concerning
them appears as I write in an account sent by Count Leo
Tolstoi to the London *Times* of the Russian sect called
Dukhobortsy (*The Times*, October 23, 1895). This sect
sprang up in the last century, and the narrative says:

" The first seeds of the teaching called afterwards ' Duk-
hoborcheskaya' were sown by a foreigner, a Quaker, who
came to Russia. The fundamental idea of his Quaker teaching was that in the soul of man dwells God himself, and
that He himself guides man by His inner word. God lives

in nature physically and in man's soul spiritually. To
Christ, as to an historical personage, the Dukhobortsy do
not ascribe great importance. . . . Christ was God's son,
but only in the sense in which we call ourselves 'sons of
God.' The purpose of Christ's sufferings was no other than
to show us an example of suffering for truth. The Quakers
who, in 1818, visited the Dukhobortsy, could not agree with
them upon these religious subjects; and when they heard
from them their opinion about Jesus Christ (that he was a
man), exclaimed 'Darkness!' . . . 'From the Old and New
Testaments,' they say, 'we take only what is useful,' mostly
the moral teaching. . . . The moral ideas of the Dukhobortsy are the following:—All men are, by nature, equal;
external distinctions, whatsoever they may be, are worth
nothing. This idea of men's equality the Dukhobortsy have
directed further, against the State authority. . . . Amongst
themselves they hold subordination, and much more, a
monarchical Government, to be contrary to their ideas."

Here is an early Hicksite Quakerism carried to Russia
long before the birth of Elias Hicks, who recovered it from
Paine, to whom the American Quakers refused burial among
them. Although Paine arraigned the union of Church and
State, his ideal Republic was religious; it was based on a
conception of equality based on the divine sonship of every
man. This faith underlay equally his burden against claims
to divine partiality by a " Chosen People," a Priesthood, a
Monarch " by the grace of God," or an Aristocracy. Paine's
" Reason " is only an expansion of the Quaker's " inner
light "; and the greater impression, as compared with previous republican and deistic writings made by his " Rights
of Man " and " Age of Reason " (really volumes of one
work), is partly explained by the apostolic fervor which made
him a spiritual successor of George Fox.

Paine's mind was by no means sceptical, it was eminently
constructive. That he should have waited until his fifty-
seventh year before publishing his religious convictions was
due to a desire to work out some positive and practicable
system to take the place of that which he believed was

crumbling. The English engineer Hall, who assisted Paine in making the model of his iron bridge, wrote to his friends in England, in 1786 : " My employer has *Common Sense* enough to disbelieve most of the common systematic theories of Divinity, but does not seem to establish any for himself." But five years later Paine was able to lay the corner-stone of his temple : " With respect to religion itself, without regard to names, and as directing itself from the universal family of mankind to the Divine object of all adoration, *it is man bringing to his Maker the fruits of his heart ;* and though those fruits may differ from each other like the fruits of the earth, the grateful tribute of every one is accepted." (" Rights of Man." See my edition of Paine's Writings, ii., p. 326.) Here we have a reappearance of George Fox confuting the doctor in America who " denied the light and Spirit of God to be in every one ; and affirmed that it was not in the Indians. Whereupon I called an Indian to us, and asked him ' whether or not, when he lied, or did wrong to any one, there was not something in him that reproved him for it ?' He said, ' There was such a thing in him that did so reprove him ; and he was ashamed when he had done wrong, or spoken wrong.' So we shamed the doctor before the governor and the people." (Journal of George Fox, September 1672.)

Paine, who coined the phrase " Religion of Humanity " (The Crisis, vii., 1778), did but logically defend it in " The Age of Reason," by denying a special revelation to any particular tribe, or divine authority in any particular creed or church ; and the centenary of this much-abused publication has been celebrated by a great conservative champion of Church and State, Mr. Balfour, who, in his " Foundations of Belief," affirms that " inspiration " cannot be denied to the great Oriental teachers, unless grapes may be gathered from thorns.

The centenary of the complete publication of " The Age of Reason," (October 25, 1795), was also celebrated at the Church Congress, Norwich, on October 10, 1895, when Professor Bonney, F. R. S., Canon of Manchester, read a paper

in which he said : " I cannot deny that the increase of scientific knowledge has deprived parts of the earlier books of the
Bible of the historical value which was generally attributed
to them by our forefathers. The story of Creation in the
Book of Genesis, unless we play fast and loose either with
words or with science, cannot be brought into harmony with
what we have learnt from geology. Its ethnological statements are imperfect, if not sometimes inaccurate. The stories
of the Fall, of the Flood, and of the Tower of Babel, are incredible in their present form. Some historical element may
underlie many of the traditions in the first eleven chapters
in that book, but this we cannot hope to recover." Canon
Bonney proceeded to say of the New Testament also, that
" the Gospels are not, so far as we know, strictly con-
temporaneous records, so we must admit the possibility of
variations and even inaccuracies in details being introduced
by oral tradition." The Canon thinks the interval too short
for these importations to be serious, but that any question
of this kind is left open proves the Age of Reason fully
upon us. Reason alone can determine how many texts are
as spurious as the three heavenly witnesses (1 John v. 7 ,
and like it " serious " enough to have cost good men their
lives, and persecutors their charities. When men interpo-
late, it is because they believe their interpolation seriously
needed. It will be seen by a note in Part II. of the work,
that Paine calls attention to an interpolation introduced
into the first American edition without indication of its
being an editorial footnote. This footnote was : " The book
of Luke was carried by a majority of one only. Vide Mosheim's Ecc. History." Dr. Priestley, then in America, answered Paine's work, and in quoting less than a page from
the " Age of Reason " he made three alterations,—one of
which changed " church mythologists " into " Christian
mythologists,"—and also raised the editorial footnote into
the text, omitting the reference to Mosheim. Having done
this, Priestley writes: " As to the gospel of Luke being carried by a majority of one only, it is a legend, if not of Mr.
Paine's own invention, of no better authority whatever."

And so on with further castigation of the author for what he
never wrote, and which he himself (Priestley) was the unconscious means of introducing into the text within the year of
Paine's publication.

If this could be done, unintentionally by a conscientious
and exact man, and one not unfriendly to Paine, if such a
writer as Priestley could make four mistakes in citing half a
page, it will appear not very wonderful when I state that in
a modern popular edition of " The Age of Reason," including both parts, I have noted about five hundred deviations
from the original. These were mainly the accumulated
efforts of friendly editors to improve Paine's grammar or
spelling; some were misprints, or developed out of such;
and some resulted from the sale in London of a copy of
Part Second surreptitiously made from the manuscript.
These facts add significance to Paine's footnote (itself altered
in some editions!), in which he says : " If this has happened
within such a short space of time, notwithstanding the aid
of printing, which prevents the alteration of copies individually; what may not have happened in a much greater
length of time, when there was no printing, and when any
man who could write, could make a written copy, and call it
an original, by Matthew, Mark, Luke, or John.

Nothing appears to me more striking, as an illustration of
the far-reaching effects of traditional prejudice, than the
errors into which some of our ablest contemporary scholars
have fallen by reason of their not having studied Paine. Professor Huxley, for instance, speaking of the freethinkers of
the eighteenth century, admires the acuteness, common
sense, wit, and the broad humanity of the best of them,
but says "there is rarely much to be said for their
work as an example of the adequate treatment of a
grave and difficult investigation," and that they shared
with their adversaries "to the full the fatal weakness of *a priori* philosophising." [1]   Professor Huxley
does not name Paine, evidently because he knows nothing
about him. Yet Paine represents the turning-point of the

[1] Science and Christian Tradition, p. 18 (Lon. ed., 1894).

historical freethinking movement, he renounced the *a
priori* method, refused to pronounce anything impossible
outside pure mathematics, rested everything on evidence,
and really founded the Huxleyan school. He plagiarized
by anticipation many things from the rationalistic leaders
of our time, from Strauss and Baur (being the first to ex-
patiate on " Christian Mythology "), from Renan (being the
first to attempt recovery of the human Jesus), and notably
from Huxley, who has repeated Paine's arguments on the
untrustworthiness of the biblical manuscripts and canon, on
the inconsistencies of the narratives of Christ's resurrection,
and various other points. None can be more loyal to the
memory of Huxley than the present writer, and it is even
because of my sense of his grand leadership that he is here
mentioned as a typical instance of the extent to which the
very elect of free-thought may be unconsciously victimized
by the phantasm with which they are contending. He says
that Butler overthrew freethinkers of the eighteenth century
type, but Paine was of the nineteenth century type ; and it
was precisely because of his critical method that he excited
more animosity than his deistical predecessors. He compelled the apologists to defend the biblical narratives in
detail, and thus implicitly acknowledge the tribunal of reason and knowledge to which they were summoned. The
ultimate answer by police was a confession of judgment. A
hundred years ago England was suppressing Paine's works,
and many an honest Englishman has gone to prison for printing and circulating his " Age of Reason." The same views
are now freely expressed ; they are heard in the seats of
learning, and even in the Church Congress ; but the suppression of Paine, begun by bigotry and ignorance, is continued
in the long indifference of the representatives of our Age of
Reason to their pioneer and founder. It is a grievous loss
to them and to their cause. It is impossible to understand
the religious history of England, and of America, without
studying the phases of their evolution represented in the
writings of Thomas Paine, in the controversies that grew
out of them with such practical accompaniments as the

foundation of the Theophilanthropist Church in Paris and
New York, and of the great rationalist wing of Quakerism
in America.

Whatever may be the case with scholars in our time,
those of Paine's time took the "Age of Reason" very seriously indeed. Beginning with the learned Dr. Richard
Watson, Bishop of Llandaff, a large number of learned men
replied to Paine's work, and it became a signal for the commencement of those concessions, on the part of theology,
which have continued to our time ; and indeed the so-called
"Broad Church" is to some extent an outcome of "The
Age of Reason." It would too much enlarge this Introduction to cite here the replies made to Paine (thirty-six are
catalogued in the British Museum), but it may be remarked
that they were notably free, as a rule, from the personalities
that raged in the pulpits. I must venture to quote one
passage from his very learned antagonist, the Rev. Gilbert
Wakefield, B.A., "late Fellow of Jesus College, Cambridge."
Wakefield, who had resided in London during all the Paine
panic, and was well acquainted with the slanders uttered
against the author of "Rights of Man," indirectly brands
them in answering Paine's argument that the original and
traditional unbelief of the Jews, among whom the alleged
miracles were wrought, is an important evidence against
them. The learned divine writes:

"But the subject before us admits of further illustration
from the example of Mr. Paine himself. In this country,
where his opposition to the corruptions of government has
raised him so many adversaries, and such a swarm of un-
principled hirelings have exerted themselves in blackening
his character and in misrepresenting all the transactions
and incidents of his life, will it not be a most difficult, nay
an impossible task, for posterity, after a lapse of 1700 years,
if such a wreck of modern literature as that of the ancient,
should intervene; to identify the real circumstances, moral
and civil, of the man? And will a true historian, such as
the Evangelists, be credited at that future period against
such a predominant incredulity, without large and mighty

accessions of collateral attestation? And how transcendantly extraordinary, I had almost said *miraculous*, will it be estimated, by candid and reasonable minds, that a writer whose object was a melioration of condition to the common people, and their deliverance from oppression, poverty, wretchedness, to the numberless blessings of upright and equal government, should be reviled, persecuted, and burned in effigy, with every circumstance of insult and execration, by these very objects of his benevolent intentions, in every corner of the kingdom?"

After the execution of Louis XVI., for whose life Paine pleaded so earnestly,—while in England he was denounced as an accomplice in the deed,—he devoted himself to the preparation of a Constitution, and also to gathering up his religious compositions and adding to them. This manuscript I suppose to have been prepared in what was variously known as White's Hotel or Philadelphia House, in Paris, No. 7 Passage des Petits Pères. This compilation of early and fresh manuscripts (if my theory be correct) was labelled, "The Age of Reason," and given for translation to François Lanthenas in March 1793. It is entered in Quérard *(La France Litéraire)* under the year 1793, but with the title "L'Age de la Raison" instead of that which it bore in 1794, "Le Siècle de la Raison." The latter, printed "Au Bureau de l'imprimérie, rue du Théâtre-Français, No. 4," is said to be by "Thomas Paine, Citoyen et cultivateur de l'Amérique septentrionale, secrétaire du Congrès du département des affaires étrangères pendant la guerre d'Amérique, et auteur des ouvrages intitulés : LA SENS COMMUN et LES DROITS DE L'HOMME."

When the Revolution was advancing to increasing terrors, Paine, unwilling to participate in the decrees of a Convention whose sole legal function was to frame a Constitution, retired to an old mansion and garden in the Faubourg St. Denis, No. 63. Mr. J. G. Alger, whose researches in personal details connected with the Revolution are original and useful, recently showed me, in the National Archives at Paris, some papers connected with the trial of Georgeit, Paine's landlord, by which it appears that the present No. 63 is not, as I had supposed, the house in which Paine resided. Mr. Alger accompanied me to the neighborhood, but we were not able to identify the house. The arrest of Georgeit is mentioned by Paine in his essay on "Forgetfulness" (Writings, iii., 319). When his trial came on one of the charges was that he had kept in his house "Paine and other Englishmen,"—Paine being then in prison,—but he (Georgeit) was acquitted of the paltry accusations brought against him by his Section, the "Faubourg du Nord." This Section took in the whole east side of the Faubourg St. Denis, whereas the present No. 63 is on the west side. After Georgeit (or Georget) had been arrested, Paine was left alone in the large mansion (said by Rickman to have been once the hotel of Madame de Pompadour), and it would appear, by his account, that it was after the execution (October 31, 1793) of his friends the Girondins, and political comrades, that he felt his end at hand, and set about his last literary bequest to the world,—"The Age of Reason,"—in the state in which it has since appeared, as he is careful to say. There was every probability, during the months in which he wrote (November and December 1793) that he would be executed. His religious testament was prepared with the blade of the guillotine suspended over him,—a fact which did not deter pious mythologists from portraying his death-bed remorse for having written the book.

In editing Part I. of "The Age of Reason," I follow closely the first edition, which was printed by Barrois in Paris from the manuscript, no doubt under the superintendence of Joel Barlow, to whom Paine, on his way to the Luxembourg, had confided it. Barlow was an American ex-clergyman, a speculator on whose career French archives cast an unfavorable light, and one cannot be certain that no liberties were taken with Paine's proofs.

I may repeat here what I have stated in the outset of my editorial work on Paine that my rule is to correct obvious misprints, and also any punctuation which seems to render the sense less clear. And to that I will now add that in following Paine's quotations from the Bible I have adopted the plan now generally used in place of his occasionally too extended writing out of book, chapter, and verse.

Paine was imprisoned in the Luxembourg on December 28, 1793, and released on November 4, 1794. His liberation was secured by his old friend, James Monroe (afterwards President), who had succeeded his (Paine's) relentless enemy, Gouverneur Morris, as American Minister in Paris. He was found by Monroe more dead than alive from semi-starvation, cold, and an abscess contracted in prison, and taken to the Minister's own residence. It was not supposed that he could survive, and he owed his life to the tender care of Mr. and Mrs. Monroe. It was while thus a prisoner in his room, with death still hovering over him, that Paine wrote Part Second of " The Age of Reason."

The work was published in London by H. D. Symonds on October 25, 1795, and claimed to be " from the Author's manuscript." It is marked as " Entered at Stationers Hall," and prefaced by an apologetic note of " The Bookseller to the Public," whose commonplaces about avoiding both prejudice and partiality, and considering " both sides," need not be quoted. While his volume was going through the press in Paris, Paine heard of the publication in London, which drew from him the following hurried note to a London publisher, no doubt Daniel Isaacs Eaton :

" SIR,—I have seen advertised in the London papers the second Edition [part] of the *Age of Reason*, printed, the advertisement says, from the *Author's Manuscript*, and entered at Stationers Hall. I have never sent any manuscript to any person. It is therefore a forgery to say it is printed from the author's manuscript ; and I suppose is done to give the Publisher a pretence of Copy Right, which he has no title to.

" I send you a printed copy, which is the only one I have sent to London. I wish you to make a cheap edition of it. I know not by what means any copy has got over to London.

If any person has made a manuscript copy I have no doubt but it is full of errors. I wish you would talk to Mr. —— upon this subject as I wish to know by what means this trick has been played, and from whom the publisher has got possession of any copy.

" T. PAINE.

"PARIS, December 4, 1795."

Eaton's cheap edition appeared January 1, 1796, with the above letter on the reverse of the title. The blank in the note was probably " Symonds " in the original, and possibly that publisher was imposed upon. Eaton, already in trouble for printing one of Paine's political pamphlets, fled to America, and an edition of the "Age of Reason" was issued under a new title; no publisher appears; it is said to be "printed for, and sold by all the Booksellers in Great Britain and Ireland." It is also said to be " By Thomas Paine, author of several remarkable performances." I have never found any copy of this anonymous edition except the one in my possession. It is evidently the edition which was suppressed by the prosecution of Williams for selling a copy of it.

A comparison with Paine's revised edition reveals a good many clerical and verbal errors in Symonds, though few that affect the sense. The worst are in the preface, where, instead of " 1793," the misleading date " 1790 " is given as the year at whose close Paine completed Part First,—an error that spread far and wide, and was fastened on by his calumnious American " biographer," Cheetham, to prove his inconsistency. The editors have been fairly demoralized by, and have altered in different ways, the following sentence of the preface in Symonds: " The intolerant spirit of religious persecution had transferred itself into politics ; the tribunals, styled Revolutionary, supplied the place of the Inquisition ; and the Guillotine of the State outdid the Fire and Faggot of the Church." The rogue who copied this little knew the care with which Paine weighed words, and that he would never call persecution " religious," nor connect the guillo-

tine with the " State," nor concede that with all its horrors
it had outdone the history of fire and faggot. What Paine
wrote was: " The intolerant spirit of church persecution had
transferred itself into politics; the tribunals, stiled Revolutionary, supplied the place of an Inquisition · and the Guillotine, of the Stake."

An original letter of Paine, in the possession of Joseph
Cowen, ex-M. P., which that gentleman permits me to bring
to light, besides being one of general interest makes clear
the circumstances of the original publication. Although the
name of the correspondent does not appear on the letter, it
was certainly written to Col. John Fellows of New York,
who copyrighted Part I. of the " Age of Reason." He published the pamphlets of Joel Barlow, to whom Paine confided
his manuscript on his way to prison. Fellows was afterwards
Paine's intimate friend in New York, and it was chiefly due
to him that some portions of the author's writings, left in
manuscript to Madame Bonneville while she was a freethinker, were rescued from her devout destructiveness after
her return to Catholicism. The letter which Mr. Cowen
sends me, is dated at Paris, January 20, 1797.

" SIR,—Your friend Mr. Caritat being on the point of his
departure for America, I make it the opportunity of writing
to you. I received two letters from you with some pamphlets a considerable time past, in which you inform me of
your entering a copyright of the first part of the Age of
Reason: when I return to America we will settle for that
matter.

" As Doctor Franklin has been my intimate friend for
thirty years past you will naturally see the reason of my continuing the connection with his grandson. I printed here
(Paris) about fifteen thousand of the second part of the Age
of Reason, which I sent to Mr. F[ranklin] Bache. I gave
him notice of it in September 1795 and the copy-right by
my own direction was entered by him. The books did not
arrive till April following, but he had advertised it long
before.

" I sent to him in August last a manuscript letter of about 70 pages, from me to Mr. Washington to be printed in a pamphlet. Mr. Barnes of Philadelphia carried the letter from me over to London to be forwarded to America. It went by the ship Hope, Cap: Harley, who since his return from America told me that he put it into the post office at New York for Bache. I have yet no certain account of its publication. I mention this that the letter may be enquired after, in case it has not been published or has not arrived to Mr. Bache. Barnes wrote to me, from London 29 August informing me that he was offered three hundred pounds sterling for the manuscript. The offer was refused because it was my intention it should not appear till it appeared in America, as that, and not England was the place for its operation.

" You ask me by your letter to Mr. Caritat for a list of my several works, in order to publish a collection of them. This is an undertaking I have always reserved for myself. It not only belongs to me of right, but nobody but myself can do it ; and as every author is accountable (at least in reputation) for his works, he only is the person to do it. If he neglects it in his life-time the case is altered. It is my intention to return to America in the course of the present year. I shall then [do] it by subscription, with historical notes. As this work will employ many persons in different parts of the Union, I will confer with you upon the subject, and such part of it as will suit you to undertake, will be at your choice. I have sustained so much loss, by disinterestedness and inattention to money matters, and by accidents, that I am obliged to look closer to my affairs than I have done. The printer (an Englishman) whom I employed here to print the second part of the Age of Reason made a manuscript copy of the work while he was printing it, which he sent to London and sold. It was by this means that an edition of it came out in London.

" We are waiting here for news from America of the state of the federal elections. You will have heard long before this reaches you that the French government has refused to receive Mr. Pinckney as minister. While Mr. Munroe was minister he had the opportunity of softening matters with this government, for he was in good credit with them tho' they were in high indignation at the infidelity of the Washington Administration. It is time that Mr. Washington retire, for he has played off so much prudent hypocrisy between France and England that neither government believes anything he says.

"Your friend, etc.,

"THOMAS PAINE."

It would appear that Symonds' stolen edition must have got ahead of that sent by Paine to Franklin Bache, for some of its errors continue in all modern American editions to the present day, as well as in those of England. For in England it was only the shilling edition—that revised by Paine—which was suppressed. Symonds, who ministered to the half-crown folk, and who was also publisher of replies to Paine, was left undisturbed about his pirated edition, and the new Society for the suppression of Vice and Immorality fastened on one Thomas Williams, who sold pious tracts, but was also convicted (June 24, 1797) of having sold one copy of the "Age of Reason." Erskine, who had defended Paine at his trial for the "Rights of Man," conducted the prosecution of Williams. He gained the victory from a packed jury, but was not much elated by it, especially after a certain adventure on his way to Lincoln's Inn. He felt his coat clutched and beheld at his feet a woman bathed in tears. She led him into the small bookshop of Thomas Williams, not yet called up for judgment, and there he beheld his victim stitching tracts in a wretched little room, where there were three children, two suffering with small-pox. He saw that it would be ruin and even a sort of murder to take away to prison the husband, who was not a freethinker, and lamented his publication of the book, and a meeting of the Society which had retained him was summoned. There was a full meeting, the Bishop of London (Porteus) in the chair. Erskine reminded them that Wil-

liams was yet to be brought up for sentence, described the
scene he had witnessed, and Williams' penitence, and, as the
book was now suppressed, asked permission to move for a
nominal sentence. Mercy, he urged, was a part of the Christianity they were defending. Not one of the Society took
his side,—not even " philanthropic " Wilberforce—and Erskine threw up his brief. This action of Erskine led the
Judge to give Williams only a year in prison instead of the
three he said had been intended.

While Williams was in prison the orthodox colporteurs
were circulating Erskine's speech on Christianity, but also
an anonymous sermon " On the Existence and Attributes of
the Deity," all of which was from Paine's " Age of Reason,"
except a brief " Address to the Deity " appended. This
picturesque anomaly was repeated in the circulation of
Paine's " Discourse to the Theophilanthropists " (their and the
author's names removed) under the title of " Atheism Refuted." Both of these pamphlets are now before me, and
beside them a London tract of one page just sent for my
spiritual benefit. This is headed " A Word of Caution."
It begins by mentioning the " pernicious doctrines of Paine,"
the first being " that there is NO GOD " (*sic*,) then proceeds
to adduce evidences of divine existence taken from Paine's
works. It should be added that this one dingy page is the
only " survival " of the ancient Paine effigy in the tract form
which I have been able to find in recent years, and to this
no Society or Publisher's name is attached.

The imprisonment of Williams was the beginning of a
thirty years' war for religious liberty in England, in the
course of which occurred many notable events, such as
Eaton receiving homage in his pillory at Charing Cross,
and the whole Carlile family imprisoned,—its head imprisoned more than nine years for publishing the " Age of
Reason." This last victory of persecution was suicidal.
Gentlemen of wealth, not adherents of Paine, helped in
setting Carlile up in business in Fleet Street, where freethinking publications have since been sold without interruption. But though Liberty triumphed in one sense, the " Age

of Reason" remained to some extent suppressed among those whose attention it especially merited. Its original prosecution by a Society for the Suppression of Vice (a device to relieve the Crown) amounted to a libel upon a morally clean book, restricting its perusal in families ; and the fact that the shilling book sold by and among humble people was alone prosecuted, diffused among the educated an equally false notion that the "Age of Reason" was vulgar and illiterate. The theologians, as we have seen, estimated more justly the ability of their antagonist, the *collaborateur* of Franklin, Rittenhouse, and Clymer, on whom the University of Pennsylvania had conferred the degree of Master of Arts,—but the gentry confused Paine with the class described by Burke as "the swinish multitude." Scepticism, or its free utterance, was temporarily driven out of polite circles by its complication with the outlawed vindicator of the "Rights of Man." But that long combat has now passed away. Time has reduced the "Age of Reason" from a flag of popular radicalism to a comparatively conservative treatise, so far as its negations are concerned. An old friend tells me that in his youth he heard a sermon in which the preacher declared that "Tom Paine" was so wicked that he could not be buried ; his bones were thrown into a box which was bandied about the world till it came to a button-manufacturer ; "and now Paine is travelling round the world in the form of buttons!" This variant of the Wandering Jew myth may now be regarded as unconscious homage to the author whose metaphorical bones may be recognized in buttons now fashionable, and some even found useful in holding clerical vestments together.

But the careful reader will find in Paine's "Age of Reason" something beyond negations, and in conclusion I will especially call attention to the new departure in Theism indicated in a passage corresponding to a famous aphorism of Kant, indicated by a note in Part II. The discovery already mentioned, that Part I. was written at least fourteen years before Part II., led me to compare the two ; and it is plain that while the earlier work is an amplification of Newtonian

Deism, based on the phenomena of planetary motion, the work of 1795 bases belief in God on " the universal display of himself in the works of the creation *and by that repugnance we feel in ourselves to bad actions, and disposition to do good ones.*"   This exaltation of the moral nature of man to be the foundation of theistic religion, though now familiar, was a hundred years ago a new affirmation ; it has led on a conception of deity subversive of last-century deism, it has steadily humanized religion, and its ultimate philosophical and ethical results have not yet been reached.

I.

THE AGE OF REASON.

CHAPTER I.

THE AUTHOR'S PROFESSION OF FAITH.

IT has been my intention, for several years past, to publish my thoughts upon religion ; I am well aware of the
difficulties that attend the subject, and from that consideration, had reserved it to a more advanced period of life. I
intended it to be the last offering I should make to my fellow-citizens of all nations, and that at a time when the purity of the motive that induced me to it could not admit of
a question, even by those who might disapprove the work.

The circumstance that has now taken place in France, of
the total abolition of the whole national order of priesthood,
and of everything appertaining to compulsive systems of
religion, and compulsive articles of faith, has not only pre-
cipitated my intention, but rendered a work of this kind
exceedingly necessary, lest, in the general wreck of superstition, of false systems of government, and false theology, we
lose sight of morality, of humanity, and of the theology that
is true.

As several of my colleagues, and others of my fellow-citizens
of France, have given me the example of making their voluntary and individual profession of faith, I also will make mine ;
and I do this with all that sincerity and frankness with which
the mind of man communicates with itself.

I believe in one God, and no more ; and I hope for happiness beyond this life.

I believe the equality of man, and I believe that religious

duties consist in doing justice, loving mercy, and endeavouring to make our fellow-creatures happy.

But, lest it should be supposed that I believe many other
things in addition to these, I shall, in the progress of this
work, declare the things I do not believe, and my reasons for
not believing them.

I do not believe in the creed professed by the Jewish
church, by the Roman church, by the Greek church, by the
Turkish church, by the Protestant church, nor by any church
that I know of.   My own mind is my own church.

All national institutions of churches, whether Jewish,
Christian, or Turkish, appear to me no other than human
inventions set up to terrify and enslave mankind, and mo-
nopolize power and profit.

I do not mean by this declaration to condemn those who
believe otherwise ; they have the same right to their belief
as I have to mine.   But it is necessary to the happiness of
man, that he be mentally faithful to himself.   Infidelity does
not consist in believing, or in disbelieving ; it consists in
professing to believe what he does not believe.

It is impossible to calculate the moral mischief, if I may
so express it, that mental lying has produced in society.
When a man has so far corrupted and prostituted the
chastity of his mind, as to subscribe his professional belief
to things he does not believe, he has prepared himself for
the commission of every other crime.   He takes up the
trade of a priest for the sake of gain, and, in order to qualify
himself for that trade, he begins with a perjury.   Can we
conceive anything more destructive to morality than this?

Soon after I had published the pamphlet COMMON SENSE,
in America, I saw the exceeding probability that a revolution in the system of government would be followed by a
revolution in the system of religion.   The adulterous connection of church and state, wherever it had taken place,
whether Jewish, Christian, or Turkish, had so effectually
prohibited, by pains and penalties, every discussion upon
established creeds, and upon first principles of religion, that
until the system of government should be changed, those

subjects could not be brought fairly and openly before the world ; but that whenever this should be done, a revolution in the system of religion would follow. Human inventions and priest-craft would be detected ; and man would return to the pure, unmixed, and unadulterated belief of one God, and no more.

CHAPTER II.

OF MISSIONS AND REVELATIONS.

EVERY national church or religion has established itself by pretending some special mission from God, communicated to certain individuals. The Jews have their Moses ; the Christians their Jesus Christ, their apostles and saints ; and the Turks their Mahomet ; as if the way to God was not open to every man alike.

Each of those churches shows certain books, which they call *revelation*, or the Word of God. The Jews say that their Word of God was given by God to Moses face to face ; the Christians say, that their Word of God came by divine inspiration ; and the Turks say, that their Word of God (the Koran) was brought by an angel from heaven. Each of those churches accuses the other of unbelief ; and, for my own part, I disbelieve them all.

As it is necessary to affix right ideas to words, I will, before I proceed further into the subject, offer some observations on the word *revelation*. Revelation when applied to religion, means something communicated *immediately* from God to man.

No one will deny or dispute the power of the Almighty to make such a communication if he pleases. But admitting, for the sake of a case, that something has been revealed to a certain person, and not revealed to any other person, it is revelation to that person only. When he tells it to a second person, a second to a third, a third to a fourth, and so on, it ceases to be a revelation to all those persons. It is revelation to the first person only, and *hearsay* to every other, and, consequently, they are not obliged to believe it.

It is a contradiction in terms and ideas to call anything a revelation that comes to us at second hand, either verbally or in writing. Revelation is necessarily limited to the first communication. After this, it is only an account of something which that person says was a revelation made to him; and though he may find himself obliged to believe it, it cannot be incumbent on me to believe it in the same manner, for it was not a revelation made to *me*, and I have only his word for it that it was made to *him*.

When Moses told the children of Israel that he received the two tables of the commandments from the hand of God, they were not obliged to believe him, because they had no other authority for it than his telling them so; and I have no other authority for it than some historian telling me so, the commandments carrying no internal evidence of divinity with them. They contain some good moral precepts such as any man qualified to be a lawgiver or a legislator could produce himself, without having recourse to supernatural intervention.*

When I am told that the Koran was written in Heaven, and brought to Mahomet by an angel, the account comes to near the same kind of hearsay evidence and second hand authority as the former. I did not see the angel myself, and therefore I have a right not to believe it.

When also I am told that a woman, called the Virgin Mary, said, or gave out, that she was with child without any cohabitation with a man, and that her betrothed husband, Joseph, said that an angel told him so, I have a right to believe them or not: such a circumstance required a much stronger evidence than their bare word for it: but we have not even this; for neither Joseph nor Mary wrote any such matter themselves. It is only reported by others that *they said so.* It is hearsay upon hearsay, and I do not chuse to rest my belief upon such evidence.

It is, however, not difficult to account for the credit that

---

* It is, however, necessary to except the declaration which says that God *visits the sins of the fathers upon the children.* This is contrary to every principle of moral justice.—*Author.*

was given to the story of Jesus Christ being the Son of God. He was born when the heathen mythology had still some fashion and repute in the world, and that mythology had prepared the people for the belief of such a story. Almost all the extraordinary men that lived under the heathen mythology were reputed to be the sons of some of their gods. It was not a new thing at that time to believe a man to have been celestially begotten ; the intercourse of gods with women was then a matter of familiar opinion. Their Jupiter, according to their accounts, had cohabited with hundreds; the story therefore had nothing in it either new, wonderful, or obscene ; it was conformable to the opinions that then prevailed among the people called Gentiles, or mythologists, and it was those people only that believed it. The Jews, who had kept strictly to the belief of one God, and no more, and who had always rejected the heathen mythology, never credited the story.

It is curious to observe how the theory of what is called the Christian Church, sprung out of the tail of the heathen mythology. A direct incorporation took place in the first instance, by making the reputed founder to be celestially begotten. The trinity of gods that then followed was no other than a reduction of the former plurality, which was about twenty or thirty thousand. The statue of Mary succeeded the statue of Diana of Ephesus. The deification of heroes changed into the canonization of saints. The Mythologists had gods for everything; the Christian Mythologists had saints for everything. The church became as crouded with the one, as the pantheon had been with the other ; and Rome was the place of both. The Christian theory is little else than the idolatry of the ancient mythologists, accommodated to the purposes of power and revenue ; and it yet remains to reason and philosophy to abolish the amphibious fraud.

CHAPTER III.

CONCERNING THE CHARACTER OF JESUS CHRIST, AND HIS HISTORY.

NOTHING that is here said can apply, even with the most distant disrespect, to the *real* character of Jesus Christ. He was a virtuous and an amiable man. The morality that he preached and practised was of the most benevolent kind; and though similar systems of morality had been preached by Confucius, and by some of the Greek philosophers, many years before, by the Quakers since, and by many good men in all ages, it has not been exceeded by any.

Jesus Christ wrote no account of himself, of his birth, parentage, or anything else. Not a line of what is called the New Testament is of his writing. The history of him is altogether the work of other people; and as to the account given of his resurrection and ascension, it was the necessary counterpart to the story of his birth. His historians, having brought him into the world in a supernatural manner, were obliged to take him out again in the same manner, or the first part of the story must have fallen to the ground.

The wretched contrivance with which this latter part is told, exceeds everything that went before it. The first part, that of the miraculous conception, was not a thing that admitted of publicity; and therefore the tellers of this part of the story had this advantage, that though they might not be credited, they could not be detected. They could not be expected to prove it, because it was not one of those things that admitted of proof, and it was impossible that the person of whom it was told could prove it himself.

But the resurrection of a dead person from the grave, and his ascension through the air, is a thing very different, as to the evidence it admits of, to the invisible conception of a child in the womb. The resurrection and ascension, supposing them to have taken place, admitted of public and ocular demonstration, like that of the ascension of a balloon, or the sun at noon day, to all Jerusalem at least. A thing which everybody is required to believe, requires that the proof and evidence of it should be equal to all, and universal , and as the public visibility of this last related act was the only evidence that could give sanction to the former part, the whole of it falls to the ground, because that evidence never was given. Instead of this, a small number of persons, not more than eight or nine, are introduced as proxies for the whole world, to say they saw it, and all the rest of the world are called upon to believe it. But it appears that Thomas did not believe the resurrection ; and, as they say, would not believe without having ocular and manual demonstration himself. *So neither will I ;* and the reason is equally as good for me, and for every other person, as for Thomas.

It is in vain to attempt to palliate or disguise this matter. The story, so far as relates to the supernatural part, has every mark of fraud and imposition stamped upon the face of it. Who were the authors of it is as impossible for us now to know, as it is for us to be assured that the books in which the account is related were written by the persons whose names they bear. The best surviving evidence we now have respecting this affair is the Jews. They are regularly descended from the people who lived in the time this resurrection and ascension is said to have happened, and they say, *it is not true.* It has long appeared to me a strange inconsistency to cite the Jews as a proof of the truth of the story. It is just the same as if a man were to say, I will prove the truth of what I have told you, by producing the people who say it is false.

That such a person as Jesus Christ existed, and that he was crucified, which was the mode of execution at that day, are historical relations strictly within the limits of probability. He preached most excellent morality, and the equality of man ; but he preached also against the corruptions and avarice of the Jewish priests, and this brought upon him the hatred and vengeance of the whole order of priesthood. The accusation which those priests brought against

him was that of sedition and conspiracy against the Roman
government, to which the Jews were then subject and tribu-
tary ; and it is not improbable that the Roman government
might have some secret apprehension of the effects of his
doctrine as well as the Jewish priests ; neither is it improbable that Jesus Christ had in contemplation the delivery of
the Jewish nation from the bondage of the Romans.   Between the two, however, this virtuous reformer and revolutionist lost his life.[1]

CHAPTER IV.

OF THE BASES OF CHRISTIANITY.

IT is upon this plain narrative of facts, together with
another case I am going to mention, that the Christian mythologists, calling themselves the Christian Church, have
erected their fable, which for absurdity and extravagance is
not exceeded by anything that is to be found in the mythology of the ancients.

The ancient mythologists tell us that the race of Giants
made war against Jupiter, and that one of them threw a
hundred rocks against him at one throw ; that Jupiter defeated him with thunder, and confined him afterwards under
Mount Etna ; and that every time the Giant turns himself,
Mount Etna belches fire.   It is here easy to see that the
circumstance of the mountain, that of its being a volcano,
suggested the idea of the fable ; and that the fable is made
to fit and wind itself up with that circumstance.

The Christian mythologists tell that their Satan made
war against the Almighty, who defeated him, and confined
him afterwards, not under a mountain, but in a pit.   It is
here easy to see that the first fable suggested the idea of the

---

[1] The French work has here : " Quoi qu'il en soit, ce verteux réformateur,
ce révolutionnaire trop peu imité, trop oublié, trop méconnu, perdit la vie pour
l'une ou pour l'autre de ces suppositions."   However this may be, for one or
the other of these suppositions this virtuous reformer, this revolutionist, too
little imitated, too much forgotten, too much misunderstood, lost his life.—*Editor.*

second ; for the fable of Jupiter and the Giants was told many hundred years before that of Satan.

Thus far the ancient and the Christian mythologists differ very little from each other. But the latter have contrived to carry the matter much farther. They have contrived to connect the fabulous part of the story of Jesus Christ with the fable originating from Mount Etna; and, in order to make all the parts of the story tye together, they have taken to their aid the traditions of the Jews ; for the Christian mythology is made up partly from the ancient mythology, and partly from the Jewish traditions.

The Christian mythologists, after having confined Satan in a pit, were obliged to let him out again to bring on the sequel of the fable. He is then introduced into the garden of Eden in the shape of a snake, or a serpent, and in that shape he enters into familiar conversation with Eve, who is no ways surprised to hear a snake talk ; and the issue of this tête-à-tête is, that he persuades her to eat an apple, and the eating of that apple damns all mankind.

After giving Satan this triumph over the whole creation, one would have supposed that the church mythologists would have been kind enough to send him back again to the pit, or, if they had not done this, that they would have put a mountain upon him, (for they say that their faith can remove a mountain) or have put him under a mountain, as the former mythologists had done, to prevent his getting again among the women, and doing more mischief. But instead of this, they leave him at large, without even obliging him to give his parole. The secret of which is, that they could not do without him ; and after being at the trouble of making him, they bribed him to stay. They promised him ALL the Jews, ALL the Turks by anticipation, nine-tenths of the world beside, and Mahomet into the bargain. After this, who can doubt the bountifulness of the Christian Mythology ?

Having thus made an insurrection and a battle in heaven, in which none of the combatants could be either killed or wounded—put Satan into the pit—let him out again—given him a triumph over the whole creation—damned all mankind by the eating of an apple, these Christian mythologists bring the two ends of their fable together. They represent this virtuous and amiable man, Jesus Christ, to be at once both God and man, and also the Son of God, celestially begotten, on purpose to be sacrificed, because they say that Eve in her longing[1] had eaten an apple.

CHAPTER V.

EXAMINATION IN DETAIL OF THE PRECEDING BASES.

PUTTING aside everything that might excite laughter by its absurdity, or detestation by its prophaneness, and confining ourselves merely to an examination of the parts, it is impossible to conceive a story more derogatory to the Almighty, more inconsistent with his wisdom, more contradictory to his power, than this story is.

In order to make for it a foundation to rise upon, the inventors were under the necessity of giving to the being whom they call Satan a power equally as great, if not greater, than they attribute to the Almighty. They have not only given him the power of liberating himself from the pit, after what they call his fall, but they have made that power increase afterwards to infinity. Before this fall they represent him only as an angel of limited existence, as they represent the rest. After his fall, he becomes, by their account, omnipresent. He exists everywhere, and at the same time. He occupies the whole immensity of space.

Not content with this deification of Satan, they represent him as defeating by stratagem, in the shape of an animal of the creation, all the power and wisdom of the Almighty. They represent him as having compelled the Almighty to the *direct necessity* either of surrendering the whole of the creation to the government and sovereignty of this Satan, or of capitulating for its redemption by coming down upon earth, and exhibiting himself upon a cross in the shape of a man.

---

[1] The French work has : " cédant à une gourmandise effrénée " (yielding to an unrestrained appetite).—*Editor.*

Had the inventors of this story told it the contrary way, that is, had they represented the Almighty as compelling Satan to exhibit *himself* on a cross in the shape of a snake, as a punishment for his new transgression, the story would have been less absurd, less contradictory. But, instead of this they make the transgressor triumph, and the Almighty fall.

That many good men have believed this strange fable, and lived very good lives under that belief (for credulity is not a crime) is what I have no doubt of. In the first place, they were educated to believe it, and they would have believed anything else in the same manner. There are also many who have been so enthusiastically enraptured by what they conceived to be the infinite love of God to man, in making a sacrifice of himself, that the vehemence of the idea has forbidden and deterred them from examining into the absurdity and profaneness of the story. The more unnatural anything is, the more is it capable of becoming the object of dismal admiration.[1]

CHAPTER VI.

OF THE TRUE THEOLOGY.

BUT if objects for gratitude and admiration are our desire, do they not present themselves every hour to our eyes? Do we not see a fair creation prepared to receive us the instant we are born—a world furnished to our hands, that cost us nothing? Is it we that light up the sun; that pour down the rain; and fill the earth with abundance? Whether we sleep or wake, the vast machinery of the universe still goes on. Are these things, and the blessings they indicate in future, nothing to us? Can our gross feelings be excited by no other subjects than tragedy and suicide? Or is the gloomy pride of man become so intolerable, that nothing can flatter it but a sacrifice of the Creator?

[1] The French work has "aveugle et" (blind and) preceding "dismal."—*Editor.*

I know that this bold investigation will alarm many, but it would be paying too great a compliment to their credulity to forbear it on that account. The times and the subject demand it to be done. The suspicion that the theory of what is called the Christian church is fabulous, is becoming very extensive in all countries; and it will be a consolation to men staggering under that suspicion, and doubting what to believe and what to disbelieve, to see the subject freely investigated. I therefore pass on to an examination of the books called the Old and the New Testament.

CHAPTER VII.

EXAMINATION OF THE OLD TESTAMENT.

THESE books, beginning with Genesis and ending with Revelations, (which, by the bye, is a book of riddles that requires a revelation to explain it) are, we are told, the word of God. It is, therefore, proper for us to know who told us so, that we may know what credit to give to the report. The answer to this question is, that nobody can tell, except that we tell one another so. The case, however, historically appears to be as follows :

When the church mythologists established their system, they collected all the writings they could find, and managed them as they pleased. It is a matter altogether of uncertainty to us whether such of the writings as now appear under the name of the Old and the New Testament, are in the same state in which those collectors say they found them ; or whether they added, altered, abridged, or dressed them up.

Be this as it may, they decided by *vote* which of the books out of the collection they had made, should be the WORD OF GOD, and which should not. They rejected several; they voted others to be doubtful, such as the books called the Apocrypha; and those books which had a majority of votes, were voted to be the word of God. Had they voted otherwise, all the people since calling themselves Christians had believed otherwise; for the belief of the one comes from the vote of the other. Who the people were that did all this, we know nothing of. They call themselves by the general name of the Church; and this is all we know of the matter.

As we have no other external evidence or authority for believing these books to be the word of God, than what I have mentioned, which is no evidence or authority at all, I come, in the next place, to examine the internal evidence contained in the books themselves.

In the former part of this essay, I have spoken of revelation. I now proceed further with that subject, for the purpose of applying it to the books in question.

Revelation is a communication of something, which the person, to whom that thing is revealed, did not know before. For if I have done a thing, or seen it done, it needs no revelation to tell me I have done it, or seen it, nor to enable me to tell it, or to write it.

Revelation, therefore, cannot be applied to anything done upon earth of which man is himself the actor or the witness; and consequently all the historical and anecdotal part of the Bible, which is almost the whole of it, is not within the meaning and compass of the word revelation, and, therefore, is not the word of God.

When Samson ran off with the gate-posts of Gaza, if he ever did so, (and whether he did or not is nothing to us,) or when he visited his Delilah, or caught his foxes, or did anything else,[1] what has revelation to do with these things? If they were facts, he could tell them himself; or his secretary, if he kept one, could write them, if they were worth either telling or writing; and if they were fictions, revelation could not make them true; and whether true or not, we are neither the better nor the wiser for knowing them.—When we contemplate the immensity of that Being, who directs and governs the incomprehensible WHOLE, of which the utmost ken of human sight can discover but a part, we ought to feel shame at calling such paltry stories the word of God.

As to the account of the creation, with which the **book**

---

[1] The French work has " frédaine " (prank).—*Editor.*

3

of Genesis opens, it has all the appearance of being a tradition which the Israelites had among them before they came
into Egypt; and after their departure from that country,
they put it at the head of their history, without telling, as it
is most probable that they did not know, how they came by
it. The manner in which the account opens, shews it to be
traditionary. It begins abruptly. It is nobody that speaks.
It is nobody that hears. It is addressed to nobody. It has
neither first, second, nor third person. It has every criterion of being a tradition. It has no voucher. Moses does
not take it upon himself by introducing it with the formality
that he uses on other occasions, such as that of saying, " *The
Lord spake unto Moses, saying.*"

Why it has been called the Mosaic account of the creation, I am at a loss to conceive. ✓Moses, I believe, was too
good a judge of such subjects to put his name to that account. He had been educated among the Egyptians, who
were a people as well skilled in science, and particularly in
astronomy, as any people of their day ; and the silence and
caution that Moses observes, in not authenticating the
account, is a good negative evidence that he neither told it
nor believed it.—The case is, that every nation of people
has been world-makers, and the Israelites had as much right
to set up the trade of world-making as any of the rest ; and
as Moses was not an Israelite, he might not chuse to contradict the tradition. The account, however, is harmless;
and this is more than can be said for many other parts of the
Bible.

Whenever we read the obscene stories, the voluptuous
debaucheries, the cruel and torturous executions, the unrelenting vindictiveness, with which more than half the Bible[1]
is filled, it would be more consistent that we called it the
word of a demon, than the Word of God. It is a history of
wickedness, that has served to corrupt and brutalize mankind ; and, for my own part, I sincerely detest it, as I detest
everything that is cruel.

[1] It must be borne in mind that by the " Bible " Paine always means the Old
Testament alone.—*Editor.*

We scarcely meet with anything, a few phrases excepted, but what deserves either our abhorrence or our contempt, till we come to the miscellaneous parts of the Bible. In the anonymous publications, the Psalms, and the Book of Job, more particularly in the latter, we find a great deal of elevated sentiment reverentially expressed of the power and benignity of the Almighty; but they stand on no higher rank than many other compositions on similar subjects, as well before that time as since.

The Proverbs which are said to be Solomon's, though most probably a collection, (because they discover a knowledge of life, which his situation excluded him from knowing) are an instructive table of ethics. They are inferior in keenness to the proverbs of the Spaniards, and not more wise and œconomical than those of the American Franklin.

All the remaining parts of the Bible, generally known by the name of the Prophets, are the works of the Jewish poets and itinerant preachers, who mixed poetry, anecdote, and devotion together—and those works still retain the air and stile of poetry, though in translation.*

There is not, throughout the whole book called the Bible, any word that describes to us what we call a poet, nor any

---

* As there are many readers who do not see that a composition is poetry, unless it be in rhyme, it is for their information that I add this note.

Poetry consists principally in two things—imagery and composition. The composition of poetry differs from that of prose in the manner of mixing long and short syllables together. Take a long syllable out of a line of poetry, and put a short one in the room of it, or put a long syllable where a short one should be, and that line will lose its poetical harmony. It will have an effect upon the line like that of misplacing a note in a song.

The imagery in those books called the Prophets appertains altogether to poetry. It is fictitious, and often extravagant, and not admissible in any other kind of writing than poetry.

To shew that these writings are composed in poetical numbers, I will take ten syllables, as they stand in the book, and make a line of the same number of syllables, (heroic measure) that shall rhyme with the last word. It will then be seen that the composition of those books is poetical measure. The instance I shall first produce is from Isaiah :—

> " *Hear, O ye heavens, and give ear, O earth !* "
> 'T is God himself that calls attention forth.

Another instance I shall quote is from the mournful Jeremiah, to which I

word that describes what we call poetry. The case is, that the word *prophet*, to which later times have affixed a new idea, was the Bible word for poet, and the word *prophesying* meant the art of making poetry. It also meant the art of playing poetry to a tune upon any instrument of music.

We read of prophesying with pipes, tabrets, and horns— of prophesying with harps, with psalteries, with cymbals, and with every other instrument of music then in fashion.[1] Were we now to speak of prophesying with a fiddle, or with a pipe and tabor, the expression would have no meaning, or would appear ridiculous, and to some people contemptuous, because we have changed the meaning of the word.

We are told of Saul being among the prophets, and also that he prophesied; but we are not told what they prophesied, nor what he prophesied. The case is, there was nothing to tell; for these prophets were a company of musicians and poets, and Saul joined in the concert, and this was called prophesying.

The account given of this affair in the book called Samuel, is, that Saul met a company of prophets; a whole company of them ! coming down with a psaltery, a tabret, a pipe, and a harp, and that they prophesied, and that he prophesied with them. But it appears afterwards, that Saul prophesied badly, that is, he performed his part badly; for it is said that an "*evil spirit from God** came upon Saul, and he prophesied."[2]

shall add two other lines, for the purpose of carrying out the figure, and shewing the intention of the poet.

> " *O, that mine head were waters and mine eyes* "
> Were fountains flowing like the liquid skies ;
> Then would I give the mighty flood release
> And weep a deluge for the human race.—*Author.*

[This footnote is not included in the French work.]—*Editor.*

* As those men who call themselves divines and commentators are very fond of puzzling one another, I leave them to contest the meaning of the first part of the phrase, that of *an evil spirit of God.* I keep to my text. I keep to the meaning of the word prophesy.—*Author.*

[1] 1 Chron. xxv., 1.—*Editor.*   [2] 1 Sam. xviii., 10.—*Editor.*

Now, were there no other passage in the book called the Bible, than this, to demonstrate to us that we have lost the original meaning of the word *prophesy*, and substituted another meaning in its place, this alone would be sufficient; for it is impossible to use and apply the word *prophesy*, in the place it is here used and applied, if we give to it the sense which later times have affixed to it. The manner in which it is here used strips it of all religious meaning, and shews that a man might then be a prophet, or he might *prophesy*, as he may now be a poet or a musician, without any regard to the morality or the immorality of his character. The word was originally a term of science, promiscuously applied to poetry and to music, and not restricted to any subject upon which poetry and music might be exercised.

Deborah and Barak are called prophets, not because they predicted anything, but because they composed the poem or song that bears their name, in celebration of an act already done. David is ranked among the prophets, for he was a musician, and was also reputed to be (though perhaps very erroneously) the author of the Psalms. But Abraham, Isaac, and Jacob are not called prophets; it does not appear from any accounts we have, that they could either sing, play music, or make poetry.

We are told of the greater and the lesser prophets. They might as well tell us of the greater and the lesser God; for there cannot be degrees in prophesying consistently with its modern sense. But there are degrees in poetry, and therefore the phrase is reconcilable to the case, when we understand by it the greater and the lesser poets.

It is altogether unnecessary, after this, to offer any observations upon what those men, stiled prophets, have written. The axe goes at once to the root, by shewing that the original meaning of the word has been mistaken, and consequently all the inferences that have been drawn from those books, the devotional respect that has been paid to them, and the laboured commentaries that have been written upon them, under that mistaken meaning, are not worth disputing about. —In many things, however, the writings of the Jewish poets deserve a better fate than that of being bound up, as they now are, with the trash that accompanies them, under the abused name of the Word of God.

If we permit ourselves to conceive right ideas of things, we must necessarily affix the idea, not only of unchangeableness, but of the utter impossibility of any change taking place, by any means or accident whatever, in that which we would honour with the name of the Word of God; and therefore the Word of God cannot exist in any written or human language.

The continually progressive change to which the meaning of words is subject, the want of an universal language which renders translation necessary, the errors to which translations are again subject, the mistakes of copyists and printers, together with the possibility of wilful alteration, are of themselves evidences that human language, whether in speech or in print, cannot be the vehicle of the Word of God.—The Word of God exists in something else.[1]

Did the book called the Bible excel in purity of ideas and expression all the books now extant in the world, I would not take it for my rule of faith, as being the Word of God; because the possibility would nevertheless exist of my being imposed upon. But when I see throughout the greatest part of this book scarcely anything but a history of the grossest vices, and a collection of the most paltry and contemptible tales, I cannot dishonour my Creator by calling it by his name.

CHAPTER VIII.

OF THE NEW TESTAMENT.

THUS much for the Bible; I now go on to the book called the New Testament. The *new* Testament! that is, the *new* Will, as if there could be two wills of the Creator.

Had it been the object or the intention of Jesus Christ to establish a new religion, he would undoubtedly have written

---

[1] This paragraph is not in the French work.—*Editor.*

the system himself, or *procured it to be written* in his life time. But there is no publication extant authenticated with his name. All the books called the New Testament were written after his death. He was a Jew by birth and by profession; and he was the son of God in like manner that every other person is; for the Creator is the Father of All.

The first four books, called Matthew, Mark, Luke, and John, do not give a history of the life of Jesus Christ, but only detached anecdotes of him. It appears from these books, that the whole time of his being a preacher was not more than eighteen months; and it was only during this short time that those men became acquainted with him. They make mention of him at the age of twelve years, sitting, they say, among the Jewish doctors, asking and answering them questions. As this was several years before their acquaintance with him began, it is most probable they had this anecdote from his parents. From this time there is no account of him for about sixteen years.[1] Where he lived, or how he employed himself during this interval, is not known. Most probably he was working at his father's trade, which was that of a carpenter.[2] It does not appear that he had any school education, and the probability is, that he could not write, for his parents were extremely poor, as appears from their not being able to pay for a bed when he was born.[3]

It is somewhat curious that the three persons whose names are the most universally recorded were of very obscure parentage. Moses was a foundling; Jesus Christ was born in a stable; and Mahomet was a mule driver. The first and the last of these men were founders of different systems of religion; but Jesus Christ founded no new sys-

---

[1] " A man named Jesus, and he about thirty years, chose us out."—*Gospel according to the Hebrews.—Editor.*

[2] τέκτων, a skilled worker in wood, stone, or iron; a builder; not necessarily a carpenter—*Editor.*

[3] One of the few errors traceable to Paine's not having a Bible at hand while writing Part I. There is no indication that the family was poor, but the reverse may in fact be inferred.—*Editor.*

tem. He called men to the practice of moral virtues, and the belief of one God. The great trait in his character is philanthropy.

The manner in which he was apprehended shews that he was not much known at that time ; and it shews also that the meetings he then held with his followers were in secret ; and that he had given over or suspended preaching publicly. Judas could no otherways betray him than by giving information where he was, and pointing him out to the officers that went to arrest him ; and the reason for employing and paying Judas to do this could arise only from the causes already mentioned, that of his not being much known, and living concealed.

The idea of his concealment, not only agrees very ill with his reputed divinity, but associates with it something of pusillanimity ; and his being betrayed, or in other words, his being apprehended, on the information of one of his followers, shews that he did not intend to be apprehended, and consequently that he did not intend to be crucified.

The Christian mythologists tell us that Christ died for the sins of the world, and that he came on *purpose to die.* Would it not then have been the same if he had died of a fever or of the small pox, of old age, or of anything else?

The declaratory sentence which, they say, was passed upon Adam, in case he ate of the apple, was not, that *thou shalt surely be crucified*, but, *thou shalt surely die*. The sentence was death, and not the *manner of dying*. Crucifixion, therefore, or any other particular manner of dying, made no part of the sentence that Adam was to suffer, and consequently, even upon their own tactic, it could make no part of the sentence that Christ was to suffer in the room of Adam. A fever would have done as well as a cross, if there was any occasion for either.

This sentence of death, which, they tell us, was thus passed upon Adam, must either have meant dying naturally, that is, ceasing to live, or have meant what these mythologists call damnation ; and consequently, the act of dying on the part of Jesus Christ, must, according to their system, apply as a prevention to one or other of these two *things* happening to Adam and to us.

That it does not prevent our dying is evident, because we all die; and if their accounts of longevity be true, men die faster since the crucifixion than before: and with respect to the second explanation, (including with it the *natural death* of Jesus Christ as a substitute for the *eternal death or damnation* of all mankind,) it is impertinently representing the Creator as coming off, or revoking the sentence, by a pun or a quibble upon the word *death.* That manufacturer of quibbles, St. Paul, if he wrote the books that bear his name, has helped this quibble on by making another quibble upon the word *Adam.* He makes there to be two Adams; the one who sins in fact, and suffers by proxy; the other who sins by proxy, and suffers in fact. A religion thus interlarded with quibble, subterfuge, and pun, has a tendency to instruct its professors in the practice of these arts. They acquire the habit without being aware of the cause.

If Jesus Christ was the being which those mythologists tell us he was, and that he came into this world to *suffer*, which is a word they sometimes use instead of *to die*, the only real suffering he could have endured would have been *to live.* His existence here was a state of exilement or transportation from heaven, and the way back to his original country was to die.—In fine, everything in this strange system is the reverse of what it pretends to be. It is the reverse of truth, and I become so tired of examining into its inconsistencies and absurdities, that I hasten to the conclusion of it, in order to proceed to something better.

How much, or what parts of the books called the New Testament, were written by the persons whose names they bear, is what we can know nothing of, neither are we certain in what language they were originally written. The matters they now contain may be classed under two heads: anecdote, and epistolary correspondence.

The four books already mentioned, Matthew, Mark, Luke, and John, are altogether anecdotal. They relate events after they had taken place. They tell what Jesus Christ

did and said, and what others did and said to him ; and in
several instances they relate the same event differently.
Revelation is necessarily out of the question with respect
to those books; not only because of the disagreement of the
writers, but because revelation cannot be applied to the
relating of facts by the persons who saw them done, nor to
the relating or recording of any discourse or conversation
by those who heard it. The book called the Acts of the
Apostles (an anonymous work) belongs also to the anecdotal
part.

All the other parts of the New Testament, except the
book of enigmas, called the Revelations, are a collection of
letters under the name of epistles ; and the forgery of letters
has been such a common practice in the world, that the probability is at least equal, whether they are genuine or forged.
One thing, however, is much less equivocal, which is, that
out of the matters contained in those books, together with
the assistance of some old stories, the church has set up a
system of religion very contradictory to the character of the
person whose name it bears. It has set up a religion of
pomp and of revenue in pretended imitation of a person
whose life was humility and poverty.

The invention of a purgatory, and of the releasing of souls
therefrom, by prayers, bought of the church with money;
the selling of pardons, dispensations, and indulgences, are
revenue laws, without bearing that name or carrying that
appearance. But the case nevertheless is, that those things
derive their origin from the proxysm of the crucifixion, and
the theory deduced therefrom, which was, that one person
could stand in the place of another, and could perform
meritorious services for him. The probability, therefore, is,
that the whole theory or doctrine of what is called the
redemption (which is said to have been accomplished by the
act of one person in the room of another) was originally
fabricated on purpose to bring forward and build all those
secondary and pecuniary redemptions upon ; and that the
passages in the books upon which the idea of theory of
redemption is built, have been manufactured and fabricated

for that purpose. Why are we to give this church credit, when she tells us that those books are genuine in every part, any more than we give her credit for everything else she has told us; or for the miracles she says she has performed? That she *could* fabricate writings is certain, because she could write; and the composition of the writings in question, is of that kind that anybody might do it; and that she *did* fabricate them is not more inconsistent with probability, than that she should tell us, as she has done, that she could and did work miracles.

Since, then, no external evidence can, at this long distance of time, be produced to prove whether the church fabricated the doctrine called redemption or not, (for such evidence, whether for or against, would be subject to the same suspicion of being fabricated,) the case can only be referred to the internal evidence which the thing carries of itself; and this affords a very strong presumption of its being a fabrication. For the internal evidence is, that the theory or doctrine of redemption has for its basis an idea of pecuniary justice, and not that of moral justice.

If I owe a person money, and cannot pay him, and he threatens to put me in prison, another person can take the debt upon himself, and pay it for me. But if I have committed a crime, every circumstance of the case is changed. Moral justice cannot take the innocent for the guilty even if the innocent would offer itself. To suppose justice to do this, is to destroy the principle of its existence, which is the thing itself. It is then no longer justice. It is indiscriminate revenge.

This single reflection will shew that the doctrine of redemption is founded on a mere pecuniary idea corresponding to that of a debt which another person might pay; and as this pecuniary idea corresponds again with the system of second redemptions, obtained through the means of money given to the church for pardons, the probability is that the same persons fabricated both the one and the other of those theories; and that, in truth, there is no such thing as redemption; that it is fabulous; and that man stands in the same relative condition with his Maker he ever did stand, since man existed ; and that it is his greatest consolation to think so.

Let him believe this, and he will live more consistently and morally, than by any other system. It is by his being taught to contemplate himself as an out-law, as an out-cast, as a beggar, as a mumper, as one thrown as it were on a dunghill, at an immense distance from his Creator, and who must make his approaches by creeping, and cringing to intermediate beings, that he conceives either a contemptuous disregard for everything under the name of religion, or becomes indifferent, or turns what he calls devout. In the latter case, he consumes his life in grief, or the affectation of it. His prayers are reproaches. His humility is ingratitude. He calls himself a worm, and the fertile earth a dunghill; and all the blessings of life by the thankless name of vanities. He despises the choicest gift of God to man, the GIFT OF REASON; and having endeavoured to force upon himself the belief of a system against which reason revolts, he ungratefully calls it *human reason*, as if man could give reason to himself.

Yet, with all this strange appearance of humility, and this contempt for human reason, he ventures into the boldest presumptions. He finds fault with everything. His selfishness is never satisfied ; his ingratitude is never at an end. He takes on himself to direct the Almighty what to do, even in the government of the universe. He prays dictatorially. When it is sunshine, he prays for rain, and when it is rain, he prays for sunshine. He follows the same idea in everything that he prays for ; for what is the amount of all his prayers, but an attempt to make the Almighty change his mind, and act otherwise than he does? It is as if he were to say—thou knowest not so well as I.

CHAPTER IX.

IN WHAT THE TRUE REVELATION CONSISTS.

BUT some perhaps will say—Are we to have no word of God—no revelation?[1] I answer yes. There is a Word of God; there is a revelation.

THE WORD OF GOD IS THE CREATION WE BEHOLD : And it is in *this word,* which no human invention can counterfeit or alter, that God speaketh universally to man.

Human language is local and changeable, and is therefore incapable of being used as the means of unchangeable and universal information. The idea that God sent Jesus Christ to publish, as they say, the glad tidings to all nations, from one end of the earth unto the other, is consistent only with the ignorance of those who know nothing·of the extent of the world, and who believed, as those world-saviours believed, and continued to believe for several centuries, (and that in contradiction to the discoveries of philosophers and the experience of navigators,) that the earth was flat like a trencher; and that a man might walk to the end of it.

But how was Jesus Christ to make anything known to all nations? He could speak but one language, which was Hebrew; and there are in the world several hundred languages. Scarcely any two nations speak the same language, or understand each other; and as to translations, every man who knows anything of languages, knows that it is impossible to translate from one language into another, not only without losing a great part of the original, but frequently of mistaking the sense; and besides all this, the art of printing was wholly unknown at the time Christ lived.

It is always necessary that the means that are to accomplish any end be equal to the accomplishment of that end, or the end cannot be accomplished. It is in this that the difference between finite and infinite power and wisdom discovers

[1] French : " Je réponds hardiment que nous ne sommes point condamnés à ce malheur." (I boldly answer that we are not condemned to this misfortune.)— *Editor.*

itself.   Man frequently fails in accomplishing his end, from a natural inability of the power to the purpose ; and frequently from the want of wisdom to apply power properly.   But it is impossible for infinite power and wisdom to fail as man faileth.   The means it useth are always equal to the end : but human language, more especially as there is not an universal language, is incapable of being used as an universal means of unchangeable and uniform information ; and therefore it is not the means that God useth in manifesting himself universally to man.

It is only in the CREATION that all our ideas and conceptions of a *word of God* can unite.   The Creation speaketh an universal language, independently of human speech or human language, multiplied and various as they be.   It is an ever existing original, which every man can read.   It cannot be forged ; it cannot be counterfeited ; it cannot be lost ; it cannot be altered ; it cannot be suppressed.   It does not depend upon the will of man whether it shall be published or not ; it publishes itself from one end of the earth to the other.   It preaches to all nations and to all worlds ; and this *word of God* reveals to man all that is necessary for man to know of God.

Do we want to contemplate his power ?   We see it in the immensity of the creation.   Do we want to contemplate his wisdom ?   We see it in the unchangeable order by which the incomprehensible Whole is governed.   Do we want to contemplate his munificence ?   We see it in the abundance with which he fills the earth.   Do we want to contemplate his mercy ?   We see it in his not withholding that abundance even from the unthankful.   In fine, do we want to know what God is ?   Search not the book called the scripture, which any human hand might make, but the scripture called the Creation.

CHAPTER X.

CONCERNING GOD, AND THE LIGHTS CAST ON HIS EXIST-
ENCE AND ATTRIBUTES BY THE BIBLE.

THE only idea man can affix to the name of God, is that
of a *first cause*, the cause of all things. And, incomprehen-
sibly difficult as it is for a man to conceive what a first
cause is, he arrives at the belief of it, from the tenfold
greater difficulty of disbelieving it. It is difficult beyond
description to conceive that space can have no end ; but it
is more difficult to conceive an end. It is difficult beyond
the power of man to conceive an eternal duration of what
we call time ; but it is more impossible to conceive a time
when there shall be no time.

In like manner of reasoning, everything we behold
carries in itself the internal evidence that it did not make
itself. Every man is an evidence to himself, that he did not
make himself ; neither could his father make himself, nor his
grandfather, nor any of his race ; neither could any tree,
plant, or animal make itself ; and it is the conviction arising
from this evidence, that carries us on, as it were, by necessity, to the belief of a first cause eternally existing, of a
nature totally different to any material existence we know
of, and by the power of which all things exist ; and this
first cause, man calls God.

It is only by the exercise of reason, that man can discover God. Take away that reason, and he would be incapable of understanding anything ; and in this case it
would be just as consistent to read even the book called the
Bible to a horse as to a man. How then is it that those
people pretend to reject reason ?

Almost the only parts in the book called the Bible, that
convey to us any idea of God, are some chapters in Job,
and the 19th Psalm ; I recollect no other. Those parts are
true *deistical* compositions ; for they treat of the *Deity*
through his works. They take the book of Creation
as the word of God ; they refer to no other book ;

and all the inferences they make are drawn from that volume.

I insert in this place the 19th Psalm, as paraphrased into English verse by Addison. I recollect not the prose, and where I write this I have not the opportunity of seeing it.

> The spacious firmament on high,
> With all the blue etherial sky,
> And spangled heavens, a shining frame,
> Their great original proclaim.
> The unwearied sun, from day to day,
> Does his Creator's power display,
> And publishes to every land
> The work of an Almighty hand.
> Soon as the evening shades prevail,
> The moon takes up the wondrous tale,
> And nightly to the list'ning earth
> Repeats the story of her birth ;
> Whilst all the stars that round her burn,
> And all the planets, in their turn,
> Confirm the tidings as they roll,
> And spread the truth from pole to pole.
> What though in solemn silence all
> Move round this dark terrestrial ball ;
> What though no real voice, nor sound,
> Amidst their radiant orbs be found,
> In reason's ear they all rejoice,
> And utter forth a glorious voice,
> Forever singing as they shine,
> THE HAND THAT MADE US IS DIVINE.[1]

What more does man want to know, than that the hand or power that made these things is divine, is omnipotent? Let him believe this, with the force it is impossible to repel if he permits his reason to act, and his rule of moral life will follow of course.

The allusions in Job have all of them the same tendency with this Psalm ; that of deducing or proving a truth that would be otherwise unknown, from truths already known.

I recollect not enough of the passages in Job to insert

---

[1] The French translator has substituted for this a version of the same psalm by Jean Baptiste Rousseau.—*Editor.*

them correctly; but there is one that occurs to me that is applicable to the subject I am speaking upon. " Canst thou by searching find out God ; canst thou find out the Almighty to perfection ? "

I know not how the printers have pointed this passage, for I keep no Bible; but it contains two distinct questions that admit of distinct answers.

First, Canst thou by *searching* find out God? Yes. Because, in the first place, I know I did not make myself, and yet I have existence ; and by *searching* into the nature of other things, I find that no other thing could make itself; and yet millions of other things exist ; therefore it is, that I know, by positive conclusion resulting from this search, that there is a power superior to all those things, and that power is God.

Secondly, Canst thou find out the Almighty to *perfection ?* No. Not only because the power and wisdom He has manifested in the structure of the Creation that I behold is to me incomprehensible ; but because even this manifestation, great as it is, is probably but a small display of that immensity of power and wisdom, by which millions of other worlds, to me invisible by their distance, were created and continue to exist.

It is evident that both of these questions were put to the reason of the person to whom they are supposed to have been addressed ; and it is only by admitting the first question to be answered affirmatively, that the second could follow. It would have been unnecessary, and even absurd, to have put a second question, more difficult than the first, if the first question had been answered negatively. The two questions have different objects ; the first refers to the existence of God, the second to his attributes. Reason can discover the one, but it falls infinitely short in discovering the whole of the other.

I recollect not a single passage in all the writings ascribed to the men called apostles, that conveys any idea of what God is. Those writings are chiefly controversial ; and the gloominess of the subject they dwell upon, that of a man dying in agony on a cross, is better suited to the gloomy genius of a monk in a cell, by whom it is not impossible they were written, than to any man breathing the open air of the Creation.   The only passage that occurs to me, that has any reference to the works of God, by which only his power and wisdom can be known, is related to have been spoken by Jesus Christ, as a remedy against distrustful care.   " Behold the lilies of the field, they toil not, neither do they spin." This, however, is far inferior to the allusions in Job and in the 19th Psalm ; but it is similar in idea, and the modesty of the imagery is correspondent to the modesty of the man.

CHAPTER XI.

OF THE THEOLOGY OF THE CHRISTIANS ; AND THE TRUE THEOLOGY.

As to the Christian system of faith, it appears to me as a species of atheism ; a sort of religious denial of God.   It professes to believe in a man rather than in God.   It is a compound made up chiefly of man-ism with but little deism, and is as near to atheism as twilight is to darkness. It introduces between man and his Maker an opaque body, which it calls a redeemer, as the moon introduces her opaque self between the earth and the sun, and it produces by this means a religious or [1] an irreligious eclipse of light.   It has put the whole orbit of reason into shade.

The effect of this obscurity has been that of turning everything upside down, and representing it in reverse ; and among the revolutions it has thus magically produced, it has made a revolution in Theology.

That which is now called natural philosophy, embracing the whole circle of science, of which astronomy occupies the chief place, is the study of the works of God, and of the power and wisdom of God in his works, and is the true theology.

---

[1] The French here has " plutôt " (rather).—*Editor*.

As to the theology that is now studied in its place, it is the study of human opinions and of human fancies *concerning* God.[1] It is not the study of God himself in the works that he has made, but in the works or writings that man has made ; and it is not among the least of the mischiefs that the Christian system has done to the world, that it has abandoned the original and beautiful system of theology,[2] like a beautiful innocent, to distress and reproach, to make room for the hag of superstition.

The Book of Job and the 19th Psalm, which even the church admits to be more ancient than the chronological order in which they stand in the book called the Bible, are theological orations conformable to the original system of theology. The internal evidence of those orations proves to a demonstration that the study and contemplation of the works of creation, and of the power and wisdom of God revealed and manifested in those works, made a great part of the religious devotion of the times in which they were written ; and it was this devotional study and contemplation that led to the discovery of the principles upon which what are now called Sciences are established ; and it is to the discovery of these principles that almost all the Arts that contribute to the convenience of human life owe their existence. Every principal art has some science for its parent, though the person who mechanically performs the work does not always, and but very seldom, perceive the connection.[3]

It is a fraud [4] of the Christian system to call the sciences *human inventions;* it is only the application of them that is human. Every science has for its basis a system of principles as fixed and unalterable as those by which the uni-

---

[1] French : " La suprême intelligence " instead of " God."—*Editor.*

[2] French : " La théologie naturelle."—*Editor.*

[3] In the French is added : " et que même, par l'ignorance que les gouvernemens modernes ont répandue, il soit très-rare aujourd'hui, que ces personnes s'en doutent " (and, such is the ignorance prevailing under modern governments, it is now even very rare for such persons to think about it).—*Editor.*

[4] French : " C'est un mensonge, une *fraude pieuse.*"—*Editor.*

verse is regulated and governed. Man cannot make principles, he can only discover them.

For example: Every person who looks at an almanack sees an account when an eclipse will take place, and he sees also that it never fails to take place according to the account there given. This shews that man is acquainted with the laws by which the heavenly bodies move. But it would be something worse than ignorance, were any church on earth to say that those laws are an human invention.

It would also be ignorance, or something worse, to say that the scientific principles, by the aid of which man is enabled to calculate and foreknow when an eclipse will take place, are an human invention. Man cannot invent any thing that is eternal and immutable; and the scientific principles he employs for this purpose must, and are, of necessity, as eternal and immutable as the laws by which the heavenly bodies move, or they could not be used as they are to ascertain the time when, and the manner how, an eclipse will take place.

The scientific principles that man employs to obtain the foreknowledge of an eclipse, or of any thing else relating to the motion of the heavenly bodies, are contained chiefly in that part of science that is called trigonometry, or the properties of a triangle, which, when applied to the study of the heavenly bodies, is called astronomy; when applied to direct the course of a ship on the ocean, it is called navigation; when applied to the construction of figures drawn by a rule and compass, it is called geometry; when applied to the construction of plans of edifices, it is called architecture; when applied to the measurement of any portion of the surface of the earth, it is called land-surveying. In fine, it is the soul of science. It is an eternal truth: it contains the *mathematical demonstration* of which man speaks, and the extent of its uses are unknown.

It may be said, that man can make or draw a triangle, and therefore a triangle is an human invention.

But the triangle, when drawn, is no other than the image of the principle: it is a delineation to the eye, and from thence to the mind, of a principle that would otherwise be imperceptible. The triangle does not make the principle, any more than a candle taken into a room that was dark, makes the chairs and tables that before were invisible. All the properties of a triangle exist independently of the figure, and existed before any triangle was drawn or thought of by man. Man had no more to do in the formation of those properties or principles, than he had to do in making the laws by which the heavenly bodies move ; and therefore the one must have the same divine origin as the other.

In the same manner as, it may be said, that man can make a triangle, so also, may it be said, he can make the mechanical instrument called a lever. But the principle by which the lever acts, is a thing distinct from the instrument, and would exist if the instrument did not ; it attaches itself to the instrument after it is made ; the instrument, therefore, can act no otherwise than it does act ; neither can all the efforts of human invention make it act otherwise. That which, in all such cases, man calls the *effect*, is no other than the principle itself rendered perceptible to the senses.

Since, then, man cannot make principles, from whence did he gain a knowledge of them, so as to be able to apply them, not only to things on earth, but to ascertain the motion of bodies so immensely distant from him as all the heavenly bodies are ? From whence, I ask, *could* he gain that knowledge, but from the study of the true theology ?

It is the structure of the universe that has taught this knowledge to man. That structure is an ever-existing exhibition of every principle upon which every part of mathematical science is founded. The offspring of this science is mechanics ; for mechanics is no other than the principles of science applied practically. The man who proportions the several parts of a mill uses the same scientific principles as if he had the power of constructing an universe, but as he cannot give to matter that invisible agency by which all the component parts of the immense machine of the universe have influence upon each other, and act in motional unison together, without any apparent contact, and to which man has given the name of attraction, gravitation, and repulsion, he supplies the place of that agency by the humble imitation of teeth and cogs. All the parts of man's microcosm must visibly touch. But could he gain a knowledge of that agency, so as to be able to apply it in practice, we might then say that another *canonical book* of the word of God had been discovered.

If man could alter the properties of the lever, so also could he alter the properties of the triangle: for a lever (taking that sort of lever which is called a steel-yard, for the sake of explanation) forms, when in motion, a triangle. The line it descends from, (one point of that line being in the fulcrum,) the line it descends to, and the chord of the arc, which the end of the lever describes in the air, are the three sides of a triangle. The other arm of the lever describes also a triangle; and the corresponding sides of those two triangles, calculated scientifically, or measured geometrically,—and also the sines, tangents, and secants generated from the angles, and geometrically measured,—have the same proportions to each other as the different weights have that will balance each other on the lever, leaving the weight of the lever out of the case.

It may also be said, that man can make a wheel and axis; that he can put wheels of different magnitudes together, and produce a mill. Still the case comes back to the same point, which is, that he did not make the principle that gives the wheels those powers. This principle is as unalterable as in the former cases, or rather it is the same principle under a different appearance to the eye.

The power that two wheels of different magnitudes have upon each other is in the same proportion as if the semi-diameter of the two wheels were joined together and made into that kind of lever I have described, suspended at the part where the semi-diameters join; for the two wheels, scientifically considered, are no other than the two circles generated by the motion of the compound lever.

It is from the study of the true theology that all our knowledge of science is derived; and it is from that knowledge that all the arts have originated.

The Almighty lecturer, by displaying the principles of science in the structure of the universe, has invited man to study and to imitation. It is as if he had said to the inhabitants of this globe that we call ours, " I have made an earth for man to dwell upon, and I have rendered the starry heavens visible, to teach him science and the arts. He can now provide for his own comfort, AND LEARN FROM MY MUNIFICENCE TO ALL, TO BE KIND TO EACH OTHER."

Of what use is it, unless it be to teach man something, that his eye is endowed with the power of beholding, to an incomprehensible distance, an immensity of worlds revolving in the ocean of space? Or of what use is it that this immensity of worlds is visible to man? What has man to do with the Pleiades, with Orion, with Sirius, with the star he calls the north star, with the moving orbs he has named Saturn, Jupiter, Mars, Venus, and Mercury, if no uses are to follow from their being visible? A less power of vision would have been sufficient for man, if the immensity he now possesses were given only to waste itself, as it were, on an immense desert of space glittering with shows.

It is only by contemplating what he calls the starry heavens, as the book and school of science, that he discovers any use in their being visible to him, or any advantage resulting from his immensity of vision. But when he contemplates the subject in this light, he sees an additional motive for saying, that *nothing was made in vain;* for in vain would be this power of vision if it taught man nothing.

CHAPTER XII.

THE EFFECTS OF CHRISTIANISM ON EDUCATION. PROPOSED REFORMS.

As the Christian system of faith has made a revolution in theology, so also has it made a revolution in the state of learning. That which is now called learning, was not learning originally. Learning does not consist, as the schools now make it consist, in the knowledge of languages, but in the knowledge of things to which language gives names.

The Greeks were a learned people, but learning with them did not consist in speaking Greek, any more than in a Roman's speaking Latin, or a Frenchman's speaking French, or an Englishman's speaking English. From what we know of the Greeks, it does not appear that they knew or studied any language but their own, and this was one cause of their becoming so learned ; it afforded them more time to apply themselves to better studies. The schools of the Greeks were schools of science and philosophy, and not of languages ; and it is in the knowledge of the things that science and philosophy teach that learning consists.

Almost all the scientific learning that now exists, came to us from the Greeks, or the people who spoke the Greek language. It therefore became necessary to the people of other nations, who spoke a different language, that some among them should learn the Greek language, in order that the learning the Greeks had might be made known in those nations, by translating the Greek books of science and philosophy into the mother tongue of each nation.

The study, therefore, of the Greek language (and in the same manner for the Latin) was no other than the drudgery business of a linguist ; and the language thus obtained, was no other than the means, or as it were the tools, employed to obtain the learning the Greeks had. It made no part of the learning itself ; and was so distinct from it as to make it exceedingly probable that the persons who had studied Greek sufficiently to translate those works, such for instance as Euclid's Elements, did not understand any of the learning the works contained.

As there is now nothing new to be learned from the dead languages, all the useful books being already translated, the languages are become useless, and the time expended in teaching and in learning them is wasted. So far as the study of languages may contribute to the progress and communication of knowledge (for it has nothing to do with the *creation* of knowledge) it is only in the living languages that new knowledge is to be found ; and certain it is, that, in general, a youth will learn more of a living language in one year, than of a dead language in seven ; and it is but seldom that the teacher knows much of it himself. The difficulty of learning the dead languages does not arise from any superior abstruseness in the languages themselves, but in their *being dead*, and the pronunciation entirely lost. It would be the same thing with any other language when it becomes dead. The best Greek linguist that now exists does not understand Greek so well as a Grecian plowman did, or a Grecian milkmaid ; and the same for the Latin, compared with a plowman or a milkmaid of the Romans ; and with respect to pronunciation and idiom, not so well as the cows that she milked. It would therefore be advantageous to the state of learning to abolish the study of the dead languages, and to make learning consist, as it originally did, in scientific knowledge.

The apology that is sometimes made for continuing to teach the dead languages is, that they are taught at a time when a child is not capable of exerting any other mental faculty than that of memory. But this is altogether erroneous. The human mind has a natural disposition to scientific knowledge, and to the things connected with it. The first and favourite amusement of a child, even before it begins to play, is that of imitating the works of man. It builds houses with cards or sticks ; it navigates the little ocean of a bowl of water with a paper boat ; or dams the stream of a gutter, and contrives something which it calls a mill ; and it interests itself in the fate of its works with a care that resembles affection. It afterwards goes to school, where its genius is killed by the barren study of a dead language, and the philosopher is lost in the linguist.

But the apology that is now made for continuing to teach the dead languages, could not be the cause at first of cutting down learning to the narrow and humble sphere of linguistry ; the cause therefore must be sought for elsewhere. In all researches of this kind, the best evidence that can be produced, is the internal evidence the thing carries with itself, and the evidence of circumstances that unites with it; both of which, in this case, are not difficult to be discovered.

Putting then aside, as matter of distinct consideration, the outrage offered to the moral justice of God, by supposing him to make the innocent suffer for the guilty, and also the loose morality and low contrivance of supposing him to change himself into the shape of a man, in order to make an excuse to himself for not executing his supposed sentence upon Adam; putting, I say, those things aside as matter of distinct consideration, it is certain that what is called the christian system of faith, including in it the whimsical account of the creation—the strange story of Eve, the snake, and the apple—the amphibious idea of a man-god—the corporeal idea of the death of a god—the mythological idea of a family of gods, and the christian system of arithmetic, [1] that three are one, and one is three, are all irreconcilable, not only to the divine gift of reason, that God has given to man, but to the knowledge that man gains of the power and wisdom of God by the aid of the sciences, and by studying the structure of the universe that God has made.

The setters up, therefore, and the advocates of the Christian system of faith, [2] could not but foresee that the continually progressive knowledge that man would gain by the aid of science, of the power and wisdom of God, manifested in the structure of the universe, and in all the works of creation, would militate against, and call into question, the truth of their system of faith; and therefore it became necessary to their purpose to cut learning down to a size less dangerous to their project, and this they effected by restricting the idea of learning to the dead [3] study of dead languages.

They not only rejected the study of science out of the christian schools, but they persecuted it; and it is only within about the last two centuries that the study has been

---

[1] French : " ce *nonsense* arithmetique." The words " christian system " do not occur in the clause.—*Editor*.

[2] Instead of " christian system of faith," the French has " ce tissu d' absur-dités."—*Editor*.

[3] French : " aride."—*Editor*.

revived. So late as 1610, Galileo, a Florentine, discovered and introduced the use of telescopes, and by applying them to observe the motions and appearances of the heavenly bodies, afforded additional means for ascertaining the true structure of the universe. Instead of being esteemed for these discoveries, he was sentenced to renounce them, or the opinions resulting from them, as a damnable heresy. And prior to that time Virgilius was condemned to be burned for asserting the antipodes, or in other words, that the earth was a globe, and habitable in every part where there was land ; yet the truth of this is now too well known even to be told.[1]

If the belief of errors not morally bad did no mischief, it would make no part of the moral duty of man to oppose and remove them. There was no moral ill in believing the earth was flat like a trencher, any more than there was moral virtue in believing it was round like a globe ; neither was there any moral ill in believing that the Creator made no other world than this, any more than there was moral virtue in believing that he made millions, and that

---

[1] I cannot discover the source of this statement concerning the ancient author whose Irish name Feirghill was Latinized into Virgilius. The British Museum possesses a copy of the work (*Decalogium*) which was the pretext of the charge of heresy made by Boniface, Archbishop of Mayence, against Virgilius, Abbot-bishop of Salzburg. These were leaders of the rival " British " and " Roman " parties, and the British champion made a countercharge against Boniface of " irreligious practices." Boniface had to express a " regret," but none the less pursued his rival. The Pope, Zachary II., decided that if his alleged " doctrine, against God and his soul, that beneath the earth there is another world, other men, or sun and moon," should be acknowledged by Virgilius, he should be excommunicated by a Council and condemned with canonical sanctions. Whatever may have been the fate involved by condemnation with " canonicis sanctionibus," in the middle of the eighth century, it did not fall on Virgilius. His accuser, Boniface, was martyred, 755, and it is probable that Virgilius harmonized his Antipodes with orthodoxy. The *gravamen* of the heresy seems to have been the suggestion that there were men not of the progeny of Adam. Virgilius was made Bishop of Salzburg in 768. He bore until his death, 789, the curious title, " Geometer and Solitary," or " lone wayfarer " (*Solivagus*). A suspicion of heresy clung to his memory until 1233, when he was raised by Gregory IX. to sainthood beside his accuser, St. Boniface.—*Editor.*

the infinity of space is filled with worlds. But when a system of religion is made to grow out of a supposed system of creation that is not true, and to unite itself therewith in a manner almost inseparable therefrom, the case assumes an entirely different ground. It is then that errors, not morally bad, become fraught with the same mischiefs as if they were. It is then that the truth, though otherwise indifferent itself, becomes an essential, by becoming the criterion that either confirms by corresponding evidence, or denies by contradictory evidence, the reality of the religion itself. In this view of the case it is the moral duty of man to obtain every possible evidence that the structure of the heavens, or any other part of creation affords, with respect to systems of religion. But this, the supporters or partizans of the christian system, as if dreading the result, incessantly opposed, and not only rejected the sciences, but persecuted the professors. Had Newton or Descartes lived three or four hundred years ago, and pursued their studies as they did, it is most probable they would not have lived to finish them; and had Franklin drawn lightning from the clouds at the same time, it would have been at the hazard of expiring for it in flames.

Later times have laid all the blame upon the Goths and Vandals, but, however unwilling the partizans of the Christian system may be to believe or to acknowledge it, it is nevertheless true, that the age of ignorance commenced with the Christian system. There was more knowledge in the world before that period, than for many centuries afterwards; and as to religious knowledge, the Christian system, as already said, was only another species of mythology; and the mythology to which it succeeded, was a corruption of an ancient system of theism.*

---

* It is impossible for us now to know at what time the heathen mythology began; but it is certain, from the internal evidence that it carries, that it did not begin in the same state or condition in which it ended. All the gods of that mythology, except Saturn, were of modern invention. The supposed reign of Saturn was prior to that which is called the heathen mythology, and was so far a species of theism that it admitted the belief of only one God. Saturn is sup-

It is owing to this long interregnum of science, *and to no other cause*, that we have now to look back through a vast chasm of many hundred years to the respectable characters we call the Ancients. Had the progression of knowledge gone on proportionably with the stock that before existed, that chasm would have been filled up with characters rising superior in knowledge to each other; and those Ancients we now so much admire would have appeared respectably in the background of the scene. But the christian system laid all waste; and if we take our stand about the beginning of the sixteenth century, we look back through that long chasm, to the times of the Ancients, as over a vast sandy desert, in which not a shrub appears to intercept the vision to the fertile hills beyond.

It is an inconsistency scarcely possible to be credited, that any thing should exist, under the name of a religion, that held it to be *irreligious* to study and contemplate the structure of the universe that God had made. But the fact is too well established to be denied. The event that served more than any other to break the first link in this long chain of despotic ignorance, is that known by the name of the Reformation by Luther. From that time, though it does not appear to have made any part of the intention of

posed to have abdicated the government in favour of his three sons and one daughter, Jupiter, Pluto, Neptune, and Juno ; after this, thousands of other gods and demi-gods were imaginarily created, and the calendar of gods increased as fast as the calendar of saints and the calendar of courts have increased since.

All the corruptions that have taken place, in theology and in religion have been produced by admitting of what man calls *revealed religion*. The mythologists pretended to more revealed religion than the christians do. They had their oracles and their priests, who were supposed to receive and deliver the word of God verbally on almost all occasions.

Since then all corruptions down from Moloch to modern predestinarianism, and the human sacrifices of the heathens to the christian sacrifice of the Creator, have been produced by admitting of what is called *revealed religion*, the most effectual means to prevent all such evils and impositions is, not to admit of any other revelation than that which is manifested in the book of Creation, and to contemplate the Creation as the only true and real word of God that ever did or ever will exist ; and every thing else called the word of God is fable and imposition.—*Author*.

Luther,[1] or of those who are called Reformers, the Sciences began to revive, and Liberality,[2] their natural associate, began to appear. This was the only public good the Reformation did; for, with respect to religious good, it might as well not have taken place. The mythology still continued the same; and a multiplicity of National Popes grew out of the downfal of the Pope of Christendom.

CHAPTER XIII.

COMPARISON OF CHRISTIANISM WITH THE RELIGIOUS IDEAS INSPIRED BY NATURE.

HAVING thus shewn, from the internal evidence of things, the cause that produced a change in the state of learning, and the motive for substituting the study of the dead languages, in the place of the Sciences, I proceed, in addition to the several observations already made in the former part of this work, to compare, or rather to confront, the evidence that the structure of the universe affords, with the christian system of religion. But as I cannot begin this part better than by referring to the ideas that occurred to me at an early part of life, and which I doubt not have occurred in some degree to almost every other person at one time or other, I shall state what those ideas were, and add thereto such other matter as shall arise out of the subject, giving to the whole, by way of preface, a short introduction.

My father being of the quaker profession, it was my good fortune to have an exceedingly good moral education, and a tolerable stock of useful learning. Though I went to the grammar school,* I did not learn Latin, not only because I had no inclination to learn languages, but because of the objection the quakers have against the books in which the language is taught. But this did not prevent me from

---

[1] French : " ce moine " (this monk) instead of " Luther."—*Editor*.

[2] French : "la civilisation" instead of "liberality."—*Editor*.

* The same school, Thetford in Norfolk, that the present Counsellor Mingay went to, and under the same master—*Author*. [This note is not in the French work.—*Editor*.]

being acquainted with the subjects of all the Latin books. used in the school.

The natural bent of my mind was to science. I had some turn, and I believe some talent for poetry ; but this I rather repressed than encouraged, as leading too much into the field of imagination. As soon as I was able, I purchased a pair of globes, and attended the philosophical lectures of Martin and Ferguson, and became afterwards acquainted with Dr. Bevis, of the society called the Royal Society, then living in the Temple, and an excellent astronomer.

I had no disposition for what was called politics. It presented to my mind no other idea than is contained in the word Jockeyship. When, therefore, I turned my thoughts towards matters of government, I had to form a system for myself, that accorded with the moral and philosophic principles in which I had been educated. I saw, or at least I thought I saw, a vast scene opening itself to the world in the affairs of America; and it appeared to me, that unless the Americans changed the plan they were then pursuing, with respect to the government of England, and declared themselves independent, they would not only involve themselves in a multiplicity of new difficulties, but shut out the prospect that was then offering itself to mankind through their means. It was from these motives that I published the work known by the name of *Common Sense*, which is the first work I ever did publish, and so far as I can judge of myself, I believe I should never have been known in the world as an author on any subject whatever, had it not been for the affairs of America. I wrote *Common Sense* the latter end of the year 1775, and published it the first of January, 1776.[1] Independence was declared the fourth of July following.

[1] The pamphlet *Common Sense* was first advertised, as "just published," on January 10, 1776. His plea for the Officers of Excise, written before leaving England, was printed, but not published until 1793. Despite his reiterated assertion that *Common Sense* was the first work he ever published the notion that he was "Junius" still finds some believers. An indirect comment on out

Any person, who has made observations on the state and progress of the human mind, by observing his own, cannot but have observed, that there are two distinct classes of what are called Thoughts ; those that we produce in ourselves by reflection and the act of thinking, and those that bolt into the mind of their own accord. I have always made it a rule to treat those voluntary visitors with civility, taking care to examine, as well as I was able, if they were worth entertaining; and it is from them I have acquired almost all the knowledge that I have. As to the learning that any person gains from school education, it serves only, like a small capital, to put him in the way of beginning learning for himself afterwards. Every person of learning is finally his own teacher ; the reason of which is, that principles, being of a distinct quality to circumstances, cannot be impressed upon the memory ; their place of mental residence is the understanding, and they are never so lasting as when they begin by conception. Thus much for the introductory part.[1]

From the time I was capable of conceiving an idea, and acting upon it by reflection, I either doubted the truth of the christian system, or thought it to be a strange affair ; I scarcely knew which it was: but I well remember, when about seven or eight years of age, hearing a sermon read by a relation of mine, who was a great devotee of the church,[2] upon the subject of what is called *Redemption by the death of the Son of God*. After the sermon was ended, I went into the garden, and as I was going down the garden steps

Paine-Junians may be found in Part 2 of this work where Paine says a man capable of writing Homer " would not have thrown away his own fame by giving it to another." It is probable that Paine ascribed the Letters of Junius to Thomas Hollis. His friend F. Lanthenas, in his translation of the Age of Reason (1794) advertises his translation of the Letters of Junius from the English " (Thomas Hollis)." This he could hardly have done without consultation with Paine. Unfortunately this translation of Junius cannot be found either in the Bibliothèque Nationale or the British Museum, and it cannot be said whether it contains any attempt at an identification of Junius—*Editor*.

[1] This sentence is not in the French work.—*Editor*.

[2] No doubt Paine's aunt, Miss Cooke, who managed to have him confirmed in the parish church at Thetford.—*Editor*.

(for I perfectly recollect the spot) I revolted at the recollection of what I had heard, and thought to myself that it was making God Almighty act like a passionate man, that killed his son, when he could not revenge himself any other way; and as I was sure a man would be hanged that did such a thing, I could not see for what purpose they preached such sermons. This was not one of those kind of thoughts that had any thing in it of childish levity; it was to me a serious reflection, arising from the idea I had that God was too good to do such an action, and also too almighty to be under any necessity of doing it. I believe in the same manner to this moment; and I moreover believe, that any system of religion that has any thing in it that shocks the mind of a child, cannot be a true system.

It seems as if parents of the christian profession were ashamed to tell their children any thing about the principles of their religion. They sometimes instruct them in morals, and talk to them of the goodness of what they call Providence; for the Christian mythology has five deities: there is God the Father, God the Son, God the Holy Ghost, the God Providence, and the Goddess Nature. But the christian story of God the Father putting his son to death, or employing people to do it, (for that is the plain language of the story,) cannot be told by a parent to a child; and to tell him that it was done to make mankind happier and better, is making the story still worse; as if mankind could be improved by the example of murder; and to tell him that all this is a mystery, is only making an excuse for the incredibility of it.

How different is this to the pure and simple profession of Deïsm! The true deist has but one Deity; and his religion consists in contemplating the power, wisdom, and benignity of the Deity in his works, and in endeavouring to imitate him in every thing moral, scientifical, and mechanical.

The religion that approaches the nearest of all others to true Deism, in the moral and benign part thereof, is that professed by the quakers: but they have contracted themselves too much by leaving the works of God out of their

5

system. Though I reverence their philanthropy, I can not help smiling at the conceit, that if the taste of a quaker could have been consulted at the creation, what a silent and drab-colored creation it would have been! Not a flower would have blossomed its gaieties, nor a bird been permitted to sing.

Quitting these reflections, I proceed to other matters. After I had made myself master of the use of the globes, and of the orrery,* and conceived an idea of the infinity of space, and of the eternal divisibility of matter, and obtained, at least, a general knowledge of what was called natural philosophy, I began to compare, or, as I have before said, to confront, the internal evidence those things afford with the christian system of faith.

Though it is not a direct article of the christian system that this world that we inhabit is the whole of the habitable creation, yet it is so worked up therewith, from what is called the Mosaic account of the creation, the story of Eve and the apple, and the counterpart of that story, the death of the Son of God, that to believe otherwise, that is, to believe that God created a plurality of worlds, at least as numerous as what we call stars, renders the christian system of faith at once little and ridiculous; and scatters it in the mind like feathers in the air. The two beliefs can not be held together in the same mind ; and he who thinks that he believes both, has thought but little of either.

Though the belief of a plurality of worlds was familiar to the ancients, it is only within the last three centuries that the extent and dimensions of this globe that we inhabit have been ascertained. Several vessels, following the tract of the

---

* As this book may fall into the hands of persons who do not know what an orrery is, it is for their information I add this note, as the ʌame gives no idea of the uses of the thing. The orrery has its name from the person who invented it. It is a machinery of clock-work, representing the universe in miniature : and in which the revolution of the earth round itself and round the sun, the revolution of the moon round the earth, the revolution of the planets round the sun, their relative distances from the sun, as the center of the whole system, their relative distances from each other, and their different magnitudes, are represented as they really exist in what we call the heavens.—*Author*.

ocean, have sailed entirely round the world, as a man may march in a circle, and come round by the contrary side of the circle to the spot he set out from. The circular dimensions of our world, in the widest part, as a man would measure the widest round of an apple, or a ball, is only twenty-five thousand and twenty English miles, reckoning sixty-nine miles and an half to an equatorial degree, and may be sailed round in the space of about three years.*

A world of this extent may, at first thought, appear to us to be great; but if we compare it with the immensity of space in which it is suspended, like a bubble or a balloon in the air, it is infinitely less in proportion than the smallest grain of sand is to the size of the world, or the finest particle of dew to the whole ocean, and is therefore but small; and, as will be hereafter shewn, is only one of a system of worlds, of which the universal creation is composed.

It is not difficult to gain some faint idea of the immensity of space in which this and all the other worlds are suspended, if we follow a progression of ideas. When we think of the size or dimensions of a room, our ideas limit themselves to the walls, and there they stop. But when our eye, or our imagination darts into space, that is, when it looks upward into what we call the open air, we cannot conceive any walls or boundaries it can have; and if for the sake of resting our ideas we suppose a boundary, the question immediately renews itself, and asks, what is beyond that boundary? and in the same manner, what beyond the next boundary? and so on till the fatigued imagination returns and says, *there is no end.* Certainly, then, the Creator was not pent for room when he made this world no larger than it is; and we have to seek the reason in something else.

If we take a survey of our own world, or rather of this, of which the Creator has given us the use as our portion in the immense system of creation, we find every part of it, the earth, the waters, and the air that surround it, filled,

* Allowing a ship to sail, on an average, three miles in an hour, she would sail entirely round the world in less than one year, if she could sail in a direct circle, but she is obliged to follow the course of the ocean.—*Author*.

and as it were crouded with life, down from the largest animals that we know of to the smallest insects the naked eye can behold, and from thence to others still smaller, and totally invisible without the assistance of the microscope. Every tree, every plant, every leaf, serves not only as an habitation, but as a world to some numerous race, till animal existence becomes so exceedingly refined, that the effluvia of a blade of grass would be food for thousands.

Since then no part of our earth is left unoccupied, why is it to be supposed that the immensity of space is a naked void, lying in eternal waste? There is room for millions of worlds as large or larger than ours, and each of them millions of miles apart from each other.

Having now arrived at this point, if we carry our ideas only one thought further, we shall see, perhaps, the true reason, at least a very good reason for our happiness, why the Creator, instead of making one immense world, extending over an immense quantity of space, has preferred dividing that quantity of matter into several distinct and separate worlds, which we call planets, of which our earth is one. But before I explain my ideas upon this subject, it is necessary (not for the sake of those that already know, but for those who do not) to shew what the system of the universe is.

CHAPTER XIV.

SYSTEM OF THE UNIVERSE.

THAT part of the universe that is called the solar system (meaning the system of worlds to which our earth belongs, and of which Sol, or in English language, the Sun, is the center) consists, besides the Sun, of six distinct orbs, or planets, or worlds, besides the secondary bodies, called the satellites, or moons, of which our earth has one that attends her in her annual revolution round the Sun, in like manner as the other satellites or moons, attend the planets or worlds to

which they severally belong, as may be seen by the assistance of the telescope.

The Sun is the center round which those six worlds or
planets revolve at different distances therefrom, and in circles
concentric to each other. Each world keeps constantly in
nearly the same tract round the Sun, and continues at the
same time turning round itself, in nearly an upright position,
as a top turns round itself when it is spinning on the ground,
and leans a little sideways.

It is this leaning of the earth (23½ degrees) that occasions
summer and winter, and the different length of days and
nights. If the earth turned round itself in a position perpendicular to the plane or level of the circle it moves in
round the Sun, as a top turns round when it stands erect
on the ground, the days and nights would be always of
the same length, twelve hours day and twelve hours night,
and the season would be uniformly the same throughout
the year.

Every time that a planet (our earth for example) turns
round itself, it makes what we call day and night; and
every time it goes entirely round the Sun, it makes what
we call a year, consequently our world turns three hundred
and sixty-five times round itself, in going once round the
Sun. *

The names that the ancients gave to those six worlds,
and which are still called by the same names, are Mercury,
Venus, this world that we call ours, Mars, Jupiter, and
Saturn.[1] They appear larger to the eye than the stars, being
many million miles nearer to our earth than any of the stars

---

[1] With reference to the omission of any mention of Uranus, see the Introduction. In the New York edition, 1794, edited by Col. John Fellows, occurs this
footnote : "Mr. Paine had made no mention of the planet Herschel, which
was first discovered, by the person whose name it bears, in 1781. It is at a
greater distance from the Sun than either of the other planets and consequently
occupies a greater length of time in performing its revolutions."—*Editor*.

* Those who supposed that the Sun went round the earth every 24 hours
made the same mistake in idea that a cook would do in fact, that should make
the fire go round the meat, instead of the meat turning round itself towards the
fire.—*Author*.

are. The planet Venus is that which is called the evening star, and sometimes the morning star, as she happens to set after, or rise before the Sun, which in either case is never more than three hours.

The Sun as before said being the center, the planet or world nearest the Sun is Mercury; his distance from the Sun is thirty-four million miles, and he moves round in a circle always at that distance from the Sun, as a top may be supposed to spin round in the tract in which a horse goes in a mill. The second world is Venus; she is fifty-seven million miles distant from the Sun, and consequently moves round in a circle much greater than that of Mercury. The third world is this that we inhabit, and which is eighty-eight million miles distant from the Sun, and consequently moves round in a circle greater than that of Venus. The fourth world is Mars; he is distant from the sun one hundred and thirty-four million miles, and consequently moves round in a circle greater than that of our earth. The fifth is Jupiter; he is distant from the Sun five hundred and fifty-seven million miles, and consequently moves round in a circle greater than that of Mars. The sixth world is Saturn; he is distant from the Sun seven hundred and sixty-three million miles, and consequently moves round in a circle that surrounds the circles or orbits of all the other worlds or planets.

The space, therefore, in the air, or in the immensity of space, that our solar system takes up for the several worlds to perform their revolutions in round the Sun, is of the extent in a strait line of the whole diameter of the orbit or circle in which Saturn moves round the Sun, which being double his distance from the Sun, is fifteen hundred and twenty-six million miles; and its circular extent is nearly five thousand million; and its globical content is almost three thousand five hundred million times three thousand five hundred million square miles. *

* If it should be asked, how can man know these things? I have one plain answer to give, which is, that man knows how to calculate an eclipse, and also how to calculate to a minute of time when the planet Venus, in making her

But this, immense as it is, is only one system of worlds. Beyond this, at a vast distance into space, far beyond all power of calculation, are the stars called the fixed stars. They are called fixed, because they have no revolutionary motion, as the six worlds or planets have that I have been describing. Those fixed stars continue always at the same distance from each other, and always in the same place, as the Sun does in the center of our system. The probability, therefore, is, that each of those fixed stars is also a Sun, round which another system of worlds or planets, though too remote for us to discover, performs its revolutions, as our system of worlds does round our central Sun.[1]

By this easy progression of ideas, the immensity of space will appear to us to be filled with systems of worlds; and that no part of space lies at waste, any more than any part of our globe of earth and water is left unoccupied.

Having thus endeavoured to convey, in a familiar and easy manner, some idea of the structure of the universe, I return to explain what I before alluded to, namely, the great benefits arising to man in consequence of the Creator having made a *plurality* of worlds, such as our system is, consisting of a central Sun and six worlds,[2] besides satellites, in preference to that of creating one world only of a vast extent.

revolutions round the Sun, will come in a strait line between our earth and the Sun, and will appear to us about the size of a large pea passing across the face of the Sun. This happens but twice in about a hundred years, at the distance of about eight years from each other, and has happened twice in our time, both of which were foreknown by calculation. It can also be known when they will happen again for a thousand years to come, or to any other portion of time. As therefore, man could not be able to do these things if he did not understand the solar system, and the manner in which the revolutions of the several planets or worlds are performed, the fact of calculating an eclipse, or a transit of Venus, is a proof in point that the knowledge exists; and as to a few thousand, or even a few million miles, more or less, it makes scarcely any sensible difference in such immense distances.—*Author.*

[1] This speculation has been confirmed by nineteenth-century astronomy. "The stars, speaking broadly, are suns "(Clarke's *System of the Stars*, ch. iii). See Herschel's *Outlines of Astronomy*, Part III. ch. xv.—*Editor.*

[2] The French work has "plusieurs planètes" (many planets) instead of "six worlds."—*Editor.*

CHAPTER XV.

ADVANTAGES OF THE EXISTENCE OF MANY WORLDS IN EACH SOLAR SYSTEM.

IT is an idea I have never lost sight of, that all our knowledge of science is derived from the revolutions (exhibited to our eye and from thence to our understanding) which those several planets or worlds of which our system is composed make in their circuit round the Sun.

Had then the quantity of matter which these six worlds contain been blended into one solitary globe, the consequence to us would have been, that either no revolutionary motion would have existed, or not a sufficiency of it to give us the ideas and the knowledge of science we now have ; and it is from the sciences that all the mechanical arts that contribute so much to our earthly felicity and comfort are derived.

As therefore the Creator made nothing in vain, so also must it be believed that he organized the structure of the universe in the most advantageous manner for the benefit of man ; and as we see, and from experience feel, the benefits we derive from the structure of the universe, formed as it is, which benefits we should not have had the opportunity of enjoying if the structure, so far as relates to our system, had been a solitary globe, we can discover at least one reason why a *plurality* of worlds has been made, and that reason calls forth the devotional gratitude of man, as well as his admiration.

But it is not to us, the inhabitants of this globe, only, that the benefits arising from a plurality of worlds are limited. The inhabitants of each of the worlds of which our system is composed, enjoy the same opportunities of knowledge as we do. They behold the revolutionary motions of our earth, as we behold theirs. All the planets revolve in sight of each other ; and, therefore, the same universal school of science presents itself to all.

Neither does the knowledge stop here. The system of worlds next to us exhibits, in its revolutions, the same prin-

ciples and school of science, to the inhabitants of their system, as our system does to us, and in like manner throughout the immensity of space.

Our ideas, not only of the almightiness of the Creator, but
of his wisdom and his beneficence, become enlarged in proportion as we contemplate the extent and the structure of the
universe. The solitary [1] idea of a solitary world, rolling or
at rest in the immense ocean of space, gives place to the
cheerful idea of a society of worlds, so happily contrived
as to administer, even by their motion, instruction to man.[2]
We see our own earth filled with abundance ; but we forget
to consider how much of that abundance is owing to the
scientific knowledge the vast machinery of the universe has
unfolded.

CHAPTER XVI.

APPLICATION OF THE PRECEDING TO THE SYSTEM OF THE CHRISTIANS.

BUT, in the midst of those reflections, what are we to
think of the christian system of faith that forms itself upon
the idea of only one world, and that of no greater extent, as
is before shewn, than twenty-five thousand miles. An extent which a man, walking at the rate of three miles an hour
for twelve hours in the day, could he keep on in a circular
direction, would walk entirely round in less than two years.
Alas! what is this to the mighty ocean of space, and the
almighty power of the Creator!

From whence then could arise the solitary and strange
conceit that the Almighty, who had millions of worlds
equally dependent on his protection, should quit the care of
all the rest, and come to die in our world, because, they say,
one man and one woman had eaten an apple! And, on the

[1] The French work has "triste."—*Editor*.

[2] The French work has : " leur mouvement même est le premier eveil, la
première instruction de la raison dans l'homme." (Their motion itself is
the first awakening, the first instruction of the reason in man).—*Editor*.

other hand, are we to suppose that every world in the boundless creation had an Eve, an apple, a serpent, and a redeemer ?   In this case, the person who is irreverently called
the Son of God, and sometimes God himself, would have
nothing else to do than to travel from world to world,
in an endless succession of death, with scarcely a momentary
interval of life.[1]

It has been by rejecting the evidence, that the word, or
works of God in the creation, affords to our senses, and the
action of our reason upon that evidence, that so many wild
and whimsical systems of faith, and of religion, have been
fabricated and set up.   There may be many systems of religion that so far from being morally bad are in many
respects morally good : but there can be but ONE that is true ;
and that one necessarily must, as it ever will, be in all things
consistent with the ever existing word of God that we behold in his works.   But such is the strange construction of the
christian system of faith, that every evidence the heavens affords to man, either directly contradicts it or renders it absurd.

It is possible to believe, and I always feel pleasure in
encouraging myself to believe it, that there have been men
in the world who persuaded themselves that what is called
a *pious fraud*, might, at least under particular circumstances,
be productive of some good.   But the fraud being once
established, could not afterwards be explained ; for it is with
a pious fraud as with a bad action, it begets a calamitous
necessity of going on.

The persons who first preached the christian system of
faith, and in some measure combined with it the morality
preached by Jesus Christ, might persuade themselves that
it was better than the heathen mythology that then prevailed.   From the first preachers the fraud went on to the
second, and to the third, till the idea of its being a pious
fraud became lost in the belief of its being true ; and that
belief became again encouraged by the interest of those
who made a livelihood by preaching it.

[1] Such constant rebirth of the Son was the doctrine of Master Eckhardt, (4th
cent.).—*Editor.*

But though such a belief might, by such means, be rendered almost general among the laity, it is next to impossible to account for the continual persecution carried on by the church, for several hundred years, against the sciences, and against the professors of science, if the church had not some record or tradition that it was originally no other than a pious fraud, or did not foresee that it could not be maintained against the evidence that the structure of the universe afforded.

CHAPTER XVII.

OF THE MEANS EMPLOYED IN ALL TIME, AND ALMOST UNIVERSALLY, TO DECEIVE THE PEOPLES.

HAVING thus shewn the irreconcileable inconsistencies between the real word of God existing in the universe, and that which is called *the word of God*, as shewn to us in a printed book that any man might make, I proceed to speak of the three principal means that have been employed in all ages, and perhaps in all countries, to impose upon mankind.

Those three means are Mystery, Miracle, and Prophecy. The first two are incompatible with true religion, and the third ought always to be suspected.

With respect to Mystery, every thing we behold is, in one sense, a mystery to us. Our own existence is a mystery: the whole vegetable world is a mystery. We cannot account how it is that an acorn, when put into the ground, is made to develop itself and become an oak. We know not how it is that the seed we sow unfolds and multiplies itself, and returns to us such an abundant interest for so small a capital.

The fact however, as distinct from the operating cause, is not a mystery, because we see it; and we know also the means we are to use, which is no other than putting the seed in the ground. We know, therefore, as much as is necessary for us to know; and that part of the operation that we do not know, and which if we did, we could not perform, the Creator takes upon himself and performs it for us. We are, therefore, better off than if we had been let into the secret, and left to do it for ourselves.

But though every created thing is, in this sense, a mystery, the word mystery cannot be applied to *moral truth*, any more than obscurity can be applied to light. The God in whom we believe is a God of moral truth, and not a God of mystery or obscurity. Mystery is the antagonist of truth. It is a fog of human invention that obscures truth, and represents it in distortion. Truth never invelops *itself* in mystery; and the mystery in which it is at any time enveloped, is the work of its antagonist, and never of itself.

Religion, therefore, being the belief of a God, and the practice of moral truth, cannot have connection with mystery. The belief of a God, so far from having any thing of mystery in it, is of all beliefs the most easy, because it arises to us, as is before observed, out of necessity. And the practice of moral truth, or, in other words, a practical imitation of the moral goodness of God, is no other than our acting towards each other as he acts benignly towards all. We cannot *serve* God in the manner we serve those who cannot do without such service; and, therefore, the only idea we can have of serving God, is that of contributing to the happiness of the living creation that God has made. This cannot be done by retiring ourselves from the society of the world, and spending a recluse life in selfish devotion.

The very nature and design of religion, if I may so express it, prove even to demonstration that it must be free from every thing of mystery, and unincumbered with every thing that is mysterious. Religion, considered as a duty, is incumbent upon every living soul alike, and, therefore, must be on a level to the understanding and comprehension of all. Man does not learn religion as he learns the secrets and mysteries of a trade. He learns the theory of religion by reflection. It arises out of the action of his own mind upon the things which he sees, or upon what he may happen to hear or to read, and the practice joins itself thereto.

When men, whether from policy or pious fraud, set up

systems of religion incompatible with the word or works of God in the creation, and not only above but repugnant to human comprehension, they were under the necessity of inventing or adopting a word that should serve as a bar to all questions, inquiries and speculations. The word *mystery* answered this purpose, and thus it has happened that religion, which is in itself without mystery, has been corrupted into a fog of mysteries.

As *mystery* answered all general purposes, *miracle* followed as an occasional auxiliary. The former served to bewilder the mind, the latter to puzzle the senses. The one was the lingo, the other the legerdemain.

But before going further into this subject, it will be proper to inquire what is to be understood by a miracle.

In the same sense that every thing may be said to be a mystery, so also may it be said that every thing is a miracle, and that no one thing is a greater miracle than another. The elephant, though larger, is not a greater miracle than a mite : nor a mountain a greater miracle than an atom. To an almighty power it is no more difficult to make the one than the other, and no more difficult to make a million of worlds than to make one. Every thing, therefore, is a miracle, in one sense ; whilst, in the other sense, there is no such thing as a miracle. It is a miracle when compared to our power, and to our comprehension. It is not a miracle compared to the power that performs it. But as nothing in this description conveys the idea that is affixed to the word miracle, it is necessary to carry the inquiry further.

Mankind have conceived to themselves certain laws, by which what they call nature is supposed to act ; and that a miracle is something contrary to the operation and effect of those laws. But unless we know the whole extent of those laws, and of what are commonly called the powers of nature, we are not able to judge whether any thing that may appear to us wonderful or miraculous, be within, or be beyond, or be contrary to, her natural power of acting.

The ascension of a man several miles high into the air, would have everything in it that constitutes the idea of a miracle, if it were not known that a species of air can be generated several times lighter than the common atmospheric air, and yet possess elasticity enough to prevent the balloon, in which that light air is inclosed, from being compressed into as many times less bulk, by the common air that surrounds it. In like manner, extracting flashes or sparks of fire from the human body, as visibly as from a steel struck with a flint, and causing iron or steel to move without any visible agent, would also give the idea of a miracle, if we were not acquainted with electricity and magnetism ; so also would many other experiments in natural philosophy, to those who are not acquainted with the subject. The restoring persons to life who are to appearance dead, as is practised upon drowned persons, would also be a miracle, if it were not known that animation is capable of being suspended without being extinct.

Besides these, there are performances by slight of hand, and by persons acting in concert, that have a miraculous appearance, which, when known, are thought nothing of. And, besides these, there are mechanical and optical deceptions. There is now an exhibition in Paris of ghosts or spectres, which, though it is not imposed upon the spectators as a fact, has an astonishing appearance. As, therefore, we know not the extent to which either nature or art can go, there is no criterion to determine what a miracle is ; and mankind, in giving credit to appearances, under the idea of their being miracles, are subject to be continually imposed upon.

Since then appearances are so capable of deceiving, and things not real have a strong resemblance to things that are, nothing can be more inconsistent than to suppose that the Almighty would make use of means, such as are called miracles, that would subject the person who performed them to the suspicion of being an impostor, and the person who related them to be suspected of lying, and the doctrine intended to be supported thereby to be suspected as a fabulous invention.

Of all the modes of evidence that ever were invented to

obtain belief to any system or opinion to which the name of religion has been given, that of miracle, however successful the imposition may have been, is the most inconsistent. For, in the first place, whenever recourse is had to show, for the purpose of procuring that belief (for a miracle, under any idea of the word, is a show) it implies a lameness or weakness in the doctrine that is preached. And, in the second place, it is degrading the Almighty into the character of a show-man, playing tricks to amuse and make the people stare and wonder. It is also the most equivocal sort of evidence that can be set up ; for the belief is not to depend upon the thing called a miracle, but upon the credit of the reporter, who says that he saw it ; and, therefore, the thing, were it true, would have no better chance of being believed than if it were a lie.

Suppose I were to say, that when I sat down to write this book, a hand presented itself in the air, took up the pen and wrote every word that is herein written ; would any body believe me ? Certainly they would not. Would they believe me a whit the more if the thing had been a fact ? Certainly they would not. Since then a real miracle, were it to happen, would be subject to the same fate as the falsehood, the inconsistency becomes the greater of supposing the Almighty would make use of means that would not answer the purpose for which they were intended, even if they were real.

If we are to suppose a miracle to be something so entirely out of the course of what is called nature, that she must go out of that course to accomplish it, and we see an account given of such a miracle by the person who said he saw it, it raises a question in the mind very easily decided, which is,—Is it more probable that nature should go out of her course, or that a man should tell a lie ? We have never seen, in our time, nature go out of her course ; but we have good reason to believe that millions of lies have been told in the same time ; it is, therefore, at least millions to one, that the reporter of a miracle tells a lie.

The story of the whale swallowing Jonah, though a whale

is large enough to do it, borders greatly on the marvellous; but it would have approached nearer to the idea of a miracle, if Jonah had swallowed the whale. In this, which may serve for all cases of miracles, the matter would decide itself as before stated, namely, Is it more probable that a man should have swallowed a whale, or told a lie?

But suppose that Jonah had really swallowed the whale, and gone with it in his belly to Nineveh, and to convince the people that it was true have cast it up in their sight, of the full length and size of a whale, would they not have believed him to have been the devil instead of a prophet? or if the whale had carried Jonah to Nineveh, and cast him up in the same public manner, would they not have believed the whale to have been the devil, and Jonah one of his imps?

The most extraordinary of all the things called miracles, related in the New Testament, is that of the devil flying away with Jesus Christ, and carrying him to the top of a high mountain; and to the top of the highest pinnacle of the temple, and showing him and promising to him *all the kingdoms of the world.* How happened it that he did not discover America? or is it only with *kingdoms* that his sooty highness has any interest.

I have too much respect for the moral character of Christ to believe that he told this whale of a miracle himself: neither is it easy to account for what purpose it could have been fabricated, unless it were to impose upon the connoisseurs of miracles, as is sometimes practised upon the connoisseurs of Queen Anne's farthings, and collectors of relics and antiquities; or to render the belief of miracles ridiculous, by outdoing miracle, as Don Quixote outdid chivalry; or to embarrass the belief of miracles, by making it doubtful by what power, whether of God or of the devil, any thing called a miracle was performed. It requires, however, a great deal of faith in the devil to believe this miracle.

In every point of view in which those things called miracles can be placed and considered, the reality of them is improbable, and their existence unnecessary. They would not, as

before observed, answer any useful purpose, even if they
were true ; for it is more difficult to obtain belief to a miracle,
than to a principle evidently moral, without any miracle.
Moral principle speaks universally for itself. Miracle could
be but a thing of the moment, and seen but by a few ; after
this it requires a transfer of faith from God to man to
believe a miracle upon man's report. Instead, therefore, of
admitting the recitals of miracles as evidence of any system
of religion being true, they ought to be considered as symptoms of its being fabulous. It is necessary to the full and
upright character of truth that it rejects the crutch ; and it
is consistent with the character of fable to seek the aid that
truth rejects. Thus much for Mystery and Miracle.

As Mystery and Miracle took charge of the past and the
present, Prophecy took charge of the future, and rounded
the tenses of *faith*.[1] It was not sufficient to know what had
been done, but what would be done. The supposed prophet
was the supposed historian of times to come ; and if he
happened, in shooting with a long bow of a thousand years,
to strike within a thousand miles of a mark, the ingenuity
of posterity could make it point-blank ; and if he happened
to be directly wrong, it was only to suppose, as in the case
of Jonah and Nineveh, that God had repented himself and
changed his mind. What a fool do fabulous systems make
of man !

It has been shewn, in a former part of this work, that the
original meaning of the words *prophet* and *prophesying* has
been changed, and that a prophet, in the sense of the word
as now used, is a creature of modern invention ; and it is
owing to this change in the meaning of the words, that the
flights and metaphors of the Jewish poets, and phrases and
expressions now rendered obscure by our not being acquainted with the local circumstances to which they applied
at the time they were used, have been erected into prophecies, and made to bend to explanations at the will and
whimsical conceits of sectaries, expounders, and commentators. Every thing unintelligible was prophetical, and

[1] In the French work : " du verbe *croire*."—*Editor.*

6

every thing insignificant was typical. A blunder would have served for a prophecy; and a dish-clout for a type.

If by a prophet we are to suppose a man to whom the Almighty communicated some event that would take place in future, either there were such men, or there were not. If there were, it is consistent to believe that the event so communicated would be told in terms that could be understood, and not related in such a loose and obscure manner as to be out of the comprehension of those that heard it, and so equivocal as to fit almost any circumstance that might happen afterwards. It is conceiving very irreverently of the Almighty, to suppose he would deal in this jesting manner with mankind; yet all the things called prophecies in the book called the Bible come under this description.

But it is with Prophecy as it is with Miracle. It could not answer the purpose even if it were real. Those to whom a prophecy should be told could not tell whether the man prophesied or lied, or whether it had been revealed to him, or whether he conceited it; and if the thing that he prophesied, or pretended to prophesy, should happen, or some thing like it, among the multitude of things that are daily happening, nobody could again know whether he foreknew it, or guessed at it, or whether it was accidental. A prophet, therefore, is a character useless and unnecessary; and the safe side of the case is to guard against being imposed upon, by not giving credit to such relations.

Upon the whole, Mystery, Miracle, and Prophecy, are appendages that belong to fabulous and not to true religion. They are the means by which so many *Lo heres!* and *Lo theres!* have been spread about the world, and religion been made into a trade. The success of one impostor gave encouragement to another, and the quieting salvo of doing *some good* by keeping up a *pious fraud* protected them from remorse

RECAPITULATION.

HAVING now extended the subject to a greater length than I first intended, I shall bring it to a close by abstracting a summary from the whole.

First, That the idea or belief of a word of God existing in print, or in writing, or in speech, is inconsistent in itself for the reasons already assigned. These reasons, among many others, are the want of an universal language; the mutability of language; the errors to which translations are subject; the possibility of totally suppressing such a word; the probability of altering it, or of fabricating the whole, and imposing it upon the world.

Secondly, That the Creation we behold is the real and ever existing word of God, in which we cannot be deceived. It proclaimeth his power, it demonstrates his wisdom, it manifests his goodness and beneficence.

Thirdly, That the moral duty of man consists in imitating the moral goodness and beneficence of God manifested in the creation towards all his creatures. That seeing as we daily do the goodness of God to all men, it is an example calling upon all men to practise the same towards each other; and, consequently, that every thing of persecution and revenge between man and man, and every thing of cruelty to animals, is a violation of moral duty.

I trouble not myself about the manner of future existence. I content myself with believing, even to positive conviction, that the power that gave me existence is able to continue it, in any form and manner he pleases, either with or without this body; and it appears more probable to me that I shall continue to exist hereafter than that I should have had existence, as I now have, before that existence began.

It is certain that, in one point, all nations of the earth and all religions agree. All believe in a God, The things in which they disagree are the redundancies annexed to that belief; and therefore, if ever an universal religion should prevail, it will not be believing any thing new, but in getting rid of redundancies, and believing as man believed at first.[1]　Adam, if ever there was such a man, was created a Deist ; but in the mean time, let every man follow, as he has a right to do, the religion and worship he prefers.

[1] " In the childhood of the world," according to the first (French) version ; and the strict translation of the final sentence is : " Deism was the religion of Adam, supposing him not an imaginary being ; but none the less must it be left to all men to follow, as is their right, the religion and worship they prefer."— *Editor.*

II.

THE AGE OF REASON.

PART II.

PREFACE.

I HAVE mentioned in the former part of *The Age of Reason* that it had long been my intention to publish my thoughts upon Religion; but that I had originally reserved it to a later period in life, intending it to be the last work I should undertake. The circumstances, however, which existed in France in the latter end of the year 1793, determined me to delay it no longer. The just and humane principles of the Revolution which Philosophy had first diffused, had been departed from. The Idea, always dangerous to Society as it is derogatory to the Almighty,—that priests could forgive sins,—though it seemed to exist no longer, had blunted the feelings of humanity, and callously prepared men for the commission of all crimes. The intolerant spirit of church persecution had transferred itself into politics; the tribunals, stiled Revolutionary, supplied the place of an Inquisition; and the Guillotine of the Stake. I saw many of my most intimate friends destroyed; others daily carried to prison; and I had reason to believe, and had also intimations given me, that the same danger was approaching myself.

Under these disadvantages, I began the former part of the Age of Reason; I had, besides, neither Bible nor Testament[1] to refer to, though I was writing against both; nor could I procure any; notwithstanding which I have pro-

[1] It must be borne in mind that throughout this work Paine generally means by " Bible " only the Old Testament, and speaks of the New as the " Testament."—*Editor*.

duced a work that no Bible Believer, though writing at his ease, and with a Library of Church Books about him, can refute. Towards the latter end of December of that year, a motion was made and carried, to exclude foreigners from the Convention. There were but two, Anacharsis Cloots and myself; and I saw I was particularly pointed at by Bourdon de l'Oise, in his speech on that motion.

Conceiving, after this, that I had but a few days of liberty, I sat down and brought the work to a close as speedily as possible ; and I had not finished it more than six hours, in the state it has since appeared,[1] before a guard came there, about three in the morning, with an order signed by the two Committees of Public Safety and Surety General, for putting me in arrestation as a foreigner, and conveying me to the prison of the Luxembourg. I contrived, in my way there, to call on Joel Barlow, and I put the Manuscript of the work into his hands, as more safe than in my possession in prison ; and not knowing what might be the fate in France either of the writer or the work, I addressed it to the protection of the citizens of the United States.

It is justice that I say, that the guard who executed this order, and the interpreter to the Committee of General Surety, who accompanied them to examine my papers, treated me not only with civility, but with respect. The keeper of the Luxembourg, Benoit, a man of good heart, shewed to me every friendship in his power, as did also all his family, while he continued in that station. He was removed from it, put into arrestation, and carried before the tribunal upon a malignant accusation, but acquitted.

After I had been in Luxembourg about three weeks, the Americans then in Paris went in a body to the Convention, to reclaim me as their countryman and friend ; but were answered by the President, Vadier, who was also President of the Committee of Surety General, and had signed the order for my arrestation, that I was born in England.[2] I

---

[1] This is an allusion to the essay which Paine wrote at an earlier part of 1793. See Introduction.—*Editor*.

[2] These excited Americans do not seem to have understood or reported the

heard no more, after this, from any person out of the walls
of the prison, till the fall of Robespierre, on the 9th of
Thermidor—July 27, 1794.

About two months before this event, I was seized with a
fever that in its progress had every symptom of becoming
mortal, and from the effects of which I am not recovered.
It was then that I remembered with renewed satisfaction,
and congratulated myself most sincerely, on having written
the former part of *The Age of Reason.* I had then but
little expectation of surviving, and those about me had less.
I know therefore by experience the conscientious trial of
my own principles.

I was then with three chamber comrades: Joseph Van-
heule of Bruges, Charles Bastíni, and Michael Robyns of
Louvain. The unceasing and anxious attention of these
three friends to me, by night and day, I remember with gratitude and mention with pleasure. It happened that a physician (Dr. Graham) and a surgeon, (Mr. Bond,) part of the
suite of General O'Hara,[1] were then in the Luxembourg: I
ask not myself whether it be convenient to them, as men
under the English Government, that I express to them my
thanks; but I should reproach myself if I did not; and also
to the physician of the Luxembourg, Dr. Markoski.

I have some reason to believe, because I cannot discover
any other, that this illness preserved me in existence.
Among the papers of Robespierre that were examined and
reported upon to the Convention by a Committee of Deputies, is a note in the hand writing of Robespierre, in the
following words:

" Démander que Thomas Paine soit décrété d'accusation, pour l'intérêt de l'Amérique autant que de la France."	Demand that Thomas Paine be de-creed of accusation, for the interest of America, as well as of France.

most important item in Vadier's reply, namely that their application was " unoffi-
cial," i. e. not made through or sanctioned by Gouverneur Morris, American
Minister.   For the detailed history of all this see vol. iii.—*Editor.*

[1] The officer who at Yorktown, Virginia, carried out the sword of Cornwallis
for surrender, and satirically offered it to Rochambeau instead of Washington.
Paine loaned him £300 when he (O'Hara) left the prison, the money he had
concealed in the lock of his cell-door.—*Editor.*

From what cause it was that the intention was not put in execution, I know not, and cannot inform myself; and therefore I ascribe it to impossibility, on account of that illness.

The Convention, to repair as much as lay in their power the injustice I had sustained, invited me publickly and unanimously to return into the Convention, and which I accepted, to shew I could bear an injury without permitting it to injure my principles or my disposition. It is not because right principles have been violated, that they are to be abandoned.

I have seen, since I have been at liberty, several publications written, some in America, and some in England, as answers to the former part of " The Age of Reason." If the authors of these can amuse themselves by so doing, I shall not interrupt them. They may write against the work, and against me, as much as they please ; they do me more service than they intend, and I can have no objection that they write on. They will find, however, by this Second Part, without its being written as an answer to them, that they must return to their work, and spin their cobweb over again. The first is brushed away by accident.

They will now find that I have furnished myself with a Bible and Testament; and I can say also that I have found them to be much worse books than I had conceived. If I have erred in any thing, in the former part of the Age of Reason, it has been by speaking better of some parts than they deserved.

I observe, that all my opponents resort, more or less, to what they call Scripture Evidence and Bible authority, to help them out. They are so little masters of the subject, as to confound a dispute about authenticity with a dispute about doctrines ; I will, however, put them right, that if they should be disposed to write any more, they may know how to begin.

THOMAS PAINE.

October, 1795.

CHAPTER I.

THE OLD TESTAMENT.

IT has often been said that any thing may be proved from the Bible; but before any thing can be admitted as proved by Bible, the Bible itself must be proved to be true; for if the Bible be not true, or the truth of it be doubtful, it ceases to have authority, and cannot be admitted as proof of any thing.

It has been the practice of all Christian commentators on the Bible, and of all Christian priests and preachers, to impose the Bible on the world as a mass of truth, and as the word of God; they have disputed and wrangled, and have anathematized each other about the supposeable meaning of particular parts and passages therein; one has said and insisted that such a passage meant such a thing, another that it meant directly the contrary, and a third, that it meant neither one nor the other, but something different from both; and this they have called *understanding* the Bible.

It has happened, that all the answers that I have seen to the former part of *The Age of Reason* have been written by priests: and these pious men, like their predecessors, contend and wrangle, and *understand* the Bible; each understands it differently, but each understands it best; and they have agreed in nothing but in telling their readers that Thomas Paine understands it not.

Now instead of wasting their time, and heating themselves in fractious disputations about doctrinal points drawn from the Bible, these men *ought to know*, and if they do not it is civility to inform them, that the first thing to be *understood* is, whether there is sufficient authority for believing the Bible to be the word of God, or whether there is not?

There are matters in that book, said to be done by the *express command* of God, that are as shocking to humanity, and to every idea we have of moral justice, as any thing done by Robespierre, by Carrier, by Joseph le Bon, in France, by the English government in the East Indies, or by any other assassin in modern times. When we read in the books ascribed to Moses, Joshua, etc., that they (the Israelites) came by stealth upon whole nations of people, who, as the history itself shews, had given them no offence; *that they put all those nations to the sword; that they spared neither age nor infancy; that they utterly destroyed men, women and childreu; that they left not a soul to breathe;* expressions that are repeated over and over again in those books, and that too with exulting ferocity; are we sure these things are facts? are we sure that the Creator of man commissioned those things to be done? Are we sure that the books that tell us so were written by his authority?

It is not the antiquity of a tale that is any evidence of its truth; on the contrary, it is a symptom of its being fabulous; for the more ancient any history pretends to be, the more it has the resemblance of a fable. The origin of every nation is buried in fabulous tradition, and that of the Jews is as much to be suspected as any other.

To charge the commission of things upon the Almighty, which in their own nature, and by every rule of moral justice, are crimes, as all assassination is, and more especially the assassination of infants, is matter of serious concern. The Bible tells us, that those assassinations were done by the *express command of God.* To believe therefore the Bible to be true, we must *unbelieve* all our belief in the moral justice of God; for wherein could crying or smiling infants offend? And to read the Bible without horror, we must undo every thing that is tender, sympathising, and benevolent in the heart of man. Speaking for myself, if I had no other evidence that the Bible is fabulous, than the sacrifice I must make to believe it to be true, that alone would be sufficient to determine my choice.

But in addition to all the moral evidence against the

Bible, I will, in the progress of this work, produce such other evidence as even a priest cannot deny ; and shew, from that evidence, that the Bible is not entitled to credit, as being the word of God.

But, before I proceed to this examination, I will shew wherein the Bible differs from all other ancient writings with respect to the nature of the evidence necessary to establish its authenticity ; and this is the more proper to be done, because the advocates of the Bible, in their answers to the former part of *The Age of Reason*, undertake to say, and they put some stress thereon, that the authenticity of the Bible is as well established as that of any other ancient book : as if our belief of the one could become any rule for our belief of the other.

I know, however, but of one ancient book that authoritatively challenges universal consent and belief, and that is *Euclid's Elements of Geometry ; * and the reason is, because it is a book of self-evident demonstration, entirely independent of its author, and of every thing relating to time, place, and circumstance. The matters contained in that book would have the same authority they now have, had they been written by any other person, or had the work been anonymous, or had the author never been known ; for the identical certainty of who was the author makes no part of our belief of the matters contained in the book. But it is quite otherwise with respect to the books ascribed to Moses, to Joshua, to Samuel, etc. : those are books of *testimony*, and they testify of things naturally incredible ; and therefore the whole of our belief, as to the authenticity of those books, rests, in the first place, upon the *certainty* that they were written by Moses, Joshua, and Samuel ; secondly, upon the credit we give to their testimony. We may believe the first, that is, may believe the certainty of the authorship, and yet not the testimony ; in the same manner that we may believe that a certain person gave evidence

---

* Euclid, according to chronological history, lived three hundred years before Christ, and about one hundred before Archimedes ; he was of the city of Alexandria, in Egypt.—*Author.*

upon a case, and yet not believe the evidence that he gave.
But if it should be found that the books ascribed to Moses,
Joshua, and Samuel, were not written by Moses, Joshua,
and Samuel, every part of the authority and authenticity of those books is gone at once; for there can be no
such thing as forged or invented testimony; neither can
there be anonymous testimony, more especially as to things
naturally incredible; such as that of talking with God face
to face, or that of the sun and moon standing still at the
command of a man.

The greatest part of the other ancient books are works
of genius; of which kind are those ascribed to Homer, to
Plato, to Aristotle, to Demosthenes, to Cicero, etc. Here
again the author is not an essential in the credit we give to
any of those works; for as works of genius they would have
the same merit they have now, were they anonymous.
Nobody believes the Trojan story, as related by Homer, to
be true; for it is the poet only that is admired, and the
merit of the poet will remain, though the story be fabulous.
But if we disbelieve the matters related by the Bible authors
(Moses for instance) as we disbelieve the things related by
Homer, there remains nothing of Moses in our estimation,
but an imposter. As to the ancient historians, from Herodotus to Tacitus, we credit them as far as they relate things
probable and credible, and no further: for if we do, we must
believe the two miracles which Tacitus relates were performed by Vespasian, that of curing a lame man, and a
blind man, in just the same manner as the same things are
told of Jesus Christ by his historians. We must also believe
the miracles cited by Josephus, that of the sea of Pamphilia
opening to let Alexander and his army pass, as is related of
the Red Sea in Exodus. These miracles are quite as well
authenticated as the Bible miracles, and yet we do not
believe them; consequently the degree of evidence necessary to establish our belief of things naturally incredible,
whether in the Bible or elsewhere, is far greater than that
which obtains our belief to natural and probable things;
and therefore the advocates for the Bible have no claim

to our belief of the Bible because that we believe things
stated in other ancient writings; since that we believe the
things stated in those writings no further than they are
probable and credible, or because they are self-evident,
like Euclid; or admire them because they are elegant, like
Homer; or approve them because they are sedate, like
Plato; or judicious, like Aristotle.

Having premised these things, I proceed to examine the
authenticity of the Bible; and I begin with what are called
the five books of Moses, *Genesis, Exodus, Leviticus, Numbers*, and *Deuteronomy*. My intention is to shew that those
books are spurious, and that Moses is not the author of
them; and still further, that they were not written in the
time of Moses nor till several hundred years afterwards;
that they are no other than an attempted history of the
life of Moses, and of the times in which he is said to have
lived, and also of the times prior thereto, written by some
very ignorant and stupid pretenders to authorship, several
hundred years after the death of Moses; as men now write
histories of things that happened, or are supposed to have
happened, several hundred or several thousand years ago.

The evidence that I shall produce in this case is from
the books themselves; and I will confine myself to this
evidence only. Were I to refer for proofs to any of the
ancient authors, whom the advocates of the Bible call pro-
phane authors, they would controvert that authority, as I
controvert theirs: I will therefore meet them on their own
ground, and oppose them with their own weapon, the Bible.

In the first place, there is no affirmative evidence that
Moses is the author of those books; and that he is the
author, is altogether an unfounded opinion, got abroad nobody knows how. The style and manner in which those
books are written give no room to believe, or even to suppose, they were written by Moses; for it is altogether the
style and manner of another person speaking of Moses. In
Exodus, Leviticus and Numbers, (for every thing in Genesis
is prior to the times of Moses and not the least allusion is
made to him therein,) the whole, I say, of these books is in

the third person; it is always, *the Lord said unto Moses, or Moses said unto the Lord ; or Moses said unto the people, or the people said unto Moses ;* and this is the style and manner that historians use in speaking of the person whose lives and actions they are writing. It may be said, that a man may speak of himself in the third person, and, therefore, it may be supposed that Moses did ; but supposition proves nothing ; and if the advocates for the belief that Moses wrote those books himself have nothing better to advance than supposition, they may as well be silent.

But granting the grammatical right, that Moses might speak of himself in the third person, because any man might speak of himself in that manner, it cannot be admitted as a fact in those books, that it is Moses who speaks, without rendering Moses truly ridiculous and absurd :—for example, Numbers xii. 3 : " *Now the man Moses was very* MEEK, *above all the men which were on the face of the earth.* If Moses said this of himself, instead of being the meekest of men, he was one of the most vain and arrogant coxcombs ; and the advocates for those books may now take which side they please, for both sides are against them : if Moses was not the author, the books are without authority ; and if he was the author, the author is without credit, because to boast of *meekness* is the reverse of meekness, and is *a lie in sentiment.*

In Deuteronomy, the style and manner of writing marks more evidently than in the former books that Moses is not the writer. The manner here used is dramatical ; the writer opens the subject by a short introductory discourse, and then introduces Moses as in the act of speaking, and when he has made Moses finish his harrangue, he (the writer) resumes his own part, and speaks till he brings Moses forward again, and at last closes the scene with an account of the death, funeral, and character of Moses.

This interchange of speakers occurs four times in this book: from the first verse of the first chapter, to the end of the fifth verse, it is the writer who speaks ; he then introduces Moses as in the act of making his harrangue, and this continues to the end of the 40th verse of the fourth

chapter; here the writer drops Moses, and speaks historically of what was done in consequence of what Moses, when
living, is supposed to have said, and which the writer has
dramatically rehearsed.

The writer opens the subject again in the first verse of
the fifth chapter, though it is only by saying that Moses
called the people of Israel together; he then introduces
Moses as before, and continues him as in the act of speaking, to the end of the 26th chapter. He does the same
thing at the beginning of the 27th chapter; and continues
Moses as in the act of speaking, to the end of the 28th
chapter. At the 29th chapter the writer speaks again
through the whole of the first verse, and the first line of
the second verse, where he introduces Moses for the last
time, and continues him as in the act of speaking, to the
end of the 33d chapter.

The writer having now finished the rehearsal on the part
of Moses, comes forward, and speaks through the whole of
the last chapter: he begins by telling the reader, that Moses
went up to the top of Pisgah, that he saw from thence
the land which (the writer says) had been promised to
Abraham, Isaac, and Jacob; that *he*, Moses, died there in
the land of Moab, that he buried him in a valley in the land
of Moab, but that no man knoweth of his sepulchre unto
this day, that is unto the time in which the writer lived who
wrote the book of Deuteronomy. The writer then tells us,
that Moses was one hundred and ten years of age when he
died—that his eye was not dim, nor his natural force abated;
and he concludes by saying, that there arose not a prophet
since in Israel like unto Moses, whom, says this anonymous
writer, the Lord knew face to face.

Having thus shewn, as far as grammatical evidence implies, that Moses was not the writer of those books, I will,
after making a few observations on the inconsistencies of
the writer of the book of Deuteronomy, proceed to shew,
from the historical and chronological evidence contained in
those books, that Moses *was not*, because *he could not be*,
the writer of them; and consequently, that there is no

authority for believing that the inhuman and horrid butch-eries of men, women, and children, told of in those books, were done, as those books say they were, at the command of God. It is a duty incumbent on every true deist, that he vindicates the moral justice of God against the calumnies of the Bible.

The writer of the book of Deuteronomy, whoever he was, for it is an anonymous work, is obscure, and also con-tradictory with himself in the account he has given of Moses.

After telling that Moses went to the top of Pisgah (and it does not appear from any account that he ever came down again) he tells us, that Moses died *there* in the land of Moab, and that *he* buried him in a valley in the land of Moab; but as there is no antecedent to the pronoun *he,* there is no knowing who *he* was, that did bury him. If the writer meant that he (God) buried him, how should *he* (the writer) know it? or why should we (the readers) believe him? since we know not who the writer was that tells us so, for certainly Moses could not himself tell where he was buried.

The writer also tells us, that no man knoweth where the sepulchre of Moses is unto this day, meaning the time in which this writer lived; how then should he know that Moses was buried in a valley in the land of Moab? for as the writer lived long after the time of Moses, as is evident from his using the expression of *unto this day*, meaning a great length of time after the death of Moses, he certainly was not at his funeral; and on the other hand, it is impossi-ble that Moses himself could say that *no man knoweth where the sepulchre is unto this day.* To make Moses the speaker, would be an improvement on the play of a child that hides himself and cries *nobody can find me* ; nobody can find Moses.

This writer has no where told us how he came by the speeches which he has put into the mouth of Moses to speak, and therefore we have a right to conclude that he either composed them himself, or wrote them from oral tradition. One or other of these is the more probable, since he has given, in the fifth chapter, a table of commandments, in which that called the fourth commandment is different from the fourth commandment in the twentieth chapter of Exodus. In that of Exodus, the reason given for keeping the seventh day is, because (says the commandment) God made the heavens and the earth in six days, and rested on the seventh; but in that of Deuteronomy, the reason given is, that it was the day on which the children of Israel came out of Egypt, and *therefore*, says this commandment, *the Lord thy God commanded thee to keep the sabbath-day.* *This* makes no mention of the creation, nor *that* of the coming out of Egypt. There are also many things given as laws of Moses in this book, that are not to be found in any of the other books; among which is that inhuman and brutal law, xxi. 18, 19, 20, 21, which authorizes parents, the father and the mother, to bring their own children to have them stoned to death for what it pleased them to call stubbornness.—But priests have always been fond of preaching up Deuteronomy, for Deuteronomy preaches up tythes; and it is from this book, xxv. 4, they have taken the phrase, and applied it to tything, that *thou shalt not muzzle the ox when he treadeth out the corn:* and that this might not escape observation, they have noted it in the table of contents at the head of the chapter, though it is only a single verse of less than two lines. O priests! priests! ye are willing to be compared to an ox, for the sake of tythes.[1]—Though it is impossible for us to know *identically* who the writer of Deuteronomy was, it is not difficult to discover him *professionally*, that he was some Jewish priest, who lived, as I shall shew in the course of this work, at least three hundred and fifty years after the time of Moses.

I come now to speak of the historical and chronological evidence. The chronology that I shall use is the Bible chronology; for I mean not to go out of the Bible for

[1] An elegant pocket edition of Paine's Theological Works (London : R. Car-lile, 1822) has in its title a picture of Paine, as a Moses in evening dress, un-folding the two tables of his " Age of Reason " to a farmer from whom the Bishop of Llandaff (who replied to this work) has taken a sheaf and a lamb which he is carrying to a church at the summit of a well-stocked hill.—*Editor*.

evidence of any thing, but to make the Bible itself prove historically and chronologically that Moses is not the author of the books ascribed to him.   It is therefore proper that I inform the readers (such an one at least as may not have the opportunity of knowing it) that in the larger Bibles, and also in some smaller ones, there is a series of chronology printed in the margin of every page for the purpose of shewing how long the historical matters stated in each page happened, or are supposed to have happened, before Christ, and consequently the distance of time between one historical circumstance and another.

I begin with the book of Genesis.—In Genesis xiv., the writer gives an account of Lot being taken prisoner in a battle between the four kings against five, and carried off; and that when the account of Lot being taken came to Abraham, that he armed all his household and marched to rescue Lot from the captors; and that he pursued them unto Dan. (ver. 14.)

To shew in what manner this expression of *pursuing them unto Dan* applies to the case in question, I will refer to two circumstances, the one in America, the other in France.   The city now called New York, in America, was originally New Amsterdam; and the town in France, lately called Havre Marat, was before called Havre-de-Grace.   New Amsterdam was changed to New York in the year 1664; Havre-de-Grace to Havre Marat in the year 1793.   Should, therefore, any writing be found, though without date, in which the name of New-York should be mentioned, it would be certain evidence that such a writing could not have been written before, and must have been written after New Amsterdam was changed to New York, and consequently not till after the year 1664, or at least during the course of that year.   And in like manner, any dateless writing, with the name of Havre Marat, would be certain evidence that such a writing must have been written after Havre-de-Grace became Havre Marat, and consequently not till after the year 1793, or at least during the course of that year.

I now come to the application of those cases, and to shew

that there was no such place as *Dan* till many years after
the death of Moses; and consequently, that Moses could
not be the writer of the book of Genesis, where this account
of pursuing them unto *Dan* is given.

The place that is called Dan in the Bible was originally
a town of the Gentiles, called Laish; and when the tribe of
Dan seized upon this town, they changed its name to Dan,
in commemoration of Dan, who was the father of that tribe,
and the great grandson of Abraham.

To establish this in proof, it is necessary to refer from
Genesis to chapter xviii. of the book called the Book of
Judges. It is there said (ver. 27) that *they* (the Danites)
*came unto Laish to a people that were quiet and secure, and
they smote them with the edge of the sword* [the Bible is filled
with murder] *and burned the city with fire; and they built a
city*, (ver. 28,) and dwelt therein, *and* [ver. 29,] *they called the
name of the city Dan, after the name of Dan, their father;
howbeit the name of the city was Laish at the first.*

This account of the Danites taking possession of Laish
and changing it to Dan, is placed in the book of Judges
immediately after the death of Samson. The death of Samson is said to have happened B. C. 1120 and that of Moses
B. C. 1451; and, therefore, according to the historical arrangement, the place was not called Dan till 331 years after
the death of Moses.

There is a striking confusion between the historical and
the chronological arrangement in the book of Judges. The
last five chapters, as they stand in the book, 17, 18, 19, 20,
21, are put chronologically before all the preceding chapters;
they are made to be 28 years before the 16th chapter, 266
before the 15th, 245 before the 13th, 195 before the 9th, 90
before the 4th, and 15 years before the 1st chapter. This
shews the uncertain and fabulous state of the Bible. According to the chronological arrangement, the taking of
Laish, and giving it the name of Dan, is made to be twenty
years after the death of Joshua, who was the successor of
Moses; and by the historical order, as it stands in the book,
it is made to be 306 years after the death of Joshua, and 331

after that of Moses; but they both exclude Moses from
being the writer of Genesis, because, according to either of
the statements, no such a place as Dan existed in the time of
Moses; and therefore the writer of Genesis must have been
some person who lived after the town of Laish had the name
of Dan; and who that person was nobody knows, and consequently the book of Genesis is anonymous, and without
authority.

I come now to state another point of historical and chronological evidence, and to shew therefrom, as in the preceding
case, that Moses is not the author of the book of Genesis.

In Genesis xxxvi. there is given a genealogy of the sons
and descendants of Esau, who are called Edomites, and also
a list by name of the kings of Edom; in enumerating of
which, it is said, verse 31, "*And these are the kings that
reigned in Edom, before there reigned any king over the children of Israel.*"

Now, were any dateless writing to be found, in which,
speaking of any past events, the writer should say, these
things happened before there was any Congress in America,
or before there was any Convention in France, it would be
evidence that such writing could not have been written
before, and could only be written after there was a Congress
in America, or a Convention in France, as the case might
be; and, consequently, that it could not be written by any
person who died before there was a Congress in the one
country, or a Convention in the other.

Nothing is more frequent, as well in history as in conversation, than to refer to a fact in the room of a date: it is
most natural so to do, because a fact fixes itself in the memory better than a date; secondly, because the fact includes
the date, and serves to give two ideas at once; and this
manner of speaking by circumstances implies as positively
that the fact alluded to is past, as if it was so expressed.
When a person in speaking upon any matter, says, it was
before I was married, or before my son was born, or before
I went to America, or before I went to France, it is absolutely
understood, and intended to be understood, that he has been

married, that he has had a son, that he has been in America, or been in France. Language does not admit of using this mode of expression in any other sense ; and whenever such an expression is found anywhere, it can only be understood in the sense in which only it could have been used.

The passage, therefore, that I have quoted—that " these are the kings that reigned in Edom, before there reigned *any* king over the children of Israel," could only have been written after the first king began to reign over them ; and consequently that the book of Genesis, so far from having been written by Moses, could not have been written till the time of Saul at least. This is the positive sense of the passage ; but the expression, *any* king, implies more kings than one, at least it implies two, and this will carry it to the time of David ; and, if taken in a general sense, it carries itself through all times of the Jewish monarchy.

Had we met with this verse in any part of the Bible that professed to have been written after kings began to reign in Israel, it would have been impossible not to have seen the application of it. It happens then that this is the case ; the two books of Chronicles, which give a history of all the kings of Israel, are *professedly*, as well as in fact, written after the Jewish monarchy began ; and this verse that I have quoted, and all the remaining verses of Genesis xxxvi. are, word for word, in 1 Chronicles i., beginning at the 43d verse.

It was with consistency that the writer of the Chronicles could say as he has said, 1 Chron. i. 43, *These are the kings that reigned in Edom, before there reigned any king over the children of Israel,* because he was going to give, and has given, a list of the kings that had reigned in Israel ; but as it is impossible that the same expression could have been used before that period, it is as certain as any thing can be proved from historical language, that this part of Genesis is taken from Chronicles, and that Genesis is not so old as Chronicles, and probably not so old as the book of Homer, or as Æsop's Fables ; admitting Homer to have been, as the tables of chronology state, contemporary with David or Solomon, and Æsop to have lived about the end of the Jewish monarchy.

Take away from Genesis the belief that Moses was the author, on which only the strange belief that it is the word of God has stood, and there remains nothing of Genesis but an anonymous book of stories, fables, and traditionary or invented absurdities, or of downright lies. The story of Eve and the serpent, and of Noah and his ark, drops to a level with the Arabian Tales, without the merit of being entertaining, and the account of men living to eight and nine hundred years becomes as fabulous as the immortality of the giants of the Mythology.

Besides, the character of Moses, as stated in the Bible, is the most horrid that can be imagined. If those accounts be true, he was the wretch that first began and carried on wars on the score or on the pretence of religion; and under that mask, or that infatuation, committed the most unexampled atrocities that are to be found in the history of any nation. Of which I will state only one instance:

When the Jewish army returned from one of their plundering and murdering excursions, the account goes on as follows (Numbers xxxi. 13): "And Moses, and Eleazar the priest, and all the princes of the congregation, went forth to meet them without the camp; and Moses was wroth with the officers of the host, with the captains over thousands, and captains over hundreds, which came from the battle; and Moses said unto them, *Have ye saved all the women alive?* behold, these caused the children of Israel, through the counsel of Balaam, to commit trespass against the Lord in the matter of Peor, and there was a plague among the congregation of the Lord. Now therefore, *kill every male among the little ones, and kill every woman that hath known a man by lying with him; but all the women-children that have not known a man by lying with him, keep alive for yourselves.*"

Among the detestable villains that in any period of the world have disgraced the name of man, it is impossible to find a greater than Moses, if this account be true. Here is an order to butcher the boys, to massacre the mothers, and debauch the daughters.

Let any mother put herself in the situation of those

mothers, one child murdered, another destined to violation, and herself in the hands of an executioner : let any daughter put herself in the situation of those daughters, destined as a prey to the murderers of a mother and a brother, and what will be their feelings? It is in vain that we attempt to impose upon nature, for nature will have her course, and the religion that tortures all her social ties is a false religion.

After this detestable order, follows an account of the plunder taken, and the manner of dividing it ; and here it is that the profaneness of priestly hypocrisy increases the catalogue of crimes. Verse 37, "*And the Lord's tribute* of the sheep was six hundred and threescore and fifteen ; and the beeves were thirty and six thousand, of which the *Lord's tribute* was threescore and twelve ; and the asses were thirty thousand, of which the *Lord's tribute* was threescore and one ; and the persons were sixteen thousand, of which the *Lord's tribute* was thirty and two.*" In short, the matters contained in this chapter, as well as in many other parts of the Bible, are too horrid for humanity to read, or for decency to hear; for it appears, from the 35th verse of this chapter, that the number of women-children consigned to debauchery by the order of Moses was thirty-two thousand.

People in general know not what wickedness there is in this pretended word of God. Brought up in habits of superstition, they take it for granted that the Bible is true, and that it is good ; they permit themselves not to doubt of it, and they carry the ideas they form of the benevolence of the Almighty to the book which they have been taught to believe was written by his authority. Good heavens! it is quite another thing, it is a book of lies, wickedness, and blasphemy ; for what can be greater blasphemy, than to ascribe the wickedness of man to the orders of the Almighty!

But to return to my subject, that of shewing that Moses is not the author of the books ascribed to him, and that the Bible is spurious. The two instances I have already given would be sufficient, without any additional evidence, to invalidate the authenticity of any book that pretended to be four or five hundred years more ancient than the matters it speaks of, or refers to, as facts ; for in the case of *pursuing them unto Dan,* and of *the kings that reigned over the children of Israel,* not even the flimsy pretence of prophecy can be pleaded. The expressions are in the preter tense, and it would be downright idiotism to say that a man could prophecy in the preter tense.

But there are many other passages scattered throughout those books that unite in the same point of evidence. It is said in Exodus, (another of the books ascribed to Moses,) xvi. 35 : "And the children of Israel did eat manna *until they came to a land inhabited;* they did eat manna *until they came unto the borders of the land of Canaan."*

Whether the children of Israel ate manna or not, or what manna was, or whether it was anything more than a kind of fungus or small mushroom, or other vegetable substance common to that part of the country, makes no part of my argument ; all that I mean to shew is, that it is not Moses that could write this account, because the account extends itself beyond the life time of Moses. Moses, according to the Bible, (but it is such a book of lies and contradictions there is no knowing which part to believe, or whether any) died in the wilderness, and never came upon the borders of the land of Canaan ; and, consequently, it could not be he that said what the children of Israel did, or what they ate when they came there. This account of eating manna, which they tell us was written by Moses, extends itself to the time of Joshua, the successor of Moses, as appears by the account given in the book of Joshua, after the children of Israel had passed the river Jordan, and came into the borders of the land of Canaan. Joshua, v. 12 : " *And the manna ceased on the morrow, after they had eaten of the old corn of the land ; neither had the children of Israel manna any more, but they did eat of the fruit of the land of Canaan that year."*

But a more remarkable instance than this occurs in Deuteronomy ; which, while it shews that Moses could not be the writer of that book, shews also the fabulous notions that prevailed at that time about giants. In Deuteronomy iii. 11, among the conquests said to be made by Moses, is an account of the taking of Og, king of Bashan : " For only Og, king of Bashan, remained of the race of giants ; behold, his bedstead was a bedstead of iron ; is it not in Rabbath of the children of Ammon? nine cubits was the length thereof, and four cubits the breadth of it, after the cubit of a man." A cubit is 1 foot $9\frac{888}{1000}$ inches ; the length therefore of the bed was 16 feet 4 inches, and the breadth 7 feet 4 inches ; thus much for this giant's bed. Now for the historical part, which, though the evidence is not so direct and positive as in the former cases, is nevertheless very presumable and corroborating evidence, and is better than the *best* evidence on the contrary side.

The writer, by way of proving the existence of this giant, refers to his bed, as an *ancient relick*, and says, is it not in Rabbath (or Rabbah) of the children of Ammon? meaning that it is ; for such is frequently the bible method of affirming a thing. But it could not be Moses that said this, because Moses could know nothing about Rabbah, nor of what was in it. Rabbah was not a city belonging to this giant king, nor was it one of the cities that Moses took. The knowledge therefore that this bed was at Rabbah, and of the particulars of its dimensions, must be referred to the time when Rabbah was taken, and this was not till four hundred years after the death of Moses ; for which, see 2 Sam. xii. 26 : " And Joab [David's general] fought against *Rabbah of the children of Ammon,* and took the royal city," etc.

As I am not undertaking to point out all the contradictions in time, place, and circumstance that abound in the books ascribed to Moses, and which prove to demonstration that those books could not be written by Moses, nor in the time of Moses, I proceed to the book of Joshua, and to shew that Joshua is not the author of that book, and that it is anonymous and without authority. The evidence I shall produce is contained in the book itself : I will not go out of the Bible for proof against the supposed authenticity of the Bible. False testimony is always good against itself.

Joshua, according to Joshua i., was the immediate successor of Moses; he was, moreover, a military man, which Moses was not; and he continued as chief of the people of Israel twenty-five years; that is, from the time that Moses died, which, according to the Bible chronology, was B.C. 1451, until B.C. 1426, when, according to the same chronology, Joshua died. If, therefore, we find in this book, said to have been written by Joshua, references to *facts done* after the death of Joshua, it is evidence that Joshua could not be the author; and also that the book could not have been written till after the time of the latest fact which it records. As to the character of the book, it is horrid; it is a military history of rapine and murder, as savage and brutal as those recorded of his predecessor in villainy and hypocrisy, Moses; and the blasphemy consists, as in the former books, in ascribing those deeds to the orders of the Almighty.

In the first place, the book of Joshua, as is the case in the preceding books, is written in the third person; it is the historian of Joshua that speaks, for it would have been absurd and vainglorious that Joshua should say of himself, as is said of him in the last verse of the sixth chapter, that "*his fame was noised throughout all the country.*"—I now come more immediately to the proof.

In Joshua xxiv. 31, it is said " And Israel served the Lord all the days of Joshua, and *all the days of the elders that over-lived Joshua.*" Now, in the name of common sense, can it be Joshua that relates what people had done after he was dead? This account must not only have been written by some historian that lived after Joshua, but that lived also after the elders that out-lived Joshua.

There are several passages of a general meaning with respect to time, scattered throughout the book of Joshua, that carries the time in which the book was written to a distance from the time of Joshua, but without marking by exclusion any particular time, as in the passage above quoted. In that passage, the time that intervened between the death of Joshua and the death of the elders is excluded descriptively and absolutely, and the evidence substantiates that the book could not have been written till after the death of the last.

But though the passages to which I allude, and which I am going to quote, do not designate any particular time by exclusion, they imply a time far more distant from the days of Joshua than is contained between the death of Joshua and the death of the elders. Such is the passage, x. 14, where, after giving an account that the sun stood still upon Gibeon, and the moon in the valley of Ajalon, at the command of Joshua, (a tale only fit to amuse children*) the passage says : "And there was no day like that, before it, nor *after it*, that the Lord hearkened to the voice of a man."

The time implied by the expression *after it*, that is, after that day, being put in comparison with all the time that passed *before it*, must, in order to give any expressive signification to the passage, mean a *great length of time :*—for example, it would have been ridiculous to have said so the next day, or the next week, or the next month, or the next year ; to give therefore meaning to the passage, comparative with the wonder it relates, and the prior time it alludes to,

---

* This tale of the sun standing still upon Mount Gibeon, and the moon in the valley of Ajalon, is one of those fables that detects itself. Such a circumstance could not have happened without being known all over the world. One half would have wondered why the sun did not rise, and the other why it did not set ; and the tradition of it would be universal ; whereas there is not a nation in the world that knows any thing about it. But why must the moon stand still ? What occasion could there be for moonlight in the daytime, and that too whilst the sun shined ? As a poetical figure, the whole is well enough ; it is akin to that in the song of Deborah and Barak, *The stars in their courses fought against Sisera ;* but it is inferior to the figurative declaration of Mahomet to the persons who came to expostulate with him on his goings on, *Wert thou*, said he, *to come to me with the sun in thy right hand and the moon in thy left, it should not alter my career.* For Joshua to have exceeded Mahomet, he should have put the sun and moon, one in each pocket, and carried them as Guy Faux carried his dark lanthorn, and taken them out to shine as he might happen to want them. The sublime and the ridiculous are often so nearly related that it is difficult to class them separately. One step above the sublime makes the ridiculous, and one step above the ridiculous makes the sublime again ; the account, however, abstracted from the poetical fancy, shews the ignorance of Joshua, for he should have commanded the earth to have stood still.—*Author.*

it must mean centuries of years; less however than one would be trifling, and less than two would be barely admissible.

A distant, but general time is also expressed in chapter viii.; where, after giving an account of the taking the city of Ai, it is said, ver. 28th, "And Joshua burned Ai, and made it an heap for ever, a desolation *unto this day;*" and again, ver. 29, where speaking of the king of Ai, whom Joshua had hanged, and buried at the entering of the gate, it is said, "And he raised thereon a great heap of stones, which remaineth *unto this day*," that is, unto the day or time in which the writer of the book of Joshua lived. And again, in chapter x. where, after speaking of the five kings whom Joshua had hanged on five trees, and then thrown in a cave, it is said, "And he laid great stones on the cave's mouth, which remain unto this very day."

In enumerating the several exploits of Joshua, and of the tribes, and of the places which they conquered or attempted, it is said, xv. 63, "As for the Jebusites, the inhabitants of Jerusalem, the children of Judah could not drive them out; but the Jebusites dwell with the children of Judah AT JERU-SALEM *unto this day.*" The question upon this passage is, At what time did the Jebusites and the children of Judah dwell together at Jerusalem? As this matter occurs again in Judges i. I shall reserve my observations till I come to that part.

Having thus shewn from the book of Joshua itself, without any auxiliary evidence whatever, that Joshua is not the author of that book, and that it is anonymous, and consequently without authority, I proceed, as before-mentioned, to the book of Judges.

The book of Judges is anonymous on the face of it; and, therefore, even the pretence is wanting to call it the word of God; it has not so much as a nominal voucher; it is altogether fatherless.

This book begins with the same expression as the book of Joshua. That of Joshua begins, chap i. 1, *Now after the death of Moses*, etc., and this of the Judges begins, *Now after*

the death of Joshua, etc. This, and the similarity of stile between the two books, indicate that they are the work of the
same author ; but who he was, is altogether unknown ; the
only point that the book proves is that the author lived long
after the time of Joshua ; for though it begins as if it followed immediately after his death, the second chapter is an
epitome or abstract of the whole book, which, according to
the Bible chronology, extends its history through a space
of 306 years ; that is, from the death of Joshua, B.C. 1426
to the death of Samson, B.C. 1120, and only 25 years before
Saul went *to seek his father's asses, and was made king.* But
there is good reason to believe, that it was not written till
the time of David, at least, and that the book of Joshua was
not written before the same time.

In Judges i., the writer, after announcing the death of
Joshua, proceeds to tell what happened between the children
of Judah and the native inhabitants of the land of Canaan.
In this statement the writer, having abruptly mentioned
Jerusalem in the 7th verse, says immediately after, in the
8th verse, by way of explanation, " Now the children of
Judah *had* fought against Jerusalem, and *taken* it ;" consequently this book could not have been written before Jerusalem had been taken. The reader will recollect the quotation I have just before made from Joshua xv. 63, where it
said that *the Jebusites dwell with the children of Judah at
Jerusalem at this day ;* meaning the time when the book of
Joshua was written.

The evidence I have already produced to prove that the
books I have hitherto treated of were not written by the
persons to whom they are ascribed, nor till many years after
their death, if such persons ever lived, is already so abundant, that I can afford to admit this passage with less weight
than I am entitled to draw from it. For the case is, that
so far as the Bible can be credited as an history, the city of
Jerusalem was not taken till the time of David ; and consequently, that the book of Joshua, and of Judges, were not
written till after the commencement of the reign of David,
which was 370 years after the death of Joshua.

The name of the city that was afterward called Jerusalem was originally Jebus, or Jebusi, and was the capital of the Jebusites. The account of David's taking this city is given in 2 Samuel, v. 4, etc.; also in 1 Chron. xiv. 4, etc. There is no mention in any part of the Bible that it was ever taken before, nor any account that favours such an opinion. It is not said, either in Samuel or in Chronicles, that they " utterly destroyed men, women and children, that they left not a soul to breathe," as is said of their other conquests; and the silence here observed implies that it was taken by capitulation; and that the Jebusites, the native inhabitants, continued to live in the place after it was taken. The account therefore, given in Joshua, that " the Jebusites dwell with the children of Judah " at Jerusalem at this day, corresponds to no other time than after taking the city by David.

Having now shown that every book in the Bible, from Genesis to Judges, is without authenticity, I come to the book of Ruth, an idle, bungling story, foolishly told, nobody knows by whom, about a strolling country-girl creeping slily to bed to her cousin Boaz.[1] Pretty stuff indeed to be called the word of God. It is, however, one of the best books in the Bible, for it is free from murder and rapine.

I come next to the two books of Samuel, and to shew that those books were not written by Samuel, nor till a great length of time after the death of Samuel; and that they are, like all the former books, anonymous, and without authority.

To be convinced that these books have been written much later than the time of Samuel, and consequently not by him, it is only necessary to read the account which the writer gives of Saul going to seek his father's asses, and of his interview with Samuel, of whom Saul went to enquire about those lost asses, as foolish people now-a-days go to a conjuror to enquire after lost things.

The writer, in relating this story of Saul, Samuel, and the asses, does not tell it as a thing that had just then happened, but as *an ancient story in the time this writer lived;* for he tells

---

[1] The text of Ruth does not imply the unpleasant sense Paine's words are likely to convey.—*Editor.*

it in the language or terms used at the time that *Samuel* lived, which obliges the writer to explain the story in the terms or language used in the time the *writer* lived.

Samuel, in the account given of him in the first of those books, chap. ix. is called *the seer;* and it is by this term that Saul enquires after him, ver. 11, " And as they [Saul and his servant] went up the hill to the city, they found young maidens going out to draw water ; and they said unto them, *Is the seer here ?* " Saul then went according to the direction of these maidens, and met Samuel without knowing him, and said unto him, ver. 18, " Tell me, I pray thee, where the *seer's house is ?* and Samuel answered Saul, and said, *I am the seer.*"

As the writer of the book of Samuel relates these questions and answers, in the language or manner of speaking used in the time they are said to have been spoken, and as that manner of speaking was out of use when this author wrote, he found it necessary, in order to make the story under-stood, to explain the terms in which these questions and answers are spoken ; and he does this in the 9th verse, where he says, " *Before-time* in Israel, when a man went to enquire of God, thus he spake, Come let us go to the seer ; for he that is now called a prophet, was *before-time* called a seer." This proves, as I have before said, that this story of Saul, Samuel, and the asses, was an ancient story at the time the book of Samuel was written, and consequently that Samuel did not write it, and that the book is without authenticity.

But if we go further into those books the evidence is still more positive that Samuel is not the writer of them ; for they relate things that did not happen till several years after the death of Samuel. Samuel died before Saul; for 1 Samuel, xxviii. tells, that Saul and the witch of Endor conjured Samuel up after he was dead ; yet the history of matters contained in those books is extended through the remaining part of Saul's life, and to the latter end of the life of David, who succeeded Saul. The account of the death and burial of Samuel (a thing which he could not write himself) is related in 1 Samuel xxv. ; and the chronology affixed to this chapter makes this to be B.C. 1060; yet the history of this *first* book is brought down to B.C. 1056, that is, to the death of Saul, which was not till four years after the death of Samuel.

The second book of Samuel begins with an account of things that did not happen till four years after Samuel was dead; for it begins with the reign of David, who succeeded Saul, and it goes on to the end of David's reign, which was forty-three years after the death of Samuel; and, therefore, the books are in themselves positive evidence that they were not written by Samuel.

I have now gone through all the books in the first part of the Bible, to which the names of persons are affixed, as being the authors of those books, and which the church, stiling itself the Christian church, have imposed upon the world as the writings of Moses, Joshua and Samuel; and I have detected and proved the falsehood of this imposition.—And now ye priests, of every description, who have preached and written against the former part of the *Age of Reason*, what have ye to say? Will ye with all this mass of evidence against you, and staring you in the face, still have the assurance to march into your pulpits, and continue to impose these books on your congregations, as the works of *inspired penmen*, and the word of God? when it is as evident as demonstration can make truth appear, that the persons who ye say are the authors, are *not* the authors, and that ye know not who the authors are. What shadow of pretence have ye now to produce for continuing the blasphemous fraud? What have ye still to offer against the pure and moral religion of deism, in support of your system of falsehood, idolatry, and pretended revelation? Had the cruel and murdering orders, with which the Bible is filled, and the numberless torturing executions of men, women, and children, in consequence of those orders, been ascribed to some friend, whose memory you revered, you would have glowed with satisfaction at detecting the falsehood of the charge, and gloried in defending his injured fame. It is because ye are sunk in the cruelty of superstition, or feel no interest in the honour of your Creator, that ye listen to the horrid tales of the Bible, or hear them with callous indifference. The evidence I have produced, and shall still produce in the course of this work, to prove that the Bible is without authority, will, whilst it wounds the stubbornness of a priest, relieve and tranquillize the minds of millions : it will free them from all those hard thoughts of the Almighty which priestcraft and the Bible had infused into their minds, and which stood in everlasting opposition to all their ideas of his moral justice and benevolence.

I come now to the two books of Kings, and the two books of Chronicles.—Those books are altogether historical, and are chiefly confined to the lives and actions of the Jewish kings, who in general were a parcel of rascals : but these are matters with which we have no more concern than we have with the Roman emperors, or Homer's account of the Trojan war. Besides which, as those books are anonymous, and as we know nothing of the writer, or of his character, it is impossible for us to know what degree of credit to give to the matters related therein. Like all other ancient histories, they appear to be a jumble of fable and of fact, and of probable and of improbable things, but which distance of time and place, and change of circumstances in the world, have rendered obsolete and uninteresting.

The chief use I shall make of those books will be that of comparing them with each other, and with other parts of the Bible, to shew the confusion, contradiction, and cruelty in this pretended word of God.

The first book of Kings begins with the reign of Solomon, which, according to the Bible chronology, was B.C. 1015 ; and the second book ends B.C. 588, being a little after the reign of Zedekiah, whom Nebuchadnezzar, after taking Jerusalem and conquering the Jews, carried captive to Babylon. The two books include a space of 427 years.

The two books of Chronicles are an history of the same times, and in general of the same persons, by another author ; for it would be absurd to suppose that the same author wrote the history twice over. The first book of

8

Chronicles (after giving the genealogy from Adam to Saul, which takes up the first nine chapters) begins with the reign of David; and the last book ends, as in the last book of Kings, soon after the reign of Zedekiah, about B.C. 588. The last two verses of the last chapter bring the history 52 years more forward, that is, to 536. But these verses do not belong to the book, as I shall shew when I come to speak of the book of Ezra.

The two books of Kings, besides the history of Saul, David, and Solomon, who reigned over *all* Israel, contain an abstract of the lives of seventeen kings and one queen, who are stiled kings of Judah; and of nineteen, who are stiled kings of Israel; for the Jewish nation, immediately on the death of Solomon, split into two parties, who chose separate kings, and who carried on most rancorous wars against each other.

These two books are little more than a history of assassinations, treachery, and wars. The cruelties that the Jews had accustomed themselves to practise on the Canaanites, whose country they had savagely invaded, under a pretended gift from God, they afterwards practised as furiously on each other. Scarcely half their kings died a natural death, and in some instances whole families were destroyed to secure possession to the successor, who, after a few years, and sometimes only a few months, or less, shared the same fate. In 2 Kings x., an account is given of two baskets full of children's heads, seventy in number, being exposed at the entrance of the city; they were the children of Ahab, and were murdered by the orders of Jehu, whom Elisha, the pretended man of God, had anointed to be king over Israel, on purpose to commit this bloody deed, and assassinate his predecessor. And in the account of the reign of Menahem, one of the kings of Israel who had murdered Shallum, who had reigned but one month, it is said, 2 Kings xv. 16, that Menahem smote the city of Tiphsah, because they opened not the city to him, *and all the women therein that were with child he ripped up.*

Could we permit ourselves to suppose that the Almighty

would distinguish any nation of people by the name of *his chosen people*, we must suppose that people to have been an example to all the rest of the world of the purest piety and humanity, and not such a nation of ruffians and cut-throats as the ancient Jews were,—a people who, corrupted by and copying after such monsters and imposters as Moses and Aaron, Joshua, Samuel, and David, had distinguished themselves above all others on the face of the known earth for barbarity and wickedness. If we will not stubbornly shut our eyes and steel our hearts it is impossible not to see, in spite of all that long-established superstition imposes upon the mind, that the flattering appellation of *his chosen people* is no other than a LIE which the priests and leaders of the Jews had invented to cover the baseness of their own characters ; and which Christian priests sometimes as corrupt, and often as cruel, have professed to believe.

The two books of Chronicles are a repetition of the same crimes; but the history is broken in several places, by the author leaving out the reign of some of their kings ; and in this, as well as in that of Kings, there is such a frequent transition from kings of Judah to kings of Israel, and from kings of Israel to kings of Judah, that the narrative is obscure in the reading. In the same book the history sometimes contradicts itself : for example, in 2 Kings, i. 17, we are told, but in rather ambiguous terms, that after the death of Ahaziah, king of Israel, Jehoram, or Joram, (who was of the house of Ahab, reigned in his stead in the *second year of* Jehoram, or Joram, son of Jehoshaphat, king of Judah ; and in viii. 16, of the same book, it is said, " And in the *fifth year* of Joram, the son of Ahab, king of Israel, Jehoshaphat being then king of Judah, Jehoram, the son of Jehoshaphat king of Judah, began to reign." That is, one chapter says Joram of Judah began to reign in the *second year* of Joram of Israel ; and the other chapter says, that Joram of Israel began to reign in the *fifth year* of Joram of Judah.

Several of the most extraordinary matters related in one history, as having happened during the reign of such or such of their kings, are not to be found in the other, in relating the reign of the same king: for example, the two first rival kings, after the death of Solomon, were Rehoboam and Jeroboam ; and in 1 Kings xii. and xiii. an account is given of Jeroboam making an offering of burnt incense, and that a man, who is there called a man of God, cried out against the altar (xiii. 2): " O altar, altar! thus saith the Lord : Behold, a child shall be born unto the house of David, Josiah by name, and upon thee shall he offer the priests of the high places that burn incense upon thee, and men's bones shall be burned upon thee." Verse 4: " And it came to pass, when king Jeroboam heard the saying of the man of God, which had cried against the altar in Bethel, that he put forth his hand from the altar, saying, *Lay hold on him ;* and his hand which he put out against him *dried up, so that he could not pull it again to him.*"

One would think that such an extraordinary case as this, (which is spoken of as a judgement,) happening to the chief of one of the parties, and that at the first moment of the separation of the Israelites into two nations, would, if it had been true, have been recorded in both histories.   But though men, in later times, have believed *all that the prophets have said unto them*, it does not appear that those prophets, or historians, believed each other: they knew each other too well.

A long account also is given in Kings about Elijah.   It runs through several chapters, and concludes with telling, 2 Kings ii. 11, " And it came to pass, as they (Elijah and Elisha) still went on, and talked, that, behold, there appeared *a chariot of fire and horses of fire*, and parted them both asunder, and Elijah *went up by a whirlwind into heaven.*" Hum ! this the author of Chronicles, miraculous as the story is, makes no mention of, though he mentions Elijah by name ; neither does he say anything of the story related in the second chapter of the same book of Kings, of a parcel of children calling Elisha *bald head ;* and that this *man of God* (ver. 24) " turned back, and looked upon them, *and cursed them in the name of the Lord ;* and there came forth two she-bears out of the wood, and tare forty and two children of them." He also passes over in silence the story told, 2 Kings xiii., that when they were burying a man in the sepulchre where Elisha had been buried, it happened that the dead man, as they were letting him down, (ver. 21) "touched the bones of Elisha, and he (the dead man) *revived, and stood up on his feet.*" The story does not tell us whether they buried the man, notwithstanding he revived and stood upon his feet, or drew him up again. Upon all these stories the writer of the Chronicles is as silent as any writer of the present day, who did not chuse to be accused of *lying*, or at least of romancing, would be about stories of the same kind.

But, however these two historians may differ from each other with respect to the tales related by either, they are silent alike with respect to those men stiled prophets whose writings fill up the latter part of the Bible. Isaiah, who lived in the time of Hezekiah, is mentioned in Kings, and again in Chronicles, when these histories are speaking of that reign; but except in one or two instances at most, and those very slightly, none of the rest are so much as spoken of, or even their existence hinted at; though, according to the Bible chronology, they lived within the time those histories were written; and some of them long before. If those prophets, as they are called, were men of such importance in their day, as the compilers of the Bible, and priests and commentators have since represented them to be, how can it be accounted for that not one of those histories should say anything about them?

The history in the books of Kings and of Chronicles is brought forward, as I have already said, to the year B.C. 588; it will, therefore, be proper to examine which of these prophets lived before that period.

Here follows a table of all the prophets, with the times in which they lived before Christ, according to the chronology affixed to the first chapter of each of the books of the prophets; and also of the number of years they lived before the books of Kings and Chronicles were written:

TABLE of the Prophets, with the time in which they lived before Christ, and also before the books of Kings and Chronicles were written:

NAMES.	Years before Christ.	Years before Kings and Chronicles.	Observations.
Isaiah	760	172	mentioned.
Jeremiah	629	41	mentioned only in the last [two] chapters of Chronicles.
Ezekiel	595	7	not mentioned.
Daniel	607	19	not mentioned.
Hosea	785	97	not mentioned.
Joel	800	212	not mentioned.
Amos	789	199	not mentioned.
Obadiah	789	199	not mentioned.
Jonah	862	274	see the note.*
Micah	750	162	not mentioned.
Nahum	713	125	not mentioned.
Habakkuk	620	38	not mentioned.
Zephaniah	630	42	not mentioned.
Haggai ⎫ Zechariah ⎬ after the year 588 Malachi ⎭			

This table is either not very honourable for the Bible historians, or not very honourable for the Bible prophets; and I leave to priests and commentators, who are very learned in little things, to settle the point of *etiquette* between the two; and to assign a reason, why the authors of Kings and of Chronicles have treated those prophets, whom, in the former part of the *Age of Reason*, I have considered as poets, with as much degrading silence as any historian of the present day would treat Peter Pindar.

I have one more observation to make on the book of Chronicles; after which I shall pass on to review the remaining books of the Bible.

In my observations on the book of Genesis, I have quoted a passage from xxxvi. 31, which evidently refers to a time, *after* that kings began to reign over the children of Israel; and I have shewn that as this verse is verbatim the same as

* In 2 Kings xiv. 25, the name of Jonah is mentioned on account of the restoration of a tract of land by Jeroboam; but nothing further is said of him, nor is any allusion made to the book of Jonah, nor to his expedition to Nineveh, nor to his encounter with the whale —*Author.*

in 1 Chronicles i. 43, where it stands consistently with the
order of history, which in Genesis it does not, that the verse
in Genesis, and a great part of the 36th chapter, have been
taken from Chronicles ; and that the book of Genesis, though
it is placed first in the Bible, and ascribed to Moses, has been
manufactured by some unknown person, after the book of
Chronicles was written, which was not until at least eight
hundred and sixty years after the time of Moses.

The evidence I proceed by to substantiate this, is regular,
and has in it but two stages. First, as I have already
stated, that the passage in Genesis refers itself for *time* to
Chronicles ; secondly, that the book of Chronicles, to which
this passage refers itself, was not *begun* to be written until
at least eight hundred and sixty years after the time of
Moses. To prove this, we have only to look into 1 Chronicles iii. 15, where the writer, in giving the genealogy of the
descendants of David, mentions *Zedekiah ;* and it was in
the time of *Zedekiah* that Nebuchadnezzar conquered Jerusalem, B.C. 588, and consequently more than 860 years
after Moses. Those who have superstitiously boasted of
the antiquity of the Bible, and particularly of the books
ascribed to Moses, have done it without examination, and
without any other authority than that of one credulous man
telling it to another : for, so far as historical and chronological evidence applies, the very first book in the Bible is not so
ancient as the book of Homer, by more than three hundred
years, and is about the same age with Æsop's Fables.

I am not contending for the morality of Homer ; on the
contrary, I think it a book of false glory, and tending to
inspire immoral and mischievous notions of honour ; and
with respect to Æsop, though the moral is in general just,
the fable is often cruel ; and the cruelty of the fable does
more injury to the heart, especially in a child, than the
moral does good to the judgment.

Having now dismissed Kings and Chronicles, I come
to the next in course, the book of Ezra.

As one proof, among others I shall produce to shew the
disorder in which this pretended word of God, the Bible,
has been put together, and the uncertainty of who the

authors were, we have only to look at the first three verses
in Ezra, and the last two in 2 Chronicles ; for by what kind
of cutting and shuffling has it been that the first three
verses in Ezra should be the last two verses in 2 Chronicles,
or that the last two in 2 Chronicles should be the first three
in Ezra? Either the authors did not know their own works
or the compilers did not know the authors.

Last Two Verses of 2 Chronicles.	*First Three Verses of Ezra.*
Ver. 22. Now in the first year of Cyrus, King of Persia, that the word of the Lord, spoken by the mouth of Jeremiah, might be accomplished, the Lord stirred up the spirit of Cyrus, king of Persia, that he made a proclamation throughout all his kingdom, and put it also in writing, saying,	Ver. 1. Now in the first year of Cyrus, king of Persia, that the word of the Lord, by the mouth of Jeremiah, might be fulfilled, the Lord stirred up the spirit of Cyrus, king of Persia, that he made a proclamation throughout all his kingdom, and put it also in writing, saying,
23. Thus saith Cyrus, king of Persia, all the kingdoms of the earth hath the Lord God of heaven given me ; and he hath charged me to build him an house in Jerusalem which is in Judah. Who is there among you of all his people? the Lord his God be with him, and let him go up.***	2. Thus saith Cyrus, king of Persia, The Lord God of heaven hath given me all the kingdoms of the earth ; and he hath charged me to build him an house at Jerusalem, which is in Judah.
	3. Who is there among you of all his people? his God be with him, and let him go up *to Jerusalem, which is in Judah, and build the house of the Lord God of Israel (he is the God) which is in Jerusalem.*

***The last verse in Chronicles is broken abruptly, and ends
in the middle of the phrase with the word *up*, without signifying to what place. This abrupt break, and the appearance of the same verses in different books, shew as I have
already said, the disorder and ignorance in which the Bible
has been put together, and that the compilers of it had no

authority for what they were doing, nor we any authority for believing what they have done.*

The only thing that has any appearance of certainty in the book of Ezra is the time in which it was written, which was immediately after the return of the Jews from the Babylonian captivity, about B.C. 536. Ezra (who, according to the Jewish commentators, is the same person as is called Esdras in the Apocrypha) was one of the persons who returned, and who, it is probable, wrote the account of that affair. Nehemiah, whose book follows next to Ezra, was

---

* I observed, as I passed along, several broken and senseless passages in the Bible, without thinking them of consequence enough to be introduced in the body of the work ; such as that, 1 Samuel xiii. 1, where it is said, " Saul reigned one year ; and when he had reigned two years over Israel, Saul chose him three thousand men," &c. The first part of the verse, that Saul reigned *one year* has no sense, since it does not tell us what Saul did, nor say any thing of what happened at the end of that one year ; and it is, besides, mere absurdity to say he reigned *one year*, when the very next phrase says he had reigned two ; for if he had reigned two, it was impossible not to have reigned one.

Another instance occurs in Joshua v. where the writer tells us a story of an angel (for such the table of contents at the head of the chapter calls him) appearing unto Joshua ; and the story ends abruptly, and without any conclusion. The story is as follows :—Ver. 13. " And it came to pass, when Joshua was by Jericho, that he lifted up his eyes and looked, and behold there stood a man over against him with his sword drawn in his hand ; and Joshua went unto him and said unto him, Art thou for us, or for our adversaries ? " Verse 14, " And he said, Nay ; but as captain of the host of the Lord am I now come. And Joshua fell on his face to the earth, and did worship and said unto him, What saith my Lord unto his servant ? " Verse 15, " And the captain of the Lord's host said unto Joshua, Loose thy shoe from off thy foot ; for the place whereon thou standeth is holy. And Joshua did so."—And what then ? nothing : for here the story ends, and the chapter too.

Either this story is broken off in the middle, or it is a story told by some Jewish humourist in ridicule of Joshua's pretended mission from God, and the compilers of the Bible, not perceiving the design of the story, have told it as a serious matter. As a story of humour and ridicule it has a great deal of point ; for it pompously introduces an angel in the figure of a man, with a drawn sword in his hand, before whom Joshua falls on his face to the earth, and worships (which is contrary to their second commandment ;) and then, this most important embassy from heaven ends in telling Joshua to *pull off his shoe.* It might as well have told him to pull up his breeches.

It is certain, however, that the Jews did not credit every thing their leaders told them, as appears from the cavalier manner in which they speak of Moses, when he was gone into the mount. As for *this* Moses, say they, *we wot not what is become of him.* Exod. xxxii. 1.—*Author.*

another of the returned persons; and who, it is also probable, wrote the account of the same affair, in the book that bears his name.   But those accounts are nothing to us, nor to any other person, unless it be to the Jews, as a part of the history of their nation; and there is just as much of the word of God in those books as there is in any of the histories of France, or Rapin's history of England, or the history of any other country.

But even in matters of historical record, neither of those writers are to be depended upon.   In Ezra ii., the writer gives a list of the tribes and families, and of the precise number of souls of each, that returned from Babylon to Jerusalem; and this enrolment of the persons so returned appears to have been one of the principal objects for writing the book; but in this there is an error that destroys the intention of the undertaking.

The writer begins his enrolment in the following manner (ii. 3): "The children of Parosh, two thousand one hundred seventy and four."   Ver. 4, "The children of Shephatiah, three hundred seventy and two."   And in this manner he proceeds through all the families; and in the 64th verse, he makes a total, and says, the whole congregation together was *forty and two thousand three hundred and threescore.*

But whoever will take the trouble of casting up the several particulars, will find that the total is but 29,818; so that the error is 12,542.*   What certainty then can there be in the Bible for any thing?

* *Particulars of the Families from Ezra ii.*

Verse			Bro't forw.	11577	Bro't forw.	15783	Bro't forw.	19444
Verse	3	2172	Ver. 13	666	Ver. 23	128	Ver. 33	725
	4	372	14	2056	24	42	34	345
	5	775	15	454	25	743	35	3630
	6	2812	16	98	26	621	36	973
	7	1254	17	323	27	122	37	1052
	8	945	18	112	28	223	38	1247
	9	760	19	223	29	52	39	1017
	10	642	20	95	30	156	40	74
	11	623	21	123	31	1254	41	128
	12	1222	22	56	32	320	42	139
							58	392
							60	652
		11,577		15,783		19,444	Total,	29,818

—*Author.*

Nehemiah, in like manner, gives a list of the returned families, and of the number of each family. He begins as in Ezra, by saying (vii. 8): "The children of Parosh, two thousand three hundred and seventy-two;" and so on through all the families. (The list differs in several of the particulars from that of Ezra.) In ver. 66, Nehemiah makes a total, and says, as Ezra had said, "The whole congregation together was forty and two thousand three hundred and threescore." But the particulars of this list make a total but of 31,089, so that the error here is 11,271. These writers may do well enough for Bible-makers, but not for any thing where truth and exactness is necessary.

The next book in course is the book of Esther. If Madam Esther thought it any honour to offer herself as a kept mistress to Ahasuerus, or as a rival to Queen Vashti, who had refused to come to a drunken king in the midst of a drunken company, to be made a shew of, (for the account says, they had been drinking seven days, and were merry,) let Esther and Mordecai look to that, it is no business of ours, at least it is none of mine; besides which, the story has a great deal the appearance of being fabulous, and is also anonymous. I pass on to the book of Job.

The book of Job differs in character from all the books we have hitherto passed over. Treachery and murder make no part of this book; it is the meditations of a mind strongly impressed with the vicissitudes of human life, and by turns sinking under, and struggling against the pressure. It is a highly wrought composition, between willing submission and involuntary discontent; and shews man, as he sometimes is, more disposed to be resigned than he is capable of being. Patience has but a small share in the character of the person of whom the book treats; on the contrary, his grief is often impetuous; but he still endeavours to keep a guard upon it, and seems determined, in the midst of accumulating ills, to impose upon himself the hard duty of contentment.

I have spoken in a respectful manner of the book of Job in the former part of the *Age of Reason*, but without knowing at that time what I have learned since; which is, that from all the evidence that can be collected, the book of Job does not belong to the Bible.

I have seen the opinion of two Hebrew commentators, Abenezra and Spinoza, upon this subject; they both say that the book of Job carries no internal evidence of being an Hebrew book; that the genius of the composition, and the drama of the piece, are not Hebrew; that it has been translated from another language into Hebrew, and that the author of the book was a Gentile; that the character represented under the name of Satan (which is the first and only time this name is mentioned in the Bible)[1] does not correspond to any Hebrew idea; and that the two convocations which the Deity is supposed to have made of those whom the poem calls sons of God, and the familiarity which this supposed Satan is stated to have with the Deity, are in the same case.

It may also be observed, that the book shews itself to be the production of a mind cultivated in science, which the Jews, so far from being famous for, were very ignorant of. The allusions to objects of natural philosophy are frequent and strong, and are of a different cast to any thing in the books known to be Hebrew. The astronomical names, Pleïades, Orion, and Arcturus, are Greek and not Hebrew names, and it does not appear from any thing that is to be found in the Bible that the Jews knew any thing of astronomy, or that they studied it, they had no translation of those names into their own language, but adopted the names as they found them in the poem.[2]

[1] In a later work Paine notes that in "the Bible" (by which he always means the Old Testament alone) the word Satan occurs also in 1 Chron. xxi. 1, and remarks that the action there ascribed to Satan is in 2 Sam. xxiv. 1, attributed to Jehovah ("Essay on Dreams"). In these places, however, and in Ps. cix. 6, Satan means "adversary," and is so translated (A. S. version) in 2 Sam. xix. 22, and 1 Kings v. 4, xi. 25. As a proper name, with the article, Satan (הַשָּׂטָן) appears in the Old Testament only in Job and in Zech. iii. 1, 2. But the authenticity of the passage in Zechariah has been questioned, and it may be that in finding the proper name of Satan in Job alone, Paine was following some opinion met with in one of the authorities whose comments are condensed in his paragraph.—*Editor.*

[2] Paine's Jewish critic, David Levi, fastened on this slip (" **Defence of the**

That the Jews did translate the literary productions of the Gentile nations into the Hebrew language, and mix them with their own, is not a matter of doubt; Proverbs xxxi. 1, is an evidence of this: it is there said, *The word of king Lemuel, the prophecy which his mother taught him.* This verse stands as a preface to the proverbs that follow, and which are not the proverbs of Solomon, but of Lemuel; and this Lemuel was not one of the kings of Israel, nor of Judah, but of some other country, and consequently a Gentile. The Jews however have adopted his proverbs; and as they cannot give any account who the author of the book of Job was, nor how they came by the book, and as it differs in character from the Hebrew writings, and stands totally unconnected with every other book and chapter in the Bible before it and after it, it has all the circumstantial evidence of being originally a book of the Gentiles.*

The Bible-makers, and those regulators of time, the Bible chronologists, appear to have been at a loss where to place and how to dispose of the book of Job; for it contains no one historical circumstance, nor allusion to any, that might

Old Testament," 1797, p. 152). In the original the names are *Ash* (Arcturus), *Kesil* (Orion), *Kimah* (Pleiades), though the identifications of the constellations in the A. S. V. have been questioned.—*Editor.*

* The prayer known by the name of *Agur's Prayer*, in Proverbs xxx.,—immediately preceding the proverbs of Lemuel,—and which is the only sensible, well-conceived, and well-expressed prayer in the Bible, has much the appearance of being a prayer taken from the Gentiles. The name of Agur occurs on no other occasion than this; and he is introduced, together with the prayer ascribed to him, in the same manner, and nearly in the same words, that Lemuel and his proverbs are introduced in the chapter that follows. The first verse says, " The words of Agur, the son of Jakeh, even the prophecy: " here the word prophecy is used with the same application it has in the following chapter of Lemuel, unconnected with anything of prediction. The prayer of Agur is in the 8th and 9th verses, " Remove far from me vanity and lies; give me neither riches nor poverty, but feed me with food convenient for me ; lest 1 be full and deny thee and say, Who is the Lord ? or lest I be poor and steal, and take the name of my God in vain." This has not any of the marks of being a Jewish prayer, for the Jews never prayed but when they were in trouble, and never for anything but victory, vengeance, or riches.—*Author.* [Prov. xxx.1, and xxxi. 1, the word "prophecy" in these verses is translated "oracle" or "burden" (marg.) in the revised version.—The prayer of Agur was quoted by Paine in his plea for the officers of Excise, 1772.—*Editor.*]

serve to determine its place in the Bible. But it would not
have answered the purpose of these men to have informed
the world of their ignorance ; and, therefore, they have
affixed it to the æra of B.C. 1520, which is during the time
the Israelites were in Egypt, and for which they have just
as much authority and no more than I should have for saying it was a thousand years before that period. The probability however is, that it is older than any book in the Bible ;
and it is the only one that can be read without indignation
or disgust.

We know nothing of what the ancient Gentile world (as
it is called) was before the time of the Jews, whose practice
has been to calumniate and blacken the character of all
other nations ; and it is from the Jewish accounts that we
have learned to call them heathens. But, as far as we know
to the contrary, they were a just and moral people, and not
addicted, like the Jews, to cruelty and revenge, but of whose
profession of faith we are unacquainted. It appears to have
been their custom to personify both virtue and vice by
statues and images, as is done now-a-days both by statuary
and by painting ; but it does not follow from this that they
worshipped them any more than we do.—I pass on to the
book of

Psalms, of which it is not necessary to make much observation. Some of them are moral, and others are very
revengeful ; and the greater part relates to certain local
circumstances of the Jewish nation at the time they were
written, with which we have nothing to do. It is, however,
an error or an imposition to call them the Psalms of David ;
they are a collection, as song-books are now-a-days, from
different song-writers, who lived at different times. The
137th Psalm could not have been written till more than
400 years after the time of David, because it is written
in commemoration of an event, the capitivity of the Jews
in Babylon, which did not happen till that distance of time.
" *By the rivers of Babylon we sat down ; yea, we wept when
we remembered Zion. We hanged our harps upon the willows,
in the midst thereof ; for there they that carried us away*

captive required of us a song, saying, sing us one of the songs of Zion." As a man would say to an American, or to a Frenchman, or to an Englishman, sing us one of your American songs, or your French songs, or your English songs. This remark, with respect to the time this psalm was written, is of no other use than to shew (among others already mentioned) the general imposition the world has been under with respect to the authors of the Bible. No regard has been paid to time, place, and circumstance; and the names of persons have been affixed to the several books which it was as impossible they should write, as that a man should walk in procession at his own funeral.

The Book of Proverbs. These, like the Psalms, are a collection, and that from authors belonging to other nations than those of the Jewish nation, as I have shewn in the observations upon the book of Job; besides which, some of the Proverbs ascribed to Solomon did not appear till two hundred and fifty years after the death of Solomon; for it is said in xxv. 1, " *These are also proverbs of Solomon which the men of Hezekiah, king of Judah, copied out."* It was two hundred and fifty years from the time of Solomon to the time of Hezekiah. When a man is famous and his name is abroad he is made the putative father of things he never said or did; and this, most probably, has been the case with Solomon. It appears to have been the fashion of that day to make proverbs, as it is now to make jest-books, and father them upon those who never saw them.[1]

The book of *Ecclesiastes*, or the *Preacher*, is also ascribed to Solomon, and that with much reason, if not with truth. It is written as the solitary reflections of a worn-out debauchee, such as Solomon was, who looking back on scenes he can no longer enjoy, cries out *All is Vanity!* A great deal of the metaphor and of the sentiment is obscure, most probably by translation; but enough is left to shew they were strongly pointed in the original.* From what is trans-

[1] A " Tom Paine's Jest Book " had appeared in London with little or nothing of Paine in it.—*Editor*.

* *Those that look out of the window shall be darkened*, is an obscure figure in translation for loss of sight.—*Author*.

mitted to us of the character of Solomon, he was witty, ostentatious, dissolute, and at last melancholy. He lived fast, and died, tired of the world, at the age of fifty-eight years.

Seven hundred wives, and three hundred concubines, are worse than none ; and, however it may carry with it the appearance of heightened enjoyment, it defeats all the felicity of affection, by leaving it no point to fix upon ; divided love is never happy. This was the case with Solomon ; and if he could not, with all his pretensions to wisdom, discover it beforehand, he merited, unpitied, the mortification he afterwards endured. In this point of view, his preaching is unnecessary, because, to know the consequences, it is only necessary to know the cause. Seven hundred wives, and three hundred concubines would have stood in place of the whole book. It was needless after this to say that all was vanity and vexation of spirit ; for it is impossible to derive happiness from the company of those whom we deprive of happiness.

To be happy in old age it is necessary that we accustom ourselves to objects that can accompany the mind all the way through life, and that we take the rest as good in their day. The mere man of pleasure is miserable in old age ; and the mere drudge in business is but little better : whereas, natural philosophy, mathematical and mechanical science, are a continual source of tranquil pleasure, and in spite of the gloomy dogmas of priests, and of superstition, the study of those things is the study of the true theology ; it teaches man to know and to admire the Creator, for the principles of science are in the creation, and are unchangeable, and of divine origin.

Those who knew Benjaman Franklin will recollect, that his mind was ever young ; his temper ever serene ; science, that never grows grey, was always his mistress. He was never without an object ; for when we cease to have an object we become like an invalid in an hospital waiting for death.

Solomon's Songs, amorous and foolish enough, but which

wrinkled fanaticism has called divine.—The compilers of the
Bible have placed these songs after the book of Ecclesiastes ;
and the chronologists have affixed to them the æra of B.C.
1014, at which time Solomon, according to the same chronology, was nineteen years of age, and was then forming his
seraglio of wives and concubines. The Bible-makers and
the chronologists should have managed this matter a little
better, and either have said nothing about the time, or
chosen a time less inconsistent with the supposed divinity
of those songs ; for Solomon was then in the honey-moon of
one thousand debaucheries.

It should also have occurred to them, that as he wrote,
if he did write, the book of Ecclesiastes, long after these
songs, and in which he exclaims that all is vanity and vexation of spirit, that he included those songs in that description.
This is the more probable, because he says, or somebody for
him, Ecclesiastes ii. 8, *I got me men-singers, and women-
singers* [most probably to sing those songs], *and musical
instruments of all sorts ;* and behold (Ver. 11), " all was
vanity and vexation of spirit." The compilers however
have done their work but by halves ; for as they have given
us the songs they should have given us the tunes, that we
might sing them.

The books called the books of the Prophets fill up all the remaining part of the Bible ; they are sixteen in number, beginning with Isaiah and ending with Malachi, of which I have
given a list in the observations upon Chronicles. Of these
sixteen prophets, all of whom except the last three lived
within the time the books of Kings and Chronicles were
written, two only, Isaiah and Jeremiah, are mentioned in the
history of those books. I shall begin with those two, reserv-
ing, what I have to say on the general character of the men
called prophets to another part of the work.

Whoever will take the trouble of reading the book ascribed to Isaiah, will find it one of the most wild and disorderly compositions ever put together ; it has neither
beginning, middle, nor end ; and, except a short historical
part, and a few sketches of history in the first two or three

9

chapters, is one continued incoherent, bombastical rant, full of extravagant metaphor, without application, and destitute of meaning ; a school-boy would scarcely have been excusable for writing such stuff ; it is (at least in translation) that kind of composition and false taste that is properly called prose run mad.

The historical part begins at chapter xxxvi., and is continued to the end of chapter xxxix. It relates some matters that are said to have passed during the reign of Hezekiah, king of Judah, at which time Isaiah lived. This fragment of history begins and ends abruptly ; it has not the least connection with the chapter that precedes it, nor with that which follows it, nor with any other in the book. It is probable that Isaiah wrote this fragment himself, because he was an actor in the circumstances it treats of ; but except this part there are scarcely two chapters that have any connection with each other. One is entitled, at the beginning of the first verse, the burden of Babylon ; another, the burden of Moab ; another, the burden of Damascus ; another, the burden of Egypt ; another, the burden of the Desert of the Sea ; another, the burden of the Valley of Vision : as you would say the story of the Knight of the Burning Mountain, the story of Cinderella, or the glassen slipper, the story of the Sleeping Beauty in the Wood, etc., etc.

I have already shewn, in the instance of the last two verses of 2 Chronicles, and the first three in Ezra, that the compilers of the Bible mixed and confounded the writings of different authors with each other ; which alone, were there no other cause, is sufficient to destroy the authenticity of any compilation, because it is more than presumptive evidence that the compilers are ignorant who the authors were. A very glaring instance of this occurs in the book ascribed to Isaiah : the latter part of the 44th chapter, and the beginning of the 45th, so far from having been written by Isaiah, could only have been written by some person who lived at least an hundred and fifty years after Isaiah was dead.

These chapters are a compliment to *Cyrus*, who permitted the Jews to return to Jerusalem from the Babylonian captivity, to rebuild Jerusalem and the temple, as is stated in Ezra. The last verse of the 44th chapter, and the beginning of the 45th [Isaiah] are in the following words : " *That saith of Cyrus, he is my shepherd, and shall perform all my pleasure ; even saying to Jerusalem, thou shalt be built ; and to the temple, thy foundations shall be laid : thus saith the Lord to his anointed, to Cyrus, whose right hand I have holden to subdue nations before him, and I will loose the loins of kings to open before him the two-leaved gates, and the gates shall not be shut ; I will go before thee,*" etc.

What audacity of church and priestly ignorance it is to impose this book upon the world as the writing of Isaiah, when Isaiah, according to their own chronology, died soon after the death of Hezekiah, which was B.C. 698 ; and the decree of Cyrus, in favour of the Jews returning to Jerusalem, was, according to the same chronology, B.C. 536 ; which is a distance of time between the two of 162 years. I do not suppose that the compilers of the Bible made these books, but rather that they picked up some loose, anonymous essays, and put them together under the names of such authors as best suited their purpose. They have encouraged the imposition, which is next to inventing it ; for it was impossible but they must have observed it.

When we see the studied craft of the scripture-makers, in making every part of this romantic book of school-boy's eloquence bend to the monstrous idea of a Son of God, begotten by a ghost on the body of a virgin, there is no imposition we are not justified in suspecting them of. Every phrase and circumstance are marked with the barbarous hand of superstitious torture, and forced into meanings it was impossible they could have. The head of every chapter, and the top of every page, are blazoned with the names of Christ and the Church, that the unwary reader might suck in the error before he began to read.

Behold a virgin shall conceive, and bear a son (Isa. vii. 14), has been interpreted to mean the person called Jesus Christ, and his mother Mary, and has been echoed through christendom for more than a thousand years; and such has been the rage of this opinion, that scarcely a spot in it but has been stained with blood and marked with desolation in consequence of it. Though it is not my intention to enter into controversy on subjects of this kind, but to confine myself to shew that the Bible is spurious,—and thus, by taking away the foundation, to overthrow at once the whole structure of superstition raised thereon,—I will however stop a moment to expose the fallacious application of this passage.

Whether Isaiah was playing a trick with Ahaz, king of Judah, to whom this passage is spoken, is no business of mine; I mean only to shew the misapplication of the passage, and that it has no more reference to Christ and his mother, than it has to me and my mother. The story is simply this:

The king of Syria and the king of Israel (I have already mentioned that the Jews were split into two nations, one of which was called Judah, the capital of which was Jerusalem, and the other Israel) made war jointly against Ahaz, king of Judah, and marched their armies towards Jerusalem. Ahaz and his people became alarmed, and the account says (Is. vii. 2), *Their hearts were moved as the trees of the wood are moved with the wind.*

In this situation of things, Isaiah addresses himself to Ahaz, and assures him in the *name of the Lord* (the cant phrase of all the prophets) that these two kings should not succeed against him; and to satisfy Ahaz that this should be the case, tells him to ask a sign. This, the account says, Ahaz declined doing; giving as a reason that he would not tempt the Lord; upon which Isaiah, who is the speaker, says, ver. 14, " Therefore the Lord himself shall give you a sign; *behold a virgin shall conceive and bear a son;* " and the 16th verse says, " *And before this child shall know to refuse the evil, and choose the good, the land* which thou abhorrest or dreadest [meaning Syria and the kingdom of Israel] shall be forsaken of both her kings." Here then was the sign, and the time limited for the completion of the assurance or promise; namely, before this child shall know to refuse the evil and choose the good.

Isaiah having committed himself thus far, it became necessary to him, in order to avoid the imputation of being a false
prophet, and the consequences thereof, to take measures to
make this sign appear. It certainly was not a difficult thing,
in any time of the world, to find a girl with child, or to make
her so ; and perhaps Isaiah knew of one beforehand ; for I
do not suppose that the prophets of that day were any more
to be trusted than the priests of this : be that, however, as
it may, he says in the next chapter, ver. 2, " And I took unto
me faithful witnesses to record, Uriah the priest, and Zechariah the son of Jeberechiah, and *I went unto the prophetess,
and she conceived and bare a son.*"

Here then is the whole story, foolish as it is, of this child
and this virgin ; and it is upon the barefaced perversion of
this story that the book of Matthew, and the impudence and
sordid interest of priests in later times, have founded a
theory, which they call the gospel; and have applied this
story to signify the person they call Jesus Christ ; begotten,
they say, by a ghost, whom they call holy, on the body of a
woman, engaged in marriage, and afterwards married, whom
they call a virgin, seven hundred years after this foolish story
was told ; a theory which, speaking for myself, I hesitate not
to believe, and to say, is as fabulous and as false as God is
true.*

But to shew the imposition and falsehood of Isaiah we
have only to attend to the sequel of this story ; which,
though it is passed over in silence in the book of Isaiah, is
related in 2 Chronicles, xxviii ; and which is, that instead of
these two kings failing in their attempt against Ahaz, king
of Judah, as Isaiah had pretended to foretel in the name of
the Lord, they *succeeded :* Ahaz was defeated and destroyed ;
an hundred and twenty thousand of his people were slaugh-
tered ; Jerusalem was plundered, and two hundred thousand
women and sons and daughters carried into captivity. Thus

---

* In Is. vii. 14, it is said that the child should be called Immanuel ; but this
name was not given to either of the children, otherwise than as a character,
which the word signifies. That of the prophetess was called Maher-shalal-
hash-baz, and that of Mary was called Jesus.—*Author.*

much for this lying prophet and imposter Isaiah, and the book of falsehoods that bears his name. I pass on to the book of

Jeremiah. This prophet, as he is called, lived in the time that Nebuchadnezzar besieged Jerusalem, in the reign of Zedekiah, the last king of Judah; and the suspicion was strong against him that he was a traitor in the interest of Nebuchadnezzar. Every thing relating to Jeremiah shews him to have been a man of an equivocal character: in his metaphor of the potter and the clay, (ch. xviii.) he guards his prognostications in such a crafty manner as always to leave himself a door to escape by, in case the event should be contrary to what he had predicted. In the 7th and 8th verses he makes the Almighty to say, " At what instant I shall speak concerning a nation, and concerning a kingdom, to pluck up, and to pull down, and destroy it, if that nation, against whom I have pronounced, turn from their evil, I will repent me of the evil that I thought to do unto them." Here was a proviso against one side of the case : now for the other side. Verses 9 and 10, " At what instant I shall speak concerning a nation, and concerning a kingdom, to build and to plant it, if it do evil in my sight, that it obey not my voice, then I will repent me of the good wherewith I said I would benefit them." Here is a proviso against the other side ; and, according to this plan of prophesying, a prophet could never be wrong, however mistaken the Almighty might be. This sort of absurd subterfuge, and this manner of speaking of the Almighty, as one would speak of a man, is consistent with nothing but the stupidity of the Bible.

As to the authenticity of the book, it is only necessary to read it in order to decide positively that, though some passages recorded therein may have been spoken by Jeremiah, he is not the author of the book. The historical parts, if they can be called by that name, are in the most confused condition ; the same events are several times repeated, and that in a manner different, and sometimes in contradiction to each other ; and this disorder runs even to the last chapter, where the history, upon which the greater part of the book has been employed, begins anew, and ends abruptly. The book has all the appearance of being a medley of un-connected anecdotes respecting persons and things of that time, collected together in the same rude manner as if the various and contradictory accounts that are to be found in a bundle of newspapers, respecting persons and things of the present day, were put together without date, order, or ex-planation. I will give two or three examples of this kind.

It appears, from the account of chapter xxxvii. that the army of Nebuchadnezzer, which is called the army of the Chaldeans, had besieged Jerusalem some time; and on their hearing that the army of Pharaoh of Egypt was marching against them, they raised the siege and retreated for a time. It may here be proper to mention, in order to understand this confused history, that Nebuchadnezzar had besieged and taken Jerusalem during the reign of Jehoakim, the predecessor of Zedekiah; and that it was Nebuchadnezzar who had make Zedekiah king, or rather vice-roy; and that this second siege, of which the book of Jeremiah treats, was in consequence of the revolt of Zedekiah against Nebuchad-nezzar. This will in some measure account for the suspicion that affixes itself to Jeremiah of being a traitor, and in the interest of Nebuchadnezzar,—whom Jeremiah calls, xliii. 10, the servant of God.

Chapter xxxvii. 11–13, says, "And it came to pass, that, when the army of the Chaldeans was broken up from Jeru-salem, for fear of Pharaoh's army, that Jeremiah went forth out of Jerusalem, to go (as this account states) into the land of Benjamin, to separate himself thence in the midst of the people; and when he was in the gate of Benjamin a captain of the ward was there, whose name was Irijah . . . and he took Jeremiah the prophet, saying, *Thou fallest away to the Chaldeans;* then Jeremiah said, *It is false; I fall not away to the Chaldeans.*" Jeremiah being thus stopt and accused, was, after being examined, committed to prison, on suspicion of being a traitor, where he remained, as is stated in the last verse of this chapter.

But the next chapter gives an account of the imprisonment of Jeremiah, which has no connection with *this* account, but ascribes his imprisonment to another circumstance, and for which we must go back to chapter xxi. It is there stated, ver. 1, that Zedekiah sent Pashur the son of Malchiah, and Zephaniah the son of Maaseiah the priest, to Jeremiah, to enquire of him concerning Nebuchadnezzar, whose army was then before Jerusalem ; and Jeremiah said to them, ver. 8, " Thus saith the Lord, Behold I set before you the way of life, and the way of death; he that abideth in this city shall die by the sword and by the famine, and by the pestilence ; *but he that goeth out and falleth to the Chaldeans that besiege you, he shall live, and his life shall be unto him for a prey.*"

This interview and conference breaks off abruptly at the end of the 10th verse of chapter xxi.; and such is the disorder of this book that we have to pass over sixteen chapters upon various subjects, in order to come at the continuation and event of this conference; and this brings us to the first verse of chapter xxxviii., as I have just mentioned. The chapter opens with saying, " Then Shaphatiah, the son of Mattan, Gedaliah the son of Pashur, and Jucal the son of Shelemiah, and Pashur the son of Malchiah, (here are more persons mentioned than in chapter xxi.) heard the words that Jeremiah spoke unto all the people, saying, Thus saith the Lord, He that remaineth in this city, shall die by the sword, by famine, and by the pestilence ; but he that goeth forth to the Chaldeans shall live; for he shall have his life for a prey, and shall live " ; [which are the words of the conference;] therefore, (say they to Zedekiah,) " We beseech thee, let this man be put to death, for thus he weakeneth the hands of the men of war that remain in this city, and the hands of all the people, in speaking such words unto them ; for this man seeketh not the welfare of the people, but the hurt:" and at the 6th verse it is said, " Then they took Jeremiah, and put him into the dungeon of Malchiah."

These two accounts are different and contradictory. The one ascribes his imprisonment to his attempt to *escape out of the city ;* the other to his *preaching and prophesying in the* *city ;* the one to his being seized by the guard at the gate ; the other to his being accused before Zedekiah by the conferees.*

In the next chapter (Jer. xxxix.) we have another instance of the disordered state of this book ; for notwithstanding the siege of the city by Nebuchadnezzar has been the subject of several of the preceding chapters, particularly xxxvii. and xxxviii., chapter xxxix. begins as if not a word had been said upon the subject, and as if the reader was still to be informed of every particular respecting it ; for it begins with saying, ver. 1, "In the ninth year of Zedekiah king of Judah, in the tenth month, came Nebuchadnezzar king of Babylon, and all his army, against Jerusalem, and besieged it," etc.

---

* I observed two chapters in 1 Samuel (xvi. and xvii.) that contradict each other with respect to David, and the manner he became acquainted with Saul ; as Jeremiah xxxvii. and xxxviii. contradict each other with respect to the cause of Jeremiah's imprisonment.

In 1 Samuel, xvi., it is said, that an evil spirit of God troubled Saul, and that his servants advised him (as a remedy) " to seek out a man who was a cunning player upon the harp." And Saul said, ver. 17, " Provide me now a man that can play well, and bring him to me. Then answered one of his servants, and said, Behold, I have seen a son of Jesse, the Bethlehemite, that is cunning in playing, and a mighty man, and a man of war, and prudent in matters, and a comely person, and the Lord is with him ; wherefore Saul sent messengers unto Jesse, and said, Send me David, thy son. And (verse 21) David came to Saul, and stood before him, and he loved him greatly, and he became his armour-bearer ; and when the evil spirit from God was upon Saul, (verse 23) David took his harp, and played with his hand, and Saul was refreshed, and was well."

But the next chapter (xvii.) gives an account, all different to this, of the manner that Saul and David became acquainted. Here it is ascribed to David's encounter with Goliah, when David was sent by his father to carry provision to his brethren in the camp. In the 55th verse of this chapter it is said, " And when Saul saw David go forth against the Philistine (Goliah) he said to Abner, the captain of the host, Abner, whose son is this youth ? And Abner said, As thy soul liveth, O king, I cannot tell. And the king said, Enquire thou whose son the stripling is. And as David returned from the slaughter of the Philistine, Abner took him and brought him before Saul, with the head of the Philistine in his hand ; and Saul said unto him, Whose son art thou, thou young man ? And David answered, I am the son of thy servant, Jesse, the Bethlehemite." These two accounts belie each other, because each of them supposes Saul and David not to have known each other before. This book, the Bible, is too ridiculous for criticism.—*Author*.

But the instance in the last chapter (lii.) is still more glaring; for though the story has been told over and over again, this chapter still supposes the reader not to know anything of it, for it begins by saying, ver. 1, "Zedekiah was one and twenty years old when he began to reign, and he reigned eleven years in Jerusalem, and his mother's name was Hamutal, the daughter of Jeremiah of Libnah." (Ver. 4,) "And it came to pass in the ninth year of his reign, in the tenth month, that Nebuchadnezzar king of Babylon came, he and all his army, against Jerusalem, and pitched against it, and built forts against it," etc.

It is not possible that any one man, and more particularly Jeremiah, could have been the writer of this book. The errors are such as could not have been committed by any person sitting down to compose a work. Were I, or any other man, to write in such a disordered manner, no body would read what was written, and every body would suppose that the writer was in a state of insanity. The only way, therefore, to account for the disorder is, that the book is a medley of detached unauthenticated anecdotes, put together by some stupid book-maker, under the name of Jeremiah; because many of them refer to him, and to the circumstances of the times he lived in.

Of the duplicity, and of the false predictions of Jeremiah, I shall mention two instances, and then proceed to review the remainder of the Bible.

It appears from chapter xxxviii. that when Jeremiah was in prison, Zedekiah sent for him, and at this interview, which was private, Jeremiah pressed it strongly on Zedekiah to surrender himself to the enemy. "If," says he, (ver. 17,) "thou wilt assuredly go forth unto the king of Babylon's princes, then thy soul shall live," etc. Zedekiah was apprehensive that what passed at this conference should be known; and he said to Jeremiah, (ver. 25,) "If the princes [meaning those of Judah] hear that I have talked with thee, and they come unto thee, and say unto thee, Declare unto us now what thou hast said unto the king; hide it not from us, and we will not put thee to death; and also what the

king said unto thee; then thou shalt say unto them, I presented my supplication before the king that he would not
cause me to return to Jonathan's house, to die there. Then
came all the princes unto Jeremiah, and asked him, and " he
told them according to all the words the king had commanded." Thus, this man of God, as he is called, could tell
a lie, or very strongly prevaricate, when he supposed it
would answer his purpose; for certainly he did not go to
Zedekiah to make this supplication, neither did he make it;
he went because he was sent for, and he employed that
opportunity to advise Zedekiah to surrender himself to
Nebuchadnezzar.

In chapter xxxiv. 2-5, is a prophecy of Jeremiah to Zedekiah in these words: " Thus saith the Lord, Behold I will
give this city into the hand of the king of Babylon, and he
will burn it with fire; and thou shalt not escape out of his
hand, but thou shalt surely be taken, and delivered into his
hand; and thine eyes shall behold the eyes of the king of
Babylon, and he shall speak with thee mouth to mouth, and
thou shalt go to Babylon. *Yet hear the word of the Lord;
O Zedekiah, king of Judah, thus saith the Lord, Thou shalt
not die by the sword, but thou shalt die in peace; and with the
burnings of thy fathers, the former kings that were before
thee, so shall they burn odours for thee, and they will lament
thee, saying, Ah, Lord! for I have pronounced the word, saith
the Lord.*"

Now, instead of Zedekiah beholding the eyes of the king
of Babylon, and speaking with him mouth to mouth, and
dying in peace, and with the burning of odours, as at the
funeral of his fathers, (as Jeremiah had declared the Lord
himself had pronounced,) the reverse, according to chapter lii., 10, 11 was the case; it is there said, that the king of
Babylon slew the sons of Zedekiah before his eyes: then he
put out the eyes of Zedekiah, and bound him in chains, and
carried him to Babylon, and put him in prison till the day of
his death.

What then can we say of these prophets, but that they
are impostors and liars?

As for Jeremiah, he experienced none of those evils. He was taken into favour by Nebuchadnezzar, who gave him in charge to the captain of the guard (xxxix, 12), "Take him (said he) and look well to him, and do him no harm ; but do unto him even as he shall say unto thee." Jeremiah joined himself afterwards to Nebuchadnezzar, and went about prophesying for him against the Egyptians, who had marched to the relief of Jerusalem while it was besieged. Thus much for another of the lying prophets, and the book that bears his name.

I have been the more particular in treating of the books ascribed to Isaiah and Jeremiah, because those two are spoken of in the books of Kings and Chronicles, which the others are not. The remainder of the books ascribed to the men called prophets I shall not trouble myself much about ; but take them collectively into the observations I shall offer on the character of the men stiled prophets.

In the former part of the *Age of Reason*, I have said that the word prophet was the Bible-word for poet, and that the flights and metaphors of Jewish poets have been foolishly erected into what are now called prophecies. I am sufficiently justified in this opinion, not only because the books called the prophecies are written in poetical language, but because there is no word in the Bible, except it be the word prophet, that describes what we mean by a poet. I have also said, that the word signified a performer upon musical instruments, of which I have given some instances ; such as that of a company of prophets, prophesying with psalteries, with tabrets, with pipes, with harps, etc., and that Saul prophesied with them, 1 Sam. x., 5. It appears from this passage, and from other parts in the book of Samuel, that the word prophet was confined to signify poetry and music ; for the person who was supposed to have a visionary insight into concealed things, was not a prophet but a *seer*,* (1 Sam.

* I know not what is the Hebrew word that corresponds to the word seer in English ; but I observe it is translated into French by Le Voyant, from the verb *voir* to *see*, and which means the person who *sees*, or the seer.—*Author*.

The Hebrew word for Seer, in 1 Samuel ix., transliterated, is *chozéh*, the gazer ; it is translated in Is. xlvii. 13, " the stargazers."—*Editor*.

ix. 9 ;) and it was not till after the word *seer* went out of use (which most probably was when Saul banished those he called wizards) that the profession of the seer, or the art of seeing, became incorporated into the word prophet.

According to the *modern* meaning of the word prophet and prophesying, it signifies foretelling events to a great distance of time ; and it became necessary to the inventors of the gospel to give it this latitude of meaning, in order to apply or to stretch what they call the prophecies of the Old Testament, to the times of the New. But according to the Old Testament, the prophesying of the seer, and afterwards of the prophet, so far as the meaning of the word "seer" was incorporated into that of prophet, had reference only to things of the time then passing, or very closely connected with it ; such as the event of a battle they were going to engage in, or of a journey, or of any enterprize they were going to undertake, or of any circumstance then pending, or of any difficulty they were then in ; all of which had immediate reference to themselves (as in the case already mentioned of Ahaz and Isaiah with respect to the expression, *Behold a virgin shall conceive and bear a son,*) and not to any distant future time. It was that kind of prophesying that corresponds to what we call fortune-telling ; such as casting nativities, predicting riches, fortunate or unfortunate marriages, conjuring for lost goods, etc. ; and it is the fraud of the Christian church, not that of the Jews, and the ignorance and the superstition of modern, not that of ancient times, that elevated those poetical, musical, conjuring, dreaming, strolling gentry, into the rank they have since had.

But, besides this general character of all the prophets, they had also a particular character. They were in parties, and they prophesied for or against, according to the party they were with ; as the poetical and political writers of the present day write in defence of the party they associate with against the other.

After the Jews were divided into two nations, that of Judah and that of Israel, each party had its prophets, who abused and accused each other of being false prophets, lying prophets, impostors, etc.

The prophets of the party of Judah prophesied against the prophets of the party of Israel; and those of the party of Israel against those of Judah. This party prophesying shewed itself immediately on the separation under the first two rival kings, Rehoboam and Jeroboam. The prophet that cursed, or prophesied against the altar that Jeroboam had built in Bethel, was of the party of Judah, where Rehoboam was king; and he was way-laid on his return home by a prophet of the party of Israel, who said unto him (1 Kings xiii.) "*Art thou the man of God that came from Judah? and he said, I am.*" Then the prophet of the party of Israel said to him "I am a prophet also, as thou art, [signifying of Judah,] and an angel spake unto me by the word of the Lord, saying, Bring him back with thee unto thine house, that he may eat bread and drink water; but (says the 18th verse) he lied unto him." The event, however, according to the story, is, that the prophet of Judah never got back to Judah; for he was found dead on the road by the contrivance of the prophet of Israel, who no doubt was called a true prophet by his own party, and the prophet of Judah a lying prophet.

In 2 Kings, iii., a story is related of prophesying or conjuring that shews, in several particulars, the character of a prophet. Jehoshaphat king of Judah, and Joram king of Israel, had for a while ceased their party animosity, and entered into an alliance; and these two, together with the king of Edom, engaged in a war against the king of Moab. After uniting and marching their armies, the story says, they were in great distress for water, upon which Jehoshaphat said, "Is there not here a prophet of the Lord, that we may enquire of the Lord by him? and one of the servants of the king of Israel said here is Elisha. [Elisha was of the party of Judah.] And Jehoshaphat the king of Judah said, The word of the Lord is with him." The story then says, that these three kings went down to Elisha; and when Elisha [who, as I have said, was a Judahmite prophet] saw the King of Israel, he said unto him,

" What have I to do with thee, get thee to the prophets of thy father and the prophets of thy mother. Nay but, said the king of Israel, the Lord hath called these three kings together, to deliver them into the hands of the king of Moab," (meaning because of the distress they were in for water;) upon which Elisha said, "As the Lord of hosts liveth before whom I stand, surely, were it not that I regard the presence of Jehoshaphat, king of Judah, I would not look towards thee nor see thee." Here is all the venom and vulgarity of a party prophet. We are now to see the performance, or manner of prophesying.

Ver. 15. " Bring me," (said Elisha), "a minstrel; and it came to pass, when the minstrel played, that the hand of the Lord came upon him." Here is the farce of the conjurer. Now for the prophecy : " And Elisha said, [singing most probably to the tune he was playing], Thus saith the Lord, Make this valley full of ditches ; " which was just telling them what every countryman could have told them without either fiddle or farce, that the way to get water was to dig for it.

But as every conjuror is not famous alike for the same thing, so neither were those prophets ; for though all of them, at least those I have spoken of, were famous for lying, some of them excelled in cursing. Elisha, whom I have just mentioned, was a chief in this branch of prophesying ; it was he that cursed the forty-two children in the name of the Lord, whom the two she-bears came and devoured. We are to suppose that those children were of the party of Israel ; but as those who will curse will lie, there is just as much credit to be given to this story of Elisha's two she-bears as there is to that of the Dragon of Wantley, of whom it is said :

> Poor children three devoured he,
> That could not with him grapple ;
> And at one sup he eat them up,
> As a man would eat an apple.

There was another description of men called prophets, that amused themselves with dreams and visions ; but whether by night or by day we know not. These, if they were not quite harmless, were but little mischievous. Of this class are

EZEKIEL and DANIEL ; and the first question upon these books, as upon all the others, is, Are they genuine? that is, were they written by Ezekiel and Daniel?

Of this there is no proof ; but so far as my own opinion goes, I am more inclined to believe they were, than that they were not. My reasons for this opinion are as follows : First, Because those books do not contain internal evidence to prove they were not written by Ezekiel and Daniel, as the books ascribed to Moses, Joshua, Samuel, etc., prove they were not written by Moses, Joshua, Samuel, etc.

Secondly, Because they were not written till after the Babylonish captivity began ; and there is good reason to believe that not any book in the bible was written before that period ; at least it is proveable, from the books themselves, as I have already shewn, that they were not written till after the commencement of the Jewish monarchy.

Thirdly, Because the manner in which the books ascribed to Ezekiel and Daniel are written, agrees with the condition these men were in at the time of writing them.

Had the numerous commentators and priests, who have foolishly employed or wasted their time in pretending to expound and unriddle those books, been carried into captivity, as Ezekiel and Daniel were, it would greatly have improved their intellects in comprehending the reason for this mode of writing, and have saved them the trouble of racking their invention, as they have done to no purpose ; for they would have found that themselves would be obliged to write whatever they had to write, respecting their own affairs, or those of their friends, or of their country, in a concealed manner, as those men have done.

These two books differ from all the rest ; for it is only these that are filled with accounts of dreams and visions : and this difference arose from the situation the writers were in as prisoners of war, or prisoners of state, in a foreign country, which obliged them to convey even the most trifling information to each other, and all their political projects or opinions, in obscure and metaphorical terms. They pretend to have dreamed dreams, and seen visions, because it was unsafe for them to speak facts or plain language. We ought, however, to suppose, that the persons to whom they wrote understood what they meant, and that it was not intended anybody else should. But these busy commentators and priests have been puzzling their wits to find out what it was not intended they should know, and with which they have nothing to do.

Ezekiel and Daniel were carried prisoners to Babylon, under the first captivity, in the time of Jehoiakim, nine years before the second captivity in the time of Zedekiah. The Jews were then still numerous, and had considerable force at Jerusalem; and as it is natural to suppose that men in the situation of Ezekiel and Daniel would be meditating the recovery of their country, and their own deliverance, it is reasonable to suppose that the accounts of dreams and visions with which these books are filled, are no other than a disguised mode of correspondence to facilitate those objects: it served them as a cypher, or secret alphabet. If they are not this, they are tales, reveries, and nonsense; or at least a fanciful way of wearing off the wearisomeness of captivity; but the presumption is, they are the former.

Ezekiel begins his book by speaking of a vision of *cherubims*, and of a *wheel within a wheel*, which he says he saw by the river Chebar, in the land of his captivity. Is it not reasonable to suppose that by the cherubims he meant the temple at Jerusalem, where they had figures of cherubims? and by a wheel within a wheel (which as a figure has always been understood to signify political contrivance) the project or means of recovering Jerusalem? In the latter part of his book he supposes himself transported to Jerusalem, and into the temple; and he refers back to the vision on the river Chebar, and says, (xliii. 3,) that this last vision was like the vision on the river Chebar; which indicates that those pretended dreams and

10

visions had for their object the recovery of Jerusalem, and nothing further.

As to the romantic interpretations and applications, wild as the dreams and visions they undertake to explain, which commentators and priests have made of those books, that of converting them into things which they call prophecies, and making them bend to times and circumstances as far remote even as the present day, it shews the fraud or the extreme folly to which credulity or priestcraft can go.

Scarcely anything can be more absurd than to suppose that men situated as Ezekiel and Daniel were, whose country was over-run, and in the possession of the enemy, all their friends and relations in captivity abroad, or in slavery at home, or massacred, or in continual danger of it ; scarcely any thing, I say, can be more absurd than to suppose that such men should find nothing to do but that of employing their time and their thoughts about what was to happen to other nations a thousand or two thousand years after they were dead ; at the same time nothing more natural than that they should meditate the recovery of Jerusalem, and their own deliverance ; and that this was the sole object of all the obscure and apparently frantic writing contained in those books.

In this sense the mode of writing used in those two books being forced by necessity, and not adopted by choice, is not irrational ; but, if we are to use the books as prophecies, they are false. In Ezekiel xxix. 11., speaking of Egypt, it is said, " No foot of man shall pass through it, nor foot of beast pass through it ; neither shall it be inhabited for forty years." This is what never came to pass, and consequently it is false, as all the books I have already reviewed are.—I here close this part of the subject.

In the former part of *The Age of Reason* I have spoken of Jonah, and of the story of him and the whale.—A fit story for ridicule, if it was written to be believed ; or of laughter, if it was intended to try what credulity could swallow ; for, if it could swallow Jonah and the whale it could swallow anything.

But, as is already shewn in the observations on the book of Job and of Proverbs, it is not always certain which of the books in the Bible are originally Hebrew, or only translations from the books of the Gentiles into Hebrew ; and, as the book of Jonah, so far from treating of the affairs of the Jews, says nothing upon that subject, but treats altogether of the Gentiles, it is more probable that it is a book of the Gentiles than of the Jews,[1] and that it has been written as a fable to expose the nonsense, and satyrize the vicious and malignant character, of a Bible-prophet, or a predicting priest.

Jonah is represented, first as a disobedient prophet, running away from his mission, and taking shelter aboard a vessel of the Gentiles, bound from Joppa to Tarshish ; as if he ignorantly supposed, by such a paltry contrivance, he could hide himself where God could not find him. The vessel is overtaken by a storm at sea ; and the mariners, all of whom are Gentiles, believing it to be a judgement on account of some one on board who had committed a crime, agreed to cast lots to discover the offender ; and the lot fell upon Jonah. But before this they had cast all their wares and merchandise over-board to lighten the vessel, while Jonah, like a stupid fellow, was fast asleep in the hold.

After the lot had designated Jonah to be the offender, they questioned him to know who and what he was ? and he told them *he was an Hebrew ;* and the story implies that he confessed himself to be guilty. But these Gentiles, instead of sacrificing him at once without pity or mercy, as a company of Bible-prophets or priests would have done by a Gentile in the same case, and as it is related Samuel had done by Agag, and Moses by the women and children, they endeavoured to save him, though at the risk of their own lives : for the account says, " Nevertheless [that is, though Jonah was a Jew and a foreigner, and the cause of all their misfortunes, and the loss of their cargo] the men rowed

[1] I have read in an ancient Persian poem (Saadi, I believe, but have mislaid the reference) this phrase : " And now the whale swallowed Jonah : the sun set."—*Editor.*

hard to bring the boat to land, but they could not, for the
sea wrought and was tempestuous against them." Still
however they were unwilling to put the fate of the lot into
execution ; and they cried, says the account, unto the Lord,
saying, "We beseech thee, O Lord, let us not perish for
this man's life, and lay not upon us innocent blood ; for
thou, O Lord, hast done as it pleased thee." Meaning
thereby, that they did not presume to judge Jonah guilty,
since that he might be innocent ; but that they considered
the lot that had fallen upon him as a decree of God, or as it
pleased God. The address of this prayer shews that the
Gentiles worshipped one *Supreme Being*, and that they were
not idolaters as the Jews represented them to be. But the
storm still continuing, and the danger encreasing, they put
the fate of the lot into execution, and cast Jonah in the sea ;
where, according to the story, a great fish swallowed him up
whole and alive !

We have now to consider Jonah securely housed from
the storm in the fish's belly. Here we are told that he
prayed ; but the prayer is a made-up prayer, taken from
various parts of the Psalms, without connection or consistency, and adapted to the distress, but not at all to the
condition that Jonah was in. It is such a prayer as a Gentile, who might know something of the Psalms, could copy
out for him. This circumstance alone, were there no other,
is sufficient to indicate that the whole is a made-up story.
The prayer, however, is supposed to have answered the
purpose, and the story goes on, (taking-off at the same time
the cant language of a Bible-prophet,) saying, "The Lord
spake unto the fish, and it vomited out Jonah upon dry
land."

Jonah then received a second mission to Nineveh, with
which he sets out ; and we have now to consider him as a
preacher. The distress he is represented to have suffered,
the remembrance of his own disobedience as the cause of it,
and the miraculous escape he is supposed to have had, were
sufficient, one would conceive, to have impressed him with
sympathy and benevolence in the execution of his mission ;

but, instead of this, he enters the city with denunciation and malediction in his mouth, crying, " Yet forty days, and Nineveh shall be overthrown."

We have now to consider this supposed missionary in the last act of his mission ; and here it is that the malevolent spirit of a Bible-prophet, or of a predicting priest, appears in all that blackness of character that men ascribe to the being they call the devil.

Having published his predictions, he withdrew, says the story, to the east side of the city.—But for what ? not to contemplate in retirement the mercy of his Creator to himself or to others, but to wait, with malignant impatience, the destruction of Nineveh. It came to pass, however, as the story relates, that the Ninevites reformed, and that God, according to the Bible phrase, repented him of the evil he had said he would do unto them, and did it not. This, saith the first verse of the last chapter, *displeased Jonah exceedingly and he was very angry.* His obdurate heart would rather that all Nineveh should be destroyed, and every soul, young and old, perish in its ruins, than that his prediction should not be fulfilled. To expose the character of a prophet still more, a gourd is made to grow up in the night, that promises him an agreeable shelter from the heat of the sun, in the place to which he is retired ; and the next morning it dies.

Here the rage of the prophet becomes excessive, and he is ready to destroy himself. " It is better, *said he*, for me to die than to live." This brings on a supposed expostulation between the Almighty and the prophet ; in which the former says, " Doest thou well to be angry for the gourd ? And Jonah said, I do well to be angry even unto death. Then said the Lord, Thou hast had pity on the gourd, for which thou hast not laboured, neither madest it to grow, which came up in a night, and perished in a night ; and should not I spare Nineveh, that great city, in which are more than threescore thousand persons, that cannot discern between their right hand and their left ? "

Here is both the winding up of the satire, and the moral

of the fable. As a satire, it strikes against the character of
all the Bible-prophets, and against all the indiscriminate
judgements upon men, women and children, with which
this lying book, the bible, is crowded ; such as Noah's flood,
the destruction of the cities of Sodom and Gomorrah, the
extirpation of the Canaanites, even to suckling infants, and
women with child ; because the same reflection ' that there
are more than threescore thousand persons that cannot discern between their right hand and their left,' meaning young
children, applies to all their cases. It satirizes also the supposed partiality of the Creator for one nation more than for
another.

As a moral, it preaches against the malevolent spirit of
prediction ; for as certainly as a man predicts ill, he becomes inclined to wish it. The pride of having his judgment right hardens his heart, till at last he beholds with
satisfaction, or sees with disappointment, the accomplishment or the failure of his predictions.—This book ends with
the same kind of strong and well-directed point against
prophets, prophecies and indiscriminate judgements, as the
chapter that Benjamin Franklin made for the Bible, about
Abraham and the stranger, ends against the intolerant spirit
of religious persecutions—Thus much for the book Jonah.[1]

Of the poetical parts of the Bible, that are called prophecies, I have spoken in the former part of *The Age of
Reason*, and already in this, where I have said that the word
prophet is the Bible-word for *poet*, and that the flights and
metaphors of those poets, many of which have become
obscure by the lapse of time and the change of circumstances, have been ridiculously erected into things called
prophecies, and applied to purposes the writers never
thought of. When a priest quotes any of those passages,
he unriddles it agreeably to his own views, and imposes

---

[1] The story of Abraham and the Fire-worshipper, ascribed to Franklin, is
from Saadi. (See my " Sacred Anthology," p. 61.) Paine has often been
called a " mere scoffer," but he seems to have been among the first to treat with
dignity the book of Jonah, so especially liable to the ridicule of superficial
readers, and discern in it the highest conception of Deity known to the Old
Testament.—*Editor*.

that explanation upon his congregation as the meaning of the writer. The *whore of Babylon* has been the common whore of all the priests, and each has accused the other of keeping the strumpet ; so well do they agree in their explanations.

There now remain only a few books, which they call books of the lesser prophets ; and as I have already shewn that the greater are impostors, it would be cowardice to disturb the repose of the little ones. Let them sleep, then, in the arms of their nurses, the priests, and both be forgotten together.

I have now gone through the Bible, as a man would go through a wood with an axe on his shoulder, and fell trees. Here they lie ; and the priests, if they can, may replant them. They may, perhaps, stick them in the ground, but they will never make them grow.—I pass on to the books of the New Testament.

CHAPTER II.

THE NEW TESTAMENT.

THE New Testament, they tell us, is founded upon the prophecies of the Old; if so, it must follow the fate of its foundation.

As it is nothing extraordinary that a woman should be with child before she was married, and that the son she might bring forth should be executed, even unjustly, I see no reason for not believing that such a woman as Mary, and such a man as Joseph, and Jesus, existed; their mere existence is a matter of indifference, about which there is no ground either to believe or to disbelieve, and which comes under the common head of, *It may be so, and what then?* The probability however is that there were such persons, or at least such as resembled them in part of the circumstances, because almost all romantic stories have been suggested by some actual circumstance; as the adventures of Robinson Crusoe, not a word of which is true, were suggested by the case of Alexander Selkirk.

It is not then the existence or the non-existence, of the persons that I trouble myself about; it is the fable of Jesus Christ, as told in the New Testament, and the wild and visionary doctrine raised thereon, against which I contend. The story, taking it as it is told, is blasphemously obscene. It gives an account of a young woman engaged to be married, and while under this engagement, she is, to speak plain language, debauched by a ghost, under the impious pretence, (Luke i. 35,) that "*the Holy Ghost shall come upon thee, and the power of the Highest shall overshadow thee.*" Notwithstanding which, Joseph afterwards marries her, cohabits with her as his wife, and in his turn rivals the ghost. This is putting the story into intelligible language, and when told in this manner, there is not a priest but must be ashamed to own it.*

Obscenity in matters of faith, however wrapped up, is always a token of fable and imposture; for it is necessary to our serious belief in God, that we do not connect it with stories that run, as this does, into ludicrous interpretations. This story is, upon the face of it, the same kind of story as that of Jupiter and Leda, or Jupiter and Europa, or any of the amorous adventures of Jupiter; and shews, as is already stated in the former part of *The Age of Reason,* that the Christian faith is built upon the heathen Mythology.

As the historical parts of the New Testament, so far as concerns Jesus Christ, are confined to a very short space of time, less than two years, and all within the same country, and nearly to the same spot, the discordance of time, place, and circumstance, which detects the fallacy of the books of the Old Testament, and proves them to be impositions, cannot be expected to be found here in the same abundance. The New Testament compared with the Old, is like a farce of one act, in which there is not room for very numerous violations of the unities. There are, however, some glaring contradictions, which, exclusive of the fallacy of the pretended prophecies, are sufficient to shew the story of Jesus Christ to be false.

I lay it down as a position which cannot be controverted, first, that the *agreement* of all the parts of a story does not prove that story to be true, because the parts may agree, and the whole may be false; secondly, that the *disagreement* of the parts of a story *proves the whole cannot be true.* The agreement does not prove truth, but the disagreement proves falsehood positively.

The history of Jesus Christ is contained in the four books ascribed to Matthew, Mark, Luke, and John.—The first chapter of Matthew begins with giving a genealogy of Jesus

* Mary, the supposed virgin, mother of Jesus, had several other children, sons and daughters. See Matt. xiii. 55, 56.—*Author.*

Christ; and in the third chapter of Luke there is also given a genealogy of Jesus Christ. Did these two agree, it would not prove the genealogy to be true, because it might nevertheless be a fabrication; but as they contradict each other in every particular, it proves falsehood absolutely. If Matthew speaks truth, Luke speaks falsehood; and if Luke speaks truth, Matthew speaks falsehood: and as there is no authority for believing one more than the other, there is no authority for believing either; and if they cannot be believed even in the very first thing they say, and set out to prove, they are not entitled to be believed in any thing they say afterwards. Truth is an uniform thing; and as to inspiration and revelation, were we to admit it, it is impossible to suppose it can be contradictory. Either then the men called apostles were imposters, or the books ascribed to them have been written by other persons, and fathered upon them, as is the case in the Old Testament.

The book of Matthew gives (i. 6), a genealogy by name from David, up, through Joseph, the husband of Mary, to Christ; and makes there to be *twenty-eight* generations. The book of Luke gives also a genealogy by name from Christ, through Joseph the husband of Mary, down to David, and makes there to be *forty-three* generations; besides which, there is only the two names of David and Joseph that are alike in the two lists.—I here insert both genealogical lists, and for the sake of perspicuity and comparison, have placed them both in the same direction, that is, from Joseph down to David.

Genealogy, according to Matthew.	Genealogy, according to Luke.
Christ	Christ
2 Joseph	2 Joseph
3 Jacob	3 Heli
4 Matthan	4 Matthat
5 Eleazer	5 Levi
6 Eliud	6 Melchi
7 Achim	7 Janna
8 Sadoc	8 Joseph
9 Azor	9 Mattathias
10 Eliakim	10 Amos

Genealogy, according to Matthew.	Genealogy, according to Luke.
11 Abiud	11 Naum
12 Zorobabel	12 Esli
13 Salathiel	13 Nagge
14 Jechonias	14 Maath
15 Josias	15 Mattathias
16 Amon	16 Semei
17 Manasses	17 Joseph
18 Ezekias	18 Juda
19 Achaz	19 Joanna
20 Joatham	20 Rhesa
21 Ozias	21 Zorobabel
22 Joram	22 Salathiel
23 Josaphat	23 Neri
24 Asa	24 Melchi
25 Abia	25 Addi
26 Roboam	26 Cosam
27 Solomon	27 Elmodam
28 David *	28 Er
	29 Jose
	30 Eliezer
	31 Jorim
	32 Matthat
	33 Levi
	34 Simeon
	35 Juda
	36 Joseph
	37 Jonan
	38 Eliakim
	39 Melea
	40 Menan
	41 Mattatha
	42 Nathan
	43 David

* From the birth of David to the birth of Christ is upwards of 1080 years; and as the life-time of Christ is not included, there are but 27 full generations. To find therefore the average age of each person mentioned in the list, at the time his first son was born, it is only necessary to divide 1080 by 27, which gives 40 years for each person. As the life-time of man was then but of the same extent it is now, it is an absurdity to suppose, that 27 following generations should all be old bachelors, before they married; and the more so, when we are told that Solomon, the next in succession to David, had a house full of wives and mistresses before he was twenty-one years of age. So far from this genealogy being a solemn truth, it is not even a reasonable lie. The list of Luke gives about twenty-six years for the average age, and this is too much.—*Author.*

Now, if these men, Matthew and Luke, set out with a
falsehood between them (as these two accounts shew they
do) in the very commencement of their history of Jesus
Christ, and of who, and of what he was, what authority (as
I have before asked) is there left for believing the strange
things they tell us afterwards? If they cannot be believed
in their account of his natural genealogy, how are we to
believe them when they tell us he was the son of God,
begotten by a ghost; and that an angel announced this in
secret to his mother? If they lied in one genealogy, why
are we to believe them in the other? If his natural genealogy be manufactured, which it certainly is, why are we not
to suppose that his celestial genealogy is manufactured also,
and that the whole is fabulous? Can any man of serious
reflection hazard his future happiness upon the belief of
a story naturally impossible, repugnant to every idea of
decency, and related by persons already detected of falsehood? Is it not more safe that we stop ourselves at the
plain, pure, and unmixed belief of one God, which is deism,
than that we commit ourselves on an ocean of improbable,
irrational, indecent, and contradictory tales?

The first question, however, upon the books of the New
Testament, as upon those of the Old, is, Are they genuine?
were they written by the persons to whom they are ascribed?
For it is upon this ground only that the strange things
related therein have been credited. Upon this point, there
is no *direct proof for or against;* and all that this state of a
case proves is *doubtfulness;* and doubtfulness is the opposite
of belief. The state, therefore, that the books are in, proves
against themselves as far as this kind of proof can go.

But, exclusive of this, the presumption is that the books
called the Evangelists, and ascribed to Matthew, Mark,
Luke, and John, were not written by Matthew, Mark,
Luke, and John; and that they are impositions. The disordered state of the history in these four books, the silence
of one book upon matters related in the other, and the disagreement that is to be found among them, implies that
they are the productions of some unconnected individuals,

many years after the things they pretend to relate, each of
whom made his own legend; and not the writings of men
living intimately together, as the men called apostles are
supposed to have done: in fine, that they have been manufactured, as the books of the Old Testament have been, by
other persons than those whose names they bear.

The story of the angel announcing what the church calls
the *immaculate conception*, is not so much as mentioned in
the books ascribed to Mark, and John; and is differently
related in Matthew and Luke. The former says the angel,
appeared to Joseph; the latter says, it was to Mary; but
either Joseph or Mary was the worst evidence that could
have been thought of; for it was others that should have
testified *for them*, and not they for themselves. Were any
girl that is now with child to say, and even to swear it, that
she was gotten with child by a ghost, and that an angel told
her so, would she be believed? Certainly she would not.
Why then are we to believe the same thing of another girl
whom we never saw, told by nobody knows who, nor when,
nor where? How strange and inconsistent is it, that the
same circumstance that would weaken the belief even of a
probable story, should be given as a motive for believing
this one, that has upon the face of it every token of absolute
impossibility and imposture.

The story of Herod destroying all the children under two
years old, belongs altogether to the book of Matthew; not
one of the rest mentions anything about it. Had such a
circumstance been true, the universality of it must have
made it known to all the writers, and the thing would have
been too striking to have been omitted by any. This writer
tell us, that Jesus escaped this slaughter, because Joseph
and Mary were warned by an angel to flee with him into
Egypt; but he forgot to make provision for John [the Bap-
tist], who was then under two years of age. John, however,
who staid behind, fared as well as Jesus, who fled; and
therefore the story circumstantially belies itself.

Not any two of these writers agree in reciting, *exactly in
the same words*, the written inscription, short as it is, which

they tell us was put over Christ when he was crucified ; and besides this, Mark says, He was crucified at the third hour, (nine in the morning ;) and John says it was the sixth hour, (twelve at noon.*)

The inscription is thus stated in those books :

> Matthew—This is Jesus the king of the Jews.
> Mark ——The king of the Jews.
> Luke ——This is the king of the Jews.
> John ——Jesus of Nazareth the king of the Jews.

We may infer from these circumstances, trivial as they are, that those writers, whoever they were, and in whatever time they lived, were not present at the scene. The only one of the men called apostles who appears to have been near to the spot was Peter, and when he was accused of being one of Jesus's followers, it is said, (Matthew xxvi. 74,) " *Then Peter began to curse and to swear, saying, I know not the man :* " yet we are now called to believe the same Peter, convicted, by their own account, of perjury. For what reason, or on what authority, should we do this?

The accounts that are given of the circumstances, that they tell us attended the crucifixion, are differently related in those four books.

The book ascribed to Matthew says *there was darkness over all the land from the sixth hour unto the ninth hour—that the veil of the temple was rent in twain from the top to the bottom—that there was an earthquake—that the rocks rent—that the graves opened, that the bodies of many of the saints that slept arose and came out of their graves after the resurrection, and went into the holy city and appeared unto many.* Such is the account which this dashing writer of the book of Matthew gives, but in which he is not supported by the writers of the other books.

The writer of the book ascribed to Mark, in detailing the

---

* According to John, (xix. 14) the sentence was not passed till about the sixth hour (noon,) and consequently the execution could not be till the afternoon ; but Mark (xv. 25) says expressly that he was crucified at the third hour, (nine in the morning,)—*Author.*

circumstances of the crucifixion, makes no mention of any earthquake, nor of the rocks rending, nor of the graves opening, nor of the dead men walking out. The writer of the book of Luke is silent also upon the same points. And as to the writer of the book of John, though he details all the circumstances of the crucifixion down to the burial of Christ, he says nothing about either the darkness—the veil of the temple—the earthquake—the rocks—the graves—nor the dead men.

Now if it had been true that these things had happened, and if the writers of these books had lived at the time they did happen, and had been the persons they are said to be —namely, the four men called apostles, Matthew, Mark, Luke, and John,—it was not possible for them, as true historians, even without the aid of inspiration, not to have recorded them. The things, supposing them to have been facts, were of too much notoriety not to have been known, and of too much importance not to have been told. All these supposed apostles must have been witnesses of the earthquake, if there had been any, for it was not possible for them to have been absent from it: the opening of the graves and resurrection of the dead men, and their walking about the city, is of still greater importance than the earthquake. An earthquake is always possible, and natural, and proves nothing; but this opening of the graves is supernatural, and directly in point to their doctrine, their cause, and their apostleship. Had it been true, it would have filled up whole chapters of those books, and been the chosen theme and general chorus of all the writers; but instead of this, little and trivial things, and mere prattling conversation of *he said this* and *she said that* are often tediously detailed, while this most important of all, had it been true, is passed off in a slovenly manner by a single dash of the pen, and that by one writer only, and not so much as hinted at by the rest.

It is an easy thing to tell a lie, but it is difficult to support the lie after it is told. The writer of the book of Matthew should have told us who the saints were that came to life again, and went into the city, and what became of them afterwards, and who it was that saw them ; for he is not hardy enough to say that he saw them himself ;—whether they came out naked, and all in natural buff, he-saints and she-saints, or whether they came full dressed, and where they got their dresses ; whether they went to their former habitations, and reclaimed their wives, their husbands, and their property, and how they were received ; whether they entered ejectments for the recovery of their possessions, or brought actions of *crim. con.* against the rival interlopers ; whether they remained on earth, and followed their former occupation of preaching or working ; or whether they died again, or went back to their graves alive, and buried themselves.

Strange indeed, that an army of saints should return to life, and nobody know who they were, nor who it was that saw them, and that not a word more should be said upon the subject, nor these saints have any thing to tell us ! Had it been the prophets who (as we are told) had formerly prophesied of these things, *they* must have had a great deal to say. They could have told us everything, and we should have had posthumous prophecies, with notes and commentaries upon the first, a little better at least than we have now. Had it been Moses, and Aaron, and Joshua, and Samuel, and David, not an unconverted Jew had remained in all Jerusalem. Had it been John the Baptist, and the saints of the times then present, everybody would have known them, and they would have out-preached and out-famed all the other apostles. But, instead of this, these saints are made to pop up, like Jonah's gourd in the night, for no purpose at all but to wither in the morning.—Thus much for this part of the story.

The tale of the resurrection follows that of the crucifixion ; and in this as well as in that, the writers, whoever they were, disagree so much as to make it evident that none of them were there.

The book of Matthew states, that when Christ was put in the sepulchre the Jews applied to Pilate for a watch or a guard to be placed over the sepulchre, to prevent the body being stolen by the disciples; and that in consequence of this request the sepulchre *was made sure, sealing the stone* that covered the mouth, and setting a watch. But the other books say nothing about this application, nor about the sealing, nor the guard, nor the watch; and according to their accounts, there were none. Matthew, however, follows up this part of the story of the guard or the watch with a second part, that I shall notice in the conclusion, as it serves to detect the fallacy of those books.

The book of Matthew continues its account, and says, (xxviii. 1,) that at the end of the Sabbath, as it began to *dawn*, towards the first day of the week, came *Mary Magdalene* and the *other Mary*, to see the sepulchre. Mark says it was sun-rising, and John says it was dark. Luke says it was Mary Magdalene and Joanna, and *Mary the mother* of James, and *other women*, that came to the sepulchre; and John states that Mary Magdalene came alone. So well do they agree about their first evidence! They all, however, appear to have known most about Mary Magdalene; she was a woman of large acquaintance, and it was not an ill conjecture that she might be upon the stroll.[1]

The book of Matthew goes on to say (ver. 2): " And behold there was a great earthquake, for the angel of the Lord descended from heaven, and came and rolled back the stone from the door, and *sat upon it.*" But the other books say nothing about any earthquake, nor about the angel rolling back the stone, and *sitting upon it ;* and, according to their account, there was no angel *sitting there.* Mark says the angel[2] was *within the sepulchre, sitting* on the right side. Luke says there were two, and they were both standing up; and John says they were both sitting down, one at the head and the other at the feet.

Matthew says, that the angel that was sitting upon the

[1] The Bishop of Llandaff, in his famous " Apology," censured Paine severely for this insinuation against Mary Magdalene, but the censure really falls on our English version, which, by a chapter-heading (Luke vii.), has unwarrantably identified her as the sinful woman who anointed Jesus, and irrevocably branded her.—*Editor.*

[2] Mark says " a young man," and Luke " two men."—*Editor.*

11

stone on the outside of the sepulchre told the two Marys that Christ was risen, and that the women went *away* quickly. Mark says, that the women, upon seeing the stone rolled away, and wondering at it, went *into* the sepulchre, and that it was the angel that was *sitting* within on the right side, that told them so. Luke says, it was the two angels that were standing up; and John says, it was Jesus Christ himself that told it to Mary Magdalene; and that she did not go into the sepulchre, but only stooped down and looked in.

Now, if the writers of these four books had gone into a court of justice to prove an *alibi*, (for it is of the nature of an alibi that is here attempted to be proved, namely, the absence of a dead body by supernatural means,) and had they given their evidence in the same contradictory manner as it is here given, they would have been in danger of having their ears cropt for perjury, and would have justly deserved it. Yet this is the evidence, and these are the books, that have been imposed upon the world as being given by divine inspiration, and as the unchangeable word of God.

The writer of the book of Matthew, after giving this account, relates a story that is not to be found in any of the other books, and which is the same I have just before alluded to. " Now," says he, [that is, after the conversation the women had had with the angel sitting upon the stone,] " behold some of the watch [meaning the watch that he had said had been placed over the sepulchre] came into the city, and shewed unto the chief priests all the things that were done; and when they were assembled with the elders and had taken counsel, they gave large money unto the soldiers, saying, Say ye, that his disciples came by night, and stole him away while we *slept ;* and if this come to the governor's ears, we will persuade him, and secure you. So they took the money, and did as they were taught; and this saying [that his disciples stole him away] is commonly reported among the Jews *until this day."*

The expression, *until this day,* is an evidence that the book ascribed to Matthew was not written by Matthew, and that it has been manufactured long after the times and things of which it pretends to treat; for the expression implies a great length of intervening time. It would be inconsistent in us to speak in this manner of any thing happening in our own time. To give, therefore, intelligible meaning to the expression, we must suppose a lapse of some generations at least, for this manner of speaking carries the mind back to ancient time.

The absurdity also of the story is worth noticing; for it shews the writer of the book of Matthew to have been an exceeding weak and foolish man. He tells a story that contradicts itself in point of possibility; for though the guard, if there were any, might be made to say that the body was taken away while they were *asleep*, and to give that as a reason for their not having prevented it, that same sleep must also have prevented their knowing how, and by whom, it was done; and yet they are made to say that it was the disciples who did it. Were a man to tender his evidence of something that he should say was done, and of the manner of doing it, and of the person who did it, while he was asleep, and could know nothing of the matter, such evidence could not be received: it will do well enough for Testament evidence, but not for any thing where truth is concerned.

I come now to that part of the evidence in those books, that respects the pretended appearance of Christ after this pretended resurrection.

The writer of the book of Matthew relates, that the angel that was sitting on the stone at the mouth of the sepulchre, said to the two Marys (xxviii. 7), "*Behold Christ is gone before you into Galilee, there ye shall see him; lo, I have told you.*" And the same writer at the next two verses (8, 9,) makes Christ himself to speak to the same purpose to these women immediately after the angel had told it to them, and that they ran quickly to tell it to the disciples; and it is said (ver. 16), "*Then the eleven disciples went away into Galilee,* into a mountain where Jesus had appointed them; and, when they saw him, they worshipped him."

But the writer of the book of John tells us a story very

different to this; for he says (xx. 19) " Then the same day
at evening, being the first day of the week, [that is, the same
day that Christ is said to have risen,] when the doors were
shut, where the disciples were assembled, for fear of the
Jews, came Jesus and stood in the midst of them."

According to Matthew the eleven were marching to
Galilee, to meet Jesus in a mountain, by his own appointment, at the very time when, according to John, they were
assembled in another place, and that not by appointment,
but in secret, for fear of the Jews.

The writer of the book of Luke xxiv. 13, 33–36, contradicts that of Matthew more pointedly than John does; for
he says expressly, that the meeting was in Jerusalem the
evening of the same day that he (Christ) rose, and that the
eleven were *there.*

Now, it is not possible, unless we admit these supposed
disciples the right of wilful lying, that the writers of these
books could be any of the eleven persons called disciples;
for if, according to Matthew, the eleven went into Galilee
to meet Jesus in a mountain by his own appointment, on the
same day that he is said to have risen, Luke and John must
have been two of that eleven; yet the writer of Luke says
expressly, and John implies as much, that the meeting was
that same day, in a house in Jerusalem; and, on the other
hand, if, according to Luke and John, the *eleven* were assembled in a house in Jerusalem, Matthew must have been
one of that eleven; yet Matthew says the meeting was in a
mountain in Galilee, and consequently the evidence given in
those books destroy each other.

The writer of the book of Mark says nothing about any
meeting in Galilee; but he says (xvi. 12) that Christ, after
his resurrection, appeared in *another form* to two of them, as
they walked into the country, and that these two told it to
the residue, who would not believe them.[1]　Luke also tells
a story, in which he keeps Christ employed the whole of the
day of this pretended resurrection, until the evening, and

[1] This belongs to the late addition to Mark, which originally ended with
xvi. 8.—*Editor.*

which totally invalidates the account of going to the mountain in Galilee. He says, that two of them, without saying which two, went that *same day* to a village called Emmaus, three score furlongs (seven miles and a half) from Jerusalem, and that Christ in disguise went with them, and staid with them unto the evening, and supped with them, and then vanished out of their sight, and re-appeared that same evening, at the meeting of the eleven in Jerusalem.

This is the contradictory manner in which the evidence of this pretended re-appearance of Christ is stated : the only point in which the writers agree, is the skulking privacy of that re-appearance ; for whether it was in the recess of a mountain in Galilee, or in a shut-up house in Jerusalem, it was still skulking. To what cause then are we to assign this skulking? On the one hand, it is directly repugnant to the supposed or pretended end, that of convincing the world that Christ was risen ; and, on the other hand, to have asserted the publicity of it would have exposed the writers of those books to public detection ; and, therefore, they have been under the necessity of making it a private affair.

As to the account of Christ being seen by more than five hundred at once, it is Paul only who says it, and not the five hundred who say it for themselves. It is, therefore, the testimony of but one man, and that too of a man, who did not, according to the same account, believe a word of the matter himself at the time it is said to have happened. His evidence, supposing him to have been the writer of Corinthians xv., where this account is given, is like that of a man who comes into a court of justice to swear that what he had sworn before was false. A man may often see reason, and he has too always the right of changing his opinion ; but this liberty does not extend to matters of fact.

I now come to the last scene, that of the ascension into heaven.—Here all fear of the Jews, and of every thing else, must necessarily have been out of the question : it was that which, if true, was to seal the whole ; and upon which the reality of the future mission of the disciples was to rest for proof. Words, whether declarations or promises, that passed in private, either in the recess of a mountain in Galilee, or in a shut-up house in Jerusalem, even supposing them to have been spoken, could not be evidence in public; it was therefore necessary that this last scene should preclude the possibility of denial and dispute; and that it should be, as I have stated in the former part of *The Age of Reason*, as public and as visible as the sun at noon-day; at least it ought to have been as public as the crucifixion is reported to have been.—But to come to the point.

In the first place, the writer of the book of Matthew does not say a syllable about it; neither does the writer of the book of John. This being the case, is it possible to suppose that those writers, who affect to be even minute in other matters, would have been silent upon this, had it been true? The writer of the book of Mark passes it off in a careless, slovenly manner, with a single dash of the pen, as if he was tired of romancing, or ashamed of the story. So also does the writer of Luke. And even between these two, there is not an apparent agreement, as to the place where this final parting is said to have been.[1]

The book of Mark says that Christ appeared to the eleven as they sat at meat, alluding to the meeting of the eleven at Jerusalem: he then states the conversation that he says passed at that meeting; and immediately after says (as a school-boy would finish a dull story,) " *So then*, after the Lord had spoken unto them, he was received up into heaven, and sat on the right hand of God." But the writer of Luke says, that the ascension was from Bethany; that *he* (Christ) *led them out as far as Bethany, and was parted from them there, and was carried up into heaven.* So also was Mahomet: and, as to Moses, the *apostle* Jude says, ver. 9, *That Michael and the devil disputed about his body.* While we believe such fables as these, or either of them, we believe unworthily of the Almighty.

I have now gone through the examination of the four

[1] The last nine verses of Mark being ungenuine, the story of the ascension rests exclusively on the words in Luke xxiv. 51, " was carried up into heaven," —words omitted by several ancient authorities.—*Editor.*

books ascribed to Matthew, Mark, Luke and John; and when it is considered that the whole space of time, from the crucifixion to what is called the ascension, is but a few days, apparently not more than three or four, and that all the circumstances are reported to have happened nearly about the same spot, Jerusalem, it is, I believe, impossible to find in any story upon record so many and such glaring absurdities, contradictions, and falsehoods, as are in those books. They are more numerous and striking than I had any expectation of finding, when I began this examination, and far more so than I had any idea of when I wrote the former part of *The Age of Reason.* I had then neither Bible nor Testament to refer to, nor could I procure any. My own situation, even as to existence, was becoming every day more precarious; and as I was willing to leave something behind me upon the subject, I was obliged to be quick and concise. The quotations I then made were from memory only, but they are correct; and the opinions I have advanced in that work are the effect of the most clear and long-established conviction, —that the Bible and the Testament are impositions upon the world;—that the fall of man, the account of Jesus Christ being the Son of God, and of his dying to appease the wrath of God, and of salvation by that strange means, are all fabulous inventions, dishonourable to the wisdom and power of the Almighty;—that the only true religion is deism, by which I then meant and now mean the belief of one God, and an imitation of his moral character, or the practice of what are called moral virtues;—and that it was upon this only (so far as religion is concerned) that I rested all my hopes of happiness hereafter. So say I now—and so help me God.

But to return to the subject.—Though it is impossible, at this distance of time, to ascertain as a fact who were the writers of those four books (and this alone is sufficient to hold them in doubt, and where we doubt we do not believe) it is not difficult to ascertain negatively that they were not written by the persons to whom they are ascribed. The contradictions in those books demonstrate two things:

First, that the writers cannot have been eye-witnesses and ear-witnesses of the matters they relate, or they would have related them without those contradictions ; and, consequently that the books have not been written by the persons called apostles, who are supposed to have been witnesses of this kind.

Secondly, that the writers, whoever they were, have not acted in concerted imposition, but each writer separately and individually for himself, and without the knowledge of the other.

The same evidence that applies to prove the one, applies equally to prove both cases; that is, that the books were not written by the men called apostles, and also that they are not a concerted imposition. As to inspiration, it is altogether out of the question ; we may as well attempt to unite truth and falsehood, as inspiration and contradiction.

If four men are eye-witnesses and ear-witnesses to a scene, they will without any concert between them, agree as to time and place, when and where that scene happened. Their individual knowledge of the *thing*, each one knowing it for himself, renders concert totally unnecessary ; the one will not say it was in a mountain in the country, and the other at a house in town ; the one will not say it was at sunrise, and the other that it was dark. For in whatever place it was, and whatever time it was, they know it equally alike.

And on the other hand, if four men concert a story, they will make their separate relations of that story agree and corroborate with each other to support the whole. *That* concert supplies the want of fact in the one case, as the knowledge of the fact supersedes, in the other case, the necessity of a concert. The same contradictions, therefore, that prove there has been no concert, prove also that the reporters had no knowledge of the fact, (or rather of that which they relate as a fact,) and detect also the falsehood of their reports. Those books, therefore, have neither been written by the men called apostles, nor by imposters in concert.—How then have they been written?

I am not one of those who are fond of believing there is

much of that which is called wilful lying, or lying originally, except in the case of men setting up to be prophets, as in the Old Testament; for prophesying is lying professionally. In almost all other cases it is not difficult to discover the progress by which even simple supposition, with the aid of credulity, will in time grow into a lie, and at last be told as a fact; and whenever we can find a charitable reason for a thing of this kind, we ought not to indulge a severe one.

The story of Jesus Christ appearing after he was dead is the story of an apparition, such as timid imaginations can always create in vision, and credulity believe. Stories of this kind had been told of the assassination of Julius Cæsar not many years before, and they generally have their origin in violent deaths, or in execution of innocent persons. In cases of this kind, compassion lends its aid, and benevolently stretches the story. It goes on a little and a little farther, till it becomes a *most certain truth.* Once start a ghost, and credulity fills up the history of its life, and assigns the cause of its appearance; one tells it one way, another another way, till there are as many stories about the ghost, and about the proprietor of the ghost, as there are about Jesus Christ in these four books.

The story of the appearance of Jesus Christ is told with that strange mixture of the natural and impossible, that distinguishes legendary tale from fact. He is represented as suddenly coming in and going out when the doors are shut, and of vanishing out of sight, and appearing again, as one would conceive of an unsubstantial vision; then again he is hungry, sits down to meat, and eats his supper. But as those who tell stories of this kind never provide for all the cases, so it is here: they have told us, that when he arose he left his grave-clothes behind him; but they have forgotten to provide other clothes for him to appear in afterwards, or to tell us what he did with them when he ascended; whether he stripped all off, or went up clothes and all. In the case of Elijah, they have been careful enough to make him throw down his mantle; how it happened not to be burnt in the chariot of fire, *they* also have not told us; but as imagination supplies all deficiencies of this kind, we may suppose if we please that it was made of salamander's wool.

Those who are not much acquainted with ecclesiastical history, may suppose that the book called the New Testament has existed ever since the time of Jesus Christ, as they suppose that the books ascribed to Moses have existed ever since the time of Moses. But the fact is historically otherwise; there was no such book as the New Testament till more than three hundred years after the time that Christ is said to have lived.

At what time the books ascribed to Matthew, Mark, Luke and John, began to appear, is altogether a matter of uncertainty. There is not the least shadow of evidence of who the persons were that wrote them, nor at what time they were written; and they might as well have been called by the names of any of the other supposed apostles as by the names they are now called. The originals are not in the possession of any Christian Church existing, any more than the two tables of stone written on, they pretend, by the finger of God, upon Mount Sinai, and given to Moses, are in the possession of the Jews. And even if they were, there is no possibility of proving the hand-writing in either case. At the time those four books were written there was no printing, and consequently there could be no publication otherwise than by written copies, which any man might make or alter at pleasure, and call them originals. Can we suppose it is consistent with the wisdom of the Almighty to commit himself and his will to man upon such precarious means as these; or that it is consistent we should pin our faith upon such uncertainties? We cannot make nor alter, nor even imitate, so much as one blade of grass that he has made, and yet we can make or alter *words of God* as easily as words of man.*

* The former part of the *Age of Reason* has not been published two years, and there is already an expression in it that is not mine. The expression is: *The book of Luke was carried by a majority of one voice only.* It may be true,

About three hundred and fifty years after the time that Christ is said to have lived, several writings of the kind I am speaking of were scattered in the hands of divers individuals; and as the church had begun to form itself into an hierarchy, or church government, with temporal powers, it set itself about collecting them into a code, as we now see them, called *The New Testament.* They decided by vote, as I have before said in the former part of the *Age of Reason,* which of those writings, out of the collection they had made, should be the *word of God,* and which should not. The Rabbins of the Jews had decided, by vote, upon the books of the Bible before.

As the object of the church, as is the case in all national establishments of churches, was power and revenue, and terror the means it used, it is consistent to suppose that the most miraculous and wonderful of the writings they had collected stood the best chance of being voted. And as to the authenticity of the books, the *vote stands in the place of it;* for it can be traced no higher.

Disputes, however, ran high among the people then calling themselves Christians, not only as to points of doctrine, but as to the authenticity of the books. In the contest between the person called St. Augustine, and Fauste, about the year 400, the latter says, " The books called the Evan-

---

but it is not I that have said it. Some person who might know of that circumstance, has added it in a note at the bottom of the page of some of the editions, printed either in England or in America ; and the printers, after that, have erected it into the body of the work, and made me the author of it. If this has happened within such a short space of time, notwithstanding the aid of printing, which prevents the alteration of copies individually, what may not have happened in a much greater length of time, when there was no printing, and when any man who could write could make a written copy and call it an original by Matthew, Mark, Luke, or John?—*Author.*

The spurious addition to Paine's work alluded to in his footnote drew on him a severe criticism from Dr. Priestley (" Letters to a Philosophical Unbeliever," p. 75), yet it seems to have been Priestley himself who, in his quotation, first incorporated into Paine's text the footnote added by the editor of the American edition (1794). The American added : "Vide Moshiem's (*sic*) Ecc. History," which Priestley omits. In a modern American edition I notice four verbal alterations introduced into the above footnote.—*Editor.*

gelists have been composed long after the times of the apostles, by some obscure men, who, fearing that the world would not give credit to their relation of matters of which they could not be informed, have published them under the names of the apostles; and which are so full of sottishness and discordant relations, that there is neither agreement nor connection between them."

And in another place, addressing himself to the advocates of those books, as being the word of God, he says, " It is thus that your predecessors have inserted in the scriptures of our Lord many things which, though they carry his name, agree not with his doctrine. This is not surprising, *since that we have often proved* that these things have not been written by himself, nor by his apostles, but that for the greatest part they are founded upon *tales*, upon *vague reports*, and put together by I know not what half Jews, with but little agreement between them; and which they have nevertheless published under the name of the apostles of our Lord, and have thus attributed to them their own *errors and their lies.**

The reader will see by those extracts that the authenticity of the books of the New Testament was denied, and the books treated as tales, forgeries, and lies, at the time they were voted to be the word of God. But the interest of the church, with the assistance of the faggot, bore down the opposition, and at last suppressed all investigation. Miracles followed upon miracles, if we will believe them, and men were taught to say they believed whether they believed or not. But (by way of throwing in a thought) the French Revolution has excommunicated the church from the power of working miracles; she has not been able, with the assistance of all her saints, to work *one* miracle since the revolution began ; and as she never stood in greater need than now, we

---

* I have taken these two extracts from Boulanger's Life of Paul, written in French ; Boulanger has quoted them from the writings of Augustine against Fauste, to which he refers.—*Author.*

This Bishop Faustus is usually styled " The Manichæan," Augustine having entitled his book, *Contra Faustum Manichæum Libri xxxiii.*, in which nearly the whole of Faustus' very able work is quoted.—*Editor.*

may, without the aid of divination, conclude that all her former miracles are tricks and lies.*

When we consider the lapse of more than three hundred years intervening between the time that Christ is said to have lived and the time the New Testament was formed into a book, we must see, even without the assistance of historical evidence, the exceeding uncertainty there is of its authenticity. The authenticity of the book of Homer, so far as regards the authorship, is much better established than that of the New Testament, though Homer is a thousand years the most ancient. It was only an exceeding good poet that could have written the book of Homer, and, therefore, few men only could have attempted it; and a man capable of doing it would not have thrown away his own fame by giving it to another. In like manner, there were but few that could have composed Euclid's Elements, because none but an exceeding good geometrician could have been the author of that work.

---

* Boulanger in his life of Paul, has collected from the ecclesiastical histories, and the writings of the fathers as they are called, several matters which shew the opinions that prevailed among the different sects of Christians, at the time the Testament, as we now see it, was voted to be the word of God. The following extracts are from the second chapter of that work:

The Marcionists (a Christian sect) asserted that the evangelists were filled with falsities. The Manichæans, who formed a very numerous sect at the commencement of Christianity, *rejected as false all the New Testament*, and shewed other writings quite different that they gave for authentic. The Cerinthians, like the Marcionists, admitted not the Acts of the Apostles. The Encratites and the Sevenians adopted neither the Acts, nor the Epistles of Paul. Chrysostom, in a homily which he made upon the Acts of the Apostles, says that in his time, about the year 400, many people knew nothing either of the author or of the book. St. Irene, who lived before that time, reports that the Valentinians, like several other sects of the Christians, accused the scriptures of being filled with imperfections, errors, and contradictions. The Ebionites, or Nazarenes, who were the first Christians, rejected all the Epistles of Paul, and regarded him as an impostor. They report, among other things, that he was originally a Pagan ; that he came to Jerusalem, where he lived some time ; and that having a mind to marry the daughter of the high priest, he had himself been circumcised ; but that not being able to obtain her, he quarrelled with the Jews and wrote against circumcision, and against the observation of the Sabbath, and against all the legal ordinances.—*Author.* [Much abridged from the *Exam. Crit. de la Vie de St. Paul*, by N. A. Boulanger, 1770.—*Editor.*]

But with respect to the books of the New Testament, particularly such parts as tell us of the resurrection and ascension of Christ, any person who could tell a story of an apparition, or of a *man's walking*, could have made such books; for the story is most wretchedly told. The chance, therefore, of forgery in the Testament is millions to one greater than in the case of Homer or Euclid. Of the numerous priests or parsons of the present day, bishops and all, every one of them can make a sermon, or translate a scrap of Latin, especially if it has been translated a thousand times before; but is there any amongst them that can write poetry like Homer, or science like Euclid? The sum total of a parson's learning, with very few exceptions, is a, b, ab, and hic, hæc, hoc; and their knowledge of science is, three times one is three; and this is more than sufficient to have enabled them, had they lived at the time, to have written all the books of the New Testament.

As the opportunities of forgery were greater, so also was the inducement. A man could gain no advantage by writing under the name of Homer or Euclid; if he could write equal to them, it would be better that he wrote under his own name; if inferior, he could not succeed. Pride would prevent the former, and impossibility the latter. But with respect to such books as compose the New Testament, all the inducements were on the side of forgery. The best imagined history that could have been made, at the distance of two or three hundred years after the time, could not have passed for an original under the name of the real writer; the only chance of success lay in forgery; for the church wanted pretence for its new doctrine, and truth and talents were out of the question.

But as it is not uncommon (as before observed) to relate stories of persons *walking* after they are dead, and of ghosts and apparitions of such as have fallen by some violent or extraordinary means; and as the people of that day were in the habit of believing such things, and of the appearance of angels, and also of devils, and of their getting into people's insides, and skaking them like a fit of an ague, and of their being cast out again as if by an emetic—(Mary Magdalene, the book of Mark tells us had brought up, or been brought to bed of seven devils;) it was nothing extraordinary that some story of this kind should get abroad of the person called Jesus Christ, and become afterwards the foundation of the four books ascribed to Matthew, Mark, Luke, and John. Each writer told a tale as he heard it, or thereabouts, and gave to his book the name of the saint or the apostle whom tradition had given as the eye-witness. It is only upon this ground that the contradictions in those books can be accounted for; and if this be not the case, they are downright impositions, lies, and forgeries, without even the apology of credulity.

That they have been written by a sort of half Jews, as the foregoing quotations mention, is discernible enough. The frequent references made to that chief assassin and impostor Moses, and to the men called prophets, establishes this point; and, on the other hand, the church has complimented the fraud, by admitting the Bible and the Testament to reply to each other. Between the Christian-Jew and the Christian-Gentile, the thing called a prophecy, and the thing prophesied of, the type and the thing typified, the sign and the thing signified, have been industriously rummaged up, and fitted together like old locks and pick-lock keys. The story foolishly enough told of Eve and the serpent, and naturally enough as to the enmity between men and serpents (for the serpent always bites about the *heel*, because it cannot reach higher, and the man always knocks the serpent about the *head*, as the most effectual way to prevent its biting;*) this foolish story, I say, has been made into a prophecy, a type, and a promise to begin with; and the lying imposition of Isaiah to Ahaz, *That a virgin shall conceive and bear a son*, as a sign that Ahaz should conquer, when the event was that he was defeated (as already noticed in the observations on the book of Isaiah), has been perverted, and made to serve as a winder up.

* "It shall bruise thy *head*, and thou shalt bruise his *heel*." Gen. iii. 15.—*Author.*

Jonah and the whale are also made into a sign and type. Jonah is Jesus, and the whale is the grave; for it is said, (and they have made Christ to say it of himself, Matt. xii. 40), "For as Jonah was *three days* and *three nights* in the whale's belly, so shall the Son of man be *three days* and *three nights* in the heart of the earth." But it happens, aukwardly enough, that Christ, according to their own account, was but one day and two nights in the grave; about 36 hours instead of 72; that is, the Friday night, the Saturday, and the Saturday night; for they say he was up on the Sunday morning by sunrise, or before. But as this fits quite as well as the *bite* and the *kick* in Genesis, or the *virgin* and her *son* in Isaiah, it will pass in the lump of *orthodox* things.—Thus much for the historical part of the Testament and its evidences.

Epistles of Paul.—The epistles ascribed to Paul, being fourteen in number, almost fill up the remaining part of the Testament. Whether those epistles were written by the person to whom they are ascribed is a matter of no great importance, since that the writer, whoever he was, attempts to prove his doctrine by argument. He does not pretend to have been witness to any of the scenes told of the resurrection and the ascension; and he declares that he had not believed them.

The story of his being struck to the ground as he was journeying to Damascus, has nothing in it miraculous or extraordinary; he escaped with life, and that is more than many others have done, who have been struck with lightning; and that he should lose his sight for three days, and be unable to eat or drink during that time, is nothing more than is common in such conditions. His companions that were with him appear not to have suffered in the same manner, for they were well enough to lead him the remainder of the journey; neither did they pretend to have seen any vision.

The character of the person called Paul, according to the accounts given of him, has in it a great deal of violence and fanaticism; he had persecuted with as much heat as he preached afterwards; the stroke he had received had changed his thinking, without altering his constitution; and either as a Jew or a Christian he was the same zealot. Such men are never good moral evidences of any doctrine they preach. They are always in extremes, as well of action as of belief.

The doctrine he sets out to prove by argument, is the resurrection of the same body: and he advances this as an evidence of immortality. But so much will men differ in their manner of thinking, and in the conclusions they draw from the same premises, that this doctrine of the resurrection of the same body, so far from being an evidence of immortality, appears to me to be an evidence againt it; for if I have already died in this body, and am raised again in the same body in which I have died, it is presumptive evidence that I shall die again. That resurrection no more secures me against the repetition of dying, than an ague-fit, when past, secures me against another. To believe therefore in immortality, I must have a more elevated idea than is contained in the gloomy doctrine of the resurrection.

Besides, as a matter of choice, as well as of hope, I had rather have a better body and a more convenient form than the present. Every animal in the creation excels us in something. The winged insects, without mentioning doves or eagles, can pass over more space with greater ease in a few minutes than man can in an hour. The glide of the smallest fish, in proportion to its bulk, exceeds us in motion almost beyond comparison, and without weariness. Even the sluggish snail can ascend from the bottom of a dungeon, where man, by the want of that ability, would perish; and a spider can launch itself from the top, as a playful amusement. The personal powers of man are so limited, and his heavy frame so little constructed to extensive enjoyment, that there is nothing to induce us to wish the opinion of Paul to be true. It is too little for the magnitude of the scene, too mean for the sublimity of the subject.

But all other arguments apart, the *consciousness of existence* is the only conceivable idea we can have of another

12

life, and the continuance of that consciousness is immortality. The consciousness of existence, or the knowing that we exist, is not necessarily confined to the same form, nor to the same matter, even in this life.

We have not in all cases the same form, nor in any case the same matter, that composed our bodies twenty or thirty years ago; and yet we are conscious of being the same persons. Even legs and arms, which make up almost half the human frame, are not necessary to the consciousness of existence. These may be lost or taken away, and the full consciousness of existence remain; and were their place supplied by wings, or other appendages, we cannot conceive that it could alter our consciousness of existence. In short, we know not how much, or rather how little, of our composition it is, and how exquisitely fine that little is, that creates in us this consciousness of existence; and all beyond that is like the pulp of a peach, distinct and separate from the vegetative speck in the kernel.

Who can say by what exceeding fine action of fine matter it is that a thought is produced in what we call the mind? and yet that thought when produced, as I now produce the thought I am writing, is capable of becoming immortal, and is the only production of man that has that capacity.

Statues of brass and marble will perish; and statues made in imitation of them are not the same statues, nor the same workmanship, any more than the copy of a picture is the same picture. But print and reprint a thought a thousand times over, and that with materials of any kind, carve it in wood, or engrave it on stone, the thought is eternally and identically the same thought in every case. It has a capacity of unimpaired existence, unaffected by change of matter, and is essentially distinct, and of a nature different from every thing else that we know of, or can conceive. If then the thing produced has in itself a capacity of being immortal, it is more than a token that the power that produced it, which is the self-same thing as consciousness of existence, can be immortal also; and that as independently of the matter it was first connected with, as the thought is of the printing or writing it first appeared in. The one idea is not more difficult to believe than the other; and we can see that one is true.

That the consciousness of existence is not dependent on the same form or the same matter, is demonstrated to our senses in the works of the creation, as far as our senses are capable of receiving that demonstration. A very numerous part of the animal creation preaches to us, far better than Paul, the belief of a life hereafter. Their little life resembles an earth and a heaven, a present and a future state; and comprises, if it may be so expressed, immortality in miniature.

The most beautiful parts of the creation to our eye are the winged insects, and they are not so originally. They acquire that form and that inimitable brilliancy by progressive changes. The slow and creeping caterpillar worm of to day, passes in a few days to a torpid figure, and a state resembling death; and in the next change comes forth in all the miniature magnificence of life, a splendid butterfly. No resemblance of the former creature remains; every thing is changed; all his powers are new, and life is to him another thing. We cannot conceive that the consciousness of existence is not the same in this state of the animal as before; why then must I believe that the resurrection of the same body is necessary to continue to me the consciousness of existence hereafter?

In the former part of *The Age of Reason*, I have called the creation the true and only real word of God; and this instance, or this text, in the book of creation, not only shews to us that this thing may be so, but that it is so; and that the belief of a future state is *a rational belief*, founded upon facts visible in the creation : for it is not more difficult to believe that we shall exist hereafter in a better state and form than at present, than that a worm should become a butterfly, and quit the dunghill for the atmosphere, if we did not know it as a fact.

As to the doubtful jargon ascribed to Paul in 1 Corinthians xv., which makes part of the burial service of some Christian sectaries, it is as destitute of meaning as the tolling of a bell at the funeral; it explains nothing to the understanding, it illustrates nothing to the imagination, but leaves the reader to find any meaning if he can. "All flesh," says he, "is not the same flesh. There is one flesh of men, another of beasts, another of fishes, and another of birds." And what then? nothing. A cook could.have said as much. "There are also," says he, "bodies celestial and bodies terrestrial; the glory of the celestial is *one* and the glory of the terrestrial is the *other*." And what then? nothing. And what is the difference? nothing that he has told. "There is," says he, "one glory of the sun, and another glory of the moon, and another glory of the stars." And what then? nothing; except that he says that *one star differeth from another star in glory*, instead of distance; and he might as well have told us that the moon did not shine so bright as the sun. All this is nothing better than the jargon of a conjuror, who picks up phrases he does not understand to confound the credulous people who come to have their fortune told. Priests and conjurors are of the same trade.

Sometimes Paul affects to be a naturalist, and to prove his system of resurrection from the principles of vegetation. "*Thou fool*," says he, "*that which thou sowest is not quickened except it die*." To which one might reply in his own language, and say, Thou fool, Paul, that which thou sowest is not quickened except it die *not;* for the grain that dies in the ground never does, nor can vegetate. It is only the living grains that produce the next crop. But the metaphor, in any point of view, is no simile. It is succession, and [not] resurrection.

The progress of an animal from one state of being to another, as from a worm to a butterfly, applies to the case; but this of a grain does not, and shews Paul to have been what he says of others, *a fool*.

Whether the fourteen epistles ascribed to Paul were written by him or not, is a matter of indifference; they are either argumentative or dogmatical; and as the argument is defective, and the dogmatical part is merely presumptive, it signifies not who wrote them. And the same may be said for the remaining parts of the Testament. It is not upon the Epistles, but upon what is called the Gospel, contained in the four books ascribed to Matthew, Mark, Luke, and John, and upon the pretended prophecies, that the theory of the church, calling itself the Christian Church, is founded. The Epistles are dependant upon those, and must follow their fate; for if the story of Jesus Christ be fabulous, all reasoning founded upon it, as a supposed truth, must fall with it.

We know from history, that one of the principal leaders of this church, Athanasius, lived at the time the New Testament was formed ; * and we know also, from the absurd jargon he has left us under the name of a creed, the character of the men who formed the New Testament ; and we know also from the same history that the authenticity of the books of which it is composed was denied at the time. It was upon the vote of such as Athanasius that the Testament was decreed to be the word of God ; and nothing can present to us a more strange idea than that of decreeing the word of God by vote. Those who rest their faith upon such authority put man in the place of God, and have no true foundation for future happiness. Credulity, however, is not a crime, but it becomes criminal by resisting conviction. It is strangling in the womb of the conscience the efforts it makes to ascertain truth. We should never force belief upon ourselves in any thing.

I here close the subject on the Old Testament and the New. The evidence I have produced to prove them forgeries, is extracted from the books themselves, and acts, like a two-edge sword, either way. If the evidence be denied, the authenticity of the Scriptures is denied with it, for it is Scripture evidence: and if the evidence be admitted, the authenticity of the books is disproved. The contradictory impossibilities, contained in the Old Testament and the New, put them in the case of a man who swears *for* and

---

* Athanasius died, according to the Church chronology, in the year 371.— *Author.*

against. Either evidence convicts him of perjury, and equally destroys reputation.

Should the Bible and the Testament hereafter fall, it is not that I have done it. I have done no more than extracted the evidence from the confused mass of matters with which it is mixed, and arranged that evidence in a point of light to be clearly seen and easily comprehended; and, having done this, I leave the reader to judge for himself, as I have judged for myself.

CHAPTER III.

CONCLUSION.

IN the former part of *The Age of Reason* I have spoken of the three frauds, *mystery, miracle,* and *prophecy ;* and as I have seen nothing in any of the answers to that work that in the least affects what I have there said upon those subjects, I shall not encumber this Second Part with additions that are not necessary.

I have spoken also in the same work upon what is called *revelation,* and have shewn the absurd misapplication of that term to the books of the Old Testament and the New; for certainly revelation is out of the question in reciting any thing of which man has been the actor or the witness. That which man has done or seen, needs no revelation to tell him he has done it, or seen it—for he knows it already—nor to enable him to tell it or to write it. It is ignorance, or imposition, to apply the term revelation in such cases; yet the Bible and Testament are classed under this fraudulent description of being all *revelation.*

Revelation then, so far as the term has relation between God and man, can only be applied to something which God reveals of his will to man; but though the power of the Almighty to make such a communication is necessarily admitted, because to that power all things are possible, yet, the thing so revealed (if any thing ever was revealed, and which, by the bye, it is impossible to prove) is revelation to the person *only to whom it is made.* His account of it to another is not revelation; and whoever puts faith in that account, puts it in the man from whom the account comes; and that man may have been deceived, or may have dreamed

it; or he may be an impostor and may lie.   There is no possible criterion whereby to judge of the truth of what he tells;
for even the morality of it would be no proof of revelation.
In all such cases, the proper answer should be, " When it is
revealed to me, I will believe it to be revelation; but it is
not and cannot be incumbent upon me to believe it to be
revelation before; neither is it proper that I should take the
word of man as the word of God, and put man in the place
of God."   This is the manner in which I have spoken of
revelation in the former part of *The Age of Reason ;* and
which, whilst it reverentially admits revelation as a possible
thing, because, as before said, to the Almighty all things are
possible, it prevents the imposition of one man upon another,
and precludes the wicked use of pretended revelation.

But though, speaking for myself, I thus admit the possibility of revelation, I totally disbelieve that the Almighty
ever did communicate any thing to man, by any mode of
speech, in any language, or by any kind of vision, or appearance, or by any means which our senses are capable of receiving, otherwise than by the universal display of himself
in the works of the creation, and by that repugnance we feel
in ourselves to bad actions, and disposition to good ones.[1]

The most detestable wickedness, the most horrid cruelties,
and the greatest miseries, that have afflicted the human race,
have had their origin in this thing called revelation, or revealed religion.   It has been the most dishonourable belief
against the character of the divinity, the most destructive
to morality, and the peace and happiness of man, that ever

[1] A fair parallel of the then unknown aphorism of Kant : " Two things fill the
soul with wonder and reverence, increasing evermore as I meditate more closely
upon them : the starry heavens above me and the moral law within me." (*Kritik
der praktischen Vernunft,* 1788).   Kant's religious utterances at the beginning
of the French Revolution brought on him a royal mandate of silence, because he
had worked out from " the moral law within " a principle of human equality precisely similar to that which Paine had derived from his Quaker doctrine of the
" inner light " of every man.   About the same time Paine's writings were suppressed in England.   Paine did not understand German, but Kant, though
always independent in the formation of his opinions, was evidently well acquainted with the literature of the Revolution, in America, England, and
France.—*Editor.*

was propagated since man began to exist. It is better, far better, that we admitted, if it were possible, a thousand devils to roam at large, and to preach publicly the doctrine of devils, if there were any such, than that we permitted one such impostor and monster as Moses, Joshua, Samuel, and the Bible prophets, to come with the pretended word of God in his mouth, and have credit among us.

Whence arose all the horrid assassinations of whole nations of men, women, and infants, with which the Bible is filled; and the bloody persecutions, and tortures unto death and religious wars, that since that time have laid Europe in blood and ashes; whence arose they, but from this impious thing called revealed religion, and this monstrous belief that God has spoken to man? The lies of the Bible have been the cause of the one, and the lies of the Testament [of] the other.

Some Christians pretend that Christianity was not established by the sword; but of what period of time do they speak? It was impossible that twelve men could begin with the sword: they had not the power; but no sooner were the professors of Christianity sufficiently powerful to employ the sword than they did so, and the stake and faggot too; and Mahomet could not do it sooner. By the same spirit that Peter cut off the ear of the high priest's servant (if the story be true) he would cut off his head, and the head of his master, had he been able. Besides this, Christianity grounds itself originally upon the [Hebrew] Bible, and the Bible was established altogether by the sword, and that in the worst use of it—not to terrify, but to extirpate. The Jews made no converts: they butchered all. The Bible is the sire of the [New] Testament, and both are called the *word of God.* The Christians read both books; the ministers preach from both books; and this thing called Christianity is made up of both. It is then false to say that Christianity was not established by the sword.

The only sect that has not persecuted are the Quakers; and the only reason that can be given for it is, that they are rather Deists than Christians. They do not believe much

about Jesus Christ, and they call the scriptures a dead let-
ter.¹ Had they called them by a worse name, they had
been nearer the truth.

It is incumbent on every man who reverences the character of the Creator, and who wishes to lessen the catalogue
of artificial miseries, and remove the cause that has sown
persecutions thick among mankind, to expel all ideas of a revealed religion as a dangerous heresy, and an impious fraud.
What is it that we have learned from this pretended thing
called revealed religion? Nothing that is useful to man,
and every thing that is dishonourable to his Maker. What
is it the Bible teaches us?—rapine, cruelty, and murder.
What is it the Testament teaches us?—to believe that the
Almighty committed debauchery with a woman engaged to
be married ; and the belief of this debauchery is called faith.

As to the fragments of morality that are irregularly and
thinly scattered in those books, they make no part of this
pretended thing, revealed religion. They are the natural
dictates of conscience, and the bonds by which society is held
together, and without which it cannot exist ; and are nearly
the same in all religions, and in all societies. The Testament teaches nothing new. upon this subject, and where it
attempts to exceed, it becomes mean and ridiculous. The
doctrine of not retaliating injuries is much better expressed
in Proverbs, which is a collection as well from the Gentiles
as the Jews, than it is in the Testament. It is there said,
(xxv. 21) "*If thine enemy be hungry, give him bread to eat ;
and if he be thirsty, give him water to drink :*" * but when it is

---

¹ This is an interesting and correct testimony as to the beliefs of the earlier
Quakers, one of whom was Paine's father.—*Editor.*

* According to what is called Christ's sermon on the mount, in the book of
Matthew, where, among some other [and] good things, a great deal of this
feigned morality is introduced, it is there expressly said, that the doctrine of
forbearance, or of not retaliating injuries, *was not any part of the doctrine of the
Jews ;* but as this doctrine is found in "Proverbs," it must, according to that
statement, have been copied from the Gentiles, from whom Christ had learned
it. Those men whom Jewish and Christian idolators have abusively called
heathen, had much better and clearer ideas of justice and morality than are to
be found in the Old Testament, so far as it is Jewish, or in the New. The
answer of Solon on the question, "Which is the most perfect popular govern-

said, as in the Testament, "*If a man smite thee on the right cheek, turn to him the other also,*" it is assassinating the dignity of forbearance, and sinking man into a spaniel.

Loving of enemies is another dogma of feigned morality, and has besides no meaning. It is incumbent on man, as a moralist, that he does not revenge an injury ; and it is equally as good in a political sense, for there is no end to retaliation ; each retaliates on the other, and calls it justice : but to love in proportion to the injury, if it could be done, would be to offer a premium for a crime. Besides, the word *enemies* is too vague and general to be used in a moral maxim, which ought always to be clear and defined, like a proverb. If a man be the enemy of another from mistake and prejudice, as in the case of religious opinions, and sometimes in politics, that man is different to an enemy at heart with a criminal intention ; and it is incumbent upon us, and it contributes also to our own tranquillity, that we put the best construction upon a thing that it will bear. But even this erroneous motive in him makes no motive for love on the other part ; and to say that we can love voluntarily, and without a motive, is morally and physically impossible.

Morality is injured by prescribing to it duties that, in the first place, are impossible to be performed, and if they could be would be productive of evil ; or, as before said, be premiums for crime. The maxim *of doing as we would be done unto* does not include this strange doctrine of loving enemies ; for no man expects to be loved himself for his crime or for his enmity.

Those who preach this doctrine of loving their enemies, are in general the greatest persecutors, and they act consistently by so doing ; for the doctrine is hypocritical, and it is natural that hypocrisy should act the reverse of what it preaches. For my own part, I disown the doctrine, and consider it as a feigned or fabulous morality ; yet the man

ment," has never been exceeded by any man since his time, as containing a maxim of political morality. " That," says he, " where the least injury done to the meanest individual, is considered as an insult on the whole constitution.' Solon lived about 500 years before Christ.—*Author.*

does not exist that can say I have persecuted him, or any man, or any set of men, either in the American Revolution, or in the French Revolution ; or that I have, in any case, returned evil for evil. But it is not incumbent on man to reward a bad action with a good one, or to return good for evil ; and wherever it is done, it is a voluntary act, and not a duty. It is also absurd to suppose that such doctrine can make any part of a revealed religion. We imitate the moral character of the Creator by forbearing with each other, for he forbears with all ; but this doctrine would imply that he loved man, not in proportion as he was good, but as he was bad.

If we consider the nature of our condition here, we must see there is no occasion for such a thing as *revealed religion*. What is it we want to know? Does not the creation, the universe we behold, preach to us the existence of an Almighty power, that governs and regulates the whole? And is not the evidence that this creation holds out to our senses infinitely stronger than any thing we can read in a book, that any imposter might make and call the word of God? As for morality, the knowledge of it exists in every man's conscience.

Here we are. The existence of an Almighty power is sufficiently demonstrated to us, though we cannot conceive, as it is impossible we should, the nature and manner of its existence. We cannot conceive how we came here ourselves, and yet we know for a fact that we are here. We must know also, that the power that called us into being, can if he please, and when he pleases, call us to account for the manner in which we have lived here ; and therefore, without seeking any other motive for the belief, it is rational to believe that he will, for we know beforehand that he can. The probability or even possibility of the thing is all that we ought to know ; for if we knew it as a fact, we should be the mere slaves of terror ; our belief would have no merit, and our best actions no virtue.

Deism then teaches us, without the possibility of being deceived, all that is necessary or proper to be known. The creation is the Bible of the deist. He there reads, in the hand-writing of the Creator himself, the certainty of his existence, and the immutability of his power; and all other Bibles and Testaments are to him forgeries. The probability that we may be called to account hereafter, will, to reflecting minds, have the influence of belief; for it is not our belief or disbelief that can make or unmake the fact. As this is the state we are in, and which it is proper we should be in, as free agents, it is the fool only, and not the philosopher, nor even the prudent man, that will live as if there were no God.

But the belief of a God is so weakened by being mixed with the strange fable of the Christian creed, and with the wild adventures related in the Bible, and the obscurity and obscene nonsense of the Testament, that the mind of man is bewildered as in a fog. Viewing all these things in a confused mass, he confounds fact with fable; and as he cannot believe all, he feels a disposition to reject all. But the belief of a God is a belief distinct from all other things, and ought not to be confounded with any. The notion of a Trinity of Gods has enfeebled the belief of *one* God. A multiplication of beliefs acts as a division of belief; and in proportion as anything is divided, it is weakened.

Religion, by such means, becomes a thing of form instead of fact; of notion instead of principle: morality is banished to make room for an imaginary thing called faith, and this faith has its origin in a supposed debauchery; a man is preached instead of a God; an execution is an object for gratitude; the preachers daub themselves with the blood, like a troop of assassins, and pretend to admire the brilliancy it gives them; they preach a humdrum sermon on the merits of the execution; then praise Jesus Christ for being executed, and condemn the Jews for doing it.

A man, by hearing all this nonsense lumped and preached together, confounds the God of the Creation with the imagined God of the Christians, and lives as if there were none.

Of all the systems of religion that ever were invented,

there is none more derogatory to the Almighty, more unedifying to man, more repugnant to reason, and more contradictory in itself, than this thing called Christianity. Too absurd for belief, too impossible to convince, and too inconsistent for practice, it renders the heart torpid, or produces only atheists and fanatics. As an engine of power, it serves the purpose of despotism; and as a means of wealth, the avarice of priests; but so far as respects the good of man in general, it leads to nothing here or hereafter.

The only religion that has not been invented, and that has in it every evidence of divine originality, is pure and simple deism. It must have been the first and will probably be the last that man believes. But pure and simple deism does not answer the purpose of despotic governments. They cannot lay hold of religion as an engine but by mixing it with human inventions, and making their own authority a part; neither does it answer the avarice of priests, but by incorporating themselves and their functions with it, and becoming, like the government, a party in the system. It is this that forms the otherwise mysterious connection of church and state; the church human, and the state tyrannic.

Were a man impressed as fully and strongly as he ought to be with the belief of a God, his moral life would be regulated by the force of belief; he would stand in awe of God, and of himself, and would not do the thing that could not be concealed from either. To give this belief the full opportunity of force, it is necessary that it acts alone. This is deism.

But when, according to the Christian Trinitarian scheme, one part of God is represented by a dying man, and another part, called the Holy Ghost, by a flying pigeon, it is impossible that belief can attach itself to such wild conceits.*

---

* The book called the book of Matthew, says, (iii. 16,) that *the Holy Ghost descended in the shape of a dove*. It might as well have said a goose ; the creatures are equally harmless, and the one is as much a nonsensical lie as the other. Acts, ii. 2, 3, says, that it descended in a mighty *rushing wind*, in the shape of *cloven tongues :* perhaps it was cloven feet. Such absurd stuff is fit only for tales of witches and wizards.—*Author*.

It has been the scheme of the Christian church, and of all the other invented systems of religion, to hold man in ignorance of the Creator, as it is of government to hold him in ignorance of his rights. The systems of the one are as false as those of the other, and are calculated for mutual support. The study of theology as it stands in Christian churches, is the study of nothing; it is founded on nothing; it rests on no principles; it proceeds by no authorities; it has no data; it can demonstrate nothing; and admits of no conclusion. Not any thing can be studied as a science without our being in possession of the principles upon which it is founded; and as this is not the case with Christian theology, it is therefore the study of nothing.

Instead then of studying theology, as is now done, out of the Bible and Testament, the meanings of which books are always controverted, and the authenticity of which is disproved, it is necessary that we refer to the Bible of the creation. The principles we discover there are eternal, and of divine origin: they are the foundation of all the science that exists in the world, and must be the foundation of theology.

We can know God only through his works. We cannot have a conception of any one attribute, but by following some principle that leads to it. We have only a confused idea of his power, if we have not the means of comprehending something of its immensity. We can have no idea of his wisdom, but by knowing the order and manner in which it acts. The principles of science lead to this knowledge; for the Creator of man is the Creator of science, and it is through that medium that man can see God, as it were, face to face.

Could a man be placed in a situation, and endowed with power of vision to behold at one view, and to contemplate deliberately, the structure of the universe, to mark the movements of the several planets, the cause of their varying appearances, the unerring order in which they revolve, even to the remotest comet, their connection and dependence on each other, and to know the system of laws estab-

lished by the Creator, that governs and regulates the whole ;
he would then conceive, far beyond what any church theology
can teach him, the power, the wisdom, the vastness, the
munificence of the Creator. He would then see that all the
knowledge man has of science, and that all the mechanical
arts by which he renders his situation comfortable here, are
derived from that source : his mind, exalted by the scene,
and convinced by the fact, would increase in gratitude as it
increased in knowledge : his religion or his worship would
become united with his improvement as a man : any employment he followed that had connection with the principles of
the creation,—as everything of agriculture, of science, and
of the mechanical arts, has,—would teach him more of God,
and of the gratitude he owes to him, than any theological
Christian sermon he now hears. Great objects inspire great
thoughts ; great munificence excites great gratitude ; but the
grovelling tales and doctrines of the Bible and the Testament are fit only to excite contempt.

Though man cannot arrive, at least in this life, at the
actual scene I have described, he can demonstrate it, because he has knowledge of the principles upon which the
creation is constructed. We know that the greatest works
can be represented in model, and that the universe can be
represented by the same means. The same principles by
which we measure an inch or an acre of ground will measure
to millions in extent. A circle of an inch diameter has the
same geometrical properties as a circle that would circum-
scribe the universe. The same properties of a triangle that
will demonstrate upon paper the course of a ship, will do it
on the ocean ; and, when applied to what are called the
heavenly bodies, will ascertain to a minute the time of an
eclipse, though those bodies are millions of miles distant
from us. This knowledge is of divine origin ; and it is from
the Bible of the creation that man has learned it, and not
from the stupid Bible of the church, that teaches man
nothing.*

* The Bible-makers have undertaken to give us, in the first chapter of
Genesis, an account of the creation ; and in doing this they have demonstrated

All the knowledge man has of science and of machinery, by the aid of which his existence is rendered comfortable upon earth, and without which he would be scarcely distinguishable in appearance and condition from a common animal, comes from the great machine and structure of the universe. The constant and unwearied observations of our ancestors upon the movements and revolutions of the heavenly bodies, in what are supposed to have been the early ages of the world, have brought this knowledge upon earth. It is not Moses and the prophets, nor Jesus Christ, nor his apostles, that have done it. The Almighty is the great mechanic of the creation, the first philosopher, and original teacher of all science. Let us then learn to reverence our master, and not forget the labours of our ancestors.

Had we, at this day, no knowledge of machinery, and were it possible that man could have a view, as I have before described, of the structure and machinery of the universe, he would soon conceive the idea of constructing some at least of the mechanical works we now have ; and the idea so conceived would progressively advance in practice. Or could a model of the universe, such as is called an orrery, be presented before him and put in motion, his mind would arrive at the same idea. Such an object and such a subject would, whilst it improved him in knowledge

nothing but their ignorance. They make there to have been three days and three nights, evenings and mornings, before there was any sun ; when it is the presence or absence of the sun that is the cause of day and night—and what is called his rising and setting, that of morning and evening. Besides, it is a puerile and pitiful idea, to suppose the Almighty to say, " Let there be light." It is the imperative manner of speaking that a conjuror uses when he says to his cups and balls, Presto, be gone—and most probably has been taken from it, as Moses and his rod is a conjuror and his wand. Longinus calls this expression the sublime ; and by the same rule the conjuror is sublime too ; for the manner of speaking is expressively and grammatically the same. When authors and critics talk of the sublime, they see not how nearly it borders on the ridiculous. The sublime of the critics, like some parts of Edmund Burke's sublime and beautiful, is like a windmill just visible in a fog, which imagination might distort into a flying mountain, or an archangel, or a flock of wild geese.—*Author.*

13

useful to himself as a man and a member of society, as well as entertaining, afford far better matter for impressing him with a knowledge of, and a belief in the Creator, and of the reverence and gratitude that man owes to him, than the stupid texts of the Bible and the Testament, from which, be the talents of the preacher what they may, only stupid sermons can be preached. If man must preach, let him preach something that is edifying, and from the texts that are known to be true.

The Bible of the creation is inexhaustible in texts. Every part of science, whether connected with the geometry of the universe, with the systems of animal and vegetable life, or with the properties of inanimate matter, is a text as well for devotion as for philosophy—for gratitude, as for human improvement. It will perhaps be said, that if such a revolution in the system of religion takes place, every preacher ought to be a philosopher. *Most certainly*, and every house of devotion a school of science.

It has been by wandering from the immutable laws of science, and the light of reason, and setting up an invented thing called "revealed religion," that so many wild and blasphemous conceits have been formed of the Almighty. The Jews have made him the assassin of the human species, to make room for the religion of the Jews. The Christians have made him the murderer of himself, and the founder of a new religion to supersede and expel the Jewish religion. And to find pretence and admission for these things, they must have supposed his power or his wisdom imperfect, or his will changeable; and the changeableness of the will is the imperfection of the judgement. The philosopher knows that the laws of the Creator have never changed, with respect either to the principles of science, or the properties of matter. Why then is it to be supposed they have changed with respect to man?

I here close the subject. I have shewn in all the foregoing parts of this work that the Bible and Testament are impositions and forgeries; and I leave the evidence I have

produced in proof of it to be refuted, if any one can do it;
and I leave the ideas that are suggested in the conclusion of
the work to rest on the mind of the reader; certain as I am
that when opinions are free, either in matters of government
or religion, truth will finally and powerfully prevail.

END OF "THE AGE OF REASON."

III.

LETTERS CONCERNING "THE AGE OF REASON."

1.

AN ANSWER TO A FRIEND.

PARIS, May 12, 1797.

IN your letter of the 20th of March, you give me several quotations from the Bible, which you call the *word of God*, to shew me that my opinions on religion are wrong, and I could give you as many, from the same book to shew that yours are not right; consequently, then, the Bible decides nothing, because it decides any way, and every way, one chooses to make it.

But by what authority do you call the Bible the *word of God?* for this is the first point to be settled. It is not your calling it so that makes it so, any more than the Mahometans calling the Koran the *word of God* makes the Koran to be so. The Popish Councils of Nice and Laodicea, about 350 years after the time the person called Jesus Christ is said to have lived, voted the books that now compose what is called the New Testament to be the *word of God*. This was done by *yeas* and *nays*, as we now vote a law. The pharisees of the second Temple, after the Jews returned from captivity in Babylon, did the same by the books that now compose the Old Testament, and this is all the authority there is, which to me is no authority at all. I am as capable of judging for myself as they were, and I think more so, because, as they made a living by their religion, they had a self-interest in the vote they gave.

You may have an opinion that a man is inspired, but you

cannot prove it, nor can you have any proof of it yourself, because you cannot see into his mind in order to know how he comes by his thoughts; and the same is the case with the word *revelation.* There can be no evidence of such a thing, for you can no more prove revelation than you can prove what another man dreams of, neither can he prove it himself.

It is often said in the Bible that God spake unto Moses, but how do you know that God spake unto Moses? Because, you will say, the Bible says so. The Koran says, that God spake unto Mahomet, do you believe that too? No. Why not? Because, you will say, you do not believe it; and so because you *do,* and because you *don't* is all the reason you can give for believing or disbelieving except that you will say that Mahomet was an impostor. And how do you know Moses was not an impostor? For my own part, I believe that all are impostors who pretend to hold verbal communication with the Deity. It is the way by which the world has been imposed upon; but if you think otherwise you have the same right to your opinion that I have to mine, and must answer for it in the same manner. But all this does not settle the point, whether the Bible be the *word of God,* or not. It is therefore necessary to go a step further. The case then is :—

You form your opinion of God from the account given of him in the Bible; and I form my opinion of the Bible from the wisdom and goodness of God manifested in the structure of the universe, and in all works of Creation. The result in these two cases will be, that you, by taking the Bible for your standard, will have a bad opinion of God; and I, by taking God for my standard, shall have a bad opinion of the Bible.

The Bible represents God to be a changeable, passionate, vindictive Being ; making a world and then drowning it, afterwards repenting of what he had done, and promising not to do so again. Setting one nation to cut the throats of another, and stopping the course of the sun till the butchery should be done. But the works of God in the Creation preach to us another doctrine. In that vast volume we see

nothing to give us the idea of a changeable, passionate, vindictive God ; everything we there behold impresses us with
a contrary idea,—that of unchangeableness and of eternal
order, harmony, and goodness. The sun and the seasons return at their appointed time, and every thing in the Creation
proclaims that God is unchangeable. Now, which am I to
believe, a book that any impostor might make and call the
word of God, or the Creation itself which none but an
Almighty Power could make ? For the Bible says one
thing, and the Creation says the contrary. The Bible represents God with all the passions of a mortal, and the Creation
proclaims him with all the attributes of a God.

It is from the Bible that man has learned cruelty, rapine,
and murder ; for the belief of a cruel God makes a cruel man.
That bloodthirsty man, called the prophet Samuel, makes
God to say, (1 Sam. xv. 3,) " Now go and smite Amaleck,
and utterly destroy all that they have, and *spare them not,
but slay both man and woman, infant and suckling, ox and
sheep, camel and ass.*"

That Samuel or some other impostor might say this, is
what, at this distance of time, can neither be proved nor disproved, but in my opinion it is blasphemy to say, or to believe, that God said it. All our ideas of the justice and
goodness of God revolt at the impious cruelty of the Bible.
It is not a God, just and good, but a devil, under the name
of God, that the Bible describes.

What makes this pretended order to destroy the Amalekites appear the worse, is the reason given for it. The
Amalekites, four hundred years before, according to the
account in Exodus xvii. (but which has the appearance of
fable from the magical account it gives of Moses holding up
his hands,) had opposed the Israelites coming into their
country, and this the Amalekites had a right to do, because
the Israelites were the invaders, as the Spaniards were the
invaders of Mexico ; and this opposition by the Amalekites,
at that time, is given as a reason, that the men, women, infants and sucklings, sheep and oxen, camels and asses, that
were born four hundred years afterwards, should be put to

death ; and to complete the horror, Samuel hewed Agag, the chief of the Amalekites, in pieces, as you would hew a stick of wood. I will bestow a few observations on this case.

In the first place, nobody knows who the author, or writer, of the book of Samuel was, and, therefore, the fact itself has no other proof than anonymous or hearsay evidence, which is no evidence at all. In the second place, this anonymous book says, that this slaughter was done by *the express command of God:* but all our ideas of the justice and goodness of God give the lie to the book, and as I never will believe any book that ascribes cruelty and injustice to God, I therefore reject the Bible as unworthy of credit.

As I have now given you my reasons for believing that the Bible is not the word of God, that it is a falsehood, I have a right to ask you your reasons for believing the contrary ; but I know you can give me none, except that *you were educated to believe the Bible ;* and as the Turks give the same reason for believing the Koran, it is evident that education makes all the difference, and that reason and truth have nothing to do in the case. You believe in the Bible from the accident of birth, and the Turks believe in the Koran from the same accident, and each calls the other *infidel.* But leaving the prejudice of education out of the case, the unprejudiced truth is, that all are infidels who believe falsely of God, whether they draw their creed from the Bible, or from the Koran, from the Old Testament, or from the New.

When you have examined the Bible with the attention that I have done, (for I do not think you know much about it,) and permit yourself to have just ideas of God, you will most probably believe as I do. But I wish you to know that this answer to your letter is not written for the purpose of changing your opinion. It is written to satisfy you, and some other friends whom I esteem, that my disbelief of the Bible is founded on a pure and religious belief in God ; for in my opinion the Bible is a gross libel against the justice and goodness of God, in almost every part of it.

THOMAS PAINE.

II.

CORRESPONDENCE WITH THE HON. SAMUEL ADAMS.[1]

[To the Editor of the " National Intelligencer," Federal City.]

TOWARDS the latter end of last December I received a letter from a venerable patriot, Samuel Adams, dated Boston, Nov. 30. It came by a private hand, which I suppose was the cause of the delay. I wrote Mr. Adams an answer, dated Jan. 1st, and that I might be certain of his receiving it, and also that I might know of that reception, I desired a

[1] The Hon. Samuel Adams (1722–1803) was from the Stamp Act agitation of 1764 to the Declaration of Independence in 1776 the pre-eminent revolutionary leader in Massachusetts, and General Gage was given orders to send him over to London, where a newspaper predicted that his head would appear on Temple Bar. He was sent by Massachusetts, with his cousin, John Adams, afterwards President, to the first Continental Congress (1774), where he was suspected, with justice, of being favorable to separation from England. When Paine published his famous appeal for American Independence (January 10, 1776), Samuel Adams was the first member of the Congress at his side, and a cordial lifelong relation existed between the two. It is to my mind certain that these two men were the real pioneers of American Independence, and they were both inspired therein by their widely different religious sentiments. Samuel Adams was the son of a deacon of the Old South Church, Boston, who sent his son to Harvard College with the hope that he would graduate into a minister. The son had no taste for theology, but he made up for it by retaining through all his career as a lawyer and public man a rigid Puritanism, of which the first article was hatred of the British system of royalty and prelacy. While Adams's desire for American independency was largely an inheritance from New England Puritans, Paine beheld in it a means of establishing a Republic based on the principles of Quakerism,—the divine Light in every man by virtue of which all were equal. Samuel Adams died October 2, 1803. The correspondence here given was printed in the *National Intelligencer*, Washington City, February 2, 1803, as one of a series of Ten Letters addressed to " The Citizens of the United States " on his return after his fifteen eventful years in Europe. These Letters were printed in a pamphlet in London, 1804, by his friend Thomas Clio Rickman, whose task, however, was achieved under sad intimidation. Rickman's preface opens with the words: " The following little work would not have been published, had there been anything in it the least offending against the government or individuals." Under this deadly fear the much prosecuted Rickman mutilated Paine's letter to Adams a good deal. I have been fortunate in being able to print the letter from Paine's own manuscript, which was recently discovered among the papers of George Bancroft, the historian, when they passed into the possession of the Lenox Library, New York, to whose excellent librarian I owe thanks for this and other favors.—*Editor*.

friend of mine at Washington to put it under cover to some friend of his at Boston, and desire him to present it to Mr. Adams. The letter was accordingly put under cover while I was present, and given to one of the clerks of the post office to seal and put in the mail. The clerk put it in his pocket book, and either forgot to put it into the mail, or supposed he had done so among other letters. The postmaster general, on learning this mistake, informed me of it last Saturday, and as the cover was then out of date, the letter was put under a new cover, with the same request, and forwarded by the post. I felt concern at this accident, lest Mr. Adams should conclude I was unmindful of his attention to me ; and therefore, lest any further accident should prevent or delay his receiving it, as well as to relieve myself from that concern, I give the letter an opportunity of reaching him by the newspapers. I am the more induced to do this, because some manuscript copies have been taken of both letters, and therefore there is a possibility of imperfect copies getting into print ; and besides this, if some of the Federal[ist] printers (for I hope they are not all base alike) could get hold of a copy, they would make no scruple of altering it, and publishing it as mine. I therefore send you the original letter of Mr. Adams, and my own copy of the answer.

THOMAS PAINE.

FEDERAL CITY.

BOSTON, Nov. 30, 1802.

SIR :

I have frequently with pleasure reflected on your services to my native and your adopted country. Your *Common Sense* and your *Crisis* unquestionably awakened the public mind, and led the people loudly to call for a Declaration of our national Independence. I therefore esteemed you as a warm friend to the liberty and lasting welfare of the human race. But when I heard that you had turned your mind to a defence of infidelity, I felt myself much astonished and more grieved that you had attempted a measure so injurious to the feelings and so repugnant to the true interest of so great a part of the citizens of the United States. The people of New England, if you will allow me to use a scripture phrase, are fast returning to their first love. Will you excite among them the spirit of angry controversy, at a time when they are hastening to unity and peace? I am told that some of our newspapers have announced your intention to publish an additional pamphlet upon the principles of your *Age of Reason*. Do you think that your pen, or the pen of any other man, can unchristianize the mass of our citizens, or have you hopes of converting a few of them to assist you in so bad a cause? We ought to think ourselves happy in the enjoyment of opinion without the danger of persecution by civil or ecclesiastical law.

Our friend, the President of the United States,[1] has been calumniated for his liberal sentiments, by men who have attributed that liberality to a latent design to promote the cause of infidelity. This and all other slanders have been made without a shadow of proof. Neither religion nor liberty can long subsist in the tumult of altercation, and amidst the noise and violence of faction.

Felix qui cautus.

Adieu.

SAMUEL ADAMS.

Mr. THOMAS PAINE.

MY DEAR AND VENERABLE FRIEND SAMUEL ADAMS:

I received with great pleasure your friendly and affectionate letter of November 30, and I thank you also for the frankness of it. Between men in pursuit of truth, and whose object is the Happiness of Man both here and hereafter, there ought to be no reserve. Even Error has a claim to indulgence, if not to respect, when it is believed to be truth.

I am obliged to you for your affectionate remembrance of what you stile my services in awakening the public mind to a declaration of Independance, and supporting it after it was declared. I also, like you, have often looked back on those

---

[1] Thomas Jefferson.

times, and have thought that if independance had not been declared at the time it was, the public mind could not have been brought up to it afterwards. It will immediately occur to you, who were so intimately acquainted with the situation of things at that time, that I allude to the black times of *seventy-six;* for though I know, and you my friend also know, they were no other than the natural consequence of the military blunders of that campaign, the country might have viewed them as proceeding from a natural inability to support its Cause against the enemy, and have sunk under the despondency of that misconceived Idea. This was the impression against which it was necessary the Country should be strongly animated.

I come now to the second part of your letter, on which I shall be as frank with you as you are with me.

" But, (say you) when I *heard* you had turned your mind to a defence of *Infidelity* I felt myself much astonished &c." —What, my good friend, do you call believing in God infidelity? for that is the great point maintained in *The Age of Reason* against all divided beliefs and *allegorical* divinities.[1] The bishop of Landaff (Doctor Watson) not only acknowledges this, but pays me some compliments upon it (in his answer to the second part of that work). " *There is* (says he) *a philosophical sublimity in some of your Ideas when speaking of the Creator of the Universe.*"

What then (my much esteemed friend for I do not respect you the less because we differ, and that perhaps not much, in religious sentiments), what, I ask, is this thing called *infidelity?* If we go back to your ancestors and mine three or four hundred years ago, for we must have had fathers and grandfathers or we should not be here, we shall find them praying to Saints and Virgins, and believing in purgatory and transubstantiation ; and therefore all of us are infidels according to our forefathers' belief. If we go back to times more ancient we shall again be infidels according to the belief of some other forefathers.

[1] The ten concluding words of this sentence were omitted from Rickman's edition, the close being " in the work alluded to."—*Editor*.

The case my friend is, that the World has been over-run with fable and creeds of human invention, with sectaries of whole Nations against all other Nations, and sectaries of those sectaries in each of them against each other. Every sectary, except the quakers, has been a persecutor. Those who fled from persecution persecuted in their turn, and it is this confusion of creeds that has filled the World with persecution and deluged it with blood. Even the depredation on your commerce by the barbary powers sprang from the Cruisades of the church against those powers. It was a war of creed against creed, each boasting of God for its author, and reviling each other with the name of Infidel. If I do not believe as you believe, it proves that you do not believe as I believe, and this is all that it proves.

There is however one point of Union wherein all religions meet, and that is in the first article of every Man's Creed, and of every Nation's Creed, that has any Creed at all : *I believe in God.* Those who rest here, and there are millions who do, cannot be wrong as far as their Creed goes. Those who chuse to go further *may be wrong,* for it is impossible that all can be right, since there is so much contradiction among them. The first therefore are, in my opinion, on the safest side.

I presume you are so far acquainted with ecclesiastical history as to know, and the bishop who has answered me has been obliged to acknowledge the fact, that the books that compose the New Testament were voted by *Yeas* and *Nays* to be the Word of God, as you now vote a law, by the popish Councils of Nice and Laodocia about 1450 years ago. With respect to the fact there is no dispute, neither do I mention it for the sake of controversy. This Vote may appear authority enough to some, and not authority enough to others. It is proper however that everybody should know the fact.[1]

---

[1] This paragraph was omitted by Rickman with a footnote saying : " A paragraph of eleven lines is here omitted, it being a principle with the Editor to offend neither the government nor individuals. Its insertion is also unnecessary, as the curious reader will find it answered in a way well worth his notice by the

With respect to *The Age of Reason*, which you so much condemn, and that I believe without having read it, for you say only that you *heard* of it, I will inform you of a Circumstance, because you cannot know it by other means.

I have said in the first page of the First Part of that work that it had long been my intention to publish my thoughts upon Religion, but that I had reserved it to a later time of life. I have now to inform you why I wrote it and published it at the time I did.

In the first place, I saw my life in continual danger. My friends were falling as fast as the guillotine could cut their heads off, and as I every day expected the same fate, I resolved to begin my Work. I appeared to myself to be on my death-bed, for death was on every side of me, and I had no time to lose. This accounts for my writing it at the time I did ; and so nicely did the time and the intention meet, that I had not finished the first part of that Work more than six hours before I was arrested and taken to prison. Joel Barlow was with me and knows the fact.

In the second place, the people of france were running headlong into Atheism, and I had the work translated and published in their own language to stop them in that carreer, and fix them to the first article (as I have before said) of every man's Creed who has any Creed at all, *I believe in God.* I endangered my own life, in the first place, by opposing in the Convention the execution of the king, and by labouring to shew they were trying the Monarchy and not the Man, and that the crimes imputed to him were the crimes of the monarchical [1] system ; and I endangered it a second time by opposing Atheism ; and yet *some* of your priests, for I do not believe that all are perverse, cry out, in the war-whoop of monarchical priestcraft, What an Infidel, what a wicked Man, is Thomas Paine ! They might as well add, for he believes in God and is against shedding blood.

bishop of Llandaff. See his apology for the Bible, from page 300 to 307." The title " Age of Reason " is also suppressed in the next paragraph, and elsewhere. —*Editor.*

[1] This word is omitted by Rickman.—*Editor.*

But all this *war-whoop* of the pulpit [1] has some concealed object. Religion is not the Cause, but is the stalking horse. They put it forward to conceal themselves behind it. It is not a secret that there has been a party composed of the leaders of the federalists, for I do not include all federalists with their leaders, who have been working by various means for several years past to overturn the federal Constitution established on the representative system, and place Government in the new World on the corrupt system of the old.[2] To accomplish this, a large standing army was necessary, and as a pretence for such an army the danger of a foreign invasion must be bellowed forth from the pulpit, from the press, and by their public orators.

I am not of a disposition inclined to suspicion. It is in its nature a mean and cowardly passion, and upon the whole, even admitting error into the case, it is better, I am sure it is more generous, to be wrong on the side of confidence than on the side of suspicion.[3] But I know as a fact that the english Government distributes annually fifteen hundred pounds sterling among the presbyterian ministers in England and one thousand among those of Ireland ;[4] and when I hear of the strange discourses of some of your ministers and professors of Colleges, I cannot, as the quakers say, find freedom in my mind to acquit them. Their anti-revolutionary doctrines invite suspicion even against one's will, and in spite of one's charity to believe well of them.

As you have given me one scripture phrase I will give you another for those ministers. It is said in Exodus xxii. 28, *"Thou shalt not revile the Gods nor curse the ruler of thy people."* But those ministers, such I mean as Dr. Emmons,[5]

---

[1] The words " of the pulpit " omitted by Rickman.—*Editor.*

[2] The preceding fourteen words omitted by Rickman.—*Editor.*

[3] The words "it is better" and "on the side of Confidence than" are dropped out of the sentence in Rickman's edition.—*Editor.*

[4] See vol. iii. p. 85, of my edition of *Paine's Writings*, where the amounts are stated as £1700 to the dissenting Ministers in England, and £800 to those of Ireland.—The preceding 29 words, and the remainder of this paragraph, are omitted by Rickman.—*Editor*

[5] Nathaniel Emmons, D.D. (1745–1840), fifty-four years minister of the

curse ruler and people both, for the majority are, politically, the people, and it is those who have chosen the ruler whom they curse. As to the first part of the verse, that of *not reviling the Gods*, it makes no part of my scripture. I have but one God.[1]

Since I began this letter, for I write it by piece-meals as I have leisure, I have seen the four letters that passed between you and John Adams. In your first letter you say, " Let divines and Philosophers, statesmen and patriots, unite their endeavours to *renovate the age* by inculcating in the minds of youth *the fear and love of the Deity and universal philanthropy.*" Why, my dear friend, this is exactly *my* religion, and is the whole of it. That you may have an Idea that *The Age of Reason* (for I believe you have not read it) inculcates this reverential fear and love of the Deity I will give you a paragraph from it.

" Do we want to contemplate his power ? We see it in the immensity of the Creation. Do we want to contemplate his wisdom : We see it in the unchangeable order by which the incomprehensible Whole is governed. Do we want to contemplate his munificence ? We see it in the abundance with which he fills the Earth. Do we want to contemplate his mercy ? We see it in his not withholding that abundance even from the unthankful."

As I am fully with you in your first part, that respecting the Deity, so am I in your second, that of *universal philanthropy ;* by which I do not mean merely the sentimental benevolence of wishing well, but the practical benevolence of doing good. We cannot serve the Deity in the manner we serve those who cannot do without that service. He needs no service from us. We can add nothing to eternity. But it is in our power to render a service *acceptable* to him, and that is not by praying, but by endeavouring to make

Franklin, Mass., Congregational Church. He was a vehement Federalist, and assailant of President Jefferson.—*Editor.*

[1] This and the preceding sentence are omitted by Rickman.—*Editor.*

his creatures happy. A man does not serve God when he
prays, for it is himself he is trying to serve ; and as to hiring
or paying men to pray, as if the Deity needed instruction, it
is, in my opinion, an abomination. One good schoolmaster
is of more use and of more value than a load of such persons
as Dr. Emmons and some others.[1]

You, my dear and much respected friend, are now far in the
vale of years ; I have yet, I believe, some years in store, for
I have a good state of health and a happy mind, and I take
care of both, by nourishing the first with temperance and
the latter with abundance. This, I believe, you will allow
to be the true philosophy of life. You will see by my third
letter to the Citizens of the United States that I have been
exposed to, and preserved through, many dangers; but instead of buffetting the Deity with prayers as if I distrusted
him, or must dictate to him,[2] I reposed myself on his protection ; and you, my friend, will find, even in your last
moments, more consolation in the silence of resignation
than in the murmuring wish of a prayer.

In every thing which you say in your second letter to
John Adams, respecting our Rights as Men and Citizens in
this World, I am perfectly with you. On other points we
have to answer to our Creator and not to each other. The
key of heaven is not in the keeping of any sect, nor ought
the road to it be obstructed by any. Our relation to each
other in this World is as Men, and the Man who is a friend
to Man and to his rights, let his religious opinions be what
they may, is a good citizen, to whom I can give, as I ought
to do, and as every other ought, the right hand of fellow-
ship, and to none with more hearty good will, my dear
friend, than to you.

THOMAS PAINE.

FEDERAL CITY, January 1, 1803.

[1] This and the preceding sentence omitted by Rickman.—*Editor.*
[2] This and the seventeen preceding words omitted by Rickman.—*Editor.*

IV.

PROSECUTION OF THE AGE OF REASON.[1]

INTRODUCTION.

IT is a matter of surprise to some people to see Mr. Erskine act as counsel for a crown prosecution commenced against the rights of opinion. I confess it is none to me, notwithstanding all that Mr. Erskine has said before ; for it is difficult to know when a lawyer is to be believed : I have always observed that Mr. Erskine, when contending as counsel for the right of political opinion, frequently took occasions, and those often dragged in head and shoulders, to lard, what he called the British Constitution, with a great deal of praise. Yet the same Mr. Erskine said to me in con-

---

[1] " A Letter to the Hon. Thomas Erskine, on the Prosecution of Thomas Williams for publishing the Age of Reason. By Thomas Paine, Author of Common Sense, Rights of Man, etc. With his Discourse at the Society of the Theophilanthropists. Paris : Printed for the Author." This pamphlet was carried through Barrois' English press in Paris, September 1797, and is here reprinted from an original copy. The Prosecution (Howells' State Trials, vol. 26,) was not technically instituted by the Crown, though in collusion with it, a Special Jury being secured. The accusers were the new " Society for carrying into effect His Majesty's Proclamation against Vice and Immorality." Erskine, who had defended Paine, on his trial for the " Rights of Man," and had gained popularity by his successful defence of others accused of sedition, was sagaciously retained by the Society, whose means were unlimited, while poor Williams sent out the following appeal :

" T. Williams, Bookseller, No. 8 Little Turnstile, Holborn, Being at this time under a prosecution *at common law*, for selling THE AGE OF REASON, and not possessing the means of legal defence, hopes he will not be deemed obtrusive in making his situation known to the Friends of Liberty, both civil and religious. His case, he presumes, requires not a long explanation. It is not whether the doctrines of the book above named are proper or improper ; nor whether the selling a book in the ordinary course of business can be considered as an evi-

versation, " were government to begin *de novo* in England, they never would establish such a damned absurdity, [it was exactly his expression] as this is." Ought I then to be surprised at Mr. Erskine for inconsistency?

In this prosecution, Mr. Erskine admits the right of controversy ; but says that the Christian religion is not to be abused. This is somewhat sophistical, because while he admits the right of controversy, he reserves the right of calling the controversy abuse : and thus, lawyer-like, undoes by one word what he says in the other. I will however in this letter keep within the limits he prescribes ; he will find here nothing about the Christian religion ; he will find only a statement of a few cases which shew the necessity of examining the books handed to us from the Jews, in order to discover if we have not been imposed upon ; together with some observations on the manner in which the trial of Williams has been conducted. If Mr. Erskine denies the right of examining those books, he had better profess himself at once an advocate for the establishment of an Inquisition, and the re-establishment of the Star-chamber.

THOMAS PAINE.

dence of his own belief ; but whether a system of prosecution, *on pretence of religion*, in direct opposition to that liberality of sentiment which, to the honour of modern times, has been so widely diffused, shall receive encouragement, by being weakly opposed. SUBSCRIPTIONS will be received by J. Ashley, shoemaker, No. 6 High Holborn ; C. Cooper, grocer, New Compton-st., Soho ; G. Wilkinson, printer, No. 115 Shoreditch ; J. Rhynd, printer, Ray-st., Clerkenwell ; R. Hodgson, hatter, No. 29 Brook-st., Holborn."

So humble were they who collected their coppers to begin the long war for religious liberty against the powerful league whose gold had taken away their leader. The defence was undertaken by Stephen Kyd (once prosecuted for sedition), the solicitor being John Martin, who served notice on the prosecution that it would be " required to produce a certain book described in the said indictment to be the Holy Bible." Erskine declared : " No man deserves to be on the Rolls of the Court, who dares, as an Attorney, to put his name to such a notice." This did not deter Kyd from referring to many of the obscene passages in the book which the protectors of morality were shielding from criticism. It was not charged by the prosecution that there was anything of that kind in Paine's work. Erskine won a victory over Williams with some results already described in my introduction to " The Age of Reason."—*Editor*.

A LETTER TO MR. ERSKINE.

OF all the tyrannies that afflict mankind, tyranny in religion is the worst: Every other species of tyranny is limited
to the world we live in, but this attempts a stride beyond
the grave, and seeks to pursue us into eternity. It is there
and not here, it is to God and not to man, it is to a heavenly
and not to an earthly tribunal, that we are to account for
our belief; if then we believe falsely and dishonorably of the
Creator, and that belief is forced upon us, as far as force can
operate by human laws and human tribunals, on whom is
the criminalty of that belief to fall; on those who impose it,
or on those on whom it is imposed?

A bookseller of the name of Williams has been prosecuted
in London on a charge of blasphemy for publishing a book
intitled the *Age of Reason*. Blasphemy is a word of vast
sound, but of equivocal and almost of indefinite signification,
unless we confine it to the simple idea of hurting or injuring
the reputation of any one, which was its original meaning.
As a word, it existed before Christianity existed, being a
Greek word, or Greek anglofied, as all the etymological
dictionaries will shew.

But behold how various and contradictory has been the
signification and application of this equivocal word: Socrates, who lived more than four hundred years before the
Christian æra, was convicted of blasphemy for preaching
against the belief of a plurality of gods, and for preaching
the belief of one god, and was condemned to suffer death
by poison: Jesus Christ was convicted of blasphemy under
the Jewish law, and was crucified. Calling Mahomet an imposter would be blasphemy in Turkey; and denying the
infallibility of the Pope and the Church would be blasphemy

at Rome. What then is to be understood by this word blasphemy? We see that in the case of Socrates truth was condemned as blasphemy. Are we sure that truth is not blasphemy in the present day? Woe however be to those who make it so, whoever they may be.

A book called the Bible has been voted by men, and decreed by human laws, to be the word of God, and the disbelief of this is called blasphemy. But if the Bible be not the word of God, it is the laws and the execution of them that is blasphemy, and not the disbelief. Strange stories are told of the Creator in that book. He is represented as acting under the influence of every human passion, even of the most malignant kind. If these stories are false, we err in believing them to be true, and ought not to believe them. It is therefore a duty which every man owes to himself, and reverentially to his Maker, to ascertain by every possible enquiry whether there be a sufficient evidence to believe them or not.

My own opinion is, decidedly, that the evidence does not warrant the belief, and that we sin in forcing that belief upon ourselves and upon others. In saying this I have no other object in view than truth. But that I may not be accused of resting upon bare assertion, with respect to the equivocal state of the Bible, I will produce an example, and I will not pick and cull the Bible for the purpose. I will go fairly to the case. I will take the first two chapters of Genesis as they stand, and shew from thence the truth of what I say, that is, that the evidence does not warrant the belief that the Bible is the word of God.

[*In the original pamphlet the first two chapters of Genesis are here quoted in full.*]

These two chapters are called the Mosaic account of the creation; and we are told, nobody knows by whom, that Moses was instructed by God to write that account.

It has happened that every nation of people has been world-makers; and each makes the world to begin his own way, as if they had all been brought up, as Hudibras says, to the trade. There are hundreds of different opinions and traditions how the world began.   My business, however, in this place, is only with those two chapters.

I begin then by saying, that those two chapters, instead of containing, as has been believed, one continued account of the creation, written by Moses, contain two different and contradictory stories of a creation, made by two different persons, and written in two different stiles of expression. The evidence that shews this is so clear, when attended to without prejudice, that did we meet with the same evidence in any Arabic or Chinese account of a creation, we should not hesitate in pronouncing it a forgery.

I proceed to distinguish the two stories from each other.

The first story begins at the first verse of the first chapter, and ends at the end of the third verse of the second chapter; for the adverbial conjunction, THUS, with which the second chapter begins, (as the reader will see,) connects itself to the last verses of the first chapter, and those three verses belong to, and make the conclnsion of, the first story.

The second story begins at the fourth verse of the second chapter, and ends with that chapter. Those two stories have been confused into one, by cutting off the last three verses of the first story, and throwing them to the second chapter.

I go now to shew that those stories have been written by two different persons.

From the first verse of the first chapter to the end of the third verse of the second chapter, which makes the whole of the first story, the word God is used without any epithet or additional word conjoined with it, as the reader will see: and this stile of expression is invariably used throughout the whole of this story, and is repeated no less than thirty-five times, viz. "In the beginning GOD created the heavens and the earth, and the spirit of GOD moved on the face of the waters, and GOD said, let there be light, and GOD saw the light," etc.

But immediately from the beginning of the fourth verse of the second chapter, where the second story begins, the stile of expression is always the *Lord God*, and this stile of expression is invariably used to the end of the chapter, and is repeated eleven times ; in the one it is always GOD, and never the *Lord God,* in the other it is always the *Lord God* and never GOD. The first story contains thirty-four verses, and repeats the single word GOD thirty-five times. The second story contains twenty-two verses, and repeats the compound word *Lord God* eleven times ; this difference of stile, so often repeated, and so uniformly continued, shews, that those two chapters, containing two different stories, are written by different persons ; it is the same in all the different editions of the Bible, in all the languages I have seen.

Having thus shewn, from the difference of style, that those two chapters, divided, as they properly divide themselves, at the end of the third verse of the second chapter, are the work of two different persons, I come to shew you, from the contradictory matters they contain, that they cannot be the work of one person, and are two different stories.

It is impossible, unless the writer was a lunatic, without memory, that one and the same person could say, as is said in i. 27, 28, " *So God created man in his own image, in the image of God created he him ; male and female created he them : and God blessed them, and God said unto them, be fruit-ful and multiply, and replenish the earth, and subdue it, and have dominion over the fish of the sea, and over the fowl of the air, and every living thing that moveth on the face of the earth* "—It is, I say, impossible that the same person who said this, could afterwards say, as is said in ii. 5, *and there was not a man to till the ground ;* and then proceed in verse 7 to give another account of the making a man for the first time, and afterwards of the making a woman out of his rib.[1]

Again, one and the same person could not write, as is written in i. 29 : " Behold I (God) have given you every herb bearing seed, which is on the face of all the earth ; and every tree, in which is the fruit of a tree bearing seed, to you it shall be for meat ; " and afterwards say, as is said in the second chapter, that the Lord God planted a tree in the midst of a garden, and forbade man to eat thereof.

[1] The original does not signify rib, but the " side " (feminine).—*Editor.*

Again, one and the same person could not say, " *Thus the heavens and the earth were finished, and all the host of them, and on the seventh day God ended all his work which he had made ;* " and immediately after set the Creator to work again, to plant a garden, to make a man and a woman, etc., as done in the second chapter.

Here are evidently two different stories contradicting each other. According to the first, the two sexes, the male and the female, were made at the same time. According to the second, they were made at different times ; the man first, and the woman afterwards. According to the first story, they were to have dominion over all the earth. According to the second, their dominion was limited to a garden. How large a garden it could be that one man and one woman could dress and keep in order, I leave to the prosecutor, the judge, the jury, and Mr. Erskine to determine.

The story of the talking serpent, and its tête-a-tête with Eve ; the doleful adventure called the *Fall of Man ;* and how he was turned out of this fine garden, and how the garden was afterwards locked up and guarded by a flaming sword, (if any one can tell what a flaming sword is,) belong altogether to the second story. They have no connection with the first story. According to the first there was no garden of Eden ; no forbidden tree : the scene was the whole earth, and the fruit of all trees were allowed to be eaten.

In giving this example of the strange state of the Bible, it cannot be said I have gone out of my way to seek it, for I have taken the beginning of the book ; nor can it be said I have made more of it than it makes of itself. That there are two stories is as visible to the eye, when attended to, as that there are two chapters, and that they have been written by different persons, nobody knows by whom. If this then is the strange condition the beginning of the Bible is in, it leads to a just suspicion that the other parts are no better, and consequently it becomes every man's duty to examine the case. I have done it for myself, and am satisfied that the Bible is *fabulous.*

Perhaps I shall be told in the cant-language of the day, as I have often been told by the Bishop of Llandaff and others, of the great and laudable pains that many pious and learned men have taken to explain the obscure, and reconcile the contradictory, or as they say the *seemingly contradictory,* passages of the Bible. It is because the Bible needs such an undertaking, that is one of the first causes to suspect it is NOT the word of God : this single reflection, when carried home to the mind, is in itself a volume.

What! does not the Creator of the Universe, the Fountain of all Wisdom, the Origin of all Science, the Author of all Knowledge, the God of Order and of Harmony, know how to write? When we contemplate the vast œconomy of the creation, when we behold the unerring regularity of the visible solar system, the perfection with which all its several parts revolve, and by corresponding assemblage form a whole ;—when we launch our eye into the boundless ocean of space, and see ourselves surrounded by innumerable worlds, not one of which varies from its appointed place— when we trace the power of a Creator, from a mite to an elephant, from an atom to an universe,—can we suppose that the mind that could conceive such a design, and the power that executed it with incomparable perfection, cannot write without inconsistence, or that a book so written can be the work of such a power? The writings of Thomas Paine, even of Thomas Paine, need no commentator to explain, compound, derange, and re-arrange their several parts, to render them intelligible ; he can relate a fact, or write an essay, without forgetting in one page what he has written in another : certainly then, did the God of all perfection condescend to write or dictate a book, that book would be as perfect as himself is perfect : The Bible is not so, and it is confessedly not so, by the attempts to amend it.

Perhaps I shall be told, that though I have produced one instance, I cannot produce another of equal force. One is sufficient to call in question the genuineness or authenticity of any book that pretends to be the word of God ; for such a book would, as before said, be as perfect as its author is perfect.

I will, however, advance only four chapters further into the book of Genesis, and produce another example that is sufficient to invalidate the story to which it belongs.

We have all heard of Noah's Flood ; and it is impossible to think of the whole human race,—men, women, children, and infants, except one family,—deliberately drowning, without feeling a painful sensation. That heart must be a heart of flint that can contemplate such a scene with tranquility. There is nothing of the ancient Mythology, nor in the religion of any people we know of upon the globe, that records a sentence of their God, or of their gods, so tremendously severe and merciless. If the story be not true, we blasphemously dishonour God by believing it, and still more so, in forcing, by laws and penalties, that belief upon others. I go now to shew from the face of the story that it carries the evidence of not being true.

I know not if the judge, the jury, and Mr. Erskine, who tried and convicted Williams, ever read the Bible or know anything of its contents, and therefore I will state the case precisely.

There was no such people as Jews or Israelites in the time that Noah is said to have lived, and consequently there was no such law as that which is called the Jewish or Mosaic Law. It is, according to the Bible, more than six hundred years from the time the flood is said to have happened, to the time of Moses, and consequently the time the flood is said to have happened was more than six hundred years prior to the Law, called the Law of Moses, even admitting Moses to have been the giver of that Law, of which there is great cause to doubt.

We have here two different epochs, or points of time— that of the flood, and that of the Law of Moses—the former more than six hundred years prior to the latter. But the maker of the story of the flood, whoever he was, has betrayed himself by blundering, for he has reversed the order of the times. He has told the story, as if the Law of Moses was prior to the flood ; for he has made God to say to Noah, Gen. vii. 2, " Of every clean beast, thou shalt take unto thee by sevens, male and his female, and of beasts that are *not clean* by two, the male and his female." This is the Mosaic Law, and could only be said after that Law was given, not before. There was no such thing as beasts clean and unclean in the time of Noah. It is no where said they were created so. They were only *declared* to be so, *as meats*, by the Mosaic Law, and that to the Jews only, and there were no such people as Jews in the time of Noah. This is the blundering condition in which this strange story stands.

When we reflect on a sentence so tremendously severe, as that of consigning the whole human race, eight persons excepted, to deliberate drowning ; a sentence, which represents the Creator in a more merciless character than any of those whom we call Pagans ever represented the Creator to be, under the figure of any of their deities, we ought at least to suspend our belief of it, on a comparison of the beneficent character of the Creator with the tremendous severity of the sentence ; but when we see the story told with such an evident contradiction of circumstances, we ought to set it down for nothing better than a Jewish fable, told by nobody knows whom, and nobody knows when.

It is a relief to the genuine and sensible soul of man to find the story unfounded. It frees us from two painful sensations at once ; that of having hard thoughts of the Creator, on account of the severity of the sentence ; and that of sympathising in the horrid tragedy of a drowning world. He who cannot feel the force of what I mean is not, in my estimation, of character worthy the name of a human being.

I have just said there is great cause to doubt, if the law, called the law of Moses, was given by Moses; the books called the books of Moses, which contain among other things what is called the Mosaic law, are put in front of the Bible, in the manner of a constitution, with a history annexed to it. Had these books been written by Moses, they would undoubtedly have been the oldest books in the Bible, and intitled to be placed first, and the law and the history they contain would be frequently referred to in the books that follow ; but this is not the case. From the time of Othniel, the first of the judges, (Judges iii. 9,) to the end of the book of Judges, which contains a period of four hundred and ten years, this law, and those books, were not in practice, nor known among the Jews ; nor are they so much as alluded to throughout the whole of that period. And if the reader will examine 2 Kings xx., xxi. and 2 Chron. xxxiv., he will find that no such law, nor any such books, were known in the time of the Jewish monarchy, and that the Jews were Pagans during the whole of that time, and of their judges.

The first time the law called the law of Moses made its appearance, was in the time of Josiah, about a thousand years after Moses was dead; it is then said to have been found by accident. The account of this finding, or pretended finding, is given 2 Chron. xxxiv. 14–18 : " Hilkiah the priest *found* the book of the law of the Lord, given by Moses, and Hilkiah answered and said to Shaphan the scribe, I have found the book of the law in the house of the Lord, and Hilkiah delivered the book to Shaphan, and Shaphan carried the book to the king, and Shaphan told the king, (Josiah,) saying, Hilkiah the priest hath given me a book."

In consequence of this finding,—which much resembles that of poor Chatterton finding manuscript poems of Rowley the Monk in the Cathedral Church at Bristol, or the late finding of manuscripts of Shakespeare in an old chest, (two well known frauds,)—Josiah abolished the Pagan religion of the Jews, massacred all the Pagan priests, though he himself had been a Pagan, as the reader will see in 2 Kings, xxiii., and thus established in blood the law that is there called the law of Moses, and instituted a Passover in commemoration thereof. The 22d verse, speaking of this passover, says, " surely there was not holden such a passover from the days of the judges that judged Israel, nor in all the days of the Kings of Israel, nor the Kings of Judah ; " and ver. 25, in speaking of this priest-killing Josiah, says, " *Like unto him, there was no king before him,* that turned to the Lord with all his heart, and with all his soul, and with all his might, according to all the law of Moses ; *neither after him arose there any like him.*" This verse, like the former one, is a general declaration against all the preceding kings without exception.

It is also a declaration against all that reigned after him, of
which there were four, the whole time of whose reigning
make but twenty-two years and six months, before the Jews
were entirely broken up as a nation and their monarchy destroyed.   It is therefore evident that the law called the law
of Moses, of which the Jews talk so much, was promulgated
and established only in the latter time of the Jewish monarchy ; and it is very remarkable, that no sooner had they
established it than they were a destroyed people, as if they
were punished of acting an imposition and affixing the name
of the Lord to it, and massacreing their former priests under
the pretence of religion.   The sum of the history of the
Jews is this—they continued to be a nation about a thousand
years, they then established a law, which they called the *law
of the Lord given by Moses*, and were destroyed.   This is not
opinion, but historical evidence.

Levi the Jew, who has written an answer to the *Age of
Reason*, gives a strange account of the Law of Moses.[1]

In speaking of the story of the sun and moon standing
still, that the Israelites might cut the throats of all their enemies, and hang all their kings, as told in Joshua x., he says,
" There is also another proof of the reality of this miracle,
which is, the appeal that the author of the book of Joshua
makes to the book of Jasher : *Is not this written in the book
of Jasher ?*   Hence," continues Levi, " it is manifest that
the book commonly called the book of Jasher existed and
was well known at the time the book of Joshua was written ;
and pray, Sir," continues Levi, " what book do you think
this was ?   *Why, no other than the law of Moses.*"   Levi, like
the Bishop of Llandaff, and many other guess-work commentators, either forgets, or does not know, what there is in
one part of the Bible, when he is giving his opinion upon
another part.

I did not, however, expect to find so much ignorance in a
Jew, with respect to the history of his nation, though I

[1] A Defence of the Old Testament, in a series of Letters addressed to
Thomas Paine, etc.   By David Levi, author of *Lingua Sacra*, Letters to Dr.
Priestley, etc.   London : 1797.—*Editor*.

might not be surprised at it in a bishop. If Levi will look into the account given in 2 Sam. i. 15–18, of the Amalekite slaying Saul, and bringing the crown and bracelets to David, he will find the following recital : " And David called one of the young men, and said, go near and fall upon him (the Amalekite,) and he smote him that he died " : " and David lamented with this lamentation over Saul and over Jonathan his son ; also he bade them teach the children the use of the bow ;—*behold it is written in the book of Jasher.*" If the book of Jasher were what Levi calls it, the law of Moses, written by Moses, it is not possible that any thing that David said or did could be written in that law, since Moses died more than five hundred years before David was born ; and, on the other hand, admitting the book of Jasher to be the law called the law of Moses, that law must have been written more than five hundred years after Moses was dead, or it could not relate anything said or done by David. Levi may take which of these cases he pleaseth, for both are against him.

I am not going in the course of this letter to write a commentary on the Bible. The two instances I have produced, and which are taken from the beginning of the Bible, shew the necessity of examining it. It is a book that has been read more, and examined less, than any book that ever existed. Had it come to us as an Arabic or Chinese book, and said to have been a sacred book by the people from whom it came, no apology would have been made for the confused and disorderly state it is in. The tales it relates of the Creator would have been censured, and our pity excited for those who believed them. We should have vindicated the goodness of God against such a book, and preached up the disbelief of it out of reverence to him. Why then do we not act as honourably by the Creator in the one case as we would do in the other ? As a Chinese book we would have examined it ; ought we not then to examine it as a Jewish book ? The Chinese are a people who have all the appearance of far greater antiquity than the Jews, and in point of permanency there is no comparison. They are also a people

of mild manners and of good morals, except where they
have been corrupted by European commerce. Yet we take
the word of a restless bloody-minded people, as the Jews of
Palestine were, when we would reject the same authority
from a better people. We ought to see it is habit and
prejudice that have prevented people from examining the
Bible. Those of the Church of England call it holy, because
the Jews called it so, and because custom and certain Acts
of Parliament call it so, and they read it from custom. Dissenters read it for the purpose of doctrinal controversy, and
are very fertile in discoveries and inventions. But none of
them read it for the pure purpose of information, and of
rendering justice to the Creator, by examining if the evidence it contains warrants the belief of its being what it is
called. Instead of doing this, they take it blindfolded, and
will have it to be the word of God whether it be so or not.
For my own part, my belief in the perfection of the Deity
will not permit me to believe that a book so manifestly obscure, disorderly, and contradictory can be his work. I can
write a better book myself. This disbelief in me proceeds
from my belief in the Creator. I cannot pin my faith upon
the *say so* of Hilkiah the priest, who said he found it, or any
part of it, nor upon Shaphan the scribe, nor upon any priest
nor any scribe, or man of the law of the present day.

As to Acts of Parliament, there are some that say there
are witches and wizzards; and the persons who made those
acts, (it was in the time of James I.,) made also some acts
which call the Bible the holy Scriptures, or word of God.
But acts of parliament decide nothing with respect to God;
and as these acts of parliament makers were wrong with
respect to witches and wizzards, they may also be wrong
with respect to the book in question. It is, therefore, necessary that the book be examined; it is our duty to examine
it; and to suppress the right of examination is sinful in any
government, or in any judge or jury. The Bible makes God
to say to Moses, Deut. vii. 2, " And when the Lord thy God
shall deliver them before thee, thou shalt smite them, and
utterly destroy them, thou shalt make no covenant with them,

nor shew mercy unto them." Not all the priests, nor scribes, nor tribunals in the world, nor all the authority of man, shall make me believe that God ever gave such a *Robesperian precept* as that of shewing *no mercy ;* and consequently it is impossible that I, or any person who believes as reverentially of the Creator as I do, can believe such a book to be the word of God.

There have been, and still are, those, who, whilst they *profess* to believe the Bible to be the word of God, affect to turn it into ridicule. Taking their profession and conduct together, they act blasphemously; because they act as if *God himself* was not to be believed. The case is exceedingly different with respect to the *Age of Reason.* That book is written to shew, from the bible itself, that there is abundant matter to suspect it is not the word of God, and that we have been imposed upon, first by Jews, and afterwards by priests and commentators.

Not one of those who have attempted to write answers to the *Age of Reason,* have taken the ground upon which only an answer could be written. The case in question is not upon any point of doctrine, but altogether upon a matter of fact. Is the book called the Bible the word of God, or is it not? If it can be proved to be so, it ought to be believed as such ; if not, it ought not to be believed as such. This is the true state of the case. The *Age of Reason* produces evidence to shew, and I have in this letter produced additional evidence, that it is *not* the word of God. Those who take the contrary side, should prove that it is. But this they have not done, nor attempted to do, and consequently they have done nothing to the purpose.

The prosecutors of Williams have shrunk from the point, as the answerers [of the *Age of Reason*] have done. They have availed themselves of prejudice instead of proof. If a writing was produced in a court of judicature, said to be the writing of a certain person, and upon the reality or non-reality of which some matter at issue depended, the point to be proved would be, that such writing was the writing of such person. Or if the issue depended upon certain words, which some certain person was said to have spoken, the point to be proved would be, that such words were spoken by such person; and Mr. Erskine would contend the case upon this ground. A certain book is said to be the word of God. What is the proof that it is so? for upon this the whole depends; and if it cannot be proved to be so, the prosecution fails for want of evidence.

The prosecution against Williams charges him with publishing a book, entitled *The Age of Reason,* which, it says, is an impious blasphemous pamphlet, tending to ridicule and bring into contempt the Holy Scriptures. Nothing is more easy than to find abusive words, and English prosecutions are famous for this species of vulgarity. The charge however is sophistical; for the charge, as growing out of the pamphlet should have stated, not as it now states, to ridicule and bring into contempt the holy scriptures, but to shew, that the book called the holy scriptures are not the holy scriptures. It is one thing if I ridicule a work as being written by a certain person; but it is quite a different thing if I write to prove that such work was not written by such person. In the first case, I attack the person through the work; in the other case, I defend the honour of the person against the work. This is what the *Age of Reason* does, and consequently the charge in the indictment is sophistically stated. Every one will admit, that if the Bible be *not* the word of God, we err in believing it to be his word, and ought not to believe it. Certainly then, the ground the prosecution should take would be to prove that the Bible is in fact what it is called. But this the prosecution has not done, and cannot do.

In all cases the prior fact must be proved, before the subsequent facts can be admitted in evidence. In a prosecution for adultery, the fact of marriage, which is the prior fact, must be proved, before the facts to prove adultery can be received. If the fact of marriage cannot be proved, adultery cannot be proved; and if the prosecution cannot prove the Bible to be the word of God, the charge of blasphemy is visionary and groundless.

In Turkey they might prove, if the case happened, that a certain book was bought of a certain bookseller, and that the said book was written against the koran. In Spain and Portugal they might prove that a certain book was bought of a certain bookseller, and that the said book was written against the infallibility of the Pope. Under the ancient Mythology they might have proved that a certain writing was bought of a certain person, and that the said writing was written against the belief of a plurality of gods, and in the support of the belief of one God: Socrates was condemned for a work of this kind.

All these are but subsequent facts, and amount to nothing, unless the prior facts be proved. The prior fact, with respect to the first case is, Is the *koran* the word of God? With respect to the second, Is the infallibility of the Pope a truth? With respect to the third, Is the belief of a plurality of gods a true belief? And in like manner with respect to the present prosecution, Is the book called the *Bible* the word of God? If the present prosecution prove no more than could be proved in any or all of these cases, it proves only as they do, or as an Inquisition would prove; and in this view of the case, the prosecutors ought at least to leave off reviling that infernal institution, the Inquisition. The prosecution however, though it may injure the individual, may promote the cause of truth; because the manner in which it has been conducted appears a confession to the world that there is no evidence to prove that the *Bible* is the word of God. On what authority then do we believe the many strange stories that the Bible tells of God?

This prosecution has been carried on through the medium of what is called a special jury, and the whole of a special jury is nominated by the master of the Crown office. Mr. Erskine vaunts himself upon the bill he brought into parliament with respect to trials for what the government party calls libels. But if in crown prosecutions the master of the Crown-office is to continue to appoint the whole special jury, which he does by nominating the forty-eight persons from which the solicitor of each party is to strike out twelve, Mr.

Erskine's bill is only vapour and smoke. The root of the grievance lies in the manner of forming the jury, and to this Mr. Erskine's bill applies no remedy.

When the trial of Williams came on, only eleven of the special jurymen appeared, and the trial was adjourned. In cases where the whole number do not appear, it is customary to make up the deficiency by taking jurymen from persons present in court. This in the law term is called a *Tales*. Why was not this done in this case? Reason will suggest, that they did not choose to depend on a man accidentally taken. When the trial re-commenced, the whole of the special jury appeared, and Williams was convicted : it is folly to contend a cause where the whole jury is nominated by one of the parties. I will relate a recent case that explains a great deal with respect to special juries in crown prosecutions.

On the trial of Lambert and others, printers and proprietors of the *Morning Chronicle*, for a libel, a special jury was struck, on the prayer of the Attorney-General, who used to be called *Diabolus Regis*, or King's Devil. Only seven or eight of the special jury appeared, and the Attorney-General not praying a *Tales*, the trial stood over to a future day ; when it was to be brought on a second time, the Attorney-General prayed for a new special jury, but as this was not admissible, the original special jury was summoned. Only eight of them appeared, on which the Attorney-General said, " As I cannot, on a second trial, have a special jury, I will pray a *Tales*." Four persons were then taken from the persons present in court, and added to the eight special jurymen. The jury went out at two o'clock to consult on their verdict, and the judge (Kenyon)[1] understanding they were divided, and likely to be some time in making up their minds, retired from the bench and went home. At seven, the jury went, attended by an officer of the court, to the judge's house, and delivered a verdict, " *Guilty of publishing, but with no malicious intention.*" The judge said, " *I cannot record*

---

[1] The judge before whom Paine, in his absence, was tried Dec. 18, 1792, for writing Part II. of " Rights of Man."—*Editor.*

this verdict : it is no verdict at all." The jury withdrew, and after sitting in consultation till five in the morning, brought in a verdict, Not Guilty. Would this have been the case, had they been all special jurymen nominated by the Master of the Crown-office? This is one of the cases that ought to open the eyes of people with respect to the manner of forming special juries.

On the trial of Williams, the judge prevented the counsel for the defendant proceeding in the defence. The prosecution had selected a number of passages from the Age of Reason, and inserted them in the indictment. The defending counsel was selecting other passages to shew that the passages in the indictment were conclusions drawn from premises, and unfairly separated therefrom in the indictment. The judge said, *he did not know how to act ;* meaning thereby whether to let the counsel proceed in the defence or not ; and asked the jury if they wished to hear the passages read which the defending counsel had selected. The jury said NO, and the defending counsel was in consequence silenced. Mr. Erskine then, (Falstaff-like,) having all the field to himself, and no enemy at hand, laid about him most heroicly, and the jury found the defendant *guilty.* I know not if Mr. Erskine ran out of court and hallooed, Huzza for the Bible and the trial by jury !

Robespierre caused a decree to be passed during the trial of Brissot and others, that after a trial had lasted three days, (the whole of which time, in the case of Brissot, was taken up by the prosecuting party,) the judge should ask the jury (who were then a packed jury) if they were satisfied? If the jury said YES, the trial ended, and the jury proceeded to give their verdict, without hearing the defence of the accused party. It needs no depth of wisdom to make an application of this case.

I will now state a case to shew that the trial of Williams is not a trial according to Kenyon's own explanation of law.

On a late trial in London (Selthens *versus* Hoossman) on a policy of insurance, one of the jurymen, Mr. Dunnage, after hearing one side of the case, and without hearing the other side, got up and said, *it was as legal a policy of insurance as ever was written.* The judge, who was the same as presided on the trial of Williams, replied, *that it was a great misfortune when any gentleman of the jury makes up his mind on a cause before it was finished.* Mr. Erskine, who in that cause was counsel for the defendant, (in this he was against the defendant,) cried out, *it is worse than a misfortune, it is a fault.* The judge, in his address to the jury in summing up the evidence, expatiated upon, and explained the parts which the law assigned to the counsel on each side, to the witnesses, and to the judge, and said, " *When all this was done*, AND NOT UNTIL THEN, *it was the business of the jury to declare what the justice of the case was; and that it was extremely rash and imprudent in any man to draw a conclusion before all the premises were laid before them upon which that conclusion was to be grounded.*" According then to Kenyon's own doctrine, the trial of Williams is an irregular trial, the verdict an irregular verdict, and as such is not recordable.

As to the special juries, they are but modern; and were instituted for the purpose of determining cases at *law* between merchants; because, as the method of keeping merchants' accounts differs from that of common tradesmen, and their business, by lying much in foreign bills of exchange, insurance, etc., is of a different description to that of common tradesmen, it might happen that a common jury might not be competent to form a judgment. The law that instituted special juries, makes it necessary that the jurors be *merchants*, or of the degree of *squires*. A special jury in London is generally composed of merchants; and in the country, of men called country squires, that is, fox-hunters, or men qualified to hunt foxes. The one may decide very well upon a case of pounds, shillings, and pence, or of the counting-house: and the other of the jockey-club or the chase. But who would not laugh, that because such men can decide such cases, they can also be jurors upon theology? Talk with some London merchants about scripture, and they will understand you mean *scrip*, and tell you how much it is worth at the Stock Exchange. Ask them about Theology, and they will say they know of no such gentleman upon 'Change. Tell some country squires of the sun and moon standing still, the one on the top of a hill, the other in a valley, and they will swear it is a lie of one's own making. Tell them that God Almighty ordered a man to make a cake and bake it with a t—d and eat it, and they will say it is one of Dean Swift's blackguard stories. Tell them it is in the Bible, and they will lay a bowl of punch it is not, and leave it to the parson of the parish to decide. Ask *them* also about Theology, and they will say, they know of no such a one on the turf. An appeal to such juries serves to bring the Bible into more ridicule than anything the author of the Age of Reason has written ; and the manner in which the trial has been conducted shews that the prosecutor dares not come to the point, nor meet the defence of the defendant. But all other cases apart, on what grounds of right, otherwise than on the right assumed by an Inquisition, do such prosecutions stand ? Religion is a private affair between every man and his Maker, and no tribunal or third party has a right to interfere between them. It is not properly a thing of this world ; it is only practised in this world ; but its object is in a future world ; and it is no otherwise an object of just laws than for the purpose of protecting the equal rights of all, however various their belief may be. If one man chuse to believe the book called the Bible to be the word of God, and another, from the convinced idea of the purity and perfection of God compared with the contradictions the book contains—from the lasciviousness of some of its stories, like that of Lot getting drunk and debauching his two daughters, which is not spoken of as a crime, and for which the most absurd apologies are made—from the immorality of some of its precepts, like that of shewing no mercy—and from the total want of evidence on the case,— thinks he ought not to believe it to be the word of God, each of them has an equal right ; and if the one has a right to give his reasons for believing it to be so, the other has an

equal right to give his reasons for believing the *contrary*,
Any thing that goes beyond this rule is an Inquisition.   Mr.
Erskine talks of his moral education: Mr. Erskine is very
little acquainted with theological subjects, if he does not
know there is such a thing as a *sincere* and *religious* belief
that the Bible is not the word of God.   This is my belief; it
is the belief of thousands far more learned than Mr. Erskine;
and it is a belief that is every day encreasing.   It is not
infidelity, as Mr. Erskine profanely and abusively calls it; it
is the direct reverse of infidelity.   It is a pure religious
belief, founded on the idea of the perfection of the Creator.
If the Bible be the word of God, it needs not the wretched
aid of prosecutions to support it, and you might with as
much propriety make a law to protect the sunshine as to
protect the Bible.   Is the Bible like the sun, or the work of
God?   We see that God takes good care of the creation he
has made.   He suffers no part of it to be extinguished: and
he will take the same care of his word, if he ever gave *one*.
But men ought to be reverentially careful and suspicious
how they ascribe books to him as his *word*, which from this
confused condition would dishonour a common scribbler,
and against which there is abundant evidence, and every
cause to suspect imposition.   Leave the Bible to itself.
God will take care of it if he has any thing to do with it, as
he takes care of the sun and the moon, which need not your
laws for their better protection.   As the two instances I have
produced in the beginning of this letter, from the book of
Genesis,—the one respecting the account called the Mosaic
account of the Creation, the other of the Flood,—sufficiently
shew the necessity of examining the Bible, in order to ascertain what degree of evidence there is for receiving or rejecting it as a sacred book, I shall not add more upon that subject; but in order to shew Mr. Erskine that there are religious
establishments for public worship which make no profession
of faith of the books called holy scriptures, nor admit of
priests, I will conclude with an account of a society lately
begun in Paris, and which is very rapidly extending
itself.

The society takes the name of Théophilantropes, which would be rendered in English by the word Theophilanthropists, a word compounded of three Greek words, signifying God, Love, and Man. The explanation given to this word is *Lovers of God and Man*, or *Adorers of God and Friends of Man*, adorateurs de dieu et amis des hommes. The society proposes to publish each year a volume, intitled ' Année Religieuse des Théophilantropes,' Year Religious of the Theophilanthropists. The first volume is just published, intitled :

RELIGIOUS YEAR OF THE THEOPHILANTHROPISTS;

OR

ADORERS OF GOD AND FRIENDS OF MAN ;

Being a collection of the discourses, lectures, hymns, and canticles, for all the religious and moral festivals of the Theophilanthropists during the course of the year, whether in their public temples or in their private families, published by the author of the Manual of the Theophilanthropists.

The volume of this year, which is the first, contains 214 pages of duodecimo. The following is the table of contents:

1. Precise history of the Theophilanthropists.
2. Exercises common to all the festivals.
3. Hymn, No. I. God of whom the universe speaks.
4. Discourse upon the existence of God.
5. Ode. II. The heavens instruct the earth.
6. Precepts of wisdom, extracted from the book of the Adorateurs.
7. Canticle, No. III. God Creator, soul of nature.
8. Extracts from divers moralists, upon the nature of God, and upon the physical proofs of his existence.
9. Canticle, No. IV. Let us bless at our waking the God who gave us light.
10. Moral thoughts extracted from the Bible.
11. Hymn, No. V. Father of the universe.
12. Contemplation of nature on the first days of the spring.
13. Ode, No. VI. Lord in thy glory adorable.

14. Extracts from the moral thoughts of Confucius.
15. Canticle in praise of actions, and thanks for the works of the creation.
16. Continuation from the moral thoughts of Confucius.
17. Hymn, No. VII. All the universe is full of thy magnificence.
18. Extracts from an ancient sage of India upon the duties of families.
19. Upon the spring.
20. Thoughts moral of divers Chinese authors.
21. Canticle, No. VIII. Every thing celebrates the glory of the eternal.
22. Continuation of the moral thoughts of Chinese authors.
23. Invocation for the country.
24. Extracts from the moral thoughts of Theognis.
25. Invocation. Creator of man.
26. Ode, No. IX. Upon death.
27. Extracts from the book of the Moral Universal, upon happiness.
28. Ode No. X. Supreme Author of Nature.

INTRODUCTION.

INTITLED

PRECISE HISTORY OF THE THEOPHILANTHROPISTS.

" Towards the month of Véndemiaire, of the year 5, (Sept. 1796,) there appeared at Paris, a small work entitled, Manual of the Théoantropophiles, since called, for the sake of easier pronunciation, Théophilantropes, (Theophilanthropists,) published by C———.[1]

" The worship set forth in this Manual, of which the origin is from the beginning of the world, was then professed by some families in the silence of domestic life. But no sooner was the Manual published, than some persons, respectable for their knowledge and their manners, saw, in the formation of a Society open to the public, an easy method of spreading moral religion, and of leading by de-

---

[1] Chemin-Dupontès.—*Editor.*

grees great numbers to the knowledge thereof, who appear to have forgotten it. This consideration ought of itself not to leave indifferent those persons who know that morality and religion, which is the most solid support thereof, are necessary to the maintenance of society, as well as to the happiness of the individual. These considerations determined the families of the Theophilanthropists to unite publicly for the exercise of their worship.

" The first society of this kind opened in the month of Nivose, year 5, (Jan. 1797,) in the street Denis, No. 34, corner of Lombard-street. The care of conducting this society was undertaken by five fathers of families. They adopted the Manual of the Theophilanthropists. They agreed to hold their days of public worship on the days corresponding to Sundays, but without making this a hindrance to other Societies to choose such other day as they thought more convenient. Soon after this, more Societies were opened, of which some celebrate on the decadi, (tenth day,) and others on the Sunday. It was also resolved that the committee should meet one hour each week for the purpose of preparing or examining the discourses and lectures proposed for the next general assembly ; that the general assemblies should be called Fêtes (festivals) religious and moral; that those festivals should be conducted in principle and form, in a manner, as not to be considered as the festivals of an exclusive worship ; and that in recalling those who might not be attached to any particular worship, those festivals might also be attended as moral exercises by disciples of every sect, and consequently avoid, by scrupulous care, every thing that might make the Society appear under the name of a sect. The Society adopts neither *rites* nor *priesthood*, and it will never lose sight of the resolution not to advance any thing, as a Society, inconvenient to any sect or sects, in any time or country, and under any government.

" It will be seen, that it is so much the more easy for the Society to keep within this circle, because that the dogmas of the Theophilanthropists are those upon which all the sects have agreed, that their moral is that upon which there has never been the least dissent; and that the name they have taken expresses the double end of all the sects, that of leading to the *adoration of God and love of man.*

" The Theophilanthropists do not call themselves the disciples of such or such a man. They avail themselves of the wise precepts that have been transmitted by writers of all countries and in all ages. The reader will find in the discourses, lectures, hymns, and canticles, which the Theophilanthropists have adopted for their religious and moral festivals, and which they present under the title of Année Religieuse, extracts from moralists, ancient and modern, divested of maxims too severe, or too loosely conceived, or contrary to piety, whether towards God or towards man."

Next follow the dogmas of the Theophilanthropists, or things they profess to believe. These are but two, and are thus expressed, *les Théophilantropes croient à l'existence de Dieu, et à l'immortalité de l'âme.* The Theophilanthropists believe in the existence of God, and the immortality of the soul.

The Manual of the Theophilanthropists, a small volume of sixty pages, duodecimo, is published separately, as is also their catechism, which is of the same size. The principles of the Theophilanthropists are the same as those published in the first part of the *Age of Reason* in 1793, and in the second part, in 1795. The Theophilanthropists, as a Society, are silent upon all the things they do not profess to believe, as the *sacredness* of the books called the Bible, etc. They profess the immortality of the soul, but they are silent on the immortality of the body, or that which the church of England calls the resurrection. The author of the *Age of Reason* gives reasons for every thing he *disbelieves*, as well as for those he *believes*; and where this cannot be done with safety, the government is a despotism, and the church an Inquisition.

It is more than three years since the first part of the Age of Reason was published, and more than a year and a half since the publication of the second part: the Bishop of

Llandaff undertook to write an answer to the second part; and it was not until after it was known that the author of the Age of Reason would reply to the bishop, that the prosecution against the book was set on foot; and which is said to be carried on by some clergy of the English Church. If the bishop is one of them, and the object be to prevent an exposure of the numerous and gross errors he has committed in his work, (and which he wrote when report said that Thomas Paine was dead,) it is a confession that he feels the weakness of his cause, and finds himself unable to maintain it. In this case he has given me a triumph I did not seek, and Mr. Erskine, the herald of the prosecution, has proclaimed it.

THOMAS PAINE.

V.

THE EXISTENCE OF GOD.

A DISCOURSE AT THE SOCIETY OF THEOPHILANTHRO-
PISTS, PARIS.[1]

RELIGION has two principal enemies, Fanatism and Infidelity, or that which is called Atheism. The first requires
to be combated by reason and morality, the other by natural philosophy.

[1] Theophilanthropy, in its six years in France, gave rise to a considerable
literature, of which Paine's account, in the Letter to Erskine, is the friendliest
chapter. The wrath with which the Catholic Church saw this Theistic Church
and Ethical Society sharing its edifices, even Notre Dame, has been transmitted
even to Protestant dictionaries, and Napoleon I. has won some repute for piety
by their ejection. As to this, an anecdote is related in the *Theophilanthropist*
(New York, 1810). M. Dupuis, author of " The Origin of all Religious Worship," reproached Napoleon for reinstating Catholicism, and Napoleon said
that " as for himself, he did not believe that such a person as Jesus Christ ever
existed ; but as the people were inclined to superstition, he thought proper not
to oppose them." " This fact," adds the *Theophilanthropist*, " Mr. Dupuis
related to Thomas Paine and Chancellor Livingston, then Minister of the
United States in Paris, as the former informed the writer of this note." This
note was probably written by Colonel John Fellows, who with other friends of
Paine had formed in New York a Society free from the defects which their departed leader had seen developed in the movement in Paris. Of the Society in
Paris he was one of the founders (Sherwin's " Life of Paine," p. 180. Henri
Grégoire's " Histoire des Sectes," tom. i., livre 2), and his Discourse was probably read at their first *public* meeting, January 16, 1797. Mr. J. G. Alger, to
whom I am indebted for various information, sends me a list of the meetings of
the Society in 1797, by which it appears that this first meeting was in the St.
Catharine Hospital, and no meeting was held elsewhere until June 25. Paine's
Discourse speaks of the Society (formed in September, 1796) as " in its infancy,"
as without enemies, and in no danger of persecution, which could hardly have
been said after the first public meeting ; he proposes a plan of procedure ; and
he does not allude to the swift development of the Society, after the President

236

The existence of a God is the first dogma of the Theo-philanthropists. It is upon this subject that I solicit your attention ; for though it has been often treated of, and that most sublimely, the subject is inexhaustible ; and there will always remain something to be said that has not been before advanced. I go therefore to open the subject, and to crave your attention to the end.

The Universe is the bible of a true Theophilanthropist. It is there that he reads of God. It is there that the proofs of his existence are to be sought and to be found. As to written or printed books, by whatever name they are called, they are the works of man's hands, and carry no evidence in themselves that God is the author of any of them. It must be in something that man could not make that we must seek evidence for our belief, and that something is the universe, the true Bible,—the inimitable work of God.

Contemplating the universe, the whole system of Creation,

Larevellière-Lépeaux had eulogized it (May 2). The first volume of the " Année Religieuse des Théophilantropes " (whose table of contents Paine enclosed with his Letter to Erskine) extends into September, 1797, and Paine's Discourse is not mentioned, nor was it ever translated into French. The probable reason of this is suggested by Count Grégoire (" Hist. des Sectes "), who says : " Thomas Payne, qui adressa une lettre aux Théophilantropes, eût été regardé comme profès s'il ne les avait censurés sur divers points." What were these different points to which Paine objected cannot be gathered from Grégoire, a rather hostile his-torian of the movement though the best authority as to its *personnel* : this very Discourse, as well as Paine's other writings, will sufficiently suggest the mis-givings he felt at the ceremonies which soon invested a religion which seemed to grow out of " Le Siècle de la Raison," and beside whose cradle he watched with his friends Bernardin St. Pierre and Dupuis. The St. Catharine Hospital had been allotted to the blind, early in the Revolution, and their instructor, M. Hauy, was also the manager of the Theophilanthropic services there. Grégoire says that Hauy never really ceased to be a Roman Catholic. Instead of the scientific lectures and apparatus of Paine's programme for the Society, the Theo-philanthropists were seen laying floral offerings on altars, and occupied with cere-monies in which those of the Church were blended with those of Robespierre's adoration of the Supreme Being. These developments had not gone very far when Paine wrote his Letter to Erskine, but it will be observed that near the close of that letter he remarks on the silence of the Theophilanthropists con-cerning the things they do not profess to believe, such as the " *sacredness* of the books called the Bible, etc," adding, " The author of the *Age of Reason* gives reasons for everything he *disbelieves* as well as for those he *believes*." (*Cf.*

in this point of light, we shall discover, that all that which is called natural philosophy is properly a divine study. It is the study of God through his works. It is the best study, by which we can arrive at a knowledge of his existence, and the only one by which we can gain a glimpse of his perfection.

Do we want to contemplate his power? We see it in the immensity of the Creation. Do we want to contemplate his wisdom? We see it in the unchangeable order by which the incomprehensible WHOLE is governed. Do we want to contemplate his munificence? We see it in the abundance with which he fills the earth. Do we want to contemplate his mercy? We see it in his not withholding that abundance even from the unthankful. In fine, do we want to know

A sentence at the end of the third paragraph of the " Precise History," in the preceding chapter.)

As for this Discourse of Paine's it appears to be a composition of early life with two or three paragraphs added. The use of the word " infidelity " in the first paragraph, to describe a philosophical opinion, could not have been written after his profound definition in the *Age of Reason* : " Infidelity does not consist in believing or disbelieving ; it consists in pretending to believe what he does not believe." It is still more crude as compared with Part II. of the *Age of Reason* in which the moral nature of man is part of the foundation of his faith in deity. The Discourse is a digest of Newton's Letters to Bentley, in which he postulates a divine power as necessary to explain planetary motion, and its literary style appears more like Paine's articles in his *Pennsylvania Magazine* in the early months of 1775 than like the works written after the American Revolution had, as he states, made him an author. In my Introduction to the *Age of Reason* I mentioned that this Discourse was circulated in England as a religious tract ("Atheism Refuted") ; my copy of which is marked with sharp contradictions by some freethinker, unaware that he is criticising Paine. A Discourse so harmless was naturally welcomed by the deistical booksellers, just after the conviction of Williams, and it was detached from the Letter to Erskine and published by Rickman (1798) with three quotations in the title, among these, "I had as lief have the foppery of Freedom, as the Morality of Imprisonment."—Shakespeare. This cheap pamphlet (4d.) had a page of inscription in capitals and uneven lines: " The following little Discourse is dedicated to the Enemies of Thomas Paine, by one who has known him long, and intimately, and who is convinced that he is the enemy of no man. By a well wisher to the whole world. By one who thinks that Discussion should be unlimited, that all coercion is error ; and that human beings should adopt no other conduct towards each other but an appeal to truth and reason.—CLIO."

In the present volume the Discourse is printed, like the Letter to Erskine, from Paine's own original Paris edition.—*Editor.*

what GOD is? Search not written or printed books, but the Scripture called the *Creation*.

It has been the error of the schools to teach astronomy, and all the other sciences, and subjects of natural philosophy, as accomplishments only; whereas they should be taught theologically, or with reference to the *Being* who is the author of them : for all the principles of science are of divine origin. Man cannot make, or invent, or contrive principles : he can only discover them ; and he ought to look through the discovery to the author.

When we examine an extraordinary piece of machinery, an astonishing pile of architecture, a well executed statue, or an highly finished painting, where life and action are imitated, and habit only prevents our mistaking a surface of light and shade for cubical solidity, our ideas are naturally led to think of the extensive genius and talents of the artist. When we study the elements of geometry, we think of Euclid. When we speak of gravitation, we think of Newton. How then is it, that when we study the works of God in the creation, we stop short, and do not think of GOD ? It is from the error of the schools in having taught those subjects as accomplishments only, and thereby separated the study of them from the *Being* who is the author of them.

The schools have made the study of theology to consist in the study of opinions in written or printed books ; whereas theology should be studied in the works or books of the creation. The study of theology in books of opinions has often produced fanatism, rancour, and cruelty of temper ; and from hence have proceeded the numerous persecutions, the fanatical quarrels, the religious burnings and massacres, that have desolated Europe. But the study of theology in the works of the creation produces a direct contrary effect. The mind becomes at once enlightened and serene, a copy of the scene it beholds : information and adoration go hand in hand ; and all the social faculties become enlarged.

The evil that has resulted from the error of the schools, in teaching natural philosophy as an accomplishment only, has been that of generating in the pupils a species of Atheism. Instead of looking through the works of creation to the Creator himself, they stop short, and employ the knowledge they acquire to create doubts of his existence. They labour with studied ingenuity to ascribe every thing they behold to innate properties of matter, and jump over all the rest by saying, that matter is eternal.

Let us examine this subject; it is worth examining; for if we examine it through all its cases, the result will be, that the existence of a SUPERIOR CAUSE, or that which man calls GOD, will be discoverable by philosophical principles.

In the first place, admitting matter to have properties, as we see it has, the question still remains, how came matter by those properties? To this they will answer, that matter possessed those properties eternally. This is not solution, but assertion; and to deny it is equally as impossible of proof as to assert it. It is then necessary to go further; and therefore I say,—if there exist a circumstance that is *not* a property of matter, and without which the universe, or to speak in a limited degree, the solar system composed of planets and a sun, could not exist a moment, all the arguments of Atheism, drawn from properties of matter, and applied to account for the universe, will be overthrown, and the existence of a superior cause, or that which man calls God, becomes discoverable, as is before said, by natural philosophy.

I go now to shew that such a circumstance exists, and what it is.

The universe is composed of matter, and, as a system, is sustained by motion. Motion is *not a property* of matter, and without this motion, the solar system could not exist. Were motion a property of matter, that undiscovered and undiscoverable thing called perpetual motion would establish itself. It is because motion is not a property of matter, that perpetual motion is an impossibility in the hand of every being but that of the Creator of motion. When the pretenders to Atheism can produce perpetual motion, and not till then, they may expect to be credited.

The natural state of matter, as to place, is a state of rest. Motion, or change of place, is the effect of an external cause acting upon matter. As to that faculty of matter that is called gravitation, it is the influence which two or more bodies have reciprocally on each other to unite and be at rest. Every thing which has hitherto been discovered, with respect to the motion of the planets in the system, relates only to the laws by which motion acts, and not to the cause of motion. Gravitation, so far from being the cause of motion to the planets that compose the solar system, would be the destruction of the solar system, were revolutionary motion to cease; for as the action of spinning upholds a top, the revolutionary motion upholds the planets in their orbits, and prevents them from gravitating and forming one mass with the sun. In one sense of the word, philosophy knows, and atheism says, that matter is in perpetual motion. But the motion here meant refers to the *state* of matter, and that only on the surface of the earth. It is either decomposition, which is continually destroying the form of bodies of matter, or recomposition, which renews that matter in the same or another form, as the decomposition of animal or vegetable substances enter into the composition of other bodies. But the motion that upholds the solar system is of an entire different kind, and is not a property of matter. It operates also to an entire different effect. It operates to *perpetual preservation,* and to prevent *any change* in the state of the system.

Giving then to matter all the properties which philosophy knows it has, or all that atheism ascribes to it, and can prove, and even supposing matter to be eternal, it will not account for the system of the universe, or of the solar system, because it will not account for motion, and it is motion that preserves it. When, therefore, we discover a circumstance of such immense importance, that without it the universe could not exist, and for which neither matter, nor any nor all the properties can account, we are by necessity forced into the rational comformable belief of the existence of a cause superior to matter, and that cause man calls GOD.

As to that which is called nature, it is no other than the laws by which motion and action of every kind, with respect to unintelligible matter, is regulated. And when we speak of looking through nature up to nature's God, we speak philosophically the same rational language as when we speak of looking through human laws up to the power that ordained them.

God is the power of first cause, nature is the law, and matter is the subject acted upon.

But infidelity, by ascribing every phænomenon to properties of matter, conceives a system for which it cannot account, and yet it pretends to demonstration. It reasons from what it sees on the surface of the earth, but it does not carry itself on the solar system existing by motion. It sees upon the surface a perpetual decomposition and recomposition of matter. It sees that an oak produces an acorn, an acorn an oak, a bird an egg, an egg a bird, and so on. In things of this kind it sees something which it calls a natural cause, but none of the causes it sees is the cause of that motion which preserves the solar system.

Let us contemplate this wonderful and stupendous system consisting of matter, and existing by motion. It is not matter in a state of rest, nor in a state of decomposition or recomposition. It is matter systematized in perpetual orbicular or circular motion. As a system that motion is the life of it: as animation is life to an animal body, deprive the system of motion, and, as a system, it must expire. Who then breathed into the system the life of motion? What power impelled the planets to move, since motion is not a property of the matter of which they are composed? If we contemplate the immense velocity of this motion, our wonder becomes increased, and our adoration enlarges itself in the same proportion. To instance only one of the planets, that of the earth we inhabit, its distance from the sun, the centre of the orbits of all the planets, is, according to observations of the transit of the planet Venus, about one hundred million miles; consequently, the diameter of the orbit, or circle in which the earth moves round the sun, is double that distance ; and the measure of the circumference of the orbit, taken as three times its diameter, is six hundred million miles. The earth performs this voyage in three hundred and sixty-five days and some hours, and consequently moves at the rate of more than one million six hundred thousand miles every twenty-four hours.

Where will infidelity, where will atheism, find cause for this astonishing velocity of motion, never ceasing, never varying, and which is the preservation of the earth in its orbit? It is not by reasoning from an acorn to an oak, from an egg to a bird, or from any change in the state of matter on the surface of the earth, that this can be accounted for. Its cause is not to be found in matter, nor in any thing we call nature. The atheist who affects to reason, and the fanatic who rejects reason, plunge themselves alike into inextricable difficulties. The one perverts the sublime and enlightening study of natural philosophy into a deformity of absurdities by not reasoning to the end. The other loses himself in the obscurity of metaphysical theories, and dishonours the Creator, by treating the study of his works with contempt. The one is a half-rational of whom there is some hope, the other a visionary to whom we must be charitable.

When at first thought we think of a Creator, our ideas appear to us undefined and confused ; but if we reason philosophically, those ideas can be easily arranged and simplified. *It is a Being whose power is equal to his will.* Observe the nature of the will of man. It is of an infinite quality. We cannot conceive the possibility of limits to the will. Observe, on the other hand, how exceedingly limited is his power of acting compared with the nature of his will. Suppose the power equal to the will, and man would be a God. He would will himself eternal, and be so. He could will a creation, and could make it. In this progressive reasoning, we see in the nature of the will of man half of that which we conceive in thinking of God ; add the other half, and we have the whole idea of a being who could make the universe, and sustain it by perpetual motion ; because he could create that motion.

We know nothing of the capacity of the will of animals, but we know a great deal of the difference of their powers. For example, how numerous are the degrees, and how immense is the difference of power, from a mite to a man. Since then every thing we see below us shews a progression of power, where is the difficulty in supposing that there is, at the *summit of all things,* a Being in whom an infinity of power unites with the infinity of the will. When this simple idea presents itself to our mind, we have the idea of a perfect Being, that man calls God.

It is comfortable to live under the belief of the existence of an infinite protecting power; and it is an addition to that comfort to know that such a belief is not a mere conceit of the imagination, as many of the theories that is called religious are; nor a belief founded only on tradition or received opinion; but is a belief deducible by the action of reason upon the things that compose the system of the universe; a belief arising out of visible facts: and so demonstrable is the truth of this belief, that if no such belief had existed, the persons who now controvert it would have been the persons who would have produced and propagated it; because by beginning to reason they would have been led to reason progressively to the end, and thereby have discovered that matter and the properties it has will not account for the system of the universe, and that there must necessarily be a superior cause.

It was the excess to which imaginary systems of religion had been carried, and the intolerance, persecutions, burnings and massacres they occasioned, that first induced certain persons to propagate infidelity; thinking, that upon the whole it was better not to believe at all than to believe a multitude of things and complicated creeds that occasioned so much mischief in the world. But those days are past, persecution hath ceased, and the antidote then set up against it has no longer even the shadow of apology. We profess, and we proclaim in peace, the pure, unmixed, comfortable, and rational belief of a God, as manifested to us in the universe. We do this without any apprehension of that belief being made a cause of persecution as other beliefs have been, or of suffering persecution ourselves.[1] To God, and not to man, are all men to account for their belief.

It has been well observed, at the first institution of this Society, that the dogmas it professes to believe are from the commencement of the world; that they are not novelties, but are confessedly the basis of all systems of religion, however numerous and contradictory they may be. All men in the outset of the religion they profess are Theophilanthropists. It is impossible to form any system of religion without building upon those principles, and therefore they are not sectarian principles, unless we suppose a sect composed of all the world.

I have said in the course of this discourse, that the study of natural philosophy is a divine study, because it is the study of the works of God in the creation. If we consider theology upon this ground, what an extensive field of improvement in things both divine and human opens itself before us! All the principles of science are of divine origin. It was not man that invented the principles on which astronomy, and every branch of mathematics, are founded and studied. It was not man that gave properties to the circle and the triangle. Those principles are eternal and immutable. We see in them the unchangeable nature of the Divinity. We see in them immortality, an immortality existing after the material figures that express those properties are dissolved in dust.

The Society is at present in its infancy, and its means are small; but I wish to hold in view the subject I allude to, and instead of teaching the philosophical branches of learning as ornamental accomplishments only, as they have hitherto been taught, to teach them in a manner that shall combine theological knowledge with scientific instruction. To do this to the best advantage, some instruments will be necessary, for the purpose of explanation, of which the Society is not yet possessed. But as the views of this

---

[1] A few years after this was uttered the Theophilanthropist Societies were suppressed by Napoleon.—*Editor.*

Society extend to public good as well as to that of the individual, and as its principles can have no enemies, means may be devised to procure them.

If we unite to the present instruction a series of lectures on the ground I have mentioned, we shall, in the first place, render theology the most delightful and entertaining of all studies. In the next place we shall give scientific instruction to those who could not otherwise obtain it. The mechanic of every profession will there be taught the mathematical principles necessary to render him a proficient in his art; the cultivator will there see developed the principles of vegetation; while, at the same time, they will be led to see the hand of God in all these things.

VI.

WORSHIP AND CHURCH BELLS.

A LETTER TO CAMILLE JORDAN.[1]

CITIZEN REPRESENTATIVE,

As everything in your Report, relating to what you call worship, connects itself with the books called the Scriptures, I begin with a quotation therefrom. It may serve to give us some idea of the fanciful origin and fabrication of those books. 2 Chronicles xxxiv. 14, etc. " Hilkiah, the priest, *found* the book of the law of the Lord given by Moses. And Hilkiah, the priest, said to Shaphan, the scribe, I have

---

[1] This pamphlet has never been published fully in English. It was printed in Paris in the summer of 1797 with the title : " Lettre de Thomas Paine sur les Cultes. A Paris, Imprimerie-Librairie du Cercle-Social, rue du Théâtre-Fran-çaise No. 4. 1797." The inner heading is : " A Jordan de Lyon, Membre du Conseil des Cinq Cents, sur les Cultes et sur les Cloches." It begins, "Citoyen, Jordan." The received English version presents so many serious divergencies from the original French Letter as to raise a doubt whether it might not be wiser to print here a translation of the whole. The first mention of it in English that I find is by Sherwin (" Life of Paine," London, 1819, p. 181), who says, "I have only seen a mutilated copy of this production." This was probably the frag-ment afterwards included in a small collection of Paine's " Theological Works " (Baldwin, Chatham-st., New York, 1821,) with a note : " The following is taken from the *Courier* (an Evening Paper) of July 13, 1797, the editor of which ob-serves, ' as the commencement of this Letter relates to Mr. Paine's opinions on the Bible, we are under the necessity, for obvious reasons, of omitting it.' " The fragment begins with the words, " It is a want of feeling to talk of priests, etc." As Jordan read his Report on June 17, Paine must have written his Letter (pp. 23 in French) at a heat to have a copy (MS.) in the hands of the London editor of the *Courier* so early as July 13. The manuscript was among the papers be-queathed by Paine to Madame Bonneville, whose return towards her former Catholic faith caused her to mutilate the manuscripts and suppress some altogether. In 1818 when she and Cobbett were preparing the outline of a memoir of Paine (published in the Appendix to my " Life of Paine ") this Letter to Jordan is re-

found the book of the law in the house of the Lord, and Hilkiah delivered the book to Shaphan. And Shaphan, the scribe, told the king, (Josiah,) saying, Hilkiah, the priest, hath given me a book."

This pretended finding was about a thousand years after the time that Moses is said to have lived. Before this pretended finding, there was no such thing practised or known in the world as that which is called the law of Moses. This being the case, there is every apparent evidence that the books called the books of Moses (and which make the first part of what are called the Scriptures) are forgeries contrived between a priest and a limb of the law,* Hilkiah, and Shaphan the scribe, a thousand years after Moses is said to have been dead.

Thus much for the first part of the Bible. Every other part is marked with circumstances equally as suspicious. We ought therefore to be reverentially careful how we ascribe books *as his word*, of which there is no evidence, and against

ferred to and Cobbett added, "which will find a place in the Appendix," but this Madame Bonneville struck out. Though she afterwards sold the MS. of the Letter, which appeared in an American edition of 1824, it was no doubt with many erasures, some of them irrecoverable. This is my conjecture as to the alterations referred to. But so many passages in the English version are clearly Paine's own writing that I can not venture to discard it, and conclude to insert as footnotes translations of the more important sentences and clauses of the French omitted from the English version.

Camille Jordan (b. at Lyons, 1771, d. at Paris, 1821,) was a royalist who in 1793 took refuge in Switzerland, and in England. Returning to Lyons in 1796 he was elected for the Department of the Rhone to the Council of Five Hundred, and, on July 17, 1797, brought in his Report for restoration of certain Catholic privileges, especially the Church Bells, which was received with ridicule by the Convention, where he was called "Jordan-Cloches." Nevertheless, he succeeded in securing relief for the unsworn priests. Although at this time professing loyalty to the Directory he united with those who attempted its overthrow, and on the 18th Fructidor (4 September, 1797) fled from a prosecution, finding a refuge in Weimar. Recalled to France in 1800 he was for some time under *surveillance*. He opposed the proposed Consular Government, and in 1814 was one of the deputation sent from Lyons to ask the Emperor of Austria to establish the Bourbons in France. Soon after he was sent to welcome Louis XVIII. in Paris, and received from him the award of nobility.—*Editor.*

* It happens that Camille Jordan is a limb of the law.—*Author.* [This note is not in the French pamphlet.—*Editor.*]

which there is abundant evidence to the contrary, and every cause to suspect imposition.[1]

In your report you speak continually of something by the name of worship, and you confine yourself to speak of one kind only, as if there were but one, and that one was unquestionably true.

The modes of worship are as various as the sects are numerous; and amidst all this variety and multiplicity there is but one article of belief in which every religion in the world agrees. That article has universal sanction. It is the belief of a God, or what the Greeks described by the word *Theism,* and the Latins by that of Deism. Upon this one article have been erected all the different superstructures of creeds and ceremonies continually warring with each other that now exist or ever existed.[2] But the men most and best informed upon the subject of theology rest themselves upon this universal article, and hold all the various superstructures erected thereon to be at least doubtful, if not altogether artificial.

The intellectual part of religion is a private affair between every man and his Maker, and in which no third party has any right to interfere. The practical part consists in our doing good to each other. But since religion has been made into a trade,[3] the practical part has been made to consist of ceremonies performed by men called priests; and the people have been amused with ceremonial shows, processions, and bells. By devices of this kind true religion has been banished; and such means have been found out to extract money even from the pockets of the poor, instead of contributing to their relief.[4]

---

[1] The French pamphlet has, instead of last sixteen words : " And when, on the contrary, we have the strongest reasons for regarding such assertions as one of the means of error and oppression invented by priests, kings, and attorneys."—*Editor.*

[2] French : "in the thousand and one religions of the four quarters of the world."—*Editor.*

[3] French : " since the most scandalous hypocrisy has made of Religion a profession and the basest trade."—*Editor.*

[4] French adds : " du superflu de la richesse." (from their superfluous wealth). —*Editor.*

No man ought to make a living by Religion. It is dishonest so to do. Religion is not an act that can be performed by proxy. One person cannot act religion for another. Every person must perform it for himself; and all that a priest can do is to take from him; he wants nothing but his money[1] and then to riot in the spoil and laugh at his credulity.

The only people who, as a professional sect of Christians provide for the poor of their society, are people known by the name of Quakers. Those men have no priests. They assemble quietly in their places of meeting, and do not disturb their neighbours with shows and noise of bells. Religion does not unite itself to show and noise. True religion is without either. Where there is both there is no true religion.[2]

The first object for inquiry in all cases, more especially in matters of religious concern, is TRUTH. We ought to inquire into the truth of whatever we are taught to believe, and it is certain that the books called the Scriptures stand, in this respect, in more than a doubtful predicament. They have been held in existence, and in a sort of credit among the common class of people, by art, terror, and persecution. They have little or no credit among the enlightened part, but they have been made the means of encumbering the world with a numerous priesthood, who have fattened on the labour of the people, and consumed the sustenance that ought to be applied to the widows and the poor.

It is a want of feeling to talk of priests and bells whilst so many infants are perishing in the hospitals, and aged and infirm poor in the streets, from the want of necessaries. The abundance that France produces is sufficient for every want, if rightly applied[3]; but priests and bells, like articles of luxury, ought to be the least articles of consideration.

[1] The ten preceding words are replaced in the French by: "to take from us not our vices but our money."—*Editor*.

[2] "A Religion uniting the two [noise and show] at the expense of the poor whose misery it should lessen, is a curious Religion; it is the Religion of kings and priests conspiring against suffering humanity."—*Editor*.

[3] "were the soil well cultivated and the cultivators not burdened with useless taxes."—*Editor*.

We talk of religion. Let us talk of truth; for that which is not truth, is not worthy of the name of religion.

We see different parts of the world overspread with different books, each of which, though contradictory to the other, is said by its partisans to be of divine origin, and is made a rule of faith and practice.[1] In countries under despotic governments, where inquiry is always forbidden, the people are condemned to believe as they have been taught by their priests.[2] This was for many centuries the case in France: but this link in the chain of slavery is happily broken by the revolution; and, that it may never be riveted again,[3] let us employ a part of the liberty we enjoy in scrutinizing into the truth. Let us leave behind us some monument, that we have made the cause and honour of our Creator[4] an object of our care. If we have been imposed upon by the terrors of government and the artifice of priests in matters of religion, let us do justice to our Creator by examining into the case. His name is too sacred to be affixed to any thing which is fabulous; and it is our duty to inquire whether we believe, or encourage the people to believe, in fables or in facts.[5]

It would be a project worthy the situation we are in, to invite an inquiry of this kind. We have committees for various objects; and, among others, a committee for bells. We have institutions, academies, and societies for various purposes; but we have none for inquiring into historical truth in matters of religious concern.

They shew us certain books which they call the Holy Scriptures, the word of God, and other names of that kind; but we ought to know what evidence there is for our believing them to be so, and at what time they originated and

---

[1] " under everlasting penalties."—*Editor.*

[2] " imposed on them, with equal arrogance and ignorance, by the idlers nourished by their blood and tears."—*Editor.*

[3] " and to prevent their discovering some new way of returning to us their absurd sermons, processions, bells, which will also restore their tithes, benefices, abbeys, and the rest."—*Editor.*

[4] " The Supreme Being" instead of " our Creator."—*Editor.*

[5] " to believe, under pain of damnation, fables that brutalise and impoverish them, or *facts* which increase their industry, general happiness, and the glory of their country."—*Editor.*

in what manner. We know that men could make books, and we know that artifice and superstition could give them a name,—could call them sacred. But we ought to be careful that the name of our Creator be not abused. Let then all the evidence with respect to those books be made a subject of inquiry. If there be evidence to warrant our belief of them, let us encourage the propagation of it ; but if not, let us be careful not to promote the cause of delusion and falsehood.

I have already spoken of the Quakers—that they have no priests, no bells—and that they are remarkable for their care of the poor of their society. They are equally as remarkable for the education of their children. I am a descendant of a family of that profession ; my father was a Quaker ; and I presume I may be admitted an evidence of what I assert. The seeds of good principles, and the literary means of advancement in the world, are laid in early life.[1] Instead, therefore, of consuming the substance of the nation upon priests, whose life at best is a life of idleness, let us think of providing for the education of those who have not the means of doing it themselves. One good schoolmaster is of more use than a hundred priests.

If we look back at what was the condition of France under the *ancien régime*, we cannot acquit the priests of corrupting the morals of the nation. Their pretended celibacy led them to carry debauchery and domestic infidelity into every family where they could gain admission ; and their blasphemous pretensions to forgive sins encouraged the commission of them. Why has the Revolution of France been stained with crimes, which the Revolution of the United States of America was not? Men are physically the same in all countries; it is education that makes them different. Accustom a people to believe that priests or any other class of men can forgive sins, and you will have sins in abundance.

I come now to speak more particularly to the object of your report.

---

[1] " Principles of humanity, of sociability, and sound instruction for advancement in society, are the first objects of studies among the Quakers."—*Editor*.

You claim a privilege incompatible with the constitution and with rights. The constitution protects equally, as it ought to do, every profession of religion ; it gives no exclusive privilege to any. The churches are the common property of all the people ; they are national goods, and cannot be given exclusively to any one profession, because the right does not exist of giving to any one that which appertains to all.[1] It would be consistent with right that the churches be sold, and the money arising therefrom be invested as a fund for the education of children of poor parents of every profession, and, if more than sufficient for this purpose, that the surplus be appropriated to the support of the aged poor. After this, every profession can erect its own place of worship, if it choose—support its own priests, if it choose to have any—or perform its worship without priests, as the Quakers do.

As to bells, they are a public nuisance. If one profession is to have bells, and another has the right to use the instruments of the same kind, or any other noisy instrument, some may choose to meet at the sound of cannon, another at the beat of drum, another at the sound of trumpets, and so on, until the whole becomes a scene of general confusion. But if we permit ourselves to think of the state of the sick, and the many sleepless nights and days they undergo, we shall feel the impropriety of increasing their distress by the noise of bells, or any other noisy instruments.

Quiet and private domestic devotion neither offends nor incommodes any body ; and the Constitution has wisely guarded against the use of externals. Bells come under this description, and public processions still more so. Streets and highways are for the accommodation of persons following their several occupations, and no sectary has a right to incommode them. If any one has, every other has the same ; and the meeting of various and contradictory processions would be tumultuous. Those who formed the Constitution had wisely reflected upon these cases ; and, whilst they were careful to reserve the equal right of every one,

[1] Added : "that which is destined for needs of the State."—*Editor.*

they restrained every one from giving offence, or incommoding another.[1]

Men who, through a long and tumultuous scene, have lived in retirement as you have done, may think, when they arrive at power, that nothing is more easy than to put the world to rights in an instant; they form to themselves gay ideas at the success of their projects; but they forget to contemplate the difficulties that attend them, and the dangers with which they are pregnant. Alas! nothing is so easy as to deceive one's self. Did all men think as you think, or as you say, your plan would need no advocate, because it would have no opposer; but there are millions who think differently to you, and who are determined to be neither the dupes nor the slaves of error or design.

It is your good fortune to arrive at power, when the sunshine of prosperity is breaking forth after a long and stormy night.[2] The firmness of your colleagues, and of those you have succeeded—the unabated energy of the Directory, and the unequalled bravery of the armies of the Republic,—have made the way smooth and easy to you. If you look back at the difficulties that existed when the Constitution commenced, you cannot but be confounded with admiration at the difference between that time and now. At that moment the Directory were placed like the forlorn hope of an army,[3] but you were in safe retirement. They occupied the post of honourable danger, and they have merited well of their country.

You talk of justice and benevolence, but you begin at the wrong end. The defenders of your country, and the deplorable state of the poor, are objects of prior consideration to priests and bells and gaudy processions.

You talk of peace, but your manner of talking of it embarrasses the Directory in making it, and serves to prevent

[1] "All such parades of vindictive and jealous priests may kindle the beginings of intestine troubles; they have been happily provided against."—*Editor*.

[2] "which seemed to bode for all Europe an eternal night."—*Editor*.

[3] "the lost children of Liberty" instead of "the forlorn hope of an army."—*Editor*.

it. Had you been an actor in all the scenes of government from its commencement, you would have been too well informed to have brought forward projects that operate to encourage the enemy. When you arrived at a share in the government, you found every thing tending to a prosperous issue. A series of victories unequalled in the world, and in the obtaining of which you had no share, preceded your arrival. Every enemy but one was subdued ; and that one, (the Hanoverian government of England,) deprived of every hope, and a bankrupt in all its resources, was sueing for peace. In such a state of things, no new question that might tend to agitate and anarchize the interior ought to have had place ; and the project you propose tends directly to that end.

Whilst France was a monarchy, and under the government of those things called kings and priests, England could always defeat her; but since France has RISEN TO BE A REPUBLIC, the GOVERNMENT OF ENGLAND crouches beneath her, so great is the difference between a government of kings and priests, and that which is founded on the system of representation. But, could the government of England find a way, under the sanction of your report, to inundate France with a flood of emigrant priests, she would find also the way to domineer as before ; she would retrieve her shattered finances at your expence, and the ringing of bells would be the tocsin of your downfall.[1]

Did peace consist in nothing but the cessation of war, it would not be difficult ; but the terms are yet to be arranged ; and those terms will be better or worse, in proportion as France and her counsels be united or divided. That the government of England counts much upon your report, and upon others of a similar tendency, is what the writer of this letter, who knows that government well, has no doubt. You are but new on the theatre of government, and you ought to suspect yourself of misjudging; the experience of those who have gone before you, should be of some service to you. But if, in consequence of such measures as you propose, you

[1] After tocsin, " which would announce to Europe your ruin."—*Editor.*

put it out of the power of the Directory to make a good peace, and force them to accept of terms you would afterwards reprobate, it is yourself that must bear the censure.

You conclude your report by the following address to your colleagues :—

" Let us hasten, representatives of the people ! to affix to these tutelary laws the seal of our unanimous approbation. All our fellow-citizens will learn to cherish political liberty from the enjoyment of religious liberty : you will have broken the most powerful arm of your enemies ; you will have surrounded this assembly with the most impregnable rampart—confidence, and the people's love. O my colleagues, how desirable is that popularity which is the offspring of good laws ! What a consolation it will be to us hereafter, when returned to our own firesides, to hear from the mouths of our fellow-citizens these simple expressions—*Blessings reward you, men of peace ! you have restored to us our temples, our ministers, the liberty of adoring the God of our fathers : you have recalled harmony to our families—morality to our hearts : you have made us adore the legislature and respect all its laws !*" [1]

Is it possible, citizen representative, that you can be serious in this address? Were the lives of the priests under the *ancien régime* such as to justify any thing you say of them ? Were not all France convinced of their immorality? Were they not considered as the patrons of debauchery and domestic infidelity, and not as the patrons of morals ? What was their pretended celibacy but perpetual adultery ? What was their blasphemous pretention to forgive sins but an encouragement to the commission of them, and a love for their own ? Do you want to lead again into France all the vices of which they have been the patrons, and to overspread the republic with English pensioners? [2] It is cheaper to corrupt than to conquer ; and the English government, unable to conquer, will stoop to corrupt. Arrogance and meanness, though in appearance opposite, are vices of the same heart.

---

[1] " Extract from the *Moniteur*, No. 275, 5 Messidor (June 23.)."—*Editor.*

[2] "pensioners of a hostile government which has already sought to plunge you into all the horrors of religious wars " instead of " English pensioners."—*Editor.*

Instead of concluding in the manner you have done, you ought rather to have said :

" O my colleagues ! we are arrived at a glorious period—a period that promises more than we could have expected, and [1] all that we could have wished. Let us hasten to take into consideration the honours and rewards due to our brave defenders. Let us hasten to give encouragement to agriculture and manufactures, that commerce may reinstate itself, and our people have employment. Let us review the condition of the suffering poor, and wipe from our country the reproach of forgetting them. Let us devise means to establish schools of instruction, that we may banish the ignorance that the *ancien régime* of kings and priests had spread among the people. Let us propagate morality, unfettered by superstition. Let us cultivate justice and benevolence, that the God of our fathers may bless us. The helpless infant and the aged poor cry to us to remember them. Let not wretchedness be seen in our streets. Let [2] France exhibit to the world the glorious example of expelling ignorance and misery together.

" Let these, my virtuous colleagues, be the subject of our care that, when we return among our fellow-citizens they may say, *Worthy representatives ! you have done well. You have done justice and honour to our brave defenders. You have encouraged agriculture, cherished our decayed manufactures, given new life to commerce, and employment to our people. You have removed from our country* [3] *the reproach of forgetting the poor—You have caused the cry of the orphan to cease—You have wiped the tear from the eye of the suffering mother—You have given comfort to the aged and infirm— You have penetrated into the gloomy recesses of wretchedness, and have banished it. Welcome among us, ye brave and virtuous representatives, and may your example be followed by your successors !* "

THOMAS PAINE.

PARIS, 1797.[4]

[1] " if not."—*Editor.*   [2] " republican."—*Editor.*
[3] " republican government."—*Editor.*
[4] The French pamphlet is without date.—*Editor.*

VII.

ANSWER TO THE BISHOP OF LLANDAFF.

EDITORIAL NOTE.

IMMEDIATELY after perusal of Bishop Watson's reply to "The Age of Reason" ("An Apology for the Bible," 1796) Paine began his answer to it. By reference to his letter to Jefferson (vol. iii. p. 377 of this edition) it will be seen that in October, 1800, he was still writing on it, and intended to publish it as Part III. of "The Age of Reason." This plan, however, was changed, and in his Will (*q. v.*) this Part III. and the "Answer" are mentioned as different manuscripts. That both were not published by Paine was due to several considerations. After his arrival in America, October 30, 1802, he found the *odium theologicum* against him so strong that it involved President Jefferson and other friends, personal and political, and it even seems doubtful whether he could have found a publisher. His last pamphlet "Examination of the Prophecies" was, it will be seen, "printed for the Author," no other publisher being named. Madame Bonneville mentions that "he left the manuscript of his Answer to the Bishop of Llandaff; the Third Part of his "Age of Reason"; several pieces on Religious Subjects, prose and verse." (See my "Life of Paine," vol. ii., p. 486.) Soon after Paine's death Madame Bonneville's reactionary religious tendencies which drew her back to the Catholic Church, led her to mutilate the manuscripts bequeathed to her. Her pious destructiveness was, however, to some extent, limited by her impecuniosity, as has been said in my introduction to "The Age of Reason," and Col. Fellows managed to rescue several fragments and restore passages that had been erased.

Fortunately another woman, without reactionary tendencies, the widow of Elihu Palmer, attended Paine during his illness in 1806, in the house of William Carver. (See *post*, note on the " Prospect Papers.") About that time he gave Mrs. Palmer a portion of the manuscript of the " Answer " which he had transcribed, and after his death she presented this to the editor of the *Theophilanthropist* (New York), in which it was published, 1810, and from which (loaned me by Mr. E. Truelove) it is here reprinted. The strange fate that brought Paine's latest religious writings under expurgation of the Catholic priesthood ultimately consigned some, though accidentally, to the flames. (See preface to my " Life of Paine.") The chief loss was, I believe, the part of his Answer alluded to in the opening fragment: " Of these things I shall speak fully when I come in another part to treat of the ancient religion of the Persians, and compare it with the modern religion of the New Testament." The incidental sentences in the further fragment, on Job, in which he accuses the Jews of dishonoring God by ascribing to him the evils of nature, rendered it certain that Paine had grappled with Bishop Butler's argument against the Deists (that the God of the Bible was no more cruel than their God of Nature) which had been pressed by Bishop Watson. Although it is clear from other passages that Paine had no belief in a personal Ahriman (as indeed Zoroaster had not) he probably adopted something like the Zoroastrian dualism.

Concerning the Bishop's " Apology " it may be remarked that those who circulated it so industriously could have hardly been aware, generally, of its heretical contents. It concedes that Paine had discovered " real difficulties " in the Old Testament, in the Christian grove some " unsightly shrubs," discrepancies in the genealogies of Christ, and inconsistencies in Ezra; it admits that a certain law in Deuteronomy is " improper," that Moses did not write some parts of the Pentateuch, and that " many learned men and good Christians " regard the Bible as fallible in matters not distinctively religious. Others who replied to Paine made large concessions in other points, the result being that when these concessions are added together they amount very nearly to a surrender of the biblical stronghold which Paine assailed. But as for Watson's "Apology," it is well known in the history of " Freethought " that the Bishop's work was second only to Paine's in the propagation of scepticism, partly, no doubt, through the extracts from the " Age of Reason " contained in it. Indeed the Bishop's own orthodoxy was suspected, his legitimate promotion was prevented, and among his papers was found (dated 1811) this bitter note : " I have treated my divinity as I twenty-five years ago treated my chemical papers : I have lighted my fire with the labour of a great portion of my life." There appears to me no doubt that both the Broad Church in England, and the rationalistic wing of the Quakers in America (Hicksites), were founded by " The Age of Reason " and the controversies raised by it.

In criticising these fragments it must be remembered that the portions published in 1810 were those thrown aside by Paine after transcribing or using them for a statement now lost, that the other portions were obtained only with Madame Bonneville's erasures, and that none of them ever received Paine's revision.

FRAGMENTS OF THE ANSWER.

GENESIS.

THE bishop says, "the oldest book in the world is Genesis." This is mere assertion ; he offers no proof of it, and I go to controvert it, and to show that the book of Job, which is not a Hebrew book, but is a book of the Gentiles translated into Hebrew, is much older than the book of Genesis.

The book of Genesis means the book of Generations ; to which are prefixed two chapters, the first and second, which contain two different cosmogonies, that is, two different accounts of the creation of the world, written by different persons, as I have shown in the preceding part of this work.

The first cosmogony begins at chapter i. 1, and ends at ii. 3 ; for the adverbial conjunction *thus*, with which chapter ii. begins, shews those three verses to belong to chapter i. The second cosmogony begins at ii. 4, and ends with that chapter.

In the first cosmogony the name of God is used without any epithet joined to it, and is repeated thirty-five times. In the second cosmogony it is always the Lord-God, which is repeated eleven times. These two different stiles of expression shew these two chapters to be the work of two different persons, and the contradictions they contain, shew they cannot be the work of one and the same person, as I have already shewn. The third chapter, in which the style of Lord God is continued in every instance except in the supposed conversation between the woman and the serpent (for in every place in that chapter where the writer speaks, it is always the Lord God) shews this chapter to belong to the second cosmogony.

This chapter gives an account of what is called the *fall of Man*, which is no other than a fable borrowed from, and constructed upon, the religious allegory of Zoroaster, or the Persians, of the annual progress of the sun through the twelve signs of the Zodiac. It is the *fall of the year*, the approach and *evil* of winter, announced by the ascension of the autumnal constellation of the *serpent* of the Zodiac, and not the moral *fall of man*, that is the key of the allegory, and of the fable in Genesis borrowed from it.

The Fall of Man in Genesis is said to have been produced by eating a certain fruit, generally taken to be an apple. The fall of the year is the season for the gathering and eating the new apples of that year. The allegory, therefore, holds with respect to the fruit, which it would not have done had it been an early summer fruit. It holds also with respect to place. The tree is said to have been placed in the *midst* of the garden. But why in the midst of the garden more than in any other place? The solution of the allegory gives the answer to this question, which is, that the fall of the year, when apples and other autumnal fruits are ripe, and when days and nights are of equal length, is the mid-season between summer and winter.

It holds also with respect to cloathing, and the temperature of the air. It is said in Genesis (iii. 21), "*Unto Adam and his wife did the Lord God make coats of skins, and cloathed them.*" But why are coats of skins mentioned? This cannot be understood as referring to anything of the nature of *moral evil*. The solution of the allegory gives again the answer to this question, which is, that the *evil of winter*, which follows the *fall of the year*, fabulously called in Genesis the *fall of man*, makes warm cloathing necessary.

But of these things I shall speak fully when I come in another part to treat of the ancient religion of the Persians, and compare it with the modern religion of the New Testament.[1] At present, I shall confine myself to the comparative

---

[1] See editorial note prefixed to these fragments. The views of Paine as to the Persian origin of the story in Genesis are those of many learned critics, among others Rosenmüller and Von Bohlen; while Julius Müller insists that

antiquity of the books of Genesis and Job, taking, at the same time, whatever I may find in my way with respect to the fabulousness of the book of Genesis ; for if what is called the Fall of Man, in Genesis, be fabulous or allegorical, that which is called the redemption in the New Testament cannot be a fact. It is logically impossible, and impossible also in the nature of things, that *moral good* can redeem *physical evil.* I return to the bishop.

If Genesis be, as the bishop asserts, the oldest book in the world, and, consequently, the oldest and first written book of the bible, and if the extraordinary things related in it ; such as the creation of the world in six days, the tree of life, and of good and evil, the story of Eve and the talking serpent, the fall of man and his being turned out of Paradise, were facts, or even believed by the Jews to be facts, they would be referred to as fundamental matters, and that very frequently, in the books of the bible that were written by various authors afterwards ; whereas, there is not a book, chapter, or verse of the bible, from the time that Moses is said to have written the book of Genesis, to the book of Malachi, the last book in the Bible, including a space of more than a thousand years, in which there is any mention made of these things, or any of them, nor are they so much as alluded to. How will the bishop solve this difficulty, which stands as a circumstantial contradiction to his assertion ?

There are but two ways of solving it :

First, that the book of Genesis is not an ancient book, that it has been written by some (now) unknown person, after the return of the Jews from the Babylonian captivity, about a thousand years after the time that Moses is said to have lived, and put as a preface or introduction to the other books when they were formed into a canon in the time of the second temple, and therefore not having existed before that time, none of these things mentioned in it could be referred to in those books.

not sin but physical suffering is connected with the Fall in the narrative. (*Doctrine of Sin*, Edinb., p. 78.) For the Eastern and Oriental legends see my *Demonology and Devil-Lore*, ii., pp. 68-104.—*Editor.*

Secondly, that admitting Genesis to have been written by Moses, the Jews did not believe the things stated in it to be true, and therefore, as they could not refer to them as facts, they would not refer to them as fables. The first of these solutions goes against the antiquity of the book, and the second against its authenticity; and the bishop may take which he please.

But be the author of Genesis whoever it may, there is abundant evidence to shew, as well from the early christian writers as from the Jews themselves, that the things stated in that book were not believed to be facts. Why they have been believed as facts since that time, when better and fuller knowledge existed on the case than is known now, can be accounted for only on the imposition of priest-craft.

Augustine, one of the early champions of the christian church, acknowledges in his *City of God* that the adventure of Eve and the serpent, and the account of Paradise, were generally considered as fiction or allegory. He regards them as allegory himself, without attempting to give any explanation, but he supposes that a better explanation might be found than those that had been offered.

Origen, another early champion of the church, says, " What man of good sense can ever persuade himself that there were a first, a second, and a third day, and that each of these days had a night when there were yet neither sun, moon, nor stars ? What man can be stupid enough to believe that God, acting the part of a gardener, had planted a garden in the east, that the tree of life was a real tree, and that its fruit had the virtue of making those who eat of it live for ever ? "

Maimonides, one of the most learned and celebrated of the Jewish Rabbins, who lived in the eleventh century (about seven or eight hundred years ago) and to whom the bishop refers in his answer to me, is very explicit in his book entitled *Moreh Nebuchim*, upon the non-reality of the things stated in the account of the Creation in the book of Genesis.

" We ought not (says he) to understand, nor take according to the letter, that which is written in the book of the creation, nor to have the same ideas of it which common men have ; otherwise our ancient sages would not have recommended with so much care to conceal the sense of it, and not to raise the allegorical veil which envelopes the truths it contains. The book of Genesis, taken according to the letter, gives the most absurd and the most extravagant ideas of the divinity. Whoever shall find out the sense of it, ought to restrain himself from divulging it. It is a maxim which all our sages repeat, and above all with respect to the work of six days. It may happen that some one, with the aid he may borrow from others, may hit upon the meaning of it. In that case he ought to impose silence upon himself ; or if he speak of it, he ought to speak obscurely, and in an enigmatical manner, as I do myself, leaving the rest to be found out by those who can understand me."

This is, certainly, a very extraordinary declaration of Maimonides taking all the parts of it. First, he declares, that the account of the Creation in the book of Genesis is not a fact, and that to believe it to be a fact gives the most absurd and the most extravagant ideas of the divinity. Secondly, that it is an allegory. Thirdly, that the allegory has a concealed secret. Fourthly, that whoever can find the secret ought not to tell it.

It is this last part that is the most extraordinary. Why all this care of the Jewish Rabbins, to prevent what they call the concealed meaning, or the secret, from being known, and if known to prevent any of their people from telling it? It certainly must be something which the Jewish nation are afraid or ashamed the world should know. It must be something personal to them as a people, and not a secret of a divine nature, which the more it is known the more it increases the glory of the creator, and the gratitude and happiness of man. It is not God's secret but their own they are keeping. I go to unveil the secret.

The case is, the Jews have stolen their cosmogony, that is, their account of the creation, from the cosmogony of the Persians, contained in the books of Zoroaster, the Persian law-giver, and brought it with them when they returned from captivity by the benevolence of Cyrus, king of Persia. For it is evident, from the silence of all the books of the bible upon the subject of the creation, that the Jews had no cosmogony before that time. If they had a cosmogony from the time of Moses, some of their judges who governed during more than four hundred years, or of their kings, the Davids and Solomons of their day, who governed nearly five hundred years, or of their prophets and psalmists, who lived in the mean time, would have mentioned it. It would, either as fact or fable, have been the grandest of all subjects for a psalm. It would have suited to a tittle the ranting poetical genius of Isaiah, or served as a cordial to the gloomy Jeremiah. But not one word, not even a whisper, does any of the bible authors give upon the subject.

To conceal the theft, the Rabbins of the second temple have published Genesis as a book of Moses, and have enjoined secresy to all their people, who by travelling or otherwise might happen to discover from whence the cosmogony was borrowed, not to tell it. The evidence of circumstances is often unanswerable, and there is no other than this which I have given that goes to the whole of the case, and this does.

Diogenes Laertius, an ancient and respectable author, whom the bishop in his answer to me quotes on another occasion, has a passage that corresponds with the solution here given. In speaking of the religion of the Persians as promulgated by their priests or magi, he says the Jewish Rabbins were the successors of their doctrine. Having thus spoken on the plagiarism, and on the non-reality of the book of Genesis, I will give some additional evidence that Moses is not the author of that book.

Aben-Ezra, a celebrated Jewish author, who lived about seven hundred years ago, and whom the bishop allows to have been a man of great erudition, has made a great many observations, too numerous to be repeated here, to shew that Moses was not, and could not be, the author of the book of Genesis, nor of any of the five books that bear his name.

Spinoza, another learned Jew, who lived about a hundred and thirty years ago, recites, in his treatise on the ceremonies of the Jews, ancient and modern, the observations of Aben-Ezra, to which he adds many others, to shew that Moses is not the author of those books. He also says, and shews his reasons for saying it, that the bible did not exist as a book till the time of the Maccabees, which was more than a hundred years after the return of the Jews from the Babylonian captivity.

In the second part of the Age of Reason, I have, among other things, referred to nine verses in Genesis xxxvi. beginning at ver. 31, (These are the kings that reigned in Edom, before there reigned any king over the children of Israel,) which it is impossible could have been written by Moses, or in the time of Moses, and which could not have been written till after the Jew kings began to reign in Israel, which was not till several hundred years after the time of Moses.

The bishop allows this, and says "I think you say true." But he then quibbles, and says, that "a small addition to a book does not destroy either the genuineness or authenticity of the whole book." This is priestcraft. These verses do not stand in the book as an addition to it, but as making a part of the whole book, and which it is impossible that Moses could write. The bishop would reject the antiquity of any other book if it could be proved from the words of the book itself that a part of it could not have been written till several hundred years after the reputed author of it was dead. He would call such a book a forgery. I am authorised, therefore, to call the book of Genesis a forgery.

Combining, then, all the foregoing circumstances together, respecting the antiquity and authenticity of the book of Genesis, a conclusion will naturally follow therefrom. Those circumstances are—

First, that certain parts of the book cannot possibly have been written by Moses, and that the other parts carry no evidence of having been written by him.

Secondly, the universal silence of all the following books

of the bible, for about a thousand years, upon the extraordinary things spoken of in Genesis, such as the creation of the world in six days—the garden of Eden—the tree of knowledge—the tree of life—the story of Eve and the Serpent—the fall of man and of his being turned out of this fine garden, together with Noah's flood, and the tower of Babel.

Thirdly, the silence of all the books of the bible upon even the name of Moses, from the book of Joshua until the second book of Kings, which was not written till after the captivity, for it gives an account of the captivity, a period of about a thousand years. Strange that a man who is proclaimed as the historian of the creation, the privy-counsellor and confidant of the Almighty—the legislator of the Jewish nation and the founder of its religion ; strange, I say, that even the name of such a man should not find a place in their books for a thousand years, if they knew or believed any thing about him or the books he is said to have written.

Fourthly, the opinion of some of the most celebrated of the Jewish commentators that Moses is not the author of the book of Genesis, founded on the reasons given for that opinion.

Fifthly, the opinion of the early christian writers, and of the great champion of Jewish literature, Maimonides, that the book of Genesis is not a book of facts.

Sixthly, the silence imposed by all the Jewish Rabbins, and by Maimonides himself, upon the Jewish nation, not to speak of any thing they may happen to know or discover respecting the cosmogony (or creation of the world) in the book of Genesis.

From these circumstances the following conclusions offer :

First, that the book of Genesis is not a book of facts.

Secondly, that as no mention is made throughout the bible of any of the extraordinary things related in [it], Genesis has not been written till after the other books were written, and put as a preface to the Bible. Every one knows that a preface to a book, though it stands first, is the last written.

Thirdly, that the silence imposed by all the Jewish Rabbins and by Maimonides upon the Jewish nation, to keep silence upon every thing related in their cosmogony, evinces a secret they are not willing should be known. The secret therefore explains itself to be, that when the Jews were in captivity in Babylon and Persia they became acquainted with the cosmogony of the Persians, as registered in the Zend-Avesta of Zoroaster, the Persian law-giver, which, after their return from captivity, they manufactured and modelled as their own, and ante-dated it by giving to it the name of Moses. The case admits of no other explanation.

From all which it appears that the book of Genesis, instead of being the *oldest book in the world*, as the bishop calls it, has been the last written book of the bible, and that the cosmogony it contains has been manufactured.

OF THE NAMES IN THE BOOK OF GENESIS. Every thing in Genesis serves as evidence or symptom that the book has been composed in some late period of the Jewish nation. Even the names mentioned in it serve to this purpose.

Nothing is more common or more natural than to name the children of succeeding generations after the names of those who had been celebrated in some former generation. This holds good with respect to all the people and all the histories we know of, and it does not hold good with the bible. There must be some cause for this.

This book of Genesis tells us of a man whom it calls Adam, and of his sons Abel and Seth; of Enoch, who lived 365 years (it is exactly the number of days in a year,) and that then God took him up. (It has the appearance of being taken from some allegory of the Gentiles on the commencement and termination of the year, by the progress of the sun through the twelve signs of the Zodiac, on which the allegorical religion of the Gentiles was founded.) It tells us of Methuselah who lived 969 years, and of a long train of other names in the fifth chapter. It then passes on to a man whom it calls Noah, and his sons, Shem, Ham, and Japhet; then to Lot, Abraham, Isaac, and Jacob and his sons, with which the book of Genesis finishes.

All these, according to the account given in that book, were the most extraordinary and celebrated of men. They were moreover heads of families. Adam was the father of the world. Enoch, for his righteousness, was taken up to heaven. Methuselah lived to almost a thousand years. He was the son of Enoch, the man of 365, the number of days in a year. It has the appearance of being the continuation of an allegory on the 365 days of the year, and its abundant productions. Noah was selected from all the world to be preserved when it was drowned, and became the second father of the world. Abraham was the father of the faithful multitude. Isaac and Jacob were the inheritors of his fame, and the last was the father of the twelve tribes.

Now, if these very wonderful men and their names, and the book that records them, had been known by the Jews before the Babylonian captivity, those names would have been as common among the Jews before that period as they have been since. We now hear of thousands of Abrahams, Isaacs, and Jacobs among the Jews, but there were none of that name before the Babylonian captivity. The Bible does not mention one, though from the time that Abraham is said to have lived to the time of the Babylonian captivity is about 1400 years.

How is it to be accounted for, that there have been so many thousands, and perhaps hundreds of thousands of Jews of the names of Abraham, Isaac, and Jacob since that period, and not one before? It can be accounted for but one way, which is, that before the Babylonian captivity the Jews had no such book as Genesis, nor knew any thing of the names and persons it mentions, nor of the things it relates, and that the stories in it have been manufactured since that time. From the Arabic name *Ibrahim* (which is the manner the Turks write that name to this day) the Jews have, most probably, manufactured their Abraham.

I will advance my observations a point further, and speak of the names of *Moses* and *Aaron*, mentioned for the first time in the book of Exodus. There are now, and have continued to be from the time of the Babylonian captivity, or soon after it, thousands of Jews of the names of *Moses* and *Aaron*, and we read not of any of that name before that time. The Bible does not mention one. The direct inference from this is, that the Jews knew of no such book as Exodus before the Babylonian captivity. In fact, that it did not exist before that time, and that it is only since the book has been invented that the names of *Moses* and *Aaron* have been common among the Jews.

It is applicable to the purpose to observe, that the picturesque work, called *Mosaic-work*, spelled the same as you would say the *Mosaic* account of the creation, is not derived from the word *Moses* but from *Muses*, (the *Muses*,) because of the variegated and picturesque pavement in the temples dedicated to the *Muses*. This carries a strong implication that the name *Moses* is drawn from the same source, and that he is not a real but an allegorical person, as Maimonides describes what is called the *Mosaic* account of the Creation to be.

I will go a point still further. The Jews now know the book of Genesis, and the names of all the persons mentioned in the first *ten chapters* of that book, from Adam to Noah: yet we do not hear (I speak for myself) of any *Jew* of the present day, of the name of Adam, Abel, Seth, Enoch, Methuselah, Noah, Shem, Ham, or Japhet, (names mentioned in the first ten chapters,) though these were, according to the account in that book, the most extraordinary of all the names that make up the catalogue of the Jewish chronology. The names the Jews now adopt, are those that are mentioned in Genesis after the tenth chapter, as Abraham, Isaac, Jacob, etc. How then does it happen that they do not adopt the names found in the first ten chapters? Here is evidently a line of division drawn between the first ten chapters of Genesis and the remaining chapters, with respect to the adoption of names. There must be some cause for this, and I go to offer a solution of the problem.

The reader will recollect the quotation I have already made from the Jewish Rabbin, Maimonides, wherein he says, " We ought not to understand nor to take according

to the letter that which is written in the book of the Creation. . . . It is a maxim (says he) which all our sages repeat,
above all with respect to the work of six days." The quali-
fying expression *above all,* implies there are other parts of
the book, though not so important, that ought not to be
understood or taken according to the letter, and as the Jews
do not adopt the names mentioned in the first ten chapters,
it appears evident those chapters are included in the injunction not to take them in a literal sense, or according to the
letter: From which it follows, that the persons or characters
mentioned in the first ten chapters, as Adam, Abel, Seth,
Enoch, Methuselah, and so on to Noah, are not real, but
fictitious or allegorical persons, and therefore the Jews do
not adopt their names into their families. If they affixed
the same idea of reality to them as they do to those that
follow after the tenth chapter, the names of Adam, Abel,
Seth, etc., would be as common among the Jews of the
present day as are those of Abraham, Isaac, Jacob, Moses,
and Aaron. In the superstition they have been in, scarcely
a Jew family would have been without an *Enoch,* as a pre-
sage of his going to Heaven as ambassador for the whole
family. Every mother who wished that the *days* of her son
might be long in the land would call him *Methuselah ;* and all
the Jews that might have to traverse the ocean would be
named Noah, as a charm against shipwreck and drowning.

This is domestic evidence against the book of Genesis,
which, joined to the several kinds of evidence before recited,
shew the book of Genesis not to be older than the Babylonian captivity, and to be fictitious. I proceed to fix the
character and antiquity of the book of

JOB. The book of Job has not the least appearance of
being a book of the Jews, and though printed among the
books of the bible, does not belong to it. There is no reference to it in any Jewish law or ceremony. On the contrary, all the internal evidence it contains shews it to be a
book of the Gentiles, either of Persia or Chaldea.

The name of Job does not appear to be a Jewish name.

There is no Jew of that name in any of the books of the bible, neither is there now that I ever heard of. The country where Job is said or supposed to have lived, or rather where the scene of the drama is laid, is called Uz, and there was no place of that name ever belonging to the Jews.[1] If Uz is the same as Ur, it was in Chaldea, the country of the Gentiles.

The Jews can give no account how they came by this book, nor who was the author, nor the time when it was written. Origen, in his work against Celsus, (in the first ages of the Christian church,) says that *the book of Job is older than Moses.* Aben-Ezra, the Jewish commentator, whom (as I have before said) the bishop allows to have been a man of great erudition, and who certainly understood his own language, says that the book of Job has been translated from another language into Hebrew. Spinoza, another Jewish commentator of great learning, confirms the opinion of Aben-Ezra, and says moreover, " *Je crois que Job était Gentil* ;* ' I believe that Job was a Gentile.'

The bishop, (in his answer to me,) says, that " the structure of the whole book of Job, in whatever light of history or drama it be considered, is founded on the belief that prevailed with the Persians and Chaldeans, and other Gentile nations, of a good and an evil spirit." In speaking of the good and evil spirit of the Persians, the bishop writes them *Arimanius* and *Oromasdes.* I will not dispute about the orthography, because I know that translated names are differently spelled in different languages. But he has nevertheless made a capital error. He has put the Devil first ; for Arimanius, or, as it is more generally written, *Ahriman*, is the *evil spirit*, and *Oromasdes* or *Ormusd* the good spirit. He has made the same mistake in the same paragraph, in speaking of the good and evil spirit of the ancient Egyptians, *Osiris* and

---

[1] The land of Uz is mentioned in Jeremiah xxv. 20, and Lamentations iv. 21 ; in both cases the indications are that it was a region of the Gentiles. Biblical geographers generally locate Uz in *Arabia Petræa.—Editor.*

* Spinoza on the Ceremonies of the Jews, p. 296, published in French at Amsterdam 1678.—*Author.*

Typho; he puts Typho before Osiris. The error is just the
same as if the bishop in writing about the christian religion,
or in preaching a sermon, were to say the *Devil* and *God.* A
priest ought to know his own trade better. We agree, however, about the structure of the book of Job, that it is Gentile. I have said in the second part of the Age of Reason,
and given my reasons for it, that *the Drama of it is not
Hebrew.*

From the Testimonies I have cited, that of Origen, who,
about fourteen hundred years ago said that the book of Job
was more ancient than Moses, that of Aben-Ezra who, in
his commentary on Job, says it has been translated from
another language (and consequently from a Gentile language)
into Hebrew; that of Spinoza, who not only says the same
thing, but that the author of it was a Gentile; and that of
the bishop, who says that the structure of the whole book is
Gentile; it follows, in the first place, that the book of Job
is not a book of the Jews originally.

Then, in order to determine to what people or nation any
book of religion belongs, we must compare it with the leading dogmas and precepts of that people or nation; and
therefore, upon the bishop's own construction, the book of
Job belongs either to the ancient Persians, the Chaldeans, or
the Egyptians; because the structure of it is consistent
with the dogma they held, that of a good and an evil spirit,
called in Job *God* and *Satan,* existing as distinct and separate beings, and it is not consistent with any dogma of the
Jews.

The belief of a good and an evil spirit, existing as distinct and separate beings, is not a dogma to be found in any
of the books of the bible. It is not till we come to the New
Testament that we hear of any such dogma. There the
person called the Son of God, holds conversation with Satan
on a mountain, as familiarly as is represented in the drama
of Job. Consequently the bishop cannot say, in this respect,
that the New-Testament is founded upon the Old. According to the Old, the God of the Jews was the God of every
thing. All good and evil came from him. According to

Exodus it was God, and not the Devil, that hardened Pha-
roah's heart. According to the book of Samuel, it was
an evil spirit from *God* that troubled Saul. And Ezekiel
makes God to say, in speaking of the Jews, " *I gave them the
statutes that were not good, and judgments by which they
should not live.*" The bible describes the God of Abraham,
Isaac, and Jacob in such a contradictory manner, and under
such a twofold character, there would be no knowing when
he was in earnest and when in irony ; when to believe, and
when not.

As to the precepts, principles, and maxims in the book of
Job, they shew that the people abusively called the heathen,
in the books of the Jews, had the most sublime ideas of
the creator, and the most exalted devotional morality. It
was the Jews who dishonoured God. It was the Gentiles
who glorified him. As to the fabulous personifications introduced by the Greek and Latin poets, it was a corruption of
the ancient religion of the Gentiles, which consisted in the
adoration of a first cause of the works of the creation, in
which the sun was the great visible agent. It appears to
have been a religion of gratitude and adoration, and not of
prayer and discontented solicitation. In Job we find adoration and submission, but not prayer. Even the Ten Commandments enjoin not prayer. Prayer has been added to
devotion by the church of Rome, as the instrument of fees
and perquisites. All prayers by the priests of the christian
Church, whether public or private, must be paid for. It
may be right, individually, to pray for virtues, or mental
instruction, but not for things.[1] It is an attempt to dictate
to the Almighty in the government of the world.—But to
return to the book of Job.

As the book of Job decides itself to be a book of the
Gentiles, the next thing is to find out to what particular
nation it belongs, and lastly, what is its antiquity.

[1] On the other hand some devout reasoners, among them Cicero, have maintained that men may pray for physical benefits which they cannot obtain by
work, but not for virtue which depends on the man himself, and is within the
reach of everyone.—*Editor.*

As a composition, it is sublime, beautiful, and scientific: full of sentiment, and abounding in grand metaphorical description. As a Drama it is regular. The Dramatis Personæ, the persons performing the several parts, are regularly introduced, and speak without interruption or confusion. The scene, as I have before said, is laid in the country of the Gentiles, and the unities, though not always necessary in a drama, are observed here as strictly as the subject would admit.

In the last act, where the Almighty is introduced as speaking from the whirlwind, to decide the controversy between Job and his friends, it is an idea as grand as poetical imagination can conceive. What follows of Job's future prosperity does not belong to it as a drama. It is an epilogue of the writer, as the first verses of the first chapter, which gave an account of Job, his country and his riches, are the prologue.

The book carries the appearance of being the work of some of the Persian Magi, not only because the structure of it corresponds to the dogma of the religion of those people, as founded by Zoroaster, but from the astronomical references in it to the constellations of the Zodiac and other objects in the heavens, of which the sun, in their religion called Mithra, was the chief. Job, in describing the power of God, (ix. 7–9,) says, " Who commandeth the sun, and it riseth not; and sealeth up the stars. Who alone spreadeth out the heavens, and treadeth upon the waves of the sea. Who maketh Arcturus, Orion, and Pleiades, and the chambers of the south." All this astronomical allusion is consistent with the religion of the Persians.

Establishing then the book of Job as the work of some of the Persian or Eastern Magi, the case naturally follows that when the Jews returned from captivity, by the permission of Cyrus king of Persia, they brought this book with them, had it translated into Hebrew, and put into their scriptural canons, which were not formed till after their return. This will account for the name of Job being mentioned in Ezekiel, (xiv. 14,) who was one of the captives, and also for its not being mentioned in any book said or supposed to have been written before the captivity.

Among the astronomical allusions in the book, there is one which serves to fix its antiquity. It is that where God is made to say to Job, in the style of reprimand, " *Canst thou bind the sweet influences of Pleiades.*" (xxxviii. 31.) As the explanation of this depends upon astronomical calculation, I will, for the sake of those who would not otherwise understand it, endeavour to explain it as clearly as the subject will admit.

The Pleiades are a cluster of pale, milky stars, about the size of a man's hand, in the constellation Taurus, or in English, the Bull. It is one of the constellations of the Zodiac, of which there are twelve, answering to the twelve months of the year. The Pleiades are visible in the winter nights, but not in the summer nights, being then below the horizon.

The Zodiac is an imaginary belt or circle in the heavens, eighteen degrees broad, in which the sun apparently makes his annual course, and in which all the planets move. When the sun appears to our view to be between us and the group of stars forming such or such a constellation, he is said to be in that constellation. Consequently the constellations he appears to be in, in the summer, are directly opposite to those he appeared in in the winter, and the same with respect to spring and autumn.

The Zodiac, besides being divided into twelve constellations, is also, like every other circle, great or small, divided into 360 equal parts, called degrees ; consequently each constellation contains 30 degrees. The constellations of the Zodiac are generally called signs, to distinguish them from the constellations that are placed out of the Zodiac, and this is the name I shall now use.

The procession of the Equinoxes is the part most difficult to explain, and it is on this that the explanation chiefly depends.

The Equinoxes correspond to the two seasons of the year when the sun makes equal day and night. [1]

[1] The fragments published by Mrs. Palmer in the *Theophilanthropist*, 1810,

SABBATH, OR SUNDAY.—The seventh day, or more properly speaking the period of seven days, was originally a numerical division of time and nothing more ; and had the bishop been acquainted with the history of astronomy, he would have known this. The annual revolution of the earth makes what we call a year. The year is artificially divided into months, the months into weeks of seven days, the days into hours, etc. The period of seven days, like any other of the artificial divisions of the year, is only a fractional part thereof, contrived for the convenience of countries. It is ignorance, imposition, and priest-craft, that have called it otherwise. They might as well talk of the Lord's month, of the Lord's week, of the Lord's hour, as of the Lord's day. All time is his, and no part of it is more holy or more sacred than another. It is, however, necessary to the trade of a priest, that he should preach up a distinction of days.

Before the science of astronomy was studied and carried to the degree of eminence to which it was by the Egyptians and Chaldeans, the people of those times had no other helps than what common observation of the very visible changes of the sun and moon afforded, to enable them to keep an account of the progress of time. As far as history establishes the point, the Egyptians were the first people who divided the year into twelve months. Herodotus, who lived above two thousand two hundred years ago, and is the most ancient historian whose works have reached our time, says, *they did this by the knowledge they had of the stars.* As to the Jews, there is not one single improvement in any science or in any scientific art that they ever produced. They were the most ignorant of all the illiterate world. If the word of the Lord had come to them, as they pretend, and as the bishop professes to believe, and that they were to be the harbingers of it to the rest of the world, the Lord would

end here, the editor adding : " We are sorry to say that it is somewhat doubtful whether the entire work will ever meet the public eye." The fragments that follow are those sold with many erasures by Madame Bonneville to an American editor, who recovered as much as he could, and printed them in 1824.— *Editor.*

have taught them the use of letters, and the art of printing; for without the means of communicating the word, it could not be communicated; whereas letters were the invention of the Gentile world, and printing of the modern world. But to return to my subject—

Before the helps which the science of astronomy afforded, the people, as before said, had no other whereby to keep an account of the progress of time, than what the common and very visible changes of the sun and moon afforded. They saw that a great number of days made a year, but the account of them was too tedious and too difficult to be kept numerically, from one to three hundred and sixty-five; neither did they know the true time of a solar year. It therefore became necessary, for the purpose of marking the progress of days, to put them into small parcels, such as are now called weeks; and which consisted as they now do of seven days. By this means the memory was assisted as it is with us at this day; for we do not say of any thing that is past, that it was fifty, sixty, or seventy days ago, but that it was so many weeks, or, if longer time, so many months. It is impossible to keep an account of time without helps of this kind.

Julian Scaliger, the inventer of the Julian period of 7,980 years, produced by multiplying the cycle of the moon, the cycle of the sun, and the years of an indiction, 19, 28, 15, into each other, says that the custom of reckoning by periods of seven days was used by the Assyrians, the Epyptians, the Hebrews, the people of India, the Arabs, and by all the nations of the east. In addition to what Scaliger says, it is evident that in Britain, in Germany, and the north of Europe, they reckoned by periods of seven days long before the book called the bible was known in those parts; and, consequently, that they did not take that mode of reckoning from any thing written in that book. That they reckoned by periods of seven days is evident from their having seven names and no more for the several days; and which have not the most distant relation to any thing in the book of Genesis, or to that which is called the fourth commandment.

Those names are still retained in England, with no other alteration than what has been produced by moulding the Saxon and Danish languages into modern English:

1. Sun-day from *Sunne* the sun, and *dag*, day, Saxon. *Sondag*, Danish. The day dedicated to the sun.

2. Monday, that is, moonday, from *Mona*, the moon Saxon. *Moano*, Danish. Day dedicated to the moon.

3. Tuesday, that is *Tuisco's-day*. The day dedicated to the Idol *Tuisco*.

4. Wednes-day, that is Woden's-day. The day dedicated to *Woden*, the Mars of the Germans.

5. Thursday, that is Thor's-day, dedicated to the Idol *Thor*.

6. Friday, that is *Friga's-day*. The day dedicated to *Friga*, the Venus of the Saxons.

7. Saturday from *Seaten* (*Saturn*) an Idol of the Saxons; one of the emblems representing time, which continually terminates and renews itself; the last day of the period of seven days.

When we see a certain mode of reckoning general among nations totally unconnected, differing from each other in religion and in government, and some of them unknown to each other, we may be certain that it arises from some natural and common cause, prevailing alike over all, and which strikes every one in the same manner. Thus all nations have reckoned arithmetically by tens, because the people of all nations have ten fingers. If they had more or less than ten, the mode of arithmetical reckoning would have followed that number, for the fingers are a natural numeration table to all the world. I now come to shew why the period of seven days is so generally adopted.

Though the sun is the great luminary of the world, and the animating cause of all the fruits of the earth, the moon by renewing herself more than twelve times oftener than the sun, which does it but once a year, served the rustic world as a natural Almanac, as the fingers served it for a numeration table. All the world could see the moon, her changes, and her monthly revolutions; and their mode of reckoning time was accommodated, as nearly as could possibly be done in round numbers, to agree with the changes of that planet, their natural Almanac. The moon performs her natural revolution round the earth in twenty-nine days and a half. She goes from a new moon to a half moon, to a full moon, to a half moon gibbous or convex, and then to a new moon again. Each of these changes is performed in seven days and nine hours ; but seven days is the nearest division in round numbers that could be taken ; and this was sufficient to suggest the universal custom of reckoning by periods of seven days, since it is impossible to reckon time without some stated period.

How the odd hours could be disposed of without interfering with the regular periods of seven days, in case the ancients recommenced a new Septenary period with every new moon, required no more difficulty than it did to regulate the Egyptian Calendar afterwards of twelve months of thirty days each, or the odd hour in the Julian Calendar, or the odd days and hours in the French Calendar. In all cases it is done by the addition of complementary days; and it can be done in no otherwise.

The bishop knows that as the solar year does not end at the termination of what we call a day, but runs some hours into the next day, as the quarter of the Moon runs some hours beyond seven days ; that it is impossible to give the year any fixed number of days that will not in course of years become wrong, and make a complementary time necessary to keep the nominal year parallel with the solar year. The same must have been the case with those who regulated time formerly by lunar revolutions. They would have to add three days to every second moon, or in that proportion, in order to make the new moon and the new week commence together, like the nominal year and the solar year.

Diodorus of Sicily, who, as before said, lived before Christ was born, in giving an account of times much anterior to his own, speaks of years of three months, of four months, and of six months. These could be of no other than years composed of lunar revolutions, and therefore, to bring the several periods of seven days to agree with such years, there must have been complementary days.

The moon was the first Almanac the world knew; and the only one which the face of the heavens afforded to common spectators. Her changes and her revolutions have entered into all the Calendars that have been known in the known world.

The division of the year into twelve months, which, as before shewn, was first done by the Egyptians, though arranged with astronomical knowledge, had reference to the twelve moons, or more properly speaking to the twelve lunar revolutions, that appear in the space of a solar year; as the period of seven days had reference to one revolution of the moon. The feasts of the Jews were, and those of the Christian church still are, regulated by the moon. The Jews observed the feasts of the new moon and full moon, and therefore the period of seven days was necessary to them.

All the feasts of the Christian church are regulated by the moon. That called Easter governs all the rest, and the moon governs Easter. It is always the first Sunday after the first full moon that happens after the vernal Equinox, or 21st of March.

In proportion as the science of astronomy was studied and improved by the Egyptians and Chaldeans, and the solar year regulated by astronomical observations, the custom of reckoning by lunar revolutions became of less use, and in time discontinued. But such is the harmony of all parts of the machinery of the universe, that a calculation made from the motion of one part will correspond with the motion of some other.

The period of seven days, deduced from the revolution of the moon round the earth, corresponded nearer than any other period of days would do to the revolution of the earth round the sun. Fifty-two periods of seven days make 364, which is within one day and some odd hours of a solar year; and there is no other periodical number that will do the same, till we come to the number thirteen, which is too great for common use, and the numbers before seven are too small. The custom therefore of reckoning by periods of seven days, as best suited to the revolution of the moon, applied with equal convenience to the solar year, and became united with it. But the decimal division of time, as regulated by the French Calendar, is superior to every other method.[1]

There is no part of the Bible that is supposed to have been written by persons who lived before the time of Josiah, (which was a thousand years after the time of Moses,) that mentions any thing about the sabbath as a day consecrated to that which is called the fourth commandment, or that the Jews kept any such day. Had any such day been kept, during the thousand years of which I am speaking, it certainly would have been mentioned frequently; and that it should never be mentioned is strong presumptive and circumstantial evidence that no such day was kept. But mention is often made of the feasts of the new-moon, and of the full-moon; for the Jews, as before shewn, worshipped the moon; and the word *Sabbath* was applied by the Jews to the feasts of that planet, and to those of their other deities. It is said in Hosea ii. 11, in speaking of the Jewish nation, " And I will cause all her mirth to cease, her feast-days, her *new-moons*, and her *sabbaths*, and all her solemn feasts." Nobody will be so foolish as to contend that the *sabbaths* here spoken of are Mosaic Sabbaths. The construction of the verse implies they are lunar sabbaths, or sabbaths of the moon. It ought also to be observed that Hosea lived in the time of Ahaz and Hezekiah, about seventy years before the time of Josiah, when the law called the law of Moses is said to have been found; and, consequently, the sabbaths that Hosea speaks of are sabbaths of the Idolatry.

When those priestly reformers, (impostors I should call them,) Hilkiah, Ezra, and Nehemiah, began to produce

---

[1] This division of time was adopted by the National Convention, in 1793. The year was divided into 12 months of 30 days each, with 5 extra days (six every fourth year) which were festivals. The months were divided by decades, and the days into 10 hours of 100 minutes each.—*Editor.*

books under the name of the books of Moses, they found the word *sabbath* in use: and as to the period of seven days, it is, like numbering arithmetically by tens, from time immemorial. But having found them in use, they continued to make them serve to the support of their new imposition. They trumped up a story of the creation being made in six days, and of the Creator resting on the seventh, to suit with the lunar and chronological period of seven days; and they manufactured a commandment to agree with both. Impostors always work in this manner. They put fables for originals, and causes for effects.

There is scarcely any part of science, or any thing in nature, which those impostors and blasphemers of science, called priests, as well Christians as Jews, have not, at some time or other, perverted, or sought to pervert to the purpose of superstition and falsehood. Every thing wonderful in appearance, has been ascribed to angels, to devils, or to saints. Every thing ancient has some legendary tale annexed to it. The common operations of nature have not escaped their practice of corrupting every thing.

FUTURE STATE. The idea of a future state was an universal idea to all nations except the Jews. At the time, and long before, Jesus Christ and the men called his disciples were born, it had been sublimely treated of by Cicero (in his book on Old Age,) by Plato, Socrates, Xenophon, and other of the ancient theologists, whom the abusive Christian Church calls heathen. Xenophon represents the elder Cyrus speaking after this manner:

" Think not, my dearest children, that when I depart from you, I shall be no more : but remember that my soul, even while I lived among you, was invisible to you ; yet by my actions you were sensible it existed in this body. Believe it therefore existing still, though it be still unseen. How quickly would the honours of illustrious men perish after death, if their souls performed nothing to preserve their fame ? For my own part, I could never think that the soul while in a mortal body lives, but when departed from it dies ; or that its consciousness is lost when it is discharged out of an unconscious habitation. But when it is freed from all corporeal alliance, it is then that it truly exists."

Since then the idea of a future existence was universal, it may be asked, what new doctrine does the New Testament contain ? I answer, that of corrupting the theory of the ancient theologists, by annexing to it the heavy and gloomy doctrine of the resurrection of the body.

As to the resurrection of the body, whether the same body or another, it is a miserable conceit, fit only to be preached to man as an animal. It is not worthy to be called doctrine. Such an idea never entered the brain of any visionary but those of the Christian church; yet it is in this that the novelty of the New Testament consists! All the other matters serve but as props to this, and those props are most wretchedly put together.

MIRACLES. The Christian church is full of miracles. In one of the churches of Brabant they shew a number of cannon balls which, they say, the Virgin Mary, in some former war, caught in her muslin *apron* as they came roaring out of the cannon's mouth, to prevent their hurting the *saints* of her favourite army. She does no such feats now-a-days. Perhaps the reason is, that the infidels have taken away her muslin apron. They show also, between Montmartre and the village of St. Denis, several places where they say St. Denis stopt with his head in his hands after it had been cut off at Montmartre. The Protestants will call those things lies ; and where is the proof that all the other things called miracles are not as great lies as those ?

CABALISM. Christ, say those Cabalists, came in the *fulness of time*. And pray what is the fulness of time ? The words admit of no idea. They are perfectly Cabalistical. Time is a word invented to describe to our conception a greater or less portion of eternity. It may be a minute, a portion of eternity measured by the vibration of a pendulum of a certain length ; it may be a day, a year, a hundred, or a thousand years, or any other quantity. Those portions are only greater or less comparatively.

The word ' fulness ' applies not to any of them. The idea of fulness of time cannot be conceived. A woman with child and ready for delivery, as Mary was when Christ was born, may be said to have gone her full time ; but it is the woman that is full, not time.

It may also be said figuratively, in certain cases, that the times are full of events ; but time itself is incapable of being full of itself. Ye hypocrites ! learn to speak intelligible language.

It happened to be a time of peace when they say Christ was born ; and what then ? There had been many such intervals ; and have been many such since. Time was no fuller in any of them than in the other. If he were he would be fuller now than he ever was before. If he was full then he must be bursting now. But peace or war have relation to circumstances, and not to time ; and those Cabalists would be at as much loss to make out any meaning to fulness of circumstances, as to fulness of time. And if they could, it would be fatal ; for fulness of circumstances would mean when there are no more circumstances to happen ; and fulness of time when there is no more time to follow.

Christ, therefore, like every other person, was neither in the fulness of one nor the other.

But though we cannot conceive the idea of fulness of time, because we cannot have conception of a time when there shall be no time ; nor of fulness of circumstance, because we cannot conceive a state of existence to be without circumstances ; we can often see, after a thing is past, if any circumstance necessary to give the utmost activity and success to that thing was wanting at the time that thing took place. If such a circumstance was wanting, we may be certain that the thing which took place was not a thing of God's ordaining ; whose work is always perfect, and his means perfect means. They tell us that Christ was the Son of God : in that case, he would have known every thing ;

and he came upon earth to make known the will of God to man throughout the whole earth. If this had been true, Christ would have known and would have been furnished with all the possible means of doing it; and would have instructed mankind, or at least his apostles, in the use of such of the means as they could use themselves to facilitate the accomplishment of the mission; consequently he would have instructed them in the art of printing, for the press is the tongue of the world, and without which, his or their preaching was less than a whistle compared to thunder. Since then he did not do this, he had not the means necessary to the mission; and consequently had not the mission.

They tell us in the book of Acts (ii.), a very stupid story of the Apostles' having the gift of tongues; and *cloven tongues of fire* descended and sat upon each of them. Perhaps it was this story of cloven tongues that gave rise to the notion of slitting Jackdaws' tongues to make them talk. Be that however as it may, the gift of tongues, even if it were true, would be but of little use without the art of printing. I can sit in my chamber, as I do while writing this, and by the aid of printing can send the thoughts I am writing through the greatest part of Europe, to the East Indies, and over all North America, in a few months. Jesus Christ and his apostles could not do this. They had not the means, and the want of means detects the pretended mission.

There are three modes of communication. Speaking, writing, and printing. The first is exceedingly limited. A man's voice can be heard but a few yards of distance; and his person can be but in one place. Writing is much more extensive; but the thing written cannot be multiplied but at great expense, and the multiplication will be slow and incorrect. Were there no other means of circulating what priests call the word of God (the Old and New Testament) than by writing copies, those copies could not be purchased at less than forty pounds sterling each; consequently, but few people could purchase them, while the writers could scarcely obtain a livelihood by it. But the art of printing changes all the cases, and opens a scene as vast as the world. It gives to man a sort of divine attribute. It gives to him mental omnipresence. He can be every where and at the same instant ; for wherever he is read he is mentally there.

The case applies not only against the pretended mission of Christ and his Apostles, but against every thing that priests call the Word of God, and against all those who pretend to deliver it ; for had God ever delivered any verbal word, he would have taught the means of communicating it. The one without the other is inconsistent with the wisdom we conceive of the Creator.

Genesis iii. 21 tells us that *God made coats of skin and cloathed* Adam and Eve. It was infinitely more important that man should be taught the art of printing, than that Adam should be taught to make a pair of leather breeches, or his wife a petticoat.

There is another matter, equally striking and important, that connects itself with these observations against this pretended word of God, this manufactured book called *Revealed Religion.* We know that whatever is of God's doing is unalterable by man beyond the laws which the Creator has ordained. We cannot make a tree grow with the root in the air and the fruit in the ground ; we cannot make iron into gold nor gold into iron ; we cannot make rays of light shine forth rays of darkness, nor darkness shine forth light. If there were such a thing, as a Word of God, it would possess the same properties which all his other works do. It would resist destructive alteration. But we see that the book which they call the Word of God has not this property. That book says, (Genesis i. 27), " *So God created man in his own image ;*" but the printer can make it say, *So man created God in his own image.* The words are passive to every transposition of them, or can be annihilated and others put in their places. This is not the case with any thing that is of God's doing ; and, therefore, this book called the Word of God, tried by the same universal rule which every other of God's works within our reach can be tried by, proves itself to be a forgery.

The bishop says, that "*miracles are proper proofs of a divine mission.*" Admitted. But we know that men, and especially priests, can tell lies and call them miracles. It is therefore necessary that the thing called a miracle be proved to be true, and also to be miraculous, before it can be admitted as proof of the thing called revelation. The Bishop must be a bad logician not to know that one doubtful thing cannot be admitted as proof that another doubtful thing is true. It would be like attempting to prove a liar not to be a liar, by the evidence of another who is as great a liar as himself.

Though Jesus Christ, by being ignorant of the art of printing, shews he had not the means necessary to a divine mission, and consequently had no such mission; it does not follow that if he had known that art the divinity of what they call his mission would be proved thereby, any more than it proved the divinity of the man who invented printing. Something therefore beyond printing, even if he had known it, was necessary *as a miracle*, to have proved that what he delivered was the word of God; and this was that the book in which that word should be contained, which is now called the Old and New Testament, should possess the miraculous property, distinct from all human books, of resisting alteration. This would be not only a miracle, but an ever existing and universal miracle; whereas, those which they tell us of, even if they had been true, were momentary and local; they would leave no trace behind, after the lapse of a few years, of having ever existed; but this would prove, in all ages and in all places, the book to be divine and not human, as effectually, and as conveniently, as aquafortis proves gold to be gold by not being capable of acting upon it, and detects all other metals and all counterfeit composition, by dissolving them. Since then the only miracle capable of every proof is wanting, and which every thing that is of a divine origin possesses, all the tales of miracles, with which the Old and New Testament are filled, are fit only for impostors to preach and fools to believe.

VIII.

ORIGIN OF FREE-MASONRY.[1]

IT is always understood that Free-Masons have a secret which they carefully conceal ; but from every thing that can be collected from their own accounts of Masonry, their real secret is no other than their origin, which but few of them understand ; and those who do, envelope it in mystery.

The Society of Masons are distinguished into three classes or degrees. 1st. The Entered Apprentice. 2d. The Fellow Craft. 3d. The Master Mason.

The Entered Apprentice knows but little more of Masonry than the use of signs and tokens, and certain steps and words by which Masons can recognize each other without being discovered by a person who is not a Mason. The Fellow Craft is not much better instructed in Masonry, than the Entered Apprentice. It is only in the Master Mason's

---

[1] This essay appeared in New York, 1818, with an anonymous preface of which I quote the opening paragraph: " This tract is a chapter belonging to the Third Part of the "Age of Reason," as will be seen by the references made in it to preceding articles, as forming part of the same work. It was culled from the writings of Mr. Paine after his death, and published in a mutilated state by Mrs. Bonneville, his executrix. Passages having a reference to the Christian religion she erased, with a view no doubt of accommodating the work to the prejudices of bigotry. These, however, have been restored from the original manuscript, except a few lines which were rendered illegible." Madame Bonneville published this fragment in New York, 1810 (with the omissions I point out) as a pamphlet.—Dr. Robinet (*Danton Emigré*, p. 7) says erroneously that Paine was a Freemason ; but an eminent member of that Fraternity in London, Mr. George Briggs, after reading this essay, which I submitted to him, tells me that " his general outline, remarks, and comments, are fairly true." Paine's intimacy in Paris with Nicolas de Bonneville and Charles François Dupuis, whose writings are replete with masonic speculations, sufficiently explain his interest in the subject.—*Editor*.

Lodge, that whatever knowledge remains of the origin of Masonry is preserved and concealed.

In 1730, Samuel Pritchard, member of a constituted lodge in England, published a treatise entitled *Masonry Dissected;* and made oath before the Lord Mayor of London that it was a true copy. "Samuel Pritchard maketh oath that the copy hereunto annexed is a true and genuine copy in every particular." In his work he has given the catechism or examination, in question and answer, of the Apprentices, the Fellow Craft, and the Master Mason. There was no difficulty in doing this, as it is mere form.

In his introduction he says, "the original institution of Masonry consisted in the foundation of the liberal arts and sciences, but more especially in Geometry, for at the building of the tower of Babel, the art and mystery of Masonry was first introduced, and from thence handed down by *Euclid*, a worthy and excellent mathematician of the Egyptians ; and he communicated it to *Hiram*, the Master Mason concerned in building Solomon's Temple in Jerusalem."

Besides the absurdity of deriving Masonry from the building of Babel, where, according to the story, the confusion of languages prevented the builders understanding each other, and consequently of communicating any knowledge they had, there is a glaring contradiction in point of chronology in the account he gives.

Solomon's Temple was built and dedicated 1004 years before the christian era ; and *Euclid*, as may be seen in the tables of chronology, lived 277 before the same era. It was therefore impossible that Euclid could communicate any thing to Hiram, since Euclid did not live till 700 years after the time of Hiram.

In 1783, Captain George Smith, inspector of the Royal Artillery Academy at Woolwich, in England, and Provincial Grand Master of Masonry for the county of Kent, published a treatise entitled, The Use and Abuse of Free-Masonry.

In his chapter of the antiquity of Masonry, he makes it to be coeval with creation, " when," says he, " the sovereign architect raised on Masonic principles the beauteous globe, and commanded the master science, Geometry, to lay the planetary world, and to regulate by its laws the whole stupendous system in just unerring proportion, rolling round the central sun."

" But," continues he, " I am not at liberty publicly to undraw the curtain, and openly to descant on this head ; it is sacred, and ever will remain so ; those who are honored with the trust will not reveal it, and those who are ignorant of it cannot betray it." By this last part of the phrase, Smith means the two inferior classes, the Fellow Craft and the Entered Apprentice, for he says in the next page of his work, " It is not every one that is barely initiated into Free-Masonry that is entrusted with all the mysteries thereto belonging; they are not attainable as things of course, nor by every capacity."

The learned, but unfortunate Doctor Dodd, Grand Chaplain of Masonry, in his oration at the dedication of Free-Mason's Hall, London, traces Masonry through a variety of stages. Masons, says he, are well informed from their own private and interior records that the building of Solomon's Temple is an important era, from whence they derive many mysteries of their art. " Now (says he,) be it remembered that this great event took place above 1000 years before the Christian era, and consequently more than a century before Homer, the first of the Grecian Poets, wrote ; and above five centuries before Pythagoras brought from the east his sublime system of truly masonic instruction to illuminate our western world. But, remote as this period is, we date not from thence the commencement of our art. For though it might owe to the wise and glorious King of Israel some of its many mystic forms and hieroglyphic ceremonies, yet certainly the art itself is coeval with man, the great subject of it. " We trace," continues he, " its footsteps in the most distant, the most remote ages and nations of the world. We find it among the first and most celebrated civilizers of the East. We deduce it regularly from the first astronomers on the plains of Chaldea, to the wise and mystic kings and priests of Egypt, the sages of Greece, and the philosophers of Rome."

From these reports and declarations of Masons of the highest order in the institution, we see that Masonry, without publicly declaring so, lays claim to some divine communication from the creator, in a manner different from, and unconnected with, the book which the christians call the bible; and the natural result from this is, that Masonry is derived from some very ancient religion, wholly independent of and unconnected with that book.

To come then at once to the point, *Masonry* (as I shall shew from the customs, ceremonies, hieroglyphics, and chronology of Masonry) is derived and is the remains of the religion of the ancient Druids ; who, like the Magi of Persia and the Priests of Heliopolis in Egypt, were Priests of the Sun. They paid worship to this great luminary, as the great visible agent of a great invisible first cause, whom they stiled " Time without limits." [1]

The christian religion and Masonry have one and the same common origin : both are derived from the worship of the Sun. The difference between their origin is, that the christian religion is a parody on the worship of the Sun, in which they put a man whom they call Christ, in the place of the Sun, and pay him the same adoration which was originally paid to the Sun, as I have shown in the chapter on the origin of the Christian religion.[*]

In Masonry many of the ceremonies of the Druids are preserved in their original state, at least without any parody. With them the Sun is still the Sun ; and his image, in the form of the sun is the great emblematical ornament of Masonic Lodges and Masonic dresses. It is the central figure on their aprons, and they wear it also pendant on the

[1] Zarvan-Akarana. This personification of Boundless Time, though a part of Parsee Theology, seems to be a later monotheistic dogma, based on perversions of the Zendavesta. See Haug's " Religion of the Parsees."—*Editor*.

[*] Referring to an unpublished portion of the work of which this chapter forms a part.—*American Editor*, 1819 [This paragraph is omitted from the pamphlet copyrighted by Madame Bonneville in 1810, as also is the last sentence of the next paragraph.—*Editor*.]

breast in their lodges, and in their processions. It has the figure of a man, as at the head of the sun, as Christ is always represented.

At what period of antiquity, or in what nation, this religion was first established, is lost in the labyrinth of unrecorded time. It is generally ascribed to the ancient Egyptians, the Babylonians and Chaldeans, and reduced afterwards to a system regulated by the apparent progress of the sun through the twelve signs of Zodiac by Zoroaster the lawgiver of Persia, from whence Pythagoras brought it into Greece. It is to these matters Dr. Dodd refers in the passage already quoted from his oration.

The worship of the Sun as the great visible agent of a great invisible first cause, " Time without limits," spread itself over a considerable part of Asia and Africa, from thence to Greece and Rome, through all ancient Gaul, and into Britain and Ireland.

Smith, in his chapter on the antiquity of Masonry in Britain, says, that " notwithstanding the obscurity which envelopes Masonic history in that country, various circumstances contribute to prove that Free-Masonry was introduced into Britain about 1030 years before Christ." It cannot be Masonry in its present state that Smith here alludes to. The Druids flourished in Britain at the period he speaks of, and it is from them that Masonry is descended. Smith has put the child in the place of the parent.

It sometimes happens, as well in writing as in conversation, that a person lets slip an expression that serves to unravel what he intends to conceal, and this is the case with Smith, for in the same chapter he says, " The Druids, when they committed any thing to writing, used the Greek alphabet, and I am bold to assert that the most perfect remains of the Druids' rites and ceremonies are preserved in the customs and ceremonies of the Masons that are to be found existing among mankind." " My brethren " says he, " may be able to trace them with greater exactness than I am at liberty to explain to the public."

This is a confession from a Master Mason, without intending it to be so understood by the public, that Masonry is the remains of the religion of the Druids; the reasons for the Masons keeping this a secret I shall explain in the course of this work.

As the study and contemplation of the Creator [is] in the works of the creation, the Sun, as the great visible agent of that Being, was the visible object of the adoration of Druids; all their religious rites and ceremonies had reference to the apparent progress of the Sun through the twelve signs of the Zodiac, and his influence upon the earth. The Masons adopt the same practices. The roof of their Temples or Lodges is ornamented with a Sun, and the floor is a representation of the variegated face of the earth either by carpeting or Mosaic work.

Free Masons Hall, in Great Queen-street, Lincoln's Inn Fields, London, is a magnificent building, and cost upwards of 12,000 pounds sterling. Smith, in speaking of this building, says (page 152,) "The roof of this magnificent Hall is in all probability the highest piece of finished architecture in Europe. In the centre of this roof, a most resplendent Sun is represented in burnished gold, surrounded with the twelve signs of the Zodiac, with their respective characters:

♈ Aries	♎ Libra
♉ Taurus	♏ Scorpio
♊ Gemini	♐ Sagittarius
♋ Cancer	♑ Capricornus
♌ Leo	♒ Aquarius
♍ Virgo	♓ Pisces "

After giving this description, he says, "The emblematical meaning of the Sun is well known to the enlightened and inquisitive Free-Mason; and as the real Sun is situated in the center of the universe, so the emblematical Sun is the center of real Masonry. We all know (continues he) that the Sun is the fountain of light, the source of the seasons, the cause of the vicissitudes of day and night, the parent of vegetation, the friend of man; hence the scientific Free-Mason only knows the reason why the Sun is placed in the center of this beautiful hall."

The Masons, in order to protect themselves from the persecution of the christian church, have always spoken in a mystical manner of the figure of the Sun in their Lodges, or, like the astronomer Lalande, who is a Mason, been silent upon the subject. It is their secret, especially in Catholic countries, because the figure of the Sun is the expressive criterion that denotes they are descended from the Druids, and that wise, elegant, philosophical religion, was the faith opposite to the faith of the gloomy Christian church. [1]

The Lodges of the Masons, if built for the purpose, are constructed in a manner to correspond with the apparent motion of the Sun. They are situated East and West.[2] The master's place is always in the East. In the examination of an Entered Apprentice, the Master, among many other questions, asks him,

" Q. How is the lodge situated?

A. East and West.

Q. Why so?

A. Because all churches and chapels are, or ought to be so."

This answer, which is mere catechismal form, is not an answer to the question. It does no more than remove the question a point further, which is, why ought all churches and chapels to be so? But as the Entered Apprentice is not initiated into the druidical mysteries of Masonry, he is not asked any questions a direct answer to which would lead thereto.

" Q. Where stands your Master?

A. In the East.

Q. Why so?

A. As the Sun rises in the East and opens the day, so the Master stands in the East, (with his right hand upon his left breast, being a sign, and the square about his neck,) to open the Lodge, and set his men at work.

---

[1] This sentence is omitted in Madame Bonneville's publication.—*Editor*.

[2] The Freemason's Hall in London, which Paine has correctly described, is situated North and South, the exigencies of the space having been too strong for Masonic orthodoxy. Though nominally eastward the Master stands at the South.—*Editor*.

" Q. Where stand your Wardens?

A. In the West.

Q. What is their business?

A. As the Sun sets in the West to close the day, so the Wardens stand in the West, (with their right hands upon their left breasts, being a sign, and the level and plumb rule about their necks,) to close the Lodge, and dismiss the men from labour, paying them their wages."

Here the name of the Sun is mentioned, but it is proper to observe that in this place it has reference only to labour or to the time of labour, and not to any religious druidical rite or ceremony, as it would have with respect to the situation of Lodges East and West. I have already observed in the chapter on the origin of the christian religion, that the situation of churches East and West is taken from the worship of the Sun, which rises in the east, and has not the least reference to the person called Jesus Christ. The christians never bury their dead on the North side of a church[1]; and a Mason's Lodge always has, or is supposed to have, three windows which are called fixed lights, to distinguish them from the moveable lights of the Sun and the Moon. The Master asks the Entered Apprentice,

" Q. How are they (the fixed lights) situated?

A. East, West, and South.

Q. What are their uses?

A. To light the men to and from their work.

Q. Why are there no lights in the North?

A. Because the Sun darts no rays from thence."

This, among numerous other instances, shows that the christian religion and Masonry have one and the same common origin, the ancient worship of the Sun.

The high festival of the Masons is on the day they call St. John's day; but every enlightened Mason must know that holding their festival on this day has no reference to the person called St. John, and that it is only to disguise the true cause of holding it on this day, that they call the day

---

[1] In many parts of Northern Europe the North was supposed to be the region of demons. Executed criminals were buried on the north side of churches.— *Editor.*

by that name. As there were Masons, or at least Druids, many centuries before the time of St. John, if such person ever existed, the holding their festival on this day must refer to some cause totally unconnected with John.

The case is, that the day called St. John's day, is the 24th of June, and is what is called Midsummer-day. The sun is then arrived at the summer solstice; and, with respect to his meridional altitude, or height at high noon, appears for some days to be of the same height. The astronomical longest day, like the shortest day, is not every year, on account of leap year, on the same numerical day, and therefore the 24th of June is always taken for Midsummer-day; and it is in honour of the sun, which has then arrived at his greatest height in our hemisphere, and not any thing with respect to St. John, that this annual festival of the Masons, taken from the Druids, is celebrated on Midsummer-day.

Customs will often outlive the remembrance of their origin, and this is the case with respect to a custom still practised in Ireland, where the Druids flourished at the time they flourished in Britain. On the eve of Saint John's day, that is, on the eve of Midsummer-day, the Irish light fires on the tops of the hills. This can have no reference to St. John; but it has emblematical reference to the sun, which on that day is at his highest summer elevation, and might in common language be said to have arrived at the top of the hill.

As to what Masons, and books of Masonry, tell us of Solomon's Temple at Jerusalem, it is no wise improbable that some Masonic ceremonies may have been derived from the building of that temple, for the worship of the Sun was in practice many centuries before the Temple existed, or before the Israelites came out of Egypt. And we learn from the history of the Jewish Kings, 2 Kings xxii. xxiii. that the worship of the Sun was performed by the Jews in that Temple. It is, however, much to be doubted if it was done with the same scientific purity and religious morality with which it was performed by the Druids, who, by all accounts that historically remain of them, were a wise, learned, and moral class of men. The Jews, on the contrary, were ignorant of astronomy, and of science in general, and if a religion founded upon astronomy fell into their hands, it is almost certain it would be corrupted. We do not read in the history of the Jews, whether in the Bible or elsewhere, that they were the inventors or the improvers of any one art or science. Even in the building of this temple, the Jews did not know how to square and frame the timber for beginning and carrying on the work, and Solomon was obliged to send to Hiram, King of Tyre (Zidon) to procure workmen; "for thou knowest, (says Solomon to Hiram, 1 Kings v. 6.) that there is not among us any that can skill to hew timber like unto the Zidonians." This temple was more properly Hiram's Temple than Solomon's, and if the Masons derive any thing from the building of it, they owe it to the Zidonians and not to the Jews.—But to return to the worship of the Sun in this Temple.

It is said, 2 Kings xxiii. 5, "And [king Josiah] put down all the idolatrous priests . . . that burned incense unto . . . the sun, the moon, the planets, and all the host of heaven." And it is said at the 11th verse: " And he took away the horses that the kings of Judah had given to the Sun, at the entering in of the house of the Lord, . . . and burned the chariots of the Sun with fire "; verse 13, " And the high places that were before Jerusalem, which were on the right hand of the mount of corruption, which Solomon the king of Israel had builded for Ashtoreth, the abomination of the Zidonians " (the very people that built the temple) " did the king defile."

Besides these things, the description that Josephus gives of the decorations of this Temple, resembles on a large scale those of a Mason's Lodge. He says that the distribution of the several parts of the Temple of the Jews represented all nature, particularly the parts most apparent of it, as the sun, the moon, the planets, the zodiac, the earth, the elements; and that the system of the world was retraced there by numerous ingenious emblems. These, in all probability, are, what Josiah, in his ignorance, calls the abominations of the Zidonians.* Every thing, however, drawn from this Temple,† and applied to Masonry, still refers to the worship of the Sun, however corrupted or misunderstood by the Jews, and consequently to the religion of the Druids.

Another circumstance, which shews that Masonry is derived from some ancient system, prior to and unconnected with the christian religion, is the chronology, or method of counting time, used by the Masons in the records of their Lodges. They make no use of what is called the christian era; and they reckon their months numerically, as the ancient Egyptians did, and as the Quakers do now. I have by me, a record of a French Lodge, at the time the late Duke of Orleans, then Duke de Chartres, was Grand Master of Masonry in France. It begins as follows: "*Le trentième jour du sixième mois de l'an de la V. L. cinq mille sept cent soixante treize;*" that is, the thirteenth day of the sixth month of the year of the Venerable Lodge, five thousand seven hundred and seventy-three. By what I observe in English books of Masonry, the English Masons use the initials A. L. and not V. L. By A. L. they mean in the *year of Light*, as the Christians by A. D. mean in the year of our Lord. But A. L. like V. L. refers to the same chronological era, that is, to the supposed time of the creation.[1] In the chapter on the origin of the Christian religion, I have shewn that the Cosmogony, that is, the account of the crea-

* Smith, in speaking of a Lodge, says, when the Lodge is revealed to an entering Mason, it discovers to him *a representation of the World;* in which, from the wonders of nature, we are led to contemplate her great original, and worship him from his mighty works; and we are thereby also moved to exercise those moral and social virtues which become mankind as the servants of the great Architect of the world.—*Author.*

† It may not be improper here to observe, that the law called the law of Moses could not have been in existence at the time of building this Temple. Here is the likeness of things in heaven above and in earth beneath. And we read in 1 Kings vi., vii., that Solomon made cherubs and cherubims, that he *carved* all the walls of the house round about with cherubims, and palm-trees, and open flowers, and that he made a molten sea, placed on twelve oxen, and the ledges of it were ornamented with lions, oxen, and cherubims: all this is contrary to the law called the law of Moses.—*Author.*

[1] V. L. are the initials of *Vraie Lumière*, true light; and A. L. of *Anno Lucis*, in the year of light. This and the three preceding sentences (of the text) are suppressed in Madame Bonneville's pamphlet, 1810.—*Editor.*

tion with which the book of Genesis opens, has been taken and mutilated from the Zend-Avesta of Zoroaster, and was fixed as a preface to the Bible after the Jews returned from captivity in Babylon, and that the Rabbins of the Jews do not hold their account in Genesis to be a fact, but mere allegory. The six thousand years in the Zend-Avesta, is changed or interpolated into six days in the account of Genesis. The Masons appear to have chosen the same period, and perhaps to avoid the suspicion and persecution of the Church, have adopted the era of the world, as the era of Masonry. The V. L. of the French, and A. L. of the English Mason, answer to the A. M. Anno Mundi, or year of the world.

Though the Masons have taken many of their ceremonies and hieroglyphics from the ancient Egyptians, it is certain they have not taken their chronology from thence. If they had, the church would soon have sent them to the stake; as the chronology of the Egyptians, like that of the Chinese, goes many thousand years beyond the Bible chronology.

The religion of the Druids, as before said, was the same as the religion of the ancient Egyptians. The priests of Egypt were the professors and teachers of science, and were styled priests of Heliopolis, that is, of the *City of the Sun.* The Druids in Europe, who were the same order of men, have their name from the Teutonic or ancient German language; the German being anciently called Teutones. The word Druid signifies a *wise man.*[1] In Persia they were called Magi, which signifies the same thing.

"Egypt," says Smith, "from whence we derive many of our mysteries, has always borne a distinguished rank in history, and was once celebrated above all others for its antiquities, learning, opulence, and fertility. In their system, their principal hero-gods, Osiris and Isis, theologically represented the Supreme Being and universal Nature; and physically the two great celestial luminaries, the Sun and the

[1] German *drud*, wizard. Cf. Milton's line : " The star-led wizards haste with odours sweet." The word Druid has also been derived from Greek δρὺς, an oak ; Celtic *deru*, an oak and *udd*, lord ; British *deruidhon*, very wise men ; Heb. *derussim*, contemplators ; etc.—*Editor.*

Moon, by whose influence all nature was actuated." " The experienced brethren of the society, [says Smith in a note to this passage] are well informed what affinity these symbols bear to Masonry, and why they are used in all Masonic Lodges." In speaking of the apparel of the Masons in their Lodges, part of which, as we see in their public processions, is a white leather apron, he says, " the Druids were apparelled in white at the time of their sacrifices and solemn offices. The Egyptian priests of Osiris wore snow-white cotton. The Grecian and most other priests wore white garments. As Masons, we regard the principles of those *who were the first worshipers of the true God*, imitate their apparel, and assume the badge of innocence."

" The Egyptians," continues Smith, " in the earliest ages constituted a great number of Lodges, but with assiduous care kept their secrets of Masonry from all strangers. These secrets have been imperfectly handed down to us by oral tradition only, and ought to be kept undiscovered to the labourers, craftsmen, and apprentices, till by good behaviour and long study they become better acquainted in geometry and the liberal arts, and thereby qualified for Masters and Wardens, which is seldom or never the case with English Masons."

Under the head of Free-Masonry, written by the astronomer Lalande, in the French Encyclopedia, I expected from his great knowledge in astronomy, to have found much information on the origin of Masonry ; for what connection can there be between any institution and the Sun and twelve signs of the Zodiac, if there be not something in that institution, or in its origin, that has reference to astronomy? Every thing used as an hieroglyphic has reference to the subject and purpose for which it is used ; and we are not to suppose the Free-Masons, among whom are many very learned and scientific men, to be such idiots as to make use of astronomical signs without some astronomical purpose. But I was much disappointed in my expectation from Lalande. In speaking of the origin of Masonry, he says, " *L' origine de la maçonnerie se perd, comme tant d'autres, dans l'obscurité des temps ;* " that is, the origin of Masonry, like many others, loses itself in the obscurity of time. When I came to this expression, I supposed Lalande a Mason, and on enquiry found he was. This *passing over* saved him from the embarrassment which Masons are under respecting the disclosure of their origin, and which they are sworn to conceal. There is a society of Masons in Dublin who take the name of Druids; these Masons must be supposed to have a reason for taking that name.

I come now to speak of the cause of secrecy used by the Masons.

The natural source of secrecy is fear. When any new religion over-runs a former religion, the professors of the new become the persecutors of the old. We see this in all instances that history brings before us. When Hilkiah the priest and Shaphan the scribe, in the reign of King Josiah, found, or pretended to find, the law, called the law of Moses, a thousand years after the time of Moses, (and it does not appear from 2 Kings, xxii., xxiii., that such a law was ever practised or known before the time of Josiah), he established that law as a national religion, and put all the priests of the Sun to death. When the christian religion over-ran the Jewish religion, the Jews were the continual subject of persecution in all christian countries. When the Protestant religion in England over-ran the Roman Catholic religion, it was made death for a Catholic priest to be found in England. As this has been the case in all the instances we have any knowledge of, we are obliged to admit it with respect to the case in question, and that when the christian religion over-ran the religion of the Druids in Italy, ancient Gaul, Britain, and Ireland, the Druids became the subject of persecution. This would naturally and necessarily oblige such of them as remained attached to their original religion to meet in secret, and under the strongest injunctions of secrecy. Their safety depended upon it. A false brother might expose the lives of many of them to destruction ; and from the remains of the religion of the Druids, thus preserved, arose the institution which, to avoid the name of Druid, took that of Mason, and practised under this new name the rites and ceremonies of Druids.

IX.

PROSPECT PAPERS.

THESE occasional pieces were contributed in 1804 to *The Prospect ; or View of the Moral World*, a monthly magazine in New York, edited by Elihu Palmer, Paine's most eminent convert. Palmer, a native of Canterbury, Connecticut, born 1754, after graduation at Dartmouth College entered the Presbyterian ministry but left it and established the " Temple of Reason" in New York. Dr. Francis, in his " Old New York," despite his dislike of Palmer's rationalism, says: " I have more than once listened to Palmer ; none could be weary within the sound of his voice; his diction was classical ; and much of his natural theology attractive by variety of illustration." Palmer said of Paine that he was " probably the most useful man that ever existed on the face of the earth." Concerning his " Principles of Nature," which was prosecuted in England along with the " Age of Reason," Paine wrote him from Paris, (" February 21, 1802, since the Fable of Christ "): " I received by Mr. Livingston the letter you wrote me, and the excellent work you have published. I see you have thought deeply on the subject, and expressed your thoughts in a strong and clear style. The hinting and intimating manner of writing that was formerly used on subjects of this kind produced scepticism, but not conviction. It is necessary to be bold." On his arrival in New York Paine joined with Palmer in founding a Theistic Church, and wrote for *The Prospect*. Palmer died suddenly in Philadelphia, March 31. I am indebted to Mr. W.

A. Hunter of Plumpton, Penrith, for the use of a letter to his grandfather from the widow of Elihu Palmer, dated New York, September 3, 1806. "Of course I am left poor indeed. I have been exceedingly distressed for the means of living. I had to sell my furniture to pay my rent the first of May, was in very bad health, and really tired of my life. But my prospects and condition are now altered for the better. Mr. Thomas Paine had a fit of apoplexy on the 27th of last July, and as soon as he recovered his senses he sent for me, and I have been with him ever since. And I expect if I outlive him to be heir to part of his property. He says I must never leave him while he lives. He is now comfortable, but so lame he cannot walk, nor get into bed without the help of two men. He stays at Mr. Carver's. . . . Mr. Paine sends his best respects to you and all your family." Of his apoplectic stroke Paine wrote to a friend : "I had neither pulse nor breathing, and the people about me supposed me dead; yet all this while my mental faculties remained as perfect as I ever enjoyed them. I consider the scene I have gone through as an experiment on dying, and I find that death has no terrors for me." Mr. Hunter also possesses a silhouette of Paine, made in his last years, which is unique among portraits as showing the great length of his head ; and at the back of this is a portrait of Elihu Palmer, with a quatrain engraved above it of which I can make out but two lines, which refer to his having become blind :

> "Though shades and darkness cloud his visual ray,
> The mind unclouded feels no loss of day ;
> In Reason's . . ."

These two men founded in New York the first purely Theistic Society in Christendom, which survives in the freethinking Fraternity, who have their halls in New York and Boston, and preserve the spirit though not the Theism of their founders.

PROSPECT PAPERS.

REMARKS ON R. HALL'S SERMON.[1]

ROBERT HALL, a protestant minister in England, preached and published a sermon against what he called *Modern Infidelity*. A copy of it was sent to a gentleman in America with a request for his opinion thereon. That gentleman sent it to a friend of his in New York, with the request written on the cover—and this last gentleman sent it to Thomas Paine, who wrote the following observations on the blank leaf at the end of the sermon :

The preacher of the foregoing sermon speaks a great deal about *infidelity*, but does not define what he means by it. His harangue is a general exclamation. Every thing, I suppose that is not in his creed is infidelity with him, and his creed is infidelity with me. Infidelity is believing falsely. If what Christians believe is not true, it is the Christians that are the infidels.

The point between deists and christians is not about doctrine, but about fact—for if the things believed by the Christians to be facts are not facts, the doctrine founded thereon falls of itself. There is such a book as the Bible, but is it a fact that the Bible is *revealed religion ?* The christians cannot prove it is. They put tradition in place of evidence, and tradition is not proof. If it were, the reality of witches could be proved by the same kind of evidence.

The Bible is a history of the times of which it speaks, and history is not revelation. The obscene and vulgar stories in

---

[1] " The following piece, obligingly communicated by Mr. Paine for The Prospect, is full of that acuteness of mind, perspicuity of expression, and clearness of discernment, for which this excellent author is so remarkable in all his writings."—*Editor of The Prospect.*

the Bible are as repugnant to our ideas of the purity of a divine Being, as the horrid cruelties and murders it ascribes to him are repugnant to our ideas of his justice. It is the reverence of the *Deists* for the attributes of the DEITY, that causes them to reject the Bible.

Is the account which the christian church gives of the person called Jesus Christ a fact, or a fable? Is it a fact that he was begotten by the Holy Ghost? The christians cannot prove it, for the case does not admit of proof. The things called miracles in the Bible, such for instance as raising the dead, admitted *if true* of occular demonstration, but the story of the conception of Jesus Christ in the womb is a case beyond miracle, for it did not admit of demonstration. Mary, the reputed mother of Jesus, who must be supposed to know best, never said so herself, and all the evidence of it is that the book of Matthew says that Joseph dreamed an angel told him so. Had an old maid two or three hundred years of age brought forth a child it would have been much better presumptive evidence of a supernatural conception, than Matthew's story of Joseph's dream about his young wife.

Is it a fact that Jesus Christ died for the sins of the world, and how is it proved? If a God he could not die, and as a man he could not redeem. How then is this redemption proved to be fact? It is said that Adam ate of the forbidden fruit, commonly called an apple, and thereby subjected himself and all his posterity for ever to eternal damnation. This is worse than visiting the sins of the fathers upon the children unto the *third and fourth generations.* But how was the death of Jesus Christ to affect or alter the case? Did God thirst for blood? If so, would it not have been better to have crucified Adam at once upon the forbidden tree, and made a new man? Would not this have been more creator-like than repairing the old one? Or did God, when he made Adam, supposing the story to be true, exclude himself from the right of making another? or impose on himself the necessity of breeding from the old stock? Priests should first prove facts, and deduce doctrines from them afterwards. But instead of this they assume every thing and prove nothing. Authorities drawn from the Bible are no more than authorities drawn from other books, unless it can be proved that the Bible is revelation.

The story of the redemption will not stand examination. That man should redeem himself from the sin of eating an apple by committing a murder on Jesus Christ, is the strangest system of religion ever set up. Deism is perfect purity compared with this. It is an established principle with the Quakers not to shed blood : suppose then all Jerusalem had been Quakers when Christ lived, there would have been no-body to crucify him, and in that case, if man is redeemed by his blood, which is the belief of the Church, there could have been no redemption ; and the people of Jerusalem must all have been damned because they were too good to commit murder. The christian system of religion is an outrage on common sense. Why is man afraid to think ?

Why do not the christians, to be consistent, make saints of Judas and Pontius Pilate ? For they were the persons who accomplished the act of salvation. The merit of a sacrifice, if there can be any merit in it, was never in the thing sacrificed, but in the persons offering up the sacrifice—and, therefore, Judas and Pontius Pilate ought to stand first on the calendar of saints.[1]

THOMAS PAINE.

OF THE WORD " RELIGION,"

AND OTHER WORDS OF UNCERTAIN SIGNIFICATION.

THE word *religion* is a word of forced application when used with respect to the worship of God. The root of the word is the latin verb *ligo*, to tie or bind. From *ligo*, comes *religo*, to tie or bind over again, or make more fast—from *religo*, comes the substantive *religio*, which, with the addition of *n* makes the English substantive *Religion*. The

---

[1] In " A Political Biography," Disraeli (Lord Beaconsfield) repeats substantially Paine's argument in this paragraph.—*Author.*

French use the word properly: when a woman enters a convent she is called a *noviciate*, that is, she is upon trial or probation. When she takes the oath, she is called a *religieuse*, that is, she is tied or bound by that oath to the performance of it. We use the word in the same kind of sense when we say we will religiously perform the promise that we make.

But the word, without referring to its etymology, has, in the manner it is used, no definite meaning, because it does not designate what religion a man is of. There is the religion of the Chinese, of the Tartars, of the Bramins, of the Persians, of the Jews, of the Turks, etc.

The word Christianity is equally as vague as the word Religion. No two sectaries can agree what it is. It is *lo here* and *lo there*. The two principal sectaries, Papists and Protestants, have often cut each other's throats about it. The Papists call the Protestants heretics, and the Protestants call the Papists idolators. The minor sectaries have shown the same spirit of rancour, but as the civil law restrains them from blood, they content themselves with preaching damnation against each other.

The word *protestant* has a positive signification in the sense it is used. It means protesting against the authority of the Pope, and this is the only article in which the Protestants agree. In every other sense, with respect to religion, the word Protestant is as vague as the word Christian. When we say an Episcopalian, a Presbyterian, a Baptist, a Quaker, we know what those persons are, and what tenets they hold ; but when we say a " Christian," we know he is not a Jew nor a Mahometan, but we know not if he be a trinitarian or an anti-trinitarian, a believer in what is called the immaculate conception or a disbeliever, a man of seven sacraments, or of two sacraments, or of none. The word " Christian " describes what a man is not, but not what he is.

The word *Theology*, from *Theos*, the Greek word for God, and meaning the study and knowledge of God, is a word that strictly speaking belongs to Theists or Deists, and not to the Christians. The head of the Christian Church is the

person called Christ, but the head of the Church of the Theists, or Deists, as they are more commonly called (from *Deus,*
the latin word for God), is God himself ; and therefore the
word " Theology " belongs to that Church which has Theos
or God for its head, and not to the Christian Church
which has the person called Christ for its head. Their
technical word is *Christianity,* and they cannot agree what
Christianity is.

The words *revealed religion,* and *natural religion,* also require explanation. They are both invented terms, contrived by the Church for the support of priestcraft. With
respect to the first, there is no evidence of any such
thing, except in the universal revelation that God has
made of his power, his wisdom, his goodness, in the structure
of the universe, and in all the works of Creation. We have
no cause or ground from any thing we behold in those works
to suppose God would deal partially by mankind, and reveal
knowledge to one nation and withhold it from another, and
then damn them for not knowing it. The sun shines an
equal quantity of light all over the world—and mankind in
all ages and countries are endued with reason, and blessed
with sight, to read the visible works of God in the creation,
and so intelligent is this book that *he that runs may read.*
We admire the wisdom of the ancients, yet they had no
bibles nor books called " revelation." They cultivated the
reason that God gave them, studied him in his works, and
arose to eminence.

As to the Bible, whether true or fabulous, it is a history,
and history is not a revelation. If Solomon had seven hundred wives, and three hundred concubines, and if Samson
slept in Delilah's lap, and she cut his hair off, the relation of
those things is mere history that needed no revelation from
heaven to tell it ; neither does it need any revelation to tell
us that Samson was a fool for his pains, and Solomon too.

As to the expressions so often used in the Bible, that *the
word of the Lord* came to such an one, or such an one, it was
the fashion of speaking in those times, like the expression
used by a Quaker, that the *spirit moveth him,* or that used

by priests, that they *have a call.* We ought not to be deceived by phrases because they are ancient. But if we admit the supposition that God would condescend to reveal himself in words, we ought not to believe it would be in such idle and profligate stories as are in the Bible; and it is for this reason, among others which our reverence to God inspires, that the Deists deny that the book called the Bible is the Word of God, or that it is revealed religion.

With respect to the term *natural religion,* it is upon the face of it, the opposite of artificial religion, and it is impossible for any man to be certain that what is called *revealed religion* is not artificial. Man has the power of making books, inventing stories of God, and calling them revelation, or the Word of God. The Koran exists as an instance that this can be done, and we must be credulous indeed to suppose that this is the only instance, and Mahomet the only impostor. The Jews could match him, and the Church of Rome could overmatch the Jews. The Mahometans believe the Koran the Christians believe the Bible, and it is education makes all the difference.

Books, whether Bibles or Korans, carry no evidence of being the work of any other power than man. It is only that which man cannot do that carries the evidence of being the work of a superior power. Man could not invent and make a universe—he could not invent nature, for nature is of divine origin. It is the laws by which the universe is governed. When, therefore, we look through nature up to nature's God, we are in the right road of happiness, but when we trust to books as the Word of God, and confide in them as revealed religion, we are afloat on the ocean of uncertainty, and shatter into contending factions. The term, therefore, *natural religion,* explains itself to be *divine religion,* and the term *revealed religion* involves in it the suspicion of being *artificial.*

To shew the necessity of understanding the meaning of words, I will mention an instance of a minister, I believe of the episcopalian church of Newark, in Jersey. He wrote and published a book, and entitled it " *An Antidote to*

Deism." [1]   An antidote to *Deism* must be *Atheism.* It has
no other antidote—for what can be an antidote to the belief
of a God, but the disbelief of God? Under the tuition of
such pastors, what but ignorance and false information can
be expected?   T. P.

OF CAIN AND ABEL.

THE story of Cain and Abel is told in Genesis iv. Cain
was the elder brother, and Abel the younger, and Cain
killed Abel. The Egyptian story of Typhon and Osiris,
and the Jewish story in Genesis of Cain and Abel, have the
appearance of being the same story differently told, and that
it came originally from Egypt.

In the Egyptian story, Typhon and Osiris are brothers;
Typhon is the elder, and Osiris the younger, and Typhon
kills Osiris. The story is an allegory on Darkness and Light:
Typhon, the elder brother, is Darkness, because Darkness was
supposed to be more ancient than Light: Osiris is the Good
Light who rules during the summer months, and brings forth
the fruits of the earth, and is the favourite, as Abel is said to
have been; for which Typhon hates him; and when the winter comes, and cold and Darkness overspread the earth,
Typhon is represented as having killed Osiris out of malice,
as Cain is said to have killed Abel.

The two stories are alike in their circumstances and their
event, and are probably but the same story. What corroborates this opinion is, that the fifth chapter of Genesis historically contradicts the reality of the story of Cain and
Abel in the fourth chapter; for though the name of *Seth,* a
son of Adam, is mentioned in the fourth chapter, he is spoken
of in the fifth chapter as if he was the firstborn of Adam.
The chapter begins thus:

" This is the book of the *generations* of Adam. In the

[1] " Antidote to Deism. The Deist unmasked; or an ample refutation of all
the objections of Thomas Paine against the Christian Religion; as contained in
a pamphlet entitled *The Age of Reason;* addressed to the citizens of these
States. By the Rev. Uzal Ogden, Rector of Trinity Church, at Newark in the
State of New Jersey. Newark, 1795."—*Editor.*

day that God created man, in the likeness of God created he him; Male and female created he them, and blessed them, and called their name Adam, in the day when they were created. And Adam lived an hundred and thirty years and begat a son, in his own likeness and after his image, and called his name *Seth.*" The rest of the chapter goes on with the genealogy.

Any body reading this chapter, cannot suppose there were any sons born before *Seth.* The chapter begins with what is called *the creation of Adam,* and calls itself the book of the *generation of Adam,* yet no mention is made of such persons as Cain and Abel. One thing however is evident on the face of these two chapters, which is, that the same person is not the writer of both; the most blundering historian could not have committed himself in such a manner.

Though I look on every thing in the first ten chapters of Genesis to be fiction, yet fiction historically told should be consistent; whereas these two chapters are not. The Cain and Abel of Genesis appear to be no other than the ancient Egyptian story of Typhon and Osiris, the Darkness and the Light, which answered very well as an allegory without being believed as a fact.

THE TOWER OF BABEL.

THE story of the tower of Babel is told in Genesis xi. It begins thus: "And the whole earth [it was but a very little part of it they knew] was of one language and of one speech. And it came to pass as they journeyed from the east, that they found a plain in the land of Shinar, and they dwelt there. And they said one to another, *Go to,* let us make brick and burn them thoroughly, and they had brick for stone, and slime had they for mortar. And they said, *Go to,* let us build us a city, and a tower whose top may reach unto heaven, and let us make us a name, lest we be scattered abroad upon the face of the whole earth. And the Lord came down to see the city and the tower which the children of men builded. And the Lord said, Behold the people is one, and they have all one language; and this they begin to do; and now nothing will be restrained from them which they have imagined to do. *Go to*, let us go down and there confound their language, that they may not understand one another's speech. So [that is, by that means] the Lord scattered them abroad from thence upon the face of all the earth; and they left off building the city."

This is the story, and a very foolish inconsistent story it is. In the first place, the familiar and irreverend manner in which the Almighty is spoken of in this chapter is offensive to a serious mind. As to the project of building a tower whose top should reach to heaven, there never could be a people so foolish as to have such a notion; but to represent the Almighty as jealous of the attempt, as the writer of the story has done, is adding prophanation to folly. "*Go to*," say the builders, "let us build us a tower whose top shall reach to heaven." "*Go to*," says God, "let us go down and confound their language." This quaintness is indecent, and the reason given for it is worse, for, "now nothing will be restrained from them which they have imagined to do." This is representing the Almighty as jealous of their getting into heaven. The story is too ridiculous, even as a fable, to account for the diversity of languages in the world, for which it seems to have been intended.

As to the project of confounding their language for the purpose of making them separate, it is altogether inconsistent; because instead of producing this effect, it would, by increasing their difficulties, render them more necessary to each other, and cause them to keep together. Where could they go to better themselves?

Another observation upon this story is, the inconsistency of it with respect to the opinion that the bible is the Word of God given for the information of mankind; for nothing could so effectually prevent such a word from being known by mankind as confounding their language. The people, who after this spoke different languages, could no more understand such a Word generally, than the builders of Babel could understand one another. It would have been necessary, therefore, had such Word ever been given or intended to be given, that the whole earth should be, as they say it was at first, of one language and of one speech, and that it should never have been confounded.

The case, however, is, that the bible will not bear examination in any part of it, which it would do if it was the Word of God. Those who most believe it are those who know least about it, and priests always take care to keep the inconsistent and contradictory parts out of sight.

T. P.

OF THE RELIGION OF DEISM COMPARED WITH THE
CHRISTIAN RELIGION, AND THE SUPERIORITY OF THE
FORMER OVER THE LATTER.

EVERY person, of whatever religious denomination he may be, is a DEIST in the first article of his Creed. Deism, from the Latin word *Deus*, God, is the belief of a God, and this belief is the first article of every man's creed.

It is on this article, universally consented to by all mankind, that the Deist builds his church, and here he rests. Whenever we step aside from this article, by mixing it with articles of human invention, we wander into a labyrinth of uncertainty and fable, and become exposed to every kind of imposition by pretenders to revelation. The Persian shews the *Zendavesta* of Zoroaster, the lawgiver of Persia, and calls it the divine law; the Bramin shews the *Shaster*, revealed, he says, by God to Brama, and given to him out of a cloud; the Jew shews what he calls the law of Moses, given, he says, by God, on the Mount Sinai; the Christian shews a collection of books and epistles, written by nobody knows who, and called the New Testament; and the Mahometan shews the Koran, given, he says, by God to Mahomet: each of these calls itself *revealed religion*, and the *only* true word of God, and this the followers of each profess to believe from the habit of education, and each believes the others are imposed upon.

But when the divine gift of reason begins to expand itself in the mind and calls man to reflection, he then reads and contemplates God in his works, and not in the books pretending to be revelation. The Creation is the bible of the true believer in God. Every thing in this vast volume inspires him with sublime ideas of the Creator. The little and paltry, and often obscene, tales of the bible sink into wretchedness when put in comparison with this mighty work. The Deist needs none of those tricks and shows called miracles to confirm his faith, for what can be a greater miracle than the Creation itself, and his own existence?

There is a happiness in Deism, when rightly understood, that is not to be found in any other system of religion. All other systems have something in them that either shock our reason, or are repugnant to it, and man, if he thinks at all, must stifle his reason in order to force himself to believe them. But in Deism our reason and our belief become happily united. The wonderful structure of the universe, and every thing we behold in the system of the creation, prove to us, far better than books can do, the existence of a God, and at the same time proclaim his attributes. It is by the exercise of our reason that we are enabled to contemplate God in his works, and imitate him in his ways. When we see his care and goodness extended over all his creatures, it teaches us our duty towards each other, while it calls forth our gratitude to him. It is by forgetting God in his works, and running after the books of pretended revelation, that man has wandered from the straight path of duty and happiness, and become by turns the victim of doubt and the dupe of delusion.

Except in the first article in the Christian creed, that of believing in God, there is not an article in it but fills the mind with doubt as to the truth of it, the instant man begins to think. Now every article in a creed that is necessary to the happiness and salvation of man, ought to be as evident to the reason and comprehension of man as the first article is, for God has not given us reason for the purpose of confounding us, but that we should use it for our own happiness and his glory.

The truth of the first article is proved by God himself, and is universal ; for *the creation is of itself demonstration of the existence of a Creator.* But the second article, that of God's begetting a son, is not proved in like manner, and stands on no other authority than that of a tale. Certain books in what is called the New Testament tell us that Joseph dreamed that the angel told him so. (Matthew i. 20.) "And behold the Angel of the Lord appeared to Joseph, in a dream, saying, Joseph, thou son of David, fear not to take unto thee Mary thy wife, for that which is conceived in her is of the Holy Ghost." The evidence upon this article bears no comparison with the evidence upon the first article, and therefore is not entitled to the same credit, and ought not to be made an article in a creed, because the evidence of it is defective, and what evidence there is, is doubtful and sus-picious. We do not believe the first article on the authority of books, whether called Bibles or Korans, nor yet on the visionary authority of dreams, but on the authority of God's own visible works in the creation. The nations who never heard of such books, nor of such people as Jews, Christians, or Mahometans, believe the existence of a God as fully as we do, because it is self evident. The work of man's hands is a proof of the existence of man as fully as his personal appearance would be. When we see a watch, we have as positive evidence of the existence of a watch-maker, as if we saw him ; and in like manner the creation is evidence to our reason and our senses of the existence of a Creator. But there is nothing in the works of God that is evidence that he begat a son, nor any thing in the system of creation that corroborates such an idea, and, therefore, we are not author-ized in believing it. What truth there may be in the story that Mary, before she was married to Joseph, was kept by one of the Roman soldiers, and was with child by him, I leave to be settled between the Jews and the Christians. The story however has probability on its side, for her hus-band Joseph suspected and was jealous of her, and was going to put her away. "Joseph, her husband, being a just man, and not willing to make her a public ex-

ample, was going to put her away privately." (Matt.
i. 19.)[1]

I have already said that " whenever we step aside from
the first article (that of believing in God), we wander into
a labyrinth of uncertainty," and here is evidence of the
justness of the remark, for it is impossible for us to decide
who was Jesus Christ's father.

But presumption can assume any thing, and therefore it
makes Joseph's dream to be of equal authority with the existence of God, and to help it on calls it revelation.   It is
impossible for the mind of man in its serious moments, however it may have been entangled by education, or beset by
priest-craft, not to stand still and doubt upon the truth of
this article and of its creed.   But this is not all.   The second
article of the Christian creed having brought the son of Mary
into the world, (and this Mary, according to the chronological tables, was a girl of only fifteen years of age when this
son was born,) the next article goes on to account for his
being begotten, which was, that when he grew a man he
should be put to death, to expiate, they say, the sin that
Adam brought into the world by eating an apple or some
kind of forbidden fruit.

But though this is the creed of the church of Rome, from
whence the protestants borrowed it, it is a creed which that
church has manufactured of itself, for it is not contained in,
nor derived from, the book called the New Testament.   The
four books called the Evangelists, Matthew, Mark, Luke and
John, which give, or pretend to give, the birth, sayings, life,
preaching, and death of Jesus Christ, make no mention of
what is called the fall of man ; nor is the name of Adam to
be found in any of those books, which it certainly would be
if the writers of them believed that Jesus was begotten, born,
and died for the purpose of redeeming mankind from the

---

[1] The literature of this story, which seems to have been known to Celsus in
one of its various forms, is referred to in detail in McClintock and Strong's
" Cyclopædia of Biblical, Theological, and Ecclesiastical Literature," article
MARY.   The Hebrew work, *Toldoth Jesu,* containing the Jewish tradition,
was published in English by Richard Carlile, London, in 1823.—*Editor.*

sin which Adam had brought into the world. Jesus never speaks of Adam himself, of the Garden of Eden, nor of what is called the fall of man.

[*Paine here repeats his citations from St. Augustine, Origen, and Maimonides, as to the mystical interpretation of the story in Genesis, given on p. 264 of this volume.*]

But the Church of Rome having set up its new religion, which it called Christianity, invented the creed which it named the Apostles' Creed, in which it calls Jesus the *only son of God, conceived by the Holy Ghost, and born of the Virgin Mary ;* things of which it is impossible that man or woman can have any idea, and consequently no belief but in words ; and for which there is no authority but the idle story of Joseph's dream in the first chapter of Matthew, which any designing impostor or foolish fanatic might make. It then manufactured the allegories in the book of Genesis into fact, and the allegorical tree of life and the tree of knowledge into real trees, contrary to the belief of the first Christians, and for which there is not the least authority in any of the books of the New Testament ; for in none of them is there any mention made of such place as the Garden of Eden, nor of any thing that is said to have happened there.

But the church of Rome could not erect the person called Jesus into a Saviour of the world without making the allegories in the book of Genesis into fact, though the New Testament, as before observed, gives no authority for it. All at once the allegorical tree of knowledge became, according to the church, a real tree, the fruit of it real fruit, and the eating of it sinful. As priest-craft was always the enemy of knowledge, because priest-craft supports itself by keeping people in delusion and ignorance, it was consistent with its policy to make the acquisition of knowledge a real sin.

The church of Rome having done this, it then brings forward Jesus the son of Mary as suffering death to redeem mankind from sin, which Adam, it says, had brought into the world by eating the fruit of the tree of knowledge. But as it is impossible for reason to believe such a story, because it can see no reason for it, nor have any evidence of it, the church then tells us we must not regard our reason, but must *believe*, as it were, and that through thick and thin, as if God had given man reason like a plaything, or a rattle, on purpose to make fun of him. Reason is the forbidden tree of priest-craft, and may serve to explain the allegory of the forbidden tree of knowledge, for we may reasonably suppose the allegory had some meaning and application at the time it was invented. It was the practice of the eastern nations to convey their meaning by allegory, and relate it in the manner of fact. Jesus followed the same method, yet nobody every supposed the allegory or parable of the rich man and Lazarus, the Prodigal Son, the ten Virgins, etc., were facts. Why then should the tree of knowledge, which is far more romantic in idea than the parables in the New Testament are, be supposed to be a real tree ? * The answer to this is, because the church could not make its new fangled system, which it called Christianity, hold together without it. To have made Christ to die on account of an allegorical tree would have been too bare-faced a fable.

But the account, as it is given of Jesus in the New Testament, even visionary as it is, does not support the creed of the church that he died for the redemption of the world. According to that account he was crucified and buried on the Friday, and rose again in good health on the Sunday morning, for we do not hear that he was sick. This cannot be called dying, and is rather making fun of death than suffering it. There are thousands of men and women also, who if they could know they should come back again in good health in about thirty-six hours, would prefer such kind of death for the sake of the experiment, and to know what the other side of the grave was. Why then should that which would be only a voyage of curious amusement to us, be magnified into merit and suffering in him ? If a God he

---

* The remark of the Emperor Julian, on the story of the Tree of Knowledge is worth observing. " If," said he, " there ever had been, or could be, a Tree of Knowledge, instead of God forbidding man to eat thereof, it would be that of which he would order him to eat the most."—*Author*.

could not suffer death, for immortality cannot die, and as a man his death could be no more than the death of any other person.

The belief of the redemption of Jesus Christ is altogether an invention of the church of Rome, not the doctrine of the New Testament. What the writers of the New Testament attempted to prove by the story of Jesus is the *resurrection of the same body from the grave*, which was the belief of the Pharisees, in opposition to the Sadducees (a sect of Jews) who denied it. Paul, who was brought up a Pharisee, labours hard at this point, for it was the creed of his own Pharisaical church : 1 Corinthians xv. is full of supposed cases and assertions about the resurrection of the same body, but there is not a word in it about redemption. This chapter makes part of the funeral service of the Episcopal church. The dogma of the redemption is the fable of priest-craft invented since the time the New Testament was compiled, and the agreeable delusion of it suited with the depravity of immoral livers. When men are taught to ascribe all their crimes and vices to the temptations of the Devil, and to believe that Jesus by his death rubs all off, and pays their passage to heaven gratis, they become as careless in morals as a spendthrift would be of money, were he told that his father had engaged to pay off all his scores. It is a doctrine not only dangerous to morals in this world, but to our happiness in the next world, because it holds out such a cheap, easy, and lazy way of getting to heaven, as has a tendency to induce men to hug the delusion of it to their own injury.

But there are times when men have serious thoughts, and it is at such times, when they begin to think, that they begin to doubt the truth of the Christian Religion ; and well they may, for it is too fanciful and too full of conjecture, inconsistency, improbability, and irrationality, to afford consolation to the thoughtful man. His reason revolts against his creed. He sees that none of its articles are proved, or can be proved. He may believe that such a person as is called Jesus (for Christ was not his name) was born and grew to be a man, because it is no more than a natural and probable case. But who is to prove he is the son of God, that he was begotten by the Holy Ghost ? Of these things there can be no proof ; and that which admits not of proof, and is against the laws of probability and the order of nature, which God himself has established, is not an object for belief. God has not given man reason to embarrass him, but to prevent his being imposed upon.

He may believe that Jesus was crucified, because many others were crucified, but who is to prove he was crucified *for the sins of the world ?* This article has no evidence, not even in the New Testament ; and if it had, where is the proof that the New Testament, in relating things neither probable nor proveable, is to be believed as true? When an article in a creed does not admit of proof nor of probability, the salvo is to call it revelation ; but this is only putting one difficulty in the place of another, for it is as impossible to prove a thing to be revelation as it is to prove that Mary was gotten with child by the Holy Ghost.

Here it is that the religion of Deism is superior to the Christian Religion. It is free from all those invented and torturing articles that shock our reason or injure our humanity, and with which the Christian religion abounds. Its creed is pure, and sublimely simple. It believes in God, and there it rests. It honours Reason as the choicest gift of God to man, and the faculty by which he is enabled to contemplate the power, wisdom and goodness of the Creator displayed in the creation ; and reposing itself on his protection, both here and hereafter, it avoids all presumptuous beliefs, and rejects, as the fabulous inventions of men, all books pretending to revelation.   T. P.

TO THE MEMBERS OF THE SOCIETY, STYLING ITSELF THE MISSIONARY SOCIETY.

The New-York Gazette of the 16th *(August) contains the following article—" On Tuesday, a committee of the Missionary Society, consisting chiefly of distinguished Clergymen, had an interview, at the City Hotel, with the chiefs of the Osage tribe of Indians, now in this City, (New York) to*

*whom they presented a Bible, together with an Address, the
object of which was, to inform them that this* good book
contained the will and laws *of the* GREAT SPIRIT."

IT is to be hoped some humane person will, on account of
our people on the frontiers, as well as of the Indians, undeceive them with respect to the present the Missionaries have
made them, and which they call a *good book*, containing,
they say, *the will and laws of the* GREAT SPIRIT. Can
those Missionaries suppose that the assassination of men,
women, and children, and sucking infants, related in the
books ascribed to Moses, Joshua, etc., and blasphemously
said to be done by the command of the Lord, the Great
Spirit, can be edifying to our Indian neighbours, or advantageous to us? Is not the Bible warfare the same kind of
warfare as the Indians themselves carry on, that of indiscriminate destruction, and against which humanity shud-
ders? Can the horrid examples and vulgar obscenity with
which the Bible abounds improve the morals or civilize the
manners of the Indians? Will they learn sobriety and decency from drunken Noah and beastly Lot; or will their
daughters be edified by the example of Lot's daughters?
Will the prisoners they take in war be treated the better by
their knowing the horrid story of Samuel's hewing Agag in
pieces like a block of wood, or David's putting them under
harrows of iron? Will not the shocking accounts of the
destruction of the Canaanites, when the Israelites invaded
their country, suggest the idea that we may serve them in
the same manner, or the accounts stir them up to do the
like to our people on the frontiers, and then justify the
assassination by the Bible the Missionaries have given them?
Will those Missionary Societies never leave off doing
mischief?

In the account which this missionary committee give of
their interview, they make the Chief of the Indians to say,
that, " as neither he nor his people could read it, he begged
that some good white man might be sent to instruct them."

It is necessary the General Government keep a strict eye

over those Missionary Societies, who, under the pretence of instructing the Indians, send spies into their country to find out the best lands.   No Society should be permitted to have intercourse with the Indian tribes, nor send any person among them, but with the knowledge and consent of the Government.   The present Administration [Jefferson's] has brought the Indians into a good disposition, and is improving them in the moral and civil comforts of life ; but if these self-created Societies be suffered to interfere, and send their speculating Missionaries among them, the laudable object of government will be defeated.   Priests, we know, are not remarkable for doing any thing gratis ; they have in general some scheme in every thing they do, either to impose on the ignorant, or derange the operations of government.

A FRIEND TO THE INDIANS.

OF THE SABBATH DAY IN CONNECTICUT.

THE word Sabbath, means REST, that is, cessation from labour, but the stupid Blue Laws * of Connecticut make a labour of rest, for they oblige a person to sit still from sunrise to sunset on a Sabbath day, which is hard work. Fanaticism made those laws, and hyprocrisy pretends to reverence them, for where such laws prevail hypocrisy will prevail also.

One of those laws says, " No person shall run on a Sabbath-day, nor walk in his garden, nor elsewhere, but reverently to and from meeting." These fanatical hypocrites forgot that God dwells not in temples made with hands, and that the earth is full of his glory.   One of the finest scenes and subjects of religious contemplation is to walk into the woods and fields, and survey the works of the God of the Creation.   The wide expanse of heaven, the earth covered with verdure, the lofty forest, the waving corn, the magnificent roll of mighty rivers, and the murmuring melody of the cheerful brooks, are scenes that inspire the mind with

* They were called Blue Laws because they were originally printed on blue paper.—*Author*.

gratitude and delight. But this the gloomy Calvinist of Connecticut must not behold on a Sabbath-day. Entombed within the walls of his dwelling, he shuts from his view the Temple of Creation. The sun shines no joy to him. The gladdening voice of nature calls on him in vain. He is deaf, dumb, and blind to every thing around that God has made. Such is the Sabbath-day of Connecticut.

From whence could come this miserable notion of devotion? It comes from the gloominess of the Calvinistic creed. If men love darkness rather than light, because their works are evil, the ulcerated mind of a Calvinist, who sees God only in terror, and sits brooding over the scenes of hell and damnation, can have no joy in beholding the glories of the Creation. Nothing in that mighty and wondrous system accords with his principles or his devotion. He sees nothing there that tells him that God created millions on purpose to be damned, and that the children of a span long are born to burn forever in hell.[1] The Creation preaches a different doctrine to this. We there see that the care and goodness of God is extended impartially over all the creatures he has made. The worm of the earth shares his protection equally with the elephant of the desert. The grass that springs beneath our feet grows by his bounty as well as the cedars of Lebanon. Every thing in the Creation reproaches the Calvinist with unjust ideas of God, and disowns the hardness and ingratitude of his principles. Therefore he shuns the sight of them on a Sabbath-day.

AN ENEMY TO CANT AND IMPOSITION.

OF THE OLD AND THE NEW TESTAMENT.

ARCHBISHOP Tillotson says: "The difference between the style of the Old and New Testament is so very remarkable, that one of the greatest sects in the primitive times, did, upon this very ground, found their heresy of two Gods, the one evil, fierce, and cruel, whom they called the God of

---

[1] This phrase, about the damnation of infants " a span long," was ascribed to Rev. Dr. Emmons and several other extreme predestinarians in America.— *Editor.*

the Old Testament; the other good, kind, and merciful, whom they called the God of the New Testament; so great a difference is there between the representations that are given of God in the books of the Jewish and Christian Religion, as to give, at least, some colour and pretence to an imagination of two Gods." Thus far Tillotson.

But the case was, that as the Church had picked out several passages from the Old Testament, which she most absurdly and falsely calls prophecies of Jesus Christ, (whereas there is no prophecy of any such person, as any one may see by examining the passages and the cases to which they apply,) she was under the necessity of keeping up the credit of the Old Testament, because if that fell the other would soon follow, and the Christian system of faith would soon be at an end. As a book of morals, there are several parts of the New Testament that are good; but they are no other than what had been preached in the Eastern world several hundred years before Christ was born. Confucius, the Chinese philosopher, who lived five hundred years before the time of Christ, says, *Acknowledge thy benefits by the return of benefits, but never revenge injuries.*

The clergy in Popish countries were cunning enough to know that if the Old Testament was made public the fallacy of the New, with respect to Christ, would be detected, and they prohibited the use of it, and always took it away wherever they found it. The Deists, on the contrary, always encouraged the reading it, that people might see and judge for themselves, that a book so full of contradictions and wickedness could not be the word of God, and that we dishonour God by ascribing it to him.

A TRUE DEIST.

HINTS TOWARDS FORMING A SOCIETY FOR INQUIRING INTO THE TRUTH OR FALSEHOOD OF ANCIENT HISTORY, SO FAR AS HISTORY IS CONNECTED WITH SYSTEMS OF RELIGION ANCIENT AND MODERN.

IT has been customary to class history into three divisions, distinguished by the names of Sacred, Profane, and Ecclesiastical. By the first is meant the Bible; by the second, the history of nations, of men and things; and by the third, the history of the church and its priesthood.

Nothing is more easy than to give names, and, therefore, mere names signify nothing unless they lead to the discovery of some cause for which that name was given. For example, *Sunday* is the name given to the first day of the week, in the English language, and it is the same in the Latin, that is, it has the same meaning, (*Dies solis,*) and also in the German, and in several other languages. Why then was this name given to that day? Because it was the day dedicated by the ancient world to the luminary which in the English we call the Sun, and therefore the day *Sun-day*, or the day of the Sun; as in the like manner we call the second day Monday, the day dedicated to the Moon.

Here the name *Sunday* leads to the cause of its being called so, and we have visible evidence of the fact, because we behold the Sun from whence the name comes; but this is not the case when we distinguish one part of history from another by the name of *Sacred*. All histories have been written by men. We have no evidence, nor any cause to believe, that any have been written by God. That part of the Bible called the Old Testament, is the history of the Jewish nation, from the time of Abraham, which begins in Genesis xi., to the downfall of that nation by Nebuchadnezzar, and is no more entitled to be called sacred than any other history. It is altogether the contrivance of priestcraft that has given it that name. So far from its being *sacred*, it has not the appearance of being true in many of the things it relates. It must be better authority than a book which any impostor might make, as Mahomet made the Koran, to make a thoughtful man believe that the sun and moon stood still, or that Moses and Aaron turned the Nile, which is larger than the Delaware, into blood, and that the Egyptian magicians did the same. These things have too much the appearance of romance to be believed for fact.

It would be of use to inquire, and ascertain the time, when that part of the Bible called the Old Testament first appeared.

From all that can be collected there was no such book till after the Jews returned from captivity in Babylon, and that it is the work of the Pharisees of the Second Temple. How they came to make Kings xix. and Isaiah xxxvii. word for word alike, can only be accounted for by their having no plan to go by, and not knowing what they were about. The same is the case with respect to the last verses in 2d Chronicles, and the first verses in Ezra ; they also are word for word alike, which shews that the Bible has been put together at random.

But besides these things there is great reason to believe we have been imposed upon with respect to the antiquity of the Bible, and especially with respect to the books ascribed to Moses. Herodotus, who is called the father of history, and is the most ancient historian whose works have reached to our time, and who travelled into Egypt, conversed with the priests, historians, astronomers, and learned men of that country, for the purpose of obtaining all the information of it he could, and who gives an account of the ancient state of it, makes no mention of such a man as Moses, though the Bible makes him to have been the greatest hero there, nor of any one circumstance mentioned in the Book of Exodus respecting Egypt, such as turning the rivers into blood, the dust into lice, the death of the first born throughout all the land of Egypt, the passage of the Red Sea, the drowning of Pharaoh and all his host, things which could not have been a secret in Egypt, and must have been generally known, had they been facts; and, therefore, as no such things were known in Egypt, nor any such man as Moses, at the time Herodotus was there, which is about two thousand two hundred years ago, it shews that the account of these things in the books ascribed to Moses is a made story of later times,—that is, after the return of the Jews from the Baby-lonian captivity,—and that Moses is not the author of the books ascribed to him.

With respect to the cosmogony, or account of the Creation, in Genesis i., of the Garden of Eden in chapter ii., and of what is called the Fall of Man in chapter iii., there is something concerning them we are not historically acquainted with. In none of the books of the Bible, after Genesis, are any of these things mentioned, or even alluded to. How is this to be accounted for? The obvious inference is, that either they were not known, or not believed to be facts, by the writers of the other books of the Bible, and that Moses is not the author of the chapters where these accounts are given.

The next question on the case is, how did the Jews come by these notions, and at what time were they written?

To answer this question we must first consider what the state of the world was at the time the Jews began to be a people, for the Jews are but a modern race compared with the antiquity of other nations. At the time there were, even by their own account, but thirteen Jews or Israelites in the world, *Jacob and his twelve sons*, and four of these were bastards, the nations of Egypt, Chaldea, Persia, and India, were great and populous, abounding in learning and science, particularly in the knowledge of astronomy, of which the Jews were always ignorant. The chronological tables mention that eclipses were observed at Babylon above two thousand years before the Christian era, which was before there was a single Jew or Israelite in the world.

All those ancient nations had their cosmogonies, that is, their accounts how the Creation was made, long before there was such people as Jews or Israelites. An account of these cosmogonies of India and Persia is given by Henry Lord, Chaplain to the East India Company at Surat, and published in London in 1630. The writer of this has seen a copy of the edition of 1630, and made extracts from it. The work, which is now scarce, was dedicated by Lord to the Archbishop of Canterbury.

We know that the Jews were carried captive into Babylon by Nebuchadnezzar, and remained in captivity several years, when they were liberated by Cyrus king of Persia. During their captivity they would have had an opportunity of acquiring some knowledge of the cosmogony of the Persians, or at least of getting some ideas how to fabricate one to put

at the head of their own history after their return from captivity. This will account for the cause, for some cause there
must have been, that no mention nor reference is made to
the cosmogony in Genesis in any of the books of the Bible
supposed to have been written before the captivity, nor is
the name of Adam to be found in any of those books.

The books of Chronicles were written after the return of
the Jews from captivity, for the third chapter of the first
book gives a list of all the Jewish kings from David to
Zedekiah, who was carried captive into Babylon, and to four
generations beyond the time of Zedekiah. In Chron. i. 1,
the name of Adam is mentioned, but not in any book in the
Bible written before that time, nor could it be, for Adam and
Eve are names taken from the cosmogony of the Persians.
Henry Lord, in his book, written from Surat and dedicated,
as I have already said, to the Archbishop of Canterbury,
says that in the Persian cosmogony the name of the first
man was *Adamoh*, and of the woman *Hevah*.* From hence
comes the Adam and Eve of the book of Genesis. In the
cosmogony of India, of which I shall speak in a future number, the name of the first man was *Pourous*, and of the
woman *Parcoutee*. We want a knowledge of the Sanscrit
language of India to understand the meaning of the names,
and I mention it in this place, only to show that it is from
the cosmogony of Persia, rather than that of India, that the
cosmogony in Genesis has been frabricated by the Jews, who
returned from captivity by the liberality of Cyrus, king of
Persia. There is, however, reason to conclude, on the authority of Sir William Jones, who resided several years in
India, that these names were very expressive in the language
to which they belonged, for in speaking of this language, he
says, (see the Asiatic Researches,) " The Sanscrit language,
whatever be its antiquity, is of wonderful structure ; it is
more perfect than the Greek, more copious than the Latin,
and more exquisitely refined than either."

These hints, which are intended to be continued, will

* In an English edition of the Bible, in 1583, the first woman is called
Hevah.—*Editor of the Prospect.*

serve to shew that a Society for inquiring into the ancient state of the world, and the state of ancient history, so far as history is connected with systems of religion ancient and modern, may become a useful and instructive institution. There is good reason to believe we have been in great error with respect to the antiquity of the Bible, as well as imposed upon by its contents. Truth ought to be the object of every man ; for without truth there can be no real happiness to a thoughtful mind, or any assurance of happiness hereafter. It is the duty of man to obtain all the knowledge he can, and then make the best use of it. T. P.

TO MR. MOORE, OF NEW YORK, COMMONLY CALLED BISHOP MOORE.[1]

I HAVE read in the newspapers your account of the visit you made to the unfortunate General Hamilton, and of administering to him a ceremony of your church which you call the *Holy Communion.*

I regret the fate of General Hamilton, and I so far hope with you that it will be a warning to thoughtless man not to sport away the life that God has given him ; but with respect to other parts of your letter I think it very reprehensible, and betrays great ignorance of what true religion is. But you are a priest, you get your living by it, and it is not your worldly interest to undeceive yourself.

After giving an account of your administering to the deceased what you call the Holy Communion, you add, " By reflecting on this melancholy event let the humble believer be encouraged ever to hold fast that precious faith which is the *only source of true consolation* in the last extremity of nature. Let the infidel be persuaded to abandon his opposition to the Gospel."

To shew you, sir, that your promise of consolation from scripture has no foundation to stand upon, I will cite to you

[1] Benjamin Moore, D.D., Rector of Trinity Church, New York, 1800, elected Bishop 1801, died 1816. Ordained by the Bishop of London, 1774. For a time President of Columbia College, New York. Alexander Hamilton fell in a duel with Aaron Burr (1804).—*Editor.*

one of the greatest falsehoods upon record, and which was given, as the record says, for the purpose, and as a promise, of consolation.

In the epistle called the First Epistle of Paul to the Thessalonians, iv., the writer consoles the Thessalonians as to the case of their friends who were already dead. He does this by informing them, and he does it he says, by the word of the Lord, (a most notorious falsehood,) that the general resurrection of the dead and the ascension of the living will be in his and their days ; that their friends will then come to life again ; that the dead in Christ will rise first.—" Then WE (says he, ver. 17, 18) which *are alive and remain* shall be *caught up* together with THEM *in the clouds, to meet the Lord in the air,* and so shall we ever be with the Lord. Wherefore *comfort* one another with these words."

Delusion and falsehood cannot be carried higher than they are in this passage. You, sir, are but a novice in the art. The words admit of no equivocation. The whole passage is in the first person and the present tense, " *We* which *are alive.*" Had the writer meant a future time, and a distant generation, it must have been in the third person and the future tense. " *They* who *shall then* be alive." I am thus particular for the purpose of nailing you down to the text, that you may not ramble from it, nor put other constructions upon the words than they will bear, which priests are very apt to do.

Now, sir, it is impossible for serious man, to whom God has given the divine gift of reason, and who employs that reason to reverence and adore the God that gave it, it is, I say, impossible for such a man to put confidence in a book that abounds with fable and falsehood as the New Testament does. This passage is but a sample of what I could give you.

You call on those whom you style " *infidels,*" (and they in return might call you an idolater, a worshipper of false gods, a preacher of false doctrine,) " to abandon their opposition to the Gospel." Prove, sir, the Gospel to be true, and the opposition will cease of itself ; but until you do this (which we know you cannot do) you have no right to expect they will notice your call. If by *infidels* you mean *Deists*, (and you must be exceedingly ignorant of the origin of the word Deist, and know but little of *Deus*, to put that construction upon it,) you will find yourself over-matched if you begin to engage in a controversy with them. Priests may dispute with priests, and sectaries with sectaries, about the meaning of what they *agree* to call scripture, and end as they began ; but when you engage with a Deist you must keep to fact. Now, sir, you cannot prove a single article of your religion to be true, and we tell you so publicly. Do it, *if you can.* The Deistical article, *the belief of a God,* with which your creed begins, has been borrowed by your church from the ancient Deists, and even this article you dishonour by putting a *dream-begotten* phantom * which you call his son, over his head, and treating God as if he was superannuated. Deism is the only profession of religion that admits of worshipping and reverencing God in purity, and the only one on which the thoughtful mind can repose with undisturbed tranquillity. God is almost forgotten in the Christian religion. Every thing, even the creation, is ascribed to the son of Mary.

In religion, as in every thing else, perfection consists in simplicity. The Christian religion of Gods within Gods, like wheels within wheels, is like a complicated machine that never goes right, and every projector in the art of Christianity is trying to mend it. It is its defects that have caused such a number and variety of tinkers to be hammering at it, and still it goes wrong. In the visible world no time-keeper can go equally true with the sun ; and in like manner, no complicated religion can be equally true with the pure and unmixed religion of Deism.

Had you not offensively glanced at a description of men

---

* The first chapter of Matthew, relates that Joseph, the betrothed husband of Mary, dreamed that the angel told him that his intended bride was with child by the Holy Ghost. It is not every husband, whether carpenter or priest, that can be so easily satisfied, for lo ! it was a dream. Whether Mary was in a dream when this was done we are not told. It is, however, a comical story. There is no woman living can understand it.—*Author*.

whom you call by a false name, you would not have been troubied nor honoured with this address ; neither has the writer of it any desire or intention to enter into controversy with you. He thinks the temporal establishment of your church politically unjust and offensively unfair[1] ; but with respect to religion itself, distinct from temporal establishments, he is happy in the enjoyment of his own, and he leaves you to make the best you can of yours.

A MEMBER OF THE DEISTICAL CHURCH.

TO JOHN MASON,[2]

ONE OF THE MINISTERS OF THE SCOTCH PRESBYTERIAN CHURCH, OF NEW YORK, WITH REMARKS ON HIS ACCOUNT OF THE VISIT HE MADE TO THE LATE GENERAL HAMILTON.

" *Come now, let us* REASON *together saith the Lord.*" This is one of the passages you quoted from your Bible, in your conversation with General Hamilton, as given in your letter, signed with your name, and published in the Commercial Advertiser, and other New-York papers, and I re-quote the passage to show that your *text* and your *Religion* contradict each other.

It is impossible to reason upon things *not comprehensible by reason ;* and therefore, if you keep to your text, which priests seldom do, (for they are generally either above it, or below it, or forget it,) you must admit a religion to which reason can apply, and this certainly is not the Christian religion.

There is not an article in the Christian religion that is cog-

---

[1] Paine's reference is to the English Church, with which the Episcopal Church in America was affiliated. After the Declaration of Independence that Church still held exceptional advantages, in some of the States, by their glebes, but it was legally established only as other denominations were, and are, by the exemption of their property from taxation.—*Editor.*

[2] John Mason, D.D., 1770–1829. This celebrated Presbyterian orator had been the particular friend of Hamilton, who was also a Presbyterian so far as he held any dogmas. In his last moments Hamilton desired Dr. Mason to administer the sacrament to him, but as this did not accord with Presbyterian usage, Bishop Moore performed that office.—*Editor.*

nizable by reason. The Deistical article of your religion, *the belief of a God*, is no more a Christian article than it is a Mahometan article. It is an universal article, common to all religions, and which is held in greater purity by Turks than by Christians; but the Deistical church is the only one which holds it in real purity; because that church acknowledges no co-partnership with God. It believes in him solely; and knows nothing of Sons, married Virgins, nor Ghosts. It holds all these things to be the fables of priest-craft.

Why then do you talk of Reason, or refer to it, since your religion has nothing to do with reason, nor reason with that? You tell people as you told Hamilton, that they must have *faith!* Faith in what? You ought to know that before the mind can have faith in any thing, it must either know it as a fact, or see cause to believe it on the probability of that kind of evidence that is cognizable by reason. But your religion is not within either of these cases; for, in the first place, you cannot prove it to be fact; and in the second place, you cannot support it by reason, not only because it is not cognizable by reason, but because it is contrary to reason. What reason can there be in supposing, or believing that God put *himself to death to satisfy himself, and be revenged on the Devil on account of Adam?* For, tell the story which way you will it comes to this at last.

As you can make no appeal to Reason in support of an unreasonable religion, you then (and others of your profession) bring yourselves off by telling people they must not believe in reason but in *revelation.* This is the artifice of habit without reflection. It is putting *words* in the place of *things;* for do you not see that when you tell people to believe in revelation, you must first prove that what you *call* revelation, *is* revelation; and as you cannot do this, you put the *word*, which is easily spoken, in the place of the *thing* you cannot prove. You have no more evidence that your Gospel is revelation than the Turks have that their Koran is revelation, and the only difference between them and you is, that they preach their delusion and you preach yours.

In your conversation with General Hamilton, you say to him, " The *simple truths* of the Gospel which require *no abstruse investigation*, but faith in the veracity of *God who cannot lie*, are best suited to your present condition."

If those matters you call "*simple truths*" are what you call them, and require no abstruse investigation, they would be so obvious that reason would easily comprehend them ; yet the doctrine you preach at other times is, *that the mysteries of the Gospel are beyond the reach of reason.* If your first position be true, that they are *simple truths*, priests are unnecessary, for we do not want preachers to tell us the sun shines ; and if your second be true, the case, as to effect, is the same, for it is waste of money to pay a man to explain unexplainable things, and loss of time to listen to him. That *God cannot lie*, is no advantage to your argument, because it is no proof that priests cannot, or that the Bible does not. Did not Paul lie when he told the Thessalonians that the general resurrection of the dead would be in his life-time, and that he should go up alive along with them into the clouds to meet the Lord in the air ? 1 Thes. iv. 17.

You spoke of what you call, " *the precious blood of Christ.*" This savage style of language belongs to the priests of the Christian religion. The professors of this religion say they are shocked at the accounts of human sacrifices of which they read in the histories of some countries. Do they not see that their own religion is founded on a human sacrifice, the blood of man, of which their priests talk like so many butchers ? It is no wonder the Christian religion has been so bloody in its effects, for it began in blood, and many thousands of human sacrifices have since been offered on the altar of the Christian religion.

It is necessary to the character of a religion, as being true, and immutable as God himself is, that the evidence of it be equally the same through all periods of time and circumstance. This is not the case with the Christian religion, nor with that of the Jews that preceded it, (for there was a time and that within the knowledge of history, when these religions did not exist,) nor is it the case with any religion we know of but the religion of Deism. In this the evidences are eternal and universal. "*The heavens declare the glory of God, and the firmament sheweth his handywork. Day unto day uttereth speech, and night unto night sheweth knowledge.*" * But all other religions are made to arise from some local circumstance, and are introduced by some temporary trifle which its partizans call a miracle, but of which there is no proof but the story of it.

The Jewish religion, according to the history of it, began in a *wilderness*, and the Christian religion in a *stable*. The Jewish book tell us of wonders exhibited upon mount Sinai. It happened that nobody lived there to contradict the account. The Christian books tell us of a star that hung over the *stable* at the birth of Jesus. There is no star there now, nor any person living that saw it. But all the stars in the heavens bear eternal evidence to the truth of Deism. It did not begin in a stable, nor in a wilderness. It began every where. The theatre of the universe is the place of its birth.

As adoration paid to any being but GOD himself is idolatry: the Christian religion by paying adoration to a man, born of a woman called Mary, belongs to the idolatrous class of religions; consequently the consolation drawn from it is delusion. Between you and your rival in communion ceremonies, Dr. Moore of the Episcopal church, you have, in order to make yourselves appear of some importance, reduced General Hamilton's character to that of a feeble minded man, who in going out of the world wanted a passport from a priest. Which of you was first or last applied to for this purpose is a matter of no consequence.

* This Psalm (19) which is a *Deistical Psalm*, is so much in the manner of some parts of the book of Job, (which is not a book of the Jews, and does not belong to the Bible,) that it has the appearance of having been translated into Hebrew from the same language in which the book of Job was originally written, and brought by the Jews from Chaldea or Persia, when they returned from captivity. The contemplation of the heavens made a great part of the religious devotion of the Chaldeans and Persians, and their religious festivals were regulated by the progress of the sun through the twelve signs of the Zodiac. But the Jews knew nothing about the Heavens, or they would not have told the foolish story of the sun's standing still upon a hill, and the moon in a valley. What could they want the moon for in the day time ?—*Author*.

The man, sir, who puts his trust and confidence in God, that leads a just and moral life, and endeavours to do good, does not trouble himself about priests when his hour of departure comes, nor permit priests to trouble themselves about him. They are in general mischievous beings where character is concerned ; a consultation of priests is worse than a consultation of physicians.

A MEMBER OF THE DEISTICAL CONGREGATION.

ON DEISM, AND THE WRITINGS OF THOMAS PAINE.[1]

THE following reflections, written last winter, were occasioned by *certain* expressions in some of the public papers against Deism and the writings of Thomas Paine on that subject.

"*Great is Diana of the Ephesians,*" was the cry of the people of Ephesus (Acts xix. 28) ; and the cry of "*our holy religion*" has been the cry of superstition in some instances, and of hypocrisy in others, from that day to this.

The Brahmin, the follower of Zoroaster, the Jew, the Mahometan, the church of Rome, the Greek church, the Protestant church, split into several hundred contradictory sectaries, preaching in some instances damnation against each other, all cry out, "*our holy religion.*" The Calvinist, who damns children of a span long to hell to burn for ever for the glory of God, (and this is called Christianity,) and the Universalist who preaches that all shall be saved and none shall be damned, (and this also is called Christianity,) boast alike of their *holy religion* and their Christian faith.[2] Something more therefore is necessary than mere *cry* and wholesale assertion, and that something is TRUTH ; and as inquiry is the road to truth, he that is opposed to inquiry is not a friend to truth.

---

[1] Though at this distance of time one paragraph in this article may seem egotistical, it should be remembered that Paine was then the object of furious attacks in religious papers and pulpits on account of his Deism.—*Editor.*

[2] Universalism in America long held strictly to orthodox dogmas, with the exception that the atonement was declared to be efficacious for the salvation of all mankind. Its doctrines are now Unitarian.—*Editor.*

The God of Truth is not the God of fable ; when, there-fore, any book is introduced into the world as the Word of God, and made a ground-work for religion, it ought to be scrutinized more than other books to see if it bear evidence of being what it is called. Our reverence to God demands that we do this, lest we ascribe to God what is not his, and our duty to ourselves demands it lest we take fable for fact, and rest our hope of salvation on a false foundation. It is not our calling a book *holy* that makes it so, any more than our calling a religion holy that entitles it to the name. In-quiry therefore is necessary in order to arrive at truth. But inquiry must have some principle to proceed on, some stand-ard to judge by, superior to human authority.

When we survey the works of Creation, the revolutions of the planetary system, and the whole economy of what is called nature, which is no other than the laws the Creator has prescribed to matter, we see unerring order and universal harmony reigning throughout the whole. No one part con-tradicts another. The sun does not run against the moon, nor the moon against the sun, nor the planets against each other. Every thing keeps its appointed time and place. This harmony in the works of God is so obvious, that the farmer of the field, though he cannot calculate eclipses, is as sensible of it as the philosophical astronomer. He sees the God of order in every part of the visible universe.

Here, then, is the standard to which every thing must be brought that pretends to be the work or Word of God, and by this standard it must be judged, independently of any thing and every thing that man can say or do. His opinion is like a feather in the scale compared with the standard that God himself has set up.

It is, therefore, by this standard, that the Bible, and all other books pretending to be the Word of God, (and there are many of them in the world,) must be judged, and not by the opinions of men or the decrees of ecclesiastical coun-cils. These have been so contradictory, that they have often rejected in one Council what they had voted to be the word of God in another ; and admitted what had been before re-

jected. In this state of uncertainty in which we are, and
which is rendered still more uncertain by the numerous contradictory sectaries that have sprung up since the time of
Luther and Calvin, what is man to do ? The answer is easy.
Begin at the root—begin with the Bible itself. Examine it
with the utmost strictness. It is our duty so to do. Compare the parts with each other, and the whole with the harmonious, magnificent order that reigns throughout the
visible universe, and the result will be, that if the same almighty wisdom that created the universe dictated also the
Bible, the Bible will be as harmonious and as magnificent in
all its parts, and in the whole, as the universe is. But if,
instead of this, the parts are found to be discordant, contradicting in one place what is said in another, (as in 2 Sam.
xxiv. 1, and 1 Chron. xxi. 1, where the same action is ascribed to God in one book and to Satan in the other,)
abounding also in idle and obscene stories, and representing
the Almighty as a passionate, whimsical Being, continually
changing his mind, making and unmaking his own works as
if he did not know what he was about, we may take it for
certainty that the Creator of the universe is not the author
of such a book, that it is not the Word of God, and that to
call it so is to dishonour his name. The Quakers, who are
a people more moral and regular in their conduct than the
people of other sectaries, and generally allowed so to be, do
not hold the Bible to be the word of God. They call it *a
history of the times*, and a bad history it is, and also a history
of bad men and of bad actions, and abounding with bad
examples.

For several centuries past the dispute has been about doctrines. It is now about fact. Is the Bible the Word of God,
or is it not? For until this point is established, no doctrine
drawn from the Bible can afford real consolation to man,
and he ought to be careful he does not mistake delusion for
truth. This is a case that concerns all men alike.

There has always existed in Europe, and also in America,
since its establishments, a numerous description of men, (I
do not here mean the Quakers,) who did not, and do not
believe the Bible to be the Word of God. These men never

formed themselves into an established society, but are to be found in all the sectaries that exist, and are more numerous than any, perhaps equal to all, and are daily increasing. From *Deus*, the Latin word for God, they have been denominated *Deists*, that is, believers in God. It is the most honourable appellation that can be given to man, because it is derived immediately from the Deity. It is not an artificial name like Episcopalian, Presbyterian, etc., but is a name of sacred signification, and to revile it is to revile the name of God.

Since then there is so much doubt and uncertainty about the Bible, some asserting and others denying it to be the Word of God, it is best that the whole matter come out. It is necessary for the information of the world that it should. A better time cannot offer than while the government,[1] patronizing no one sect or opinion in preference to another, protects equally the rights of all ; and certainly every man must spurn the idea of an ecclesiastical tyranny, engrossing the rights of the press, and holding it free only for itself.

Whilst the terrors of the Church, and the tyranny of the State, hung like a pointed sword over Europe, men were commanded to believe what the Church told them, or go to the stake. All inquiries into the authenticity of the Bible were shut out by the Inquisition. We ought therefore to suspect that a great mass of information respecting the Bible, and the introduction of it into the world, has been suppressed by the united tyranny of Church and State, for the purpose of keeping people in ignorance, and which ought to be known.

The Bible has been received by the Protestants on the authority of the Church of Rome, and on no other authority. It is she that has said it is the Word of God. We do not admit the authority of that Church with respect to its pretended *infallibility*, its manufactured miracles, its setting itself up to forgive sins, its amphibious doctrine of transubstantiation, etc. ; and we ought to be watchful with respect to any book introduced by her, or her ecclesiastical Councils, and called by her the Word of God : and the more so, be-

[1] Under the presidency of Jefferson.—*Editor.*

cause it was by propagating that belief and supporting it by fire and faggot, that she kept up her temporal power. That the belief of the Bible does no good in the world, may be seen by the irregular lives of those, as well priests as laymen, who profess to believe it to be the Word of God, and the moral lives of the Quakers who do not. It abounds with too many ill examples to be made a rule for moral life, and were a man to copy after the lives of some of its most celebrated characters, he would come to the gallows.

Thomas Paine has written to show that the Bible is not the Word of God, that the books it contains were not written by the persons to whom they are ascribed, that it is an anonymous book, and that we have no authority for calling it the Word of God, or for saying it was written by inspired penmen, since we do not know who the writers were. This is the opinion not only of Thomas Paine, but of thousands and tens of thousands of the most respectable characters in the United States and in Europe. These men have the same right to their opinions as others have to contrary opinions, and the same right to publish them. Ecclesiastical tyranny is not admissible in the United States.

With respect to morality, the writings of Thomas Paine are remarkable for purity and benevolence ; and though he often enlivens them with touches of wit and humour, he never loses sight of the real solemnity of his subject. No man's morals, either with respect to his Maker, himself, or his neighbour, can suffer by the writings of Thomas Paine.[1]

It is now too late to abuse Deism, especially in a country where the press is free, *or where free presses can be established.* It is a religion that has God for its patron and derives its name from him. The thoughtful mind of man, wearied with the endless contentions of sectaries against sectaries, doctrines against doctrines, and priests against priests, finds its repose at last in the contemplative belief and worship of one God and the practice of morality; for as Pope wisely says,

> " He can't be wrong, whose life is in the right."

[1] This article was anonymous.—*Editor.*

OF THE BOOKS OF THE NEW TESTAMENT.

ADDRESS TO THE BELIEVERS IN THE BOOK CALLED THE SCRIPTURES.

THE New Testament contains twenty-seven books, of which four are called Gospels; one called the Acts of the Apostles; fourteen called the Epistles of Paul; one of James; two of Peter; three of John; one of Jude; one called the Revelation.

None of those books have the appearance of being written by the persons whose names they bear, neither do we know who the authors were. They come to us on no other authority than the Church of Rome, which the Protestant Priests, especially those of New England, call the *Whore of Babylon.* This church, or to use their own vulgar language, *this whore,* appointed sundry Councils to be held, to compose creeds for the people, and to regulate Church affairs. Two of the principal of these Councils were that of Nice, and of Laodicea (names of the places where the Councils were held,) about three hundred and fifty years after the time that Jesus is said to have lived. Before this time there was no such book as the New Testament. But the Church could not well go on without having something to show, as the Persians showed the Zendavesta, revealed they say by God to Zoroaster; the Bramins of India, the Shaster, revealed, they say, by God to Brama, and given to him out of a dusky cloud; the Jews, the books they call the Law of Moses, given they say also out of a cloud on Mount Sinai. The Church set about forming a code for itself out of such materials as it could find or pick up. But where they got those materials, in what language they were written, or whose handwriting they were, or whether they were originals or copies, or on what authority they stood, we know nothing of, nor does the New Testament tell us. The Church was resolved to have a New Testament, and as, after the lapse of more than three hundred years, no handwriting could be proved or disproved, the Church, which like former impostors had then gotten possession of the State, had every

thing its own way. It invented creeds, such as that called
the Apostles Creed, the Nicean Creed, the Athanasian
Creed, and out of the loads of rubbish that were presented
it voted four to be Gospels, and others to be Epistles, as we
now find them arranged.

Of those called Gospels, above forty were presented, each
pretending to be genuine. Four only were voted in, and
entitled : the Gospel *according* to St. Matthew—the Gospel
according to St. Mark—the Gospel *according* to St. Luke—
the Gospel *according* to St. John.

This word *according*, shews that those books have not
been written by Matthew, Mark, Luke, and John, but according to some accounts or traditions, picked up concerning them. The word " according" means agreeing with,
and necessarily includes the idea of two things, or two persons. We cannot say, *The Gospel written by Matthew according to Matthew ;* but we might say, the Gospel of some
other person according to what was reported to have been
the opinion of Matthew. Now we do not know who those
other persons were, nor whether what they wrote accorded
with any thing that Matthew, Mark, Luke, and John might
have said. There is too little evidence, and too much
contrivance, about those books to merit credit.

The next book after those called Gospels, is that called
the Acts of the Apostles. This book is anonymous ; neither
do the Councils that compiled or contrived the New Testament tell us how they came by it. The Church, to supply
this defect, say it was written by Luke, which shews that
the Church and its priests have not compared that called the
Gospel according to St. Luke and the Acts together, for
the two contradict each other. The book of Luke, xxiv.,
makes Jesus ascend into heaven the very same day that it
makes him rise from the grave.[1] The book of Acts, i. 3, says
that he remained on earth forty days after his crucifix-
tion. There is no believing what either of them says.

The next to the book of Acts is that entitled, " The

[1] With reference to Luke xxiv. 51, it is said in the Revised Version, " Some
ancient authorities omit *and was carried up into heaven.*"—*Editor.*

Epistle of Paul the Apostle* to the Romans." This is not an Epistle, or letter, written by Paul or signed by him. It is an Epistle, or letter, written by a person who signs himself TERTIUS, and sent, as it is said in the end, by a servant woman called Phebe. The last chapter, ver. 22, says, "I Tertius, who wrote this Epistle, salute you." Who Tertius or Phebe were, we know nothing of. The Epistle is not dated. The whole of it is written in the first person, and that person is Tertius, not Paul. But it suited the Church to ascribe it to Paul. There is nothing in it that is interesting except it be to contending and wrangling sectaries. The stupid metaphor of the potter and the clay is in chapter ix.

The next book is entitled " The First Epistle of Paul the Apostle to the Corinthians." This, like the former, is not an Epistle written by Paul, nor signed by him. The conclusion of the Epistle says, " The first epistle to the Corinthians was written from Philippi, by Stephanas, and Fortunatus, and Achaicus, and Timotheus." The second epistle entitled, " The second Epistle of Paul the Apostle to the Corinthians," is in the same case with the first. The conclusion of it says, " It was written from Philippi, a city of Macedonia, by Titus and Lucas."

A question may arise upon these cases, which is, are these persons the writers of the epistles originally, or are they the writers and attestors of copies sent to the Councils who compiled the code or canon of the New Testament ? If the epistles had been dated this question could be decided ; but in either of the cases the evidences of Paul's hand writing and of their being written by him is wanting, and, therefore, there is no authority for calling them Epistles of Paul. We know not whose Epistles they were, nor whether they are genuine or forged.

The next is entitled, " The Epistle of Paul the Apostle to

---

* According to the criterion of the Church, Paul was not an Apostle ; that appellation being given only to those called the Twelve. Two sailors belonging to a man of war got into a dispute upon this point, whether Paul was an Apostle or not, and they agreed to refer it to the boatswain, who decided very *canonically* that Paul was an *acting* Apostle but not *rated.*—*Author.*

the Galatians." It contains six short chapters, yet the writer
of it says, vi. 11, "Ye see how large a letter I have written
to you with my own hand." If Paul was the writer of this
it shews he did not accustom himself to write long epistles;
yet the epistle to the Romans and the first to the Corinthians contain sixteen chapters each; the second to the
Corinthians and that to the Hebrews thirteen each. There
is something contradictory in these matters. But short as
the Epistle is, it does not carry the appearance of being
the work or composition of one person. Chapter v. 2 says,
"If ye be circumcised Christ shall avail you nothing." It
does not say circumcision shall profit you nothing, but
Christ shall profit you nothing. Yet in vi. 15 it says, "For
in Christ Jesus neither circumcision availeth any thing nor
uncircumcision, but a new creature." These are not reconcilable passages, nor can contrivance make them so. The
conclusion of the Epistle says it was written from Rome,
but it is not dated, nor is there any signature to it, neither
do the compilers of the New Testament say how they came
by it. We are in the dark upon all these matters.

The next is entitled, " The Epistle of Paul the Apostle to
the Ephesians." [1] Paul is not the writer. The conclusion
of it says, "Written from Rome unto the Ephesians by
Tychicus."

The next is entitled, " The Epistle of Paul the Apostle
to the Philippians." Paul is not the writer. The conclusion of it says, " It was written to the Philippians from Rome
by Epaphroditus." It is not dated. Query, were those
men who wrote and signed those Epistles journeymen
Apostles, who undertook to write in Paul's name, as Paul
is said to have preached in Christ's name?

The next is entitled, " The Epistle of Paul the Apostle to
the Colossians." Paul is not the writer. Doctor Luke is
spoken of in this Epistle as sending his compliments.
" Luke, the beloved physician, and Demas, greet you."
(iv. 14.) It does not say a word about his writing any Gos-

---

[1] Here, and in each of the succeeding paragraphs concerning the Epistles,
Paine gives the number of their " short chapters," which I omit.—*Editor*.

pel. The conclusion of the Epistle says, " Written from Rome to the Colossians by Tychicus and Onesimus."

The next is entitled, " The first and the second Epistles of Paul the Apostle to the Thessalonians." Either the writer of these Epistles was a visionary enthusiast, or a direct impostor, for he tells the Thessalonians, and, he says, he tells them by the word of the Lord, that the world will be at an end in his and their time ; and after telling them that those who are already dead shall rise, he adds, iv. 17, " Then we which are alive and remain shall be caught up with them into the clouds to meet the Lord in the air, and so shall we be ever with the Lord." Such detected lies as these, ought to fill priests with confusion, when they preach such books to be the Word of God. These two Epistles are said in the conclusion of them, to be written from Athens. They are without date or signature.

The next four Epistles are private letters. Two of them are to Timothy, one to Titus, and one to Philemon. Who they were, nobody knows.

The first to Timothy, is said to be written from Laodicea. It is without date or signature. The second to Timothy, is said to be written from Rome, and is without date or signature. The Epistle to Titus is said to be written from Nicopolis in Macedonia. It is without date or signature. The Epistle to Philemon is said to be written from Rome by Onesimus. It is without date.

The last Epistle ascribed to Paul is entitled, " The Epistle of Paul the Apostle to the Hebrews," and is said in the conclusion to be written from Italy, by Timothy. This Timothy (according to the conclusion of the Epistle called the second Epistle of Paul to Timothy) was Bishop of the church of the Ephesians, and consequently this is not an Epistle of Paul.

On what slender cob-web evidence do the priests and professors of the Christian religion hang their faith ! The same degree of hearsay evidence, and that at third and fourth hand, would not, in a court of justice, give a man title to a cottage, and yet the priests of this profession presumptuously promise their deluded followers the kingdom of Heaven. A little reflection would teach men that those books are not to be trusted to; that so far from there being any proof they are the Word of God, it is unknown who the writers of them were, or at what time they were written, within three hundred years after the reputed authors are said to have lived. It is not the interest of priests, who get their living by them, to examine into the insufficiency of the evidence upon which those books were received by the popish Councils who compiled the New Testament. But if Messrs. Linn and Mason would occupy themselves upon this subject (it signifies not which side they take, for the event will be the same) they would be better employed than they were last presidential election, in writing jesuitical electioneering pamphlets. The very name of a priest attaches suspicion on to it the instant he becomes a dabbler in party politics. The New England priests set themselves up to govern the state, and they are falling into contempt for so doing. Men who have their farms and their several occupations to follow, and have a common interest with their neighbours in the public prosperity and tranquillity of their country, neither want nor choose to be told by a priest who they shall vote for, nor how they shall conduct their temporal concerns.

The cry of the priests that the Church is in danger, is the cry of men who do not understand the interest of their own craft ; for instead of exciting alarms and apprehensions for its safety, as they expect, it excites suspicion that the foundation is not sound, and that it is necessary to take down and build it on a surer foundation. Nobody fears for the safety of a mountain, but a hillock of sand may be washed away! Blow then, O ye priests, " the Trumpet in Zion," for the Hillock is in danger.

DETECTOR—P.

BIBLICAL BLASPHEMY.

THE Church tells us that the books of the Old and New Testament are divine revelation, and without this revelation we could not have true ideas of God.

The Deist, on the contrary, says that those books are *not* divine revelation ; and that were it not for the light of reason and the religion of Deism, those books, instead of teaching us true ideas of God, would teach us not only false but blasphemous ideas of him.

Deism teaches us that God is a God of truth and justice. Does the Bible teach the same doctrine? It does not.

The Bible says, (Jeremiah xx. 5, 7,) that God is a de-ceiver. "O Lord (says Jeremiah) thou hast deceived me, and I was deceived. Thou art stronger than I, and hast prevailed."

Jeremiah not only upbraids God with deceiving *him*, but, in iv. 9, he upbraids God with deceiving the people of Jerusalem. "Ah! Lord God, (says he,) surely thou hast greatly deceived this people and Jerusalem, saying, ye shall have peace, whereas the sword reacheth unto the soul."

In xv. 8, the Bible becomes more impudent, and calls God in plain language, a *liar.* "Wilt thou, (says Jeremiah to God,) be altogether unto me as a liar and as waters that fail."

Ezekiel xiv. 9, makes God to say—"If the prophet be deceived when he hath spoken a thing, *I the Lord have de-ceived that prophet.*" All this is downright blasphemy.

The prophet Micaiah, as he is called, 2 Chron. xviii. 18–21, tells another blasphemous story of God. "I saw," says he, "the Lord sitting on his throne, and all the hosts of heaven standing on his right hand and on his left. And the Lord said, who shall entice Ahab, king of Israel, to go up and *fall* at Ramoth Gilead? And one spoke after this man-ner, and another after that manner. Then there came out a spirit [Micaiah does not tell us where he came from] and *stood before the Lord*, [what an impudent fellow this spirit was,] and said, I will entice him. And the Lord said unto him, wherewith? And he said, I will go out and be a lying spirit in the mouth of all his prophets. And the Lord said, Thou shalt entice him, and thou shalt also prevail ; go out, and do even so,"

We often hear of a gang of thieves plotting to rob and

murder a man, and laying a plan to entice him out that they may execute their design, and we always feel shocked at the wickedness of such wretches; but what must we think of a book that describes the Almighty acting in the same manner, and laying plans in heaven to entrap and ruin mankind? Our ideas of his justice and goodness forbid us to believe such stories, and therefore we say that a lying spirit has been in the mouth of the writers of the books of the Bible.

T. P.

BIBLICAL ANACHRONISM.

In addition to the judicious remarks in your 12th number, on the absurd story of Noah's flood, in Genesis vii. I send you the following:

The second verse makes God to say unto Noah, "Of every *clean* beast thou shalt take to thee by sevens, the male and his female, and of every beast that are *not clean*, by two, the male and his female."

Now, there was no such thing as beasts *clean* and *unclean* in the time of Noah. Neither were there any such people as Jews or Israelites at that time, to whom that distinction was a law. The law, called the the law of Moses, by which a distinction is made, beasts clean and unclean, was not until several hundred years after the time that Noah is said to have lived. The story, therefore, detects itself, because the inventor forgot himself, by making God make use of an expression that could not be used at the time. The blunder is of the same kind, as if a man in telling a story about America a hundred years ago, should quote an expression from Mr. Jefferson's inaugural speech as if spoken by him at that time.

My opinion of this story is the same as what a man once said to another, who asked him in a drawling tone of voice, "Do you believe the account about No-ah?" The other replied in the same tone of voice, *ah-no.*

T. P.

RELIGIOUS INTELLIGENCE.

THE following publication, which has appeared in several newspapers in different parts of the United States, shews in the most striking manner the character and effects of religious fanaticism, and to what extravagant lengths it will carry its unruly and destructive operations. We give it a place in the Prospect, because we think the perusal of it will be gratifying to our subscribers ; and, because, by exposing the true character of such frantic zeal, we hope to produce some influence upon the reason of man, and induce him to rise superior to such dreadful illusions. The judicious remarks at the end of this account were communicated to us by a very intelligent and faithful friend to the cause of Deism.

Extract from a Letter of the Rev. George Scott, of Mill Creek, Washington County, Pennsylvania, to Col. William M'Farran, of Mount Bethel, Northampton County, Pa., dated November 3, 1802.

" My Dear Friend,
We have wonderful times here. God has been pleased to visit this barren corner with abundance of his grace. The work began in a neighbouring congregation, at a sacramental occasion, about the last of September. It did not make its appearance in my congregation till the first Tuesday of October. After society in the night, there appeared an evident stir among the young people, but nothing of the appearance of what appeared afterwards. On Saturday evening following we had society, but it was dull throughout. On Sabbath-day one cried out, but nothing else extraordinary appeared.—That evening I went part of the way to the Raccoon congregation, where the sacrament of the supper was administered ; but on Monday morning a very strong impression of duty constrained me to return to my congregation in the Flats, where the work was begun. We met in the afternoon at the meeting-house where we had a warm society. In the evening we removed to a neighbouring

house, where we continued in society till midnight; numbers
were falling all the time of society.—After the people were
dismissed, a considerable number staid and sung hymns, till
perhaps two o'clock in the morning, when the work began to
the astonishment of all.   Only five or six were left able to
take care of the rest, to the number perhaps of near forty.—
They fell in all directions, on benches, on beds, and on the
floor.   Next morning the people began to flock in from all
quarters.   One girl came early in the morning, but did not
get within one hundred yards of the house before she fell
powerless, and was carried in.   We could not leave the
house, and, therefore, continued society all that day and all
that night, and on Wednesday morning I was obliged to
leave a number of them on the spot.   On Thursday evening
we met again, when the work was amazing ; about twenty
persons lay to all appearance dead for near two and a half
hours, and a great number cried out with sore distress.—
Friday I preached at Mill Creek.   Here nothing appeared
more than an unusual solemnity.   That evening we had
society, where great numbers were brought under conviction, but none fell.   On sabbath-day I preached at Mill
Creek.   This day and evening was a very solemn time but
none fell.   On Monday I went to attend presbytery, but returned on Thursday evening to the Flats, where society was
appointed, when numbers were struck down.   On Saturday
evening we had society, and a very solemn time—about a
dozen persons lay dead three and a half hours by the watch.
On sabbath a number fell, and we were obliged to continue
all night in society, as we had done every evening we had
met before.   On Monday a Mr. Hughes preached at Mill
Creek, but nothing extraordinary appeared, only a great
deal of falling.   We concluded to divide that evening into
two societies, in order to accommodate the people.   Mr. H.
attended the one and I the other.   Nothing strange appeared
where Mr. H. attended ; but where I attended God was
present in the most wonderful manner.   I believe there was
not one present but was more or less affected.   A considerable number fell powerless, and two or three, after laying

some time, recovered with joy, and spoke near half an hour. One, especially, declared in a surprising manner the wonderful view she had of the person, character, and offices of Christ, with such accuracy of language, that I was astonished to hear it. Surely this must be the work of God! On Thursday evening we had a lively society, but not much falling down. On Saturday we all went to the Cross Roads, and attended a sacrament. Here were, perhaps, about 4000 people collected. The weather was uncomfortable ; on the Sabbath-day it rained, and on Monday it snowed. We had thirteen ministers present. The exercises began on Saturday, and continued on night and day with little or no intermission. Great numbers fell; to speak within bounds, there were upwards of 150 down at one time, and some of them continued three or four hours with but little appearance of life. Numbers came to, rejoicing, while others were deeply distressed.—The scene was wonderful ; the cries of the distressed, and the agonising groans, gave some faint representation of the awful cries and the bitter screams which will no doubt be extorted from the damned in hell. But what is to me the most surprising, of those who have been subjects among my people with whom I have conversed, but three had any terrors of hell during their exercise. The principal cry is, O how long have I rejected Christ! O how often have I embrued my hands in his precious blood! O how often have I waded through his precious blood by stifling conviction! O this dreadful hard heart! O what a dreadful monster sin is! It was my sin that nailed Jesus to the cross! &c.

The preaching is various ; some thunder the terrors of the law—others preach the mild invitation of the gospel. For my part, since the work began, I have confined myself chiefly to the doctrines of our fallen state by nature, and the way of recovery through Christ ; opening the way of salvation ; showing how God can be just and yet be the justifier of them that believe, and also the nature of true faith and repentance ; pointing out the difference between true and false religion, and urging the invitations of the gospel in the most engaging manner that I am master of, without any strokes of terror. The convictions and cries appear to be, perhaps, nearly equal under all these different modes of preaching, but it appears rather most when we preach on the fulness and freeness of salvation."

REMARKS BY MR. PAINE.

In the fifth chapter of Mark, we read a strange story of the Devil getting into the swine after he had been turned out of a man, and as the freaks of the Devil in *that* story and the tumble-down description in *this* are very much alike, the two stories ought to go together. [*Paine here quotes in full Mark v.* 1–13.]

The force of the imagination is capable of producing strange effects.—When Animal Magnetism began in France, which was while Doctor Franklin was Minister to that country, the wonderful accounts given of the wonderful effects it produced on the persons who were under operation, exceeded any thing related in the foregoing letter from Washington County. They tumbled down, fell into trances, roared and rolled about like persons supposed to be bewitched. The government, in order to ascertain the fact, or detect the imposition, appointed a Committee of physicians to inquire into the case, and Doctor Franklin was requested to accompany them, which he did.

The Committee went to the operator's house, and the persons on whom an operation was to be performed were assembled. They were placed in the position in which they had been when under former operations, and *blind-folded.* In a little time they began to show signs of agitation, and in the space of about two hours they went through all the frantic airs they had shewn before ; but the case was, that no operation was performing upon them, neither was the operator in the room, for he had been ordered out of it by the physicians ; but as the persons did not know this, they supposed him present and operating upon them. It was the effect of imagination only. Doctor Franklin, in relating this account to the writer of this article, said, that he thought the government might as well have let it gone on, for that as imagination sometimes produced disorders it might also cure some. It is fortunate, however, that this falling down and crying out scene did not happen in New England a century ago, for if it had the preachers would have been hung for witchcraft, and in more ancient times the poor falling down folks would have been supposed to be possessed of a devil, like the man in Mark, among the tombs. The progress that reason and Deism make in the world lessen the force of superstition, and abate the spirit of persecution.

X.

EXAMINATION OF PROPHECIES.[1]

AUTHOR'S PREFACE.

To the Ministers and Preachers of all Denominations of Religion.

IT is the duty of every man, as far as his ability extends, to detect and expose delusion and error. But nature has not given to every one a talent for the purpose ; and among

[1] This was the last work that Paine ever gave to the press. It appeared in New York in 1807 with the following title : "An Examination of the Passages in the New Testament, quoted from the Old and called Prophecies concerning Jesus Christ. To which is prefixed an Essay on Dream, shewing by what operation of the mind a Dream is produced in sleep, and applying the same to the account of Dreams in the New Testament. With an Appendix containing my private thoughts of a Future State. And Remarks on the Contradictory Doctrine in the Books of Matthew and Mark. By Thomas Paine, New York : Printed for the Author." Pp. 68.

This work is made up from the unpublished Part III. of the "Age of Reason," and the answer to the Bishop of Llandaff. In the Introductory chapter, on Dream, he would seem to have partly utilized an earlier essay, and this is the only part of the work previously printed. Nearly all of it was printed in Paris, in English, soon after Paine's departure for America. This little pamphlet, of which the only copy I have seen or heard of is in the Bodleian Library, has never been mentioned by any of Paine's editors, and perhaps he himself was not aware of its having been printed. Its title is : "Extract from the M. S. Third Part of Thomas Paine's Age of Reason. Chapter the Second : Article, Dream. Paris : Printed for M. Chateau, 1803." It is possible that it was printed for private circulation. I have compared this Paris pamphlet closely with an original copy of Paine's own edition (New York, 1807) with results indicated in footnotes to the Essay.

Dr. Clair J. Grece, of Redhill, has shown me a copy of the "Examination" which Paine presented to his (Dr. Grece's) uncle, Daniel Constable, in New

those to whom such a talent is given, there is often a want of disposition or of courage to do it.

The world, or more properly speaking, that small part of it called christendom, or the christian world, has been amused for more than a thousand years with accounts of Prophecies in the Old-Testament about the coming of the person called Jesus Christ, and thousands of sermons have been preached, and volumes written, to make man believe it.

In the following treatise I have examined all the passages in the New-Testament, quoted from the Old, and called prophecies concerning Jesus Christ, and I find no such thing as a prophecy of any such person, and I deny there are any. The passages all relate to circumstances the Jewish nation was in at the time they were written or spoken, and not to any thing that was or was not to happen in the world several hundred years afterwards; and I have shewn what the circumstances were to which the passages apply or refer. I have given chapter and verse for every thing I have said, and have not gone out of the books of the Old and New Testament for evidence that the passages are not prophecies of the person called Jesus Christ.

The prejudice of unfounded belief, often degenerates into the prejudice of custom, and becomes at last rank hypocrisy. When men, from custom or fashion or any worldly motive, profess or pretend to believe what they do not believe, nor can give any reason for believing, they unship the helm of their morality, and being no longer honest to their own minds they feel no moral difficulty in being unjust to others.

York, July 21, 1807, with the prediction, " It is too much for the priests, and they will not touch it." It is rudely stitched in brown paper cover, and without the Preface and the Essay on Dream. It would appear from a note, which I quote at the beginning of the " Examination," by an early American editor that Paine detached that part as the only fragment he wished to be circulated.

This pamphlet, with some omissions, was published in London, 1811, as Part III. of the " Age of Reason," by Daniel Isaacs Eaton, for which he was sentenced to eighteen months imprisonment, and to stand in the pillory for one hour in each month. This punishment drew from Shelley his celebrated letter to Lord Ellenborough, who had given a scandalously prejudiced charge to the jury.—*Editor.*

It is from the influence of this vice, hypocrisy, that we see so many church-and-meeting-going professors and pretenders to religion so full of trick and deceit in their dealings, and so loose in the performance of their engagements that they are not to be trusted further than the laws of the country will bind them. Morality has no hold on their minds, no restraint on their actions.

One set of preachers make salvation to consist in believing. They tell their congregations that if they believe in Christ their sins shall be forgiven. This, in the first place, is an encouragement to sin, in a similar manner as when a prodigal young fellow is told his father will pay all his debts, he runs into debt the faster, and becomes the more extravagant. Daddy, says he, pays all, and on he goes: just so in the other case, *Christ pays all*, and on goes the sinner.

In the next place, the doctrine these men preach is not true. The New Testament rests itself for credibility and testimony on what are called prophecies in the Old-Testament of the person called Jesus Christ ; and if there are no such things as prophecies of any such person in the Old-Testament, the New-Testament is a forgery of the Councils of Nice and Laodicea, and the faith founded thereon delusion and falsehood.*

Another set of preachers tell their congregations that God predestinated and selected, from all eternity, a certain number to be saved, and a certain number to be damned eternally. If this were true, *the day of Judgment* IS PAST : *their preaching* is in vain, and they had better work at some useful calling for their livelihood.

This doctrine, also, like the former, hath a direct tendency to demoralize mankind. Can a bad man be reformed by telling him, that if he is one of those who was decreed to be

---

* The councils of Nice and Laodicea were held about 350 years after the time Christ is said to have lived ; and the books that now compose the New Testament, were then voted for by YEAS and NAYS, as we now vote a law. A great many that were offered had a majority of nays, and were rejected. This is the way the New-Testament came into being.—*Author*.

damned before he was born his reformation will do him no good ; and if he was decreed to be saved, he will be saved whether he believes it or not ?   For this is the result of the doctrine.   Such preaching and such preachers do injury to the moral world.   They had better be at the plough.

As in my political works my motive and object have been to give man an elevated sense of his own character, and free him from the slavish and superstitious absurdity of monarchy and hereditary government, so in my publications on religious subjects my endeavours have been directed to bring man to a right use of the reason that God has given him, to impress on him the great principles of divine morality, justice, mercy, and a benevolent disposition to all men, and to all creatures, and to inspire in him a spirit of trust, confidence, and consolation in his creator, unshackled by the fables of books pretending to be *the word of God.*

THOMAS PAINE.

INTRODUCTORY CHAPTER.

AN ESSAY ON DREAM.

As a great deal is said in the New Testament about dreams, it is first necessary to explain the nature of Dream, and to shew by what operation of the mind a dream is produced during sleep. When this is understood we shall be the better enabled to judge whether any reliance can be placed upon them; and consequently, whether the several matters in the New Testament related of dreams deserve the credit which the writers of that book and priests and commentators ascribe to them.

In order to understand the nature of Dream, or of that which passes in ideal vision during a state of sleep, it is first necessary to understand the composition and decomposition of the human mind.

The three great faculties of the mind are IMAGINATION, JUDGMENT, and MEMORY. Every action of the mind comes under one or the other of these faculties.[1] In a state of wakefulness, as in the day-time, these three faculties are all active; but that is seldom the case in sleep, and never perfectly: and this is the cause that our dreams are not so regular and rational as our waking thoughts.

The seat of that collection of powers or faculties that constitute what is called the mind, is in the brain. There is not, and cannot be, any visible demonstration of this anatomically, but accidents happening to living persons shew it to be so. An injury done to the brain by a fracture of the scull, will sometimes change a wise man into a childish idiot, —a being without a mind. But so careful has nature been

---

[1] This sentence is not in Paris edition.—*Editor*.

of that Sanctum Sanctorum of man, the brain, that of all the external accidents to which humanity is subject, this occurs the most seldom. But we often see it happening by long and habitual intemperance.

Whether those three faculties occupy distinct apartments of the brain, is known only to that ALMIGHTY POWER that formed and organized it. We can see the external effects of muscular motion in all the members of the body, though its primum mobile, or first moving cause, is unknown to man. Our external motions are sometimes the effect of intention, sometimes not. If we are sitting and intend to rise, or standing and intend to sit or to walk, the limbs obey that intention as if they heard the order given. But we make a thousand motions every day, and that as well waking as sleeping, that have no prior intention to direct them. Each member acts as if it had a will or mind of its own. Man governs the whole when he pleases to govern, but in the interim the several parts, like little suburbs, govern themselves without consulting the sovereign.

And all these motions, whatever be the generating cause, are external and visible. But with respect to the brain, no occular observation can be made upon it. All is mystery; all is darkness in that womb of thought.

Whether the brain is a mass of matter in continual rest; whether it has a vibrating pulsative motion, or a heaving and falling motion like matter in fermentation ; whether different parts of the brain have different motions according to the faculty that is employed, be it the imagination, the judgment, or the memory, man knows nothing of. He knows not the cause of his own wit. His own brain conceals it from him.

Comparing invisible by visible things, as metaphysical can sometimes be compared to physical things, the operations of these distinct and several faculties have some resemblance to a watch. The main spring which puts all in motion corresponds to the imagination ; the pendulum which corrects and regulates that motion, corresponds to the judgment; and the hand and dial, like the memory, record the operation.

Now in proportion as these several faculties sleep, slumber, or keep awake, during the continuance of a dream, in that proportion the dream will be reasonable or frantic, remembered or forgotten.

If there is any faculty in mental man that never sleeps, it is that volatile thing the imagination. The case is different with the judgment and memory. The sedate and sober constitution of the judgment easily disposes it to rest ; and as to the memory, it records in silence and is active only when it is called upon.

That the judgment soon goes to sleep may be perceived by our sometimes beginning to dream before we are fully asleep ourselves. Some random thought runs in the mind, and we start, as it were, into recollection that we are dreaming between sleeping and waking. [If a pendulum of a watch by any accident becomes displaced, that it can no longer control and regulate the elastic force of the spring, the works are instantly thrown into confusion, and continue so as long as the spring continues to have force. In like manner][1] if the judgment sleeps whilst the imagination keeps awake, the dream will be a riotous assemblage of misshapen images and ranting ideas, and the more active the imagination is the wilder the dream will be. The most inconsistent and the most impossible things will appear right ; because that faculty whose province it is to keep order is in a state of absence. The master of the school is gone out and the boys are in an uproar.

If the memory sleeps, we shall have no other knowledge of the dream than that we have dreamt, without knowing what it was about. In this case it is sensation rather than recollection that acts. The dream has given us some sense of pain or trouble, and we feel it as a hurt, rather than remember it as vision.

If the memory slumbers we shall have a faint remembrance of the dream, and after a few minutes it will sometimes happen that the principal passages of the dream will occur to us more fully. The cause of this is that the memory

---

[1] The words within crotchets are only in the Paris edition. In the New York edition (1807) the next word " If " begins a new paragraph.—*Editor.*

will sometimes continue slumbering or sleeping after we are awake ourselves, and that so fully, that it may and sometimes does happen, that we do not immediately recollect where we are, nor what we have been about, or have to do. But when the memory starts into wakefulness it brings the knowledge of these things back upon us like a flood of light, and sometimes the dream with it.

But the most curious circumstance of the mind in a state of dream, is the power it has to become the agent of every person, character and thing of which it dreams. It carries on conversation with several, asks questions, hears answers, gives and receives information, and it acts all these parts itself.

Yet however various and eccentric the imagination may be in the creating of images and ideas, it cannot supply the place of memory with respect to things that are forgotten when we are awake. For example, if we have forgotten the name of a person, and dream of seeing him and asking him his name, he cannot tell it ; for it is ourselves asking ourselves the question.

But though the imagination cannot supply the place of real memory, it has the wild faculty of counterfeiting memory. It dreams of persons it never knew, and talks to them as if it remembered them as old acquaintance. It relates circumstances that never happened, and tells them as if they had happened. It goes to places that never existed, and knows where all the streets and houses are, as if we had been there before. The scenes it creates are often as scenes remembered. It will sometimes act a dream within a dream, and, in the delusion of dreaming, tell a dream it never dreamed, and tell it as if it was from memory. It may also be remarked, that the imagination in a dream has no idea of time, *as time.* It counts only by circumstances ; and if a succession of circumstances pass in a dream that would require a great length of time to accomplish them, it will appear to the dreamer that a length of time equal thereto has passed also.

As this is the state of the mind in a dream, it may rationally be said that every person is mad once in twenty-four hours, for were he to act in the day as he dreams in the night, he would be confined for a lunatic. In a state of wakefulness, those three faculties being all active, and acting in unison, constitute the rational man. In dream it is otherwise, and, therefore, that state which is called insanity appears to be no other than a dismission of those faculties, and a cessation of the judgment during wakefulness, that we so often experience during sleep; and idiocity, into which some persons have fallen, is that cessation of all the faculties of which we can be sensible when we happen to wake before our memory.

In this view of the mind, how absurd it is to place reliance upon dreams, and how much more absurd to make them a foundation for religion ; yet the belief that Jesus Christ is the Son of God, begotten by the Holy Ghost, a being never heard of before, stands on the foolish story of an old man's dream. " *And behold the angel of the Lord appeared unto him in a dream, saying, Joseph, thou son of David, fear not thou to take unto thee Mary thy wife, for that which is conceived in her is of the Holy Ghost.*"—Matt. i. 20.

After this we have the childish stories of three or four other dreams: about Joseph going into Egypt; about his coming back again; about this, and about that, and this story of dreams has thrown Europe into a dream for more than a thousand years. All the efforts that nature, reason, and conscience have made to awaken man from it, have been ascribed by priestcraft and superstition to the working of the devil, and had it not been for the American Revolution, which, by establishing the universal right of conscience,[1] first opened the way to free discussion, and for the French Revolution that followed, this Religion of Dreams had continued to be preached, and that after it had ceased to be believed. Those who preached it and did not believe it, still believed the delusion necessary. They were not bold enough to be honest, nor honest enough to be bold.[2]

[1] The words " right of " are not in the Paris edition.—*Editor*.

[2] The remainder of this essay, down to the last two paragraphs, though contained in the Paris pamphlet, was struck out of the essay by Paine when he

I shall conclude this Essay on Dream with the first two verses of Ecclesiasticus xxxiv. one of the books of the Aprocrypha. " *The hopes of a man void of understanding are vain and false ; and dreams lift up fools. Whoso regardeth*

published it in America ; it was restored by an American editor who got hold of the original manuscript, with the exception of two sentences which he supposed caused the author to reserve the nine paragraphs containing them. It is probable, however, that this part was omitted as an interruption of the essay on Dream. The present Editor therefore concludes to insert the passage, without any omission, in this footnote :

" Every new religion, like a new play, requires a new apparatus of dresses and machinery, to fit the new characters it creates. The story of Christ in the New Testament brings a new being upon the stage, which it calls the Holy Ghost ; and the story of Abraham, the father of the Jews, in the Old Testament, gives existence to a new order of beings it calls Angels. There was no Holy Ghost before the time of Christ, nor Angels before the time of Abraham. We hear nothing of these winged gentlemen, till more than two thousand years, according to the Bible chronology, from the time they say the heavens, the earth, and all therein were made. After this, they hop about as thick as birds in a grove. The first we hear of, pays his addresses to Hagar in the wilderness ; then three of them visit Sarah ; another wrestles a fall with Jacob ; and these birds of passage having found their way to earth and back, are continually coming and going. They eat and drink, and up again to heaven. What they do with the food they carry away in their bellies, the Bible does not tell us. Perhaps they do as the birds do, discharge it as they fly ; for neither the scripture nor the church hath told us there are necessary houses for them in heaven. One would think that a system loaded with such gross and vulgar absurdities as scripture religion is could never have obtained credit ; yet we have seen what priestcraft and fanaticism could do, and credulity believe.

From Angels in the Old Testament we get to prophets, to witches, to seers of visions, and dreamers of dreams ; and sometimes we are told, as in 1 Sam. ix. 15, that God whispers in the ear. At other times we are not told how the impulse was given, or whether sleeping or waking. In 2 Sam. xxiv. 1, it is said, "*And again the anger of the Lord was kindled against Israel, and he moved David against them to say, Go number Israel and Judah.*" And in 1 Chron. xxi. 1, when the same story is again related, it is said, "*And Satan stood up against Israel, and moved David to number Israel.*"

Whether this was done sleeping or waking, we are not told, but it seems that David, whom they call " a man after God's own heart," did not know by what spirit he was moved ; and as to the men called inspired penmen, they agree so well about the matter, that in one book they say that it was God, and in the other that it was the Devil.

Yet this is trash that the church imposes upon the world as the WORD OF GOD ; this is the collection of lies and contradictions called the HOLY BIBLE ! this is the rubbish called REVEALED RELIGION !

The idea that writers of the Old Testament had of a God was boisterous, con-

dreams is like him that catcheth at a shadow, and followeth after the wind."

I now proceed to an examination of the passages in the Bible, called prophecies of the coming of Christ, and to shew

temptible, and vulgar. They make him the Mars of the Jews, the fighting God of Israel, the conjuring God of their Priests and Prophets. They tell us as many fables of him as the Greeks told of Hercules. They pit him against Pharaoh, as it were to box with him, and Moses carries the challenge. They make their God to say insultingly, " *I will get me honour upon Pharaoh and upon all his Host, upon his chariots and upon his Horsemen.*" And that he may keep his word, they make him set a trap in the Red Sea, in the dead of the night, for Pharaoh, his host, and his horses, and drown them as a rat-catcher would do so many rats. Great honour indeed! the story of Jack the giant-killer is better told!

They match him against the Egyptian magicians to conjure with them, and after hard conjuring on both sides (for where there is no great contest there is no great honour) they bring him off victorious. The first three essays are a dead match : each party turns his rod into a serpent, the rivers into blood, and creates frogs : but upon the fourth, the God of the Israelites obtains the laurel, he covers them all over with lice! The Egyptian magicians cannot do the same, and this lousy triumph proclaims the victory!

They make their God to rain fire and brimstone upon Sodom and Gomorrah, and belch fire and smoak upon mount Sinai, as if he was the Pluto of the lower regions. They make him salt up Lot's wife like pickled pork ; they make him pass like Shakespeare's Queen Mab into the brain of their priests, prophets, and prophetesses, and tickle them into dreams,[1] and after making him play all kinds of tricks they confound him with Satan, and leave us at a loss to know what God they meant!

This is the descriptive God of the Old Testament ; and as to the New, though the authors of it have varied the scene, they have continued the vulgarity.

Is man ever to be the dupe of priestcraft, the slave of superstition ? Is he never to have just ideas of his Creator ? It is better not to believe there is a God, than to believe of him falsely. When we behold the mighty universe that surrounds us, and dart our contemplation into the eternity of space, filled with innumerable orbs revolving in eternal harmony, how paltry must the tales of the Old and New Testaments, prophanely called the word of God, appear to thoughtful man ! The stupendous wisdom and unerring order that reign and govern throughout this wonderous whole, and call us to reflection, *put to shame the Bible !* The God of eternity and of all that is real, is not the God of passing dreams and shadows of man's imagination. The God of truth is not the God of fable ; the belief of a God begotten and a God crucified, is a God blasphemed. It is making a profane use of reason."—*Author.*

[1] " Tickling a parson's nose as 'a lies asleep,
       Then dreams he of another benefice." (Rom. and Jul.)—*Editor.*

there are no prophecies of any such person ; that the passages clandestinely stiled prophecies are not prophecies ;
and that they refer to circumstances the Jewish nation was
in at the time they were written or spoken, and not to any
distance of future time or person.

EXAMINATION OF THE PROPHECIES.[1]

THE passages called Prophecies of, or concerning, Jesus Christ, in the Old Testament may be classed under the two following heads.

First, those referred to in the four books of the New Testament, called the four Evangelists, Matthew, Mark, Luke, and John.

Secondly, those which translators and commentators have, of their own imagination, erected into prophecies, and dubbed with that title at the head of the several chapters of the Old Testament. Of these it is scarcely worth while to waste time, ink, and paper upon; I shall, therefore, confine

---

[1] An early American Editor, Col. Fellows, Paine's personal friend, adds after the title of this " Examination " the following interesting Note : " This work was first published by Mr. Paine, at New-York, in 1807, and was the last of his writings edited by himself. It is evidently extracted from his answer to the bishop of Llandaff, or from his third part of the Age of Reason, both of which, it appears by his will, he left in manuscript. The term, ' *The Bishop,*' occurs in this examination six times without designating what bishop is meant. Of all the replies to his second part of the Age of Reason, that of bishop Watson was the only one to which he paid particular attention; and he is, no doubt, the person here alluded to. Bishop Watson's Apology for the Bible had been published some years before Mr. P. left France, and the latter composed his answer to it, and also his third part of the Age of Reason, while in that country.

" When Mr. Paine arrived in America, and found that liberal opinions on religion were in disrepute, through the influence of hypocrisy and superstition, he declined publishing the entire of the works which he had prepared ; observing that ' An author might lose the credit he had acquired by writing too much.' He however gave to the public the Examination before us, in a pamphlet form. But the apathy which appeared to prevail at that time in regard to religious inquiry, fully determined him to discontinue the publication of his theological writings. In this case, taking only a portion of one of the works before mentioned, he chose a title adapted to the particular part selected."— *Editor*.

myself chiefly to those referred to in the aforesaid four books of the New Testament. If I shew that these are not prophecies of the person called Jesus Christ, nor have reference to any such person, it will be perfectly needless to combat those which translators or the church have invented, and for which they had no other authority than their own imagination.

I begin with the book called the Gospel according to St. Matthew.

In i. 18, it is said, " *Now the birth of Jesus Christ was on this wise : When his mother Mary was espoused to Joseph, before they came together,* SHE WAS FOUND WITH CHILD OF THE HOLY GHOST."—This is going a little too fast ; because to make this verse agree with the next it should have said no more than that *she was found with child ;* for the next verse says, " *Then Joseph her husband, being a just man, and not willing to make her a public example, was minded to put her away privately."* Consequently Joseph had found out no more than that she was with child, and he knew it was not by himself.

Ver. 20, 21. " *And while he thought of these things,* [that is whether he should put her away privately, or make a public example of her,] *behold the Angel of the Lord appeared to him* IN A DREAM [that is, Joseph *dreamed* that an angel appeared unto him] *saying, Joseph, thou son of David, fear not to take unto thee Mary thy wife, for that which is conceived in her is of the Holy Ghost. And she shall bring forth a son, and call his name Jesus ; for he shall save his people from their sins."*

Now, without entering into any discussion upon the merits or demerits of the account here given, it is proper to observe, that it *has no higher authority than that of a dream ;* for it is impossible to a man to behold any thing in a dream but that which he dreams of. I ask not, therefore, whether Joseph if there was such a man had such a dream or not, because admitting he had, it proves nothing. So wonderful and irrational is the faculty of the mind in dream, that it acts the part of all the characters its imagination creates, and what it thinks it hears from any of them is no other than what the roving rapidity of its own imagination invents. It is therefore nothing to me what Joseph dreamed of; whether of the fidelity or infidelity of his wife. I pay no regard to my own dreams, and I should be weak indeed to put faith in the dreams of another.

The verses that follow those I have quoted, are the words of the writer of the book of Matthew. "*Now*, [says he,] *all this* [that is, all this dreaming and this pregnancy] *was done that it might be fulfilled which was spoken of the Lord by the Prophet, saying, Behold a virgin shall be with child, and shall bring forth a son, and they shall call his name Emmanuel, which being interpreted, is, God with us.*

This passage is in Isaiah vii. 14, and the writer of the book of Matthew endeavours to make his readers believe that this passage is a prophecy of the person called Jesus Christ. It is no such thing, and I go to shew it is not. But it is first necessary that I explain the occasion of these words being spoken by Isaiah. The reader will then easily perceive that so far from their being a prophecy of Jesus Christ, they have not the least reference to such a person, nor to any thing that could happen in the time that Christ is said to have lived, which was about seven hundred years after the time of Isaiah. The case is this;

On the death of Solomon the Jewish nation split into two monarchies: one called the kingdom of Judah, the capital of which was Jerusalem: the other the kingdom of Israel, the capital of which was Samaria. The kingdom of Judah followed the line of David, and the kingdom of Israel that of Saul; and these two rival monarchies frequently carried on fierce wars against each other.

At the time Ahaz was king of Judah, which was in the time of Isaiah, Pekah was king of Israel; and Pekah joined himself to Rezin, king of Syria, to make war against Ahaz, king of Judah; and these two kings marched a confederated and powerful army against Jerusalem. Ahaz and his people became alarmed at their danger, and "*their hearts were moved as the trees of the wood are moved with the wind.*" Isaiah vii. 3.

In this perilous situation of things, Isaiah addresses himself to Ahaz, and assures him in the name of the Lord, (the
cant phrase of all the prophets,) that these two kings should
not succeed against him ; and to assure him that this should
be the case, (the case was however directly contrary,*) tells
Ahaz to ask a sign of the Lord. This Ahaz declined doing,
giving as a reason, that he would not tempt the Lord ; upon
which Isaiah, who pretends to be sent from God, says, ver.
14, " Therefore the Lord himself shall give you a sign, *behold
a virgin shall conceive and bear a son*—Butter and honey
shall he eat, that he may know to refuse the evil and chuse
the good—For before the child shall know to refuse the evil
and chuse the good, the land which thou abhorrest shall be
forsaken of both her kings "—meaning the king of Israel
and the king of Syria who were marching against him.

Here then is the sign, which was to be the birth of a child,
and that child a son ; and here also is the time limited for
the accomplishment of the sign, namely, before the child
should know to refuse the evil and chuse the good.

The thing, therefore, to be a sign of success to Ahaz, must
be something that would take place before the event of the
battle then pending between him and the two kings could be
known. A thing to be a sign must precede the thing signified. The sign of rain must be before the rain.

It would have been mockery and insulting nonsense for
Isaiah to have assured Ahaz as a sign that these two kings
should not prevail against him, that a child should be born
seven hundred years after he was dead, and that before the
child so born should know to refuse the evil and choose the
good, he, Ahaz, should be delivered from the danger he was
then immediately threatened with.

---

* II. Chron. xxviii. 1. *Ahaz was twenty years old when he began to reign,
and he reigned sixteen years in Jerusalem, but he did not that which was right
in the sight of the Lord.*—ver. 5. *Wherefore the Lord his God delivered him
into the hand of the king of Syria, and they smote him, and carried away a
great multitude of them captive and brought them to Damascus ; and he was also
delivered into the hand of the king of Israel, who smote him with a great
slaughter.* Ver. 6. *And Pekah* (king of Israel) *slew in Judah an hundred and
twenty thousand in one day.*—ver. 8. *And the children of Israel carried away
captive of their brethren two hundred thousand women, sons, and daughters.*

But the case is, that the child of which Isaiah speaks *was his own child*, with which his wife or his mistress was then pregnant; for he says in the next chapter, (Is. viii. 2), "*And I took unto me faithful witnesses to record, Uriah the priest, and Zechariah the son of Jeberechiah; and I went unto the prophetess, and she conceived and bear a son;*" and he says, at ver. 18 of the same chapter, "*Behold I and the children whom the Lord hath given me are for signs and for wonders in Israel.*"

It may not be improper here to observe, that the word translated *a virgin* in Isaiah, does not signify a virgin in Hebrew, but merely a *young woman*. The tense is also falsified in the translation. Levi gives the Hebrew text of Isaiah vii. 14, and the translation in English with it—"*Behold a young woman is with child and beareth a son.*" [1] The expression, says he, is in the present tense. This translation agrees with the other circumstances related of the birth of this child which was to be a sign to Ahaz. But as the true translation could not have been imposed upon the world as a prophecy of a child to be born seven hundred years afterwards, the christian translators have falsified the original: and instead of making Isaiah to say, behold a *young woman is* with child and *beareth* a son, they have made him to say, " Behold a *virgin shall* conceive and *bear* a son. It is, however, only necessary for a person to read Isaiah vii. and viii., and he will be convinced that the passage in question is no prophecy of the person called Jesus Christ. I pass on to the second passage quoted from the Old Testament by the New, as a prophecy of Jesus Christ.

Matthew ii. 1–6. " Now when Jesus was born in Bethlehem of Judea, in the days of Herod the king, behold there came wise men from the East to Jerusalem, saying, where is he that is born king of the Jews? for we have seen his star in the East, and are come to worship Him. When Herod the king heard these things he was troubled, and all Jerusalem with him ; and when he had gathered all the chief

[1] "A Defence of the Old Testament." By David Levi. London, 1797.—*Editor.*

priests and scribes of the people together, he demanded of them where Christ should be born. And they said unto him, In Bethlehem, in the land of Judea : for thus it is written by the prophet, *And thou Bethlehem, in the land of Judea, art not the least among the princes of Judah, for out of thee shall come a Governor that shall rule my people Israel.*" This passage is in Micah v. 2.

I pass over the absurdity of seeing and following a star in the day time, as a man would a *Will with the whisp*, or a candle and lanthorn at night ; and also that of seeing it in the east, when themselves came from the east ; for could such a thing be seen at all to serve them for a guide, it must be in the west to them. I confine myself solely to the passage called a prophecy of Jesus Christ.

The book of Micah, in the passage above quoted, v. 2, is speaking of some person, without mentioning his name, from whom some great atchievements were expected ; but the description he gives of this person, ver. 5, 6, proves evidently that it is not Jesus Christ, for he says, "and *this man* shall be the peace, when the Assyrian shall come into our land : and when he shall tread in our palaces, then shall we raise up against him [that is, against the Assyrian] seven shepherds and eight principal men. And they shall waste the land of Assyria with the sword, and the land of Nimrod on the entrance thereof ; thus shall *He* [the person spoken of at the head of the second verse] deliver us from the Assyrian, when he cometh into our land, and when he treadeth within our borders."

This is so evidently descriptive of a military chief, that it cannot be applied to Christ without outraging the character they pretend to give us of him. Besides which, the circumstances of the times here spoken of, and those of the times in which Christ is said to have lived, are in contradiction to each other. It was the Romans, and not the Assyrians that had conquered and *were in the land* of Judea, and *trod in their palaces* when Christ was born, and when he died, and so far from his driving them out, it was they who signed the warrant for his execution, and he suffered under it.

Having thus shewn that this is no prophecy of Jesus Christ, I pass on to the third passage quoted from the Old Testament by the New, as a prophecy of him. This, like the first I have spoken of, is introduced by a dream. Joseph dreameth another dream, and dreameth that he seeth another angel. The account begins at Matthew ii. 13. "The angel of the Lord appeared to Joseph in a dream, saying, Arise and take the young child and his mother and flee into Egypt, and be thou there until I bring thee word: For Herod will seek the life of the young child to destroy him. When he arose he took the young child and his mother by night and departed into Egypt: and was there until the death of Herod, that it might be fulfilled which was spoken of the Lord by the prophet, saying, *Out of Egypt have I called my son.*"

This passage is in the book of Hosea, xi. 1. The words are, "When Israel was a child then I loved him and *called my son out of Egypt.* As they called them so they went from them, they sacrificed unto Baalim and burnt incense to graven images."

This passage, falsely called a prophecy of Christ, refers to the children of Israel coming out of Egpyt in the time of Pharaoh, and to the idolatry they committed afterwards. To make it apply to Jesus Christ, he then must be the person who *sacrificed unto Baalim and burnt incense to graven images;* for the person called out of Egypt by the collective name, Israel, and the persons committing this idolatry, are the same persons, or the descendants of them. This then can be no prophecy of Jesus Christ, unless they are willing to make an idolator of him. I pass on to the fourth passage called a prophecy by the writer of the book of Matthew.

This is introduced by a story told by nobody but himself, and scarcely believed by any body, of the slaughter of all the children under two years old, by the command of Herod. A thing which it is not probable should be done by Herod, as he only held an office under the Roman government, to which appeals could always be had, as we see in the case of Paul.

Matthew, however, having made or told his story, says, ii.
17, 18, "Then was fulfilled that which was spoken by
Jeremy the prophet, saying,—*In Ramah was there a voice
heard, lamentation, and weeping and great mourning, Rachel
weeping for her children, and would not be comforted because
they were not.*"

This passage is in Jeremiah xxxi. 15 ; and this verse, when
separated from the verses before and after it, and which
explain its application, might with equal propriety be
applied to every case of wars, sieges, and other violences,
such as the Christians themselves have often done to the
Jews, where mothers have lamented the loss of their children. There is nothing in the verse, taken singly, that
designates or points out any particular application of it,
otherwise than it points to some circumstances which, at the
time of writing it, had already happened, and not to a thing
yet to happen, for the verse is in the preter or past tense.
I go to explain the case and shew the application of the
verse.

Jeremiah lived in the time that Nebuchadnezar besieged,
took, plundered, and destroyed Jerusalem, and led the Jews
captive to Babylon. He carried his violence against the
Jews to every extreme. He slew the sons of king Zedekiah
before his face, he then put out the eyes of Zedekiah, and
kept him in prison till the day of his death.

It is of this time of sorrow and suffering to the Jews that
Jeremiah is speaking. Their Temple was destroyed, their
land desolated, their nation and government entirely broken
up, and themselves, men, women and children, carried into
captivity. They had too many sorrows of their own, immediately before their eyes, to permit them, or any of their
chiefs, to be employing themselves on things that might, or
might not, happen in the World seven hundred years
afterwards.

It is, as already observed, of this time of sorrow and suffering to the Jews that Jeremiah is speaking in the verse in
question. In the next two verses (16, 17), he endeavours to
console the sufferers by giving them hopes, and, according

to the fashion of speaking in those days, assurances from the Lord, that their sufferings should have an end, and that *their children should return again to their own children.* But I leave the verses to speak for themselves, and the Old Testament to testify against the New.

Jeremiah xxxi. 15.—" Thus saith the Lord, a voice *was* heard in Ramah [it is in the preter tense], lamentation and bitter weeping : Rachel, weeping for her children, refused to be comforted for her children because they were not." Ver. 16, " Thus saith the Lord : Refrain thy voice from weeping, and thine eyes from tears ; for thy work shall be rewarded, saith the Lord ; and THEY *shall come again from the land of the enemy.*" Ver. 17.—" And there is hope in thine end, saith the Lord, that *thy children shall come again to their own border.*"

By what strange ignorance or imposition is it, that the children of which Jeremiah speaks, (meaning the people of the Jewish nation, scripturally called *children of Israel,* and not mere infants under two years old,) and who were to return again from the land of the enemy, and come again into their own borders, can mean the children that Matthew makes Herod to slaughter ? Could those return again from the land of the enemy, or how can the land of the enemy be applied to them ? Could they come again to their own Borders ? Good heavens ! How has the world been imposed upon by testament-makers, priestcraft, and pretended prophecies. I pass on to the fifth passage called a prophecy of Jesus Christ.

This, like two of the former, is introduced by dream. Joseph dreamed another dream, and dreameth of another Angel. And Matthew is again the historian of the dream and the dreamer. If it were asked how Matthew could know what Joseph dreamed, neither the Bishop nor all the Church could answer the question. Perhaps it was Matthew that dreamed, and not Joseph ; that is, Joseph dreamed by proxy, in Matthew's brain, as they tell us Daniel dreamed for Nebuchadnezar.—But be this as it may, I go on with my subject.

The account of this dream is in Matthew, ii. 19–23. " But when Herod was dead, behold an Angel of the Lord appeared in a dream to Joseph in Egypt, saying, Arise, and take the young child and his mother and go into the land of Israel ; for they are dead which sought the young child's life. And he arose and took the young child and his mother, and came into the land of Israel. But when he heard that Archelaus did reign in Judea in the room of his father Herod, he was afraid to go thither. Notwithstanding being warned of God in a *dream* [here is another dream] he turned aside into the parts of Galilee ; and he came and dwelt in a city called *Nazareth, that it might be fulfilled which was spoken by the prophets, He shall be called a Nazarene.*"

Here is good circumstantial evidence that Matthew dreamed, for there is no such passage in all the Old Testament ; and I invite the bishop,[1] and all the priests in Christendom, including those of America, to produce it. I pass on to the sixth passage, called a prophecy of Jesus Christ.

This, as Swift says on another occasion, is *lugged in head and shoulders ;* it need only to be seen in order to be hooted as a forced and far-fetched piece of imposition.

Matthew iv. 12–16, " Now when Jesus heard that John was cast into prison, he departed into Galilee : and leaving Nazareth, he came and dwelt in Capernaum, which is upon the sea coast, in the borders of Zebulon and Nephthalim : That it might be fulfilled which was spoken by Esaias [Isaiah] the prophet, saying, *The land of Zebulon and the land of Nephthalim, by the way of the sea, beyond Jordan, Galilee of the Gentiles, the people which sat in darkness saw great light, and to them which sat in the region and shadow of death, light is springing upon them.*

I wonder Matthew has not made the cris-cross-row, or the christ-cross-row (I know not how the priests spell it) into a prophecy. He might as well have done this as cut out these unconnected and undescriptive sentences from the place

---

[1] Dr. Watson, Bishop of Llandaff, who had replied to " The Age of Reason."
—*Editor*.

they stand in and dubbed them with that title. The words however, are in Isaiah, ix. 1, 2, as follows: " Nevertheless the dimness shall not be such as was in her vexation, when at the first he lightly afflicted *the land of Zebulon and the land of Naphtali, and afterwards did more grievously afflict her by the way of the sea beyond Jordan in Galilee of the nations.*"

All this relates to two circumstances that had already happened at the time these words in Isaiah were written. The one, where the land of Zebulon and Naphtali had been lightly afflicted, and afterwards more grievously by the way of the sea.

But observe, reader, how Matthew has falsified the text. He begins his quotation at a part of the verse where there is not so much as a comma, and thereby cuts off every thing that relates to the first affliction. He then leaves out all that relates to the second affliction, and by this means leaves out every thing that makes the verse intelligible, and reduces it to a senseless skeleton of names of towns.

To bring this imposition of Matthew clearly and immediately before the eye of the reader, I will repeat the verse, and put between crotchets [ ] the words he has left out, and put in *Italics* those he has preserved.

" [Nevertheless the dimness shall not be such as was in her vexation when at the first he lightly afflicted] *the land of Zebulon and the land of Naphtali,* [and did afterwards more grievously afflict her] *by the way of the sea beyond Jordan in Galilee of the nations.*"

What gross imposition is it to gut, as the phrase is, a verse in this manner, render it perfectly senseless, and then puff it off on a credulous world as a prophecy. I proceed to the next verse.

Ver. 2. " The people that walked in darkness have seen a great light ; they that dwell in the land of the shadow of death, upon them hath the light shined." All this is historical, and not in the least prophetical. The whole is in the preter tense : it speaks of things that *had been accomplished* at the time the words were written, and not of things to be accomplished afterwards.

As then the passage is in no possible sense prophetical, nor intended to be so, and that to attempt to make it so is not only to falsify the original but to commit a criminal imposition, it is matter of no concern to us, otherwise than as curiosity, to know who the people were of which the passage speaks that sat in darkness, and what the light was that had shined in upon them.

If we look into the preceding chapter, Is. viii., of which ix. is only a continuation, we shall find the writer speaking, at verse 19 of "*witches and wizards who peep about and mutter,*" and of people who made application to them ; and he preaches and exhorts them against this darksome practice. It is of this people, and of this darksome practice, or *walking in darkness*, that he is speaking at ix. 2 ; and with respect to *the light that had shined in upon them*, it refers entirely to his own ministry, and to the boldness of it, which opposed itself to that of *the witches and wizards who peeped about and muttered*.

Isaiah is, upon the whole, a wild disorderly writer, preserving in general no clear chain of perception in the arrangement of his ideas, and consequently producing no defined conclusions from them. It is the wildness of his stile, the confusion of his ideas, and the ranting metaphors he employs, that have afforded so many opportunities to priestcraft in some cases, and to superstition in others, to impose those defects upon the world as prophecies of Jesus Christ. Finding no direct meaning in them, and not knowing what to make of them, and supposing at the same time they were intended to have a meaning, they supplied the defect by inventing a meaning of their own, and called it *his*. I have however in this place done Isaiah the justice to rescue him from the claws of Matthew, who has torn him unmercifully to pieces, and from the imposition or ignorance of priests and commentators, by letting Isaiah speak for himself.

If the words *walking in darkness*, and *light breaking in*, could in any case be applied prophetically, which they cannot be, they would better apply to the times we now live in than to any other. The world has "*walked in darkness*" for eighteen hundred years, both as to religion and government, and it is only since the American Revolution began that light has broken in. The belief of *one God*, whose attributes are revealed to us in the book or scripture of the creation, which no human hand can counterfeit or falsify, and not in the written or printed book which, as Matthew has shewn, can be altered or falsified by ignorance or design, is now making its way among us: and as to government, *the light is already gone forth*, and whilst men ought to be careful not to be blinded by the excess of it, as at a certain time in France when everything was Robespierrean violence, they ought to reverence, and even to adore it, with all the perseverance that true wisdom can inspire.

I pass on to the seventh passage, called a prophecy of Jesus Christ.

Matthew viii. 16, 17. "When the evening was come, they brought unto him [Jesus] many that were possessed with devils, and he cast out the spirits with his word, and healed all that were sick: That it might be fulfilled which was spoken by Esaias (Isaiah) the prophet, saying, *himself took our infirmities, and bare our sickness.*"

This affair of people being possessed by devils, and of casting them out, was the fable of the day when the books of the New Testament were written. It had not existence at any other time. The books of the Old Testament mention no such thing; the people of the present day know of no such thing; nor does the history of any people or country speak of such a thing. It starts upon us all at once in the book of Matthew, and is altogether an invention of the New Testament-makers and the Christian church. The book of Matthew is the first book where the word *Devil* is mentioned.* We read in some of the books of the Old Testament of things called familiar spirits, the supposed companions of people called witches and wizards. It was no other than the trick of pretended conjurers to obtain money from credulous and ignorant people, or the fabricated charge

---

* The word *devil* is a personification of the word *evil.—Author*.

of superstitious malignancy against unfortunate and decrepid old age. But the idea of a familiar spirit, if we can affix any idea to the term, is exceedingly different to that of being possessed by a devil. In the one case, the supposed familiar spirit is a dexterous agent, that comes and goes and does as he is bidden ; in the other, he is a turbulent roaring monster, that tears and tortures the body into convulsions. Reader, whoever thou art, put thy trust in thy creator, make use of the reason he endowed thee with, and cast from thee all such fables.

The passage alluded to by Matthew, for as a quotation it is false, is in Isaiah, liii. 4, which is as follows : " Surely *he* [the person of whom Isaiah is speaking] *hath borne* our griefs and carried our sorrows." It is in the preter tense.

Here is nothing about casting out devils, nor curing of sicknesses. The passage, therefore, so far from being a prophecy of Christ, is not even applicable as a circumstance.

Isaiah, or at least the writer of the book that bears his name, employs the whole of this chapter, liii., in lamenting the sufferings of some deceased persons, of whom he speaks very pathetically. It is a monody on the death of a friend ; but he mentions not the name of the person, nor gives any circumstance of him by which he can be personally known ; and it is this silence, which is evidence of nothing, that Matthew has laid hold of, to put the name of Christ to it ; as if the chiefs of the Jews, whose sorrows were then great, and the times they lived in big with danger, were never thinking about their own affairs, nor the fate of their own friends, but were continually running a Wild-Goose chase into futurity.

To make a monody into a prophecy is an absurdity. The characters and circumstances of men, even in the different ages of the world, are so much alike, that what is said of one may with propriety be said of many ; but this fitness does not make the passage into a prophecy ; and none but an impostor, or a bigot, would call it so.

Isaiah, in deploring the hard fate and loss of his friend,

mentions nothing of him but what the human lot of man is subject to. All the cases he states of him, his persecutions, his imprisonment, his patience in suffering, and his perseverance in principle, are all within the line of nature; they belong exclusively to none, and may with justness be said of many. But if Jesus Christ was the person the church represents him to be, that which would exclusively apply to him must be something that could not apply to any other person; something beyond the line of nature, something beyond the lot of mortal man; and there are no such expressions in this chapter, nor any other chapter in the Old Testament.

It is no exclusive description to say of a person, as is said of the person Isaiah is lamenting in this chapter, *He was oppressed and he was afflicted, yet he opened not his mouth; he is brought as a Lamb to the slaughter, and as a sheep before his shearers is dumb, so he openeth not his mouth.* This may be said of thousands of persons, who have suffered oppressions and unjust death with patience, silence, and perfect resignation.

Grotius, whom the Bishop [of Llandaff] esteems a most learned man, and who certainly was so, supposes that the person of whom Isaiah is speaking, is Jeremiah. Grotius is led into this opinion from the agreement there is between the description given by Isaiah and the case of Jeremiah, as stated in the book that bears his name. If Jeremiah was an innocent man, and not a traitor in the interest of Nebuchadnezar when Jerusalem was besieged, his case was hard; he was accused by his countrymen, was persecuted, oppressed, and imprisoned, and he says of himself, (see Jer. xi. 19,) " *But as for me, I was like a lamb or an ox that is brought to the slaughter.*"

I should be inclined to the same opinion with Grotius, had Isaiah lived at the time when Jeremiah underwent the cruelties of which he speaks; but Isaiah died about fifty years before; and it is of a person of his own time whose case Isaiah is lamenting in the chapter in question, and which imposition and bigotry, more than seven hundred years afterwards, perverted into a prophecy of a person they call Jesus Christ.

I pass on to the eighth passage called a prophecy of Jesus Christ.

Matthew xii. 14–21 : " Then the Pharisees went out and held a council against him, how they might destroy him. But when Jesus knew it he withdrew himself ; and great numbers followed him and he healed them all ; and he charged them they should not make him known : That it might be fulfilled which was spoken by Esaias (Isaiah) the prophet, saying, Behold my servant, whom I have chosen ; my beloved, in whom my soul is well pleased ; I will put my spirit upon him, and he shall shew judgment to the Gentiles. He shall not strive nor cry ; neither shall any man hear his voice in the streets.   A bruised reed shall he not break, and smoking flax shall he not quench, till he send forth judgment unto victory.   And in his name shall the Gentiles trust."

In the first place, this passage hath not the least relation to the purpose for which it is quoted.

Matthew says, that the Pharisees held a council against Jesus to destroy him—that Jesus withdrew himself—that great numbers followed him—that he healed them—and that he charged them they should not make him known.   But the passage Matthew has quoted as being fulfilled by these circumstances does not so much as apply to any one of them. It has nothing to do with the Pharisees holding a council to destroy Jesus—with his withdrawing himself—with great numbers following him—with his healing them—nor with his charging them not to make him known.

The purpose for which the passage is quoted, and the passage itself, are as remote from each other, as nothing from something.   But the case is, that people have been so long in the habit of reading the books called the Bible and Testament with their eyes shut, and their senses locked up, that the most stupid inconsistencies have passed on them for truth, and imposition for prophecy.   The allwise creator hath been dishonoured by being made the author of Fable, and the human mind degraded by believing it.

In this passage, as in that last mentioned, the name of the person of whom the passage speaks is not given, and we are left in the dark respecting him. It is this defect in the history that bigotry and imposition have laid hold of, to call it prophecy.

Had Isaiah lived in the time of Cyrus, the passage would descriptively apply to him. As king of Persia, his authority was great among the Gentiles, and it is of such a character the passage speaks ; and his friendship for the Jews, whom he liberated from captivity, and who might then be compared to a *bruised reed*, was extensive. But this description does not apply to Jesus Christ, who had no authority among the Gentiles ; and as to his own countrymen, figuratively described by the bruised reed, it was they who crucified him. Neither can it be said of him that he did not cry, and that his voice was not heard in the street. As a preacher it was his business to be heard, and we are told that he travelled about the country for that purpose. Matthew has given a long sermon, which (if his authority is good, but which is much to be doubted since he imposes so much,) Jesus preached to a multitude upon a mountain, and it would be a quibble to say that a mountain is not a street, since it is a place equally as public.

The last verse in the passage (the 4th) as it stands in Isaiah, and which Matthew has not quoted, says, " He shall not fail nor be discouraged till he have set judgment in the Earth and the Isles shall wait for his law." This also applies to Cyrus. He was not discouraged, he did not fail, he conquered all Babylon, liberated the Jews, and established laws. But this cannot be said of Jesus Christ, who in the passage before us, according to Matthew, [xii. 15], withdrew himself for fear of the Pharisees, and charged the people that followed him not to make it known where he was ; and who, according to other parts of the Testament, was continually moving from place to place to avoid being apprehended.*

* In the second part of the *Age of Reason*, I have shewn that the book ascribed to Isaiah is not only miscellaneous as to matter, but as to authorship ;

But it is immaterial to us, at this distance of time, to know who the person was : it is sufficient to the purpose I am upon, that of detecting fraud and falsehood, to know who it was not, and to shew it was not the person called Jesus Christ.

I pass on to the ninth passage called a prophecy of Jesus Christ.

Matthew xxi. 1–5. "And when they drew nigh unto Jerusalem, and were come to Bethphage, unto the mount of Olives, then Jesus sent two of his disciples, saying unto

that there are parts in it which could not be written by Isaiah, because they speak of things one hundred and fifty years after he was dead. The instance I have given of this, in that work, corresponds with the subject I am upon, *at least a little better than Matthew's introduction and his question.*

Isaiah lived, the latter part of his life, in the time of Hezekiah, and it was about one hundred and fifty years from the death of Hezekiah to the first year of the reign of Cyrus, when Cyrus published a proclamation, which is given in Ezra i., for the return of the Jews to Jerusalem. It cannot be doubted, at least it ought not to be doubted, that the Jews would feel an affectionate gratitude for this act of benevolent justice, and it is natural they would express that gratitude in the customary stile, bombastical and hyperbolical as it was, which they used on extraordinary occasions, and which was and still is in practice with all the eastern nations.

The instance to which I refer, and which is given in the second part of the Age of Reason, Is. xliv. 28 and xlv. 1, in these words : " *That saith of Cyrus, he is my shepherd and shall perform all my pleasure : even saying to Jerusalem, Thou shalt be built, and to the Temple, Thy foundation shall be laid. Thus saith the Lord to his anointed, to Cyrus, whose right hand I have holden to subdue nations before him ; and I will loose the loins of kings, to open before him the two-leaved gates, and the gates shall not be shut.*"

This complimentary address is in the present tense, which shews that the things of which it speaks were in existence at the time of writing it ; and consequently that the author must have been at least one hundred and fifty years later than Isaiah, and that the book which bears his name is a compilation. The Proverbs called Solomon's, and the Psalms called David's, are of the same kind. The last two verses of the second book of Chronicles, and the first three verses of Ezra i. are word for word the same ; which shew that the compilers of the Bible mixed the writings of different authors together, and put them under some common head.

As we have here an instance in Isaiah xliv. and xlv. of the introduction of the name of Cyrus into a book to which it cannot belong, it affords good ground to conclude, that the passage in chapter xlii., in which the character of Cyrus is given without his name, has been introduced in like manner, and that the person there spoken of is Cyrus.—*Author.*

them, Go into the village over against you, and straightway ye shall find an Ass tied, and a colt with her ; loose them and bring them unto me. And if any man say ought to you, ye shall say, the Lord hath need of them, and straightway he will send them. All this was done that it might be fulfilled which was spoken by the prophet, saying, *Tell ye the daughter of Sion, Behold thy King cometh unto thee, meek, and sitting upon an Ass, and a colt the foal of an Ass.*"

Poor ass ! let it be some consolation amidst all thy sufferings, that if the heathen world erected a Bear into a constellation, the christian world has elevated thee into a prophecy.

This passage is in Zechariah ix. 9, and is one of the whims of friend Zechariah to congratulate his countrymen, who were then returning from captivity in Babylon, and himself with them, to Jerusalem. It has no concern with any other subject. It is strange that apostles, priests, and commentators, never permit, or never suppose, the Jews to be speaking of their own affairs. Every thing in the Jewish books is perverted and distorted into meanings never intended by the writers. Even the poor ass must not be a Jew-ass but a Christian-ass. I wonder they did not make an apostle of him, or a bishop, or at least make him speak and prophesy. He could have lifted up his voice as loud as any of them.

Zechariah, in the first chapter of his book, indulges himself in several whims on the joy of getting back to Jerusalem. He says at the 8th verse, " I saw by night [Zechariah was a sharp-sighted seer] and behold a man setting on a *red horse,* [yes reader, a *red horse,*] and he stood among the myrtle trees that were in the bottom, and behind him were *red horses, speckled and white.*" He says nothing about green horses, nor blue horses, perhaps because it is difficult to distinguish green from blue by night, but a christian can have no doubt they were there, because "*faith is the evidence of things not seen.*"

Zechariah then introduces an angel among his horses, but he does not tell us what colour the angel was of, whether black or white, nor whether he came to buy horses, or only to look at them as curiosities, for certainly they were of that kind. Be this however as it may, he enters into conversation with this angel on the joyful affair of getting back to Jerusalem, and he saith at the 16th verse, " *Therefore, thus saith the Lord*, I AM RETURNED *to Jerusalem with mercies; my house shall be built in it saith the Lord of hosts, and a line shall be stretched forth upon Jerusalem.*" An expression signifying the rebuilding the city.

All this, whimsical and imaginary as it is, sufficiently proves that it was the entry of the Jews into Jerusalem from captivity, and not the entry of Jesus Christ seven hundred years afterwards, that is the subject upon which Zechariah is always speaking.

As to the expression of riding upon an ass, which commentators represent as a sign of humility in Jesus Christ, the case is, he never was so well mounted before. The asses of those countries are large and well proportioned, and were anciently the chief of riding animals. Their beasts of burden, and which served also for the conveyance of the poor, were camels and dromedaries. We read in Judges x. 4, that Jair [one of the Judges of Israel] " had thirty sons that *rode on thirty ass-colts*, and they had thirty cities." But commentators distort every thing.

There is besides very reasonable grounds to conclude that this story of Jesus riding publicly into Jerusalem, accompanied, as it is said at verses 8 and 9, by a great multitude, shouting and rejoicing and spreading their garments by the way, is a story altogether destitute of truth.

In the last passage called a prophecy that I examined, Jesus is represented as withdrawing, that is, running away, and concealing himself for fear of being apprehended, and charging the people that were with him not to make him known. No new circumstance had arisen in the interim to change his condition for the better ; yet here he is represented as making his public entry into the same city from which he had fled for safety. The two cases contradict each other so much, that if both are not false, one of them at

least can scarcely be true. For my own part, I do not believe there is one word of historical truth in the whole book.
I look upon it at best to be a romance: the principal personage of which is an imaginary or allegorical character
founded upon some tale, and in which the moral is in many
parts good, and the narrative part very badly and blunder-
ingly written.

I pass on to the tenth passage called a prophecy of Jesus
Christ.

Matthew xxvi. 51–56: "And behold one of them which
was with Jesus [meaning Peter] stretched out his hand, and
drew his sword, and struck a servant of the high priest, and
smote off his ear. Then said Jesus unto him, put up again
thy sword into its place: for all they that take the sword
shall perish with the sword. Thinkest thou that I cannot
now pray to my Father, and he shall presently give me more
than twelve legions of angels? But how then shall the
scriptures be fulfilled that thus it must be? In that same
hour Jesus said to the multitudes, Are ye come out as against
a thief, with swords and with staves for to take me? I sat
daily with you teaching in the temple, and ye laid no hold
on me. But all this was done that the scriptures of the
prophets might be fulfilled."

This loose and general manner of speaking, admits neither
of detection nor of proof. Here is no quotation given, nor
the name of any bible author mentioned, to which reference
can be had.

There are, however, some high improbabilities against the
truth of the account.

First—It is not probable that the Jews, who were then a
conquered people, and under subjection to the Romans,
should be permitted to wear swords.

Secondly—If Peter had attacked the servant of the high
priest and cut off his ear, he would have been immediately
taken up by the guard that took up his master and sent to
prison with him.

Thirdly—What sort of disciples and preaching apostles
must those of Christ have been that wore swords?

Fourthly—This scene is represented to have taken place the same evening of what is called the Lord's supper, which makes, according to the ceremony of it, the inconsistency of wearing swords the greater.

I pass on to the eleventh passage called a prophecy of Jesus Christ.

Matthew xxvii. 3–10: " Then Judas, which had betrayed him, when he saw that he was condemned, repented himself, and brought again the thirty pieces of silver to the chief priests and elders, saying, I have sinned in that I have betrayed the innocent blood. And they said, What is that to us, see thou to that. And he cast down the thirty pieces of silver, and departed, and went and hanged himself. And the chief priests took the silver pieces and said, it is not lawful to put them in the treasury, because It is the price of blood. And they took counsel, and bought with them the potter's field, to bury strangers in. Wherefore that field is called the field of blood unto this day. Then was fulfilled that which was spoken by Jeremiah the prophet, saying, And they took the thirty pieces of silver, the price of him that was valued, whom they of the children of Israel did value, and gave them for the potter's field, as the Lord appointed me."

This is a most barefaced piece of imposition. The passage in Jeremiah which speaks of the purchase of a field, has no more to do with the case to which Matthew applies it, than it has to do with the purchase of lands in America. I will recite the whole passage :

Jeremiah xxxii. 6–15 : " And Jeremiah said, The word of the Lord came unto me, saying, Behold Hanameel, the son of Shallum thine uncle, shall come unto thee, saying, Buy thee my field that is in Anathoth, for the right of redemption is thine to buy it. So Hanameel mine uncle's son came to me in the court of the prison, according to the word of the Lord, and said unto me, Buy my field I pray thee that is in Anathoth, which is in the country of Benjamin ; for the right of inheritance is thine, and the redemption is thine ; buy it for thyself. Then I knew this was the word of the Lord. And I bought the field of Hanameel mine uncle's son, that was in Anathoth, and weighed him the money, even seventeen shekels of silver. And I subscribed the evidence and sealed it, and took witnesses and weighed him the money in the balances. So I took the evidence of the purchase, both that which was sealed according to the law and custom, and that which was open ; and I gave the evidence of the purchase unto Baruch the son of Neriah, the son of Maaseiah, in the sight of Hanameel mine uncle's son, and in the presence of the witnesses that subscribed [the book of the purchase,] before all the Jews that sat in the court of the prison. And I charged Baruch before them, saying, Thus saith the Lord of hosts, the God of Israel: Take these evidences, this evidence of the purchase, both which is sealed, and this evidence which is open, and put them in an earthen vessel, that they may continue many days. For thus saith the Lord of hosts, the God of Israel : Houses and fields and vineyards shall be possessed again in this land."

I forbear making any remark on this abominable imposition of Matthew. The thing glaringly speaks for itself. It is priests and commentators that I rather ought to censure, for having preached falsehood so long, and kept people in darkness with respect to those impositions. I am not contending with these men upon points of doctrine, for I know that sophistry has always a city of refuge. I am speaking of facts ; for wherever the thing called a fact is a falsehood, the faith founded upon it is delusion, and the doctrine raised upon it not true. Ah, reader, put thy trust in thy creator, and thou wilt be safe ; but if thou trustest to the book called the scriptures thou trustest to the rotten staff of fable and falsehood. But I return to my subject.

There is among the whims and reveries of Zechariah, mention made of thirty pieces of silver given to a Potter. They can hardly have been so stupid as to mistake a potter for a field : and if they had, the passage in Zechariah has no more to do with Jesus, Judas, and the field to bury strangers in, than that already quoted. I will recite the passage.

Zechariah xi. 7–14 : "And I will feed the flock of slaughter, even you, O poor of the flock. And I took unto me two staves; the one I called *Beauty*, and the other I called *Bands;* and I fed the flock. Three shepherds also I cut off in one month ; and my soul lothed them, and their soul also abhorred me. Then said I, I will not feed you ; that which dieth, let it die ; and that which is to be cut off, let it be cut off ; and let the rest eat every one the flesh of another.— And I took my staff, even *Beauty*, and cut it asunder, that I might break my covenant which I had made with all the people. And it was broken in that day ; and so the poor of the flock who waited upon me knew that it was the word of the Lord. And I said unto them, If ye think good, give me my price, and if not, forbear. So they weighed for my price *thirty pieces of silver*. And the Lord said unto me, Cast it unto the *potter ;* a goodly price that I was prised at of them. And I took the thirty pieces of silver, and cast them to the potter in the house of the Lord. Then I cut asunder mine other staff, even *Bands*, that I might break the brotherhood between Judah and Israel." *

* Whiston, in his Essay on the Old Testament, says, that the passage of Zechariah of which I have spoken, was, in the copies of the Bible of the first century, in the book of Jeremiah, from whence, says he, it was taken and inserted without coherence in that of Zechariah. Well, let it be so, it does not make the case a whit the better for the New Testament ; but it makes the case a great deal the worse for the Old. Because it shews, as I have mentioned respecting some passages in a book ascribed to Isaiah, that the works of different authors have been so mixed and confounded together, they cannot now be discriminated, except where they are historical, chronological, or biographical, as in the interpolation in Isaiah. It is the name of Cyrus, inserted where it could not be inserted, as he was not in existence till one hundred and fifty years after the time of Isaiah, that detects the interpolation and the blunder with it.

Whiston was a man of great literary learning, and what is of much higher degree, of deep scientific learning. He was one of the best and most celebrated mathematicians of his time, for which he was made professor of mathematics of the University of Cambridge. He wrote so much in defence of the Old Testament, and of what he calls prophecies of Jesus Christ, that at last he began to suspect the truth of the Scriptures, and wrote against them ; for it is only those who examine them, that see the imposition. Those who believe them most, are those who know least about them.

Whiston, after writing so much in defence of the Scriptnres, was at last prosecuted for writing against them. It was this that gave occasion to Swift, in

There is no making either head or tail of this incoherent gibberish. His two staves, one called *Beauty* and the other *Bands*, is so much like a fairy tale, that I doubt if it had any other origin. There is, however, no part that has the least relation to the case stated in Matthew; on the contrary, it is the reverse of it. Here the *thirty pieces* of silver, whatever it was for, is called a *goodly price*, it was as much as the thing was worth, and according to the language of the day, was approved of by the Lord, and the money given to the potter in the house of the Lord. In the case of Jesus and Judas, as stated in Matthew, the thirty pieces of silver were the price of blood; the transaction was condemned by the Lord, and the money when refunded was refused admittance into the Treasury. Every thing in the two cases is the reverse of each other.

Besides this, a very different and direct contrary account to that of Matthew, is given of the affair of Judas, in the book called the *Acts of the Apostles;* according to that book the case is, that so far from Judas repenting and returning the money, and the high priest buying a field with it to bury strangers in, Judas kept the money and bought a field with it for himself; and instead of hanging himself as Matthew says, that he fell headlong and burst asunder. Some commentators endeavour to get over one part of the contradiction by ridiculously supposing that Judas hanged himself first and the rope broke.

Acts i. 16–18 : " Men and brethren, this scripture must needs have been fulfilled which the Holy Ghost by the mouth of David spake before concerning Judas, which was guide to them that took Jesus, [David says not a word about Judas,] for he [Judas] was numbered among us and obtained part of our ministry. *Now this man purchased a*

his ludicrous epigram on Ditton and Whiston, each of which set up to find out the longitude, to call the one *good master Ditton* and the other *wicked Will Whiston*. But as Swift was a great associate with the Freethinkers of those days, such as Bolingbroke, Pope, and others, who did not believe the book called the scriptures, there is no certainty whether he wittily called him *wicked* for defending the scriptures, or for writing against them. The known character of Swift decides for the former.—AUTHOR.

field with the reward of iniquity, and falling headlong, he burst asunder in the midst and his bowels gushed out."

Is it not a species of blasphemy to call the New Testament *revealed religion*, when we see in it such contradictions and absurdities? I pass on to the twelfth passage called a prophecy of Jesus Christ.

Matthew xxvii. 35. "And they crucified him, and parted his garments, casting lots; that it might be fulfilled which was spoken by the prophet, *They parted my garments among them, and upon my vesture did they cast lots."* This expression is in Psalm xxii. 18. The writer of that Psalm (whoever he was, for the Psalms are a collection and not the work of one man) is speaking of himself and his own case, and not that of another. He begins this Psalm with the words which the New Testament writers ascribed to Jesus Christ : " *My God, my God, why hast thou forsaken me "*— words which might be uttered by a complaining man without any great impropriety, but very improperly from the mouth of a reputed God.

The picture which the writer draws of his own situation, in this Psalm, is gloomy enough. He is not prophesying, but complaining of his own hard case. He represents himself as surrounded by enemies and beset by persecutions of every kind; and by way of shewing the inveteracy of his persecutors he says, " *They parted my garments among them, and cast lots upon my vesture."* The expression is in the present tense ; and is the same as to say, they pursue me even to the clothes upon my back, and dispute how they shall divide them. Besides, the word *vesture* does not always mean clothing of any kind, but *property*, or rather the admitting a man to, or *investing* him with property ; and as it is used in this Psalm distinct from the word garment, it appears to be used in this sense. But Jesus had no property ; for they make him say of himself, " *The foxes have holes and the birds of the air have nests, but the Son of Man hath not where to lay his head."*

But be this as it may, if we permit ourselves to suppose the Almighty would condescend to tell, by what is called the spirit of prophecy, what could come to pass in some future age of the world, it is an injury to our own faculties, and to our ideas of his greatness, to imagine that it would be about an old coat, or an old pair of breeches, or about any thing which the common accidents of life, or the quarrels which attend it, exhibit every day.

That which is in the power of man to do, or in his will not to do, is not a subject for prophecy, even if there were such a thing, because it cannot carry with it any evidence of divine power, or divine interposition. The ways of God are not the ways of men. That which an almighty power performs, or wills, is not within the circle of human power to do, or to controul. But any executioner and his assistants might quarrel about dividing the garments of a sufferer, or divide them without quarrelling, and by that means fulfil the thing called a prophecy, or set it aside.

In the passages before examined, I have exposed the falsehood of them. In this I exhibit its degrading meanness, as an insult to the creator and an injury to human reason.

Here end the passages called prophecies by Matthew.

Matthew concludes his book by saying, that when Christ expired on the cross, the rocks rent, the graves opened, and the bodies of many of the saints arose; and Mark says, there was darkness over the land from the sixth hour until the ninth. They produce no prophecy for this; but had these things been facts, they would have been a proper subject for prophecy, because none but an almighty power could have inspired a fore-knowledge of them, and afterwards fulfilled them. Since then there is no such prophecy, but a pretended prophecy of an old coat, the proper deduction is, there were no such things, and that the book of Matthew was fable and falsehood.

I pass on to the book called the Gospel according to St. Mark.

THE BOOK OF MARK.

There are but few passages in Mark called prophecies; and but few in Luke and John. Such as there are I shall examine, and also such other passages as interfere with those cited by Matthew.

Mark begins his book by a passage which he puts in the shape of a prophecy. Mark i. 1, 2.—" The beginning of the Gospel of Jesus Christ, the Son of God ; As it is written in the prophets, *Behold I send my messenger before thy face, which shall prepare thy way before thee.*" (Malachi iii. 1.) The passage in the original is in the first person. Mark makes this passage to be a prophecy of John the Baptist, said by the Church to be a forerunner of Jesus Christ. But if we attend to the verses that follow this expression, as it stands in Malachi, and to the first and fifth verses of the next chapter, we shall see that this application of it is erroneous and false.

Malachi having said, at the first verse, " Behold I will send my messenger, and he shall prepare the way before me," says, at the second verse, " But who may abide the day of his coming ? And who shall stand when he appeareth ? for he is like a refiner's fire, and like fuller's soap." This description can have no reference to the birth of Jesus Christ, and consequently none to John the Baptist. It is a scene of fear and terror that is here described, and the birth of Christ is always spoken of as a time of joy and glad tidings.

Malachi, continuing to speak on the same subject, explains in the next chapter what the scene is of which he speaks in the verses above quoted, and whom the person is whom he calls the messenger.

" Behold," says he, (iv. 1,) " the day cometh that shall burn like an oven, and all the proud, yea, and all that do wickedly, shall be stubble ; and the day cometh that shall burn them up, saith the Lord of hosts, that it shall leave them neither root nor branch." Verse 5. " Behold I will send you Elijah the prophet before the coming of the great and dreadful day of the Lord."

By what right, or by what imposition or ignorance Mark
has made Elijah into John the Baptist, and Malachi's description of the day of judgment into the birth day of Christ,
I leave to the Bishop [of Llandaff] to settle.

Mark, (i. 2, 3), confounds two passages together, taken
from different books of the Old Testament. The second
verse, " Behold I send my messenger before thy face, which
shall prepare thy way before thee," is taken, as I have said
before, from Malachi. The third verse, which says, " The
voice of one crying in the wilderness, Prepare ye the way of
the Lord, make his paths straight," is not in Malachi, but in
Isaiah, xl. 3, Whiston says that both these verses were
originally in Isaiah. If so, it is another instance of the disordered state of the Bible, and corroborates what I have
said with respect to the name and description of Cyrus
being in the book of Isaiah, to which it cannot chronologically belong.

The words in Isaiah,—" *The voice of him that cryeth in
the wilderness, Prepare ye the way of the Lord, make his paths
straight*,"—are in the present tense, and consequently not pre-
dictive. It is one of those rhetorical figures which the Old
Testament authors frequently used. That it is merely rhetorical and metaphorical, may be seen at the 6th verse:
" And the voice said, cry; and he said what shall I cry?
All flesh is grass." This is evidently nothing but a figure ;
for flesh is not grass otherwise than as a figure or metaphor,
where one thing is put for another. Besides which, the
whole passage is too general and too declamatory to be applied exclusively to any particular person or purpose.

I pass onto the eleventh chapter.

In this chapter, Mark speaks of Christ riding into Jerusalem upon a colt, but he does not make it the accomplishment of a prophecy, as Matthew has done, for he says nothing about a prophecy. Instead of which he goes on the
other tack, and in order to add new honours to the ass, he
makes it to be a miracle ; for he says, ver. 2, it was a colt
" *whereon never man sat ;* " signifying thereby, that as the ass
had not been broken, he consequently was *inspired into good*

manners, for we do not hear that he kicked Jesus Christ off. There is not a word about his kicking in all the four Evangelists.

I pass on from these feats of *horsemanship* performed upon a Jack-ass, to the 15th chapter. At the 24th verse of this chapter Mark speaks of *parting Christ's garments and casting lots upon them,* but he applies no prophecy to it as Matthew does. He rather speaks of it as a thing then in practice with executioners, as it is at this day.

At the 28th verse of the same chapter, Mark speaks of Christ being crucified between two thieves; that, says he, the scripture might be fulfilled, " *which saith, and he was numbered with the transgressors."* The same might be said of the thieves.

This expression is in Isaiah liii. 12. Grotius applies it to Jeremiah. But the case has happened so often in the world, where innocent men have been numbered with transgressors, and is still continually happening, that it is absurdity to call it a prophecy of any particular person. All those whom the church calls martyrs were numbered with transgressors. All the honest patriots who fell upon the scaffold in France, in the time of Robespierre, were numbered with transgressors; and if himself had not fallen, the same case according to a note in his own handwriting, had befallen me;[1] yet I suppose the Bishop [of Leandaff] will not allow that Isaiah was prophesying of Thomas Paine.

These are all the passages in Mark which have any reference to prophecies.

Mark concludes his book by making Jesus to say to his disciples, (xvi. 16–18), "Go ye into all the world and preach the Gospel to every creature; he that believeth and is baptized shall be saved, but he that believeth not shall be damned, [fine popish stuff this,] and these signs shall follow them that believe : in my name they shall cast out devils ; they shall speak with new tongues ; they shall take up serpents ; and if they drink any deadly thing it shall not hurt

[1] See vol. iii. p. 222 of this edition of Paine's Writings; also Preface to Part II. of " The Age of Reason "—*Editor.*

them; they shall lay hands on the sick, and they shall recover." [1]

Now, the Bishop, in order to know if he has all this saving and wonder-working faith, should try those things upon himself. He should take a good dose of arsenick, and if he please, I will send him a rattle-snake from America.

As for myself, as I believe in God and not at all in Jesus Christ, nor in the books called the scriptures, the experiment does not concern me.

I pass on to the book of Luke.

THE BOOK OF LUKE.

There are no passages in Luke called prophecies, excepting those which relate to the passages I have already examined.

Luke speaks of Mary being espoused to Joseph, but he makes no references to the passage in Isaiah, as Matthew does. He speaks also of Jesus riding into Jerusalem upon a colt, but he says nothing about a prophecy. He speaks of John the baptist and refers to the passage in Isaiah of which I have already spoken.

At chapter xiii. 31, 32, he says, " *The same day there came certain of the Pharisees, saying unto him* [*Jesus*] *Get thee out and depart hence, for Herod will kill thee.   And he said unto them, Go ye and tell that fox, Behold I cast out devils, and I do cures to-day and to-morrow, and the third day I shall be perfected.*"

Matthew makes Herod to die whilst Christ was a child in Egypt, and makes Joseph to return with the child on the news of Herod's death, who had sought to kill him. Luke makes Herod to be living, and to seek the life of Jesus after Jesus was thirty years of age: for he says, (iii. 23), " And Jesus began to be about thirty years of age, being, as was supposed, the son of Joseph."

The obscurity in which the historical part of the New Testament is involved, with respect to Herod, may afford to priests and commentators a plea, which to some may ap-

---

[1] These are among the twelve apocryphal verses added to Mark.—*Editor.*

pear plausible, but to none satisfactory, that the Herod of which Matthew speaks, and the Herod of which Luke speaks, were different persons. Matthew calls Herod a king; and Luke (iii. 1) calls Herod Tetrarch (that is, Governor) of Galilee. But there could be no such person as *a king Herod*, because the Jews and their country were then under the dominion of the Roman Emperors who governed then by Tetrarchs, or Governors.

Luke ii. makes Jesus to be born when Cyrenius was Governor of Syria, to which government Judea was annexed; and according to this, Jesus was not born in the time of Herod. Luke says nothing about Herod seeking the life of Jesus when he was born; nor of his destroying the children under two years old; nor of Joseph fleeing with Jesus into Egypt; nor of his returning from thence. On the contrary, the book of Luke speaks as if the person it calls Christ had never been out of Judea, and that Herod sought his life after he commenced preaching, as is before stated. I have already shewn that Luke, in the book called the Acts of the Apostles, (which commentators ascribe to Luke,) contradicts the account in Matthew with respect to Judas and the thirty pieces of silver. Matthew says that Judas returned the money, and that the high priests bought with it a field to bury strangers in; Luke says that Judas kept the money, and bought a field with it for himself.

As it is impossible the wisdom of God should err, so it is impossible those books should have been written by divine inspiration. Our belief in God and his unerring wisdom forbids us to believe it. As for myself, I feel religiously happy in the total disbelief of it.

There are no other passages called prophecies in Luke than those I have spoken of. I pass on to the book of John.

THE BOOK OF JOHN.

John, like Mark and Luke, is not much of a prophecy-monger. He speaks of the ass, and the casting lots for Jesus's clothes, and some other trifles, of which I have already spoken.

John makes Jesus to say., (v. 46), " *For had ye believed Moses, ye would have believed me, for he wrote of me.*" The book of the Acts, in speaking of Jesus says, (iii. 22), " *For Moses truly said unto the fathers, A prophet shall the Lord your God raise up unto you of your brethren, like unto me; him shall ye hear in all things whatsoever he shall say unto you.*"

This passage is in Deuteronomy, xviii. 15. They apply it as a prophecy of Jesus. What imposition! The person spoken of in Deuteronomy, and also in Numbers, where the same person is spoken of, is *Joshua,* the minister of Moses, and his immediate successor, and just such another Robespierrean character as Moses is represented to have been. The case, as related in those books, is as follows:

Moses was grown old and near to his end, and in order to prevent confusion after his death, for the Israelites had no settled system of government, it was thought best to nominate a successor to Moses whilst he was yet living. This was done, as we are told, in the following manner: Numbers xxvii. 12, 13: "And the Lord said unto Moses, Get thee up into this mount Abarim, and see the land which I have given unto the children of Israel. And when thou hast seen it thou also shalt be gathered unto thy people, as Aaron thy brother is gathered." Ver. 15-20. "And Moses spake unto the Lord, sayi1g, Let the Lord, the God of the spirits of all flesh, set a man over the congregation, which may go out before them, and which may go in before them, and which may lead them out, and which may bring them in; that the congregation of the Lord be not as sheep that have no shepherd. And the Lord said unto Moses, take thee *Joshua,* the son of Nun, a man in whom is the spirit, and lay thine hand upon him; and set him before Eleazar the priest, and before all the congregation; and give him a charge in their sight. And thou shalt put some of thine honor upon him, that all the congregation of the children of Israel may be obedient." Ver. 22, 23. "And Moses did as the Lord commanded him; and he took Joshua, and set him before Eleazar the priest, and before all the congregation ; and he laid hands upon him, and gave him a charge, as the Lord commanded by the hand of Moses."

I have nothing to do, in this place, with the truth, or the conjuration here practised, of raising up a successor to Moses like unto himself. The passage sufficiently proves it is Joshua, and that it is an imposition in John to make the case into a prophecy of Jesus. But the prophecy-mongers were so inspired with falsehood, that they never speak truth.*

* Newton, Bishop of Bristol in England, published a work in three volumes, entitled, " *Dissertations on the Prophecies.*" The work is tediously written and tiresome to read. He strains hard to make every passage into a prophecy that suits his purpose. Among others, he makes this expression of Moses, " the Lord shall raise thee up a prophet like unto me," into a prophecy of Christ, who was not born, according to the Bible chronologies, till fifteen hundred and fifty-two years after the time of Moses ; whereas it was an immediate successor to Moses, who was then near his end, that is spoken of in the passage above quoted. This Bishop, the better to impose this passage on the world as a prophecy of Christ, has entirely omitted the account in the book of Numbers which I have given at length, word for word, and which shews, beyond the possibility of a doubt, that the person spoken of by Moses is Joshua, and no other person. Newton is but a superficial writer. He takes up things upon *hear-say*, and inserts them without either examination or reflection, and the more extraordinary and incredible they are, the better he likes them. In speaking of the walls of Babylon, (vol. i. p. 263,) he makes a quotation from a traveller of the name of *Tavernier*, whom he calls, (by way of giving credit to what he says,) *a celebrated traveller*, that those walls *were made of burnt brick, ten feet square and three feet thick.* If Newton had only thought of calculating the weight of such a brick, he would have seen the impossibility of their being used or even made. A brick ten feet square, and three feet thick, contains 300 cubic feet, and allowing a cubic foot of brick to be only one hundred pounds, each of the Bishop's bricks would weigh 30,000 pounds ; and it would take about thirty cart loads of clay (one horse carts) to make one brick. But his account of the stones used in the building of Solomon's temple, (vol. ii. p. 211,) far exceeds his bricks of ten feet square in the walls of Babylon ; these are but brick-bats compared to them. The stones (says he) employed in the foundation, were in magnitude forty cubits, (that is above sixty feet, a cubit, says he, being somewhat more than one foot and a half, (a cubit is one foot nine inches,) and the superstructure (says this Bishop) was worthy of such foundations. There were some stones, says he, of the whitest marble forty-five cubits long, five cubits high, and six cubits broad. These are the dimensions this Bishop has given, which, in measure of twelve inches to a foot, is 78 feet 9 inches long, 10 feet 6 inches broad, and 8 feet 3 inches thick, and contains 7,234 cubic feet.

I now go to demonstrate the imposition of this Bishop. A cubic foot of

I pass to the last passage, in these fables of the Evangelists, called a prophecy of Jesus Christ.

John, having spoken of Jesus expiring on the cross between two thieves, says, (xix. 32, 33), " Then came the soldiers and brake the legs of the first [meaning one of the thieves] and of the other which was crucified with him. But when they came to Jesus, and saw that he was dead already, they brake not his legs." Verse 36. " For these things were done that the Scripture should be fulfilled, *A bone of him shall not be broken.*"

The passage here referred to is in Exodus, and has no more to do with Jesus than with the ass he rode upon to Jerusalem; nor yet so much, if a roasted jack-ass, like a roasted he-goat, might be eaten at a Jewish passover. It might be some consolation to an ass to know that though his bones might be picked, they would not be broken. I go to state the case.

The book of Exodus, in instituting the Jewish passover, in which they were to eat a he-lamb, or a he-goat, says, (xii. 5), " Your lamb shall be without blemish, a male of the

water weighs sixty-two pounds and a half. The specific gravity of marble to water is as 2 1-2 is to one. The weight, therefore, of a cubic foot of marble is 156 pounds, which, multiplied by 7,234, the number of cubic feet in one of those stones, makes the weight of it to be 1,128,504 pounds, which is 503 tons. Allowing then a horse to draw about half a ton, it will require a thousand horses to draw one such stone on the ground ; how then were they to be lifted into the building by human hands? The Bishop may talk of faith removing mountains, but all the faith of all the Bishops that ever lived could not remove one of those stones, and their bodily strength given in.

This Bishop also tells of *great guns* used by the Turks at the taking of Constantinople, one of which, he says, was drawn by seventy yoke of oxen, and by two thousand men. (Vol. iii. p. 117.) The weight of a cannon that carries a ball of 43 pounds, which is the largest cannon that are cast, weighs 8,000 pounds, about three tons and a half, and may be drawn by three yoke of oxen. Any body may now calculate what the weight of the Bishop's *great gun* must be, that required seventy yoke of oxen to draw it. This Bishop beats Gulliver.

When men give up the use of the divine gift of reason in writing on any subject, be it religious or any thing else, there are no bounds to their extravagance, no limit to their absurdities. The three volumes which this Bishop has written on what he calls the prophecies, contain above 1,200 pages, and he says in vol. iii. p. 117, " *I have studied brevity.*" This is as marvellous as the Bishop's great gun.—*Author.*

first year ; ye shall take it from the *sheep* or from the *goats*."
The book, after stating some ceremonies to be used in
killing and dressing it, (for it was to be roasted, not boiled,)
says, (ver. 43–48), " And the Lord said unto Moses and
Aaron, This is the ordinance of the passover : there shall no
stranger eat thereof ; but every man's servant that is bought
for money, when thou hast circumcised him, then shall he
eat thereof. A foreigner shall not eat thereof. In one
house shall it be eaten ; thou shalt not carry forth ought of
the flesh thereof abroad out of the house ; *neither shall ye
break a bone thereof.*"

We here see that the case as it stands in Exodus is a
ceremony and not a prophecy, and totally unconnected with
Jesus's bones, or any part of him.

John, having thus filled up the measure of apostolic fable,
concludes his book with something that beats all fable ; for
he says at the last verse, " And there are also many other
things which Jesus did, the which if they could be written
every one, *I suppose that even the world itself could not contain
the books that should be written.*" [1]

This is what in vulgar life is called a *thumper ;* that is, not
only a lie, but a lie beyond the line of possibility ; besides
which it is an absurdity, for if they should be written in the
world, the world would contain them.—Here ends the examination of the passages called prophecies.

I HAVE now, reader, gone through and examined all the
passages which the four books of Matthew, Mark, Luke,
and John, quote from the Old Testament and call them
prophecies of Jesus Christ. When I first sat down to this
examination, I expected to find cause for some censure, but
little did I expect to find them so utterly destitute of truth,
and of all pretensions to it, as I have shewn them to be.

The practice which the writers of these books employ is
not more false than it is absurd. They state some trifling
case of the person they call Jesus Christ, and then cut out a

---

[1] This belongs to the part of John now admitted to be spurious.—*Editor.*

sentence from some passage of the Old Testament and call it a prophecy of that case. But when the words thus cut out are restored to the place they are taken from, and read with the words before and after them, they give the lie to the New Testament. A short instance or two of this will suffice for the whole.

They make Joseph to dream of an angel, who informs him that Herod is dead, and tells him to come with the child out of Egypt. They then cut out a sentence from the book of Hosea, " *Out of Egypt have I called my Son*," and apply it as a prophecy in that case. The words, " *And called my Son out of Egypt*," are in the Bible. But what of that? They are only part of a passage, and not a whole passage, and stand immediately connected with other words which shew they refer to the children of Israel coming out of Egypt in the time of Pharaoh, and to the idolatry they committed afterwards.

Again, they tell us that when the soldiers came to break the legs of the crucified persons, they found Jesus was already dead, and, therefore, did not break his. They then, with some alteration of the original, cut out a sentence from Exodus, " *a bone of him shall not be broken*," and apply it as a prophecy of that case. The words " *Neither shall ye break a bone thereof*," (for they have altered the text,) are in the Bible. But what of that? They are, as in the former case, only part of a passage, and not a whole passage, and when read with the words they are immediately joined to, shew it is the bones of a he-lamb or a he-goat of which the passage speaks.

These repeated forgeries and falsifications create a well-founded suspicion that all the cases spoken of concerning the person called Jesus Christ are *made cases*, on purpose to lug in, and that very clumsily, some broken sentences from the Old Testament, and apply them as prophecies of those cases; and that so far from his being the Son of God, he did not exist even as a man—that he is merely an imaginary or allegorical character, as Apollo, Hercules, Jupiter, and all the deities of antiquity were. There is no history written at the time Jesus Christ is said to have lived that speaks of the existence of such a person, even as a man.

Did we find in any other book pretending to give a system of religion, the falsehoods, falsifications, contradictions, and absurdities, which are to be met with in almost every page of the Old and New Testament, all the priests of the present day, who supposed themselves capable, would triumphantly shew their skill in criticism, and cry it down as a most glaring imposition. But since the books in question belong to their own trade and profession, they, or at least many of them, seek to stifle every inquiry into them and abuse those who have the honesty and the courage to do it.

When a book, as is the case with the Old and New Testament, is ushered into the world under the title of being the WORD OF GOD, it ought to be examined with the utmost strictness, in order to know if it has a well founded claim to that title or not, and whether we are or are not imposed upon : for as no poison is so dangerous as that which poisons the physic, so no falsehood is so fatal as that which is made an article of faith.

This examination becomes more necessary, because when the New Testament was written, I might say invented, the art of printing was not known, and there were no other copies of the Old Testament than written copies. A written copy of that book would cost about as much as six hundred common printed bibles now cost. Consequently the book was in the hands of very few persons, and these chiefly of the Church. This gave an opportunity to the writers of the New Testament to make quotations from the Old Testament as they pleased, and call them prophecies, with very little danger of being detected. Besides which, the terrors and inquisitorial fury of the Church, like what they tell us of the flaming sword that turned every way, stood sentry over the New Testament ; and time, which brings every thing else to light, has served to thicken the darkness that guards it from detection.

Were the New Testament now to appear for the first time, every priest of the present day would examine it line by line, and compare the detached sentences it calls prophecies with the whole passages in the Old Testament from whence they are taken. Why then do they not make the same examination at this time, as they would make had the New Testament never appeared before? If it be proper and right to make it in one case, it is equally proper and right to do it in the other case. Length of time can make no difference in the right to do it at any time. But, instead of doing this, they go on as their predecessors went on before them, to tell the people there are prophecies of Jesus Christ, when the truth is there are none.

They tell us that Jesus rose from the dead, and ascended into heaven. It is very easy to say so; a great lie is as easily told as a little one. But if he had done so, those would have been the only circumstances respecting him that would have differed from the common lot of man; and, consequently, the only case that would apply exclusively to him, as prophecy, would be some passage in the Old Testament that foretold such things of him. But there is not a passage in the Old Testament that speaks of a person who, after being crucified, dead, and buried, should rise from the dead, and ascend into heaven. Our prophecy-mongers supply the silence the Old Testament guards upon such things, by telling us of passages they call prophecies, and that falsely so, about Joseph's dream, old cloaths, broken bones, and suchlike trifling stuff.

In writing upon this, as upon every other subject, I speak a language full and intelligible. I deal not in hints and intimations. I have several reasons for this: First, that I may be clearly understood. Secondly, that it may be seen I am in earnest; and thirdly, because it is an affront to truth to treat falsehood with complaisance.

I will close this treatise with a subject I have already touched upon in the First Part of the Age of Reason.

The world has been amused with the term *revealed religion*, and the generality of priests apply this term to the books called the Old and New Testament. The Mahometans apply the same term to the Koran. There is no man that believes in revealed religion stronger than I do ; but it is not the reveries of the Old and New Testament, nor of the Koran, that I dignify with that sacred title. That which is revelation to me, exists in something which no human mind can invent, no human hand can counterfeit or alter.

The *Word of God* is the *Creation* we behold ; and this word of God revealeth to man all that is necessary for man to know of his creator. Do we want to contemplate his power? We see it in the immensity of his creation. Do we want to contemplate his wisdom? We see it in the unchangeable order by which the incomprehensible whole is governed. Do we want to contemplate his munificence? We see it in the abundance with which he fills the earth. Do we want to contemplate his mercy? We see it in his not withholding that abundance, even from the unthankful. Do we want to contemplate his will, so far as it respects man ? The goodness he shews to all is a lesson for our conduct to each other.

In fine—Do we want to know what God is? Search not the book called the Scripture, which any human hand might make, or any impostor invent ; but the SCRIPTURE CALLED THE CREATION.

When, in the first part of the Age of Reason, I called the Creation the true revelation of God to man, I did not know that any other person had expressed the same idea. But I lately met with the writings of Doctor Conyers Middleton, published the beginning of last century, in which he expresses himself in the same manner, with respect to the Creation, as I have done in the Age of Reason. He was principal librarian of the University of Cambridge, in England, which furnished him with extensive opportunities of reading, and necessarily required he should be well acquainted with the dead as well as the living languages. He was a man of a strong original mind, had the courage to think for himself, and the honesty to speak his thoughts. He made a journey to Rome, from whence he wrote letters to shew that the forms and ceremonies of the Romish Christian Church were taken from the degenerate state of the

heathen mythology, as it stood in the latter times of the
Greeks and Romans. He attacked without ceremony the
miracles which the Church pretended to perform ; and in
one of his treatises, he calls the *creation a revelation.* The
priests of England, of that day, in order to defend their
citadel, by first defending its out-works, attacked him for
attacking the Roman ceremonies ; and one of them censures
him for calling the *creation a revelation.* He thus replies
to him :

" One of them," says he, " appears to be scandalized by
the title of *revelation* which I have given to that discovery
which God made of himself in the visible works of his creation. Yet it is no other than what the wise in all ages have
given to it, who consider it as the most authentic and indisputable revelation which God has ever given of himself,
from the beginning of the world to this day. It was this by
which the first notice of him was revealed to the inhabitants
of the earth, and by which alone it has been kept up ever
since among the several nations of it. From this the reason
of man was enabled to trace out his nature and attributes,
and, by a gradual deduction of consequences, to learn his
own nature also, with all the duties belonging to it, which
relate either to God or to his fellow-creatures. This constitution of things was ordained by God, as an universal law,
or rule of conduct to man ; the source of all his knowledge ;
the test of all truth, by which all subsequent revelations,
which are supposed to have been given by God in any other
manner must be tried, and cannot be received as divine any
further than as they are found to tally and coincide with
this original standard.

" It was this divine law which I referred to in the passage
above recited, [meaning the passage on which they had
attacked him,] being desirous to excite the reader's attention
to it, as it would enable him to judge more freely of the
argument I was handling. For by contemplating this law,
he would discover the genuine way which God himself has
marked out to us for the acquisition of true knowledge ;
not from the authority or reports of our fellow-creatures,

but from the information of the facts and material objects which, in his providential distribution of worldly things, he hath presented to the perpetual observation of our senses. For as it was from these that his existence and nature, the most important articles of all knowledge, were first discovered to man, so that grand discovery furnished new light towards tracing out the rest, and made all the inferior subjects of human knowledge more easily discoverable to us by the same method.

" I had another view likewise in the same passage, and applicable to the same end, of giving the reader a more enlarged notion of the question in dispute, who, by turning his thoughts to reflect on the works of the Creator, as they are manifested to us in this fabric of the world, could not fail to observe that they are all of them great, noble, and suitable to the majesty of his nature ; carrying with them the proofs of their origin, and shewing themselves to be the production of an all-wise and almighty being ; and by accustoming his mind to these sublime reflections, he will be prepared to determine whether those miraculous interpositions, so confidently affirmed to us by the primitive fathers, can reasonably be thought to make a part in the grand scheme of the Divine administration, or whether it be agreeable that God, who created all things by his will, and can give what turn to them he pleases by the same will, should, for the particular purposes of his government and the services of the church, *descend to the expedient of visions and revelations*, granted sometimes to boys for the instruction of the elders, and sometimes to women to settle the fashion and length of their veils, and sometimes to Pastors of the Church to enjoin them to ordain one man a lecturer, another a priest ; or that he should scatter a profusion of miracles around the stake of a martyr, yet all of them vain and insignificant, and without any sensible effect, either of preserving the life or easing the sufferings of the saint, or even of mortifying his persecutors, who were always left to enjoy the full triumph of their cruelty, and the poor martyr to expire in a miserable death. When these things, I say, are brought to the original test, and compared with the genuine and indisputable works of the Creator, how minute, how trifling, how contemptible must they be? And how incredible must it be thought that, for the instruction of his Church, God should employ ministers so precarious, unsatisfactory, and inadequate, as the extacies of women and boys, and the visions of interested priests, which were derided at the very time by men of sense to whom they were proposed.

"That this universal law [continues Middleton, meaning the law revealed in the works of the creation] was actually revealed to the heathen world long before the gospel was known, we learn from all the principal sages of antiquity, who made it the capital subject of their studies and writings.

" Cicero [says Middleton] has given us a short abstract of it, in a fragment still remaining from one of his books on government, which [says Middleton] I shall here transcribe in his own words, as they will illustrate my sense also, in the passages that appear so dark and dangerous to my antagonist :

" ' The true law, [it is Cicero who speaks] is right reason, conformable to the nature of things, constant, eternal, diffused through all, which calls us to duty by commanding, deters us from sin by forbidding ; which never loses its influence with the good, nor ever preserves it with the wicked. This law cannot be over-ruled by any other, nor abrogated in whole or in part ; nor can we be absolved from it either by the senate or by the people ; nor are we to seek any other comment or interpreter of it but himself ; nor can there be one law at Rome and another at Athens ; one now and another hereafter ; but the same eternal immutable law comprehends all nations at all times, under one common master and governor of all—GOD. He is the inventor, propounder, enacter of this law ; and whoever will not obey it must first renounce himself, and throw off the nature of man ; by doing which, he will suffer the greatest punishments though he should escape all the other torments which are commonly believed to be prepared for the wicked.' Here ends the quotation from Cicero.

" Our Doctors [continues Middleton] perhaps will look on this as RANK DEISM ; but let them call it what they will, I shall ever avow and defend it as the fundamental, essential, and vital part of all true religion." Here ends the quotation from Middleton.

I have here given the reader two sublime extracts from men who lived in ages of time far remote from each other, but who thought alike. Cicero lived before the time in which they tell us Christ was born. Middleton may be called a man of our own time, as he lived within the same century with ourselves.

In Cicero we see that vast superiority of mind, that sublimity of right reasoning and justness of ideas, which man acquires, not by studying bibles and testaments, and the theology of schools built thereon, but by studying the creator in the immensity and unchangeable order of his creation, and the immutability of his law. " *There cannot*," says Cicero, " *be one law now, and another hereafter; but the same eternal immutable law comprehends all nations, at all times, under one common master and governor of all*—GOD." But according to the doctrine of schools which priests have set up, we see one law, called the *Old Testament*, given in one age of the world, and another law, called the *New Testament*, given in another age of the world. As all this is contradictory to the eternal immutable nature, and the unerring and unchangeable wisdom of God, we must be compelled to hold this doctrine to be false, and the old and the new law, called the Old and the New Testament, to be impositions, fables, and forgeries.

In Middleton, we see the manly eloquence of an enlarged mind and the genuine sentiments of a true believer in his Creator. Instead of reposing his faith on books, by whatever name they may be called, whether Old Testament or New, he fixes the creation as the great original standard by which every other thing called the word or work of God is to be tried. In this we have an indisputable scale whereby to measure every word or work imputed to him. If the thing so imputed carries not in itself the evidence of the same Almightiness of power, of the same unerring truth and wisdom, and the same unchangeable order in all its parts, as are visibly demonstrated to our senses, and comprehensible by our reason, in the magnificent fabric of the universe, that word or that work is not of God.   Let then the two books called the Old and New Testament be tried by this rule, and the result will be that the authors of them, whoever they were, will be convicted of forgery.

The invariable principles, and unchangeable order, which regulate the movements of all the parts that compose the universe, demonstrate both to our senses and our reason that its creator is a God of unerring truth.   But the Old Testament, beside the numberless absurd and bagatelle stories it tells of God, represents him as a God of deceit, a God not to be confided in.   Ezekiel makes God to say, (xiv. 9), " And if the prophet be deceived when he hath spoken a thing, I, *the Lord have deceived that prophet.*" And at xx. 25, he makes God, in speaking of the children of Israel, to say "*Wherefore I gave them statutes that were not good, and judgments by which they should not live.*"   This, so far from being the word of God, is horrid blasphemy against him.   Reader, put thy confidence in thy God, and put no trust in the bible.

The same Old Testament, after telling us that God created the heavens and the earth in six days, makes the same almighty power and eternal wisdom employ itself in giving directions how a priest's garments should be cut, and what sort of stuff they should be made of, and what their offerings should be, Gold, and Silver, and Brass, and blue, and purple, and scarlet, and fine linen, and goats' hair, and rams' skins dyed red, and badger skins, etc. (xxv. 3); and in one of the pretended prophecies I have just examined, God is made to give directions how they should kill, cook, and eat a he-lamb or a he-goat.   And Ezekiel, (iv.,) to fill up the measure of abominable absurdity, makes God to order him to take *wheat, and barley, and beans, and lentiles, and millet, and fitches, and make a loaf or a cake thereof, and bake it with human dung and eat it ;* but as Ezekiel complained that this mess was too strong for his stomach, the matter was compromised from man's dung to cow-dung. Compare all this ribaldry, blasphemously called the word of God, with the Almighty power that created the universe, and whose eternal wisdom directs and governs all its mighty movements, and we shall be at a loss to find a name sufficiently contemptible for it.

In the promises which the Old Testament pretends that God made to his people, the same derogatory ideas of him prevail. It makes God to promise to Abraham that his seed should be like the stars in heaven and the sand on the sea shore for multitude, and that he would give them the land of Canaan as their inheritance for ever. But observe, reader, how the performance of this promise was to begin, and then ask thine own reason, if the wisdom of God, whose power is equal to his will, could, consistently with that power and that wisdom, make such a promise. The performance of the promise was to begin, according to that book, by four hundred years of bondage and affliction. Genesis xv. 13, "*And he said unto Abraham, Know of a surety that thy seed shall be a stranger in a land that is not theirs, and shall serve them ; and they shall afflict them four hundred years.*" This promise then to Abraham and his seed for ever, to inherit the land of Canaan, had it been a fact instead of a fable, was to operate, in the commencement of it, as a curse upon all the people and their children, and their children's children, for four hundred years.

But the case is, the book of Genesis was written after the bondage in Egypt had taken place ; and in order to get rid of the disgrace of the Lord's chosen people, as they called themselves, being in bondage to the Gentiles, they make God to be the author of it, and annex it as a condition to a pretended promise ; as if God, in making that promise, had exceeded his power in performing it, and consequently his wisdom in making it, and was obliged to compromise with them for one half, and with the Egyptians, to whom they were to be in bondage, for the other half.

Without degrading my own reason by bringing those wretched and contemptible tales into a comparative view with the Almighty power and eternal wisdom, which the Creator hath demonstrated to our senses in the creation of the universe, I will confine myself to say, that if we compare them with the divine and forcible sentiments of Cicero, the result will be that the human mind has degenerated by believing them. Man, in a state of grovelling superstition from which he has not courage to rise, loses the energy of his mental powers.

I will not tire the reader with more observations on the Old Testament.

As to the New Testament, if it be brought and tried by that standard which, as Middleton wisely says, God has revealed to our senses, of his Almighty power and wisdom in the creation and government of the visible universe, it will be found equally as false, paltry, and absurd, as the Old.

Without entering, in this place, into any other argument, that the story of Christ is of human invention and not of divine origin, I will confine myself to shew that it is derogatory to God, by the contrivance of it; because the means it supposes God to use, are not adequate to the end to be obtained; and, therefore, are derogatory to the Almightiness of his power, and the eternity of his wisdom.

The New Testament supposes that God sent his Son upon earth to make a new covenant with man, which the Church calls *the covenant of grace ;* and to instruct mankind in a new doctrine, which it calls *Faith,* meaning thereby, not faith in God, for Cicero and all true Deists always had and always will have this, but faith in the person called Jesus Christ ; and that whoever had not this faith should, to use the words of the New Testament, be DAMNED.

Now, if this were a fact, it is consistent with that attribute of God called his *goodness,* that no time should be lost in letting poor unfortunate man know it ; and as that goodness was united to Almighty power, and that power to Almighty wisdom, all the means existed in the hand of the

Creator to make it known immediately over the whole earth, in a manner suitable to the Almightiness of his divine nature, and with evidence that would not leave man in doubt; for it is always incumbent upon us, in all cases, to believe that the Almighty always acts, not by imperfect means as imperfect man acts, but consistently with his Almightiness. It is this only that can become the infallible criterion by which we can possibly distinguish the works of God from the works of man.

Observe now, reader, how the comparison between this supposed mission of Christ, on the belief or disbelief of which they say man was to be saved or damned—observe, I say, how the comparison between this, and the Almighty power and wisdom of God demonstrated to our senses in the visible creation, goes on.

The Old Testament tells us that God created the heavens and the earth, and everything therein, in six days. The term *six days* is ridiculous enough when applied to God; but leaving out that absurdity, it contains the idea of Almighty power acting unitedly with Almighty wisdom, to produce an immense work, that of the creation of the universe and every thing therein, in a short time. Now as the eternal salvation of man is of much greater importance than his creation, and as that salvation depends, as the New Testament tells us, on man's knowledge of and belief in the person called Jesus Christ, it necessarily follows from our belief in the goodness and justice of God, and our knowledge of his Almighty power and wisdom, as demonstrated in the Creation, that ALL THIS, if true, would be made known to all parts of the world, in as little time at least, as was employed in making the world. To suppose the Almighty would pay greater regard and attention to the creation and organization of inanimate matter, than he would to the salvation of innumerable millions of souls, which himself had created, "*as the image of himself,*" is to offer an insult to his goodness and his justice.

Now observe, reader, how the promulgation of this pretended salvation by a knowledge of, and a belief in Jesus

Christ went on, compared with the work of creation. In the first place, it took longer time to make the child than to make the world, for nine months were passed away and totally lost in a state of pregnancy; which is more than forty times longer time than God employed in making the world, according to the bible account. Secondly, several years of Christ's life were lost in a state of human infancy. But the universe was in maturity the moment it existed. Thirdly, Christ, as Luke asserts, was thirty years old before he began to preach what they call his mission. Millions of souls died in the mean time without knowing it. Fourthly, it was above three hundred years from that time before the book called the New Testament was compiled into a written copy, before which time there was no such book. Fifthly, it was above a thousand years after that before it could be circulated; because neither Jesus nor his apostles had knowledge of, or were inspired with, the art of printing: and, consequently, as the means for making it universally known did not exist, the means were not equal to the end, and therefore it is not the work of God.

I will here subjoin the nineteenth Psalm, which is truly deistical, to shew how universally and instantaneously the works of God make themselves known, compared with this pretended salvation by Jesus Christ:

" The heavens declare the glory of God, and the firmament showeth his handywork. Day unto day uttereth speech, and night unto night showeth knowledge. There is no speech nor language where their voice is not heard. Their line is gone out through all the earth, and their words to the end of the world. In them hath he set a chamber for the sun, which is as a bridegroom coming out of his chamber, and rejoiceth as a strong man to run a race. His going forth is from the end of the heaven, and his circuit unto the ends of it, and there is nothing hid from the heat thereof."

Now, had the news of salvation by Jesus Christ been inscribed on the face of the Sun and the Moon, in characters that all nations would have understood, the whole earth had known it in twenty-four hours, and all nations would have believed it ; whereas, though it is now almost two thousand years since, as they tell us, Christ came upon earth, not a twentieth part of the people of the earth know any thing of it, and among those who do, the wiser part do not believe it.

I have now, reader, gone through all the passages called prophecies of Jesus Christ, and shewn there is no such thing.

I have examined the story told of Jesus Christ, and compared the several circumstances of it with that revelation which, as Middleton wisely says, God has made to us of his Power and Wisdom in the structure of the universe, and by which every thing ascribed to him is to be tried. The result is, that the story of Christ has not one trait, either in its character or in the means employed, that bears the least resemblance to the power and wisdom of God, as demonstrated in the creation of the universe. All the means are human means, slow, uncertain, and inadequate to the accomplishment of the end proposed ; and therefore the whole is a fabulous invention, and undeserving of credit.

The priests of the present day profess to believe it. They gain their living by it, and they exclaim against something they call infidelity. I will define what it is. HE THAT BELIEVES IN THE STORY OF CHRIST IS AN INFIDEL TO GOD.

THOMAS PAINE.

AUTHOR'S APPENDIX.

CONTRADICTORY DOCTRINES BETWEEN MATTHEW AND MARK.

IN the New Testament (Mark xvi. 16), it is said " He that believeth and is baptized shall be saved, but he that believeth not shall be damned."[1] This is making salvation, or, in other words, the happiness of man after this life, to depend entirely on believing, or on what Christians call faith.

---

[1] One of the concluding twelve verses not found in the earlier manuscripts of the second gospel.—*Editor.*

But *The Gospel according to Matthew* makes Jesus Christ preach a direct contrary doctrine to *The Gospel according to Mark;* for it makes salvation, or the future happiness of man, to depend entirely on *good works;* and those good works are not works done to God, for he needs them not, but good works done to man. The passage referred to in Matthew is the account there given of what is called the last day, or the day of judgment, where the whole world is represented to be divided into two parts, the righteous and the unrighteous, mataphorically called the *sheep* and the *goats.* To the one part called the righteous, or the sheep, it says, " Come, ye blessed of my father, inherit the kingdom prepared for you from the beginning of the world : for I was an hungered, and ye gave me meat: I was thirsty, and ye gave me drink: I was a stranger, and ye took me in : naked, and ye clothed me : I was sick, and ye visited me : I was in prison, and ye came unto me. Then shall the righteous answer him, saying, Lord, when saw we thee an hungered, and fed thee ? or thirsty, and gave thee drink ? When saw we thee a stranger, and took thee in ? or naked, and clothed thee ? Or when saw we thee sick, or in prison, and came unto thee ? And the king shall answer and say unto them, *Verily I say unto you, Inasmuch as ye have done it unto one of the least of these my brethren, ye have done it unto me.*"

Here is nothing about believing in Christ—nothing about that phantom of the imagination called *Faith.* The works here spoken of are works of humanity and benevolence, or, in other words, an endeavour to make God's creation happy. Here is nothing about preaching and making long prayers, as if God must be dictated to by man ; nor about building churches and meetings, nor hiring priests to pray and preach in them. Here is nothing about predestination, that lust which some men have for damning one another. Here is nothing about baptism, whether by sprinkling or plunging, nor about any of those ceremonies for which the Christian Church has been fighting, persecuting, and burning each other ever since the Christian Church began.

If it be asked, why do not priests preach the doctrine contained in this chapter, the answer is easy : they are not fond of practising it themselves. It does not answer for their trade. They had rather get than give. Charity with them begins and ends at home.

Had it been said, *Come ye blessed, ye have been liberal in paying the preachers of the word, ye have contributed largely towards building churches and meeting-houses,* there is not a hired priest in Christendom but would have thundered it continually in the ears of his congregation. But as it is altogether on good works done to men, the priests pass over it in silence, and they will abuse me for bringing it into notice.

THOMAS PAINE.

MY PRIVATE THOUGHTS ON A FUTURE STATE.

I HAVE said, in the first part of the Age of Reason, that " *I hope for happiness after this life.*" This hope is comfortable to me, and I presume not to go beyond the comfortable idea of hope, with respect to a future state.

I consider myself in the hands of my creator, and that he will dispose of me after this life consistently with his justice and goodness. I leave all these matters to him, as my creator and friend, and I hold it to be presumption in man to make an article of faith as to what the creator will do with us hereafter.

I do not believe because a man and a woman make a child, that it imposes on the creator the unavoidable obligation of keeping the being so made in eternal existence hereafter. It is in his power to do so, or not to do so, and it is not in our power to decide which he will do.

The book called the New Testament, which I hold to be fabulous and have shewn to be false, gives an account in Matthew xxv. of what is there called the last day, or the day of judgment. The whole world, according to that account, is divided into two parts, the righteous and the unrighteous, figuratively called the sheep and the goats. They are then to receive their sentence. To the one, figuratively called the sheep, it says, " *Come ye blessed of my Father, inherit the kingdom prepared for you from the foundation of the world.*" To the other, figuratively called the goats, it says, "*Depart from me, ye cursed, into everlasting fire, prepared for the devil and his angels.*"

Now the case is, the world cannot be thus divided : the moral world, like the physical world, is composed of numerous degrees of character, running imperceptibly one into the other, in such a manner that no fixed point of division can be found in either. That point is no where, or is every where. The whole world might be divided into two parts numerically, but not as to moral character ; and therefore the metaphor of dividing them, as sheep and goats can be divided, whose difference is marked by their external figure, is absurd. All sheep are still sheep ; all goats are still goats ; it is their physical nature to be so. But one part of the world are not all good alike, nor the other part all wicked alike. There are some exceedingly good ; others exceedingly wicked. There is another description of men who cannot be ranked with either the one or the other—they belong neither to the sheep nor the goats ; and there is still another description of them who are so very insignificant, both in character and conduct, as not to be worth the trouble of damning or saving, or of raising from the dead.

My own opinion is, that those whose lives have been spent in doing good, and endeavouring to make their fellow-mortals happy, for this is the only way in which we can serve God, *will be happy hereafter ;* and that the very wicked will meet with some punishment. But those who are neither good nor bad, or are too insignificant for notice, will be dropt entirely. This is my opinion. It is consistent with my idea of God's justice, and with the reason that God has given me, and I gratefully know that he has given me a large share of that divine gift.

THOMAS PAINE.

XI.

A LETTER TO ANDREW DEAN.[1]

RESPECTED FRIEND,

I received your friendly letter, for which I am obliged to you. It is three weeks ago to day (Sunday, Aug. 15,) that I was struck with a fit of an apoplexy, that deprived me of all sense and motion. I had neither pulse nor breathing, and the people about me supposed me dead. I had felt exceedingly well that day, and had just taken a slice of bread and butter for supper, and was going to bed. The fit took me on the stairs, as suddenly as if I had been shot through the head; and I got so very much hurt by the fall, that I have not been able to get in and out of bed since that day, otherwise than being lifted out in a blanket, by two persons; yet all this while my mental faculties have remained as perfect as I ever enjoyed them. I consider the scene I have passed through as an experiment on dying, and I find that death has no terrors for me. As to the people called Christians, they have no evidence that their religion is true. There is no more proof that the Bible is the word of God, than that the Koran of Mahomet is the word of God. It is education makes all the difference. Man, before he begins to think for himself, is as much the child of habit in *Creeds* as he is in ploughing and sowing. Yet creeds, like opinions, prove nothing.

[1] Mr. Dean, who rented Paine's farm at New Rochelle, had written : " I have read with good attention your manuscript on Dreams, and Examination on the Prophecies in the Bible. I am now searching the old prophecies and comparing the same to those said to be quoted in the New Testament. I confess the comparison is a matter worthy of our serious attention ; I know not the result till I finish ; then, if you be living, I shall communicate the same to you ; I hope to be with you soon."—*Editor*.

Where is the evidence that the person called Jesus Christ is the begotten Son of God? The case admits not of evidence either to our senses or our mental faculties: neither has God given to man any talent by which such a thing is comprehensible. It cannot therefore be an object for faith to act upon, for faith is nothing more than an assent the mind gives to something it sees cause to believe is fact. But priests, preachers, and fanatics, put imagination in the place of faith, and it is the nature of the imagination to believe without evidence.

If Joseph the carpenter dreamed, (as the book of Matthew (i) says he did,) that his betrothed wife, Mary, was with child by the Holy Ghost, and that an angel told him so, I am not obliged to put faith in his dreams; nor do I put any, for I put no faith in my own dreams, and I should be weak and foolish indeed to put faith in the dreams of others.

The Christian religion is derogatory to the Creator in all its articles. It puts the Creator in an inferior point of view, and places the Christian Devil above him. It is he, according to the absurd story in Genesis, that outwits the Creator in the garden of Eden, and steals from him his favourite creature, Man, and at last obliges him to beget a son, and put that son to death, to get Man back again; and this the priests of the Christian religion call redemption.

Christian authors exclaim against the practice of offering up human sacrifices, which, they say, is done in some countries; and those authors make those exclamations without ever reflecting that their own doctrine of salvation is founded on a Human Sacrifice. They are saved, they say, by the blood of Christ. The Christian religion begins with a dream and ends with a murder.

As I am now well enough to sit up some hours in the day, though not well enough to get up without help, I employ myself as I have always done, in endeavouring to bring man to the right use of the reason that God has given him, and to direct his mind immediately to his Creator, and not to fanciful secondary beings called **mediators, as if God was superannuated or ferocious.**

As to the book called the Bible, it is blasphemy to call it the word of God. It is a book of lies and contradictions, and a history of bad times and bad men. There are but a few good characters in the whole book. The fable of Christ and his twelve apostles, which is a parody on the Sun and the twelve signs of the Zodiac, copied from the ancient religions of the Eastern world, is the least hurtful part. Every thing told of Christ has reference to the Sun. His reported resurrection is at sunrise, and that on the first day of the week ; that is, on the day anciently dedicated to the Sun, and from thence called Sunday—in Latin *Dies Solis,* the day of the Sun ; as the next day, Monday, is Moon-day. But there is no room in a letter to explain these things.

While man keeps to the belief of one God, his reason unites with his creed. He is not shocked with contradictions and horrid stories. His bible is the heavens and the earth. He beholds his Creator in all his works, and every thing he beholds inspires him with reverence and gratitude. From the goodness of God to all, he learns his duty to his fellow-man, and stands self-reproved when he trangresses it. Such a man is no persecutor.

But when he multiplies his creed with imaginary things, of which he can have neither evidence nor conception, such as the tale of the garden of Eden, the Talking Serpent, the Fall of Man, the Dreams of Joseph the Carpenter, the pretended Resurrection and Ascension, of which there is even no historical relation,—for no historian of those times mentions such a thing,—he gets into the pathless region of confusion, and turns either fanatic or hypocrite. He forces his mind, and pretends to believe what he does not believe. This is in general the case with the Methodists. Their religion is all creed and no morals.

I have now, my friend, given you a *fac simile* of my mind on the subject of religion and creeds, and my wish is, that you make this letter as publicly known as you find opportunities of doing.

Yours, in friendship,
THOMAS PAINE.

N. Y. Aug. 15, 1806.

XII.

PREDESTINATION.

REMARKS ON ROMANS IX. 18–21.[1]

Addressed to the Ministers of the Calvinistic Church.

PAUL, in speaking of God, says, " Therefore hath he mercy on whom he will have mercy, and whom he will he hardeneth. Thou wilt say, why doth he yet find fault? For who hath resisted his will? Nay, but who art thou, O man, that repliest against God? Shall the thing formed say to him that formed it, Why hast thou made me thus? Hath not the potter power over the clay of the same lump, to make one vessel unto honour and another unto dishonour?"

I shall leave it to Calvinists and Universalists to wrangle about these expressions, and to oppose or corroborate them by other passages from other books of the Old or New Testament. I shall go to the root at once, and say, that the whole passage is presumption and nonsense. Presumption, because it pretends to know the private mind of God : and nonsense, because the cases it states as parallel cases have no parallel in them, and are opposite cases.

The first expression says, " Therefore hath he (God) mercy on whom he will have mercy, and whom he will he hardeneth." As this is ascribing to the attribute of God's power, at the expence of the attribute of his justice, I, as a believer in the justice of God, disbelieve the assertion of Paul. The Predestinarians, of which the loquacious Paul was one, appear to acknowledge but one attribute in God, that of

[1] Reprinted from an Appendix to Paine's Theological Works, published in London, by Mary Ann Carlile, in 1820. This I believe to be the last piece written by Paine.—*Editor.*

power, which may not improperly be called the *physical
attribute*. The Deists, in addition to this, believe in his
moral attributes, those of justice and goodness.

In the next verses, Paul gets himself into what in vulgar
life is called a hobble, and he tries to get out of it by nonsense and sophistry ; for having committed himself by saying
that " God hath mercy on whom he will have mercy, and
whom he will he hardeneth," he felt the difficulty he was in,
and the objections that would be made, which he anticipates
by saying, " Thou wilt say then unto me, Why doth he
(God) yet find fault ? for who hath resisted his will ? Nay,
but, O man, who art thou, that repliest against God ! " This
is neither answering the question, nor explaining the case.
It is down right quibbling and shuffling off the question,
and the proper retort upon him would have been, " Nay,
but who art thou, presumptuous Paul, that puttest thyself
in God's place ! " Paul, however, goes on and says, " Shall
the thing formed say to him that formed it, why hast thou
made me thus ? " Yes, if the thing felt itself hurt, and
could speak, it would say it. But as pots and pans have not
the faculty of speech, the supposition of such things speaking is putting nonsense in the place of argument, and is too
ridiculous even to admit of apology. It shews to what
wretched shifts sophistry will resort.

Paul, however, dashes on, and the more he tries to reason
the more he involves himself, and the more ridiculous he appears. " Hath not," says he, " the potter power over the
clay of the same lump, to make one vessel unto honour and
another unto dishonour "? In this metaphor, and a most
wretched one it is, Paul makes the potter to represent God ;
the lump of clay the whole human race ; the vessels unto
honour those souls " on whom he hath mercy because he
will have mercy ; " and the vessels unto dishonour, those
souls " whom he hardeneth (for damnation) because he will
harden them." The metaphor is false in every one of its
points, and if it admits of any meaning or conclusion, it is
the reverse of what Paul intended and the Calvinists understand.

In the first place a potter doth not, because he cannot, make vessels of different qualities, from the same lump of clay; he cannot make a fine china bowl, intended to ornament a side-board, from the same lump of clay that he makes a coarse pan, intended for a close-stool. The potter selects his clays for different uses, according to their different qualities, and degrees of fineness and goodness.

Paul might as well talk of making gun-flints from the same stick of wood of which the gun-stock is made, as of making china bowls from the same lump of clay of which are made common earthen pots and pans. Paul could not have hit upon a more unfortunate metaphor for his purpose, than this of the potter and the clay; for if any inference is to follow from it, it is that as the potter selects his clay for different kinds of vessels according to the different qualities and degrees of fineness and goodness in the clay, so God selects for future happiness those among mankind who excel in purity and good life, which is the reverse of predestination.

In the second place there is no comparison between the souls of men, and vessels made of clay; and, therefore, to put one to represent the other is a false position. The vessels, or the clay they are made from, are insensible of honour or dishonour. They neither suffer nor enjoy. The clay is not punished that serves the purpose of a close-stool, nor is the finer sort rendered happy that is made up into a punch-bowl. The potter violates no principle of justice in the different uses to which he puts his different clays; for he selects as an artist, not as a moral judge; and the materials he works upon know nothing, and feel nothing, of his mercy or his wrath. Mercy or wrath would make a potter appear ridiculous, when bestowed upon his clay. He might kick some of his pots to pieces.

But the case is quite different with man, either in this world or the next. He is a being sensible of misery as well as of happiness, and therefore Paul argues like an unfeeling idiot, when he compares man to clay on a potter's wheel, or to vessels made therefrom: and with respect to God, it is an offence to his attributes of justice, goodness, and wisdom, to suppose that he would treat the choicest work of creation like inanimate and insensible clay. If Paul believed that God made man after his own image, he dishonours it by making that image and a brick-bat to be alike.

The absurd and impious doctine of predestination, a doctrine destructive of morals, would never have been thought of had it not been for some stupid passages in the Bible, which priestcraft at first, and ignorance since, have imposed upon mankind as revelation. Nonsense ought to be treated as nonsense, wherever it be found ; and had this been done in the rational manner it ought to be done, instead of intimating and mincing the matter, as has been too much the case, the nonsense and false doctrine of the Bible, with all the aid that priestcraft can give, could never have stood their ground against the divine reason that God has given to man.

Doctor Franklin gives a remarkable instance of the truth of this, in an account of his life, written by himself. He was in London at the time of which he speaks. " Some volumes," says he, " against Deism, fell into my hands. They were said to be the substance of Sermons preached at Boyle's Lectures. It happened that they produced on me an effect precisely the reverse of what was intended by the writers ; for the arguments of the Deists, which were cited in order to be refuted, appeared to me more forcible than the refutation itself. In a word I soon became a perfect Deist."—New York Edition of Franklin's Life, page 93.

All America, and more than all America, knows Franklin. His life was devoted to the good and improvement of man. Let, then, those who profess a different creed, imitate his virtues, and excel him if they can.

THOMAS PAINE.

APPENDIX A.

ATUOBIOGRAPHICAL SKETCH.

PREFATORY NOTE BY THE EDITOR.—For this recently discovered paper I am indebted to the Lenox Library, New York, into whose possession the original came with the papers of the Hon. George Bancroft. It was enclosed in a letter of January 14, 1779, to Hon. Henry Laurens, which was published in 1861 (Frank Moore's " Materials of History," p. 129) and is here reprinted, as connected with the autobiographical sketch which has so long been buried among the papers of the late historian. The circumstances under which the communication was made may be gathered from the last three chapters of vol. ii. of this edition, and from my " Life of Paine," i., chapters 10 and 11. The exposure of Silas Deane's frauds by Paine led to his resignation of his office of Secretary to the Foreign Affairs Committee, and also to the resignation of the presidency of Congress by the Hon. Henry Laurens, who had stood shoulder to shoulder with Paine in breaking up the " ring " in Paris. The Secretary had resigned on January 8, 1779. There were rumors of duels at the time, and Paine's expression of apprehensions about his nearest friend probably refers to them ; or it may even be that there were grounds for fearing assassination, so large were the money interests baffled. The subjoined account that Paine gives of himself after his arrival in America (November 30, 1774), written probably at the request of Laurens, may appear egotistical, but in fact he omits facts that would have shed great honor upon him, and, in this entirely confidential letter to an intimate friend, limits himself to services that involved pecuniary losses. These had just culminated in a service which saved much money to the Treasury, but had been requited with an ill-treatment that led him to resign office, being thereby left without means.

THOMAS PAINE TO HON. HENRY LAURENS.

SIR : My anxiety for your *personal* safety has not only fixed a profound silence upon me, but prevents my asking you a great many questions, lest I should be the unwilling, unfortunate cause of new difficulties or fatal consequences to you, and in such a case I might indeed say, " *'T is the survivor dies.*"

I omitted sending the inclosed in the morning as I intended. It will serve you to parry ill nature and ingratitude with, when undeserved reflections are cast upon me.

I certainly have some awkward natural feeling, which I never shall get rid of. I was sensible of a kind of shame at the Minister's door to-day, lest any one should think I was going to solicit a pardon or a pension. When I come to you I feel only an *unwillingness* to be seen, on your account. I shall never make a courtier, I see that.

I am your obedient humble servant,

THOMAS PAINE.

January 14, 1779.

429

Sir,—For your amusement I give you a short history of my conduct since I have been in America.

I brought with me letters of introduction from Dr. Franklin. These letters were with a flying seal, that I might, if I thought proper, close them with a wafer. One was to Mr. Bache of this city. The terms of Dr. Franklin's recommendation were "*a worthy, ingenious, etc.*" My particular design was to establish an academy on the plan they are conducted in and about London, which I was well acquainted with.[1] I came some months before Dr. Franklin, and waited here for his arrival. In the meantime a person of this city desired me to give him some assistance in conducting a magazine, which I did without making any bargain.[2] The work turned out very profitable. Dr. Witherspoon had likewise a concern [in] it. At the end of six months I thought it necessary to come to some contract. I agreed to leave the matters to arbitration. The bookseller mentioned two on his own part—Mr. Duché, your late chaplain, and Mr. Hopkinson. I agreed to them and declined mentioning any on my part. But the bookseller getting information of what Mr. Duché's private opinion was, withdrew from the arbitration, or rather refused to go into it, as our agreement to abide by it was only verbal. I was requested by several literary gentlemen in this city to undertake such a work on my own account, and I could have rendered it very profitable.

As I always had a taste to science, I naturally had friends of that cast in England; and among the rest George Lewis Scott, esq., through whose formal introduction my first acquaintance with Dr. Franklin commenced.[3] I esteem Mr. Scott as one of the most amiable characters I know of, but his particular situation had been, that in the minority of the present King he was his sub-preceptor, and from the occasional traditionary accounts yet remaining in the family of Mr. Scott, I obtained the true character of the present King from his childhood upwards, and, you may naturally suppose, of the present ministry. I saw the people of this country were all wrong, by an ill-placed confidence. After the breaking out of hostilities I was confident their design was a total conquest. I wrote to Mr. Scott in May, 1775, by Captain James Josiah, now in this city. I read the letter to him before I closed it. I used in it this free expression : " Surely the ministry are all mad ; they never will be able to conquer America." The reception which the last petition of Congress met with put it past a doubt that such was their design, on which I determined with myself to write the pamphlet ' [Common] Sense.' As I knew the time of the Parliament meeting, and had no doubt what sort of King's speech it would produce, my contrivance was to have the pamphlet come out just at the time the speech might arrive in America, and so fortunate was I in this cast of policy that both of them made their appearance in this city on the same day.[4] The first edition was printed by Bell on the recommendation of Dr. Rush. I gave him the pamphlet on the following conditions : That if any loss should arise I would pay it—and in order to make him industrious in circulating it, I gave him one-half the profits, if it should produce any. I gave a written order to Col. Joseph Dean and Capt. Thos. Prior, both of this city, to receive the other half, and lay it out for mittens for the troops that were going to Quebec. I did this to do honour to the cause. Bell kept the whole, and abused me into the bargain. The price he set upon them was two shillings. I then enlarged the pamphlet with an appendix and an address to the Quakers, which made it one-third bigger than before, printed 6,000 at my own expense, 3,000 by B. Towne, 3,000 by Cist & Steyner, and delivered them ready stitched and fit for sale to Mr. Bradford at the Coffee-house ; and though the work was thus increased, and consequently should have borne a higher price, yet, in order that it might produce the general service I wished, I confined Mr. Bradford to sell them at only one shil-

---

[1] In 1767 Paine was usher in a school in Kensington, London. For Franklin's letter see my " Life of Paine," i., p. 40.—*Editor*.

[2] Robert Aitkin. This was the *Pennsylvania Magazine.—Editor*.

[3] Scott was a Commissioner of the Board of Excise, by which Paine had been employed. See my " Life of Paine," i. p. 30.—*Editor*.

[4] " Common Sense " appeared January 10, 1776.—*Editor*.

ling each, or tenpence by the dozen, and to enable him to do this, with sufficient advantage to himself, I let him have the pamphlets at 8½d. Pennsylvania currency each.

The sum of 8½d. each was reserved to defray the expense of printing, paper, advertising, etc., and such as might be given away. The state of the account at present is that I am £39 11s. out of pocket, being the difference between what I have paid for printing, etc., and what I have received from Bradford. He has a sufficiency in his hands to balance with and clear me, which is all I aimed at, but by his unaccountable dilatoriness and unwillingness to settle accounts, I fear I shall be obliged to sustain a real loss exclusive of my trouble.

I think the importance of that pamphlet was such that if it had not appeared, and that at the exact time it did, the Congress would not now have been sitting where they are. The light which that performance threw upon the subject gave a turn to the politics of America which enabled her to stand her ground. Independence followed in six months after it, although before it was published it was a dangerous doctrine to speak of, and that because it was not understood.

In order to accommodate that pamphlet to every man's purchase and to do honour to the cause, I gave up the profits I was justly entitled to, which in this city only would at the usual price of books [have] produced me £1,000 at that time a day, besides what I might have made by extending it to other States. I gave permission to the printers in other parts of this State [Pennsylvania] to print it on their own account. I believe the number of copies printed and sold in America was not short of 150,000—and is the greatest sale that any performance ever had since the use of letters,—exclusive of the great run it had in England and Ireland.

The doctrine of that book was opposed in the public newspapers under the signature of Cato, who, I believe, was Dr. Smith,[1] and I was sent for from New York to reply to him, which I did, and happily with success. My letters are under the signature of "The Forester." It was likewise opposed in a pamphlet signed "Plain Truth," but the performance was too weak to do any hurt or deserve any answer. In July following the publication of 'Common Sense' the Associators of this State[2] marched to Amboy under the command of Gen. Roberdeau. The command was large, yet there was no allowance for a secretary. I offered my service voluntarily, only that my expenses should be paid, all the charges I put Gen. Roberdeau to was $48; although he frequently pressed me to make free with his private assistance. After the Associators returned I went to Fort Lee, and continued with Gen. [Nathaniel] Greene till the evacuation.

A few days after our army had crossed the Delaware on the 8th of December, 1776, I came to Philadelphia on public service, and, seeing the deplorable and melancholy condition the people were in, afraid to speak and almost to think, the public presses stopt, and nothing in circulation but fears and falsehoods, I sat down, and in what I may call a passion of patriotism, wrote the first number of the *Crisis.* It was published on the 19th of December, which was the very blackest of times, being before the taking of the Hessians at Trenton. I gave that piece to the printer gratis, and confined him to the price of two coppers, which was sufficient to defray his charge.

I then published the second number, which being as large again as the first number, I gave it to him on the condition of his taking only four coppers each. It contained sixteen pages.

I then published the third number, containing thirty-two pages, and gave it to the printer, confining him to ninepence.

When the account of the battle of Brandywine got to this city, the people were again in a state of fear and dread. I immediately wrote the fourth number [of the *Crisis*]. It contained only four pages, and as there was no less money than the sixth of dollars in general circulation, which would have been

---

[1] The Rev. William Smith, D.D., President of the University of Philadelphia.—*Editor.*
[2] The Flying Camp.—*Editor.*

too great a price, I ordered 4,000 to be printed at my own private charge and given away.

The fifth number I gave Mr. Dunlap, at Lancaster. He, very much against my consent, set half a crown upon it ; he might have done it for a great deal less. The sixth and seventh numbers I gave in the papers. The seventh number would have made a pamphlet of twenty-four pages, and brought me in $3,000 or $4,000 in a very few days, at the price which it ought to have borne. Monies received since I have been in America :

Salary for 17 months at 70 dollars per month [1]................1,190 dollars	
For rations and occasional assistance at Fort Lee..............	141 ditto
For defraying the expense of a journey from East Town round by Morriss when secretary to the Indian Commission,[2] and some other matters, about 140 or 145 dollars...............	145 ditto

Total of public money.......................................1,476

In the spring, 1776, some private gentleman, thinking it was too hard that I should, after giving away my profits for a public good, be money out of pocket on account of some expense I was put to—sent me by the hands of Mr. Christopher Marshall 108 dollars.

You have here, sir, a faithful history of my services and my rewards.

[1] As Secretary of the Congressional Committee of Foreign Affairs, to which he was appointed April 17, 1777.—*Editor.*
[2] This commission met the Indian chiefs at Easton, Pa., in January, 1777.—*Editor.*

APPENDIX B.

A LETTER FROM LONDON.[1]

LONDON, January 5, 1789.

·' I sincerely thank you for your very friendly and welcome letter. I was in the country when it arrived and did not receive it soon enough to answer it by the return of the vessel.

" I very affectionately congratulate Mr. and Mrs. Few on their happy marriage, and every branch of the families allied by that connection ; and I request my fair correspondent to present me to her partner, and to say, for me, that he has obtained one of the highest Prizes on the wheel. Besides the pleasure which your letter gives me to hear you are all happy and well, it relieves me from a sensation not easy to be dismissed ; and if you will excuse a few dull thoughts for obtruding themselves into a congratulatory letter I will tell you what it is. When I see my female friends drop off by matrimony I am sensible of something that affects me like a loss in spite of all the appearance of joy : I cannot help mixing the sincere compliment of regret with that of congratulation. It appears as if I had outlived or lost a friend. It seems to me as if the original was no more, and that which she is changed to forsakes the circle and forgets the scenes of former society. Felicities are cares superior to those she formerly cared for, create to her a new landscape of Life that excludes the little friendships of the past. It is not every Lady's mind that is sufficiently capacious to prevent those greater objects crowding out the less, or that can spare a thought to former friendships after she has given her hand and heart to the man who loves her. But the sentiment your letter contains has prevented these dull Ideas from mixing with the congratulations I present you, and is so congenial with the enlarged opinion I have always formed of you, that at the time I read your letter with pleasure, I read it with pride because it convinces me that I have some judgment in that most difficult science—a Lady's mind. Most sincerely do I wish you all the good that Heaven can bless you with, and as you have in your own family an example of domestic happiness you are already in the knowledge of obtaining it. That no condition we can enjoy is an exemption from care— that some shade will mingle itself with the brightest sunshine of Life—that even our affections may become the instruments of our own sorrows —that the sweet felicities of home depend on good temper as well as on good sense, and that there is always something to forgive even in the nearest and dearest of our friends,—are truths which, tho' too obvious to be told, ought never to be forgotten ; and I know you will not esteem my friendship the less for impressing them upon you.

" Though I appear a sort of wanderer, the married state has not a sincerer friend than I am. It is the harbour of human life, and is, with respect to the things of this world, what the next world is to this. It is *home ;* and that one

[1] This letter was written to Miss Kitty Nicholson, whom Paine had petted as a school girl in Bordentown, New Jersey, and who had written to him of her approaching marriage with Colonel Few, an eminent Southern Congressman. I am indebted to a member of that family for the use of this letter, remarkable for its historical as well as personal interest.—*Editor.*

word conveys more than any other word can express. For a few years we may glide along the tide of youthful single life and be wonderfully delighted ; but it is a tide that flows but once, and what is still worse, it ebbs faster than it flows, and leaves many a hapless voyager aground. I am one, you see that have experienced the fate, I am describing.[1] I have lost my tide ; it passed by while every thought of my heart was on the wing for the salvation of my dear America, and I have now as contentedly as I can, made myself a little bower of willows on the shore that has the solitary resemblance of a home. Should I always continue the tenant of this home, I hope my female acquaintance will ever remember that it contains not the churlish enemy of their sex, not the cold inaccessible hearted mortal, nor the capricious tempered oddity, but one of the best and most affectionate of their friends.

"I did not forget the Dunstable hat, but it was not on wear here when I arrived. That I am a negligent correspondent I freely confess, and I always reproach myself for it. You mention only one letter, but I wrote twice ; once by Dr. Derby, and another time by the Chevalier St. Triss—by whom I also wrote to Gen. Morris, Col. Kirkbride, and several friends in Philadelphia, but have received no answers. I had one letter from Gen. Morris last winter, which is all I have received from New York till the arrival of yours.

"I thank you for the details of news you give. Kiss Molly Field for me and I wish her joy,—and all the good girls of Bordentown. How is my favorite Sally Morris, my boy Joe, and my horse Button? Pray let me know. Polly and Nancy Rogers,—are they married ? or do they intend to build bowers as I have done? If they do, I wish they would twist their green willows somewhere near to mine.

"I am very much engaged here about my Bridge. There is one building of my construction at Messrs. Walkers Iron Works in Yorkshire, and I have direction of it. I am lately come from thence and shall return again in two or three weeks.

"As to news on this side the water, the King is mad, and there is great bustle about appointing a Regent. As it happens, I am in pretty close intimacy with the heads of the opposition—The Duke of Portland, Mr. Fox and Mr. Burke. I have sent your letter to Mrs. Burke as a specimen of the accomplishments of the American Ladies. I sent it to Miss Alexander, a lady you have heard me speak of, and I asked her to give me a few of her thoughts how to answer it. She told me to write as I felt, and I have followed her advice.

"I very kindly thank you for your friendly invitation to Georgia and if I am ever within a thousand miles of you, I will come and see you ; though it be but for a day.

"You touch me on a very tender part when you say my friends on your side the water 'cannot be reconciled to the idea of my resigning my adopted America, even for my native England.' They are right. Though I am in as elegant style of acquaintance here as any American that ever came over, my heart and myself are 3000 miles apart ; and I had rather see my horse Button in his own stable, or eating the grass of Bordentown or Morrisania, than see all the pomp and show of Europe.

"A thousand years hence (for I must indulge in a few thoughts), perhaps in less, America may be what England now is ! The innocence of her character that won the hearts of all nations in her favor may sound like a romance, and her inimitable virtue as if it had never been. The ruin of that liberty which thousands bled for, or suffered to obtain, may just furnish materials for a vil-

---

[1] Paine's marriage and separation from his wife had been kept a secret in America, where the "Tories" would have used it to break the influence of his patriotic writings. In the absence of any divorce law in England, a separation under the Common Law was generally held as pronouncing the marriage a nullity *ab initio.* According to Chalmers, Paine was dissatisfied with articles of separation drawn up by an attorney, Josias Smith, May 24, 1774, and insisted on new ones to which the clergyman was a party. The "common lawyers" regarded the marriage as completely annulled, and Paine, in America certainly, was free to marry again. However, he evidently never thought of doing so, and that his relations with ladies were chaste as affectionate appears in this letter to Mrs. Few, and in his correspondence generally.—*Editor.*

lage tale or extort a sigh from rustic sensibility, while the fashionable of that day, enveloped in dissipation, shall deride the principle and the fact.

" When we contemplate the fall of Empires and the extinction of nations of the ancient world, we see but little to excite our regret than the mouldering ruins of pompous palaces, magnificent monuments, lofty pyramids, and walls and towers of the most costly workmanship. But when the Empire of America shall fall, the subject for contemplative sorrow will be infinitely greater than crumbling brass or marble can inspire. It will not then be said, here stood a temple of vast antiquity,—here rose a Babel of invisible height, or there a palace of sumptuous extravagance ; but here, ah painful thought ! the noblest work of human wisdom, the grandest scene of human glory, the fair cause of freedom rose and fell !

" Read this and then ask if I forget America—But I 'll not be dull if I can help it, so I leave off, and close my letter to-morrow, which is the day the mail is made up for America.

" January 7th. I have heard this morning with extreme concern of the death of our worthy friend Capt. Read. Mrs. Read lives in a house of mine at Bordentown, and you will much oblige me by telling her how much I am affected by her loss ; and to mention to her, with that delicacy which such an offer and situation require, and which no one knows better how to convey than yourself, that the two years' rent which is due I request her to accept of, and to consider herself at home till she hears further from me.

" This is the severest winter I ever knew in England ; the frost has continued upwards of five weeks, and is still likely to continue. All the vessels from America have been kept off by contrary winds. The Polly and the " Pigeon " from Philadelphia and the Eagle from Charleston are just got in.

" If you should leave New York before I arrive (which I hope will not be the case) and should pass through Philadelphia, I wish you would do me the favor to present my compliments to Mrs. Powell, the lady whom I wanted an opportunity to introduce you to when you were in Philadelphia, but was prevented by your being at a house where I did not visit.

" There is a Quaker favorite of mine at New York, formerly Miss Watson of Philadelphia ; she is now married to Dr. Lawrence and is an acquaintance of Mrs. Oswald ; be so kind as to make her a visit for me. You will like her conversation. She has a little of the Quaker primness—but of the pleasing kind—about her.

" I am always distressed at closing a letter, because it seems like taking leave of my friends after a parting conversation.—Captain Nicholson, Mrs. Nicholson, Hannah, Fanny, James, and the little ones, and you my dear Kitty, and your partner for life—God bless you all ! and send me safe back to my much loved America !

Thomas Paine = aet. 52
or if you better like it
Common Sense.

" This comes by the packet which sails from Falmouth, 300 miles from London ; but by the first vessel from London to New York I will send you some magazines. In the mean time be so kind as to write to me by the first opportunity. Remember me to the family at Morrisiana, and all my friends at New York and Bordentown. Desire Gen. Morris, to take another guinea of Mr. Constable, who has some money of mine in his hands, and give it to my boy Joe. Tell Sally to take care of ' Button.' Then direct for me at Mr. Peter Whiteside's London. When you are at Charleston remember me to my dear old friend Mrs. Laurens, Col. and Mrs. L. Morris, and Col. Washington ; and at Georgia, to Col. Walton. Adieu."

APPENDIX C.

SCIENTIFIC MEMORANDA.

Trees and Fountains.[1]

DEAR SIR : I enclose you a Problem, not about Bridges but Trees ; and to explain my meaning I begin with a fountain. The Idea seems far-fetched,— but Fountains and Trees are in my walk to Challiot. Suppose Fig. 1. a fountain. It is evident that no more water can pass thro' the branching Tubes than pass thro' the trunk. Secondly that, admitting all the water to pass with equal freedom, the sum of the squares of the diameters of the two first branches must be equal to the square of the diameter of the Trunk ; also the sum of the squares of the four Branches must be equal to the two ; and the sum of the squares of the eight Branches must be equal to the four. And therefore 8, 4, 2, and the Trunk, being reciprocally equal, the solid content of the whole will be equal to the Cylinder (Fig. 2) of the same diameter of the trunk, and height of the fountain.

Carry the Idea of a fountain to a Tree growing. Consider the sap ascending in capillary tubes like the water in the fountain, and no more sap will pass thro' the Branches than passes thro' the Trunk. Secondly, consider the Branches as so many divisions and sub-divisions of the Trunk, as they are in the fountain, and that their contents are to be found by some rule—with the difference only of a Pyramidal figure instead of a Cylindrical one. Therefore, to find the quantity of timber (or rather loads) in the Tree (figure 3,) draw a Pyramid equal to the height of the Tree (as in Fig 4), taking for the inclination of the Pyramid, the diameter at the bottom, and at any discretionary height above it (which in this is as 3 and 2.)

P. S.—As sensible men should never guess, and as it is impossible to judge without some point to begin at, this appears to me to be that point ; and [one] by which a person may ascertain near enough the quantity [of] Timber and loads of wood in any quantity of land. And he may distinguish them into Timber, wood and faggots.

Attraction.[2]

YOUR saying last evening that Sir Isaac Newton's principle of gravitation would not explain, or could not apply as a rule to find, the quantity of the at-traction of cohesion, and my replying that I never could comprehend any meaning in the term " Attraction of Cohesion "—the result must be, that either I have a dull comprehension, or that the term does not admit of comprehension. It appears to me an Athanasian jumble of words, each of which admits of a clear and dis-tinct Idea, but of no Idea at all when compounded.[3]

[1] Undated, but written at Paris, in 1788, and left with Jefferson, residing at Challiot.— *Editor*.
[2] Left with Jefferson at Paris, undated.
[3] This phrase " Athanasian jumble of words," used more than five years before Paine had published any theological heresies, suggests that the creeds had been discussed with his friend at Challiot.—*Editor*.

The immense difference there is between the attracting power of two Bodies, at the least possible distance the mind is capable of conceiving, and the great power that instantly takes place to resist separation when the two Bodies are incorporated, prove to me that there is something else to be considered in the case than can be comprehended by attraction or gravitation. Yet this matter appears sufficiently luminous to me, according to my own line of Ideas.

Attraction is to matter, what desire is to the mind ; but cohesion is an entirely different thing, produced by an entirely different cause—it is the effect of the figure of matter.

Take two iron hooks,—the one strongly magnetical,—and bring them to touch each other, and a very little force will separate them for they are held together only by attraction. But their figure renders them capable of holding each other with infinitely more power to resist separation than attraction can ; by hooking them.

Now if we suppose the particles of Matter to have figures capable of interlocking and embracing each other we shall have a clear distinct Idea between cohesion and attraction, and that they are things totally distinct from each other and arise from as different causes.

The welding of two pieces of Iron appears to me no other than entangling the particles in much the same manner as turning a key within the wards of a lock,—and if our eyes were good enough we should see how it was done.

I recollect a scene at one of the Theatres that very well explains the difference between attraction and cohesion. A condemned lady wishes to see her child and the child its mother—this call attraction. They were admitted to meet, but when ordered to part they threw their arms round each other and fastened their persons together. This is what I mean by cohesion,—which is a mechanical contact of the figures of their persons, as I believe all cohesion is.

Tho' the term " *attraction of cohesion* " has always appeared to me like the Athanasian Creed, yet I think I can help the Philosophers to a better explanation of it than what they give themselves—which is, to suppose the attraction to continue in such a direction as to produce the mechanical interlocking of the figure of the particles of the bodies attracted.

Thus suppose a male and female screw lying on a table, and attracting each other with a force capable of drawing them together. The direction of the attracting power to be a right line till the screws begin to touch each other, and then, if the direction of the attracting power be circular, the screws will be screwed together. But even in this explanation, the cohesion is mechanical, and the attraction serves only to produce the contact.

While I consider attraction as a quality of matter capable of acting at a distance from the visible presence of matter, I have as clear an Idea of it as I can have of invisible things.

And while I consider cohesion as the mechanical interlocking of the particles of matter, I can conceive the possibility of it much easier than I can attraction, because I can, by crooking my fingers, see figures that will interlock—but no visible figure can explain attraction. Therefore to endeavour to explain the less difficulty by the greater appears to me unphilosophical. The cohesion which others attribute to attraction and which they cannot explain, I attribute to figure, which I can explain.

A number of fish hooks attracting and moving towards each other will shew me there is such a thing as attraction, but I see not how it is performed, but their figurative hooking together shews cohesion visibly. And a handful of fish hooks thrown together in a heap explains cohesion better than all the Newtonian Philosophy. It is with Gravitation, as it is with all new discoveries, it is applied to explain too many things.

It is a rainy morning, and I am waiting for Mr. Parker, and in the mean time, having nothing else to do, I have amused myself with writing this.

On the Means of Generating Motion for Mechanical Uses.[1]

As the limit of the Mechanical powers, properly so called, is fixt—in Nature no addition or improvement otherwise than in the application of them, can be made. To obtain a still greater quantity of power we must have recourse to the natural powers, and for usefulness, combine them with the Mechanical powers. Of this kind are wind and water, to which has since been added steam. The first two cannot be generated at pleasure. We must take them where and when we find them. It is not so with the Steam Engine. It can be erected in any place and act in all times where a well can be dug and fuel can be obtained. Attempts have been made to apply this power to the purpose of transportation, as that of moving carriages on land and vessels on the water. The first I believe to be impracticable, because I suppose, that the weight of the apparatus necessary to produce steam is greater than the power of the steam to remove that weight and consequently that the steam engine cannot move itself.

The thing wanted for purposes of this kind, and if applicable to this may be applicable to many others, is something that contains the greatest quantity of power in the least quantity of weight and bulk, and we find this property in gunpowder. When I consider the wisdom of nature I must think that she endowed matter with this extraordinary property for other purposes than that of destruction. Poisons are capable of other uses than that of killing.

If the power which an ounce of Gun-powder contains could be detailed out as steam or water can be, it would be a most commodious natural power, because of its small weight, and little bulk ; but gun powder acts, as to its force, by explosion. In most machinery operations the generating power is applied to produce a rotary motion on a wheel, and I think that gun powder can be applied to this purpose. But as an ounce of Gun powder or any other quantity when on fire, cannot be detailed out so as to act with equal force thro' any given space of time, the substitute in this case is, to divide the gun powder into a number of equal parts, and discharge them in equal spaces of time on the wheel, so as to keep it in nearly an equal and continual motion ; as a boy's whipping top is kept up by repeated floggings. Every separate stroke given to the top acts with the suddenness of explosion, but produces, as to continual motion, the effect of uninterrupted power.

When a stream of water strikes on a water wheel, it puts it in motion, and continues it. Suppose the water removed and that discharges of Gunpowder were made on the periphery of the wheel where the water strikes, would they not produce the same effect ?

I mention this merely for the simplicity of the case. But the wheel on which Gunpowder is to act must be fitted for the purpose. The buckets or boards placed on the periphery of a water wheel are the whole breadth of the stream of water ; but the parts corresponding to them on a gunpowder wheel should be of Iron and concave like a cup, and of no larger size than to receive the whole of the explosion. The back of them should be convex and oval, because in that shape they meet with less resistance from the air. The barrels from which the discharges are to be made, should, I think, be in the direction of a tangent with the cups. But if it should be found better to make the discharge on the solid periphery of the Wheel the barrels should be a tangent of a circle something less than the periphery of the wheel. A wheel put and continued in motion in this manner is represented by holding the axis of a wheel in one hand and striking the periphery with the other.

If acting on the solid periphery of the wheel should be found preferable to acting on the cups, the wheel should be shod with Iron, the edges should be turned up, and the middle part fluted cross. By this means the explosion cannot well escape sideways and the fluting will be preferable to a plain surface.

That the power of any given quantity of Gun powder can be detailed out by this means to act thro' any given quantity of time, and that a wheel can be put

Sent to Jefferson, from Paris, June 25, 1801. —*Editor.*

and continued in motion thereby, there is I think no doubt. Whether it will answer profitably in practice is another question. But the experiment, I think is worth making, and the more so, because it appears one of things in which a small experiment decides almost positively for a large one, which is not the case in many other small experiments. I think the wheel for a great work should be large, 30 or 40 feet diameter, because the explosions would give too much velocity to a small one, and because the larger the wheel is, the longer the explosion would rest upon it and the motion will be less irregular.

The machine which it seems to come into competition with is the steam engine. In the first place a steam engine is very expensive to erect. In this only a few Iron barrels are required. In a steam engine the expence and consumption of fuel is great, and this is to be compared to the expence of Gun powder, with the advantage that the interest of the money expended in erecting a steam engine goes towards the expence of the Gunpowder. A steam engine is subject to be out of order, and for this reason they frequently have two, that when one is repairing the other can suppy its place, or all the works dependent upon it must stand still. But nothing of this kind can happen to the gunpowder engine, because if a barrel burst, which is all that can happen, its place can be immediately supplied by another ; but if a boiler bursts there must be a new one. But I will not take up your time with calculations of this kind. The first thing to know is, if the experiment will succeed.

If in your retirement from business you should be disposed to vary your mechanical amusements, I wish you would try the effect of gunpowder on a wheel of two or three feet diameter ; the smallest bored pistol there is, about the size of a quill would give it considerable velocity. The first experiment will be to observe how long it will revolve with one impulse, and then with two. If the wheel revolves perpendicularly fast to its axis, and a cord be fastened to the axis with a weight to the end of the cord which, when the wheel is in motion, will wind on the axis and draw up the weight, the force with which it revolves will be known.

Perhaps there may be some difficulty in starting a great wheel into motion at first, because Gunpowder acts with a shock. In this case, might not Gunpowder be mixed with some other material, such as is used to make sky rockets ascend, because this lessens the shock and prolongs the force. But I conceive that after the wheel is in motion, there will be scarcely any sensible shock from the Gunpowder.

As it is always best to say nothing about new concerts till we know something of their effects I shall say nothing of this till I have the happiness to see you, which I hope will not be long, and which I anxiously wish for.

T. P.

APPENDIX D.

THE IRON BRIDGE.

LETTER TO SIR GEORGE STAUNTON, BART.[1]

SIR :—As I know you interest yourself in the success of the useful arts, and are a member of the society for the promotion thereof, I do myself the pleasure to send you an account of a small experiment I have been making at Messrs. Walker's iron works at this place. You have already seen the model I constructed for a bridge of a single arch, to be made of iron, and erected over the river Schuylkill, at Philadelphia ; but as the dimensions may have escaped your recollection, I will begin with stating those particulars.

The vast quantity of ice and melted snow at the breaking up of the frost in that part of America, render it impracticable to erect a bridge on piers. The river can conveniently be contracted to four hundred feet, the model, therefore, is for an arch of four hundred feet span ; the height of the arch in the centre, from the chord thereof, is to be about twenty feet, and to be brought off on the top, so as to make the ascent about one foot in eighteen or twenty.

The judgment of the Academy of Sciences at Paris, has been given on the principles and practicability of the construction. The original, signed by the Academy, is in my possession ; and in which they fully approve and support the design. They introduce their opinion by saying :

" It is certain that when such a project as that of making an iron arch of four hundred feet span is thought of, and when we consider the effects resulting from an arch of such vast magnitude, it would be strange if doubts were not raised as to the success of such an enterprise, from the difficulties which at first present themselves. But if such be the disposition of the various parts, and the method of uniting them, that the collective body should present a whole both firm and solid, we should then no longer have the same doubts of the success of the plan."

The Academy then proceed to state the reasons on which their judgment is founded, and conclude with saying :

" We conclude from what we have just remarked that Mr. Paine's Plan of an Iron Bridge is ingeniously imagined, that the construction of it is simple, solid, and proper to give it the necessary strength for resisting the effects resulting from its burden, and that it is deserving of a trial. In short, it may furnish a new example of the application of a metal, which has not hitherto been used in any works on an extensive scale, although on many occasions it is employed with the greatest success."

As it was my design to pass some time in England before I returned to America, I employed part of it in making the small essay I am now to inform you of.

My intention, when I came to the iron works, was to raise an arch of at least two hundred feet span ; but as it was late in the fall of last year, the season was too far advanced to work out of doors, and an arch of that extent too great to be worked within doors, and as I was unwilling to lose time, I

---

[1] Sir George Leonard Staunton, LL.D. (died 1801), an eminent physician, diplomatist, and author of a work on China.—*Editor.*

moderated my ambition with a little " common sense," and began with such an arch as could be compassed within some of the buildings belonging to the works. As the construction of the American arch admits, in practice, any species of curve with equal facility, I set off in preference to all others a catenarian arch of ninety feet span and five feet high. Were this arch converted into an arch of a circle, the diameter of its circle would be four hundred and ten feet. From the ordinates of the arch taken from the wall where the arch was struck, I produced a similar arch on the floor whereon the work was to be fitted and framed, and there was something so apparently just when the work was set out, that the looking at it promised success.

You will recollect that the model is composed of four parallel arched ribs, and as the number of ribs may be increased at pleasure to any breadth an arch sufficient for a road-way may require, and the arches to any number the breadth of a river may require, the construction of one rib would determine for the whole ; because if one rib succeeded, all the rest of the work, to any extent, is a repetition.

In less time than I expected, and before the winter set in, I had fitted and framed the arch, or properly the rib, completely together on the floor ; it was then taken in pieces and stowed away during the winter, in a corner of a work shop, used in the meantime by the carpenters, where it occupied so small a compass as to be hid among the shavings ; and though the extent of it is ninety feet, the depth of the arch at the centre two feet nine inches, and the depth at the branches six feet, the whole of it might, when in pieces, be put in an ordinary stage wagon, and sent to any part of England.

I returned to the works in April, and began to prepare for erecting ; we chose a situation between a steel furnace and a workshop, which served for butments. The distance between those buildings was about four feet more than the span of the arch, which we filled up with chumps of wood at each end. I mention this as I shall have occasion to refer to it hereafter.

We soon ran up a centre to turn the arch upon, and began our erections. Every part fitted to a mathematical exactness. The raising an arch of this construction is different to the method of raising a stone arch. In a stone arch they begin at the bottom, on the extremities of the arch, and work upwards, meeting at the crown. In this we began at the crown by a line perpendicular thereto and worked downward each way. It differs likewise in another respect. A stone arch is raised by sections of the curve, each stone being so, and this by concentric curves. The effect likewise of the arch upon the centre is different, for as stone arches sometimes break down the centre by their weight, this, on the contrary, grew lighter on the centre as the arch increased in thickness, so much so, that before the arch was completely finished, it rose itself off the centre the full thickness of the blade of a knife from one butment to the other. and is, I suppose, the first arch of ninety feet span that ever struck itself.

I have already mentioned that the spaces between the ends of the arches and the butments were filled up with chumps of wood, and those rather in a damp state ; and though we rammed them as close as we could, we could not ram them so close as the drying, and the weight of the arch, or rib, especially when loaded, would be capable of doing ; and we had now to observe the effects which the yielding and pressing up of the wood, and which corresponds to the giving away of the butments, so generally fatal to stone arches, would have upon this.

We loaded the rib with six tons of pig iron, beginning at the centre, and proceeding both ways, which is twice the weight of the iron in the rib, as I shall hereafter more particularly mention. This had not the least visible effect on the strength of the arch, but it pressed the wood home, so as to gain in three or four days, together with the drying and the shrinking of the wood, above a quarter of an inch at each end, and consequently the chord or span of the arch was lengthened above half an inch. As this lengthening was more than double the feather of the keystone in a stone arch of these dimensions, such an alteration at the butment would have endangered the safety of the stone arch, while it produced on this no other than the proper mathematical effect. To evidence this, I had recourse to the cord still swinging on the wall from which the curve of the arch was taken. I set the cord to ninety feet span, and five feet for the height of the arch, and marked the curve on the wall. I then removed the ends of the cords horizontally something more than a quarter of an inch at each end. The cord should then describe the exact catenarian curve which the rib had assumed by the same lengthening at the butments; that is, the rising of the cord should exactly correspond to the lowering of the arch, which it did through all their corresponding ordinates. The cord had risen something more than two inches at the centre, diminishing to nothing each way, and the arch had descended the same quantity, and in the same proportion. I much doubt whether a stone arch, could it be constructed as flat as this, could sustain such an alteration; and, on the contrary, I see no reason to doubt but an arch on this construction and dimensions, or corresponding thereto, might be let down to half its height, or as far as it would descend, with safety. I say "as far as it would descend," because the construction renders it exceedingly probable that there is a point beyond which it would not descend, but retain itself independent of butments; but this cannot be explained but by a sight of the arch itself.

In four or five days, the arch having gained nearly all it could gain on the wood, except what the wood would lose by a summer's drying, the lowering of the arch began to be scarcely visible. The weight still continues on it, to which I intend to add more, and there is not the least visible effect on the perfect curvature or strength of the arch. The arch having thus gained nearly a solid bearing on the wood and the butments, and the days beginning to be warm, and the nights continuing to be cool, I had now to observe the effects of the contraction and expansion of the iron.

The Academy of Sciences at Paris, in their report on the principles and construction of this arch, state these effects as a matter of perfect indifference to the arch, or to the butments, and the experience establishes the truth of their opinion. It is probable the Academy may have taken, in part, the observations of M. Peronnet, architect to the King of France, and a member of the Academy, as some ground for that opinion. From the observations of M. Peronnet, all arches, whether of stone or brick, are constantly ascending or descending by the changes of the weather, so as to render the difference perceptible by taking a level, and that all stone and brick buildings do the same. In short, that matter is never stationary, with respect to its dimensions, but when the atmosphere is so; but that as arches, like the tops of houses, are open to the air, and at freedom to rise, and all their weight in all changes of heat and cold is the same, their pressure is very little or nothing affected by it.

I hung a thermometer to the arch, where it has continued several days, and by what I can observe it equals, if not exceeds, the thermometer in exactness.

In twenty-four hours it ascends and descends two and three tenths of an inch at the centre, diminishing in exact mathematical proportion each way; and no sooner does an ascent or descent of half a hair's breadth appear at the centre, but it may be proportionally discovered through the whole span of ninety feet. I have affixed an index which multiplies ten times, and it can as easily be multiplied an hundred times: could I make a line of fire on each side the arch, so as to heat it in the same equal manner through all its parts, as the natural air does, I would try it up to blood heat. I will not attempt a description of the construction; first, because you have already seen the model; and, secondly, that I have often observed that a thing may be so very simple as to baffle description. On this head I shall only say, that I took the idea of constructing it from a spider's web, of which it resembles a section, and I naturally supposed, that when Nature enabled that insect to make a web, she taught it the best method of putting it together.

Another idea I have taken from Nature is, that of increasing the strength of matter by causing it to act over a larger space than it would occupy in a solid state, as is evidenced in the bones of animals, quills of birds, reeds, canes, etc., which, were they solid with the same quantity of matter, would have the same weight with a much less degree of strength.

I have already mentioned that the quantity of iron in this rib is three tons : that an arch of sufficient width for a bridge is to be composed of as many ribs as that width requires ; and that the number of arches, if the breadth of a river requires more than one, may be multiplied at discretion.

As the intention of this experiment was to ascertain, first, the practicability of the construction, and secondly, what degree of strength any given quantity of iron would have when thus formed into an arch, I employed in it no more than three tons, which is as small a quantity as could well be used in the experiment. It has already a weight of six tons constantly lying on it, without any effect on the strength or curvature of the arch. What greater weight it will bear cannot be judged of ; but taking even these as data, an arch of any strength, or capable of bearing a greater weight than can ever possibly come upon any bridge, may be easily calculated.

The river Schuylkill, at Philadelphia, as I have already mentioned, requires a single arch of four hundred feet span. The vast quantities of ice render it impossible to erect a bridge on piers, and is the reason why no bridge has been attempted. But great scenes inspire great ideas. The natural mightiness of America expands the mind, and it partakes of the greatness it contemplates. Even the war, with all its evils, had some advantages. It energized invention and lessened the catalogue of impossibilities. At the conclusion of it every man returned to his home to repair the ravages it had occasioned, and *to think of war no more.* As one amongst thousands who had borne a share in that memorable revolution, I returned with them to the re-enjoyment of quiet life, and, that I might not be idle, undertook to construct a bridge of a single arch for this river. Our beloved General had engaged in rendering another river, the Patowmac, navigable. The quantity of iron I had allowed in my plan for this arch was five hundred and twenty tons, to be distributed into thirteen ribs, in commemoration of the Thirteen United States, each rib to contain forty tons ; but although strength is the first object in works of this kind, I shall, from the success of this experiment, very considerably lessen the quantity of iron I had proposed.

The Academy of Sciences, in their report upon this construction, say, '' there is one advantage in the construction of M. Paine's bridge that is singular and important, which is, that the success of an arch to any span can be determined before the work be undertaken on the river, and with a small part of the expense of the whole, by erecting part on the ground."

As to its appearance, I shall give you an extract of a letter from a gentleman in the neighborhood, member in the former parliament for this county, who, in speaking of the arch, says, '' In point of elegance and beauty, it far exceeds my expectations, and it is certainly beyond anything I ever saw." I shall likewise mention that it is much visited and exceedingly admired by the ladies, who, though they may not be much acquainted with mathematical principles, are certainly judges of taste.

I shall close my letter with a few other observations, naturally and necessarily connected with the subject.

That, contrary to the general opinion, the most preservative situation in which iron can be placed is within the atmosphere of water, whether it be that the air is less saline and nitrous than that which arises from the filth of streets, and the fermentation of the earth, I am not undertaking to prove ; I speak only of fact, which any body may observe by the rings and bolts in wharfs and other watery situations. I never yet saw the iron chain affixed to a well-bucket consumed or injured by rust ; and I believe it is impossible to find iron exposed to the open air in the same preserved condition as that which is exposed over water.

A method of extending the span and lessening the height of arches has always been the *desideratum* of bridge architecture. But it has other advantages. It renders bridges capable of becoming a portable manufacture, as they may, on this construction, be made and sent to any part of the world ready to be erected; and at the same time it greatly increases the magnificence, elegance, and beauty of bridges, it considerably lessens their expense, and their appearance by re-painting will be ever new ; and as they may be erected in all situations where stone bridges can be erected, they may, moreover, be erected in certain situations where, on account of ice, infirm foundations in the beds of rivers, low shores, and various other causes, stone bridges cannot be erected. The last convenience, and which is not inconsiderable, that I shall mention is, that after they are erected, they may very easily be taken down without any injury to the materials of the construction, and be re-erected elsewhere.

I am, sir,

Your much obliged and obedient humble servant,

THOMAS PAINE.

(Rotherham, spring of 1789.)

APPENDIX E.

THE CONSTRUCTION OF IRON BRIDGES.

As bridges, and the method of constructing them, are becoming objects of great importance throughout the United States, and as there are at this time proposals for a bridge over the Delaware, and also a bridge beginning to be erected over the Schuylkill at Philadelphia, I present the public with some account of the construction of iron bridges.

The following memoir on that subject written last winter at the Federal City, was intended to be presented to Congress. But as the session would necessarily be short, and as several of its members would be replaced by new elections at the ensuing session, it was judged better to let it lie over. In the mean time, on account of the bridges now in contemplation, or begun, I give the memoir the opportunity of appearing before the public, and the persons concerned in those works.

N.B.—The two models mentioned in this memoir will, I expect, arrive at Philadelphia by the next packet, from the federal city and will remain for some time in Mr. Peale's museum.

THOMAS PAINE.

BORDENTOWN, June, 1803.

TO THE CONGRESS OF THE UNITED STATES.

I HAVE deposited in the office of the Secretary of State, and under the care of the Patent Office, two models of iron bridges; the one in pasteboard, the other cast in metal.[1] As they will show, by inspection, the manner of constructing iron bridges, I shall not take up the time of Congress with a description of them.

My intention in presenting this memoir to Congress, is to put the country in possession of the means and of the right of making use of the construction freely; as I do not intend to take any patent right for it.

As America abounds in rivers that interrupt the land communication, and as by violence of floods, and the breaking up of the ice in the spring, the bridges depending for support from the bottom of the river are frequently carried away, I turned my attention, after the revolutionary war was over, to find a method of constructing an arch, that might, without rendering the height inconvenient or the ascent difficult, extend at once from shore to shore, over rivers of three, four, or five hundred feet, and probably more.

The principle I took to begin with, and work upon, was that the small segment of a large circle was preferable to the great segment of a small circle. The appearance of such arches, and the manner of forming and putting the parts together, admit of many varieties, but the principle will be the same in all. The bridge architects that I conversed with in England denied the principle, but it was generally supported by mathematicians, and experiment has now established the fact.

In 1786, I made three models, partly at Philadelphia, but mostly at Bordentown in the state of New-Jersey. One model was in wood, one in cast iron,

---

[1] For an account of the making of these models see vol. iii., p. 376, of this work.—*Editor*.

and one in wrought iron connected with blocks of wood, representing cast iron blocks, but all on the same principle, that of the small segment of a large circle.

I took the last mentioned one with me to France in 1787, and presented it to the Academy of Sciences at Paris for their opinion of it, The Academy appointed a committee of three of their own body—Mons. Le Roy, the abbé Bossou, and Mons. Borda. The first was an acquaintance of Dr. Franklin, and of Mr. Jefferson, then Minister at Paris. The two others were celebrated as mathematicians. I presented it as a model for a bridge of a single arch of 400 feet span over the river Schuylkill at Philadelphia. The committee brought in a report which the Academy adopted—that an arch on the principle and construction of the model, in their opinion, might be extended 400 feet, the extent proposed.

In September of the same year, I sent the model to Sir Joseph Banks, president of the Royal Society in England, and soon after went there myself.

In order to ascertain the truth of the principle on a larger scale than could be shown by a portable model five or six feet in length, I went to the iron foundery of Messrs. Walker, at Rotherham, county of Yorkshire, in England, and had a complete rib of 90 feet span, and 5 feet of height from the cord line to the centre of the arch, manufactured and erected.[1] It was a segment of a circle of 410 feet diameter ; and until this was done, no experiment on a circle of such an extensive diameter had ever been made in architecture, or the practicability of it supposed.

The rib was erected between a wall of a furnace belonging to the iron works, and the gable end of a brick building, which served as butments. The weight of iron in the rib was three tons, and we loaded it with double its weight in pig iron. I wrote to Mr. Jefferson who was then at Paris, an account of this experiment, and also to Sir Joseph Banks in London, who in his answer to me says—" I look for many other bold improvements from your countrymen, the Americans, who think with vigour, and are not fettered with the trammels of science before they are capable of exerting their mental faculties to advantage." On the success of this experiment, I entered into an agreement with the ironfounders at Rotherham to cast and manufacture a complete bridge, to be composed of five ribs of 210 feet span, and 5 feet of height from the cord line, being a segment of a circle 610 feet diameter, and send it to London, to be erected as a specimen for establishing a manufactory of iron bridges, to be sent to any part of the world. The bridge was erected at the village of Paddington, near London, but being in a plain field, where no advantage could be taken of butments without the expense of building them, as in the former case, it served only as a specimen of the practicability of a manufactory of iron bridges. It was brought by sea, packed in the hold of a vessel, from the place where it was made ; and after standing a year was taken down, without injury to any of its parts, and might be erected any where else.

At this time my bridge operations became suspended. Mr. Edmund Burke published his attack on the French revolution and the system of representative

---

[1] See Guest's " Historic Notices of Rotherham," where two letters of Paine appear. The tradition that Paine wrote there his " Age of Reason," and the similar one at Bromley, Kent, suggest that Paine may already have given expression in conversation to his deistical views. With regard to the model arch the following extract from an unpublished letter, written from London by Paine (Feb. 26, 1789) to Thomas Walker, Rotherham, will be read with interest : " I wrote to the President of the Board of Works last Monday wishing him to begin making preparations for erecting the arch. I am so confident of his judgment that I can safely rely upon his going on as far as he pleases without me, and at any rate I shall not be long before I visit Rotherham.—I had a letter yesterday from Mr. Foljambe apologizing for his being obliged unexpectedly to leave town without calling on me, but that he should be in London again in a few days. He concludes his letter by saying : " I saw the Rib of your Bridge. In point of eloquence and beauty it far exceeded my expectations, and is certainly beyond anything I ever saw." You will please to inform the President what Mr. Foljambe says, as I think him entitled to participate in the applause. Mr. Fox of Derby called again on me last evening respecting the Bridge, but I was not at home. There is a project of erecting a Bridge at Dublin, which will be a large undertaking ; and as the Duke of Leinster and the other deputies from Ireland are arrived, I intend making an opportunity of speaking to them on that business."—*Editor.*

government, and in defence of government by hereditary succession, a thing which is in its nature an absurdity, because it is impossible to make wisdom hereditary ; and therefore, so far as wisdom is necessary in a government, it must be looked for where it can be found, sometimes in one family, sometimes in another. History informs us that the son of Solomon was a fool. He lost ten tribes out of twelve (2 Chron. ch. x.). There are those in later times who lost thirteen.[1]

The publication of this work by Mr. Burke, absurd in its principles and outrageous in its manner, drew me, as I have said, from my bridge operations, and my time became employed in defending a system then established and operating in America, and which I wished to see peaceably adopted in Europe. I therefore ceased my work on the bridge to employ myself on the more necessary work, *Rights of Man*, in answer to Mr. Burke.

In 1792, a Convention was elected in France for the express purpose of forming a Constitution on the authority of the people, as had been done in America, of which Convention I was elected a member. I was at this time in England, and knew nothing of my being elected till the arrival of the person who was sent officially to inform me of it.

During my residence in France, which was from 1792 to 1802, an iron bridge of 236 feet span, and 34 of height from the cord line, was erected over the river Wear near the town of Sunderland, in the county of Durham, England. It was done chiefly at the expense of the two Members of Parliament for that county, Milbanke and Burdon.

It happened that a very intimate friend of mine, Sir Robert Smyth (who was also an acquaintance of Mr. Monroe, the American Minister, and since of Mr. Livingston) was then at Paris. He had been a colleague in Parliament with Milbanke, and supposing that the persons who constructed the iron bridge at Sunderland had made free with my model, which was at the iron works where the Sunderland bridge was cast, he wrote to Milbanke on the subject, and the following is that gentleman's answer.

" With respect to the iron bridge over the river Wear at Sunderland, it certainly is a work well deserving admiration, both for its structure and utility, and I have good grounds for saying that the first idea was suggested by Mr. Paine's bridge exhibited at Paddington. What difference there may be in some part of the structure, or in the proportion of wrought and cast iron, I cannot pretend to say, Burdon having undertaken to build the bridge, in consequence of his having taken upon himself whatever the expense might be beyond between three and four thousand pounds sterling, subscribed by myself and some other gentlemen. But whatever the mechanism might be, it did not supersede the necessity of a centre."* (The writer has here confounded a centre with a scaffolding.) "Which centre (continues the writer) was esteemed a very ingenious piece of workmanship, and taken from a plan sketched out by Mr. Nash, an architect of great merit, who had been consulted in the outset of the business, when a bridge of stone was in contemplation.

" With respect therefore to any gratuity to Mr. Paine, though ever so desirous of rewarding the labours of an ingenious man, I do not feel how, under the circumstances already described, I have it in my power, having had nothing to do with the bridge after the payment of my subscription, Mr. Burdon then becoming accountable for the whole. But if you can point out any mode according to which it would be in my power to be instrumental in procuring him any compensation for the advantages the public may have derived from his ingenious model, from which certainly the outline of the Bridge at Sunderland was taken, be assured it will afford me very great satisfaction.†

" RA. MILBANKE."

[1] The thirteen American colonies.—*Editor.*
* It is the technical term, meaning the boards and numbers which form the arch upon which the permanent materials are laid ; when a bridge is finished the workmen say they are ready to strike centre, that is to take down the scaffolding.—*Author.*
† The original is in my possession.—*Author.*

The year before I left France, the government of that country had it in contemplation to erect an iron bridge over the river Seine, at Paris. As all edifices of public construction came under the cognizance of the Minister of the Interior, (and as their plan was to erect a bridge of five iron arches of one hundred feet span each, instead of passing the river with a single arch, and which was going backward in practice, instead of forward, as there was already an iron arch of 230 feet in existence), I wrote the Minister of the Interior, the citizen Chaptal, a memoir on the construction of iron bridges. The following is his answer :

"*The Minister of the Interior to the citizen Thomas Paine.*—I have received, Citizen, the observations that you have been so good as to address to me upon the construction of iron bridges. They will be of the greatest utility to us, when the new kind of construction goes to be executed for the first time. With pleasure, I assure you, Citizen, that you have rights of more than one kind to the thankfulness of nations, and I give you, cordially, the particular expression of my esteem.—CHAPTAL." *

A short time before I left France, a person came to me from London with plans and drawings for an iron bridge of one arch over the river Thames at London, of 600 feet span, and sixty feet of height from the cord line. The subject was then before a committee of the House of Commons, but I know not the proceedings thereon.

As this new construction of an arch for bridges, and the principles on which it is founded, originated in America, as the documents I have produced sufficiently prove, and is becoming an object of importance to the world, and to no part of it more than to our own country, on account of its numerous rivers, and as no experiment has been made in America to bring it into practice, further than on the model I have executed myself, and at my own expense, I beg leave to submit a proposal to Congress on the subject, which is,

To erect an experiment rib of about 400 feet span, to be the segment of a circle of at least 1000 feet diameter, and to let it remain exposed to public view, that the method of constructing such arches may be generally known.

It is an advantage peculiar to the construction of iron bridges that the success of an arch of a given extent and height, can be ascertained without being at the expense of building the bridge ; which is, by the method I propose, that of erecting an experiment rib on the ground where advantage can be taken of two hills for butments.

I began in this manner with the rib of 90 feet span and 5 feet of height, being a segment of a circle of 410 feet diameter. The undertakers of the Sunderland bridge began in the same manner. They contracted with the iron-founder for a single rib, and, finding it to answer, had five more manufactured like it, and erected into a bridge consisting of six ribs, the experiment rib being one. But the Sunderland bridge does not carry the principle much further into practice than had been done by the rib of 90 feet span and 5 feet in height, being, as before said, a segment of a circle of 410 feet diameter : the Sunderland bridge, being 206 feet span and 34 feet of height, gives the diameter of the circle of which it is a segment to be 444 feet, within a few inches, which is but a larger segment of a circle of 30 feet more diameter.

The construction of those bridges does not come within the line of any established practice of business. The stone architect can derive but little from the theory or practice of his art that enters into his construction of an iron bridge ; and the iron-founder, though he may be expert in moulding and casting the parts, when the models are given him, would be at a loss to proportion them, unless he was acquainted with all the lines and properties belonging to a circle.

If it should appear to Congress that the construction of iron bridges will be of utility to the country, and they should direct that an experiment rib be made for that purpose, I will furnish the proportions for the several parts of the work, and give my attendance to superintend the erection of it.

But, in any case, I have to request that this memoir may be put on the journals of Congress, as an evidence hereafter, that this new method of constructing bridges originated in America.

THOMAS PAINE.

FEDERAL CITY, Jan. 3, 1803.

Editorial Note.—Paine's Specification is given in vol. ii., chap. 10, of this work, and some facts about his bridge in chap. 11. (See also my "Life of Paine," Index.) For the convenience of those who wish to pursue the subject I quote Burdon's declaration : " My Invention consists in applying iron or other metallic compositions to the purpose of constructing arches, upon the same principle as stone is now employed, by a substitution into blocks, easily portable, answering to the keystones of a common arch, which being brought to bear on each other, gives them all the firmness of the solid stone arch, whilst by the great vacuities in the blocks and their respective distances in their lateral position, the arch becomes infinitely lighter than that of stone, and, by the tenacity of the metal, the parts are so intimately connected that the accurate calculation of the extrados and intrados, so necessary in stone arches of magnitude, is rendered of much less consequence." (*Specification of Rowland Burdon*, A.D. *1795, No. 2066.*) Those who are aware of the extent to which Paine's discoveries and "materials" have been utilized in political and religious structures, while their originator's effigy (alone known to many people) has been held up to execration, will not wonder that while the literal effigy was being burnt throughout England (1792–93) his Paddington model (210 feet span) was following the usual course, as is stated by Dr. Smiles : " In the meantime the bridge exhibited at Paddington had produced important results. The manufacturers agreed to take it back as part of their debt, and the materials were afterwards used in the construction of the noble bridge over the Wear at Sunderland, which was erected in 1796. The project . . . is due to Mr. Rowland Burdon, under whom Mr. T. Wilson served as engineer. The details differed in several important respects from the proposed bridge of Paine, Mr. Burdon introducing several new and original features, more particularly as regarded the framed iron panels radiating towards the centre in the form of voussoirs, for the purpose of resisting compression. Mr. Phipps, C. E., in a report prepared by him at the instance of the late Robert Stephenson . . . observes, with regard to the original design,—' We should probably make a fair division of the honour connected with this unique bridge, by conceding to Mr. Burdon all that belongs to a careful elaboration and improvement upon the designs of another, to the boldness of taking upon himself the responsibility of applying this idea on so magnificent a scale, and to his liberality and public spirit in furnishing the requisite funds ; but we must not deny to Paine the credit of conceiving the construction of iron bridges of far larger span than had been made before his time, or of the important examples both as models and large constructions which he caused to be made and publicly exhibited.'"—Smiles' "Life of Telford."—*Editor*.

APPENDIX F.

TO THE PEOPLE OF ENGLAND ON THE INVASION OF ENGLAND.

EDITOR'S PREFACE.—It may appear at this distance of time inconsistent with Paine's humane and peaceful principles that he should desire the invasion of England by Napoleon, for it is difficult to see behind the England of to-day the country of Pitt which was harrying the world by land and sea, seizing American ships and seamen, and at home imprisoning every patriot who protested against royal outrages. It had become the firm faith of best men, in many countries, that the English people would never rise in their strength and stop these outrages until they could look upon the horrid face of war at their own doors. On the return of Napoleon from his brilliant campaign in Italy, December, 1797, he consulted Paine, said the author of *Rights of Man* should have a statue of gold, and invited him to accompany him on his invasion of England, and assist his purpose of liberating the English people. Flushed with the great hope of giving, as he wrote to Jefferson, " the people of England an opportunity of forming a government for themselves, and thereby bring about peace," Paine wrote a letter read by Coupé to the Council of Five Hundred, January 28, 1798 :

" CITIZENS REPRESENTATIVES : Though it is not convenient to me, in the present situation of my affairs, to subscribe to the loan towards the descent upon England, my economy permits me to make a small patriotic donation. I send a hundred livres, and with it all the wishes of my heart for the success of the descent, and a voluntary offer of any service I can render to promote it. There will be no lasting peace for France, nor for the world, until the tyranny and corruption of the English government be abolished, and England, like Italy, become a sister republic. As to those men, whether in England, Scotland, or Ireland, who, like Robespierre in France, are covered with crimes, they, like him, have no other resource than committing more. But the mass of the people are the friends of liberty : tyranny and taxation oppress them, but they deserve to be free.

" Accept, Citizens Representatives, the congratulations of an old colleague in the dangers we have passed and on the happy prospect before us. Salut et respect."

Paine accompanied the expedition to Belgium, and discovered that it was, as he wrote to Jefferson, " only a feint." He also discovered that Napoleon's enthusiasm for *Rights of Man* and its author was a feint. A London paper, quoted in the New York *Theophilanthropist* (1801, No. 1) says :

" He [Paine] continued in Paris long after Bonaparte rendered himself supreme in the State, and spoke as freely as ever. He told the writer of this article, at Paris, on the peace of Amiens, that he was preparing for America ; that he could not reside in comfort in the dominions of Bonaparte ; that if he was to govern like an angel, he should always remember that he had perjured himself ; that he had heard him swear that France should be a pure republic ; and that he himself would rather die than endure the authority of a single individual : he would end his days in America, for he thought there was no liberty anywhere else."

When Paine reached America, towards the close of 1802, he found his friend Jefferson, now President, almost an enthusiast for Napoleon, and soon afterwards the First Consul's Civil Code, his provisions for education and Science, and the declaration of war against him (May 18, 1803) by England, somewhat restored Paine's confidence in him. The revival of the plan for a descent on England, whose fleets were paralyzing the commerce of the world, made Napoleon appear, if not a republican, a "scourge of God" to arrest the aggressions of monarchy. But Paine little dreamed that at the very moment when this pamphlet was appearing in America (May, 1804,) Napoleon was assuming at St. Cloud the title of Emperor !

TO THE PEOPLE OF ENGLAND

IN casting my eye over England and America, and comparing them together, the difference is very striking. The two countries were created by the same power, and peopled from the same stock. What then has caused the difference ? Have those who emigrated to America improved, or those whom they left behind degenerated ? There are as many degrees of difference in the political morality of the two people as there are of longitude between the two countries.

In the science of cause and effect, every thing that enters into the composition of either must be allowed its proportion of influence. Investigating, therefore, into the cause of this difference, we must take into the calculation the difference of the two systems of government, the *hereditary* and the *representative*. Under the hereditary system, it is the government that forms and fashions the political character of the people. In the representative system, it is the people that form the character of the government. Their own happiness as citizens forms the basis of their conduct, and the guide of their choice. Now, is it more probable that an hereditary government should become corrupt, and corrupt the people by its example, or that a whole people should become corrupt, and produce a corrupt government ? For the point where the corruption begins, becomes the source from whence it afterwards spreads.

While men remained in Europe as subjects of some hereditary potentate, they had ideas conformable to that condition ; but when they arrived in America, they found themselves in possession of a new character, the character of sovereignty ; and, like converts to a new religion, they became inspired with new principles. Elevated above their former rank, they considered government and public affairs as part of their own concern, for they were to pay the expence and they watched them with circumspection. They soon found that government was not that complicated thing, enshrined in mystery, which church and state, to play into each other's hands, had represented ; and that to conduct it with proper effect, was to conduct it justly. Common sense, common honesty, and civil manners, qualify a man for government ; and besides this, put man in a situation that requires new thinking, and the mind will grow up to it, for, like the body, it improves by exercise. Man is but a learner all his life-time.

But whatever be the cause of the difference of character between the government and people of England and those of America, the effect arising from that difference is as distinguishable as the sun from the moon. We see America flourishing in peace, cultivating friendship with all nations, and reducing her public debt and taxes, incurred by the revolution. On the contrary, we see England almost perpetually in war, or warlike disputes, and her debt and taxes continually encreasing. Could we suppose a stranger, who knew nothing of the origin of the two countries, he would from observation conclude that America was the *old* country, experienced and sage, and England the *new*, eccentric and wild.

Scarcely had England drawn home her troops from America, after the revolutionary war, than she was on the point of plunging herself into a war with Holland, on account of the Stadtholder ; then with Russia ; then with Spain, on the account of Nootka *cat-skins ;* and actually with France to prevent her revolution. Scarcely had she made peace with France, and before she had fulfilled her own part of the treaty, than she declared war again to avoid fulfilling the treaty. In her treaty of peace with America, she engaged to evacuate the western posts within six months, but having obtained peace she refused to fulfil the conditions, and kept possession of the posts and embroiled us in an Indian war. In her treaty of peace with France, she engaged to evacuate Malta within three months, but having obtained peace she refused to evacuate Malta, and began a new war.[1]

All these matters pass before the eyes of the world, who form their own opinion thereon, regardless of what English newspapers may say of France, or French papers say of England. The non-fulfilment of a treaty is a case that every body can understand. They reason upon it as they would on a contract between two individuals, and in so doing they reason from a right foundation. The affected pomp and mystification of courts make no alteration in the principle. Had France declared war to compel England to fulfil the treaty, as a man would commence a civil action to compel a delinquent party to fulfil a contract, she would have stood acquitted in the opinion of nations. But that England still holding Malta, should go to war for Malta, is a paradox not easily solved, unless it be supposed that the peace was insidious from the beginning, that it was concluded with the expectation that the military ardour of France would cool, or a new order of things arise, or a national discontent prevail, that would favour a non-execution of the treaty, and leave England arbiter of the fate of Malta.

Something like this, which was like a vision in the clouds, must have been the calculation of the British ministry ; for certainly they did not expect the war would take the turn it has. Could they have foreseen, and they ought to have foreseen, that a declaration of war was the same as sending a challenge to Bonaparte to invade England and make it the seat of war, they hardly would have done it unless they were mad ; for in any event such a war might produce, in a military view, it is England would be the sufferer unless it terminated in a wise revolution. One of the causes assigned for this declaration of war by the British Ministry, was that Bonaparte had cramped their commerce. If by cramping their commerce is to be understood that of encouraging and extending the commerce of France, he had a right, and it was his duty to do it. The prerogative of monopoly belongs to no nation. But to make this one of the causes of war, considering their commerce in consequence of that declaration is now cramped ten times more, is like the case of a foolish man who, after losing an eye in fight, renews the combat to revenge the injury, and loses the other eye.

Those who never experienced an invasion, by suffering it, which the English people have not, can have but little idea of it. Between the two armies the country will be desolated, wherever the armies are, and that as much by their own army as by the enemy. The farmers on the coast will be the first sufferers ; for, whether their stock of cattle, corn, &c. be seized by the invading army, or driven off, or burnt, by orders of their own government, the effect will be the same to them. As to the revenue, which has been collected altogether in paper, since the bank stopped payment, it will go to destruction the instant an invading army lands ; and as to effective government, there can be but little where the two armies are contending for victory in a country small as England is.

With respect to the general politics of Europe, the British Ministry could not have committed a greater error than to make Malta the ostensible cause of the

---

[1] With regard to the Western Posts, Paine was not fully informed. The United States had failed to fulfil the Treaty as to the payment of their debts to English creditors. For the Treaty with France see *Parl. Hist.*, xxxvi., p. 558. Among the reasons for the Declaration of May, 1803, is that His Majesty has learned that the French Government had "even suggested the idea of a partition of the Turkish empire !"—*Editor.*

war ; for though Malta is an unproductive rock, and will be an expence to any nation that possesses it, there is not a power in Europe will consent that England should have it. It is a situation capable of annoying and controuling the commerce of other nations in the Mediterranean ; and the conduct of England on the seas and in the Baltic, has shewn the danger of her possessing Malta. Bonaparte, by opposing her claim, has all Europe with him : England, by asserting it, loses all. Had the English Ministry studied for an object that would put them at variance with all nations, from the north of Europe to the south, they could not have done it more effectually.

But what is Malta to the people of England, compared with the evils and dangers they already suffer in consequence of it ? It is their own government that has brought this upon them. Were Burke now living, he would be deprived of his exclamation, that " *the age of chivalry is gone ;* " for this declaration of war is like a challenge sent from one knight of the sword to another knight of the sword to fight him on the challenger's ground, and England is staked as the prize.

But though the British Ministry began this war for the sake of Malta, they are now artful enough to keep Malta out of sight. Not a word is now said about Malta in any of their parliamentary speeches and messages. The King's speech is silent upon the subject, and the invasion is put in its place, as if the invasion was the cause of the war, and not the consequence of it. This policy is easily seen through. The case is, they went to war *without counting the cost*, or calculating upon events, and they are now obliged to shift the scenes to conceal the disgrace.

If they were disposed to try experiments upon France, they chose for it the worst possible time, as well as the worst possible object. France has now for its chief the most enterprising and fortunate man, either for deep project or daring execution, the world has known for many ages. Compared with him, there is not a man in the British government, or under its authority, has any chance with him. That he is ambitious, the world knows, and he always was so ; but he knew where to stop. He had reached the highest point of probable expectation, and having reduced all his enemies to peace, had set himself down to the improvement of agriculture, manufactures, and commerce at home ; and his conversation with the English ambassador, Whitworth, shewed he wished to continue so. In this view of his situation, could anything be worse policy than to give to satisfied ambition a new object, and provoke it into action ? Yet this the British Ministry have done.

The plan of a descent upon England by gun-boats, began after the first peace with Austria, and the acquisition of Belgium by France. Before that acquisition, France had no territory on the North Sea, and it is there the descent will be carried on. Dunkirk was then her northern limit. The English coast opposite to France, on the Channel, from the straits between Dover and Calais to the Land's End, about three hundred miles, is high, bold, and rocky, to the height, in many places, perpendicular, of three, four, or five hundred feet, and it is only where there are breaks in the rocks, as at Portsmouth, Plymouth, &c., that a landing can be made ; and as those places could be easily protected, because England was mistress of the Channel, France had no opportunity of making an invasion, unless she could first defeat the English fleet. But the union of Belgium to France makes a new order of things.

The English coast on the North Sea, including the counties of Essex, Suffolk, Norfolk, and Lincolnshire, is as level as a bowling green, and approachable in every part for more than two hundred miles. The shore is a clean firm sand, where a flat-bottomed boat may row dry a-ground. The country people use it as a race-ground, and for other sports, when the tide is out. It is the weak and defenceless part of England, and it is impossible to make it otherwise : and besides this, there is not a port or harbour in it where ships of the line or large frigates can rendezvous for its protection. The Belgic coast, and that of Holland, which joins it, are directly opposite this defenceless part, and opens a new passage for invasion. The Dutch fishermen knew this coast better than the

English themselves, except those who live upon it; and the Dutch smugglers know every creek and corner in it.

The original plan, formed in the time of the Directory, (but now much more extensive,) was to build one thousand boats, each sixty feet long, sixteen feet broad, to draw about two feet water, to carry a twenty-four or thirty-six pounder in the head, and a field-piece in the stern, to be run out as soon as they touched ground. Each boat was to carry an hundred men, making in the whole one hundred thousand, and to row with twenty or twenty-five oars on a side. Bonaparte was appointed to the command, and by an agreement between him and me, I was to accompany him, as the intention of the expedition was to give the people of England an opportunity of forming a government for themselves, and thereby bring about peace. I have no reason to suppose this part of the plan is altered, because there is nothing better Bonaparte can do. As to the clamour spread by some of the English newspapers, that he comes for plunder, it is absurd. Bonaparte is too good a general to undiscipline and dissolute his army by plundering, and too good a politician, as well as too much accustomed to great achievements, to make plunder his object. He goes against the government that has declared war against him.

As the expedition could choose its time of setting off, either after a storm, when the English would be blown off, or in a calm, or in a fog ; and as thirty-six hours' rowing would be able to carry it over, the probability is it would arrive, and when arrived no ship of the line or large frigate could approach it, on account of the shoalness of the coast ; and besides this, the boats would form a floating battery, close in with the shore, of a thousand pieces of heavy artillery ; and the attempt of Nelson against the gun-boats at Boulogne shews the insufficiency of ships in such situations. About two hundred and fifty gun-boats were built, when the expedition was abandoned for that of Egypt, to which the preparations had served as a feint.

The present impolitic war by the English government has now renewed the plan, and that with much greater energy than before, and with national unanimity. All France is alive to chastise the English government for recommencing the war, and all Europe stands still to behold it. The preparations for the invasion have already demonstrated to France what England ought never to have suffered her to know, which is, that she can hold the English government in terror, and the whole country in alarm, whenever she pleases, and as long as she pleases, and that without employing a single ship of the line, and more effectually than if she had an hundred sail. The boasted navy of England is outdone by gun-boats ! It is a revolution in naval tactics ; but we live in an age of revolutions.

The preparations in England for defence are also great, but they are marked with an ominous trait of character. There is something sullen on the face of affairs in England. Not an address has been presented to the king by any county, city, town, or corporation, since the declaration of war. The people unite for the protection of themselves and property against whatever events may happen, but they are *not pleased*, and their silence is the expression of their discontent.

Another circumstance, curious and awkward, was the conduct of the House of Commons with respect to their address to the king, in consequence of the king's speech at the opening of the Parliament. The address, which is always an echo of the speech, was voted without opposition, and this equivocal silence passed for unanimity. The next thing was to present it, and it was made the order for the next day that the House should go up in a body to the king, with the Speaker at their head, for that purpose. The time fixed was half after three, and it was expected the procession would be numerous, three or four hundred at least, in order to shew their zeal and their loyalty and their thanks to the king for his intention of taking the field. But when half after three arrived, only thirty members were present, and without forty (the number that makes a House) the address could not be presented. The serjeant was then sent out, with the authority of a press-warrant, to search for members, and by four o'clock he returned with just enough to make up forty, and the procession set off with the slowness of a funeral ; for it was remarked it went slower than usual.

Such a circumstance in such a critical juncture of affairs, and on such an occasion, shews at least a great indifference towards the government. It was like saying, you have brought us into a great deal of trouble, and we have no *personal* thanks to make to you. We have voted the address, as a customary matter of form, and we leave it to find its way to you as well as it can.

If the invasion succeed, I hope Bonaparte will remember that this war has not been provoked by the people. It is altogether the act of the government, without their consent or knowledge ; and though the late peace appears to have been insidious from the first, on the part of the government, it was received by the people with a sincerity of joy.

There is yet, perhaps, one way, if it be not too late, to put an end to this burthensome state of things, and which threatens to be worse ; which is, for the people, now they are embodied for their own protection, to instruct their representatives in Parliament to move for the fulfilment of the treaty of Amiens, for a treaty ought to be fulfilled. The present is an uncommon case, accompanied with uncommon circumstances, and it must be got over by means suited to the occasion. What is Malta to them ? The possession of it might serve to extend the patronage and influence of the Crown, on the appointment to new offices, and the part that would fall to the people would be to pay the expence. The more acquisitions the government makes abroad, the more taxes the people have to pay at home. This has always been the case in England.

The non-fulfilment of a treaty ruins the honour of a government, and spreads a reproach over the character of a nation. But when a treaty of peace is made with the concealed design of not fulfilling it, and war is declared for the avowed purpose of avoiding it, the case is still worse. The representative system does not put it in the power of an individual to declare war of his own will. It must be the act of the body of the representatives, for it is their constituents who are to pay the expence. The state which the people of England are now in shews the extreme danger of trusting this power to the caprice of an individual, whatever title he may bear. In that country this power is assumed by what is called the Crown, for it is not constituted by any legal authority. It is a branch from the trunk of monarchical despotism.

By this impolitic declaration of war the government of England have put every thing to issue ; and no wise general would commence an action he might avoid, where nothing is to be gained by gaining a battle, and every thing is to be lost by losing it. An invasion and a revolution, which consequently includes that of Ireland, stand now on the same ground. What part the people may finally take in a contest pregnant with such an issue is yet to be known. By the experiment of raising the country *in mass* the government have put arms into the hands of men whom they would have sent to Botany Bay but a few months before, had they found a pike in their possession. The honour of this project, which is copied from France, is claimed by Mr. Pitt ; and no project of his has yet succeeded, in the end, except that of raising the taxes, and ruining the Bank. All his schemes in the revolutionary war of France failed of success, and finished in discredit. If Bonaparte is remarkable for an unexampled series of good fortune, Mr. Pitt is remarkable for a contrary fate, and his want of popularity with the people, whom he deserted and betrayed on the question of a reform of Parliament, sheds no beams of glory round his projects.

If the present eventful crisis, for an eventful one it is, should end in a revolution, the people of England have, within their glance, the benefit of experience both in theory and fact. This was not the case at first. The American revolution began on untried ground. The representative system of government was then unknown in practice, and but little thought of in theory. The idea that man must be governed by effigy and show, and that superstitious reverence was necessary to establish authority, had so benumbed the reasoning faculties of men, that some bold exertion was necessary to shock them into reflection. But the experiment has now been made. The practice of almost thirty years, the last twenty of which have been of peace, notwithstanding the wrong-headed tumultuous administration of John Adams, has proved the excellence of the representative system, and the NEW WORLD is now the preceptor of the OLD. The children are become the fathers of their progenitors.

With respect to the French revolution, it was begun by good men and on good principles, and I have always believed it would have gone on so, had not the provocative interference of foreign powers, of which Pitt was the principal and vindictive agent, distracted it into madness, and sown jealousies among the leaders.

The people of England have now two revolutions before them. The one as an example ; the other as a warning. Their own wisdom will direct them what to choose and what to avoid, and in every thing which regards their happiness, combined with the common good of mankind, I wish them honour and success.

THOMAS PAINE.

NEW YORK, May, 1804.

APPENDIX G.

CONSTITUTIONAL REFORM.[1]

To the Citizens of Pennsylvania on the Proposal for calling a Convention.

As I resided in the capital of your state, Philadelphia, in the *time that tried mens souls*, and all my political writings, during the revolutionary war, were written in that city,[2] it seems natural for me to look back to the place of my political and literary birth, and feel an interest for its happiness. Removed as I now am from the place, and detached from every thing of personal party, I address this token to you on the ground of principle, and in remembrance of former times and friendships.

The subject now before you, is the call of a Convention, to examine, and, if necessary, to reform the Constitution of the State ; or to speak in the correct language of constitutional order, to propose written articles of reform to be accepted or rejected by the people by vote, in the room of those now existing, that shall be judged improper or defective. There cannot be, on the ground of reason, any objection to this ; because if no reform or alteration is necessary, the sense of the country will permit none to be made ; and, *if necessary*, it *will* be made because it *ought* to be made. Until, therefore, the sense of the country can be collected, and made known by a Convention elected for that purpose, all opposition to the call of a Convention not only passes for nothing, but serves to create a suspicion that the opposers are conscious that the Constitution will not bear an examination.

The Constitution formed by the Convention of 1776, of which Benjamin Franklin (the greatest and most useful man America has yet produced,) was president, had many good points in it which were overthrown by the Convention of 1790, under the pretence of making the Constitution conformable to that of the United States ; as if the forms and periods of election for a territory extensive as that of the United States is could become a rule for a single State.

The principal defect in the Constitution of 1776 was, that it was subject, in practice, to too much precipitancy ; but the ground-work of that Constitution was good. The present Constitution appears to me to be clogged with inconsistencies of a hazardous tendency, as a supposed remedy against a precipitancy that might not happen. Investing any individual, by whatever name or official title he may be called, with a negative over the formation of the laws, is copied from the English government, without ever perceiving the inconsistency and absurdity of it, when applied to the representative system, or understanding the origin of it in England.[3]

The present form of government in England, and all those things called pre-

---

[1] This was Paine's last political pamphlet. It was printed at the *Aurora* office, Philadelphia. The gubernatorial election of 1805 turned on this proposal, and the " new constitutionalists " were defeated by the election of McKean over Snyder.—*Editor.*
[2] The fifth " Crisis," was written at Lancaster, Pennsylvania.—*Editor.*
[3] *Cf.* an important note by Paine on the single executive, vol. iii., p. 214.—*Editor.*

rogatives of the Crown, of which this negative power is one, was established by conquest, not by compact. Their origin was the conquest of England by the Normans, under William of Normandy, surnamed the Conqueror, in 1066, and the genealogy of its kings takes its date from him. He is the first of the list. There is no historical certainty of the time when Parliaments began ; but be the time when it may, they began by what are called grants or charters from the Norman Conqueror, or his successors, to certain towns, and to counties, to elect members to meet and serve in Parliament,* subject to his controul ; and the custom still continues with the king of England calling the parliament *my Parliament ;* that is, a Parliament originating from his authority, and over which he holds controul in right of himself, derived from that conquest. It is from this assumed right, derived from conquest, and not from any constitutional right by compact, that kings of England hold a negative over the formation of the laws ; and they hold this for the purpose of preventing any being enacted that might abridge, invade, or in any way affect or diminish what they claim to be their hereditary or family rights and prerogatives, derived originally from the conquest of the country.† This is the origin of the king of England's negative. It is a badge of disgrace which *his* Parliaments are obliged to wear, and to which they are abject enough to submit.

But what has this case to do with a Legislature chosen by freemen, on their own authority, in right of themselves ? Or in what manner does a person styled Governor or Chief Magistrate resemble a conqueror subjugating a country, as William of Normandy subjugated England, and saying to it, *you shall have no laws but what I please ?* The negativing power in a country like America, is of that kind, that a wise man would not choose to be embarrassed with it, and a man fond of using it will be overthrown by it. It is not difficult to see that when Mr. M'Kean negatived the Arbitration Act, he was induced to it as a *lawyer*, for the benefit of the profession, and not as a *magistrate*, for the benefit of the people ; for it is the office of a Chief Magistrate to compose differences and *prevent* law-suits. If the people choose to have arbitrations instead of law-suits, why should they not have them ? It is a matter that concerns them as individuals, and not as a State or community, and is not a proper case for a Governor to interfere in, for it is not a State or government concern : nor does it concern the peace thereof, otherwise than to make it more peaceable by making it less contentious.

This negativing power in the hands of an individual ought to be constitutionally abolished. It is a dangerous power. There is no prescribing rules for the use of it. It is discretionary and arbitrary ; and the will and temper of the person at any time possessing it, is its only rule. There must have been great want of reflection in the Convention that admitted it into the Constitution. Would that Convention have put the Constitution it had formed (whether good or bad) in the power of any individual to negative ? It would not. It would have treated such a proposal with disdain. Why then did it put the Legislatures thereafter to be chosen, and all the laws, in that predicament ? Had that Convention, or the law members thereof, known the origin of the negativing power used by kings of England, from whence they copied it, they must have seen the inconsistency of introducing it into an American Constitution. We are not a conquered people ; we know no conqueror ; and the negativing power used by kings in England is for the defence of the personal and family prerogatives of the successors of the conqueror against the Parliament and the People. What is all this to us ? We know no prerogatives but what belong to the sovereignty of ourselves.

At the time this Constitution was formed, there was a great departure from

---

* *Parliament* is a French word, brought into England by the Normans. It comes from the French verb *parler*—to speak.—*Author.*

† When a king of England (for they are not an English race of kings) negatives an act passed by the Parliament, he does it in the Norman or French language, which was the language of the conquest, the literal translation of which is, *the king will advise himself of it.* It is the only instance of a king of England speaking French in Parliament ; and shews the **origin of the negative.**—*Author.*

the principles of the revolution, among those who then assumed the lead, and the country was grossly imposed upon. This accounts for some inconsistencies that are to be found in the present constitution, among which is the negativing power inconsistently copied from England. While the exercise of the power over the State remained dormant, it remained unnoticed ; but the instant it began to be active it began to alarm ; and the exercise of it against the rights of the People to settle their private pecuniary differences by the peaceable mode of arbitration, without the interference of lawyers, and the expence and tediousness of courts of law, has brought its existence to a crisis. Arbitration is of more importance to society than courts of law, and ought to have precedence of them in all cases of pecuniary concerns between individuals or parties of them. Who are better qualified than merchants to settle disputes between merchants, or who better than farmers to settle disputes between farmers ? And the same for every other description of men. What do lawyers or courts of law know of these matters ? They devote themselves to forms rather than to principles, and the merits of the case become obscure and lost in a labyrinth of verbal perplexities. We do not hear of lawyers going to law with each other, though they could do it cheaper than other people, which shews they have no opinion of it for themselves. The principle and rule of arbitration ought to be constitutionally established. The honest sense of a country collected in Convention will find out how to do this without the interference of lawyers, who may be hired to advocate any side of any cause ; for the case is, the practice of the bar is become a species of prostitution that ought to be controuled. It lives by encouraging the injustice it pretends to redress.

Courts in which law is practised are of two kinds. The one for criminal cases, the other for civil cases, or cases between individuals respecting property of any kind, or the value thereof. I know not what may be the numerical proportion of these two classes of cases to each other ; but that the civil cases are far more numerous than the criminal cases, I make no doubt of. Whether they be ten, twenty, thirty, or forty to one, or more, I leave to those who live in the State, or in the several counties thereof, to determine. But be the proportion what it may, the expence to the public of supporting a Judiciary for both will be, in some relative degree, according to the number of cases the one bears to the other ; yet it is only one of them that the public, as a public, have any concern with. The criminal cases, being breaches of the peace, are consequently under the cognizance of the government of the State, and the expence of supporting the courts thereof belong to the public, because the preservation of the peace is a public concern. But civil cases, that is, cases of private property between individuals, belong wholly to the individuals themselves ; and all that government has consistently to do in the matter, is to establish the process by which the parties concerned shall proceed and bring the matter to decision themselves, by referring it to impartial and judicious men of the neighbourhood, of their own choosing. This is by far the most convenient, as to time and place, and the cheapest method to them ; for it is bringing *justice home to their own doors*, without the chicanery of law and lawyers. Every case ought to be determined on its own merits, without the farce of what are called precedents, or reports of cases ; because, in the first place, it often happens that the decision upon the case brought as a precedent is bad, and ought to be shunned instead of imitated ; and, in the second place, because there are no two cases perfectly alike in all their circumstances, and therefore the one cannot become a rule of decision for the other. It is justice and good judgment that preside by right in a court of arbitration. It is forms, quoted precedents, and contrivances for delay and expence to the parties, that govern the proceedings of a court of law.

By establishing arbitrations in the room of courts of law for the adjustment of private cases, the public will be eased of a great part of the expence of the present judiciary establishment ; for certainly such a host of judges, associate judges, presidents of circuits, clerks, and criers of courts, as are at present supported at the public expence, will not then be necessary. There are, perhaps, more of them than there are criminals to try in the space of a year. Arbitration will lessen the sphere of patronage, and it is not improbable that this was one of the private reasons for negativing the arbitration act ; but public economy, and the convenience and ease of the individuals, ought to have outweighed all such considerations. The present administration of the United States has struck off a long list of useless officers, and economised the public expenditure, and it is better to make a precedent of this, than to imitate its forms and long periods of election, which require reform themselves. A great part of the people of Pennsylvania make a principle of not going to law, and others avoid it from prudential reasons ; yet all those people are taxed to support a Judiciary to which they never resort, which is as inconsistent and unjust as it is in England to make the Quakers pay tythes to support the Episcopal church. Arbitration will put an end to this imposition.

Another complaint against the Constitution of Pennsylvania, is the great quantity of patronage annexed to the office of Governor.

Patronage has a natural tendency to increase the public expence, by the temptation it leads to (unless in the hands of a wise man like Franklin) to multiply offices within the gift or appointment of that patronage. John Adams, in his administration, went upon the plan of increasing offices and officers. He expected by thus increasing his patronage, and making numerous appointments, that he should attach a numerous train of adherents to him who would support his measures and his future election. He copied this from the corrupt system of England ; and he closed his midnight labours by appointing sixteen new unnecessary judges, at an expence to the public of thirty-two thousand dollars annually. John counted only on one side of the case. He forgot that where there was *one* man to be benefited by an appointment, all the rest had to pay the cost of it ; and that by attaching *the one* to him by patronage, he ran the risk of losing *the many* by disgust. And such was the consequence ; and such will ever be the consequence in a free country, where men reason *for* themselves and *from* themselves, and not from the dictates of others.

The less quantity of patronage a man is *incumbered* with the safer he stands. He cannot please everybody by the use of it ; and he will have to refuse, and consequently to displease, a greater number than he can please. Mr. Jefferson gained more friends by dismissing a long train of officers, than John Adams did by appointing them. Like a wise man, Mr. Jefferson dismantled himself of patronage.

The Constitution of New-York, though like all the rest it has its defects, arising from want of experience in the representative system of government at the time it was formed, has provided much better, in this case, than the Constitution of Pennsylvania has done. The appointments in New-York are made by a *Council of Appointment*, composed of the Governor and a certain number of members of the Senate, taken from different parts of the State. By this means they have among them a personal knowledge of whomsoever they appoint. The Governor has one vote, but no negative. I do not hear complaints of the abuse of this kind of patronage.

The Constitution of Pennsylvania, instead of being an improvement in the representative system of government, is a departure from the principles of it. It is a copy in miniature of the government of England, established at the conquest of that country by William of Normandy. I have shewn this in part in the case of the king's negative, and I shall shew it more fully as I go on. This brings me to speak of the Senate.

The complaint respecting the Senate is the length of its duration, being four years. The sage Franklin has said, " Where annual election ends, tyranny begins ; " and no man was a better judge of human nature than Franklin, nor has any man in our time exceeded him in the principles of honour and honesty.

When a man ceases to be accountable to those who elected him, and with whose public affairs he is entrusted, he ceases to be their representative, and is put in a condition of being their despot. He becomes the representative of nobody but himself. *I am elected*, says he, *for four years ; you cannot turn me out, neither am I responsible to you in the meantime. All that you have to do with me is to pay me.*

The conduct of the Pennsylvania Senate in 1800, respecting the choice of electors for the Presidency of the United States, shews the impropriety and danger of such an establishment. The manner of choosing electors ought to be fixed in the Constitution, and not be left to the caprice of contention. It is a matter equally as important, and concerns the rights and interests of the people as much as the election of members for the State Legislature, and in some instances much more. By the conduct of the Senate at that time, the people were deprived of their right of suffrage, and the State lost its consequence in the Union. It had but one vote. The other fourteen were paired off by compromise,—seven and seven. If the people had chosen the electors, which they had a right to do, for the electors were to represent *them* and not to represent the Senate, the State would have had fifteen votes which would have counted.

The Senate is an imitation of what is called the House of Lords in England, and which Chesterfield, who was a member of it, and therefore knew it, calls "*the Hospital of Incurables.*" The Senate in Pennsylvania is not quite an hospital of incurables, but it took almost four years to bring it to a *state of convalescence.*

Before we imitate any thing, we ought to examine whether it be worth imitating, and had this been done by the Convention at that time, they would have seen that the model from which their mimic imitation was made, was no better than unprofitable and disgraceful lumber.

There was no such thing in England as what is called the House of Lords until the conquest of that country by the Normans, under William the Conqueror, and like the king's negative over the laws, it is a badge of disgrace upon the country ; for it is the effect and evidence of its having been reduced to unconditional submission.

William, having made the conquest, dispossessed the owners of their lands, and divided those lands among the chiefs of the plundering army he brought with him, and from hence arose what is called the *House of Lords*. Daniel de Foe, in his historical satire entitled "*The True-born Englishman,*" has very concisely given the origin and character of this House, as follows :

> The great invading Norman let them know
> What conquerors, in after times, might do ;
> To every musketeer he brought to town,
> He gave the lands that never were his own—
> He cantoned out the country to his men,
> And every soldier was a denizen ;
> No parliament his army could disband.
> He raised no money, for he paid in land ;
> The rascals, thus enriched, he called them *Lords,*
> To please their upstart pride with new made words,
> And Domesday Book his tyranny records ;
> Some show the sword, the bow, and some the spear,
> Which their great ancestor, forsooth, did wear ;
> But who the hero was, no man can tell,
> Whether a colonel or a-corporal ;
> The silent record blushes to reveal
> Their undescended dark original ;
> Great ancestors of yesterday they show,
> And Lords whose fathers were—*the Lord knows who !*

This is the disgraceful origin of what is called the House of Lords in England, and it still retains some tokens of the plundering baseness of its origin. The swindler Dundas was lately made a lord, and is now called *noble lord !* [1] Why do they not give him his proper title, and call him *noble swindler*, for he swindled by wholesale. But it is probable he will escape punishment ; for Blackstone, in his commentary on the laws, recites an Act of Parliament, passed in 1550, and not since repealed, that extends what is called the benefit of clergy,

---

[1] Lord Melville, impeached in 1805, but, as Paine predicted, acquitted by the Lords. It was to the same man that Paine addressed two public letters (vol iii., chaps. 5 and 10 of this edition).—*Editor.*

that is, exemption from punishment for all clerical offences, to all lords and peers of the realm who could not read, as well as those who could, and also for "the crimes of *house-breaking, highway-robbing, horse-stealing, and robbing of churches*." This is consistent with the original establishment of the House of Lords, for it was originally composed of robbers. This is aristocracy. This is one of the pillars of John Adams' "stupendous fabric of human invention." A privilege for house-breaking, highway-robbing, horse-stealing, and robbing of churches! John Adams knew but little of the origin and practice of the government of England. As to Constitution, it has none.

The Pennsylvania Convention of 1776 copied nothing from the English government. It formed a Constitution on the basis of honesty. The defect, as I have already said, of that constitution was the precipitancy to which the Legislatures might be subject in enacting laws. All the members of the Legislature established by that Constitution sat in one chamber, and debated in one body, and this subjected them to precipitancy. This precipitancy was provided against, but not effectually. The Constitution ordered that the laws, before being finally enacted, should be published for public consideration. But as no given time was fixed for that consideration, nor any means for collecting its effects, nor were there then any public newspapers in the State but what were printed in Philadelphia, the provision did not reach the intention of it, and thus a good and wise intention sank into mere form, which is generally the case when the means are not adequate to the end.

The ground work, however, of that Constitution was good, and deserves to be resorted to, Every thing that Franklin was concerned in producing merits attention. He was the wise and benevolent friend of man. Riches and honours made no alteration in his principles or his manners.

The Constitution of 1776 was conformable to the Declaration of Independence and the Declaration of Rights, which the present Constitution is not ; for it makes artificial distinctions among men in the right of suffrage, which the principles of equity know nothing of ; neither is it consistent with sound policy We every day see the rich becoming poor, and those who were poor before becoming rich. Riches, therefore, having no stability, cannot and ought not to be made a criterion of right. Man is man in every condition of life, and the varieties of fortune and misfortune are open to all.

Had the number of representatives in the Legislature established by that Constitution been increased, and instead of their sitting together in one chamber, and debating and voting all at one time, been divided by lot into two equal parts, and sat in separate chambers, the advantage would have been, that one half, by not being entangled in the first debate, nor having committed itself by voting, would be silently possessed of the arguments, for and against, of the former part, and be in a calm condition to review the whole. And instead of one Chamber, or one House, or by whatever name they may be called, negativing the vote of the other, which is now the case, and which admits of inconsistencies even to absurdities, to have added the votes of both chambers together, and the majority of the whole to be the final decision,—there would be reason in this, but there is none in the present mode. The instance that occurred in the Pennsylvania Senate, in the year 1800, on the bill for choosing electors, where a small majority in that house controuled and negatived a large majority in the other House, shews the absurdity of such a division of legislative power.

To know if any theory or position be true or rational, in practice, the method is, to carry it to its greatest extent ; if it be not true upon the whole, or be absurd, it is so in all its parts, however small. For instance, if one House consists of two hundred members and the other fifty, which is about the proportion they are in some of the States, and if a proposed law be carried on the affirmative in the larger House with only one dissenting voice, and be negatived in the smaller House by a majority of one, the event will be, that twenty-seven controul and govern two hundred and twenty-three, which is too absurd even for argument, and totally inconsistent with the principles of representative government, which know no difference in the value and importance of its members but what arises from their virtues and talents, and not at all from the name of the House or Chamber they sit in.

As the practice of a smaller number negativing a greater is not founded in reason, we must look for its origin in some other cause.

The Americans have copied it from England, and it was brought into England by the Norman Conqueror, and is derived from the ancient French practice of voting by ORDERS, of which they counted three ; *the Clergy*, (that is, Roman Catholic clergy,) the *Noblesse*, (those who had titles,) and the *Tiers État*, or third estate,* which included all who were not of the two former orders, and which in England are called the *Commons*, or *common people*, and the house in which they are represented is from thence called the *House of Commons*.

The case with the Conqueror was, in order to complete and secure the conquest he had made, and hold the country in subjection, he cantoned it out among the chiefs of his army, to whom he gave castles, and whom he dubbed with the title of *Lords*, as is before shewn. These being dependent on the Conqueror, and having a united interest with him, became the defenders of his measures, and the guardians of his assumed prerogative against the people ; and when the house called the *Commons House of Parliament* began by grants and charters from the Conqueror and his successors, these Lords, claiming to be a distinct ORDER from the Commons, though smaller in number, held a controuling or negativing vote over them, and from hence arose the irrational practice of a smaller number negativing a greater.

But what are these things to us, or why should we imitate them ? We have but one ORDER in America, and that of the highest degree, the ORDER OF SOVEREIGNTY, and of this ORDER every citizen is a member in his own personal right. Why then have we descended to the base imitation of inferior things ? By the event of the Revolution we were put in a condition of thinking originally. The history of past ages shews scarcely anything to us but instances of tyranny and antiquated absurdities. We have copied some of them, and experienced the folly of them.

Another subject of complaint in Pennsylvania is the Judiciary, and this appears to require a thorough reform. Arbitration will of itself reform a great part, but much will remain to require amendment. The courts of law still continue to go on, as to practice, in the same manner as when the State was a British colony. They have not yet arrived at the dignity of independence. They hobble along by the stilts and crutches of English and antiquated precedents. Their pleadings are made up of cases and reports from English law books ; many of which are tyrannical, and all of them now foreign to us. Our courts require to be domesticated, for as they are at present conducted, they are a dishonour to the national sovereignty. Every case in America ought to be determined on its own merits, according to American laws, and all reference to foreign adjudications prohibited. The introduction of them into American courts serves only to waste time, embarrass causes, and perplex juries. This reform alone will reduce cases to a narrow compass easily understood.

The terms used in courts of law, in sheriffs' sales, and on several other occasions, in writs, and other legal proceedings, require reform. Many of those terms are Latin, and others French. The Latin terms were brought into Britain by the Romans, who spoke Latin, and who continued in Britain between four and five hundred years, from the first invasion of it by Julius Cæsar, fifty-two years before the Christian era. The French terms were brought by the Normans when they conquered England in 1066, as I have before shewn, and whose language was French.

---

* The practice of voting by *orders* in France, whenever the States-General met, continued until the late Revolution. It was the present Abbé Sieyès who made the motion, in what was afterwards called the National Assembly, for abolishing the vote by *orders*, and established the rational practice of deciding by a majority of numbers.—*Author.*

These terms being still used in English law courts, show the origin of those courts, and are evidence of the country having been under foreign jurisdiction. But they serve to *mystify*, by not being generally understood, and therefore they serve the purpose of what is called law, whose business is to perplex ; and the courts in England put up with the disgrace of recording foreign jurisdiction and foreign conquest, for the sake of using terms which the clients and the public do not understand, and from thence to create the false belief that law is a learned science, and lawyers are learned men. The English pleaders, in order to keep up the farce of the profession, always compliment each other, though in contradiction, with the title of *my learned brother*. Two farmers or two merchants will settle cases by arbitration which lawyers cannot settle by law. Where then is the learning of the law, or what is it good for ?

It is here necessary to distinguish between *lawyer's law*, and *legislative law*. Legislative law is the law of the land, enacted by our own legislators, chosen by the people for that purpose. Lawyer's law is a mass of opinions and decisions, many of them contradictory to each other, which courts and lawyers have instituted themselves, and is chiefly made up of law-reports of cases taken from English law books. The case of every man ought to be tried by the laws of his own country, which he knows, and not by opinions and authorities from other countries, of which he may know nothing. A lawyer, in pleading, will talk several hours about law, but it is *lawyer's law*, and not *legislative law*, that he means.

The whole of the Judiciary needs reform. It is very loosely appointed in most of the States, and also in the general government. The case, I suppose, has been, that the judiciary department in a Constitution has been left to the lawyers, who might be in a Convention, to form, and they have taken care to leave it loose. To say, that a judge shall hold his office during *good behaviour*, is saying nothing ; for the term *good behaviour* has neither a legal nor a moral definition. In the common acceptation of the term, it refers rather to a style of manners than to principles, and may be applied to signify different and contradictory things. A child of good behaviour, a judge of good behaviour, a soldier of good behaviour in the field, and a dancing-master of good behaviour in his school, cannot be the same good behaviour. What then is the good behaviour of a judge ?

Many circumstances in the conduct and character of a man may render him unfit to hold the office of a judge, yet not amount to cause of impeachment, which always supposes the commission of some known crime. Judges ought to be held to their duty by continual responsibility, instead of which the constitution releases them from all responsibility, except by impeachment, from which, by the loose, undefined establishment of the judiciary, there is always a hole to creep out. In annual elections for legislators, every legislator is responsible every year, and no good reason can be given why those entrusted with the execution of the laws should not be as responsible, at stated periods, as those entrusted with the power of enacting them.

Releasing the judges from responsibility, is in imitation of an act of the English Parliament, for rendering the judges so far independent of what is called the Crown, as not to be removable by it. The case is, that judges in England are appointed by the Crown, and are paid out of the king's civil list, as being his representatives when sitting in court ; and in all prosecutions for treason and criminal offences, the king is the prosecutor. It was therefore reasonable that the judge, before whom a man was to be tried, should not be dependent, for the tenure of his office, on the will of the prosecutor. But this is no reason that in a government founded on the representative system a judge should not be responsible, and also removable by some constitutional mode, without the tedious and expensive formality of impeachment. We remove or turn out presidents, governors, senators, and representatives, without this formality. Why then are judges, who are generally lawyers, privileged with duration ? It is, I suppose, because lawyers have had the formation of the judiciary part of the Constitution.

The term, " contempt of court," which has caused some agitation in Pennsylvania, is also copied from England ; and in that country it means *contempt of the king's authority or prerogative in court*, because the judges appear there as his representatives, and are styled in their commissions, when they open a court, "His Majesty the King's Justices."

This now undefined thing, called *contempt of court*, is derived from the Norman conquest of England, as is shown by the French words used in England, with which proclamation for silence, "on pain of imprisonment," begins, "Oyez, Oyez, Oyez." * This shows it to be of Norman origin. It is, however, a species of despotism ; for contempt of court is now any thing a court imperiously pleases to call so, and then it inflicts punishment as by prerogative without trial, as in Passmore's case, which has a good deal agitated the public mind. This practice requires to be constitutionally regulated, but not by lawyers.

Much yet remains to be done in the improvement of Constitutions. The Pennsylvania Convention, when it meets, will be possessed of advantages which those that preceded it were not. The ensuing Convention will have two Constitutions before them ; that of 1776, and that of 1790, each of which continued about fourteen years. I know no material objection against the Constitution of 1776, except that in practice it might be subject to precipitancy ; but this can be easily and effectually remedied, as the annexed essay, respecting "Constitutions, Governments, and Charters," will show. But there have been many and great objections and complaints against the present Constitution and the practice upon it, arising from the improper and unequal distribution it makes of power.

The circumstance that occurred in the Pennsylvania Senate in the year 1800, on the bill passed by the House of Representatives for choosing electors, justifies Franklin's opinion, which he gave by request of the Convention of 1776, of which he was president, respecting the propriety or impropriety of two houses negativing each other. "It appears to me," said he, "like putting one horse before a cart and the other behind it, and whipping them both. If the horses are of equal strength, the wheels of the cart, like the wheels of government, will stand still ; and if the horses are strong enough, the cart will be torn to pieces." It was only the moderation and good sense of the country, which did not engage in the dispute raised by the Senate, that prevented Pennsylvania from being torn to pieces by commotion.

Inequality of rights has been the cause of all the disturbances, insurrections, and civil wars, that ever happened in any country, in any age of mankind. It was the cause of the American revolution, when the English Parliament sat itself up *to bind America in all cases whatsoever*, and to reduce her to unconditional submission. It was the cause of the French revolution ; and also of the civil wars in England, in the time of Charles and Cromwell, when the House of Commons voted the House of Lords useless.

The fundamental principle in representative government is, that *the majority governs ;* and as it will be always happening that a man may be in the minority on one question, and in the majority on another, he obeys by the same principle that he rules. But when there are two houses of unequal numbers, and the smaller number negativing the greater, it is the minority that governs, which is contrary to the principle. This was the case in Pennsylvania in 1800.

America has the high honour and happiness of being the first nation that gave to the world the example of forming written Constitutions by Conventions elected expressly for the purpose, and of improving them by the same procedure, as time and experience shall shew necessary. Government in other nations, vainly calling themselves civilized, has been established by bloodshed. Not a drop of blood has been shed in the United States in consequence of establishing Constitutions and governments by her own peaceful system. The silent vote, or the simple *yea* or *nay*, is more powerful than the bayonet, and decides the strength of numbers without a blow.

* Hear ye, hear ye, hear ye.—*Author.*

I have now, citizens of Pennsylvania, presented you, in good will, with a collection of thoughts and historical references, condensed into a small compass, that they may circulate the more conveniently.   They are applicable to the subject before you, that of calling a Convention, in the progress and completion of which I wish you success and happiness, and the honour of shewing a profitable example to the States around you, and to the world.

Yours, in friendship,

THOMAS PAINE.

NEW ROCHELLE, NEW-YORK,
August, 1805.

APPENDIX H.

CONSTITUTIONS, GOVERNMENTS, AND CHARTERS.

THE people of Pennsylvania are, at this time, earnestly occupied on the subject of calling a Convention to revise their State Constitution, and there can be but little doubt that a revision is necessary. It is a Constitution, they say, for the emolument of lawyers.

It has happened that the Constitutions of all the States were formed before any experience had been had on the representative system of government ; and it would be a miracle in human affairs that mere theory without experience should start into perfection at once. The Constitution of New-York was formed so early as the year 1777. The subject that occupied and engrossed the mind of the public at that time was the revolutionary war, and the establishment of Independence, and in order to give effect to the Declaration of Independence by Congress it was necessary that the States severally should make a practical beginning by establishing State Constitutions, and trust to time and experience for improvement. The general defect in all the Constitutions is that they are modelled too much after the system, if it can be called a system, of the English government, which in practice is the most corrupt system in existence, for it is corruption systematized.

An idea also generally prevailed at that time of keeping what were called the Legislative, the Executive, and the Judicial powers distinct and separated from each other. But this idea, whether correct or not, is always contradicted in practice ; for where the consent of a Governor, or Executive, is required to an Act before it can become a law, or where he can by his negative prevent an act of the legislature becoming a law, he is effectually a part of the Legislature, and possesses full one half of the powers of a whole Legislature.

In this state, (New-York,) this power is vested in a select body of men, composed of the Executive, by which is to be understood the Governor, the Chancellor, and the Judges, and called the Council of Revision. This is certainly better than vesting that power in an individual, if it is necessary to invest it any where ; but is a direct contradiction to the maxim set up, that those powers ought to be kept separate ; for here the Executive and the Judiciary are united into one power, acting legislatively.

When we see maxims that fail in practice, we ought to go to the root, and see if the maxim be true. Now it does not signify how many nominal divisions, and sub-divisions, and classifications we make, for the fact is, *there are but two powers in any government, the power of willing or enacting the laws, and the power of executing them ;* for what is called the *Judiciary* is a branch of Executive power ; it executes the laws ; and what is called the *Executive* is a superintending power to see that the laws are executed.[1]

Errors in theory are, sooner or later, accompanied with errors in practice ; and this leads me to another part of the subject, that of considering a Constitution and a Government relatively to each other.

A Constitution is the act of the people in their orginal character of sovereignty. A Government is a creature of the Constitution ; it is produced and

[1] *Cf.* vol. ii., pp. 238–239.—*Editor.*

brought into existence by it. A Constitution defines and limits the powers of the Government it creates. It therefore follows, as a natural and also a logical result, that the governmental exercise of any power not authorized by the Constitution is an assumed power, and therefore illegal.

There is no article in the Constitution of this State, nor of any of the States, that invests the Government in whole or in part with the power of granting charters or monopolies of any kind ; the spirit of the times was then against all such speculation ; and therefore the assuming to grant them is unconstitutional, and when obtained by bribery and corruption is criminal. It is also contrary to the intention and principle of annual elections. Legislatures are elected annually, not only for the purpose of giving the people, in their elective character, the opportunity of showing their approbation of those who have acted right, by re-electing them, and rejecting those who have acted wrong ; but also for the purpose of correcting the wrong (where any wrong has been done) of a former Legislature. But the very intention, essence, and principle of annual election would be destroyed, if any one Legislature, during the year of its authority, had the power to place any of its acts beyond the reach of succeeding Legislatures ; yet this is always attempted to be done in those acts of a Legislature called charters. Of what use is it to dismiss Legislators for having done wrong, if the wrong is to continue on the authority of those who did it? Thus much for things that are wrong. I now come to speak of things that are right, and may be necessary.

Experience shows that matters will occasionally arise, especially in a new country, that will require the exercise of a power differently constituted to that of ordinary legislation ; and therefore there ought to be in a Constitution an article, defining how that power shall be constituted and exercised. Perhaps the simplest method, that which I am going to mention, is the best ; because it is still keeping strictly within the limits of annual elections, makes no new appointments necessary, and creates no additional expense. For example,

That all matters of a different quality to matters of ordinary legislation, such, for instance, as sales or grants of public lands, acts of incorporation, public contracts with individuals or companies beyond a certain amount, shall be proposed in one legislature, and published in the form of a bill. with the yeas and nays, after the second reading, and in that state shall lie over to be taken up by the succeeding Legislature ; that is. there shall always be, on all such matters, one annual election take place between the time of bringing in the bill and the time of enacting it into a permanent law.[1]

It is the rapidity with which a self-interested speculation, or a fraud on the public property, can be carried through within the short space of one session, and before the people can be apprised of it, that renders it necessary that a precaution of this kind, unless a better can be devised, should be made an article of the Constitution. Had such an article been originally in the Constitution, the bribery and corruption employed to seduce and manage the members of the late Legislature, in the affair of the Merchants' Bank, could not have taken place. It would not have been worth while to bribe men to do what they had not the power of doing. That Legislature could only have proposed, but not have enacted the law ; and the election then ensuing would, by discarding the proposers, have negatived the proposal without any further trouble.

This method has the appearance of doubling the value and importance of annual elections. It is only by means of elections, that the mind of the public can be collected to a point on any important subject ; and as it is always the interest of a much greater number of people in a country, to have a thing right than to have it wrong, the public sentiment is always worth attending to. It may sometimes err, but never intentionally, and never long. The experiment of the Merchants' Bank shows it is possible to bribe a small body of men, but it is always *impossible* to bribe a whole nation ; and therefore in all legislative matters that by requiring permanency differ from acts of ordinary legislation,

---

[1] *Cf.* the distinction drawn between *acts* and laws, vol. ii., p. 142.—*Editor.*

which are alterable or repealable at all times, it is safest that they pass through two legislatures, and a general election intervene between. The elections will always bring up the mind of the country on any important proposed bill; and thus the whole state will be its own *Council of Revision.* It has already passed its *veto* on the Merchants' Bank bill, notwithstanding the *minor* Council of Revision approved it.

COMMON SENSE.

NEW ROCHELLE, June 21, 1805.

APPENDIX I.

THE CAUSE OF THE YELLOW FEVER,

AND THE MEANS OF PREVENTING IT IN PLACES NOT YET INFECTED WITH IT.

Addressed to the Board of Health in America.[1]

A GREAT deal has been written respecting the Yellow Fever. First, with respect to its causes, whether domestic or imported. Secondly, on the mode of treating it.

What I am going to suggest in this essay is, to ascertain some point to begin at, in order to arrive at the cause, and for this purpose some preliminary observations are necessary.

The Yellow Fever always begins in the lowest part of a populous mercantile town near the water, and continues there, without affecting the higher parts. The sphere or circuit it acts in is small, and it rages most where large quantities of new ground have been made by banking out the river, for the purpose of making wharfs. The appearance and prevalence of the Yellow Fever in these places, being those where vessels arrive from the West Indies, has caused the belief that the Yellow Fever was imported from thence: but here are two cases acting in the same place : the one, the condition of the ground at the wharves, which being new made on the muddy and filthy bottom of the river, is different from the natural condition of the ground in the higher parts of the city, and consequently subject to produce a different kind of effluvia or vapour ; the other case is the arrival of vessels from the West Indies.

In the State of Jersey neither of these cases has taken place ; no shipping arrive there, and consequently there have been no embankments for the purpose

---

[1] The distinguished physician, Dr. Francis, in his recollections of " Old New York," makes honorable mention of this " timely " essay, to which indeed Paine had given a good deal of time and study. In a letter to Jefferson, September 23, 1803, he says : " We are still afflicted with the Yellow Fever, and the Doctors are disputing whether it is an imported or domestic disease. Would it not be a good measure to prohibit the arrival of all vessels from the West Indies from the last of June to the middle of October ? If this was done this session of Congress, and we escaped the fever next summer, we should always know how to escape it. I question if performing quarantine is sufficient guard. The disease may be in the cargo, especially that part which is barrelled up, and not in the persons on board, and when that cargo is opened on our wharfs, the hot steaming air in contact with the ground imbibes the infection. I can conceive that infected air can be barrelled up, not in a hogshead of rum, nor perhaps sucre, but in a barrel of coffee." Paine's pamphlet was printed in London, in 1807, by Clio Rickman, with the following lines (his own) on the title-page :

> " Friend, to whate'er is good, and great, and free,
> All comes appropriate and clear from THEE ;
> And did Diogenes, in this our day,
> Seeking an Honest Man, pursue his way,
> Light but on THEE, no farther would he pry,
> But smile with joy—and throw his Lanthorn by ! "

Rickman says in his note " To the Reader " :—" I know it will gratify many to have anything from his pen ; and to hear that the Author, though above seventy, possesses health, fortune, and happiness ; and that he is held in the highest estimation amongst the most exalted and best characters in America—that America which is indebted for almost every blessing she knows to HIS labours and exertions."—*Editor*.

of wharfs ; and the Yellow Fever has never broke out in Jersey. This, however, does not decide the point, as to the immediate cause of the fever, but it shows that this species of fever is not common to the country in its natural state ; and, I believe the same was the case in the West Indies before embankments began for the purpose of making wharfs, which always alter the natural condition of the ground. No old history, that I know of, mentions such a disorder as the Yellow Fever.

A person seized with the Yellow Fever in an affected part of the town, and brought into the healthy part, or into the country, and among healthy persons, does not communicate it to the neighbourhood, or to those immediately around him ; why then are we to suppose it can be brought from the West Indies, a distance of more than a thousand miles, since we see it cannot be carried from one town to another, nor from one part of a town to another, at home ? Is it in the air ? This question on the case requires a minute examination. In the first place, the difference between air and wind is the same as between a stream of water and a standing water. A stream of water is water in motion, and wind is air in motion. In a gentle breeze the whole body of air, as far as the breeze extends, moves at the rate of seven or eight miles an hour ; in a high wind, at the rate of seventy, eighty, or an hundred miles an hour : when we see the shadow of a cloud gliding on the surface of the ground, we see the rate at which the air moves, and it must be a good trotting horse that can keep pace with the shadow, even in a gentle breeze ; consequently, a body of air that is in and over any place of the same extent as the affected part of a city may be, will, in the space of an hour, even at the moderate rate I speak of, be moved seven or eight miles to leeward ; and its place, in and over the city, will be supplied by a new body of air coming from a healthy part, seven or eight miles distant the contrary way ; and then on in continual succession. The disorder, therefore, is not in the air, considered in its natural state, and never stationary. This leads to another consideration of the case.

An impure effluvia, arising from some cause in the ground, in the manner that fermenting liquors produce near their surface an effluvia that is fatal to life, will become mixed with the air contiguous to it, and as fast as that body of air moves off it will impregnate every succeeding body of air, however pure it may be when it arrives at the place.

The result from this state of the case is, that the impure air, or vapour, that generates the Yellow Fever, issues from the earth, that is, from the new made earth, or ground raised on the muddy and filthy bottom of the river ; and which impregnates every fresh body of air that comes over the place, in like manner as air becomes heated when it approaches or passes over fire, or becomes offensive in smell when it approaches or passes over a body of corrupt vegetable or animal matter in a state of putrefaction.

The muddy bottom of rivers contains great quantities of impure and often inflammable air, (carburetted hydrogen gas,) injurious to life ; and which remains entangled in the mud till let loose from thence by some accident. This air is produced by the dissolution and decomposition of any combustible matter falling into the water and sinking into the mud, of which the following circumstance will serve to give some explanation.

In the fall of the year that New York was evacuated (1783,) General Washington had his headquarters at Mrs. Berrian's, at Rocky Hill, in Jersey, and I was there : the Congress then sat at Prince Town.[1] We had several times been told that the river or creek, that runs near the bottom of Rocky Hill, and over which there is a mill, might be set on fire, for that was the term the country people used ; and as General Washington had a mind to try the experiment, General Lincoln, who was also there, undertook to make preparation for it against the next evening, November 5th. This was to be done, as we were told, by disturbing the mud at the bottom of the river, and holding something in a blaze, as paper or straw, a little above the surface of the water.

[1] See vol. ii., p. 464, also my " Life of Paine," vol. i., p. 199.—*Editor.*

Colonels Humphreys and Cobb were at that time Aids-de-Camp of General Washington, and those two gentlemen and myself got into an argument respecting the cause. Their opinion was that, on disturbing the bottom of the river, some bituminous matter arose to the surface, which took fire when the light was put to it ; I, on the contrary, supposed that a quantity of inflammable air was let loose, which ascended through the water, and took fire above the surface. Each party held to his opinion, and the next evening the experiment was to be made.

A scow had been stationed in the mill dam, and General Washington, General Lincoln, and myself, and I believe Colonel Cobb, (for Humphreys was sick,) and three or four soldiers with poles, were put on board the scow. General Washington placed himself at one end of the scow, and I at the other ; each of us had a roll of cartridge paper, which we lighted and held over the water, about two or three inches from the surface, when the soldiers began disturbing the bottom of the river with the poles.

As General Washington sat at one end of the scow, and I at the other, I could see better any thing that might happen from his light, than I could from my own, over which I was nearly perpendicular. When the mud at the bottom was disturbed by the poles, the air bubbles rose fast, and I saw the fire take from General Washington's light and descend from thence to the surface of the water, in a similar manner as when a lighted candle is held so as to touch the smoke of a candle just blown out, the smoke will take fire, and the fire will descend and light up the candle. This was demonstrative evidence that what was called setting the river on fire was setting on fire the inflammable air that arose out of the mud.

I mentioned this experiment to Mr. Rittenhouse of Philadelphia [1] the next time I went to that city, and our opinion on the case was, that the air or vapour that issued from any combustible matter, (vegetable or otherwise,) that underwent a dissolution and decomposition of its parts, either by fire or water in a confined place, so as not to blaze, would be inflammable, and would become flame whenever it came in contact with flame.

In order to determine if this was the case, we filled up the breech of a gun barrel about five or six inches with saw dust, and the upper part with dry sand to the top, and after spiking up the touch hole, put the breech into a smith's furnace, and kept it red hot, so as to consume the saw dust ; the sand of consequence would prevent any blaze. We applied a lighted candle to the mouth of the barrel ; as the first vapour that flew off would be humid, it extinguished the candle ; but after applying the candle three or four times, the vapour that issued out began to flash ; we then tied a bladder over the mouth of the barrel, which the vapour soon filled, and then tying a string round the neck of the bladder, above the muzzle, took the bladder off.

As we could not conveniently make experiments upon the vapour while it was in the bladder, the next operation was to get it into a phial. For this purpose, we took a phial of about three or four ounces, filled it with water, put a cork slightly into it, and introducing it into the neck of the bladder, worked the cork out, by getting hold of it through the bladder, into which the water then emptied itself, and the air in the bladder ascended into the phial ; we then put the cork into the phial, and took it from the bladder. It was now in a convenient condition for experiment.

We put a lighted match into the phial, and the air or vapour in it blazed up in the manner of a chimney on fire ; we extinguished it two or three times, by stopping the mouth of the phial ; and putting the lighted match to it again it repeatedly took fire, till the vapour was spent, and the phial became filled with atmospheric air.

These two experiments, that in which some combustible substance (branches and leaves of trees) had been decomposed by water, in the mud ; and this, where the decomposition had been produced by fire, without blazing, shews

[1] David Rittenhouse (1732–1796) who succeeded Franklin as President of the Philosophical Society.—*Editor.*

that a species of air injurious to life, when taken into the lungs, may be generated from substances which, in themselves, are harmless.

It is by means similar to these that charcoal, which is made by fire without blazing, emits a vapour destructive to life. I now come to apply these cases, and the reasoning deduced therefrom, to account for the cause of the Yellow Fever.*

First :—The Yellow Fever is not a disorder produced by the climate naturally, or it would always have been here in the hot months. The climate is the same now as it was fifty or a hundred years ago ; there was no Yellow Fever then, and it is only within the last twelve years, that such a disorder has been known in America.

Secondly :—The low grounds on the shores of the rivers, at the cities, where the Yellow Fever is annually generated, and continues about three months without spreading, were not subject to that disorder in their natural state, or the Indians would have forsaken them ; whereas, they were the parts most frequented by the Indians in all seasons of the year, on account of fishing. The result from these cases is, that the Yellow Fever is produced by some new circumstance not common to the country in its natural state, and the question is, what is that new circumstance ?

It may be said, that everything done by the white people, since their settlement in the country, such as building towns, clearing lands, levelling hills, and filling vallies, is a new circumstance ; but the Yellow Fever does not accompany any of these new circumstances. No alteration made on the dry land produces the Yellow Fever ; we must therefore look to some other new circumstances, and we now come to those that have taken place between wet and dry, between land and water.

The shores of the rivers at New York, and also at Philadelphia, have on account of the vast increase of commerce, and for the sake of making wharfs, undergone great and rapid alterations from their natural state within a few years ; and it is only in such parts of the shores where those alterations have taken place that the Yellow Fever has been produced. The parts where little or no alteration has been made, either on the East or North River, and which continue in their natural state, or nearly so, do not produce the Yellow Fever. The fact therefore points to the cause.

Besides several new streets gained from the river by embankment, there are upwards of eighty new wharfs made since the war, and the much greater part within the last ten or twelve years ; the consequence of which has been that great quantities of filth or combustible matter deposited in the muddy bottom of the river contiguous to the shore, and which produced no ill effect while exposed to the air, and washed twice every twenty-four hours by the tide water, have been covered over several feet deep with new earth, and pent up, and the tide excluded. It is in these places, and in these only, that the Yellow Fever is produced.

Having thus shewn, from the circumstances of the case, that the cause of the Yellow Fever is in the place where it makes its appearance, or rather, in the pernicious vapour issuing therefrom, I go to shew a method of constructing wharfs, where wharfs are yet to be constructed (as on the shore on the East River at Corlder's Hook, and also on the North River) that will not occasion the Yellow Fever, and which may also point out a method of removing it from places already infected with it. Instead, then, of embanking out the river and raising solid wharves of earth on the mud bottom of the shore, the better method would be to construct wharfs on arches, built of stone ; the tide will then flow in under the arch, by which means the shore, and the muddy bottom, will be washed and kept clean, as if they were in their natural state, without wharves.

When wharfs are constructed on the shore lengthways, that is without cut-

* The author does not mean to infer that the inflammable air or carburetted hydrogen gas, is the cause of the Yellow Fever ; but that perhaps it enters into some combination with miasm generated in low grounds, which produces the disease.—*Author.*

ting the shore up into slips, arches can easily be turned, because arches joining each other lengthways serve as buttments to each other ; but when the shore is cut up into slips there can be no buttments ; in this case wharfs can be formed on stone pillars, or wooden piles planked over on the top.   In either of these cases, the space underneath will be commodious shelter or harbour for small boats, which can come in and go out always, except at low water, and be secure from storms and injuries.   This method besides preventing the cause of the Yellow Fever, which I think it will, will render the wharfs more productive than the present method, because of the space preserved within the wharf.

I offer no calculation of the expence of constructing wharfs on arches or piles ; but on a general view, I believe they will not be so expensive as the present method.   A very great part of the expence of making solid wharfs of earth is occasioned by the carriage of materials, which will be greatly reduced by the methods here proposed, and still more so were the arches to be constructed of cast iron blocks.   I suppose that one ton of cast iron blocks would go as far in the construction of an arch as twenty tons of stone.

If, by constructing wharfs in such a manner that the tide water can wash the shore and bottom of the river contiguous to the shore, as they are washed in their natural condition, the Yellow Fever can be prevented from generating in places where wharfs are yet to be constructed, it may point out a method of removing it, at least by degrees, from places already infected with it ; which will be by opening the wharfs in two or three places in each, and letting the tide water pass through ; the parts opened can be planked over, so as not to prevent the use of the wharf.

In taking up and treating this subject, I have considered it as belonging to natural philosophy, rather than medicinal art ; and therefore I say nothing about the treatment of the disease, after it takes place ; I leave that part to those whose profession it is to study it.

THOMAS PAINE.

NEW YORK, June 27, 1806.

APPENDIX J.

LIBERTY OF THE PRESS.[1]

THE writer of this remembers a remark made to him by Mr. Jefferson concerning the English newspapers, which at that time, 1787, while Mr. Jefferson was Minister at Paris, were most vulgarly abusive. The remark applies with equal force to the Federal papers of America. The remark was, that " the licentiousness of the press produces the same effect as the restraint of the press was intended to do. if the restraint was to prevent things being told, and the licentiousness of the press prevents things being believed when they are told." We have in this state an evidence of the truth of this remark. The number of Federal papers in the city and state of New-York are more than five to one to the number of Republican papers, yet the majority of the elections go always against the Federal papers ; which is demonstrative evidence that the licentiousness of those papers is destitute of credit.

Whoever has made observation on the characters of nations will find it generally true that the manners of a nation, or of a party, can be better ascertained from the character of its press than from any other public circumstance. If its press is licentious, its manners are not good. Nobody believes a common liar, or a common defamer.

Nothing is more common with printers, especially of newspapers, than the continual cry of the *Liberty of the Press*. as if because they are printers they are to have more privileges than other people. As the term *Liberty of the Press* is adopted in this country without being understood, I will state the origin of it, and show what it means. The term comes from England, and the case was as follows :

Prior to what is in England called *the Revolution*, which was in 1688, no work could be published in that country without first obtaining the permission of an officer appointed by the government for inspecting works intended for publication. The same was the case in France, except that in France there were forty who were called *Censors*, and in England there was but one, called Imprimateur.

At the Revolution, the office of Imprimateur was abolished, and as works could then be published without first obtaining the permission of the government officer, the press was, in consequence of that abolition, said to be free, and it was from this circumstance that the term *Liberty of the Press* arose. The press, which is a tongue to the eye, was then put exactly in the case of the human tongue. A man does not ask liberty before hand to say something he has a mind to say, but he becomes answerable afterwards for the atrocities he may utter. In like manner, if a man makes the press utter atrocious things, he becomes as answerable for them as if he had uttered them by word of mouth. Mr. Jefferson has said in his inaugural speech, that " *error of opinion might be tolerated, when reason was left free to combat it.*" This is sound philosophy in cases of error. But there is a difference between error and licentiousness.

Some lawyers in defending their clients, (for the generality of lawyers, like

[1] From the *American Citizen*, October 20, 1806. Paine had witnessed in France (see vol. iii. p. 138) the terrible effects of personal libels shielded under the liberty of press.—*Editor.*

Swiss soldiers, will fight on either side,) have often given their opinion of what they defined the liberty of the press to be. One said it was this, another said it was that, and so on, according to the case they were pleading. Now these men ought to have known that the term *liberty of the press* arose from a FACT, the abolition of the office of Imprimateur, and that opinion has nothing to do in the case. The term refers to the fact of printing *free from prior restraint*, and not at all to the matter printed, whether good or bad. The public at large,— or in case of prosecution, a jury of the country—will be judges of the matter.

THOMAS PAINE.

October 19, 1806.

APPENDIX K.

SONGS AND RHYMES.

THE DEATH OF GENERAL WOLFE.[1]

In a mouldering cave where the wretched retreat,
　　Britannia sat wasted with care ;
She mourned for her Wolfe, and exclaim'd against fate
　　And gave herself up to despair.
The walls of her cell she had sculptured around
　　With the feats of her favourite son ;
And even the dust, as it lay on the ground,
　　Was engraved with the deeds he had done.

The sire of the Gods, from his crystalline throne,
　　Beheld the disconsolate dame,
And moved with her tears, he sent Mercury down,
　　And these were the tidings that came :
' Britannia forbear, not a sigh nor a tear
　　For thy Wolfe so deservedly loved,
Your tears shall be changed into triumphs of joy,
　　For thy Wolfe is not dead but removed.

' The sons of the East, the proud giants of old,
　　Have crept from their darksome abodes,
And this is the news as in Heaven it was told,
　　They were marching to war with the Gods ;
A Council was held in the chambers of Jove,
　　And this was their final decree,
That Wolfe should be called to the armies above,
　　And the charge was entrusted to me.

' To the plains of Quebec with the orders I flew,
　　He begg'd for a moment's delay ;
He cry'd, ' Oh ! forbear, let me victory hear,
　　And then thy command I 'll obey.'
With a darksome thick film I encompass'd his eyes,
　　And bore him away in an urn,
Lest the fondness he bore to his own native shore,
　　Should induce him again to return.'

---

[1] This song was written at the time of Wolfe's death, and is said to have been sung at the Headstrong Club, in Lewes, England. In several editions it is said to have been printed in *The Gentleman's Magazine*. Such is not the fact. It first appeared in Paine's *Pennsylvania Magazine*, March, 1775, with the music. It is the earliest composition of Paine which has been preserved. Paine never collected any of his poems.—*Editor.*

FARMER SHORT'S DOG PORTER: A TALE.[1]

The following story, ridiculous as it is, is a fact. A farmer at New Shoreham, near Bright-helmstone, in England, having voted at an election for a member of Parliament, contrary to the pleasure of three neighboring justices, they took revenge upon his dog, which they caused to be hung, for starting a hare upon the road. The piece has been very little seen, never published, nor any copies taken.

THREE Justices (so says my tale)
Once met upon the public weal.
For learning, law, and parts profound,
Their fame was spread the county round;
Each by his wondrous art could tell
Of things as strange as Sydrophel;
Or by the help of sturdy ale,
So cleverly could tell a tale,
That half the gaping standers by
Would laugh aloud. The rest would cry.
Or by the help of nobler wine,
Would knotty points so nice define,
That in an instant right was wrong,
Yet did not hold that station long,
For while they talk'd of wrong and right,
The question vanish'd out of sight.
Each knew by practice where to turn
To every powerful page in Burn,
And could by help of note and book
Talk law like Littleton and Coke.
Each knew by instinct when and where
A farmer caught or kill'd a hare;
Could tell if any man had got
One hundred pounds per ann. or not;
Or what was greater, could divine
If it was only ninety-nine.
For when the hundred wanted one,
They took away the owner's gun.
Knew by the leering of an eye
If girls had lost their chastity,
And if they had not—would divine
Some way to make their virtue shine.

---

[1] This incident was made the subject of a prose drama, by Mr. Justice Edward Long: " The Trial of Farmer Carter's Dog Porter, for Murder. Taken down verbatim et literatim in Short-hand (*sic*), and now published by Authority, from the corrected Manuscript of Counsellor Clear-point, Barrister at Law. N. B. This is the only true and authentic copy; and all others are spurious.

'——— Manet altâ mente repostum
Judicium."

VIRGIL.

" LONDON : Printed for T. LOWNDES, in Fleet-Street. MDCCLXXI. Price One Shilling."

Nichols (" Literary Anecdotes," viii., p. 435) says that Long's pamphlet " has been attributed to Tom Paine, some of whose admirers assert that he did write a pamphlet on that subject, founded on a real event which actually took place, 1771, in the neighbourhood of Chichester, where the actors in the tragedy were well known by their nicknames given in Mr. Long's pamphlet."

Regarding the genuineness of the incident, it seems to be sufficiently attested by the fact of its having engaged the attention of two different writers, Justice Long and Paine, neither of whom seems (for I have carefully compared the two) to have seen the composition of the other; nor need it be wondered at by those who recall that, so recently as 1888, a Welsh jury ordered the destruction of a gun which had killed a man. (*Folklore*, March, 1895, p. 70.) There is little doubt that this piece, like the Song on Wolfe, was written by Paine to amuse his fellows of the Headstrong Club, at Lewes, where he resided until the autumn of 1774. It was first printed in the *Pennsylvania Magazine* (edited by Paine), July, 1775.—*Editor.*

These learned brothers being assembled,
(At which the county feared and trembled,)
A warrant sent to bring before 'em,
One Farmer Short, who dwelt at Shoreham,
Upon a great and heavy charge,
Which we shall here relate at large,
That those who were not there may read,
In after days, the mighty deed :

Viz.

" That he, the 'foresaid Farmer Short,
Being by the devil moved, had not
One hundred pounds per annum got ;
That having not (in form likewise)
The fear of God before his eyes,
By force and arms did keep and cherish,
Within the aforesaid town and parish,
Against the statute so provided,
A dog.   And there the dog abided.
That he, this dog, did then and there
Pursue, and take, and kill a hare ;
Which treason was, or some such thing,
Against our SOVEREIGN LORD THE KING."

The constable was bid to jog,
And bring the farmer—not the dog.

But fortune, whose perpetual wheel
Grinds disappointment sharp as steel,
On purpose to attack the pride
Of those who over others ride,
So nicely brought the matter round,
That Farmer Short could not be found,
Which plunged the bench in so much doubt
They knew not what to go about.
But after pondering pro and con,
And mighty reasonings thereupon,
They found, on opening of the laws,
That he, the dog aforesaid, was
By being privy to the fact,
Within the meaning of the act,
And since the master had withdrawn,
And was the Lord knows whither gone,
They judged it right, and good in law,
That he, the dog, should answer for
Such crimes as they by proof could show,
Were acted by himself and Co.
The constable again was sent,
To bring the dog ; or dread the event.

POOR PORTER, right before the door,
Was guarding of his master's store ;
And as the constable approach'd him,
He caught him by the leg and broach'd him ;
Poor Porter thought (if dogs can think)
He came to steal his master's chink.

The man, by virtue of his staff,
Bid people help ; not stand and laugh ;
On which a mighty rout began ;
Some blamed the dog, and some the man.
Some said he had no business there,
Some said he had business every where.
At length the constable prevail'd,
And those who would not help were jail'd ;
And taking Porter by the collar,
Commanded all the guards to follow.

The justices received the felon,
With greater form than I can tell on,
And quitting now their wine and punch,
Began upon him all at once.

At length a curious quibble rose,
How far the law could interpose,
For it was proved, and rightly too,
That he, the dog, did not pursue
The hare with any ill intent,
But only followed by the scent ;
And she, the hare, by running hard,
Thro' hedge and ditch, without regard,
Plunged in a pond, and there was drown'd,
And by a neighboring justice found ;
Wherefore, though he the hare annoy'd,
It can't be said that he destroy'd ;
It even can't be proved he beat her,
And " to destroy " must mean " to eat her."
Did you e'er see a gamester struck,
With all the symptoms of ill luck ?
Or mark the visage which appears,
When even Hope herself despairs ?
So look'd the bench, and every brother
Sad pictures drew of one another ;
Till one more learned than the rest
Rose up, and thus the court address'd :

" Why, gentlemen, I 'll tell ye how,
Ye may clear up this matter now,
For I am of opinion strong
The dog deserves, and should be hung.
I 'll prove it by as plain a case,
As is the nose upon your face.

" Now if, suppose, a man, or so,
Should be obliged, or not, to go
About, or not about, a case,
To this, or that, or t' other place ;
And if another man, for fun,
Should fire a pistol (viz.) a gun,
And he, the first, by knowing not
That he, the second man, had shot,
Should undesign'dly meet the bullet,
Against the throat (in Greek) the gullet,
And get such mischief by the hit

As should unsense him of his wit,
And if that, after that he died,
D' ye think the other may n't be tried ?
Most sure he must, and hang'd, because
He fired his gun against the laws :
For 't is a case most clear and plain,
Had A not shot, B had not been slain :
So had the dog not chased the hare,
She never had been drown'd—that 's clear."

This logic, rhetoric, and wit,
So nicely did the matter hit,
That Porter, though unheard, was cast,
And in a halter breathed his last.
The justices adjourned to dine,
And whet their logic up with wine.

THE SNOWDROP AND THE CRITIC,[1]

To the Editor of the Pennsylvania Magazine, 1775.

SIR—

I have given your very modest " Snow Drop " what, I think, Shakespeare
calls " a local habitation and a name ; " that is, I have made a poet of him,
and have sent him to take possession of a page in your next Magazine : here he
comes, disputing with a critic about the propriety of a prologue.

Enter CRITIC *and* SNOW DROP.

CRITIC.

Prologues to magazines !—the man is mad,
No magazine a prologue ever had ;
But let us hear what new and mighty things
Your wonder working magic fancy brings.

SNOW DROP.

Bit by the muse in an unlucky hour,
I 've left myself at home, and turn'd a flower,
And thus disguised came forth to tell my tale,
A plain white Snow Drop gathered from the vale :
I come to sing that summer is at hand,
The summer time of wit you 'll understand ;
And that this garden of our Magazine
Will soon exhibit such a pleasing scene,
That even critics shall admire the show
If their good grace will give us time to grow ;
Beneath the surface of the parent earth
We 've various seeds just struggling into birth ;

---

[1] In the Introduction to the *Pennsylvania Magazine*, No. 1, it was said that " like the snow-
drop it comes forth in a barren season, and contents itself with foretelling that choicer flowers
are preparing to appear." Paine was the Editor, and wrote both the Introduction and this
poetic response.—*Editor.*

Plants, fruits, and flowers, and all the smiling race,
That can the orchard or the garden grace ;
Our numbers, Sir, so fast and endless are,
That when in full complexion we appear,
Each eye, each hand, shall pluck what suits its taste,
And every palate shall enjoy a feast ;
The Rose and Lily shall address the fair,
And whisper sweetly out, " My dears, take care " ;
With sterling worth, the Plant of Sense shall rise,
And teach the curious to philosophize ;
The keen eyed wit shall claim the Scented Briar,
And sober cits the Solid Grain admire ;
While generous Juices sparkling from the Vine,
Shall warm the audience until they cry—divine !
And when the scenes of one gay month are o'er,
Shall clap their hands, and shout—encore, encore !

CRITIC.

All this is mighty fine ! but prithee, when
The frost returns, how fight you then your men ?

SNOW DROP.

I 'll tell you, Sir : we 'll garnish out the scenes
With stately rows of hardy Evergreens,
Trees that will bear the frost, and deck their tops
With everlasting flowers, like diamond drops ;
We'll draw, and paint, and carve, with so much skill,
That wondering wits shall cry,—diviner still !

CRITIC.

Better, and better, yet ! but now suppose,
Some critic wight, in mighty verse or prose,
Should draw his gray goose weapon, dipt in gall,
And mow ye down, Plants, Flowers, Trees, and all.

SNOW DROP.

Why, then we 'll die like Flowers of sweet Perfume,
And yield a fragrance even in the tomb !

THE MONK AND THE JEW.

AN unbelieving Jew one day
Was skating o'er the icy way,
Which being brittle let him in,
Just deep enough to catch his chin ;
And in that woful plight he hung,
With only power to move his tongue.
  A brother skater near at hand,
A Papist born in foreign land,

With hasty strokes directly flew
To save poor Mordecai the Jew—
" But first, quoth he, I must enjoin
That you renounce your faith for mine ;
There 's no entreaties else will do,
'T is heresy to help a Jew——"
  " Forswear mine fait ! No ! Cot forbid !
Dat would be very base indeed,
Come never mind such tings as deeze,
Tink, tink, how fery hard it freeze.
More coot you do, more coot you be,
Vat signifies your fait to me ?
Come tink agen, how cold and vet,
And help me out von little bit."
  " By holy mass, 't is hard, I own,
To see a man both hang and drown,
And can't relieve him from his plight
Because he is an Israelite ;
The church refuses all assistance,
Beyond a certain pale and distance ;
And all the service I can lend
Is praying for your soul my friend."
  " Pray for my soul, ha ! ha ! you make me **laugh.**
You petter help me out py half :
Mine soul I farrant vill take care,
To pray for her own self, my tear :
So tink a little now for me,
'T is I am in de hole not she."
  " The church forbids it, friend, and saith
That all shall die who have no faith."
  " Vell, if I must pelieve, I must,
But help me out von little first."
  " No, not an inch without Amen
That seals the whole "—" Vell, hear me **den,**
I here renounce for coot and all
De race of Jews both great and small ;
'Tis de vurst trade peneath the sun,
Or vurst religion ; dat 's all von.
Dey cheat, and get deir living py 't,
And lie, and swear the lie is right.
I'll co to mass as soon as ever
I get to toder side the river.
So help me out, dow Christian friend,
Dat I may do as I *intend*."
  " Perhaps you do intend to cheat,
If once you get upon your feet."
  " No, no, I do intend to be
A *Christian*, such a one as *dee*."
For, thought the Jew, he is as much
A Christian man as I am such.
  The bigot Papist joyful hearted
To hear the heretic converted,
Replied to the *designing* Jew,
" This was a happy fall for you :
You 'd better die a Christian now,
For if you live you 'll break your vow."
Then said no more, but in a trice
Popp'd Mordecai beneath the ice.

BACHELORS' HALL,

At Philadelphia, being destroyed by Lightning, 1775.

FAIR Venus so often was miss'd from the skies,
And Bacchus as frequently absent likewise,
That the synod began to inquire out the reason,
Suspecting the culprits were plotting of treason ;
At length it was found they had open'd a ball
At a place by the mortals call'd Bachelors' Hall ;
Where Venus disclosed every fun she could think of,
And Bacchus made nectar for mortals to drink of.
Jove, highly displeas'd at such riotous doings,
Sent Time to reduce the whole building to ruins ;
But Time was so slack with his traces and dashes,
That Jove in a passion consumed it to ashes.

LIBERTY TREE.

A Song, written early in the American Revolution.

Tune—The gods of Greece.

IN a chariot of light, from the regions of day,
　The Goddess of Liberty came,
Ten thousand celestials directed her way,
　And hither conducted the dame.
A fair budding branch from the gardens above,
　Where millions with millions agree,
She brought in her hand as a pledge of her love,
　And the plant she named Liberty Tree.

The celestial exotic stuck deep in the ground,
　Like a native it flourished and bore ;
The fame of its fruit drew the nations around,
　To seek out this peaceable shore.
Unmindful of names or distinctions they came,
　For freemen like brothers agree ;
With one spirit endued, they one friendship pursued,
　And their temple was Liberty Tree.

Beneath this fair tree, like the patriarchs of old.
　Their bread in contentment they ate,
Unvexed with the troubles of silver or gold,
　The cares of the grand and the great.
With timber and tar they Old England supplied,
　And supported her power on the sea :
Her battles they fought, without getting a groat,
　For the honour of Liberty Tree.

But hear, O ye swains, ('t is a tale most profane,)
　How all the tyrannical powers,
Kings, Commons, and Lords, are uniting amain
　To cut down this guardian of ours.

From the east to the west blow the trumpet to arms,
Thro' the land let the sound of it flee :
Let the far and the near all unite with a cheer,
In defence of our Liberty Tree.

AN ADDRESS TO LORD HOWE.[1]

THE rain pours down, the city looks forlorn,
And gloomy subjects suit the howling morn ;
Close by my fire, with door and window fast,
And safely shelter'd from the driving blast,
To gayer thoughts I bid a day's adieu,
To spend a scene of solitude with you.

So oft has black revenge engross'd the care
Of all the leisure hours man finds to spare ;
So oft has guilt, in all her thousand dens,
Call'd for the vengeance of chastising pens ;
That while I fain would ease my heart on you,
No thought is left untold, no passion new.

From flight to flight the mental path appears,
Worn with the steps of near six thousand years,
And fill'd throughout with every scene of pain,
From George the murderer down to murderous Cain
Alike in cruelty, alike in hate,
In guilt alike, but more alike in fate,
Cursèd supremely for the blood they drew,
Each from the rising world, while each was new.

Go, man of blood ! true likeness of the first,
And strew your blasted head with homely dust :
In ashes sit—in wretched sackcloth weep,
And with unpitied sorrows cease to sleep.
Go haunt the tombs, and single out the place
Where earth itself shall suffer a disgrace.
Go spell the letters on some mouldering urn,
And ask if he who sleeps there can return.
Go count the numbers that in silence lie,
And learn by study what it is to die ;
For sure your heart, if any heart you own,
Conceits that man expires without a groan ;
That he who lives receives from you a grace,
Or death is nothing but a change of place :
That peace is dull, that joy from sorrow springs
And war the most desirable of things.
Else why these scenes that wound the feeling mind,
This sport of death—this cockpit of mankind !
Why sobs the widow in perpetual pain ?
Why cries the orphan, " Oh ! my father 's slain ! "
Why hangs the sire his paralytic head,
And nods with manly grief—" My son is dead ! "

[1] The British Commander to whom Paine addressed " Crisis No. II.," January 13, 1777.—
Editor.

Why drops the tear from off the sister's cheek,
And sweetly tells the misery she would speak ?
Or why, in sorrow sunk, does pensive John
To all the neighbors tell, " Poor master's gone ! "

Oh ! could I paint the passion that I feel,
Or point a horror that would wound like steel,
To thy unfeeling, unrelenting mind,
I 'd send destruction and relieve mankind.
You that are husbands, fathers, brothers, all
The tender names which kindred learn to call ;
Yet like an image carved in massy stone,
You bear the shape, but sentiment have none ;
Allied by dust and figure, not with mind,
You only herd, but live not with mankind,

Since then no hopes to civilize remain,
And mild Philosophy has preached in vain,
One prayer is left, which dreads no proud reply,
That he who made you breathe will make you die.

THE BOSTON PATRIOTIC SONG.

Tune—Anacreon in Heaven.

YE sons of Columbia who bravely have fought,
   For those rights which unstain'd from your sires have descended.
May you long taste the blessings your valor has bought,
   And your sons reap the soil which their fathers defended ;
      'Mid the reign of mild peace,
      May your nation increase,
With the glory of Rome, and the wisdom of Greece ;
   And ne'er may the sons of Columbia be slaves,
    While the earth bears a plant or the sea rolls its waves.

In a clime whose rich vales feed the marts of the world,
   Whose shores are unshaken by Europe's commotion,
The trident of commerce should never be hurl'd,
   To increase the legitimate power of the ocean ;
      But should pirates invade,
      Though in thunder array'd,
Let your cannon declare the free charter of trade.
    For ne'er shall the sons, etc.

The fame of our arms, of our laws the mild sway,
   Had justly ennobled our nation in story,
Till the dark clouds of faction obscured our bright day,
   And envelop'd the sun of American glory ;
      But let traitors be told,
      Who their country have sold,
And barter'd their God for his image in gold,
      That ne'er shall the sons, etc.

While France her huge limbs bathes recumbent in blood,
    And society's base threats with wide dissolution,
May Peace, like the dove who return'd from the flood,
    Find an Ark of abode in our mild Constitution ;
        But tho' peace is our aim,
        Yet the boon we disclaim,
If bought by our Sovereignty, Justice, or Fame.
    For ne'er shall the sons, etc.

'T is the fire of the flint each American warms,
    Let Rome's haughty victors beware of collision !
Let them bring all the vassals of Europe in arms,
    We're a World by ourselves, and disdain a division ;
        While with patriot pride,
        To our laws we're allied,
No foe can subdue us, no faction divide ;
    For ne'er shall the sons, etc.

Our mountains are crown'd with imperial oak,
    Whose roots like our Liberty ages have nourish'd,
But long e'er the nation submits to the yoke,
    Not a tree shall be left on the soil where it flourish'd.
        Should invasion impend,
        Every grove would descend,
From the hill tops they shaded, our shores to defend.
    For ne'er shall the sons, etc.

Let our patriots destroy vile anarchy's worm,
    Lest our Liberty's growth should be check'd by corrosion,
Then let clouds thicken round us, we heed not the storm,
    Our earth fears no shock but the earth's own explosion ;
        Foes assail us in vain,
        Tho' their fleets bridge the main,
For our altars, and claims, with our lives we'll maintain.
    For ne'er shall the sons, etc.

Should the tempest of war overshadow our land,
    Its bolts can ne'er rend Freedom's temple asunder ;
For unmoved at its portals would Washington stand
    And repulse with his breast the assaults of the thunder.
        His sword from its sleep,
        In its scabbard would leap,
And conduct with its point every flash to the deep.
    For ne'er shall the sons, etc.

Let Fame to the world sound America's voice,
    No intrigue her sons from their government can sever ;
Its wise regulations and laws are their choice,
    And shall flourish till Liberty slumber forever.
        Then unite heart and hand,
        Like Leonidas' band ;
And swear by the God of the ocean and land,
        That ne'er shall the sons of Columbia be slaves,
        While the earth bears a plant, or the sea rolls its waves.

HAIL GREAT REPUBLIC.

Tune—Rule Britannia.

HAIL great Republic of the world,
　Which rear'd her empire in the west,
Where fam'd Columbus' flag unfurl'd,
　Gave tortured Europe scenes of rest ;
　　Be thou forever great and free,
　　The land of Love, and Liberty !

Beneath thy spreading, mantling vine,
　Beside each flowery grove and spring,
And where thy lofty mountains shine,
　May all thy sons and fair ones sing.
　　　　　　Be thou forever, &c.

From thee may hellish Discord prowl,
　With all her dark and hateful train ;
And whilst thy mighty waters roll,
　May heaven-descended Concord reign.
　　　　　　Be thou forever, &c.

Where'er the Atlantic surges lave,
　Or sea the human eye delights,
There may thy starry standard wave,
　The Constellation of thy Rights !
　　　　　　Be thou forever, &c.

May ages as they rise proclaim
　The glories of thy natal day ;
And States from thy exalted name
　Learn how to rule, and to obey.
　　　　　　Be thou forever, &c.

Let Laureats make their birthdays known,
　Or how war's thunderbolts are hurl'd ;
Tis ours the charter, ours alone,
　To sing the birthday of a world !
　　Be thou forever great and free,
　　The land of Love and Liberty !

COLUMBIA.

Tune—Anacreon in Heaven.

To Columbia who, gladly reclined at her ease
On Atlantic's broad bosom, lay smiling in peace,
Minerva flew hastily sent from above,
And addrest her this message from thundering Jove :
　　" Rouse, quickly awake !
　　Your Freedom 's at stake,
　Storms arise, your renown'd Independence to shake,

Then lose not a moment, my aid I will lend,
If your sons will assemble your Rights to defend.

Roused Columbia rose up, and indignant declared,
That no nation she'd wrong'd and no nation she fear'd,
That she wished not for war, but if war were her fate,
She would rally up souls independent and great :
   Then tell mighty Jove,
   That we quickly will prove,
 We deserve the protection he 'll send from above ;
For ne'er shall the sons of America bend,
But united their Rights and their Freedom defend.

Minerva smiled cheerfully as she withdrew,
Enraptured to find her Americans true,
" For," said she, " our sly Mercury ofttimes reports,
That your sons are divided "—Columbia retorts,
   " Tell that vile god of thieves,
   His report but deceives,
 And we care not what madman such nonsense believes,
For ne'er shall the sons of America bend,
But united their Rights and their Freedom defend."

Jove rejoiced in Columbia such union to see,
And swore by old Styx she deserved to be free ;
Then assembled the Gods, who all gave consent,
Their assistance if needful her ill to prevent ;
   Mars arose, shook his armour,
   And swore his old Farmer [1]
 Should ne'er in his country see aught that could harm her,
For ne'er should the sons of America bend,
But united their Rights and their Freedom defend.

Minerva resolved that her Ægis she 'd lend,
And Apollo declared he their cause would defend,
Old Vulcan an armour would forge for their aid,
More firm than the one for Achilles he made.
   Jove vow'd he 'd prepare,
   A compound most rare,
 Of courage and union, a bountiful share ;
And swore ne'er shall the sons of America bend,
But their Rights and their Freedom most firmly defend.

Ye sons of Columbia, then join hand in hand,
Divided we fall, but united we stand ;
'T is ours to determine, 't is ours to decree,
That in peace we will live Independent and Free ;
   And should from afar
   Break the horrors of war,
 We 'll always be ready at once to declare,
That ne'er will the sons of America bend,
But united their Rights and their Freedom defend.

[1] Washington.—*Editor.*

FROM THE CASTLE IN THE AIR,

TO THE LITTLE CORNER OF THE WORLD.[1]

In the region of clouds, where the whirlwinds arise,
　　My Castle of Fancy was built ;
The turrets reflected the blue from the skies,
　　And the windows with sunbeams were gilt.

The rainbow sometimes, in its beautiful state,
　　Enamell'd the mansion around ;
And the figures that fancy in clouds can create,
　　Supplied me with gardens and ground.

I had grottoes, and fountains, and orange tree groves,
　　I had all that enchantment has told ;
I had sweet shady walks, for the Gods and their Loves,
　　I had mountains of coral and gold.

But a storm that I felt not, had risen and roll'd,
　　While wrapp'd in a slumber I lay ;
And when I look'd out in the morning, behold
　　My Castle was carried away.

It pass'd over rivers, and vallies, and groves,
　　The world it was all in my view ;
I thought of my friends, of their fates, of their loves,
　　And often, full often of you.

At length it came over a beautiful scene,
　　That nature in silence had made ;
The place was but small, but 't was sweetly serene,
　　And chequer'd with sunshine and shade.

I gazed and I envied with painful goodwill,
　　And grew tired of my seat in the air ;
When all of a sudden my Castle stood still,
　　As if some attraction was there.

Like a lark from the sky it came fluttering down,
　　And placed me exactly in view,
When whom should I meet in this charming retreat,
　　This corner of calmness, but you.

Delighted to find you in honour and ease,
　　I felt no more sorrow, nor pain ;
But the wind coming fair, I ascended the breeze,
　　And went back with my Castle again.

[1] **Addressed** to Lady Smyth (see vol. iii., chap. 27). While in prison in Paris, Paine received sympathetic letters from " The Little Corner of the World." He responded from " The Castle in the Air," and afterwards found her to be Lady Smyth.—*Editor*.

TO SIR ROBERT SMYTH.

Paris, 1800.

As I will not attempt to rival your witty description of Love, (in which you say, " Love is like paper, with a fool it is wit, with a wit it is folly,") I will retreat to sentiment, and try if I can match you there ; and that I may start with a fair chance, I will begin with your own question,

WH*I T* IS LOVE ?

'T is that delights me transport we can feel
Which painters cannot paint, nor words reveal,
Nor any art we know of can conceal.

Canst thou describe the sunbeams to the blind,
Or make him feel a shadow with his mind ?
So neither can we by description shew
This first of all Felicities below.

When happy Love pours magic o'er the soul,
And all our thoughts in sweet delirium roll ;
When Contemplation spreads her rainbow wings,
And every flutter some new rapture brings ;
How sweetly then our moments glide away,
And dreams repeat the raptures of the day :
We live in ecstacy, to all things kind,
For Love can teach a moral to the mind.

But are there not some other marks that prove,
What is this wonder of the soul, call'd Love ?
O yes there are, but of a different kind,
The dreadful horrors of a dismal mind :
Some jealous Fury throws her poison'd dart,
And rends in pieces the distracted heart.

When Love 's a tyrant, and the soul a slave,
No hope remains to thought, but in the grave ;
In that dark den it sees an end to grief,
And what was once its dread becomes relief.

What are the iron chains that hands have wrought ?
The hardest chain to break is made of thought.
Think well of this, ye Lovers, and be kind,
Nor play with torture on a tortured mind.

NOTE.—The above poem, that which precedes, and those which follow it, with the exception of " Lines Extempore," were never intended for publication, and are altogether posthumous.—*Editor.*

CONTENTMENT; OR, IF YOU PLEASE, CONFESSION.

To Mrs. Barlow, on her pleasantly telling the author, that after writing against the superstition of the Scripture religion, he was setting up a religion capable of more bigotry and enthusiasm, and more dangerous to its votaries —that of making a religion of Love.

> O COULD we always live and love,
>   And always be sincere,
> I would not wish for heaven above,
>   My heaven would be here.
>
> Though many countries I have seen,
>   And more may chance to see,
> *My Little Corner of the World*
>   Is half the world to me ;
>
> The other half, as you may guess,
>   America contains ;
> And thus, between them, I possess
>   The whole world for my pains.
>
> I 'm then contented with my lot,
>   I can no happier be ;
> For neither world I 'm sure has got
>   So rich a man as me.
>
> Then send no fiery chariot down
>   To take me off from hence,
> But leave me on my heavenly ground—
>   This prayer is *common-sense.*
>
> Let others choose another plan,
>   I mean no fault to find ;
> The true theology of man
>   Is *happiness of mind.*

IMPROMPTU

ON A LONG-NOSED FRIEND.

> GOING along the other day,
>   Upon a certain plan ;
> I met a nose upon the way,
>   Behind it was a man.
>
> I called unto the nose to stop,
>   And when it had done so,—
> The man behind it—he came up ;
>   They made Zenobio.

Paris, 1800.

A FEDERALIST FEAST.[1]

From Mr. Paine to Mr. Jefferson, on the occasion of a toast being given at a federal dinner at Washington, of, " May they never know pleasure who love Paine."

I SEND you, Sir, a tale about some ' Feds,'
Who, in their wisdom, got to loggerheads.
The case was this, they felt so flat and sunk,
They took a glass together and got drunk.
Such things, you know, are neither new nor rare,
For some will harry themselves when in despair.
It was the natal day of Washington,
And that they thought a famous day for fun ;
For with the learnéd world it is agreed,
The better day the better deed.
They talked away, and as the glass went round
They grew, in point of wisdom, more profound ;
For at the bottom of the bottle lies
That kind of sense we overlook when wise.
'Come, here 's a toast,' cried one, with roar immense,
May none know pleasure who love (Common Sense).
'Bravo !' cried some,—no, no ! some others cried,
But left it to the waiter to decide.
' I think, said he, the case would be more plain,
To leave out (Common Sense), and put in Paine.'
On this a mighty noise arose among
This drunken, bawling, senseless throng :
Some said that common sense was all a curse,
That making people wiser made them worse—
It learned them to be careful of their purse,
And not be laid about like babes at nurse,
Nor yet believe in stories upon trust,
Which all mankind, to be well governed, must ;
And that the toast was better at the first,
And he that did n't think so might be cursed.
So on they went, till such a fray arose
As all who know what Feds are may suppose.

LINES EXTEMPORE.

July, 1803.

QUICK as the lightning's vivid flash
  The poet's eye o'er Europe rolls ;
Sees battles rage, hears tempests crash,
  And dims at horror's threatening scowls—

Marks ambition's ruthless king,
  With crimson'd banners scathe the globe,
While trailing after conquest's wing,
  Man's festering wounds his demons probe.

[1] 1802. I found these lines among some manuscripts of William Cobbett.—*Editor.*

Palléd with streams of reeking gore
  That stain the proud imperial day ;
He turns to view the western shore,
  Where freedom holds her boundless sway.

'T is here her sage[1] triumphant sways
  An empire in the people's love,
'T is here the sovereign will obeys
  No King but Him who rules above.

THE STRANGE STORY OF

KORAH, DATHAN, AND ABIRAM.

Numbers, chap. xvi., accounted for.

OLD ballads sing of Chevy Chace,
  Beneath whose rueful shade,
Full many a valiant man was slain
  And many a widow made.

But I will tell of one much worse,
  That happ'd in days of yore,
All in the barren wilderness,
  Beside the Jordan shore,

Where Moses led the children forth,
  Call'd chosen tribes of God,
And fed them forty years with quails,
  And ruled them with a rod.

A dreadful fray once rose among
  These self named tribes of I Am ;
Where Korah fell, and by his side
  Fell Dathan and Abiram.

An earthquake swallowed thousands up,
  And fire came down like stones,
Which slew their sons and daughters all,
  Their wives and little ones.

'T was all about old Aaron's tythes
  This murdering quarrel rose ;
For tythes are worldly things of old,
  That led from words to blows.

A Jew of Venice has explained,
  In the language of his nation,
The manner how this fray began,
  Of which here is translation.

[1] President Jefferson.—*Editor.*

There was a widow old and poor,
    Who scarce herself could keep ;
Her stock of goods was very small,
    Her flock one single sheep.

And when her time of shearing came,
    She counted much her gains ;
For now, said she, I shall be blest
    With plenty for my pains.

When Aaron heard the sheep was shear'd
    And gave a good increase,
He straightway sent his tything man
    And took away the fleece.

At this the weeping widow went
    To Korah to complain.
And Korah he to Aaron went
    In order to explain.

But Aaron said, in such a case,
    There can be no forbearing,
The law ordains that thou shalt give
    The first fleece of thy shearing.

When lambing time was come about,
    This sheep became a dam,
And bless'd the widow's mournful heart,
    By bringing forth a lamb.

When Aaron heard the sheep had young,
    He staid till it was grown,
But then he sent his tything man,
    And took it for his own.

Again the weeping widow went
    To Korah with her grief,
But Aaron said, in such a case
    There could be no relief ;

For in the holy law 't is writ,
    That whilst thou keep'st the stock,
Thou shalt present unto the Lord
    The firstling of thy flock.

The widow then, in deep distress,
    And having naught to eat,
Against her will she killed the sheep,
    To feed upon the meat.

When Aaron heard the sheep was killed
    He sent and took a limb ;
Which by the holy law, he said,
    Pertainéd unto him :

For in the holy law 't is writ,
That when thou kill'st a beast,
Thou shalt a shoulder and a breast
Present unto the priest.

The widow then, worn out with grief,
Sat down to mourn and weep ;
And in a fit of passion said,
The devil take the sheep !

Then Aaron took the whole away,
And said, the laws record
That all and each devoted thing
Belongs unto the Lord.

The widow went among her kin,
The tribes of Israel rose,
And all the widows, young and old,
Pull'd Aaron by the nose.

But Aaron called an earthquake up,
And fire from out the sky ;
And all the consolation is—
The Bible tells a lie.

A COMMENTARY ON

THE EASTERN WISE MEN,

*Travelling to Bethlehem, guided by a Star, to see the little Jesus in a Manger,
as recorded in the Gospel of Matthew.*

THREE pedlars travelling to a fair,
To see the fun and what was there,
And sell their merchandise ;
They stopp'd upon the road to chat,
Refresh, and ask of this and that,
That they might be more wise.

" And pray," the landlord says to them,
" Where go ye, sirs ? " " To Bethlehem,"
The citizens replied.
" You 're merchants, sirs," to them said he,
" We are," replied the pedlars three,
" And eastern men beside."

" I pray, what have you in your packs ?
If worth the while I will go snacks,"
To them quoth Major Domo ;
" We 've buckles, buttons, spectacles,
And every thing a merchant sells,"
Replied the travelling trio.

" These things are very well," said he,
" For beaux and those who cannot see
 Much further than their knuckles ;
But Bethlehem Fair 's for boys and girls
Who never think of spectacles,
 And cannot buy your buckles :

" I have a pack of toys," quoth he,
" A travelling merchant left with me,
 Who could not pay his score,
And you shall have them on condition
You sell them at a cheap commission,
 And make the money sure."

" There 's one of us will stay in pawn,
Until the other two return,
 If you suspect our faith," said they ;
The landlord thought this was a plan
To leave upon his hands the man,
 And therefore he said " Nay."

They truck'd however for the pack,
Which one of them took on his back,
 And off the merchants travelled ;
And here the tale the apostles told
Of wise men and their gifts of gold,
 Will fully be unravelled.

The star in the east that shines so bright,
As might be seen both day and night,
 If you will credit them,
It was no other than a sign
To a public house where pedlars dine,
 In East Street, Bethlehem.

These wise men were the pedlars three,
As you and all the world may see,
 By reading to the end ;
For commentators have mistook,
In paraphrasing on a book
 They did not understand.

Our travellers coming to a house,
Scarce fit to entertain a mouse,
 Enquired to have a room ;
The landlord said he was not able,
To give them any but a stable,
 So many folks were come.

" I pray, whom have you here," say they,
" And how much money must we pay,
 For we have none to spare."
" Why, there 's one Joseph and a wench,
Who are to go before the bench
 About a love affair.

" Some how or other, in a manger,
A child exposed to every danger
    Was found, as if 't was sleeping :
The girl she swears that she 's a maid,
So says the man, but I 'm afraid
    On me will fall the keeping :

" Now if you 'll set your wits about
To find this knotty matter out,
    I 'll pay whate'er it may be."
Then on the trav'lling pedlars went,
To pay their birthday compliment,
    And talk about the baby.

They then unpack'd their pack of toys,
Some were for show and some for noise,
    But mostly for the latter ;
One gave a rattle, one a whistle,
And one a trumpet made of gristle,
    To introduce the matter :

One squeaked away, the other blew,
The third played on the rattle too,
    To keep the bantling easy ;
And hence this story comes to us,
Of which some people make such fuss,
    About the Eastern Magi.

NOTE.—The above has long been published as Paine's, but was first printed by Cheetham (in his libellous biography of Paine) who got it from Carver, a treacherous parasite of Paine, and there is no certainty that it was written by Paine.—*Editor*.

APPENDIX L.[1]

CASE OF THE OFFICERS OF EXCISE ; WITH REMARKS ON THE QUALIFICATIONS OF OFFICERS, AND ON THE NUMEROUS EVILS ARISING TO THE REVE-NUE, FROM THE INSUFFICIENCY OF THE PRES-ENT SALARY : HUMBLY ADDRESSED TO THE MEMBERS OF BOTH HOUSES OF PARLIAMENT.

THE INTRODUCTION.

As a Design among the Excise Officers throughout the Kingdom is on Foot, for an humble Application to Parliament next Session, to have the State of their Salaries taken into Consideration ; it has been judged not only expe-dient, but highly necessary, to present a State of their Case, previous to the Presentation of their Petition.

There are some Cases so singularly reasonable, that the more they are con-sidered, the more Weight they obtain. It is a strong Evidence both of Sim-plicity and honest Confidence, when Petitioners in any Case ground their Hopes of Relief on having their Case fully and perfectly known and under-stood.

Simple as this Subject may appear at first, it is a Matter, in my humble Opinion, not unworthy a Parliamentary Attention. 'T is a Subject interwoven with a Variety of Reasons from different Causes. New Matter will arise on every Thought. *If the Poverty of the Officers of Excise, if the Temptations arising from their Poverty, if the Qualifications of Persons to be admitted into Employment, if the Security of the Revenue itself,* are Matters of any Weight, then I am conscious that my voluntary Services in this Business, will produce some good Effect or other, either to the better Security of the Revenue, the Relief of the Officers, or both.

THE STATE OF THE SALARY OF THE OFFICERS OF EXCISE.

When a Year's Salary is mentioned in the Gross, it acquires a Degree of Consequence from its *Sound*, which it would not have if separated into daily Payments, and if the Charges attending the receiving and other unavoidable Expences were considered with it. Fifty Pounds a Year, and One Shilling and Ninepence Farthing a Day, carry as different Degrees of Significancy with them, as My Lord's Steward, and the Steward's Labourer ; and yet an Out-Ride Officer in the Excise, under the Name of Fifty Pounds a Year, receives for himself no more than One Shilling and Ninepence Farthing a Day.

---

[1] I place at the end of my edition Paine's earliest prose composition and his last,—his Plea for Excisemen, and his Will. This Plea was a petition to Parliament ; it was printed and widely distributed in 1772, but not published until 1793. Its interest being now mainly biographical, I have reproduced it with exactness, including its multiplicity of capitals. Con-cerning the circumstances under which it was written, see my " Life of Paine," vol. i., ch. 2. —*Editor.*

After Tax, Charity, and sitting Expences are deducted, there remains very little more than Forty-six pounds ; and the expences of Horse-keeping in many Places cannot be brought under Fourteen Pounds a Year, besides the Purchase at first, and the Hazard of Life, which reduces it to Thirty-two Pounds *per Annum*, or One Shilling and Ninepence Farthing *per* Day.

I have spoken more particularly of the Out-Rides, as they are by far the most numerous, being in Proportion to the Foot-Walks as Eight is to Five throughout the Kingdom. Yet in the latter the same Misfortunes exist ; the Channel of them only is altered. The excessive dearness of House-rent, the great Burthen of Rates and Taxes, and the excessive Price of all Necessaries of Life, in Cities and large Trading Towns, nearly counter-balance the expences of Horse-keeping. Every Office has its Stages of Promotions, but the pecuniary Advantages arising from a Foot-walk are so inconsiderable, and the Loss of disposing of Effects, or the Charges of removing them to any considerable Distance so great, that many Out-ride Officers with a Family remain as they are, from an Inability to bear the Loss, or support the expence.

The Officers resident in the Cities of *London* and *Westminster*, are exempt from the particular Disadvantages of Removals. This seems to be the only Circumstance which they enjoy superior to their Country Brethren. In every other respect they lay under the same Hardships, and suffer the same Distresses.

There are no Perquisites or Advantages in the least, annexed to the Employment. A few Officers who are stationed along the Coast, may sometimes have the good Fortune to fall in with a Seizure of contraband Goods, and yet, that frequently at the Hazard of their Lives : But the inland Officers can have no such Opportunities. Besides, the surveying Duty in the Excise is so continual, that without Remissness from the real Business itself, there is no Time to seek after them. With the Officers of the Customs it is quite otherwise ; their whole Time and Care is appropriated to that Service, and their Profits are in proportion to their Vigilance.

If the Increase of Money in the Kingdom is one Cause of the high Price of Provisions, the Case of the Excise-Officers is peculiarly pitiable. No Increase comes to them—They are shut out from the general Blessing—They behold it like a map of *Peru*. The answer of Abraham to Dives is somewhat applicable to them, " *There is a great Gulf fix'd.*"

To the Wealthy and Humane, it is a Matter worthy of Concern that their Affluence should become the Misfortune of others. Were the Money in the Kingdom to be increased double, the Salary would in Value be reduced one half. Every Step upwards, is a Step downwards with them. Not to be Partakers of the Increase would be a little hard, but to be Sufferers by it exceedingly so. The Mechanic and the Labourer may in a great Measure ward off the Distress, by raising the Price of their Manufactures or their Work, but the Situation of the Officers admits of no such Relief.

Another Consideration in their Behalf, (and which is peculiar to the Excise,) is, that as the Law of their Office removes them far from all their natural Friends and Relations, it consequently prevents those occasional Assistances from them, which are serviceably felt in a Family, and which even the poorest among the poor enjoys. Most poor Mechanics, or even common Labourers, have some Relations or Friends, who, either out of Benevolence or Pride, keep their Children from Nakedness, supply them occasionally with perhaps half a Hog, a Load of Wood, a Chaldron of Coals, or something or other which abates the Severity of their Distress ; and yet those Men thus relieved will frequently earn more than the daily Pay of an Excise Officer.

Perhaps an Officer will appear more reputable with the same Pay, than a Mechanic or Labourer. The difference arises from Sentiment, not Circumstances. A something like reputable Pride makes all the Distinction, and the thinking Part of Mankind well knows that none suffer so much as they who endeavour to conceal their Necessities.

The frequent Removals which unavoidably happen in the Excise are attended with such an Expence, especially where there is a Family, as few Officers are able to support. About two Years ago, an Officer with a Family, under Orders for removing, and rather embarrassed Circumstances, made his Application to me, and from a conviction of his Distress I advanced a small Sum to enable him to proceed. He ingenuously declared, that without the Assistance of some Friend, he should be driven to do Injustice to his Creditors, and compelled to desert the Duty of his Office. He has since honestly paid me, and does as well as the Narrowness of such Circumstances can admit of.

There is one general allowed Truth which will always operate in their favour, which is, that no Set of Men under his Majesty earn their Salary with any Comparison of Labour and Fatigue with that of the Officers of Excise. The Station may rather be called a Seat of constant Work, than either a Place or an Employment. Even in the different Departments of the general Revenue, they are unequalled in the Burthen of Business; a Riding-Officer's place in the Customs, whose Salary is 60 *l.* a Year, is *Ease* to theirs; and the Work in the Window-Light Duty, compared with the Excise, is Lightness itself; yet their Salary is subject to no Tax, they receive Forty-nine pounds Twelve shillings and Sixpence, without Deduction.

The Inconveniences which affect an Excise Officer are almost endless; even the Land Tax Assessment upon their Salaries, which though the Government pays, falls often with Hardship upon them. The Place of their Residence, on account of the Land Tax, has in many Instances, created frequent Contentions between Parishes, in which the Officer, though the innocent and unconcerned Cause of the Quarrel, has been the greater Sufferer.

To point out particularly the Impossibility of an Excise Officer supporting himself and Family, with any proper Degree of Credit and Reputation, on so scanty a Pittance, is altogether unnecessary. The Times, the Voice of general Want, is Proof itself. Where Facts are sufficient, Arguments are useless; and the Hints which I have produced are such as affect the Officers of Excise *differently* to any other set of Men. A single Man may barely live; but as it is not the Design of the Legislature, or the Honourable Board of Excise, to impose a State of Celibacy on them, the Condition of much the greater Part is truly wretched and pitiable.

Perhaps it may be said, Why do the Excise Officers complain; they are not pressed into the Service, and may relinquish it when they please; if they can mend themselves, why don't they? Alas! what a Mockery of Pity would it be, to give such an Answer to an honest, faithful old Officer in the Excise, who had spent the Prime of his Life in the Service, and was become unfit for any Thing else. The Time limited for an Admission into an Excise Employment, is between twenty-one and thirty Years of Age—the very Flower of Life. Every other Hope and Consideration is then given up, and the Chance of establishing themselves in any other Business becomes in a few Years not only lost to them, but they become lost to it. " There is a Tide in the Affairs of Men," which if embraced, leads on to Fortune—*That neglected*, all beyond is Misery or Want.

When we consider how few in the Excise arrive at any comfortable Eminence, and the Date of Life when such Promotions only can happen, the great Hazard there is of ill rather than good Fortune in the Attempt, and that all the Years antecedent to that is a State of mere Existence, wherein they are shut out from the common Chance of Success in any other Way: a Reply like that can be only a Derision of their Wants. 'T is almost impossible after any long Continuance in the Excise, that they *can* live any other way. Such as are of Trades, would have their Trade to learn over again; and People would have but little Opinion of their Abilities in any Calling, who had been ten, fifteen, or twenty Years absent from it. Every Year's Experience gained in the Excise, is a Year's Experience lost in Trade; and by the Time they become wise Officers, they become foolish Workmen.

Were the Reasons for augmenting the Salary grounded only on the Charitableness of so doing, they would have great Weight with the Compassionate.

But there are Auxiliaries of such a powerful Cast, that in the Opinion of Policy they obtain the Rank of Originals. The first is truly the Case of the Officers, but this is rather the Case of the Revenue.

The Distresses in the Excise are so generally known, that Numbers of Gentlemen, and other Inhabitants in Places where Officers are resident, have generously and humanely recommended their Case to the Members of the Honourable House of Commons: And Numbers of Traders of Opulence and Reputation, well knowing that the Poverty of an Officer may subject him to the fraudulent Designs of some selfish Persons under his Survey, to the great Injury of the fair Trader, and Trade in general, have, from Principles both of Generosity and Justice, joined in the same Recommendation.

THOUGHTS ON THE CORRUPTION OF PRINCIPLES, AND ON THE NUMEROUS EVILS ARISING TO THE REVENUE, FROM THE TOO GREAT POVERTY OF THE OFFICERS OF EXCISE.

IT has always been the Wisdom of Government to consider the Situation and Circumstances of Persons in Trust. Why are large Salaries given in many Instances, but to proportion it to the Trust, to set Men above Temptation, and to make it even literally worth their while to be honest? The Salaries of the Judges have been augmented, and their Places made independent even on the Crown itself, for the above wise Purposes.

Certainly there can be nothing unreasonable in supposing there is such an Instinct as Frailty among the Officers of Excise, in common with the rest of Mankind; and that the most effectual Method to keep Men honest is to enable them to live so. The Tenderness of Conscience is too often overmatched by the Sharpness of Want; and Principle, like Chastity, yields with just Reluctance enough to excuse itself. There is a powerful Rhetorick in Necessity, which exceeds even a *Dunning* or a *Wedderburne.* No Argument can satisfy the feelings of Hunger, or abate the Edge of Appetite. Nothing tends to a greater Corruption of Manners and Principles, than a too great Distress of Circumstances; and the Corruption is of that Kind, that it spreads a Plaister for itself: Like a Viper, it carries a Cure, though a false one, for its own Poison. *Agur*, without any Alternative, has made Dishonesty the immediate Consequence of Poverty. "Lest I be poor and steal."[1] A very little Degree of that dangerous Kind of Philosophy, which is the almost certain Effect of involuntary Poverty, will teach men to believe that to starve is more criminal than to steal, by as much as every Species of Self-Murder exceeds every other Crime; that true Honesty is sentimental, and the Practice of it dependent upon Circumstances. If the Gay find it difficult to resist the Allurements of Pleasure, the Great the temptations of Ambition, or the Miser the Acquisition of Wealth, how much stronger are the Provocations of Want and Poverty? The Excitements to Pleasure, Grandeur, or Riches, are mere "Shadows of a Shade," compared to the irresistible Necessities of Nature. Not to be led into temptation, is the prayer of Divinity itself; and to guard against, or rather to prevent, such insnaring Situations, is one of the greatest Heights of Human Prudence: In private life it is partly religious; and in a Revenue Sense, it is truly political.

The Rich, in Ease and Affluence, may think I have drawn an unnatural Portrait; but could they descend to the cold Regions of Want, the Circle of Polar Poverty, they would find their Opinions changing with the Climate. There are Habits of Thinking peculiar to different Conditions, and to find them out is truly to study Mankind.

That the situation of an Excise Officer is of this dangerous Kind, must be allowed by every one who will consider the Trust unavoidably reposed in him, and compare the Narrowness of his Circumstances with the Hardship of the

---

[1] See *ante*, p. 125.—*Editor.*

Times. If the Salary was judged competent an Hundred Years ago, it cannot be so now. Should it be advanced, that it the present Set of Officers are dissatisfied with the Salary, that enow may be procured not only for the present Salary, but for less ; the Answer is extremely easy. The question needs only be put ; it destroys itself. Were Two or Three Thousand Men to offer to execute the Office without any Salary, would the Government accept them ? No. Were the same Number to offer the same Service for a Salary less than can possibly support them, would the government accept them ? Certainly No ; for while Nature, in spite of Law or Religion, makes it a ruling Principle not to starve, the event would be this, that if they could not live on the Salary, they would discretionarily live out of the Duty. Quære, whether Poverty has not too great an Influence now ? Were the Employment a Place of direct Labour, and not of Trust, then Frugality in the Salary would be sound Policy : But when it is considered that the greatest single Branch of the Revenue, a Duty amounting to near Five Millions Sterling, is annually charged by a Set of Men, most of whom are wanting even the common Neccessaries of Life, the thought must, to every Friend to Honesty, to every Person concerned in the Management of the Public Money, be strong and striking. Poor and in Power, are powerful Temptations ; I call it Power, because they have it in their Power to defraud. The trust unavoidably reposed in an Excise Officer is so great, that it would be an Act of Wisdom, and perhaps of Interest, to secure him from the Temptations of downright Poverty. To relieve their Wants would be Charity, but to secure the Revenue by so doing, would be Prudence. Scarce a Week passes at the Office but some Detections are made of fraudulent and collusive proceedings. The Poverty of the Officers is the fairest Bait for a designing Trader that can possibly be ; such introduce themselves to the Officer under the common Plea of the Insufficiency of the Salary. Every considerate Mind must allow, that Poverty and Opportunity corrupt many an honest Man. I am not at all surprised that so many opulent and reputable Traders have recommended the Case of the Officers to the good favour of their Representatives. They are sensible of the pinching Circumstances of the Officers, and of the injury to Trade in general, from the Advantages which are taken of them. The welfare of the fair Trader and the Security of the Revenue are so inseparably one, that their Interest or Injuries are alike. It is the Opinion of such whose Situation give them a perfect Knowledge in the Matter, that the Revenue suffers more by the Corruption of a few Officers in a County, than would make a handsome Addition to the Salary of the whole Number in the same Place.

I very lately knew an Instance where it is evident, on Comparison of the Duty charged since, that the Revenue suffered by one Trader, (and he not a very considerable one,) upwards of One Hundred and Sixty Pounds *per Annum* for several Years ; and yet the Benefit to the Officer was a mere trifle, in Consideration of the Trader's. Without Doubt the Officer would have thought himself much happier to have received the same Addition another Way. The Bread of Deceit is a Bread of Bitterness ; but alas ! how few in Times of Want and Hardship are capable of thinking so : Objects appear under new Colours, and in Shapes not naturally their own ; Hunger sucks in the Deception, and Necessity reconciles it to Conscience.

The Commissioners of Excise strongly enjoin that no Officer accept any Treaty, Gratuity, or, in short, lay himself under any kind of Obligation to the Traders under their Survey : The wisdom of such an Injunction is evident ; but the Practice of it, to a Person surrounded with Children and Poverty, is scarcely possible ; and such Obligations, wherever they exist, must operate, directly or indirectly, to the Injury of the Revenue. Favours will naturally beget their Likenesses, especially where the Return is not at our own Expence.

I have heard it remarked by a Gentleman whose Knowledge in Excise Business is indisputable, that there are Numbers of Officers who are even afraid to look into an unentered Room, lest they should give Offence. Poverty and Obligation tye up the Hands of Office, and give a prejudicial Bias to the Mind.

There is another kind of Evil, which, though it may never amount to what may be deemed Criminality in Law, yet it may amount to what is much worse in Effect, and that is, *a constant and perpetual leakage in the revenue :* A Sort of Gratitude in the Dark, a distant Requital for such Civilities as only the lowest Poverty would accept, and which are a Thousand *per Cent.* above the Value of the Civility received. Yet there is no immediate Collusion ; the Trader and Officer are both safe ; the Design, if discovered, passes for Error.

These, with numberless other Evils, have all their Origin in the Poverty of the Officers. Poverty, in Defiance of Principle, begets a Degree of Meanness that will stoop to almost any Thing. A thousand Refinements of Argument may be brought to prove, that the Practice of Honesty will be still the same, in the most trying and necessitous Circumstances. He who never was an hunger'd may argue finely on the Subjection of his Appetite ; and he who never was distressed, may harangue as beautifully on the Power of Principle. But Poverty, like Grief, has an incurable Deafness, which never hears ; the Oration loses all its Edge ; and " *To be, or not to be,*" becomes the only Question.

There is a striking Difference between Dishonesty arising from Want of Food, and Want of Principle. The first is worthy of Compassion, the other of Punishment. Nature never produced a Man who would starve in a well stored Larder, because the Provisions were not his own : But he who robs it from Luxury of Appetite deserves a Gibbet.

There is another Evil which the Poverty of the Salary produces, and which nothing but an Augmentation of it can remove ; and that is Negligence and Indifference. These may not appear of such dark Complexion as Fraud and Collusion, but their Injuries to the Revenue are the same. It is impossible that any Office or Business can be regarded as it ought, where this ruinous Disposition exists. It requires no sort of Argument to prove that the Value set upon any Place or Employment will be in Proportion to the Value of it ; and that Diligence or Negligence will arise from the same Cause.[1] The continual Number of Relinquishments and Discharges always happening in the Excise, are evident Proofs of it.

Persons first coming into the Excise form very different Notions of it, to what they have afterwards. The gay Ideas of Promotion soon expire. The Continuance of Work, the Strictness of the Duty, and the Poverty of the Salary, soon beget Negligence and Indifference : The Course continues for a while, the Revenue suffers, and the Officer is discharged : The Vacancy is soon filled up, new ones arise to produce the same Mischief, and share the same Fate.

What adds still more to the Weight of this Grievance is, that this destructive Disposition reigns most among such as are otherwise the most proper and qualified for the Employment ; such as are neither fit for the Excise, or any Thing else, are glad to hold in by any Means : But the Revenue lies at as much Hazard from their Want of Judgment, as from the others' Want of Diligence.

In private Life, no Man would trust the Execution of any important Concern to a Servant who was careless whether he did it or not, and the same Rule must hold good in a Revenue Sense. The Commissioners may continue discharging every Day, and the Example will have no Weight while the Salary is an Object so inconsiderable, and this Disposition has such a general Existence. Should it be advanced, that if Men will be careless of such Bread as is in their Possession, they will still be the same were it better ; I answer that, as the Disposition I am speaking of is not the Effect of natural Idleness, but of Dissatisfaction in point of Profit, they would *not* continue the same. A good Servant will be careful of a good Place, though very indifferent about a bad one. Besides, this Spirit of Indifference, should it procure a discharge, is no ways

---

[1] The documents connected with Paine's own discharge from office in 1776, his restoration, and final dismissal in 1774, are given in my Life of Paine, vol. i. ch. 2. No dishonesty was charged. Cobbett held that this dismissal of Paine cost England her American Colonies !— *Editor.*

affecting to their Circumstances   The easy Transition of a qualified Officer to a 'Compting-House, or at least to a School-Master, at any Time, as it naturally supports and backs his Indifference about the Excise, so it takes off all Punishment from the Order whenever it happens.

I have known Numbers discharged from the Excise who would have been a Credit to their Patrons and the Employment, could they have found it worth their while to have attended to it.   No Man enters into Excise with any higher Expectations than a competent Maintenance ; but not to find even that, can produce nothing but *Corruption, Collusion* and *Neglect.*

REMARKS ON THE QUALIFICATIONS OF OFFICERS.

In Employments where direct Labour only is wanted, and Trust quite out of the Question, the Service is merely animal or mechanical.   In cutting a River, or forming a Road, as there is no Possibility of Fraud, the Merit of Honesty is but of little Weight.   Health, Strength, and Hardiness are the Labourer's Virtues.   But where Property depends on the Trust, and lies at the Discretion of the Servant, the Judgement of the Master takes a different Channel, both in the Choice and the Wages.   The Honest and the Dissolute have here no Comparison of Merit.   A known Thief may be trusted to gather Stones ; but a Steward ought to be Proof against the Temptations of uncounted Gold.

The Excise is so far from being of the Nature of the first, that it is all and more than can commonly be put together in the last :   'T is a place of *Poverty, of Trust, of Opportunity, and Temptation.*   A Compound of Discords, where the more they harmonize, the more they offend.   Ruin and Reconcilement are produced at once.

To be properly qualified for the Employment, it is not only necessary that the Person should be honest, but that he be sober, diligent, and skilful : Sober, that he may be always capable of Business ; diligent, that he may be always in his business ; and skilful, that he may be able to prevent or detect Frauds against the Revenue.   The Want of any of these Qualifications is a Capital Offence in the Excise.   A Complaint of Drunkenness, Negligence, or Ignorance, is certain Death by the Laws of the Board.   It cannot then be all Sorts of Persons who are proper for the Office.   The very notion of procuring a sufficient Number for even less than the present Salary, is so destitute of every Degree of sound Reason, that it needs no Reply.   The Employment, from the Insufficiency of the Salary, is *already* become so inconsiderable in the general Opinion, that Persons of any Capacity or Reputation will keep out of it ; for where is the Mechanic, or even the Labourer, who cannot earn at least 1s. 9¼d. *per* day ?   It certainly cannot be proper to take the Dregs of every Calling, and to make the Excise the common Receptacle for the Indigent, the Ignorant, and the Calamitous.

A truly worthy Commissioner, lately dead, made a public Offer a few Years ago, of putting any of his Neighbours' Sons into the Excise ; but though the Offer amounted almost to an Invitation, one only, whom seven Years Apprenticeship could not make a Taylor, accepted it ; who, after a Twelvemonth's Instruction, was ordered off, but in a few Days finding the Employment beyond his Abilities, he prudently deserted it, and returned Home, where he now remains in the Character of an Husbandman.

There are very few Instances of Rejection even of persons who can scarce write their own names legibly ; for as there is neither Law to compel, nor Encouragement to incite, no other can be had than such as offer, and none will offer who can see any other Prospect of Living.   Every one knows that the Excise is a Place of Labour, not of Ease ; of Hazard, not of Certainty ; and that downright Poverty finishes the Character.

It must strike every considerate Mind to hear a Man with a large Family faithful enough to declare, that he cannot support himself on the Salary with that honest Independance he could wish.   There is a great Degree of affecting

Honesty in an ingenuous Confession. Eloquence may strike the Ear, but the Language of Poverty strikes the Heart ; the first may charm like Music, but the second alarms like a Knell.

Of late Years there has been such an Admission of improper and ill qualified Persons into the Excise, that the Office is not only become contemptible, but the Revenue insecure. Collectors, whose long Services and Qualifications have advanced them to that Station, are disgraced by the Wretchedness of new Supers continually. Certainly some Regard ought to be had to Decency, as well as Merit.

These are some of the capital Evils which arise from the wretched Poverty of the Salary. Evils they certainly are ; for what can be more destructive in a Revenue Office, than CORRUPTION, COLLUSION, NEGLECT, AND ILL QUALIFI- CATIONS.

Should it be questioned whether an Augmentation of Salary would remove them, I answer, there is scarce a Doubt to be made of it. Human Wisdom may possibly be deceived in its wisest Designs ; but here, every Thought and Circumstance establish the Hope. They are Evils of such a ruinous Tendency, that they must, by some Means or other, be removed. Rigour and Severity have been tried in vain ; for Punishment loses all its Force where Men expect and disregard it.

Of late Years, the Board of Excise has shewn an extraordinary Tenderness in such Instances as might otherwise have affected the Circumstances of their Officers. Their compassion has greatly tended to lessen the Distresses of the Employment : But as it cannot amount to a total Removal of them, the Officers of Excise throughout the Kingdom have (as the Voice of one Man) prepared Petitions to be laid before the Hon. House of Commons on the ensuing Par- liament.

An Augmentation of Salary, sufficient to enable them to live honestly and competently, would produce more good Effect than all the Laws of the Land can enforce. The Generality of such Frauds as the Officers have been de- tected in, have appeared of a Nature as remote from inherent Dishonesty as a temporary Illness is from an incurable Disease. Surrounded with *Want*, *Children*, and *Despair*, what can the *Husband* or the *Father* do? No Laws compel like Nature—No Connections bind like Blood.

With an Addition of Salary, the Excise would wear a new Aspect, and recover its former Constitution. Languor and Neglect would give Place to Care and Chearfulness. Men of Reputation and Abilities would seek after it, and finding a comfortable Maintenance, would stick to it. The unworthy and the incapable would be rejected ; the Power of Superiors be re-established, and Laws and Instructions receive new Force. The Officers would be secured from the Temptations of Poverty, and the Revenue from the Evils of it ; the Cure would be as extensive as the Complaint, and new Health out-root the present CORRUPTIONS.

THOMAS PAINE.

APPENDIX M.

THE WILL OF THOMAS PAINE.

NOTE BY THE EDITOR.—The fact that Paine's wife (*née* Elizabeth Ollive) is not mentioned in his Will may be explained by the fact that she pre-deceased him. In the *Monthly Repository* (London) of September, 1808, is the following obituary : " MRS. PAINE. On Sunday July 27, at her brother's house, at Cranbrook in Kent, in the 68th year of her age, Mrs. Paine, wife of the celebrated Thomas Paine, author of the ' Rights of Man,' ' Age of Reason,' &c. &c. She was the daughter of Mr. Ollive, a respectable tradesman in Lewes, Essex, in whose house Mr. Paine lived before his marriage as some time after. The marriage took place at Lewes in the year 1771 ; but brought the parties little satisfaction or comfort. After living together three years Mr. and Mrs. Paine, convinced it would seem that they were unsuited to each other, agreed mutually to separate, and accordingly a legal deed of separation was executed. Mrs. Paine's family were Dissenters of the Calvinistic persuasion. It may be considered unfortunate that Mr. Paine knew little of Christians in England but as Calvinists, or in France but as Papists. His attack on Christianity was indeed directed against the gross corruptions of it, as exhibited by those two great Christian parties. Few or none of his sneers affect the religion of the New Testament. Mrs. Paine lived amongst her friends, maintaining a respectable and Christian character. Some of her time was passed in London, where she communicated with the Calvinistic church under Dr. Rippon, meeting in Carter Lane, Tooley-st, Southwark ; the rest of it at Cranbrook, where she attended on the ministry of Mr. Stonehouse of the same denomination.—The death of Mrs. Paine has given occasion for much abuse of her husband. This was needless, ungenerous, and we believe in a great measure unjustifiable. Husbands and wives may live uncomfortably together where there is no deism or republicanism to favour dissension." Paine's domestic troubles are detailed, so far as known, in my biography of him. He gave to his wife all of his possessions, and went to America penniless. When he had secured means he sent money to her anonymously. Madame Bonneville and her children, to whom most of his property was left, were its proper recipients. She and her husband (detained in France under surveillance, by Napoleon) had given Paine a home, 1797-1802, for which he could partly pay, but also care and affection which his always warm gratitude could not forget.

The People of the State of New York, by the Grace of God, Free and Independent, to all to whom these presents shall come, or may concern, SEND GREETING :

KNOW YE, That the annexed is a true copy of the Will of THOMAS PAINE, deceased, as recorded in the office of the surrogate, in and for the city and county of New York. In testimony whereof, we have caused the seal of office of our said surrogate to be hereunto affixed. Witness, Silvanus Miller, Esq., surrogate of said county, at the city of New York, the twelfth day of July, in the year of our Lord one thousand eight hundred and nine, and of our Independence the thirty-fourth.

SILVANUS MILLER.

THE WILL.

THE last Will and Testament of me, the subscriber, Thomas Paine, reposing confidence in my Creator, God, and in no other being, for I know of no other, nor believe in any other. I, Thomas Paine, of the State of New York, author of the work entitled *Common Sense,* written in Philadelphia, in 1775, and published in that city the beginning of January, 1776, which awaked America to a declaration of Independence on the fourth of July following, which was as fast as the work could spread through such an extensive country ; author also of the several numbers of the *American Crisis,* thirteen in all ; published occasionally during the progress of the revolutionary war—the last is on the peace ; author also of *Rights of Man,* parts the first and second, written and published in London, in 1791 and 1792 ; author also of a work on religion, *Age of Reason,* parts the first and second—N. B. I have a third part by me in manuscript, and an answer to the bishop of Llandaff ; author also of a work, lately published, entitled *Examination of the Passages in the New Testament, Quoted from the Old, and called Prophecies concerning Jesus Christ, and showing there are no Prophecies of any such Person ;* author also of several other works not here enumerated, *Dissertations on First Principles of Government,—Decline and Fall of the English System of Finance,—Agrarian Justice,* &c. &c., make this my last Will and Testament, that is to say : I give and bequeath to my executors hereinafter appointed, Walter Morton and Thomas Addis Emmet, thirty shares I hold in the New York Phœnix Insurance Company, which cost me fourteen hundred and seventy dollars, they are worth now upwards of fifteen hundred dollars, and all my moveable effects, and also the money that may be in my trunk or elsewhere at the time of my decease, paying thereout the expenses of my funeral, IN TRUST as to the said shares, moveables, and money, for Margaret Brazier Bonneville, wife of Nicholas Bonneville, of Paris, for her own sole and separate use, and at her own disposal, notwithstanding her coverture. As to my farm in New Rochelle, I give, devise, and bequeath the same to my said executors, Walter Morton and Thomas Addis Emmet, and to the survivor of them, his heirs and assigns forever, IN TRUST nevertheless, to sell and dispose of the north side thereof, now in the occupation of Andrew A. Dean, beginning at the west end of the orchard, and running in a line with the land sold to —— Coles, to the end of the farm, and to apply the money arising from such sale as hereinafter directed. I give to my friends Walter Morton, of the New York Phœnix Insurance Company, and Thomas Addis Emmet, Counsellor at Law, late of Ireland, two hundred dollars each, and one hundred dollars to Mrs. Palmer, widow of Elihu Palmer, late of New York, to be paid out of the money arising from said sale ; and I give the remainder of the money arising from that sale, one half thereof to Clio Rickman, of High or Upper Mary-le-Bone Street, London, and the other half to Nicholas Bonneville, of Paris, husband of Margaret B. Bonneville, aforesaid : and as to the south part of the said farm, containing upwards of one hundred acres, in trust to rent out the same, or otherwise put it to profit, as shall be found most adviseable, and to pay the rents and profits thereof to the said Margaret B. Bonneville, in trust for her children, Benjamin Bonneville, and Thomas Bonneville, their education and maintenance, until they come to the age of twenty-one years, in order that she may bring them well up, give them good and useful learning, and instruct them in their duty to God, and the practice of morality ; the rent of the land, or the interest of the money for which it may be sold, as hereinafter mentioned, to be employed in their education. And after the youngest of the said children shall have arrived at the age of twenty-one years, in further trust to convey the same to the said children, share and share alike, in fee simple. But if it shall be thought advisable by my executors and executrix, or the survivors of them, at any time before the youngest of the said children shall come of age, to sell and dispose of the said south side of the said farm, in that case I hereby authorize and empower my said executors to sell and dispose of the same, and I direct that the money arising from such sale be put into stock, either in the United States Bank stock, or New York Phœnix Insurance Company stock, the interest or dividends thereof to be applied as is already directed for the education and maintenance of the said children, and the principal to be transferred to the said children, or the survivor of them, on his or their coming of age. I know not if the society of people, called Quakers, admit a person to be buried in their burying ground, who does not belong to their society, but if they do, or will admit me, I would prefer being buried there ; my father belonged to that profession, and I was partly brought up in it. But if it is not consistent with their rules to do this, I desire to be buried on my own farm at New Rochelle. The place where I am to be buried, to be a square of twelve feet, to be enclosed with rows of trees, and a stone or post and rail fence, with a headstone with my name and age engraved upon it, author of *Common Sense.* I nominate, constitute, and appoint Walter Morton, of the New York Phœnix Insurance Company, and Thomas Addis Emmet, Counsellor at Law, late of Ireland, and Margaret B. Bonneville, executors and executrix to this my last Will and Testament, requesting the said Walter Morton and Thomas Addis Emmet, that they will give what assistance they conveniently can to Mrs. Bonneville, and see that the children be well brought up. Thus placing confidence in their friendship, I herewith take my final leave of them and of the world. I have lived an honest and useful life to mankind ; my time has been spent in doing good, and I die in perfect composure and resignation to the will of my Creator, God. Dated the eighteenth day of January, in the year one thousand eight hundred and nine ; and I have also signed my name to the other sheet of this Will, in testimony of its being a part thereof.

Thomas Paine.

Signed, sealed, published, and declared by the testator, in our presence, who, at his request, and in the presence of each other, have set our names as witnesses thereto, the words " published and declared " first interlined.

Wm. Keese,
James Angevine,
Cornelius Ryder.

INDEX.